WORLD INFORMATION TECHNOLOGY MANUAL

Volume II:
Systems and Services

WORLD INFORMATION TECHNOLOGY MANUAL

Volume II:
Systems and Services

Edited by

A.E.CAWKELL

CITECH Ltd
P.O. Box 565
Iver, Buckinghamshire
England

1991
ELSEVIER
AMSTERDAM • LONDON • NEW YORK • TOKYO

ELSEVIER SCIENCE PUBLISHERS B.V.
Sara Burgerhartstraat 25
P.O. Box 211, 1000 AE Amsterdam, The Netherlands

Distributors for the United States and Canada:

ELSEVIER SCIENCE PUBLISHING COMPANY INC.
655 Avenue of the Americas
New York N.Y. 10010, U.S.A.

```
         Library of Congress Cataloging-in-Publication Data


World information technology manual / [edited by] A.E. Cawkell.
      p.    cm.
    Rev. and expanded ed. of: Handbook of information technology and
  office systems / edited by A.E. Cawkell. 1986.
    Includes bibliographical references and index.
    Contents: v. 1. Computers, telecommunications, and information
  processing -- v. 2. Systems and services.
    ISBN 0-444-89314-8 (set). -- ISBN 0-444-87488-7 (v. 1). -- ISBN
  0-444-89313-X (v. 2)
    1. Electronic data processing.  2. Information storage and
  retrieval systems.  3. Office practice--Automation.  4. Information
  technology.   I. Cawkell, A. E.   II. Handbook of information
  technology and office systems.
  QA76.W663  1991
  004--dc20                                                91-32678
                                                               CIP
```

ISBN Volume II : 0 444 89313 X
ISBN Volume I : 0 444 87488 7
ISBN Set   : 0 444 89314 8

Printed in The Netherlands

PREFACE II

Although Volume I of "The World Information Technology Manual" contains information about some of the rapidly expanding segments of the "industry", if that it be, Volume II contains most of them. The opportunity has been taken in this volume, mainly written a little later than the first, to include "last minute" developments before going to press to make the book as current as possible.

Volume II also contains the guest author chapters - 33 to 43. Since Chapters 1 to 32 claim to cover the major areas of the subject it is not surprising that some of these authors cover similar topics. However they supplement the earlier chapters quite well, providing an alternative view and some additional information.

There are also one or two guest author chapters about subjects covered very briefly in the earlier chapters - Kingscott on the re-born topic "Language Translation by Computer", for example. Kingscott provides a rather nice example of the computer's difficulties. Try it with:- "No electric passenger carrying vehicles allowed past this point".

It is in Volume II that you will find information about new activities, some requiring whole chapters, which received no mention in the book's 1986 predecessor the "Handbook of Information Technology and Office Systems". Such subjects as Hypertex, Desktop Publishing, Multimedia, High Definition Television, VDUs and Health, and Telecommuting are included here.

Each new subject makes its debut accompanied by the standard IT rosy forecasts - for example none of us will be able to do without multimedia. You will get an overview of these new areas in this volume accompanied by a range of opinions taken from the current literature about their uses and future prospects.

A.E.Cawkell.

ACKNOWLEDGEMENTS

The following organisations have provided information, illustrations, and in some cases specially composed illustrations. I acknowledge
their co-operation with many thanks.

Abaton
Adobe (Illustrator)
Aldus (Pagemaker)
Apple
Associated Knowledge Systems
     (Assassin)
Audio Digital Imaging
Banyan
BBC
Blast Software
British Telecom
Case
Compuadd
Compuserve
Comshare
Conner
Crosfield
DEC
Dowty
Dragon Systems (Cherry)
Epson
Farallon
Formscan
Gemini
Glaxo
Hewlett Packard
Heyden & Son
Howtek
Hughes
IBM
ICI
ICL
IEA Coal Research

Institute for Scientific
     Information (Scimate)
Intel
Intelligent Computers
Interleaf
Kurzweil
Kodak
Letraset (Image Studio)
Macromind (Director)
Mentor
Mercury
Metro Software
Microsoft
Mnemos
Monklands Library
Multimedia Corporation
National Library of Medicine
NEC
Optiram
Pacific Telesis
PCO (Corning)
Philips
Polytechnic of Central London
Que Corporation
Sharp
Siemens
Sony
Surrey County Libraries
Taxan
Texas Instruments
Toshiba
University of Strathclyde
Wireless World
Xerox (Ventura)

This book took a long time to compile. It would have taken far
longer without the support of an efficient assistant editor - my wife,
Kathleen. Many many thanks Kathy (did I hear you say "never again"?).

TABLE OF CONTENTS

VOLUME I

	Preface for volume I	v
	Acknowledgements	vi
Chapter 1.	Reference Data	3
Chapter 2.	Semiconductor Technology and Electronics	10
Chapter 3.	Principles of Digital Computing	29
Chapter 4.	Magnetic Storage Systems	49
Chapter 5.	Input and Output Technology Part 1: Inputs Part 2: Outputs	 60 90
Chapter 6.	Telecommunications and Information Transmission Part 1: History, Principles, Methods, and Systems	 122
Chapter 7.	Telecommunications and Information Transmission Part 2: Networks, Systems, Protocols, and Futures	 146
Chapter 8.	Fibreoptic Technology and Transmission Systems	195
Chapter 9.	Satellite Communication Technology	208
Chapter 10.	Document Processing and Delivery Systems Part 1. Telecommunication-Based Systems	227
Chapter 11.	Document Processing and Delivery Systems Part 2. Disc-Based Systems	253
Chapter 12.	Speech Recognition and Synthesis	289
Chapter 13.	Expert Systems and Artificial Intelligence	305
Chapter 14.	Theoretical and Applied Information Science	326
Chapter 15.	Personal Information Systems	372
Chapter 16.	The Man-Machine Interface	392
Chapter 17.	Online Information Systems and Databases	417
	Abbreviations and Acronyms*	A1
	Glossary*	G1
	Subject Index*	I1

viii

VOLUME II

Preface for volume II   v

Acknowledgements   vi

Chapter 18. Microcomputer Systems
             Part 1: Hardware   441

Chapter 19. Microcomputer Systems
             Part 2: Software   474

Chapter 20. Information Technology and Information Management   506

Chapter 21. Office Systems
             Part 1: Introduction, Systems, & Word Processing   529

Chapter 22. Office Systems
             Part 2: Services and Effectiveness   550

Chapter 23. Information Technology in Banking, Retailing, and Publishing   567

Chapter 24. Desktop Publishing   585

Chapter 25. Cable Systems and Markets   615

Chapter 26. Television-Based Information Systems:
             Videotex and High Definition Television (HDTV)   638

Chapter 27. Microform Systems   663

Chapter 28. Multimedia and Hypertext   674

Chapter 29. The Information Society   709

Chapter 30. Privacy, Freedom, and Data Protection   770

Chapter 31. The Value of Information   790

Chapter 32. Copyright and Patents   802

Contributed Chapters

Chapter 33. Broadband ISDN
             D. Fisher   813

Chapter 34. Electronic Displays
             K.G. Freeman   833

Chapter 35. The Transformation of Colour Printing
             A. Tribute   846

Chapter 36. Designing Hypertext Systems
             C. McKnight, A. Dillon and J. Richardson   853

Chapter 37. Network & PC Development:
             The Security Problems – and a few answers
             K. Slater   872

Chapter 38.   Language Translation by Computer
              G. Kingscott   885

Chapter 39.   Document Supply Systems
              A. Braid   897

Chapter 40.   Library Systems
              L. Tedd   916

Chapter 41.   Coping with Technological Innovation:
              Regulating the European Telecommunications Marketplace
              R. Mansell   932

Chapter 42.   Integrated Office System of the Future
              H. Watanabe   948

Chapter 43.   The Artificial Intelligence Society.
              C.J. Hinde and J. Edwards   965

              Abbreviations and Acronyms*   A1

              Glossary*   G1

              Subject Index*   I1

* Combined for volume 1 and 2

CHAPTER 18. MICROCOMPUTER SYSTEMS. PART 1: HARDWARE

Introduction

This chapter, in which the major features and functions of today's complete machines are described, is complemented by the previous chapters mentioned below, where the principles and component parts and units were discussed.

Some aspects of hardware have already been covered under appropriate headings in earlier chapters. Semiconductor components and memories were discussed in Chapter 2. In Chapter 3 - "Principles of Digital Computing"- the operation of the Central Processing Unit, timing principles, and associated circuits were described. Also in Chapter 3 other commonly used circuits such as Buffers, Cache memory, Gates etc., were listed and described. Most of the principles and circuit elements covered in Chapter 3 are applicable to microcomputers.

Magnetic storage including discs were described in Chapter 4 and input and output components in Chapter 5. Again, most of the topics covered in that chapter are applicable to microcomputers. Formerly there were substantial differences between microcomputers, minicomputers, and mainframes. Today the differences are preserved only because of the sheer power of large mainframes.

Certain techniques associated with that power are still essential for large scale data processing and number crunching applications. In most other respects the differences between the three classes of machines are fast disappearing.

The basic arrangement of a 1990/1991 microcomputer still resembles the microcomputer of 1978/1980. However a new word should really have been invented because the specification which identifies a machine as being recognisably a microcomputer today is a considerable advance even on the mainframes of that earlier period.

HISTORY OF MICROCOMPUTERS AND SOME CURRENT DESIGNS

Introduction and Early History

At the lower end the distinction between micros and programmable calculators is blurred.

Microcomputers, as opposed to mini-computers - the "next size up" - are probably most easily defined in terms of price; it is otherwise becoming increasingly difficult to distinguish between them. The price of a micro starts at a few hundred dollars and extends upwards to about $5000, or even to $10,000 or more if various power-extending add-ons and peripheral units, which are steadily becoming available, are added.

A **Microcomputer** consists of a CPU and other electronics with peripherals (e.g. keyboard, display unit, etc). The peripherals enable data to be fed into and out of the machine, and provide a visual, and to a lesser extent, audible, interface with the user. The user issues commands by typing or by voice and the micro performs useful tasks under program control.

The **Central Processor Unit** (CPU) of a microcomputer is an integrated

1924. IBM printer cylinder

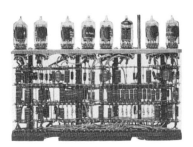

1952 IBM 701 assembly

1975. The Altair 880

1977. The TRS-80

1977. The Commodore Pet

1990. IBM PS/2 50

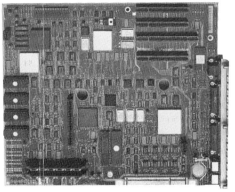

1983. Apple Lisa

FIGURE 18.1. STAGES OF DEVELOPMENT

circuit of components and connections deposited on a very small slice or chip, usually of silicon, called a **Microprocessor**. At one time the CPU was the only major controlling device in the machine but other microprocessors may be included in present generation microcomputers for certain processing-intensive subsidiary tasks. These processors work semi-autonomously, with the CPU in overall control.

Few technologies have moved from first experiments to widespread use in so short a time. Favourable political, economic, and engineering factors have combined to beat the "10 year rule" which says that a period of at least ten years will pass before a major new technology will take off. The devices mentioned and the terms used in this potted history of the microcomputer will be explained later in this chapter.

The PDP-8 minicomputer, sold by the Digital Equipment Corporation in 1965 at about $20,000, provided a foretaste of what would soon become possible. The major enabling developments were the transistor (first patent filed 1948), improvements in photolithography and diffusion techniques enabling transistors and other circuit elements to be manufactured as integrated circuits (Fairchild 1959), US government subsidisation of semiconductor developments amounting to about $1000M in 1958-1974, and subsequently a large local computer market capable of absorbing and encouraging improved devices.

The arrival of the Intel 4004 4-bit microprocessor on one chip in 1971, priced at $200, was the first indication of the impending advances in chips. It contained 2000 transistors on one chip and was later developed into the 8080 and the 8080A. Intel announced the 8-bit 8080 microprocessor - destined to be the CPU work-horse for some years - in 1973.

The 8080

The 8080A is an MOS technology chip internally programmed by code stored in its own read-only memory to perform arithmetic and logical functions. It circulates information internally as 8 bits in parallel on an 8 line bi-directional **"bus"**. A bus is simply an interconnecting line carrying the same information to or from a number of different circuits (See later section).

The 8080A contains a number of **registers** which are simply small storage units, an **Arithmetic Logic Unit (ALU)** to perform the operations required by instructions stored in the registers, an **Instruction Decoder** to decode external program instructions and an **Accumulator** register temporarily to store the results. More information about the functioning of these circuits is given in Chapter 3.

The 8080A also contains an eight line **Multiplexer** to connect a selected register to the internal data bus. The Timing and control unit receives timing pulses from the external clock and controls the machine cycles. It also generates signals to control external operations at the right instant.

An 8 bit register can store up to 256 decimal numbers implying that when used to indicate an address - say a memory location - the memory could have up to 256 locations. This is too small for many purposes. In the 8080A 16 bit numbers can be represented by using registers in pairs so that one out of 2^{16} = 65,636 ("64K") addresses can be located. 16 connections for external addressing are provided so that 16 address bits can be moved in parallel via a 16 line address bus.

Control over the 8080A is exerted by means of an **Instruction Set** of over 50 commands or instructions (sometimes known as OPcodes), recognised by the instruction decoder, such as ADD (Add contents of register to accumulator) and LDA (Load accumulator from memory). A program consists of a sequence of OP codes each followed by supplementary data which are stored in external memory and called into the CPU when the program is executed.

The actual movement and control of data between registers and other elements within the microprocessor after decoding by the instruction decoder is controlled by "microprograms" inherent in the way the circuits are connected together.

Data is processed and conveyed to other parts of a microcomputer in short bursts when all circuits are periodically switched by impulses generated from a master timing clock.

8080A machine cycles are synchronised from clock (See Chapter 3) impulses at about 0.5 us intervals (2 MHz). Some of the more complex instructions may take up to five clock cycles to complete. This does not mean that all activities in a machine controlled by an 8080A are limited to a repetition rate of 0.5 us (500 ns).

For example even in vintage 1977 microcomputers a 14 MHz clock oscillator was fitted with dividing circuits to generate impulses at 2 MHz for 8080A timing. The display of characters on the CRT was controlled by a character generator chip to which the 14 MHz clock was connected. This chip stored a character set as dot patterns and was programmed to feed out the dots at 14 MHz (70 ns intervals)) to represent a character on a CRT.

The arrival of the microcomputer

IBM introduced a terminal incorporating the FD-11 floppy disk providing cheap bulk storage in 1971. Competitors announced copies almost immediately, but in September 1972 IBM announced the 3740 data entry station incorporating a "diskette", and a host of competitors followed.

In 1974, Gary Kildall was asked by Imsai, then a floppy disk supplier, to design managing software and the first version of CP/M, labelled 1.3, became available. Hardware dependent functions were concentrated in one section of it enabling it to be adapted for use with any microcomputer using the 8080 and the Zilog Z80 - a strong competitor for the 8080 - which appeared in 1975. Kildall founded Digital Research in 1976 and more CP/M versions were released later, including one for 16 bit machines, CP/M 86. The C programming language was developed in the same year.

1975 was a milestone year. The first commercially available machine to be produced in any quantity - the Altair 8800 - was supplied as a kit by MITS early in that year for $395. It was advertised as "The world's first minicomputer kit to rival commercial models". An improved copy of the Altair made by Imsai was announced in August. At about the same type MOS Technology were advertising their MC6000 series of microprocessors at about $20.

For a short time the Altair and its successors were limited by small memories and the absence of disk storage, to a market composed of enthusiastic hobbyists. Software for useful applications was non-existent. Demand increased with increasing software availability, improved reliability, and falling costs.

In 1976 microcomputers with CP/M and floppy disks offering 250 Kbytes and later up to 1 Mbyte Random Access Storage were manufactured at reasonable prices and the "business microcomputer" was born. The pioneering companies were Ohio Scientific, Cromemco, and Polymorphic.

At the end of the year the Sol computer was designed by Lee Felsenstein of Processor Technology. Some thousands of this machine were sold, and two were purchased by the Institute for Scientific Information, on which Primate, the forerunner of the Scimate personal information, was

developed (Cawkell 1979). It was a CP/M machine using the 8080 with a 64K
memory and dual 8" disk drives.

In 1977 Commodore, Apple, and Radio Shack/Tandy introduced personal
computers selling complete with Cathode Ray Tube display, cassette tape data
recorder, keyboard and Basic software for below $1000.

Parallel developments of larger disks started with the IBM Ramac
"hard disk" introduced in 1956, and in 1973 IBM announced the 3340
"Winchester Disk" a sealed unit with the heads flying 20 microinches above
the disk surface. In due course engineering developments were put in hand to
miniaturise and mass produce Winchesters and in 1978 Shugart announced the
SA4000 Winchester for microcomputers. In 1980 Seagate introduced a 5 Mbyte
5.25 inch Winchester selling for $925. Tandon replied in 1982 with the same
unit for $400.

The 1980s

In the 1980s hardware development showed some signs of slowing up
as the physical limits of optical resolution in chip layout appeared to be
approaching. The problem of the
man-hours required to write
software capable of capitalising
on the hardware also started to
receive increasing attention.
Some machine language software
started to be built into the
chips. The software writer
could use a terse statement
where previously lines of code
were needed.

Processor	Address space (bytes)	Bus width (bits)	Bus speed (us./transfer)	Bandwidth (Megabytes/sec.)
6502	64K	8	1	1
6809	64K	8	1	1
8088	1M	8	.4	2.5
68000	16M	16	.25	8
80286	16M	16	.33	6
68020	4G	32	.25	16
80386	4G	32	.25	16

Year	320x200 (4 bits/pixel)	640x480 (4 bits/pixel)	1024x768 (8 bits/pixel)
1979	$125	$560	$3000
1981	$60	$280	$1500
1983	$30	$145	$740
1985	$15	$70	$370
1987	$8	$35	$185

**PROGRESS IN SPEEDS AND DISPLAYS
FIGURE 18.2**

Since the 8080 the major
developments have been increases
in clock speeds, number of elements per chip, and number of
bits per word. Clock speeds went
up to 5 MHz in the Intel 8086
and to 8 MHz in the Motorola
68000. The increase in word
length means that more information is moved per cycle. 16 bit
microprocessors are already being overtaken by 32 bit, although the amount
of software available for longer word microprocessors limits the rate
of introduction. 64 bit words were introduced in 1990.

The number of instructions in an instruction set have increased, so
has the power of instructions. A single instruction replaces several
previously separate instructions. In the 16 bit Motorola MC68000 there are
two levels of instruction enabling internal microprograms, stored within the
chip on a 22K store, to be installed by the manufacturer.

With the NCR 32000 32 bit 4 chip microprocessor, external
microprogramming became possible, enabling mini or mainframe instruction
sets to be emulated. Extra sophistication has been introduced by
"pipe-lining" meaning that the next instruction is fetched in the same
machine cycle used for the execution of the previous one. 32 bit busses with
pipelining enable bit transfer rates at 36 Mbytes/sec.

A major benefit of using a longer word is the larger addressing capability. A 32 bit microprocessor, or a 16 bit using two registers, can potentially address 2^{32} storage elements which is over four thousand million. In practice the address range provided is usually up to 16 Mbytes.

By 1984 the most popular microprocessors fitted in microcomputers were the Intel 8080 series (including the 8085, 8086, 8087, 8088). Next came the Zilog 80, followed some way behind by the Motorola 68000 and 6800, and the Zilog Z8000. Microprocessor cycle times are 330 ns for the Texas 99000, and 400 ns for the 68000 or 8086. However the actual "performance", "speed", "work done", or "instructions per second" of a microprocessor/memory combination also depend on other things such as instruction efficiency and transmission delays.

In 1987 the next generation of microprocessors were announced - the 32 bit Intel 80386 and the Motorola 68020, to be followed in 1989 by the 80486 and the 68040 chips containing over one million transistors. The net result in current (1990) microcomputers is that speeds have gone up from the 5 Mhz of the IBM PC to 33 Mhz, but because of other additional refinements, power has gone up by about 13 times.

The Xerox Star and the Macintosh

If 1975 was the first milestone year, 1981 was the second. In that year the Xerox Star first became commercially available and so did the IBM PC.

The Xerox Star machine and its Smalltalk software was first demonstrated at the Palo Alto Research Centre (PARC), California, in 1978. The concept was ahead of its time. Many of the concepts which it pioneered were taken up in Apple's Lisa microcomputer including something called the "Desktop Manager" with 2.5 Mbytes of software - unheard of in contemporary micros. It included a "point and select" cursor controller called a Mouse, bypassing the need to learn special commands.

Selectable functions were represented as Ikons (small images). Overlapping pages called "Windows" on which active or temporarily suspended tasks were visible, appeared on the CRT screen, and a 720 x 364 pixel display was used - much better than was then available on other machines. A new word was coined for it - WYSIWYG - What You See (on the screen) Is What You Get (on the printer).

Microprocessor developments came at the right time for Apple. The 5 Mhz Motorola 68000 processor, with its 24 bit internal and 16 bit external busses became available in 1979 - the year in which the Lisa project started. Apple developed a unique memory management system for re-locating large blocks of code controllable by the 68000. However the potential of the Word Processing and graphics software called LisaWrite and LisaDraw respectively, was not immediately obvious, and the system was expensive.

In May 1984 Apple announced the Macintosh at $3000. This machine together with the development of the laser scanner, page formatting software, and other devices and software gave rise to the Desktop Publishing idea.

The Macintosh was Apple's last chance to get its policy right and the company built a new factory with automated production capable of manufacturing 350,000 machines a year. This volume coupled with a "just in

time" scheme for scheduling the delivery of supplies as required, rather
than holding stocks, was needed to produce the machine at the advertised
price.

A fundamental part of the design lies in the idea of providing a
standard user interface software contained in two Read Only Memory (ROM)
chips. This software includes the usual operating system functions and the
Quickdraw and Toolbox software (described in the next chapter). The result
is cheap fast storage, no delay in loading from disc, and more space
available on the disc for users.

Early in 1985 a Macintosh with a 512K memory was introduced selling
for $3495, and a whole range of improvements were announced aimed at the
office market including the Zilog 8530 SCC chip with Appletalk software
enabling Macintoshes to communicate on a twisted pair LAN at up to 230 Kbps,
with a laser printer and file printer for added resources.

Later Apple introduced the Mac Plus with more memory, the SE and the
Mac II. The latter includes a 15Mhz 68020 processor, with a 68881
co-processor to speed up operations and facilities for handling colour.

The Latest Mac II is the IIx (compact version the IIcx) based on the
32 bit 68030 microprocessor running at 15.7 MHz. Arithmetic-intensive
applications are speeded up by a 68882 co-processor. A US company called
Mercury Computer Systems (Lowell, MA) can supply a co-processor board for
the Mac to make it run at 10 Million Instructions Per Second (MIPS) -
considerably faster than a Sun 4 or a DEC VAX 11/780 computer.

Standard memory is 4 Mbytes expandible to 8. 1.44 Mbyte 3.5" floppy
and 80 Mbyte hard disc drives are fitted internally. Analogue monochrome or
colour monitors are available with 640 x 480 pel resolution; with video card
expansion, 256 shades of grey, or 256 colours chosen from a palette of 16M
colours may be displayed.

The IIx has 6 slots for plug-in boards and six ports - 2 serial, 2
Apple desktop (for up to 16 daisy-chained small peripherals), 1 sound, and 1
SCSI (Small Computer Systems Interface). Up to seven SCSI devices such as
scanners, optical disc drives, tape drives etc., may be connected to this
interface. The standard set of SCSI commands eases communications between
computer and peripherals. The machine will run on MS-DOS or a Unix operating
system as well as Apple's own operating system.

The Macintosh is one of the best - many would say the very best -
microcomputers available. It is also one
of the most expensive. Until September
1989, in the UK the IIx ranged from around
£5000 (about £2850) for a model with a 4 Mbyte
memory and floppy, to about £8000 (about £4500)
with 8 Mbyte memory and 80 Mbyte hard disc.

However in September 1990 Apple introduced three new machines as shown in Table 18.1.

These prices make these Macs competitive
with IBM PC clones, but with the advantage of the
Apple operating system integrated with the graphic interface and generally simpler installation
and operation.

THE MAC CLASSIC
FIGURE 18.3

Name	Processor	Mem.	Floppy	Hard Disc	Approx. UK. Price	Monitor Pixels	Details
Classic	8 MHz	1 Mbyte	1.44 Mbyte		575	512 x 342	Mono
		2 Mbyte	1.44 Mbyte	40 Mbyte	895		
LC	16 MHz	2 Mbyte	1.44 Mbyte	40 Mbyte	1375	512 x 342	Mono
		2 Mbyte	1.44 Mbyte	40 Mbyte	1495	640 x 480	Colour (13")
IIsi	20 MHz	2 Mbyte	1.44 Mbyte	40 Mbyte	2695	512 x 342	Mono
					3000	640 x 480	Colour (13")
		5 Mbyte	1.44 Mbyte	80 Mbyte	3395	512 x 342	Mono
					3700	640 x 480	Colour (13")

TABLE 18.1 1990 INEXPENSIVE MACINTOSHES

The IBM PC

IBM's entry into microcomputers late in 1981 made micros respectable. The IBM PC was developed in a relatively short time, and was and is being marketed through retailers - a new departure for IBM at the time. It uses operating systems written by other companies - IBM realised that the "all home-grown treatment" accorded to its other products was inappropriate for the PC market and acted accordingly.

The PC was launched in the US first; people in the UK realised something unusual was going on when IBM turned its attention to this country in 1983. Regular full page advertisements in the national press followed by extensive TV advertising for microcomputers was something new.

The IBM PC runs on the MS-DOS operating system. MS-DOS-based computers - that is IBM PCs and clones - outsell Apple Mcintoshes by about 10 to 1. What other microcomputer manufacturer can finance an advertising budget to compare with a company with a turnover of $44KM (44 billion dollars)? We must hope that indigenous industries will continue to be ableto offer choices.

The IBM PC uses the Intel 8088 16 bit processor and was similar to other 16 bit machines available at the time. There were a number of machines at £3000 - £4000 in the UK when compared on a like-with-like basis - that is which include 128K memory, hard disk, and operating system. The PC could run on several different operating systems, but a preferred system soon emerged - a version of Microsoft's PC/DOS.

A range of application programs soon became available from well known software houses, and verions of Visicalc, Wordstar and other programs were offered. Hard disk units up to 27 Mbytes, a huge range of plug-in alternative boards and disk drives, and all sorts of accessories and software are now available from dozens of suppliers hanging on to IBM's coat-tails.

For example the CompuAdd 325, competing with recent versions of the PC, runs at 25 MHz with its 80486 processor and a co-processor, includes 4 Mbytes of RAM, a 3.5" 1.44 Mbyte diskette drive and 80 MByte hard disc drive, and comes bundled with software (Figure 8.4). At £4995 CompuAdd claims that this is "less than half" the price of IBM or Compaq 386 technology.

FIGURE 18.4 THE COMPUADD 325

The advent of this machine had a strong influence on other microcomputer manufacturers who produced machines advertised as "fully compatible with the IBM personal computer", "IBM circuit board compatible expansion slots" etc.

Mach. Type	Proces. (F. MHz)	Mem.(Kb) Stan.	Max.	Discs (Mb) Flop.	Hard	Screen Resolution	Col- ours	Ports Slots	Price ($K)
PC	8088 (4.77)	64	640	2x0.32 5.25"	No	320 x 200 (min) 640 x 200 (max)	16	1 Ser. 5	3.0
PC/ XT	8088 (4.77)	128	640	2x0.32 5.25"	10	..	16	1 Ser. 6 + 2	4.4
PC/ AT	80286 (6.0)	256	3M	1x1.2 5.25"	20	..	16	1 Ser. 8 1 Par.	5.8

TABLE 18.2. IBM PCs

Subsequently IBM introduced an improved PC, the PC/XT, and in 1985 the IBM/AT, a considerably more advanced machine (See Table 18.2). The AT has a 16 bit instead of an 8 bit data bus, as on the previous models, and its 80286 requires about half the number of clock cycles per instruction execution compared with the 8088; the net effect is that the AT is two to three times faster than the PC or PC/XT. Options available on the AT include an 80287 co-processor, up to 16 Mbytes of memory, and a new version 3.0 of the PC-DOS software.

Amstrad

Many well known microcomputer companies went out of business in the period 1981 to 1984 mainly due to the impact of the IBM PC. But a number of manufacturers who argued "If you can't beat 'em, join 'em" succeeded. They were able to offer machines which were compatible with or virtually identical to the IBM models ("clones"), but at a lower price and often with a performance edge. Compaq is probably the most successful.

However one manufacturer, Amstrad, adopted a different, highly successful, formula, based on the policy of boss Alan Sugar - rock-bottom prices without much sacrifice of performance. In 1985 Amstrad produced the CPC 464 which was successful when most companies were having a bad time.

In 1986 the company introduced the PCW 8256 selling at £399 including built-in disc drive, keyboard, monitor, and printer - by 1986 Amstrad's sales had reached nearly half a million machines. One reviewer found that with the printer operating in "letter quality" mode, the quality was as good as that obtainable from an Epson printer which cost more than the entire Amstrad system. The 8256 came with a Z80 4 MHz processor, 256K RAM, a 3" disc drive with an optional second drive, and the CP/M operating system. Sales advanced from £136M in 1985 to £304M in 1986.

In late 1986 Amstrad launched its IBM compatible PC1512 using the 8086 running at twice the speed of the IBM PC, again at £399, undercutting IBM PC clones from Taiwan. The company continued to launch machines which were good value for the money; by the end of 1987 it had taken 10% of the European market, rising later to 24%, second to IBM's 35%.

In 1988 Amstrad was hit by the chip shortage and its expected satellite receiver sales - another pioneering venture - did not materialise. Its PC business seemed to be well passed its peak and its profits announced in February 1989 were well down.

Ebullient as ever, in September 1989 Sugar announced a facsimile machine with advanced features selling at £599, and new computers, the 1286 and 1386, filling in gaps in the range, at prices between £700 and £1700.

In September 1990 it launched its "Generation 3" PC compatible machines in an attempt to break in to the corporate market with inexpensive but reliable machines. The PC3386SX, for example, costs £1600 complete with 640K RAM, 40 Mbyte hard disc, and VGA monitor. Its 30386SX processor runs at 20 MHz.

The IBM PS/2 range

By 1986 IBM PC and PC/XT compatibles/clones had taken an estimated 48% of the total IBM PC market, and AT clones had taken well over 30%. The introduction of the PS/2 in mid-1987 has been seen as IBM's attempt to regain control of the market. To discourage cloners no details of the PS/2's BIOS (Basic Input/Output System) in Read Only Memory (ROM) are published, only details of its points of entry and electronic waveforms.

Models 50 and 60 incorporate a 16 bit bus and model 80 a 32 bit bus using Micro Channel Architecture (MCA) which is not compatible with the bus used on IBM PCs. For more details about the bus, see the section headed "Buses" in this chapter. The OS/2 software for the PS/2 is described in Chapter 19.

Details of the range are given in Table 18.3. In terms of speed, the 70-A21 (the fastest machine in the range) is nearly four times faster than the 8 MHz PC/AT, the fastest machine in the PC range, which appeared at the beginning of 1987.

Mach. Type	Proces. (F. MHz)	Mem.(Mb) Stan.	Max.	Discs (Mb) Flop.	Hard	Screen Resol.	Col-ours	Ports	Slots	Price ($K)
PS2 30*	8086 (8)	.64	2.64	1x.72	No	MCGA !			3 8 bit	1695
PS2 50+	80286 (10)	1	16	1x1.44 2nd opt.	20	VGA &	16	1 ser 1 par	3 16 bit	3595
PS2 60à	80286 (10)	1	16	1x1.44 2nd opt.	44 2nd opt.	VGA	16		7 16 bit	5295
PS2 70$	80386 (16)	2	16	1x1.44 2nd opt.	60	VGA	16		2 32 bit 1 16 bit	5995
PS2 80%	80386 (16)	1	16	1x1.44 2nd opt.	44 2nd opt.	VGA	16		3 32 bit 4 16 bit	6995
PS2 90	80486 (25)	8	33	1x1.44	160	XGA	256 (64000 VGA)		3 32 bit	£8500
PS2 95?	80486 (25)	8	33	1x1.44	160	XGA	256 (64000 VGA)		6 32 bit	£8960

* 30-21. 30-022 has 2 x 720K floppies and 20 Mbyte hard disc.
+ 50-Z. 50-021 has 60 Mbyte hard disc.
à 60-041. 60-071 has 70 Mbyte hard disc and up to 115 mbytes optional.
$ 70-F61 70-121 has 20 Mhz speed and 120 Mbyte hard disk.
        70-A21 has 25 MHz speed, 64 cache mem., 120 Mbyte hard disc.
% 80-041 80-071 has 70 Mbyte hard disc, up to 314 Mbyte optional.
        80-111 has 20 MHz speed, 115 Mbyte hard disc, up to 314 opt.
        80-311 has 20 MHz speed, 314 Mbyte hard disc, up to 314 opt.
! MCGA is Multi Colour Graphics Display 640 x 400 (max) with 16 on-screen colours from a palette of 262,144 colours.
& VGA provides a 640 x 480 resolution (max) with 16 on-screen colours from a palette of 262,144 colours, or 320 x 200 with 256 colours.
? The mechanical construction of the 95 is different from the 90 to allow for more up-grading.

TABLE 18.3. IBM PS/2 PCs

The PS/2 incorporates 3.5" floppy disk drives and considerable hard disk capacity. It includes the VGA high resolution/colour display system (discussed in more detail in Chapter 5) based on an Inmos transputer chip. The range contains a number of sophisticated features making PS/2s much more difficult to copy.

FIGURE 18.5. IBM PS/2 MODEL 90

Certain other features might infringe copyright if copied and IBM's financial muscle is bound to make potential infringers nervous. However in April 1988, IBM announced that it would negotiate patent license agreements at a rate up to 5% of sales revenue, compared with a flat rate of 1% for earlier licenses. Incidentally the first PS/2 MCA-compatible clone appeared in June 1988 in the shape of the Tandy 5000 MC with an 80386 processor running at 20 MHz, selling for $4999 or $6499 with 40 Mbyte hard disc. Tandy has an exchange of patents agreement with IBM.

The IBM PS/1

IBM introduced the PS/1 in late 1990 selling in the UK from £600 to £1200 and the in the US at $1000 to $2000. It uses a 10 Mhz 80286 with a 512K or 1 Mbyte RAM, 3.5 inch floppy disc and 30 Mbyte hard disk. A VGA monitor and mouse are included. The bundled software is IBM DOS 4.01 and Microsoft Works (Word processor, spreadsheet, database, and communications). The machine is aimed at small businesses.

Portables

The last few years have seen the arrival of portables - truly portable machines, which were preceded by "luggables" - machines which were portable but too heavy to be easily carried. Their arrival has been made possible by the development of chips consuming low current, low current thin displays to replace the CRT, and general advances in technology at lower costs.

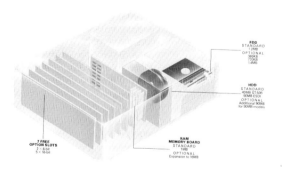

FIGURE 18.6. STORAGE ARRANGEMENTS IN EPSON MICROCOMPUTERS

To emphasise the portability the current in-phrase is "laptops", and within the last few months "palmtops".

1989 portables cost in the range $3000 to $9000, typically use the 80386 processor running at 16 Mhz, include 2 Mbytes of memory and a 40 Mbyte disc drive, and weigh 22 pounds inclusive of battery. Batteries last for about two and a half hours and the machines can be used from a mains power pack. The display will either be backlit LED or gas plasma, hinged to the machine and folding down flat for carrying. Figure 18.7 shows the Toshiba T5200.

In September 1989 Psion introduced a PC compatible portable manufactured in the UK using a liquid crystal display and plug in Flash EPROM chips for storage. These units are used until they are full, and then another is plugged in. Erasure of the whole memory chip is carried out with a 2 second 12 volt pulse. The battery lasts for 60 hours, the weight is 5 pounds, and the machine costs £1500 plus £195 per flash memory.

At about the same time the 1" x 8.75" x 4" Poqet PC appeared weighing 1 pound with a 6.8" x 2.7" LCD screen, priced at $2000. It uses two standard AA size alkaline batteries claimed to last for 100 hours. This life is achieved by reducing consumption to about one tenth of other portables by a power management system which shuts down those parts of the machine which are not actually in use. It has a 77 key plus 12 function keys keyboard, runs at 7 MHz, and uses 512K memory cards.

Several new types of battery (Reinhardt 1990) are expected to be a considerable improvement over the nickel-cadmium rechargeable batteries currently used (although some use conventional dry lead-acid or alkaline batteries). The nickel hydride battery is expected to last 50% longer per charge and may be available in 1991.

Also expected in 1991 is the zinc aerobic battery which uses atmospheric oxygen and is expected to last four times longer than nickel-cadmium and will be lighter and cheaper.

FIGURE 18.7 TOSHIBA T5200 PORTABLE

Further into the future is a new type of lithium battery said to be capable of seven times the capacity of nickel-cadmium.

MICROCOMPUTER TECHNOLOGY AND OPERATIONS

The CPU and basic operations

Microcomputer operations typically consist of a succession of "fetch-execute" cycles operating in a step-by-step manner, initiated, say, by a typed command from the operator, which continue until the required program sequence is completed. The appropriate buses are switched to interconnect the appropriate units during data transfer, and a Program Counter keeps track of each step.

Bytes of data are moved from memory to various parts of the machine - say to a peripheral device via a port. Alternatively a byte might have to be moved into the CPU to be added to another number stored in the arithmetic circuits as the result of an earlier instruction.

The CPU interacts with peripheral units by "polling". It is periodically switched round to each peripheral to check readiness for data transfer. If readiness is indicated, the CPU completes the current instruction, branches to a program for data transfer, and then returns to the interrupted program. Alternatively a peripheral may generate an **Interrupt** signal to indicate readiness. In accordance with pre-arranged rules about priorities, the CPU will run a routine to transfer the data.

If a long run of data has to be transferred to or from a peripheral in a given time period, a series of CPU-controlled byte by byte processes would be too laborious and time-consuming. Many microcomputers include a **Direct Memory Access (DMA)** routine. Direct memory Transfer is a fast method of exchanging data between memory and a peripheral device. The CPU temporarily surrenders control of the I/O - memory data exchange to the input/output controller.

A **Microprocessor** is a collection of components arranged in a circuit capable of executing program instructions. It is used in various ways - for instance to control a sequence of operations in a washing machine. However the aspect which has received the greatest attention, and with which the word "microprocessor" has almost become synonymous, is when it forms the **Central Processing Unit (CPU)** of a computer. Much of the effort in chip technology has been directed towards developing faster, smaller, cheaper, more comprehensive CPU microprocessors.

The operation of a typical CPU was described in Chapter 3 in conjunction with Figure 3.2. The CPU performs step by step manipulations of data by arithmetical and logical operations in order to achieve the results demanded by a program.

It controls the flow of data to and from external (peripheral) devices, most of which provide the means for humans to input data, interact with the machine, and view or read processed data. It manages the reception, processing, and delivery of data under program control to and from specifically addressed parts of the computer such as storage.

The main sections of a microcomputer are shown in figure 18.8. A **program,** stored in the computer's mem -ory, directs the CPU to fetch as many instructions as may be needed to conduct operations such as reading in data from a peripheral unit - say a scanner, moving data between storage units, processing data by perform- ing a logical or arithmet- ical function on the content of a storage unit and so on.

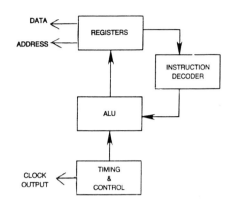

FIGURE 18.8. BASIC MICROCOMPUTER

Data is moved about in successive **Machine Cycles** - synchronised bursts of activity - between parts of the CPU and between units of the computer via multiple connecting wires called **Busses** (see below). "Data" means both program instructions, and data retrieved from storage, originally having been received, say, via an input/output **port,** the point of connection to a peripheral such as a disc store.

A microcomputer CPU is characterised by its architecture, instruction set, word length, and speed. The **Instruction Set** is the repertoire of permanently stored instructions that the CPU can execute. An instruction is initiated when an instruction word is received from the Instruction Decoder. The word consists of the **Opcode** which is the name of the instruction and the **Operand** - the object to be operated upon. The operand may be a data value or the address of a value.

The **Word Length** is the size of a unit of data. Words are moved about in each machine cycle so the volume of data moved per second depends on the repetition rate or **speed** of the cycle and the amount of data per word - i.e. the word length. Provided that other parts of the computer can accommodate higher speeds, and various other factors being equal, the "power" of the computer is related to the word length and the cycle rate.

Here is an example (after Stanley) of the events occurring in the first part of a program for moving some input data into the accumulator ready for further operations:-

> Program Counter having been reset to 0000, CPU addresses memory
> location 0000 (Hex) and then increments to 0001.
> CPU sends out "memory read" command on the address bus.
> Memory places contents of addressed location on to data bus.
> CPU reads data into Instruction Decoder - it knows the first byte
> after a reset will be an Opcode requiring decoding.
> CPU detects that the instruction contains two bytes - an
> INPUT opcode instruction and an address; the Program Counter
> having been set to 0001, the CPU fetches the second byte, "00",
> via the data bus from that address and places it in an
> address register.
> Since "00" represents input port "0" the CPU sends out the address
> of that port on the address bus and an "I/O read" command on the
> I/O read line. Data from the port is routed to the accumulator -
> the automatic destination of all input data.

The series of events handled by the CPU are accurately timed. **Timimg and Synchronisation** with **Clock** pulses, is described in Chapter 3.

Buses

CPU's have internal buses; the buses discussed here are Systems Busses - computer data communications highways. Sometimes parts of the Systems Bus are labelled "Input/Output (I/O)", and "Memory" - both self-evident names associated with their functions.

In larger computers the most usual arrangement is a "multi-master" system where a particular unit of the machine assumes bus control for the duration of a particular operation; but the bus concept is now less important as logic functions are becoming decentralised. The bus came into its own in microcomputers where functions are usually concentrated on a controlling **Motherboard** bus-connected to slots into which boards or cards performing special functions are plugged.

Buses may be **Synchronously** controlled - timing impulses are derived from a single clock - the usual system in microcomputers. Alternatively they may be **Asynchronous** where timing between units is arranged by a preliminary exchange of timing data known as "handshaking". Bus **Protocol** refers to the rules provided for the orderly exchange of data.

The **Bus Width** is the number of wires or lines used for conveying the bits of a word in parallel. In the expression "2^n", "n" describes the number of lines, the addressing capability, and the capacity of storage on the bus.Thus a 32 line bus can carry the addresses for 2^{32} = 4.3 billion storage elements.

With this mass of interconnecting lines it obviously makes sense to standardise the purpose of each line, together with its identification, numbering and connection. If this was not done, each type of machine would need a different program simply to distribute information correctly to the right place.

A popular method of construction is associated with the adoption of buses - the **Backplane.** A degree of standardisation has occurred as needs have become evident. An early example was the adoption of a standard set of 100 lines with designated functions called "S-100" defined by the US IEEE in specification 696.

Its practical realisation is a line of 100 sockets spaced along a thin plastic strip. Several of these socket-strips are fixed above each other along one side of a "cage" and each socket on a strip is wired to the same socket on every other strip - e.g. each socket numbered 83 will be connected to socket number 83 on all other strips. Printed circuit cards have 100 gold plated flat pins spaced along one edge in order to fit into a 100-socket-strip.

The completed assembly consists of a number of cards plugged into the socket strips and retained in the cage, with each bus line carried round to all cards via the described arrangement. Any card may be plugged in to any socket.

But the backplane imposed by the introduction of the IBM PC soon became the most widely used (Karanassios 1985). The IBM PC has five 62-contact slots for plug-in cards. There are 8 data lines, 20 address lines, 4 power supply lines and ground, and a number of other lines such as "memory write", "memory read", "I/O write", "I/O read", "Clock", "Interrupt", "Address Enable (DMA controls bus)" and so on.

The Apple Mac II microcomputer uses the 32 bit Nubus originally designed at MIT. The system was designed for large machines with multi-mastering. In the Mac II any board/slot can assume temporary control of the bus by generating an **Interrupt** signal - for instance for an I/O data transfer. The bus is an IEEE/ANSI standard bus, meaning that any supplier can offer a plug-in card to be used in the Mac II, if it is designed to function in the non-proprietary Nubus.

In mid-1989 a series of claims and counter-claims were being made for the merits of IBM Micro Channel Architecture (MCA) Bus, and a bus design called Extended Industry Standard Architecture (EISA) sponsored by a number of IBM's competitors of whom Compaq and Olivetti were the most active. MCA is the proprietary bus used in IBM's PS/2 range of microcomputers, probably protected by Copyright. EISA is based on the widely used bus used in IBM's PC/AT and clones which preceded PS/2.

PS/2 Models 50 and 60 incorporate a 16 bit bus and model 80 a 32 bit bus using MCA which is not compatible with the bus used on IBM PCs. The bus uses TTL signalling and separate lines without multiplexing, with particular attention paid to interference minimisation by special grounding ("earthing") arrangements. MCA is FCC Class B certified even at the highest clock speeds. Data and addresses are transferred at rates up to 20 Mbps.

The bus is a new departure for microcomputers where designs have been developed for CPU intensive operations such as spreadsheets and local databases. MCA is oriented towards Input/Output intensive applications as encountered in distributed processing.

In September 1989 IBM announced new MCA data transmission modes at up to 160 Mbps. The normal rate is doubled by eliminating the need for transmitting address data in second and subsequent data transfers. It is doubled again by multiplexing data through the address bus when the latter is idle. In due course a further doubling will be effected by decreasing the intervals between data transfers so that the data rate will then become 160 Mbps.

Co-processor

A co-processor, also called an FPU (Floating Point Unit) when it handles floating point arithmetic, is a processor to which certain tasks, normally carried out by the CPU, are allocated. A co-processor may have as much or more power than the main CPU - in effect it is a small computer in its own right.

Typical co-processor functions are to deal with floating point operations, or to handle all special graphic operations, particularly for good quality colour which requires extra processing. Co-processors need additional software to tell them when to take over specific operations, and their own instruction software.

A plug-in card called the DSI co-processor, for instance, includes a 16 MHz 68020 processor, a 68881 maths co-processor, and a 4 Mbyte RAM. As used with the Apple Mac SE it increases the speed of maths-intensive operations by several times.

458

Display functions

Bright dots can be formed on the screen by electronically switching on the electron beam of a CRT as it reaches particular positions during its traverse. The beam scans continuously, zig-zag fashion, generating closely spaced rows of dots, sweeping out the entire pattern repeatedly at a high speed so that the eye sees an apparently permanent image.

A character set, usually of at least 128 characters to include upper and lower case, numerals and symbols, is permanently stored, each character as a 7 x 9 dot pattern, in 8 rows of 16 characters within an "8K" bit Character Generator (CG) ROM (7 x 9 x 8 x 16 = 8064 bits). It is these patterns, read out when needed and forming bright dots on the CRT screen, which represent displayed characters.

The addresses of the characters to be successively displayed are called by the program as the CRT beam progresses. The time taken for the beam to reach any position on the screen is accurately known, so provided character information is released for spot brightness control purposes from the CG ROM at the correct moment by the Display RAM (which contains all the data for a current screen) all will be well.

Microcomputers are often designed to display 24 rows of 80 characters per row - a total of 1920 characters - built up by a pattern of dots formed line by line as the beam traverses. To be easily readable a character requires to be about 9 dots high - that is 9 scanning lines are required - and 7 dots wide. "G", "H" and "E" formed in this manner would appear as in Fig. 18.9.

There has to be a space between characters and a two-line space between each row requiring a total number of 8 x 11 = 88 dots per character. A screenful of 1920 characters therefore requires over 169,000 controllable dots.

Since a "page" of characters has to be displayed for as long as the viewer needs it, about 170 Kbits of storage with associated control circuits would apparently be required just for this purpose, quite apart from extra memory for dot patterns representing each character. Various techniques are used to reduce this

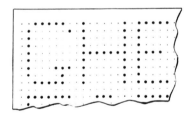

FIGURE 18.9
BRIGHT-DOT CHARACTER DISPLAY

complexity. The most popular works by scanning out permanently stored dot patterns which form characters. An 8K Display RAM is provided to receive and temporarily store, in the form of 7 bit ASCII code, as many characters received from the keyboard as may be needed up to a screenful, together with data about cursor co-ordinates, to determine where each character is to be positioned.

The CRT beam is initially cut-off so several lines may be traced by the spot with the screen remaining black. Eventually the moment comes for a line to be scanned which will carry some bright blobs representing the top strip of the first row of characters. Say there are just three characters in the first row - G,H,E, as in Figure 18.9.

The program calls the address in Display RAM where data about the first character is stored. The data is ASCII code for G - in other words the address of the matrix representing G in the CG ROM. The dot pattern for the top of the G - five dots - is clocked out from the CG ROM to the CRT beam as fast successive switch-on pulses.

The beam then cuts-off for a time interval corresponding to two spot-clocked intervals for inter-character spacing, and then the second character matrix, H, in display RAM is addressed. One switch-on pulse, five clocked off intervals, and then another switch-on pulse are clocked out from the H matrix in CG ROM, forming the top of the H as two spaced bright blobs.

The beam continues, having switched on for very short intervals to produce a succession of bright spots, until the scan line is complete, flies back, and starts on the next line. The same sequence occurs to produce the next strip of blobs for the same characters with the next scanning line and so on. After nine lines (See Figure 18.9) the characters are complete.

All that is present on the screen at any instant when the beam is on is a single spot which stays there for 50 nanoseconds or less. To produce an image which is visible to the eye the whole screen is scanned usually 50 (UK) or 60 (US) time per second. The blob pattern is continuously overlaid so the tube phosphor glows continuously at each point where the beam is switched on to form rows of visible characters.

Keyboard functions

In capacity-actuated keyboards each key operates a variable capacitor, and all capacitors are arranged in a matrix. The rows and columns of the matrix are continuously scanned and counted. When, say, the "H" key is depressed, the capacitance change at the row/column intersection is detected by the scanner and the row and column counters "note" that a change has occurred at the point "H". The same principle is used in other types of keyboard.

The scanner/counter is connected to a small ROM in which is permanently stored the ASCII code for each character. In this case the code for H is extracted and moved into a register ready for transmission. Information about the position required for the character on the display is derived from cursor movement. The cursor, displayed as a bright blob, is stepped along each time a key is depressed or may be placed anywhere on the screen by using special "arrowed" keys to indicate direction.

Cursor positioning keys control up-down counters which provide coordinate information for positioning the cursor. If the H is required to be the second character in the third row, and the cursor is placed in that position, keying H will cause it to appear in the same position as the cursor.

Memories and memory chips

The development of semiconductor memories is discussed in Chapter 2.

Non-volatile **Read Only Memory (ROM),** has data permanently written into it which does not disappear when the power is switched off. The data is usually supplied in the ROM with the machine. This ROM is used for programs needed to be routinely and repeatedly called into operation - for example to load data from disk into memory when the machine is switched on and **"Booted"**.

Such a program is "hard-wired" into the ROM chip at the design stage. Upon receipt of a triggering impulse a series of inter-connected circuits generate a sequence of impulses representing the program code.

ROMs are divisible into three classes according to programming - those programmed irreversibly by the manufacturer (Masked ROMs), those programmable once irreversibly by the user (PROMs), and those which can be erased and re-programmed by the user (EPROMs). "Black Boxes" are commercially available for programming or erasure. The PROM or EPROM is plugged into the box which is connected to a computer by a cable plugging into a standard RS232 port (socket on the machine for peripheral devices).

A **Programmable Read Only Memory (PROM)** chip contains a number of fuseable links interconnecting a large number of possible circuit arrangements. The links are individually addressable. To implant a permanent program, the "fuses" can be selectively blown leaving a permanent particular kind of circuit arrangement, and so a "hard wired" program.

In **Erasable PROMs (EPROMs)** the "fuses" are replaced by electrical charges positioned to block or unblock addressable gates. Gates can be blocked or unblocked in order to arrange the circuit network as required. All the charges can be removed (making the device ready to receive a different program) by the energy contained in ultraviolet light.

A window is left in the chip for exposing it to UV light for erasing purposes. A major function of ROMs and PROMs is to retain program instructions and control data when the microcomputer is switched off, ready for use when power is again applied.

Volatile read-and-write RAM (**Dynamic** RAM or DRAM) is used in the main memory for storing programs and data which continually change as the microcomputer carries out its tasks. The contents of the memory disappear when the equipment is switched off.

Its contents also disappear relatively slowly even when power is applied, rather like the slow discharge of a voltage stored in a capacitor. To combat this, the memory is automatically **Refreshed** by the periodic scanning and reinforcement of whichever state the memory cells may be in - that is they are either "on" or "off". In the early eighties access times were around 300 ns. Today this has decreased to less than 50 ns in some chips.

Alternatively **Static** RAM storage elements may be used consisting, for instance, of a flip-flop which stores a 0 or a 1, according to the state to which it is switched, for as long as the supply voltage is switched on. SRAMs do not require refreshing periodically - the stored data endures. They are relatively expensive. SRAM access times have decreased to 35 ns (average) with the fastest down to below 10 ns.

Developments in memories have been towards increasing the number of elements per chip from around 4K capacity to 16, 32, 64, 256, 512K , up to 1 or 4 Mbytes, and 16 Mbytes in the near future, each occupying less space and costing less per bit than its predecessor.

It now costs about $2 per K of dynamic RAM memory when purchasing up to 128K on a ready to use memory board, and about $1 per K to plug in extra chips into the empty sockets provided on the board for expansion. Memory access times have been substantially reduced - a small bipolar RAM can be accessed in about 40 ns.

If the memory forms part of a microcomputer it will be controlled by the CPU. Signals on the Chip Select/enable (CS) lines and Read/Write (R/W) lines consist of a change of voltage to a high or low value for a specific period of time. A typical memory cycle starts with CS going low enabling the memory to be written or read. For large memories CS may activate a specified part of the memory only. The address of a wanted data byte is then output to the address bus from the CPU as the column and row number of the required storage location.

This is followed by one byte of data being written to or read from the location on to the data bus as controlled by the CPU. Finally CS goes high, ending the cycle, and only then can another cycle be initiated.

Semiconductor memory used to come as "1K" per chip - that is with a capacity of 2^{10} = 1024 bytes, but "16K" (16,384 byte) chips were soon developed. Beyond that, new problems were encountered in manufacturing the extremely small transistor cells required.

In 1980 three manufacturers were producing 64K chips in quantity but at a higher price per bit compared with 16K chips. 256K RAMs were introduced by the Japanese experimentally in 1980 with 100 nanosecond access times and connections about 1 micrometer wide. One Japanese company even produced a 1Mbit chip with only about twice the physical size of a 64K. Current advances up to 16 Mbyte chips are described in Chapter 2.

Memory management: expanded and extended memory and protected mode

As soon as you consider the "80" series of processors - and that means IBM PCs, which means the DOS operating systems, which means Microsoft - you cannot avoid considering memory management. If you are a user, who quite rightly doesn't want to know about the details, memory limitations unfortunately impose themselves upon you. To assess these limitations it helps to have some knowledge about the basics.

64 Kbytes of memory sufficed for the CP/M operating system with 8080 or Z80 processors. But "better", more comprehensive software with more "features", able to deal with an even wider range of faster applications requires more semiconductor memory.

The DOS operating system, described in the next chapter, was designed to work with 8088 or 8068 16 bit processors as used on the IBM PC. These processors could handle "1 Mbyte" (actually 2^{20} = 1.0486 Mbytes) of memory which was allocated as 640K for application programmes, 128K for display purposes, 192K various, and 64K for boot and other input/output codes. The 640K reserved for applications was thought to be enormous at the time of introduction.

16 bit processors can address memory with 20 bit addresses by juggling about with registers to add an "address offset" to 16 bits in order to provide the necessary 20 bits.

462

Lotus/Intel introduced their Expanded Memory System, known as LIM/EMS or EMS, in 1985. Version 4.0 enables you to plug in up to 8 Mbytes of memory on a board, and use that memory for applications with DOS by swapping programs stored there in and out of the main 640K area (McAuliffe, 1990. Raja, 1990).

The arrival of the 80286 processor enables 16 Mbytes to be directly addressed with a virtual address space of 1 Gbyte (= 1000 Mbytes). The 80386 provides for 4 Gbytes of direct addressing, and 10 Tbytes (= 10M Mbytes) of virtual.

DOS is still restricted to addressing 1 Mbyte - an address specifies a position in physical memory. To deal with these huge memory increases a technique called virtual addressing has been introduced. Virtual addressing enables segments (variable length blocks) to be moved within RAM, extended RAM, or swapped in and out of disc (**"Virtual Memory"**).

Virtual memory is a memory management system enabling programs to be executed which reside only partially in main memory, and whose size is limited only by the addressing capability of the processor. Systems of this kind are fully explained by Milenkovic (1990).

The addresses and other information about segments are stored as segment descriptors called selectors in an index. The selectors listing all the segments in an application remain the same, but the corresponding segment addresses change as the segments are moved about. This index is the means by which required segments are shifted into memory addressable by DOS. Extended addressing is a major function of Protected Mode, as this process is called.

The reason for its name is that several other functions to do with the protection of system resources and the watertight separation of processes is inherent in the system via a hierarchy of privilege and protection arrangements.

Faster processors working with longer words accessing large amounts of memory are a necessary resource to deal with multitasking user programmes of ever increasing complexity.

Mouse

The mouse was invented by Douglas Engelbart, working at Stanford University in 1963. It was developed from an analogue into a digital device by the Xerox PARC staff and became widely used with IBM PCs and Apple Mac machines following software support introduced by Microsoft. According to Alford (1990) over five million mice were sold in 1989.

A mouse is a small container hand-held by the user against a flat surface such a desk. The edge of a ball projects slightly from its under surface and the ball can rotate in any direction as the user slides the mouse about. A cursor/pointer on the screen follows its motion so the user can watch the screen and quickly move the mouse so that it points at any displayed object.

A major purpose of a mouse is to enable the user to execute a function by pointing it at a displayed item - for instance an ikon (pictorial object), or one out of a number of choices displayed on a menu - symbolising the function, and pressing a button situated on the top of the mouse. This eliminates the need to memorise and type a command line to execute the function.

A mouse contains a mechanism for separating the ball's motion into horizontal and vertical components, for example by arranging two rollers at right angles bearing against it. Rotational movement is digitized by passing a current through a contact which slides over conductive points arranged round the circumference of a disc attached to the rollers, or by detecting the interruptions in a beam of light shining through holes round the disc.

The **resolution** of a mouse is the number of small steps made by the cursor per inch of mechanical motion. It is usually between 200 and 400 steps per inch. Some mice include a refinement called **ballistic tracking** where the resolution is inversely proportional to the speed of motion. When the mouse is moved rapidly the cursor moves rapidly in large steps, but as the user slows down to home in to an object the cursor's steps become smaller.

Pipelining

Pipelining is a technique used to avoid the bottleneck when a computer handles data as a process-by-process procedure - that is when each process must be completed before the unit starts on a new process. With pipelining the steps in a process are handled by different units; when a unit has completed a step, the next step may be carried out by another unit, freeing the first unit to start a new process.

Given several units and appropriate arrangements for controlling processes handled piecemeal in this fashion, each process will be completed in a shorter time and in fewer machine cycles. Pipelining requires that data is available from memory at the necessary rate, so it is often associated with Cache memories (See Chapter 3).

RISC technology

During the last few years, many microprocessors and microcomputers have embodied certain techniques collectively referred to as **RISC (Reduced Instruction Set Computer)** originated at the University of California at Berkeley in the seventies. RISC represents a fairly considerable change from the "pre-RISC" CPU. RISC was briefly discussed in Chapter 2. Some operational details are added here.

Formerly, instruction sets provided a comprehensive set of instructions; each instruction word triggered a small ROM stored microcode program which could take many machine cycles to execute - hence the title of this system - Complex Instruction Set Computer (CISC). At least 20 cycles could be taken just to load a register and 100 or more to do simple arithmetic. When memories were slow there was not much incentive for speed improvements.

IBM did some experimental work in the early eighties and used a RISC chip in a workstation introduced in 1986. Hewlett-Packard also took up this technology in 1986 in its 3000 series in which the instruction set was reduced from the normal 300 or more instructions, to 140 shorter instructions. Inmos was an early adopter of RISC with only 70 instructions for its transputer processor. For further information about RISC semiconductor developments see Chapter 2.

RISC techniques using small instruction sets, imply more, faster, register-to-register operations, and fewer register-to-memory operations, consequently it makes sense to separate and optimise the transmission paths for these two kinds of transaction (Allison 1988). For example the average number of machine cycles needed to complete an instruction for the Motorola 68010 is 12. With RISC ideas as implemented on the 68030, sometimes referred to as "streamlining", an average of only 5.5 cycles are needed.

In April 1989 Intel announced the 80860 RISC chip with several new features enabling it to complete an instruction in one machine cycle. Sheer speed is often a major requirement whether or not RISC is used; in the 860 most of the units associated with the processor are on the same chip so circuit path lengths are minimised. The 80860 is physically relatively large but it contains well over one million transistors; it is a 64 bit chip, but some data are moved round internally as 128 bit words at a rate exceeding one billion bps.

The 80860 uses parallel processing – it contains three separate mathematical sections which can work at the same time on integer maths, floating point addition, and floating point multiplication. With the aid of pipelining (described above) each maths section can produce a result once per machine cycle, so when operating at 40 MHz (it will run at up to 50 MHz), these sections can theoretically generate 120 million results per second. In order to feed data into the system for results to be generated at this rate, on-chip cache memories are provided.

Small Computer Systems Interface (SCSI)

This fast parallel flexible interface is a semi-standardised input/output bus for compatible computer to peripheral connection. It is described in chapter 4.

Wait-states

A wait-state is a non-operational clock period. One reason for a wait state in a microcomputer is that processor speeds exceed memory access speeds and the processor waits for one or more clock cycles until the memory has been read.

RAM access speeds have not kept pace with microprocessors. In practice the speed of access of RAM would have had to have been as shown in Table 18.4 at the time a microprocessor, also shown below, became available, for there to be no wait states. In fact the "no wait state" condition was rarely achieved until very recently.

Processor	Speed (MHzu	Required access (ns) for no wait-states
Z80	4	200
8088	5	450
80286	8	120
	12	80
80386	16	60
	25	40
80486	33	30

TABLE 18.4. MICROPROCESSOR/MEMORY WAIT-STATES

MICROCOMPUTER SPEEDS AND BENCHMARKS

There are endless discussions about measuring the speed and "power" of microcomputers. Although the speed of a machine in a particular application depends on a number of other factors as well, fast hardware is an important basis for the fast completion of a job.

The table shows the bit-widths of the internal and external busses, and the rounded-off clocking frequencies and repetition rates of some popular processors, together with some of the machines which use them.

Processor	Bus bit-width Int/ext	Usual Frequency = (MHz)	Repetition Rate (Nanosecs.)	Microcomputers
Z80	8/8	2	500	
8080	8/8	2	500	
8088	16/8	5	200	IBM PC, PC/XT
8086	16/16	5 - 8	200 - 125	IBM PS/2 Model 30
68000	24/16	8	125	Apple Macintosh, Mac SE
80286	16/16	6 - 10	166 - 100	IBM PC/AT, PS/2 50 & 60
68020	32/16	16	62.5	Mac II
80386	32/32	16	62.5	IBM PS/2 80, Kaypro 386, Compaq Deskpro 386, Apricotv XEN-i 386
80386	32/32	20	50.0	Compaq Deskpro 386/20
80486	32/32	33	30.0	AST Premium

TABLE 18.5. MICROCOMPUTER SPEEDS

The wider the internal bus the more quickly can the processor exchange data between its different units - fast handling by the Arithmetic Logic Unit (ALU), for example, is important in mathematical operations. The external bus width is arguably more important because not only is it the main data highway between the major parts of the machine, but its width also determines the different number of memory storage locations that can be directly addressed.

Thus 8, 16, and 32 bits enable stores of 2^8, 2^{16}, and 2^{32} bytes, that is 256, 65.5K (usually rounded to"64K"), and 4.3 Gbytes (thousands of megabytes) to be controlled, assuming 1 byte of data per location. In 8 bit machines 16 bits formed from two successive 8 bit bytes are usually used to address a 64K memory.

The "Repetition rate" column in the table simply shows the time interval between clock pulses coming from the processor's clocking oscillator. It is easy to remember that 1 Mhz = 1 million pulses per second = 1 pulse every microsecond, so 4 Mhz = 1/4 microsecond = 250 ns pulses, etc. Each time a clock pulse is generated numerous different circuits in the machine are switched synchronously to execute some function.

The basic speed concepts for a bus are simple - a bus, or data transfer channel, which can handle 16 bits simultaneously at a rate of 4 MHz - that is 16 bits every quarter millionth of a second or every 250 nanoseconds - is handling twice as much data, twice as quickly, as an 8 bit

2 MHz (500 ns) bus. All other things being equal, machines near the bottom of the table will be the most "powerful", and machines with the same buses and processor frequencies will be equally powerful.

In practice all things are not equal. It may take several clock cycles for an instruction to be completed and executed. For example many of the instructions used by a 68000 processor take from 7 to 11 cycles to be completed. The performance of machines with the same bus widths and clock speeds is affected by whatever other speed-inducing methods are added by designers - and new ideas proliferate.

The following facilities affect speeds:-

RISC architecture reduces the number of cycles per instruction and reduces the need for memory accesses since some instructions can be executed by register to register communication only. IBM introduced a machine in January 1986 called the RT PC incorporating its own RISC processor. In 1987 Acorn announced the Archimedes machine using its own 32 bit chip with RISC. Acorn claims that the machine outperforms the Compaq 386 in benchmark (see below) tests.

Wait-states - caused, for example, by the processor having to wait for a slower memory - are non-operational clock periods. Thus the IBM PS/2 Model 50 which uses an 80286 processor operating at 10 MHz - a 100ns clock - adds one wait-state to both memory access and Input/Output (I/O) operations. A memory access in the Model 50 takes two clock periods plus one wait-state, or 300 ns.

Cache memories controlled by software designed to access whatever data is most likely to be needed next and to fetch it from main memory into cache. The objective is to obtain a high "hit ratio" - i.e. to make as many accesses to cache and as few to main memory as possible. Small caches have access times as fast as 20 ns.

Pipelining - the overlapping of operations normally taking place at different times, or even the simultaneous occurrence of operations otherwise occurring in successive clock cycles.

Static Random Access Memories (RAMs), unlike dynamic RAMs which are widely used for memories, do not require refreshing periodically - the stored data endures. They are expensive but the latest static RAMs have access times below 10 ns.

Co-processors, which may be equal in power to the main processor (CPU), and are effectively small computers in their own right.

Memory Size. Continually falling prices encourage the trend to provide large memories providing more space for large files such as image files with consequently fewer disk accesses.

Disc Drive Interface. There is a degree of standardisation in disc drive interfaces, type ST506 being the slowest, then SCSI, ESDI, and SMD which is the fastest.

Data Transfer Method. Disc controllers may work 1 byte at a time, a method used with the IBM PC, or Direct Memory Access (DMA) (discussed earlier) may be used. Differences between the way memory is handled by the processor will affect large files particularly. For example the 8088 and 80286 processors deal with memory in 64K segments which makes graphics handling awkward but the 68000 series of processors treat memory as a large linear address space.

Machines which embody a fast processor and incorporate several of these techniques will be faster. Thus the **PCs Limited 386** machine uses the 80386 but also embodies a pre-fetch cache which holds the next instructions, arranges for memory to be accessed and instructions to be executed at the same time, and embodies no wait-state no-refresh fast static RAM. Consequently its supplier claims that it out-performs the Compaq and Kaypro 386 machines.

As can be seen from Table 18.6 a variety of benchmarks have been devised in an attempt to establish standards so that various aspects of the performance of machines can be compared. Since the figure generated by most benchmarks is "time to complete the test", the smaller the figure, the better. However for Dhrystones, MIPs, MFLOPS, and Whetstones the figure given is for the amount of work done per second, so the **larger** the figure the better.

If the same benchmark is used to test two machines but the language used and compiler optimisation is different, as it often necessarily must be, then the tests are not identical and the results will be affected. (A compiler is a program which translates a higher-level language, designed for programming convenience, into the code which actually runs the machine).

MIPS has been used for a long time although it is a rough and ready indicator. Instructions may be long or short and may take up one or many clock periods. As some measure of the rate of progress the IBM PC (1981) rated about 0.5 MIPS, the PC/AT (1984) 1.2, Apple Mac (1984) 1.5, 80386 (16 Mhz) processor 4.

A further weakness of mips arises because the complexity of a CISC instruction varies, so mips varies according to the instructions used in a particular application. A RISC instruction is hardly comparable with a CISC instruction, so again a mips comparison between RISC and CISC machines is un-likely to be helpful. Several of the benchmarks in the table have been devised by computer magazines for providing on-going comparisons on the same basis when reviewing new machines.

BF CALC	Basic performance test. Multiply 10,000 and divide 10,000 prime numbers
BF SIEVE	Basic performance test: "Sieve of Eratosthenes" test to find 1899 prime numbers
DHRYSTONES/ SEC.	General purpose test of system-programming non-numeric performance of processors in medium size and small machines
DA READ	Disk Access. Read 64K sequential file
DA WRITE	Disk Access. Write 64K sequential file
FIBONACCI	Compute first 24 numbers in a specified sequence. Iterate 100 times
FILE COP	Copy a 40K disk file from one hard disk location to another
FLOAT	10,000 repeats of 14 double-precision multiplication and division
GRAFSCRN	Repeat specified pixel plot 100 times
INTMATH	Repeat specified calculation 1000 times
LINPACK	Linear Algebra Software Library (for large machines)
LIV LOOP	Livermore National Laboratory scalar and vector floating point performance measurement (for large machines)
MFLOPS	Million Floating Point calculations per Second. Not a benchmark but a "unit of measurement" used in benchmarking
MIPS	Million Processor Instructions per Second. (Misleading). Not a benchmark but a "unit of performance" used in benchmarking
SAVAGE	Floating point test. 25,000 iterations of nested sequence of trigonometric functions
SIEVE	See BF SIEVE
SORT	Perform "Quicksort" algorithm 100 times on array of 1000 long integers
SS LOAD	Load 100 row 25 column spreadsheet with specified cell values
SS RECALC	Recalculate the values in the SS LOAD spreadsheet
STORE	Write a specified record to disk 1000 times.
TEXTSCRN	Write specified characters 1000 times
WHETSTONES/ SEC.	Basic arithmetic test for medium size and small machines. Used for testing CPU's with Floating Point Processor Units (FPUs)

TABLE 18.6. EXAMPLES OF BENCHMARKS

Use of benchmarks

If a "large machine" benchmark was to be used to show how small computers compare with large ones, the IBM RT and the Sun workstation (one of the most powerful available) work at about 0.1 MFLOPS when Linpack tested, a DEC8700 at 0.9, CDC 875 at 4, IBM 3090-200 at 11 and a Cray XMP4 at 40.

The benchmarks most suitable for assessing performance for page formatting and graphic file applications, such as in Desktop Publishing, are likely to be Dhrystones/sec, Textscrn, Grafscrn, Store, and Disk Access. Table 18.7 shows a list of machines in Dhrystone order. More than one value in the same column indicates different figures obtained from different sources.

The unsatisfactory situation for benchmarking larger machines was highlighted at the beginning of 1989 in a dispute between IBM and DEC in connection with transaction processing machines and software. IBM uses its own benchmark Ramp-C, details of which have not been published.

IBM and DEC differed in their assessment of debit/credit transactions measured on the IBM 9377/90 machine by a factor of three times. This has prompted critical comments to the effect that benchmarking needs serious attention if companies of this standing cannot obtain results in reasonable agreement.

	Dhrystones per sec		Textscrn	Grafscrn	DA read	DA write
IBM PC	400		60	30	54	30
Mac SE	574					
PC/AT (8 MHz) + 80287 FPU	1748	1590				
PC/AT (8 MHz) + DSI 780	1748.9		25.4		9.3	14.0
Mac II + 68881 FPU	2083	2106			6.3	15
Mac SE + Hypercharger	2114	2176				
Mac SE + Prodigy	2380					
Kaypro 386	3271				4.9	7.3
PS/2 Model 80 + 80387 FPU	3125	3626				
Compaq 386 + 80287 FPU	3707	3748	25.5	4.8	4.8	7.2
Acorn Archimedes	4901		4.2	6.3		

TABLE 18.7 SELECTED MICROCOMPUTERS RANKED BY THE DHRYSTONE BENCHMARK

MICROCOMPUTER CHOICE AND AVOIDING DISASTERS

Choice

These remarks apply to microcomputers for business and possibly home use when considering file management, information storage and retrieval and text processing but not to more specialised applications such as "number crunching", process control, robotics, etc.

Microcomputers suitable for office use cost from about £500 or $500 upwards, but at this price the size of the memory and disk storage would be rather small. You can narrow down the choice simply by eliminating those machines above your price range and those which have a performance which is either superior (on paper) or inferior to your requirements.

This assumes that you know enough about micros to know what to look for in the manufacturer's blurb. If you don't, there are lots of books for beginners available in most bookshops. Weekly and monthly magazines abound and some have unbiased reviews and lists of machines with performance and price data in them - for example Which Computer and Personal Computer World in the UK and Byte in the US. Some list the machine reviews which appeared in earlier issues and will provide reprints.

When searching a UK magazine recently I found I could buy Apples all over the place - from Claisse-Allen at £8,000, Parr Computer Services at £4,000, and Action Computers at £2,000. Parr offer 9 application packages - the maximum number which where inclusively listed by any supplier. Obviously once a feel for the type of computer, the peripherals, and the software have been established, quotes should be obtained for the identical combination from several suppliers.

Best of all get comments from everybody you know who uses a computer.

Maintenance

If you've chosen a machine and programs which do the job well you may become more and more dependent upon them, so a breakdown will become more and more of a nuisance or even a disaster. A good, fast, maintenance service is important. Find out from others what maintenance organisation they use.

A good maintenance agreement is expensive - it may cost up to 12.5% of the machine's purchase price per year. Alternatively, are you prepared to find out enough to be able to diagnose the area in which a fault probably lies and do repairs at least on a "plug in a new board and try it" basis (if the form of construction permits it)? Is it worth buying a spare set of plug in circuit boards for this purpose? Find out the cost of spares and consider the idea.

Unfortunately this approach will not identify a software fault - for example a bug which does not appear until you use the combination of processes which are affected by it.

Alternatively, is the acquisition of enough knowledge to identify faults of any kind the right use of your time? Some people like being "handymen/women", others prefer to pay someone else to do it, particularly if they, personally, don't have to pay!

If you use floppy disks buy the best. Use long life disks for heavy use and cheap ones for copies kept as insurance. The latter may only get used twice. Wear and dirt are the enemies. The cost of a good disk easily outweighs the agro and cost of time wasted in only one "incident".

On the acquisition of knowledge

Although 60% of a sample of people in Britain over 14, when asked by Gallup back in 1983 whether they understood the words "software" and "micro" said "never heard of them", the business community can hardly escape them. The well cultivated "progressive" Information Technology image makes us feel inefficient, or even fossilised, if we do not adopt it.

The UK Sunday Times "Living with the Computer" supplement dated May 13th 1984 contained an article headed "Instant information: tidy, efficient, paper-free", which is typical of thousands of articles still being published.

Surely small and medium size businesses should be able to find something to match their requirements from an enormous choice of hardware and software packages, and rejoice in the benefits? The answer may well be yes, but to get to the operational stage, time must be spent absorbing new knowledge for a two-stage process - purchasing and using. But there is a chicken and egg problem.

In order to ask the right questions at the time of purchase, knowledge which can best be gained from experience following hands-on operation is needed. You can ask people who you think may have the required knowledge and experience before buying, but beware of computer buffs disguised as bona fide users.

These people love messing about with computers regardless of time. Their attitude towards doing anything useful is beside the point. Fiddling with the thing is an end in itself. They will never admit to having had learning problems or unreliable equipment. Their job is to purvey the mystique using a language designed to conceal. Don't listen. To them, experimentation and achievement is rewarding fun, and time rushes by. For you, fiddling about time will soon exhaust your budget and ruin your schedule.

Purchasing policy

Buying and installing a system needs sufficient knowledge both about the job to be done **and** computers to be able to ask the right questions about hardware/software performance, operating systems, etc., and assess the value for money of suitable offerings.

When you buy a car, vendors will be pleased to take you for a trial run. There used not be any way you can take a comparable trial run on your computer. You require suitable software, an appropriate volume of on-board data resembling your own, and your accumulated expertise in order to try out some typical tasks.

In the absence of such a test you will have to assess the suitability of the software available; it may need modifying. You will also need to consider reliability, the storage requirements, backup, and maintenance arrangements, and the probability that the vendor will be in business next year.

You may require communications (Note. All communications are a hassle). Having purchased the system you will have to learn how to get everything to work, polish up your perception of the strengths and weaknesses of paper-based and machine-based systems, understand computer file organisation, and organise work methods combining paper and machine based data.

But note the words three paragraphs ago "there used not to be....". In 1990, competition is fiercer than ever and vendors want orders. You may be able to get everything you need on a 14 days sale or return basis. I did. The penalty you pay is your time in testing. But you may find out about a problem which was almost impossible to anticipate. The success of this approach depends on whether you know enough to conduct tests rapidly.

There are three aspects which I have found particularly important when attempting to help people with computer problems. They do not usually receive much attention in "proceed carefully" or "which one to buy" publications.

Firstly, try and get a software package ("application program") which is known to work well on the chosen machine and which will do your job, or most of it, without modification. The intensely competitive software market brings with it "bells and whistles" salesmanship. 50 "features" look better than 25 in advertisements, but are the extra 25 any use to you?

Have a good look at the Instruction Manual before purchasing. A good manual is worth its weight in gold and it's well worth spending some time in examining it. A good, easily understandable, manual is an exception. Does the vendor offer a telephone help line for both hardware and software problem queries for at least six months after purchase?

Don't ask someone to write a new software package if it can be avoided. Some people possess one kind of occupational knowledge (e.g. Accountants, Librarians, Chemists, etc.). Others (computer software writers) have another kind. These two groups find it very hard to communicate. For a chemist it is a great advantage to go to a computer person who knows some chemistry - each can then understand the other's jargon.

If you must get a package modified or get a new one written, go to someone with a verifiable track record for software for your kind of application. It won't be cheap. Negotiate a satisfactory arrangement inclusive of "complete" (an unsatisfactory word, but I cannot think of a better one) documentation including an instruction manual, ideally with enough leeway to add a bonus for adherence to delivery date.

Try and get all the details down in writing and avoid changing your mind later (it may give rise to unquoted cost-uncontrolled modifications).

The designer may later become "unavailable" for any one of a number of reasons and if after delivery something doesn't work properly, or if a modification is later required, it's unhelpful if all the relevant information resides only in the designer's head.

Take every precaution against getting into a situation where the software, almost complete, requires an unforseen change and you have to decide whether to put good money after what may already be bad money. Never have there been so many "software experts" about. Modifying someone else's software is often very difficult; if good documentation does not exist it may be well-nigh impossible.

The current situation regarding operating systems, and the computers on which they will run needs some homework. An operating system is software which manages machine functions and allocates the resources of the machine for the job to be done by the application program (the one which does your specific job).

472

Operating systems and machine size

The most likely choice will be between MS-DOS, Unix, and Apple with its integrated software. These systems are discussed in the next chapter. An application program will be written to run in conjunction with a designated operating system, but there may be versions for different operating systems. The benefit of the application - operating system "co-operation" is that application program writers, knowing that the "housekeeping" will be taken care of by the operating system, can concentrate on the job in hand without needing to spend time on housekeeping.

You will need to acquire two kinds of knowledge - about the application software and about the operating system. Operating system commands are used for general organisation. In systems with good graphic user-interfaces.

A 64K memory, once considered large, is now virtually useless, so is a system with a floppy disk drive of less than 500 Kbytes. A 640K memory for MSDOS machines and a 1.4 Mbyte floppy must be reckoned as the minimum. Provision for more plug-in memory, a hard disk of 20 Mbytes or more, and several within-machine sockets for cards, are desirable.

Information retrieval applications

One particular aspect requires special attention in information retrieval applications. Information storage and retrieval can bring great benefits (regardless of occupational specialty) in small/medium sized offices - the biggest market for microcomputers. This aspect really has two parts - adjusting your ingrained paper-based information habits to cope with machine files, and a re-consideration of indexing principles.

Nobody has yet succeeded in designing computer software which follows the curious ways in which paperwork is shuffled about and the way people interact, decisions are made, and office work gets done. This system has evolved over many years and somehow creaks along.

A computer-based small-office system on the other hand - let us say a combination of file management, personnel and customer record storage and processing, word processing, information retrieval, accounting and invoicing - is an exercise in systematic formality. It forces concentration upon and changes in working methods which can be beneficial in themselves. It takes some time to re-organise, face up to ways of combining paper and machine-based operations, and appreciate how to make the most of new possibilities.

Unless a particular procedure out of the many provided in a software package is used regularly its complication may require it to be learnt all over again when it is next used. For instance, try remembering the significance of the way you set up a "spreadsheet" financial model (e.g. Visicalc) when you want to use it again with some different figures after an interval of a few weeks.

Notes in your own words and your own list of most frequently used commands are almost essential. Many packages contain all kinds of "interesting time-saving procedures". Never experiment unless you are a computer buff and time is no object. Learn only the procedures for which the payoff is predictably beneficial.

For information retrieval rudimentary indexing may suffice for some office paperwork. Other papers - for example reports - may require as much attention as scientific articles. Many clues are available about the contents of papers. Visible shelves, drawers, the colour of covers, and even strategically placed piles all help.

Few office software people have heard of Indexing. It is a boring overhead which is never listed among the "features" in glossy software leaflets. Tangible clues are lost when information is electrically stored. Good indexing becomes essential in personal information systems, but vital in central filing systems to avoid the unacceptable penalty of many people's idiosyncratic indexing.

Indexing in offices is rarely considered to be a professional activity. It is usually someone's incidental chore - a notion which must be changed unless the office is very small.

References.

The references for this chapter are combined with those for Chapter 19 and will be found at the end of that chapter.

CHAPTER 19. MICROCOMPUTER SYSTEMS PART 2: SOFTWARE.

Operating system functions

An operating system enables housekeeping jobs to be executed, usually in conjunction with an application program. An example of a job is the printing of a line of type; to print a line, data must be transmitted from a specified address in storage, at a specified rate through a specified port to the printer until the line is complete.

An operating system is a set of programs stored as named files. Programs are loaded as needed into memory from disc. The operating system disc is kept in the drive. In micros with hard disc drives the operating system will probably be loaded initially via the micro's floppy disc drive into the hard disc where it will be permanently stored and called into memory as needed; the floppy disc is removed after loading.

If a microcomputer user possesses a machine with a "standard" operating system, the probability of finding a program for the application in hand which will work is greatly increased. The operative words here are "standard" and "which will work".

There are no actual standards but certain operating systems are in widespread use - as **de facto** standards. A machine capable of running on one or more operating systems should also be capable of running on the application programs supported by those operating systems provided that the version of the machine which is available embodies the right hardware.

Every operating system supports one or more popular high level languages - meaning that the operating system and a program written in that language can be used together. To use a program supplied on a disc in the language, or to write a program in it, Compiler or Interpreter (see Glossary) programs for the language must also be available on disc and be called into memory so that the machine can execute data in machine language. Thus a program in the language can be stored on disc in a named file which can be manipulated by the operating system and executed, provided the Compiler or Interpreter programs have been loaded.

Microcomputers were once only able to be used by one person at a time, but many are now available using time-sharing - an arrangement by which it appears to each person that he or she has almost independent and unrestricted use of the machine.

Most operating systems were designed to run on a particular CPU. Often, modified versions were designed later for other CPUs or to accommodate the change from 8 bit to 16 bit words in the same CPU family. This became particularly important when microcomputer disc systems came into widespread use and a number of them embody the words Disc Operating System (DOS) into their name for that reason. An operating system is designed to respond to a user's requirements via a command language and much depends on the repertoire of commands which can be displayed on the screen and executed. Commands are usually self-evident words e.g. "CREATE".

Alternatively commands may be symbolised by ikons so that a user does not need to know sets of symbols but can simply select an ikon.

To an operating system almost everything is a "file". That means that a file is not only a set of your records or your text stored on disc - it is an entity which can be manipulated via the operating system. A file may also be a software routine to control some part of the system - for example an "output file" which is a program for managing the display of characters on a CRT, or for managing a printer.

An operating system command (OSC) may often itself be a file because when the command is typed a small program must be called up in readiness to handle any of a number of symbols expected to be typed to follow the command. OSC's are words like COPY (copy contents of one named file to another named file) or FILES (display a directory of the names of the files in storage). Other commands are available for the use of a person who may wish to change the software, for example EXEC (execute code at a named address).

As an example of the functioning of an operating system, say you want to write a short program in the assembly language of the machine. After booting (starting up and loading software automatically) the machine, a "*" appears meaning "ready to accept a typed OSC".

The appearance of the "*" also implies that a file has already been called up - namely the keyboard, (an input file) so the machine is ready to accept data from that source. Another file will also have been called up automatically as well - the display output file - in order that typed characters will be displayed in the right places on the screen.

When CREATE is typed the machine expects instructions in a certain order from the current input file - in this case the keyboard. The first expected item is the file name - let us call the file which will contain a new program "TRIAL". The disc directory is first searched for a file called CREATE containing the CREATE program, which already exists and is loaded into memory at an address specified in the file's heading.

At the same time instructions are sent to the CPU to arrange for the CREATE program to be in control. When the name TRIAL is typed, a special file on disc which contains data about available disc space, is called from disc into memory. This file is up-dated to show that space has been allocated for TRIAL at a particular address, and is then read back to disc.

The disc directory file is now called into memory, the data required to up-date the directory about TRIAL is added to it and it is then read back on to disc. The CREATE program is still in command and any data typed into TRIAL will be read on to that disc file. The machine will possess facilities to execute programs in the Assembly language of the particular CPU fitted.

Assuming a programmer now starts to write his or her program into the TRIAL file, the program will consist of line numbers for reference purposes followed by program source code on each line.

Upon completion of the program the operating system command ASSM is typed followed by the file name TRIAL. The assembler software is now loaded into memory and processes the source code to translate it into machine readable binary object code. When that is done the programmer can use another OSC - DEBUG which calls up a special program for debugging the code previously input on the TRIAL file.

As an example of the use of a simple program with the CP/M operating

system, following the prompt ">A" (indicating that drive A is in use), a
typed command "TYPE LISTC.MEM" would call up a command program named "TYPE"
and display the contents of a user's file called "LISTC.MEM". The "TYPE"
program, executed by typing "TYPE", is one of the many programs contained in
the operating system which will always be loaded into storage in response to
"TYPE", and will control the sequence of processes needed to call up a named
file and display it, line by line, on the screen.

Operating systems, word lengths, and addressing.

A "word" in an 8 bit device is a sequence of 8 bits, in a 16 bit
device, 16 bits etc. 8 bits = 2^8 and 16 = 2^{16} so 8 bits can represent 256
different numbers, and 16 bits 65536 (often called "64K") numbers.

Microcomputer word lengths started at 4 bits, then 8 bits became
widely adopted to be followed by 16, 32, and very recently 64. This has
become possible because improvements in technology, particularly in the
packing density of semiconductor elements, have enabled the extra complexity
needed to handle longer words to be introduced without proportional
increases in cost, space, or unreliability.

Longer word lengths are needed in order to be able to address each
cell of the larger memories which are now available in microcomputers. The
address word can be formed from smaller words - for example in 8 bit
microcomputers the 16 bit word needed to address the 65,536 locations of a
"64K" memory is composed of one 8 bit word for the 8 "lower order" bits and
a second 8 bit word for the 8 "higher order" bits. The 16 bits of the two
words are transmitted simultaneously along 16 lines to memory as if they
were one 16 bit word. A 32 bit word potentially can address over four
thousand million locations.

One advantage of machines working with longer words is that single
word addressing of larger memories becomes possible without the extra
complexity and cost of organising two or more words for the purpose. Larger
memories can accommodate more sophisticated programs and more of the user's
data which otherwise would have to be accommodated on disc which takes much
longer to access than semiconductor memory.

Another advantage is that data can be moved about in larger chunks.
If each 16 bit data word is moved around at the same speed as an 8 bit data
word, any task involving the movement of numbers of data words will be
completed in a shorter time, and if 32 bit words are used, in a still
shorter time. For example, a row of 32 pixels (picture elements)
representing black or white parts of an image will be processed in four
cycles by an 8 bit, 2 cycles by a 16 bit, and in one by a 32 bit machine -
i.e. four times faster by the latter.

In some computer system applications it may be necessary to allocate
a unique code to describe each item in a collection of n different items.
The shortest single code word to uniquely describe each item must contain 2^n
bits. Thus an 8 bit word can describe up to 256 items, 9 bits 512 items, 16
bits 65536 etc. Again there is an advantage if the word length is long
enough to describe each item in a large collection with one word.

The penalty to be paid is the cost of the extra bandwidth (for buses
this means more lines) needed to move longer words at the same speed as
shorter words, and of the additional circuits and storage. However

improvements in manufacturing techniques and rapid adoption on a big scale
enable these performance improvements to be incorporated into microcomputers
with the machine selling for less than the previous generation of machines
which it displaced.

The size of memory routinely fitted to most microcomputers is around
1.05 Mbytes, usually known as "1 Mbyte"". 16 bit processors such as the
Intel 8086 and 8088, Motorola 68000, and Zilog Z8001 and Z8002 have become
widely used. The realisation of the full potential of a microcomputer is
strongly dependent upon the operating system which manages the facilities
provided.

MSDOS was originally able to access a memory of 1 Mbyte maximum size
and could control up to 100 Mbytes of disc storage. Xenix could access 1
Mbyte of memory, and up to 230 Mbytes of disc. Motorola's Versados could
access 16 Mbytes and up to 192 Mbytes of disc. Versados and Xenix are
multi-user multi-task operating systems, while MSDOS is single user single
task.

When 16 bit systems were introduced there was nothing like the
volume of software available for 16 bit machines as there was for 8 bit.
Moreover the 16 bit software did not necessarily capitalise on all aspects
of 16 bit potential - much of it was developed at minimum cost from 8
bit.

But improvements in clock and cycle times soon reinforced the
benefits of 16 bit CPUs. Clock oscillators increased to 12 MHz, compared
with up to about 4 MHz for most 8-bit systems, providing cycle times of less
than 100 nanoseconds (0.1 microseconds or over 10 million cycles per second)
compared with 250 ns, in theory.

The arrival of 16 bits or more removed the 8 bit addressing
bottleneck, enabling many more stored items to be addressed. Semiconductor
memory and disc storage steadily became cheaper so that 125K, 256K, and
upwards directly addressable memories could be fitted at low cost. This
large memory enables effective multi-user and multi-task systems to be used.
One of the first new operating systems was Concurrent CP/M, capable of
running several jobs simultaneously, developed mainly in consequence of the
availability of larger useable memories.

The difference between 8 bit and 16 bit systems is well illustrated
by the difference between CP/M and CP/M 86. CP/M could manage up to 64K of
memory and 64,000 records occupying up to 8 Mbytes in a single user database
system. CP/M 86 could manage up to 1 Mbyte of memory and 16 disc drives each
containing 8 Mbytes, with multiple users.

Single user applications also benefit from large memories - notably
in image processing and high resolution graphic applications. Large amounts
of data can reside in cheap Winchesters, but data must be brought into
memory for high speed processing - larger quantities than before at one
time. This enables faster processing to be carried out in certain
applications as, for instance, when strings of text fetched from disc are
matched against query strings stored in memory during database searches.

When memory gets still more compact and yet cheaper, all data could
reside in memory and this would result in yet faster processing and shorter
response times.

478

Operating systems in general use

Operating systems are closely associated with the instruction set available on the microprocessor used in the Central Processing Unit (CPU). The designer of the operating system will probably have written it in a high level language which has been translated into machine code by a special program (compiler).

The compiler uses appropriate codes ("opcodes") selected from the instruction set for the particular microprocessor, followed by data, addresses etc., specifying what has to be done. The microprocessor uses its permanent internal micro-instructions to translate the opcodes into operation sequences.

The CP/M operating system was designed to be used originally with the 8080, and later the Z80. The instruction sets for 16 bit processors such as the Intel 8086 or 8088, Motorola MC-68000, and Zilog Z8000 are larger and different. CP/M 86, Concurrent CP/M 86, MS-DOS, MSX-DOS - a variation of MS-DOS written by Microsoft for Japanese micro manufacturers, Unix/Xenix, and UCSDp are the best known operating systems for use with machines containing these CPUs.

Versions of any of these operating systems seem to be available for use on machines with any of the CPUs just mentioned, although it will always be necessary to check just what runs on what.

CP/M, usually believed to stand for "Control Program for Microcomputers" originally stood for "Control Program Monitor" is shown in Figure 19.1. It was developed in 1975 by Gary Kidall, founder of Digital Research who own and licence the use of the system. The advent of floppy disc drives following the introduction of the 8080 and Z80 CPUs prompted the widespread introduction of low cost microcomputer systems. CP/M arrived at the right moment for mass adoption in the rapidly growing microcomputer market.

Although CP/M is now obsolete its simple organisation is useful for the purpose of explaining functions still found in other systems. Referring to Figure 19.1, CCP, the Console Command Processor, does some processing, but is primarily used to interpret commands received from the keyboard. It calls up the resources of BIOS and BDOS as necessary. BIOS (Basic Input/ Output System) handles the communication routines carried out by driver programs, and BDOS (Basic Disc Operating System) manages disc files.

Different zones of the memory (minimum 16K) are allocated to modules. Programs are loaded into TPA (Transient Program Area). The 16K memory space is arranged as shown in the figure. Each additional 16K of memory purchased by the user is made available for programs (TPA) at the bottom of memory, the top being reserved for the system.

To maximise storage utilisation, the memory is re-arranged when the micro is running a program. For instance after a command has been received and a program is being executed, CCP is emptied and that space is made available as an increase in the capacity of TPA. CCP is made available for its original purpose when the program is finished by calling it in again from disc. Some micro manufacturers purchased CP/M and modified and re-named it - for instance Cromemco amd Processor Technology (now defunct) - but the major functions remain as just described.

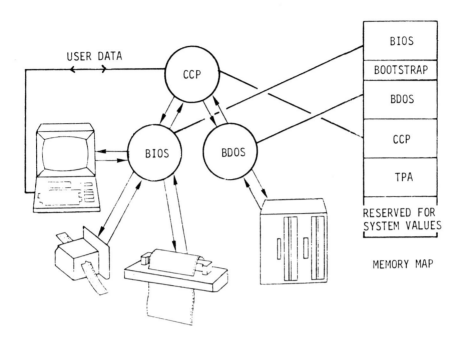

FIGURE 19.1 ARRANGEMENT OF THE CP/M OPERATING SYSTEM

CP/M 80's adoption as a **de facto** standard was accompanied by the development of compiler software for many languages including Basic, Fortran, Cobol, Pascal, APL and Pl/1. At one time CP/M became standardised at version 1.4, but further enhancements were soon introduced - 2.2 was a widely used version.

MP/M, a multi-user version of CP/M allowing a single machine to be used for several tasks, followed later by the **CP/M 86** operating system for the 16 bit 8086 CPU. MP/M was partly superseded by **CP/NET** for networked distributed processing - for instance for the use of a master computer and its resources, files, etc by any of a number of micros each with its own private files.

Files can, in principle, be transferred from one CP/M machine to another without MP/M or CP/NET provided they have identical disc drives, by inter-changing discs. If they do not have matching floppy disc drives, two machines, with appropriate local communications software, can be interconnected by means of their RS232 ports and the files transmitted as ASCII code. In practice, differences in application programs may require that software changes be made before this can be done.

The versatility of the various versions of CP/M 86 was certainly considerable. That part of CP/M which needed to be changed to suit the hardware of 8 bit Z80, 8080 or 8085 machines, or 16 bit 8086 or 8088 is located in the BIOS section occupying 12K of memory. This is "easily" done - but not by your average user.

MS-DOS

The selection of Microsoft's 16-bit MS-DOS as the standard operating system for the IBM-PC and the success of that machine was a major factor in displacing CP/M. It was claimed that special attention had been paid to ease of "transportability" between different hardware arrangements - particularly to take care of apparently similar machines which do in fact have differences between methods of display, cursor codes, and input/output arrangements. With MS-DOS a range of "driver" software was introduced to provide for compatibility between MS-DOS and hardware items.

The use of MS-DOS in the IBM PC and Microsoft's considerable resources was enough to establish MS-DOS as a de facto standard. MS-DOS maintains files in a hierarchical structure for ease of organisation and indexing and the directory is easy to use.

Another feature of MS-DOS is the adoption of ANSI standard terminal codes describing terminal types. MS-DOS recognises the identity code from a terminal and adapts itself to suit the one being used - another idea to improve transportability. A formatting standard was not introduced when 5.25" discs started to be used. Consequently you cannot necessarily use any disc.

The 640K addressability limitation of DOS is imposed by 8088 and 8086 chips which can address only 1 Mbyte of memory, of which 360K is occupied by BIOS. This limitation became a nuisance in view of the steady increase in the size of programs. Some large Desktop Publishing programs have to be complex and slow in order to "overlay" programs - that is to swap parts of the program to and from disc as they are needed.

Various additions to memory management in MD-DOS were introduced to mitigate this problem with "extended" and "virtual" memory arrangements as already described in Chapter 18.

UNIX

Unix was developed by K. Thompsons at the Bell Telephone Laboratories in 1970 specifically as a time sharing system for the popular 16 bit DEC PDP-7 minicomputer - a machine which was in widespread use in Universities and research establishments.

Thompsons found that a system widely used at the time called Multics was too complex for small machines so he chose the name UN (single user) + IX (borrowed from Multics). Unix was licensed by Western Electric, both Bell and WE, being, of course, AT&T affiliates, at prices the market would stand from $30,000 for big users to $300 for universities. It was supplied by WE on disc for PDP11s but by others in various versions. For instance, Cromemco offered a variation of it with its machines, and Onyx computers offered another variation, ONIX, for its machines.

Since Unix was a 16 bit system from the outset, not a conversion from something else, and because it has many very useful features it is a contender for a 16 bit **de facto** standard. Although it started as a single user system, a multi-user version was soon developed and a huge fund of experience with Unix has accumulated - by 1974 it was already used on over 600 PDP11 installations. Since then it has been modified to run on 16 bit 8086, Z8000, 80286/386/486, 68000, or RISC 16/32-bit multi-tasking multi-user operating system.

Its virtues have been enumerated by Pappas (1990) as outstanding for software development with many built-in tools, and very good for advanced text preparation and choice of terminal types by "virtual terminal" selection. Other virtues include its ease of transfer of applications ("portability") across machines with different architectures, the fact that it is ready for LAN and WAN communications, and, of course, its multi-user facility. Its disadvantages are its lack of operational messages and its complexity.

The traditional rivalry between operating systems being what it is the Unix plaudits by Papas prompted a vigorous response about the virtues of DOS (Jude 1990) and the disadvantages of Unix. Jude thinks that "Unix is a pain to work with..., has never made the slightest concession to the user... was developed by programmers for programmers. It offers no significant applications.. have you ever tried using its powerful text macros? You'll spend a week writing your next memo. User friendly they aren't".

However Silicon Graphics's Personal Iris 4D/23 workstation (Smith 1990) is reviewed in Byte as "The Dream Maker... displays models on a computer with as much detail and flexibility as in the mind... most impressive graphics performance can't be measured by benchmarks.. will emulate DOS but even the most complex DOS program would seem simple by comparison". It is a Unix machine, but the cheapest version costs $13,500.

Unix's strong feature is the hierarchical structure of its file store and directories, with a facility for moving file stores to different levels in the tree structure. This has particular significance in a multi-user system where each file has an owner with unique password access; any file owner can be linked to any other file if he has permission from the owner.

The flavour of Unix becomes obvious when reading the specification for one version, Microsoft's Xenix 3.0, by arrangement with Western Electric, offered at about $250 to individual users and available from Logica in the UK. It includes a software development and text processing system with commands such as "typset mathematics", "permuted index", and "find spelling errors". An inter-Xenix machine electronic mail system is also provided. Xenix is a multi-user system with time sharing software included as part of the package.

Xenix is an up-market microcomputer operating system. It requires 512K of memory and a 10 Mbyte disc, assuming that time sharing is to be used with a small number of users. When 16 bit micromputers emerged, Unix was already a sophisticated well tested 16 bit operating system backed by the clout of Bell/ AT&T. AT&T's policy of low-fee licencing for Unix at Universities looks like paying off.

In May 1983 Intel and National Semiconductor followed Motorola in announcing microprocessors suitable for Unix machines. Later, Hewlett Packard and NCR stated that Unix would be the operating system for their new micros. Some manufacturers are hedging their bets by fitting two CPU's and offering two operating systems on the same machine.

Another major virtue claimed for Unix is its portability; two of the

steps required when modifying it for use with a particular machine -
recoding and debugging - are carried out in the high level language C. C is
well known as being a "programmer's" language, containing special features
for software development, and the same may be said for Unix.

AIX, which will run on PS/2 Model 80, is a version of UNIX designed
by IBM for industrial applications. AIX already runs on factory/engineering
oriented 370, 43XX, and the 9370 and the PS/2 80 will be able to communicate
with them.

OS/2

When a new computer with an entirely new operating system is
introduced it must compete against established machines and operating
systems for which a huge fund of tested and tried applicational software
exists. At the end of 1988, not unexpectedly, it was reported that it might
take five years for a critical mass of software for the PS/2 with its OS/2
operating system to become available and for the necessary in-house back-up
resources and skills to become established.

Meanwhile many PS/2 users continue to use DOS. The PS/2 will also
run on UNIX and IBM AIX operating systems.

The OS/2 80286/386 16-bit single-user multi-tasking operating system
was introduced by Microsoft in 1987 with the emphasis on communications.
Memory is 8 MBytes directly addressable, extendible to 16 Mbytes per
process. The meaning of multi-tasking is self evident. Spreadsheet
re-calculations can be proceeding in the background while new data is being
entered. As another, perhaps more important example, at least one
application can be running with communications in progress as well. In
"protected mode", applications are kept separate from each other and from
the operating system.

The main features of OS/2 are:-

1. An 80286-based Standard edition 1.0 which runs on the PC AT, PC
XT 286, and PS/2 models 50, 60, and 80. It requires 2 Mbytes of memory. The
user command interface is quite similar to DOS. Theoretically capable of
addressing over a gigabyte of virtual memory, in practice the software
provides virtual addressing for 48 Mbytes. The price when introduced in 1988
was $325.

2. A version called 1.1., to be issued free, including a
Presentation Manager graphics interface.

3. Support of multi-tasking with applications protection. 16 Mbytes
of directly addressable memory available, in contrast to its single-task DOS
predecessor capable of directly addressing 640 Kbytes.

4. An Extended edition version 1.0, priced at $795, which includes a
Communications Manager with provision for linking with programs running on
other IBM systems, and a Database Manager using the Structured Query
Language (SQL) for relational databases. IBM's Systems Application
Architecture (SAA) is included with the object of enabling common user
interfaces with IBM mainframes.

OS/2 embodies a minicomputer-like task scheduling system where all users get a fair share of system use. Real-time requirements automatically receive priority with 255 assignable priority levels. The memory management system includes software protection that restricts the access of programs to areas of memory in order to provide security during multi-user operations.

The memory limitations of MS-DOS are removed in the PS/2 range, except for low-end machines, where 80286 and 80386 chips are used in the protected mode. The 80286 provides for 16 Mbytes and the 80386 for over 1 Gigabyte addressing.

The Apple System

The Mac is well known for its WIMP - Windows, Ikons, Mouse, Popup menu approach - another legacy from the Xerox Altos/Star. Everyone else has copied it. Partly because of its "all-of-a-piece" design - it does not have a separate operating system, - most people would say that Apple's elegant way of doing things has resulted in a user-oriented system easier to learn and use than any other.

The Toolbox forms part of the kernel or nucleus of a kind of operating system. The kernel allocates hardware resources for programs running under the operating system. The toolbox includes Quickdraw for image creation and text appearance, Font Manager and font creation routines, Event Manager which is a mouse/keyboard interface, and the "Windows" Manager (described later in the chapter).

The Mac's graphics, Quickdraw, creates virtually everything that appears on the screen, including the various fonts and styles of text. It took three years to develop, and being part of the operating system provides very fast interactive service. Quickdraw also performs the clipping and control of overlapping windows, and saves any sequence of operations needed during the compiling of a picture.

Johnson (1988) quotes Schneiderman (1983) who described the "pre-Apple - WIMP/GUI" command situation as follows:-

"Imagine driving a car that has no steering wheel, accelerator, brake pedal... you have only a typewriter keyboard. Anytime you want to turn a corner, change lanes, slow down... you have to type a command sequence on the keyboard. Unfortunately the car can't understand English sentences.. you must type in some letters and numbers... why bother to learn to drive such a car when so many cars (e.g. Apple-cars) use familiar controls"?

In 1989 Apple released a 32 bit version of Quickdraw which provides for 24 bit colour and full colour screen refresh in one pass. When taking full advantage of this version with a Radius Direct Colour 24 board, 256 colours appear on a 1152 x 882 pixel screen at one time, drawn from a palette of 16.7 million colours.

As the Toolbox forms part of the kernel it will only run on Apple Macs. It is not "portable". The benefits are that any new application run on a Mac has a familiar look and feel to it - the same direct manipulation is used. Moreover because the Toolbox design is simple and requires only a small program it is very fast.

However the Toolbox did not provide for multitasking. What it provided was a scheme called Clipboard for the exchange of data between applications. This is a kind of non-automatic "cut and paste" technique which must be performed by the user. For example a spreadsheet section can be "pasted" in to a WP page, but if spreadsheet data is changed, the pasting-in must be done again with the new version.

Apple introduced its answer to OS/2 - System 7.0, which includes multi-tasking - in late 1990. It brings many improvements with its re-designed Toolbox, including inter-application Communications Architecture enabling another Mac anywhere on a network to extract a file from a particular host computer and send it in a specified format. Suppliers of new software products will now be able to design-in multitasking features.

System 7.0 embodies a very interesting "publishers update system". A named document can be broadcast to "subscribers" on the network from a Mac, and subsequently that document can be automatically up-dated by broadcast from the originating Mac to the subscribers.

Microcomputer Languages

BASIC. (Tiny Basic, Basic, Extended Basic, MBasic and other variations). BASIC was developed in 1964 by Kemeny and Kurz at Dartmouth College in the United States and generally introduced by Microsoft Inc., in 1975. It is easily the most popular microcomputer language, being suitable for first-time users and also for more advanced work with subroutines, strings etc. A version of it, often in the form of an Interpreter program on disc, is available for nearly all microcomputers and operating systems.

FORTRAN (FORmula TRANslation) was introduced many years ago for scientific and engineering numerical applications in batch mode for mainframe computers. Later, interactive versions became available, and later still microcomputer versions for numerical work. Available on a number of machines, it is efficient in terms of machine code generated per statement and strong on arithmetic routines.

COBOL (COmmon Business Oriented Language) also introduced years ago for mainframe computers, is more suitable for "information" handling (that is for "human" information not "data" information). Cobol is structured to handle business applications and is generally available for most microcomputers as Cobol-80.

PASCAL is named after the French mathematician Blaise Pascal who invented a calculating machine in 1642. Pascal's sister stated that he discovered for himself most of Euclid's theorems when he was 12 years old. Developed by Wirth and confined for some time to academia, it was made available for microcomputer use at the University of California (San Diego) in 1970 and versions became available available from Intel, Zilog, Texas and others. It is favoured by some teachers in preference to Basic, as a starting language for newcomers and is becoming increasingly popular for micros, allowing problems to be solved in the way natural thought problems are solved - from the top downwards..

C a language closely associated with the UNIX operating system, which owes some of its origins to BCPL - a high level language originated at Cambridge University. The language was called C by Bell Laboratories when developed for use with Unix on their own PDP machines. C is very suitable for general work, is economic to use and easy to write and has come into wide use particularly because of the increasing popularity of Unix.

Popularity of operating systems

By 1981 Basic was supported on 75% of the available operating systems (meaning that it could be used on microcomputers in conjunction with those operating systems) although it was starting to be displaced by other languages. Fortran had spurted from 35% to over 50% presumably because of the increasing use of small machines for scientific purposes in universities. Pascal's operating system support had grown from 45 to 50%, and Cobol from 22 to 33% reflecting the growth of business applications.

The most popular language used in microcomputers in 1984 was Basic (all versions) followed by Pascal, Cobol, and Fortran.

Windows: 1. With the CP/M operating systems

Most people are familiar with Windows either because they have seen them on pictures of computer screens - a favourite eye-catcher in advertisements - or they have seen or used them on a microcomputer.

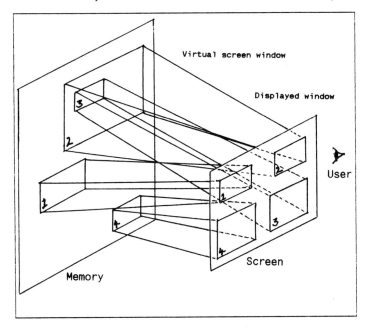

FIGURE 19.2. WINDOWS - IN MEMORY AND ON SCREEN

Several vendors of software for CP/M systems released packages for providing multi-tasking facilities. Multi-tasking means that several programs can be running instantaneously on one machine - as with Concurrent CP/M 86. The user interface enabled several "windows" - small boxed sub-displays - to be used, the data in each being controlled by a different program.

For example one window might be handling telephone numbers, blown up to a size capable of containing a scrollable list of names and numbers large enough to read, or reduced at will to a size just large enough to contain the title "telephone directory". When the number is selected and auto-dialled - perhaps simply by pointing at it, WP software is loaded so that the main area of the screen is available for electronic mail messages.

Vendors included Visicorp ("VisiOn"), Microsoft ("Windows"), and Digital Research. Windows and other improvements to the user interface were considered to be a step forward to the long touted "executive work station".

Windows: 2. Integrated program windowing systems with MS-DOS and Apple

The computer resources made available by MS-DOS greatly increased the popularity of windows. The way in which windows are arranged is shown in Figure 19.2. They are stored as a bit mapped "virtual screen" in memory and means are provided for the user to position them anywhere on the screen.

The co-ordinates of the windows are specified as part of an application, or are under the control of windows supervisory software - the "windows manager". They can be altered in size or overlapped. Windows where overlapping is not possible are called "tiled windows".

In a multi-tasking system a number of applications may be running in different windows by sharing processor time. Message passing may be scheduled so that each application gets its fair share of processor cycles. Alternatively different priorities may be assigned to different applications and a process may be interrupted by a higher priority process.

There must be some arrangement for the user to select a "listener" - that is the window which is currently under the control of the keyboard. A simple way of doing it is for the listening window to be the one which contains the cursor. In many systems the mouse is used to control the window's position on the screen.

In operational details of this kind, numerous differences or extras are available from different suppliers of window software. Myers (1988) lists some of the alternatives - tiled or overlapped windows, with or without title lines, with different kinds of ikons or without ikons, variety of window shapes, etc. He suggests two ways of classifying windows software - by the operational functions of the windows manager, and by the methods provided for user's control.

Myers also differentiates between the presentation - the pictures displayed by the window manager, and the operations - the command arrangements provided for the user.

The Myers article is mandatory reading if you wish to know more about windows:- "Window managers have become popular because they allow separate activities to be put in physically separate parts of the computer screen. Before window managers, people had to remember various activities and how to switch back & forth between them".

"Window managers allow each activity to have its own separate area of the screen. Switching from one window to another is usually very simple. This physical separation is even more important when the system allows multiple activities to operate at the same time ("multiprocessing" or "multitasking") ... window managers can support much higher quality user interfaces. For example the window managers on the Star and Macintosh help support the metaphor that using the computer is like doing operations on a physical desk".

Microsoft Windows brings to the IBM PC a graphics user interface akin to those available on the Mac. It replaces the MS-DOS "command line" type of control. However the first version, launched in 1983, was a failure. Its claims to multitasking were frustrated by the 640 Kbyte memory limit of MS-DOS which severely limited the size of each task. When it was re-designed it incorporated "paging" - that is the provision of "virtual memory" by swapping pages of data between memory and disc.

The package enables information from unrelated application software packages to be viewed in different windows, and information may be cross-transferred and merged. Microsoft Windows arranges for application programs to be brought into memory so that inter-package operations are fast. In late 1984 it became available on DEC Rainbow, Wang Professional, Zenith Z100, HP 150, and certain Altos and NCR machines.

Other windowing system competed against Microsoft in this period - for instance "DesQ" from a US company called Quarterdeck (Santa Monica). General principles and facilities were similar to Microsoft Windows. To be effective such systems require substantial amounts of memory and disc storage. DesQ code takes up to 150K of memory, and the user may wish to have simultaneous access to several application programs.

Speed and effectiveness will depend on the amount of memory in a user's machine. With an IBM PC, an absolute minimum of 250K is required with 512K preferred, together with a 5 Mbyte hard disc. DesQ includes a zoom and unzoom feature - that is identifiable windows/programs can be available on the screen for blowing up, working on, and "pushing away to a corner of the desk" as required.

The potential of systems like this is considerable. On a big screen and in theory, at least, window systems seem to represent real progress. Questions asked at the time were how easy would they be to use, and how much better would they be for office tasks? How much ingenuity in software selection, task design, and related paperwork changes would be needed to make them really useful?

Once you got to grips with them, will you wonder how on earth you managed before, or will windows become another new toy syndrome casualty because you need a course on them each time you use them?

Re-launched as "Windows 1.0". Microsoft windows still had its shortcomings; although it would run on 256 Kbytes of memory, paging made it very slow unless 640K of memory was used. Fortunately the Lotus-Intel Expanded Memory Specification (EMS) was introduced at about the same time. In Windows 1.0 tiled windows were used. A "zoom" button controlled expansion or reduction to alter the sizes of the non-overlapping windows.

When Windows 2.0 came out in 1987, overlapping windows were provided, control from the keyboard was improved, and Dynamic Data Exchange (DDE) - useable multitasking - was introduced, which was not available at that time from Apple. Apple did not introduce full multitasking until 1990.

When windows are allowed to overlap, as in the Macintosh, the overlapped visible area must be stored; in the case of multiple overlaps a tree structure of overlaps must be stored.

Witten et al (1985) reason:- "At some extra cost in storage it may be easier to save complete windows instead of overlapped fragments. However then it will take longer to redraw when the window pile is altered, and redrawing time is usually a critical resource. We know of no published work which assesses the costs and benefits of overlapped windows in real applications; overlaps seem to be fashionable rather than provably beneficial".

There was not much you could do with Windows 2 unless you were prepared to write applications programmes yourself because few such programmes were available. It was followed by Windows 286 which is Windows 2.0 for running on a micro with a 80286 processor.

The memory management provided with Windows 286 enables the "virtual 80286" mode to be used which allows several MS-DOS programs to run apparently simultaneously, each using 640K of RAM. The processor has sufficient power to run in this mode without too much user waiting time.

A major feature of Windows 2.0 is that it connects with hardware via a "driver". A driver is a software package interposed between Windows 2.0 and hardware. To make Windows 2.0 run with a particular hardware item, you load the driver specific to that hardware. In other words Windows 2.0 is hardware independent. Many drivers are available for different printers, video boards, etc.

Microsoft stated that the Windows 2.0 user interface was very similar to "Presentation Manager", at that time under discussion for IBM's OS/2 software, to be integrated into it to provide the advantage of Apple's approach.

For Windows 3.0, launched by Microsoft in 1990, a wide range of programmes were made available at the launch date for Desktop Publishing (including Page-maker 3.01), Telecoms, Graphics design, Word Processing, Databases, etc. 52 software packages were said to be available. The editor of Byte (Lange 1990) thinks that Microsoft's Windows 3.0 is sensational:- "We expect end users and corporations to flock to Windows by the millions" he says. "The ripples will be felt in almost every corner of the desktop computing world".

Presumably Merle Martin, who commented about windows in the IBM Journal of Systems Management (1990) is less enthusiastic. "There is nothing so confounding as windows exploding upon windows. Watch end user's eyes explode at this exponential complexity! See how many windows you can pack into one screen (all with different colours of course)" says Martin.

And according to Manchester (1990) "GUI's (Graphic User Interfaces)... can be distracting for some applications and mean changes in working practices... they use up resources - Windows 3 consumes about 7 Mbytes of hard disc... For these and other reasons GUI's have made little impact outside the obvious areas such as DTP and CASE... a senior Microsoft executive admitted that only 5% of MS-DOS users were also using the earlier version, Windows 2.0".

The discerning user will no doubt distinguish between the actual benefits of windows, and the bells, whistles, and other lurid accoutrements included at the insistence of an enthusiastic sales department.

When a window is not in use it is represented as a small ikon available for retrieval. A windows system may be single-tasking or multi-tasking. Ikons representing windows are shown in Figure 19.3 - an illustration of the facilities provided by Microsoft's Windows 3.0 (I am indebted to Microsoft for permission to use this and other illustrations).

More memory is a major benefit. On 80286 machines it can be up to 16 Mbytes and more on 80386's. The memory management provided with Windows 3.0 to use this memory evidently removes most of the restrictions in multitasking.

Differences of opinion about the benefits of the windows concept notwithstanding, Microsoft Windows 3.0 appears to be a great improvement over Windows 2.0. There is more memory, effective multitasking, protection between tasks, and support for a number of LANs.

The kind of application where the benefits should be felt are those involving Megabytes of data such as multi-page documents with graphics. Englowstein (1990) reviews Pagemaker with Windows 3.C. It took over 90 seconds to flow about 10 Mbytes of data into 35 pages using Windows 286 which involves much swapping between memory and disc. However with Windows 3.0 on the same machine with 4 Mbytes of memory called into play the job took 35 seconds.

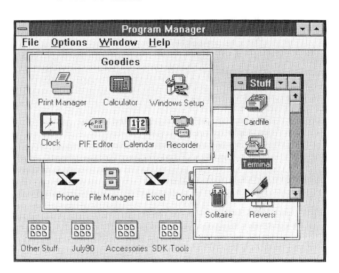

FIGURE 19.3 IKONS AND WINDOWS 3.0

The other area where more memory and faster operation is required is for colour applications. Windows 3.0 includes a palette manager enabling exact colours to be generated by combining known proportions of red, green, and blue, or by the adjustment of hue, saturation, and luminosity (See Cawkell Feb 1990).

In the illustrations of Windows 3.0 here it is not possible to do justice to the very good colour of the originals. Figure 19.3 shows the Program Manager window where applications are denoted by ikons, with applications sub-divided into groups. One item "Solitaire" can be seen (bottom right) in a partly obscured group. Figure 19.4 shows the game in progress. Figure 19.5 shows a window displaying the colour selection program in which pre-defined or "customised" colours can be chosen.

The August 1990 issue of Byte contains a list of over 80 Windows 3.0

software packages in Communications, Databases, Spreadsheets, Multimedia, Networking, OCR, Personal information systems and many others (Anon 1990).

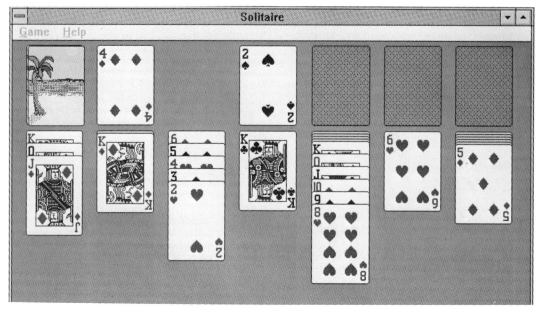

FIGURE 19.4. WINDOWS 3.0: SOLITAIRE IN PROGRESS

Apple introduced System 7.0 software in mid-1990. It brings many improvements and a re-designed Toolkit. Apple windows in System 7.0 includes the introduction of Interapplication Communications Architecture (ICA) programming interfaces.

Suppliers of new software products will now be able to design-in multitasking features. For example a spreadsheet moved into a WP document can be automatically up-dated without user intervention. Improved communications in System 7.0 enable such changes or add-on items to be broadcast to network-interconnected machines to modify automatically selected files on those machines.

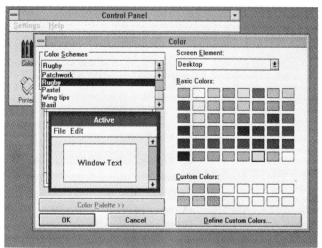

FIGURE 19.5 WINDOWS 3.0: COLOUR CUSTOMISING

X Windows

X Windows was developed at MIT and consists of the server software with device-dependent code which controls the display, the user's application program, and the interprocess communication protocol which inter-connects them. Any application will run on a particular machine once a server has been implemented for it.

X Windows does not include a "look and feel design" - the intention is to enable a range of applications to run with a range of designs. However "tool-kits" are available, and so is ready-to-use X Windows software with an already designed graphic users interface.

X Windows seems to have found its particular niche in association with the TCP/IP protocol for interprocess communication and the Unix operating system. For instance a user with a micro requiring a workstation to connect to a Unix application on a host computer network can buy X Windows server software with TCP/IP to convert his micro to an "X terminal".

Note this special feature of X windows - the server and the "client" application are on two different network-connected machines. Such an arrangement would make particularly good sense if the client application required expensive software running on a large machine, and a number of remote users can access it via their X terminals. However the server, protocol, and application can all be on the same machine if required.

Note also that as if there were not enough confusion in the jargon already, the usually understood meanings of the terms "server" and "client" seem to have been reversed here.

A software package called X Vision, available in the UK from Visionware, will convert a micro into a network-connected X terminal and arranges for it to run DOS with remote client X window applications at the same time. Consequently mixed Microsoft Windows and X windows can be displayed together on the same screen.

Transferring files: 1. Basic method

Transferring files between two side by side machines running on the same operating system is about the most basic exercise in telecoms that there is. This might be necessary if it cannot be done by transferring a disc - as for example when the machines contain drives for different types of disc, a by no means uncommon problem. Otherwise identical microcomputers - PS/2s, for instance - come with either 3.5" or 5.25" drives. Sending a disc to a media conversion bureaux is another way of dealing with the problem.

To transfer files via a link between two adjacent machines, the method is to interconnect the RS232 serial communication ports of the machines using a specially made-up "null-modem" cable, available from computer shops. If you are handy with a small soldering iron you can buy the parts and do the job yourself. The cable should be fitted with standard 25 pin plugs in which the inter-connections between pins 2 and 3 have been transposed (receive to send and send to receive). No modem is necessary.

With CP/M machines the procedure was to designate the sending port for a printer and the receiving port for a tape reader, reserve up to 16

Kbytes of RAM as a buffer store, and then use the PIP command for file transfer. Provided that the baud rates of the two machines were the same, the receiving machine was started first, less than 16 Kbytes were sent at a time, and the file was ASCII only, the arrangement worked.

With this simple system the file will be displayed on the second machine as ASCII decoded characters. If a file contains special characters as it nearly always will, they will not be correctly interpreted by the receiving machine since it contains no instructions for dealing with them. For instance with a file composed using a WP package, an underlined word, or bold characters, will not appear as such. For this to happen a special programme must be installed.

Transferring files: 2. Terms used in technology and telecommunications.

Before continuing further, a number of the special terms used in the file transfer area will be explained here for convenience so that reference need not be made to the glossary or to other chapters.

APPC.

Advanced Program to Program Communication. See LU6.2.

Asynchronous transmission

A method of transmitting data suited to sending characters spaced at unknown intervals, for example when someone is sending direct from a keyboard. Each fixed length byte, normally of 8 bits, is preceded by a single bit going high (e.g. forming a positive pulse) to warn the receiver that an 8 bit byte follows. The receiver clock then counts in 8 data bits. The transmitter concludes with a stop bit going low so that the receiver will know that the next bit going high is a start bit.

Bridge

A bridge interconnects two LANs. It reads all packets on LAN A, and retransmits on LAN B, which uses the same protocol, all packets addressed to a host on B. It also performs the reverse B to A functions. See also Router.

Coaxial cable

A cable consisting of a central conductor spaced from an outer conducting sheath by a low loss material with a touch protective covering. The data rate of co-ax is up to about 500 Mbps per Km without repeaters. The most widely used wideband cable until the advent of fibreoptic cable (q.v.). Expected to become less used now that the costs of fibre are becoming comparable.

CSMA/CD

Carrier Sense Multiple Access/Collision Detection. A method of packet transmission used in LANs where a station checks the channel before sending. If in use it tries again after a delay. Every station checks passing packets, only capturing those addressed to it. In the event of a collision, both stations retransmit after a delay.

Fibreoptic cable

Cable made by depositing compounds in vapour from (which will become the core) on to the inside of a silica tube (which will become the cladding), subsequently collapsed and drawn out into a thin fibre. When the core diameter is about 4.1 microns, light introduced at a particular angle is propagated (monomode) with little energy loss along the fibre providing a data transmission capable of at least 1000 Mbps per Km without repeaters.

Gateway

The term gateway is currently applied (although it may have been previously used in a more general sense) to a network interconnection device which is a step-up in the progression bridge (q.v.) router (q.v.) gateway. A gateway interconnects two networks employing different architectures using all seven layers of the OSI model in the process. For example it would be used to interconnect a network using a proprietary architecture to an OSI network.

Kermit

Kermit was devised at Columbia University in the early eighties and was named (for a reason that escapes me, although it brings to telecoms a vague but welcome sense of humour) after the frog in the Muppet Show.

It is a more or less successful comprehensive attempt to set a de facto standard for file transfers since it has become quite widely used. As one of its designers says (Da Cruz 1984): "Kermit accommodates itself to many systems by conforming to a common subset of their features. But the resulting simplicity and generality allow Kermit on any machine to communicate with Kermit or any other machine - microcomputer or mainframe.

The back and forth exchange of packets keeps the two sides synchronised; the protocol can be called asynchronous because the communication hardware itself operates asynchronously".

LU 6.2

IBM software for communication between programs in distributed processing. It replaces the idea of intelligent mainframes and dumb terminals by distributing intelligence around the network and providing secure communications within IBM's SNA scheme.

Netbios

The IBM PC Application Program Interface designed to ease LAN communications. Its major facilities are the provision for naming the LAN adaptor cards in machines connected to the network (in addition to the unique name provided by IBM for all adaptor cards) and a set of commands providing for the transmission of information to any other machine.

Netbios commands are hardware independent - they can be used with various network e.g. Ethernet, Token Ring, Arcnet etc., - and are also independent of LAN software such as Banyan Vines, Novell Netware, 3 Com, etc., which include a Netbios interface.

Packet

A group of bits of defined size conforming to an address and sequence protocol, being a part of a message which has been sub-divided for transmission purposes.

Pipe

A one-way communication mechanism for passing a character stream from one task to another in multitasking software such as OS/2. Named Pipes are a variation for communicating large blocks of data in both directions across a network. One useful application is the use of a pipe to feed a long output from one application directly to the input of another.

Router

A router is a Bridge (q.v.) with a difference. It interconnects two dissimilar LANs, using an internet protocol, taking care, among other things, of different forms of address, packet sizes, and interface differences.

Script file

A small file for setting up the operational telecommunication requirements of a computer.

A script file can range in comprehensivity from setting basic requirements like bit rates, modem designation etc., to controlling quite elaborate tasks, as in the Hayes Smartcom III (Hayes, Atlanta, USA) such as automatically logging on to and polling a remote database periodically, querying the database, and downloading data, all in 'background mode' - that is while the machine is being used for some other task.

A script file may consist of a form in which the user is prompted to enter the various parameters required, which then automatically becomes a telecoms control file, or it may be written as a program in a script programming language to control specific requirements.

A script file may also include passwords, telephone numbers, etc., which are used automatically as needed.

Server

A station (node) on a network that provides a service by managing a communal resource such as storage, printing etc.

SNA

Systems Network Architecture IBM's layered communications architecture which has been closely, but not exactly, followed in the OSI model.

Synchronous transmission

A method of sending data suited to continuous transmission where the receiving clock is usually pulled into exact synchronism with the sending clock by sending unique signals (e.g. a succession of half-length bits).

When the transmitter sends data, the receiver distinguishes between successive bytes (normally of 8 bits) by counting. The method is more complex than asynchronous transmission (q.v.) because of the need for precise timing.

Token Ring

A method of transmission used in LANs where a station wishing to transmit awaits the arrival of an empty packet. Packets circulate round a ring channel in one direction. A station receiving a packet addressed to it copies the data, and the packet circulates to its transmitting station. The station checks it for errors, removes it if correct, and re-tries if not.

There are several variations of the method, notably the "slotted-ring" and the "permission token ring".

Twisted pair cable

Cheapest communication link available. The data rate without repeaters is about 16 Mbps per Km. Telephone lines between subscribers and the local exchange - the most common type of twisted pair connection - are usually able to transmit data far above the rate required for analogue speech for which they were designed. Consequently they will usually not need to be replaced when connection to the ISDN is made.

X, Y and Z modem

X modem is the easily implemented de-facto file transfer checking standard, introduced as long ago as 1977. Its simplicity is responsible for its longevity. It, or one of its descendants, is still often incorporated in today's elaborate telecom software packages.

It is a half-duplex method of checking whether a block of data is correct - the receiving station has to wait until a block of 128 bytes has been received.

A block is checked by the "checksum" method; the simplest is to add bits at the sending end so that the addition of the bits in a byte or, in this case, block, always adds up to an even or odd number, as agreed.

The receiver checks the total and replies after each block has been sent with either an ACK, or a NAK calling for re-transmission.

X modem was improved by using a more sophisticated block-checking method for longer blocks. Y modem is a further improvement - it uses 1 Kbyte blocks and files may be sent in batches, not just singly as in X modem. Also it takes account of error-correcting modems by including the option to omit ACK and NAK altogether. With Z-modem a highly effective error correction was re-introduced.

X, Y or Z protocols must be in place at both ends of the communication channel for the method to function, except in the case of Z modem, where if the transmitter finds the Z modem is not supported but X and Y are, it automatically steps down to a "lower" protocol.

XON, XOFF

A simple method of bit flow control, used to control incoming bits during transmission according to the capacity of a buffer store. The receiver sends either XON or XOFF back to the transmitter as necessary.

Transfering files: 3. Organising software and telecoms.

When computers were used only by large organisations they were usually confined to, and managed by the Data Processing department. Microcomputers arrived and tended to be "managed" by their users. They were purchased by individuals and in due course permeated into small organisations and homes. There was no overall control and no specific purchasing policy. All were single-user systems, and there was no intercommunication.

As microcomputer useage increased and inter-machine communications were introduced, communication networks were required and it became essential to deal with actual or potential chaos by organising and managing software and telecoms. System requirements will vary according to occupational needs. Here I will discuss "library systems" by way of example.

When telecommunications first appeared in the library world they were usually associated with online access to remote databases. In due course microcomputers, telecoms, Local Area Networks (LANs) etc., arrived. No doubt Wachter's comment (1990):- "You need the best technical support you can get, especially in the beginning" represent the feelings of many.

For inter-computer communications some kind of interface - usually a plug-in card - is needed between the computer and the telecoms channel or LAN, together with either separate software which handles inter-computer transactions on a "peer-to-peer" basis, or networked communications software which usually comes as part of the operating system.

As an example of a working system, Figure 19.6 shows a library network on four sites (Polytechnic of Central London) - one of the largest of its kind in the UK. The box marked "yak libertas" represents a VAX machine running the Libertas library system; it has 36 Mb of memory and 1.8 Gb of disc. (Conroy 1990). The main purpose of the system is to transfer information files between computers so that they are correctly received, stored, and are retrievable in their original form.

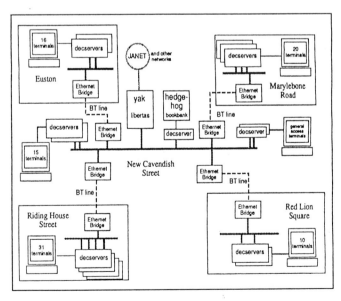

FIGURE 19.6. LIBRARY NETWORK

From the system management viewpoint, the operational situation will probably lie between two extremes:-

(1)   Easy. The communicating computers are on the same site where all equipment has been purchased from one vendor and identical software is installed on all machines.

(2)   Difficult. Communication is between different sites owned by different organisations with multi-vendor procurement policies.

Under situation 2, a correctly stored file received from another organisation may not necessarily be presented by the recipient as the sender intended. For example the text in a text file composed using Wordstar WP software might be stored exactly as sent but when called up might not appear at all on the screen. Alternatively it might appear as one continuous paragraph interspersed with meaningless symbols, or it might appear perfectly.

Communications software is available which may go some way to dealing with complexity by anticipating problems and providing solutions. For example a terminal may contain emulating software for altering itself so that it appears to the remote computer as if it is a terminal known to be compatible with that computer.

Extra facilities of this kind are a growth industry designed to capture a share of an intensely competitive market where increasing choice and complexity provide the opportunity to offer extra "features" to "make life easier". Whether a "facility" will succeed in this respect or whether it's put there to pad out the list on a sales glossy is a matter for the discriminating buyer.

If local support is unavailable and the library is not already lumbered with a quantity of assorted microcomputers, it makes sense to buy from a single vendor, and pay for installation and testing. However that policy may mean becoming locked in with that vendor. When expansion is needed, his range may be limited or uncompetitive.

Transfering files: 4. Managing microcomputer networks

The management problem depends upon the library's computer and telecoms expertise. Many libraries in universities, public libraries, and special libraries in larger organisations have a computer department within the organisation. They will be able to arrange their technical management policy according to their relationship with that department.

The importance of technical management is evident with reference to Figure 19.7. This layout is representative of a simple situation where an organisation possessing a collection of microcomputers has provided telecommunications for general internal and external communications.

The figure is taken from a sheet supplied by Blast - a supplier of communications software. A number of Ethernet connected microcomputers are shown with their differing operating systems all of which could have come from different suppliers and which may be incompatible with each other.

The technical requirements are that any micro should be able to exchange files with any other, should be able to exchange files with the VAX minicomputer, and should be able to access external databases via a modem. The Blast software provides the necessary protocol changes and automatic text conversion for files exchanged via different operating systems.

The figure is probably fairly representative of a situation presented by an un-coordinated purchasing policy, or even by a co-ordinated policy if specific requirements have dictated the purchase of machines with a specific performance. The problem is to decide, on the basis of a specification for the required network services, how to organise a system purchased (in this case) from several suppliers, use what exists, make it work, maintain it, be kept informed about the need updates, and add to it as necessary.

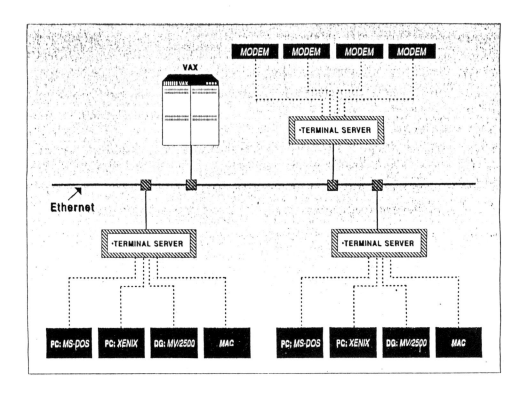

FIGURE 19.7. NETWORK INTER-CONNECTING ASSORTED DEVICES

Technical management has to pin down the responsibility for any kind of malfunction to a specific supplier during any stage of the current or expansion programmes. This may not be at all easy. But it is all too easy, in view of the diffusion of functions across the system, for Competent Computers Ltd., to say "not in our part, you obviously need to talk to Safe Software Inc.", and so the buck passes round the various suppliers.

There are three parties in the file transfer software package business - the sellers, who will usually say that their software does the job easily and effectively, and the informed users, who know that the file transfer process is a notoriously difficult problem area. Heaven help the third party - the uninformed user.

An article about this topic appeared in Byte six years ago (Barr, 1984). Two more articles appeared later (Crabb, 1990 and Van Name, 1990). Dozens, if not hundreds, of software packages have appeared in this six year period - surely things must have improved?

These three authors are computer professionals. David Barr says "We have used everything from the earlier commercial microcomputers with their severely restricted memories to new lap-size portables and high powered jobs with hard discs and RAM discs. We have spent (or misspent) countless hours communicating with all kinds of hosts and we've used dedicated and dumb terminals as well as microcomputers that were configured as both dumb and smart terminals. As a consequence we've spent more time than we care to remember scratching our heads and wondering why nothing will work".

On the subject of getting ready to use a Local Area Network - now one of the most likely telecom routes for file transfers - Van Name says "The source of all this confusion, of course, is the PC architecture, which doesn't automatically recognise add-in boards (or much of anything else attached to the system for that matter).. worse, you need a different combination of drivers and client software for every board configuration and LAN operating system combination".

Continuing, Van Name asks the question "Why, after all, should millions of PC users have to work so much harder than Mac users to use a LAN?". He is contrasting the Apple world with the IBM PC world to the detriment of the latter.

As Van Name says:- "The Mac world is a benevolent dictatorship - Apple, love it or hate it, set the Mac LAN standards... ". But for PC users "... each product uses different client software and works with a different subset of the many available LAN adaptors". But Apple gets low marks for high prices and slowness in enabling Macintosh-LAN connections.

Having had some experience of PCs versus Macs, the cobbled together aspect of PC software compared with the "all-of-a-piece" feel of a Mac seems to me to be very obvious.

However Crabb is critical of Apple: "The real reason for connecting computers is simple: sharing information". He continues with praise for Claris, an Apple subsidiary, to the detriment of Apple. "Claris... is well aware that connectivity really means transparent data exchange and update among applications... Claris envisions you sitting in front of your computer and working with information rather than worrying about the tool".

So what has happened to computer information sharing during the six years spanned by these authors? Increases in complexity, added facilities, and "new features" (per se) do not seem to have been accompanied by an increase in ease of use.

Exchanging files between machines is dealt with largely automatically - a range of software packages are available for the purpose. A package called Rapid Relay Easy for example, for PC XTs or ATs, will transfer data at speeds up to 115 Kbps.

The Blast package is representative of the many more elaborate packages available. It will "allow any two computers on which it has been implemented, regardless of vendor, to communicate through RS232 serial ports, using either a hard-wire or telephone-line link with asynchronous modems. It can transmit and receive binary or text files and console commands. It provides easy to use menu screens auto-dial/auto logon and unattended operation".

Inter-computer communications supported by operating systems

By involving operating systems in inter-computer communications a user is enabled to do much more than simply exchange files. In effect a remote machine on a network appears to the user almost as if it is his own machine. Traditional 3270 terminal emulation and basic file transfer is replaced by arrangements where the mainframe looks after the corporate database, and networked workstations provide user-friendly information presentation.

According to Dataquest (end of 1988 forecast), 60% of PCs will be connected to a LAN by 1992. LAN networking, or any kind of networking for that matter, introduces several new considerations. A fairly heavy memory overhead is added to participating micros and unless they are sufficiently powerful, operations are likely to be slow. For accessing databases outside the networks a shared gateway needs organising with sufficient ports to provide adequate service per user assuming that some maximum fraction of users will require simultaneous service.

Once two or more users are able to access the same file, all users except the user making changes must be locked-out until they are completed. In the case of shared access to a database, special arrangements need to be made if lockouts are not to seriously slow up access. Methods include locking out on an individual record basis, read locks for queries and write locks when the database is being up-dated, or better still, lockouts on a row by row basis.

Such arrangements require database re-organisation - for instance the database and the database management software reside in a server, while each PC contains a database user interface.

Today, a very few people will still be using the 8-bit single-user CP/M operating system. If you have a quantity of CP/M-created files and don't want to become involved in file conversion problems when you buy a DOS machine, you can buy a card to run CP/M on it. Back in 1987, Microsolutions brought out an 8-bit 8MHz no-wait-states Z80 half-size card (at $195) to plug in to a PC compatible. It included DOS/CP/M emulator software. No doubt there are others.

The dominance of IBM PC compatible microcomputers means that most people will be using the MS-DOS single-user operating system. DOS has some resemblance to CP/M but there are certain big differences - notably DOS's 8088/16-bit word length and its directory structure. When DOS 4.0 came out it extended the 640K memory limitation to the equivalent of 5 Mbytes using fast look-ahead buffers with hashed entries.

An important software package which became available with DOS is IBM's NETBIOS with its own set of commands for controlling LAN messages, as used in and/or augmented by compatible LAN control systems such as "IBM PC

LAN", "3 Com 3 + open and + share", "Novell Netware", etc.

Most operating systems, discussed earlier in this chapter, now cater for telecommunications.

The OS/2 80286/386 16-bit single-user multi-tasking operating system was introduced by Microsoft in 1987 with the emphasis on communications; at least one application can be running with communications in progress as well.

Unix, a 80286/386/486, 68000, or RISC 16/32-bit multi-tasking multi-user operating system, includes the means for LAN and WAN communications, A Unix-to-Unix communication subsystem for automatic file servers, E-Mail, remote printing etc., are part of the system and the only extra needed is a modem.

File sharing among users takes place in such a way that different machines can combine their file systems and users can work with any files in any machine regardless of its location.

Apple provide communications with their "Appletalk" system which runs on Ethernet CSMA/CD network or on Token Ring. Novell and 3 Com provide compatible networking systems so that Macs can be used as workstations and share data with PCs, Unix, DEC and IBM minis/mainframes.

Apple have just introduced its answer to OS/2 - System 7.0. It includes inter-application Communications Architecture enabling another Mac anywhere on a network to extract a file from a particular host computer and send it in a specified format. Macs can work simultaneously as servers and clients on all-Mac networks.

The System 7.0 communications toolbox handles hardware, e.g. drivers to emulate different terminals, and also alternative protocols. User selection is made very easy - you simply choose the Apple "folder" icon labelled with the required terminal or protocol.

System 7.0 includes a very interesting "publishers update system". A named document can be broadcast to "subscribers" on the network from a Mac, and subsequently that document can be automatically up-dated by broadcast from the originating Mac to the subscribers.

Mac-DOS-Mac file transfers are relatively easy when software such as Word Perfect, Pagemaker, etc., exists (as it does) in both Mac and DOS versions because both versions use the same file formats. Otherwise file conversion is necessary. Additional software is needed for Mac/DOS printers. This can be useful if a DOS user wants to use, say, a MAC laser printer. A package called TOPS will deal with the matters described in this paragraph.

In late 1990 Apple introduced a software package called A/UX 2.0 to enable users to use their Macs as low cost Unix workstations. Ethernet boards and X-window can be added to a Mac, and with this combination the combined benefits of Apple's familiar user interface and Unix can become available.

References

Adams, R.
  Gower, Aldershot, 1990.
    Communication and delivery systems for librarians.
Alford, Roger.
  Byte 15(12), 395-401, November 1990.
    The mouse that roared.
Allison, Andrew.
  Mini-Micro Systems, 49-62, January 1988.
    Where there's RISC there's opportunity.
Ambler, Allen L., and Burnett, M.M.
  Computer 22(1)), 9-22, October 1989.
    Influence of visual technology on the evolution of language environ-
    ments.
Anderson, C.
  Microsoft Systems Journal 4(4), 17-26, July 1989.
    Extended memory specification 2.Taking advantage of the 80286 pro-
    tected mode.
Anon.
  Byte 15(8), 125-128, August 1990.
    Windows shopping resource guide.
Arnow, B.J.
  Byte, 9(12), 187-194, December 1984.
    Writing communications in Basic: easy terminal emulation and file
    transfer
Barr, David and De W. Rogers, G.
  Byte, 9(12), 199-210, December 1984.
    Looking for the perfect programme.
Bass, F.M.
  Management Sci., 15, page 215, 1969.
    A new product growth model for consumer durables.
Beynon, J.D.E.
  Radio & Electronic Engineer, 50(5), pps 201-204, May 1980.
    Charge coupled devices: concepts, technology and limitations.
Cannon, Don L.
  Texas Instruments Learning Centre, PO Box 225012, MS-54, Dallas, Texas
  75265, USA.
    Fundamentals of microcomputer design. 1982.
Carpenter, James; Deloria, Dennis; Morganstein, David.
  Byte 9(4), 234-264, April 1984.
    Statistical software for microcomputers.
Cawkell, Anthony E.
  In 4th International Online Information Meeting, London, December 1980.
  pps 377-386. Pub. by Learned Information Ltd., Besselsleigh Rd.,
  Abingdon, Oxford OX13 6EF.
    A personal microcomputer for office use.
Cawkell, A.E.
  Critique 2(1), 1-12 October/November 1989. Aslib, London.
    Advances in word processing.
Cawkell, A.E.
  Critique, 2(3), 1-12, January 1990.
    Machines and human communication.
Cawkell, A.E.
  Critique, 2(4), 1-12, February 1990.
    The reproduction of colour.

Cawkell A.E.
  Critique, 2(6), 1-12, 1990.
    Information theory is thriving.
Clements, Alan.
  Microprocessors & Microsystems, 8(7), 324-337 ,September 1984.
    The 68000 and its interface.
Cobb, Alan, and Weiner, J.
  Microsoft Systems Journal 4(6), 1-18, November 1989.
    Examining New Wave, Hewlett-Packard's graphical object-oriented
    environment.
Condroy, J.
  In Computers in Libraries International, Meckler, 1990. pps 79-83.
    Networking for a multi-site service.
Da Cruz, F. and Catchings, B.
  Byte, 9(6), 255-278, June 1984.
     Kermit: a file-transfer protocol for universities.
Crabb, Don.
  Byte 15(5), 103-106, May 1990.
    The fruits of connectivity.
Dickerson, Connie J. (Ed)
  Elsevier Science Publishing, Published twice each year.
    The software catalogue: microcomputers. (28,000 software packages).
Eden, Richard C., Livingston, Anthony R., Welch, Bryant M.
  IEEE Spectrum, 20(12), December 1983, pps 30-37.
    Integrated circuits: the case for Gallium Arsenide.
Eglowstein, Howard.
  Byte 15(8), page 122, July 1990.
    Pagemaker revs up under Windows 3.0.
Fullagar, David.
  IEEE Spectrum, 17(12), pps 24-27, December 1980.
    CMOS comes of age.
Furht, Borivoje and Milutinovic, V.
  Computer 20(3), 48-67, March 1987.
    A survey of microprocessor architectures for memory management.
Glass, B.
  Byte, 13(7), 251-257, July 1988.
    Weighing the options: comparing the many flavours of multitasking.
Goldman, Phil.
  Byte 14(11), 350-357, November 1989.
    Mac Virtual memory revealed.
Gray, Paul; Carlson, Ray,
  IEEE Trans. Syst. Man. & Cyber. SMC-10(8), 484-501, 1980.
    Analysing the future impact of personal computers.
Gupta, Amar; Toong, H.D.
  Proc IEEE, 71(11), 1236-1256, 1983.
    Microprocessors - the first twelve years.
Guteri, Fred et al.
  IEEE Spectrum 22(1), 43-55, January 1985.
    Personal computers; software; microprocessors.
Heffer, D.E., King, G.A., Keith, D.C.
  Edward Arnold, London. 1981.
    Basic principles and practice of microprocessors.
Hyde, Randall L.
  Byte 13(4), 219-225, April 1988.
    Overview of memory management.

Johnson, Jeff, Roberts T.L., et al.
  Computer 22(9), 11-26, September 1989.
    The Xerox Star: a retrospective.
Jude, Michael R.
  Computer 23(3), page 4, 1990.
    In defense of DOS.
Karanassios, V., Horlick, G.
  Talanta 32(8A), 615-631, 1985.
    Smart Backplanes II. The IBM PC.
Krajewski, Rich.
  Byte 10(5), 171-198, May 1985.
    Multiprocessing - an overview.
Learn, L.L.
  OCLC Library Centre, Dublin, Ohio 1989.
    Telecommunications for information specialists.
Lemmons, Phil.
  Byte 8(12), 48-54, December 1983.
    Microsoft windows.
Lemmons Phil, et al.
  Byte 9(12), A3-A138, December 1984.
    Guide to the Apple personal computers: Apple IIE, Apple IIc,
    Macintosh, Lisa.
Malloy, R.
  Byte, 13(7), 111-115, July 1988.
    IBM's OS/2 extended edition.
Markoff, John and Shapiro, Ezra.
  Byte 9(8), 347-356, August 1984.
    Macintosh's other designers.
Martin, Merle P.
  IBM Journal of Systems Management, 22-24, April 1990.
    Instant screen design.
McAuliffe, Daniel.
  Computer 23(4), 105-109, April 1990.
    Breaking the DOS 640 Kbyte barrier.
Mead, Carver, and Conway, Lynn A.
  Addison-Wesley, Reading, Mass., USA, 1980.
    Introduction to VLSI systems.
Milenkovic, Milan.
  IEEE Micro, 70-85, April 1990.
    Microprocessor memory management units.
Miller, Alan R.
  Byte, 9(11), 143-154. November 1984
    Introduction to semiconductors.
Moote, Robert.
  Byte 14(11), 342-350, November 1989.
    Virtual memory: the next generation.
Moran, Tom.
  Mini-micro Systems, 47-49, June 15 1984.
    Personal computer spotlight shifts to portables.
Myers, Brad A.
  IEEE Computer Graphics & Applications, 65-84, September 1988.
    A taxonomy of window manager user interface.
Nirmal, Barry; Nutter, Jean.
  J.Syst. Management, 12-15, March 1985.
    Present state of personal computing - challenges and concerns.

Pappas, T.L.
  Computer 23(1), 103-108, January 1990.
    Unix on the PC AT/386.
Pohm, A.V, Smay, T.A
  Computer, pps 93-110, October 1981 .
    Tutorial series 13: Computer memory systems.
Raja, Arif.
  Personal Computer World, 190-194, July 1990.
    Exceeding the limits.
Raskin, Jeff., Whitney, Tom.
  Computer, 62-73, January 1981.
    Perspectives on personal computing.
Reinhardt, Andy.
  Byte 15(5), 273-276, May 1990.
    Power to the portables.
Schneiderman, B.
  Computer 16(8), 57-68, August 1983.
    Direct manipulation: a step beyond programming languages.
Schofield, Jack et al.
  Practical Computing 8(6), 96-106, June 1985.
    The IBM PC success.
Slater, J.A.
  In Microsoftware - A symposium, University of Sussex, England, July
  1980. Published by the Institution of Electronic & Radio Engineers,
  99 Gower St., London WC1E 6AZ. Pps 113-127.
    Software quality assurance.
Smith, Alan Jay.
  Computing Surveys 14(3), September 1982, pps 474-530.
    Cache Memories.
Tabak, Daniel.
  Computer 22(8), page 105, August 1989.
    Definitions of RISC.
Thompson, Lester E.
  Byte 9(9), 147, 436-443, September 1984.
    Floppy disk formats.
Vail, Hollis.
  The Futurist, 52-58, December 1980.
    The home computer terminal: transforming the household of tomorrow.
Van Name, Mark L., and Catchings, B.
  Byte 15(7), 105-108, July 1990.
    Networks shouldn't be this hard.
Wachter, M.
  In Computers in Libraries International, Meckler. pps. 77-78, 1990.
    Planning your library automation project.
White, Webster, Bruce F.
  Byte 9(8), 238-251, August 1984.
    The Macintosh.
Williams, Gregg.
  Byte 9(2), 30-54, February 1984.
    The Apple Macintosh Computer.
Witten, Ian H., and Greenberg, S.
  Oxford Surveys in Information Technology, 2, 69-104, 1985.
    User interfaces for office systems.
Zorpette, Glenn.
  IEEE Spectrum 22(1), 53-55, January 1985.
    Microprocessors.

CHAPTER 20. INFORMATION TECHNOLOGY AND INFORMATION MANAGEMENT

Under pressure decision makers discard information and
avoid bringing in expertise and new alternatives. They
simplify a problem to the point where it becomes manageable
H.L.Wilensky 1967

I believe that by 1975 the computer will have had
a substantial impact on top executives decision
making in large R&D and manufacturing companies
R.H. Brady, Harvard Business Review, 1967.

Nor are man-machine dialogs via desk-side consoles likely to become
a feature of life in the executive suite in the forseeable future
McKinsey Report 1968.

A few years from now a single book will be
too small to even sketch out the uses of Artificial Intelligence techniques in management
Herbert Simon in Foundations of Decision Support Systems 1981.

Despite all the excitement and the apparently stunning breakthroughs, the impact of computerised information systems
on top management has been and will continue to be negligible
J. Dearden, Sloan Manag. Rev., 1983.

Although the system at the US Government Printing Office....
used sophisticated voice output and touchscreen technologies
it was never actively used and was eventually abandoned
Jeff Moad, Datamation, 1988.

Even one-time EIS sceptics, such as
Quaker Oats president Frank Morgan
are now among its biggest backers
Jeff Moad, (about an EIS running for 5 years), Datamation, 1986.

Office Automation - Acts of Faith or measurement of results?

Early discussions about "Office Automation" or "Office Systems"
frequently covered the activities of managers, and "Management Information
Systems" (MIS) and "Decision Support Systems" (DSS) were self-evidently
management tools. The idea of "Information Management" per se, was a later
concept.

However the notion of Information Management was born out of MIS and
DSS so it is appropriate at this stage to review the enthusiasm and later
disillusionment with the whole "Office System" area. Office Systems
themselves are discussed in the next chapter.

In 1977 Higgins & Finn reported the results of the attitudes of
British Chief Executives towards their Information Systems. They came from
56 organisations chosen randomly from the Times Top 1000 companies. Although
over half performed calculations, albeit infrequently, they usually did them

with "back of an envelope" sophistication.

The majority received analytical computer reports with which they were satisfied; 88% delegated decision analysis to their staff. Some thought that non-quantifiable factors were more important than quantifiable analysis, but most agreed (with reservations) that computer based-aids were indispensable.

In 1980 Booz Allen & Hamilton Inc., reported the results of a study on the activities of 300 US managers and other professionals. The results are shown opposite. Booz Allen consider that time-saving of up to 30% could be achieved for some groups. The systems which should be introduced included Teleconferencing, Multi-media store and forward communications, Large screen displays, Micrographics and digital storage, Databases and electronic publishing, Portable terminals, and Continuous speech recognition systems. Booz Allen obviously did not agree with Peter Drucker who a year or two previously had suggested that "All great ideas ultimately degenerate into hardware".

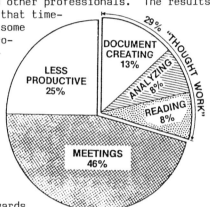

Evidently manager's attitudes towards computer based-systems were changing, and with 71% of their time poorly used or spent in meetings, there appeared to be scope for helpful systems of some kind. Above all, while US estimates for the average capitalization per factory worker was $25,000, estimates per office worker were from $2000 to $6000. In the last ten years industrial productivity had increased by 90%, office productivity by 4%. All in all it seemed to the suppliers that the time for a sales drive had arrived.

It remained difficult to acquire information about successful in-the-field systems. Why should anybody tell you about the success of their office system? While there was an excessive amount of information from the suppliers about what their systems were supposed to do, there was very little from the users about what they **actually** did. Unlike suppliers, users have no great incentive to broadcast their activities.

The computer magazines frequently publish comparative tables about the off-site performance of microcomputers, printers, desktop publishing systems, facsimile machines, Local Area Networks, etc. Unfortunately it is far harder, if not impractical, to devise a test for a **collection of people and equipment forming a system** in order to provide answers to the really important questions. These include how long does it take to learn how to use system X for the particular applications you have in mind, how reliable is it, what is the supplier's support like, and what are the benefits?

However most comments in the early days were enthusiastic. A 1964 article in Fortune is typical:- "Computerised information systems enable top management to know everything important that happens as soon as it happens".

Moving forward to the seventies the arrival of Word Processing machines provided more ammunition for "office of the future" hype. In 1978 Edwards extrapolated to the "remote management" concept:- "Distance is irrelevant....it makes no difference whether the manager is at a terminal in the office, at home, or in another city".

     But some cautionary voices were also heard. Michael Zisman of MIT (1978) considered that in the first stage, organisations would perceive opportunities for cost reduction or productivity increases using un-integrated office equipment. The second stage, which would start in the eighties, would be to replace paper flow with electronic information flow by the integration of tools. Tasks but not functions, such as office procedures, would be mechanised.

     The third stage would be to devise computer systems which would handle office processes - that is they would perform a particular job by controlling a sequence of tools. Zisman suggested that "knowledge-based systems" would be developed - an early use of a phrase which has since become commonplace. The main problems would be human; there would probably be a period of employee resistance and alienation, but "Systems might become available in five to ten years".

     There were a few more vigorous dissenters. James Driscoll, a Professor at the Sloan School of Management at MIT at the time, heads his chapter in a book about the subject (1982) "Office automation: the dynamics of a technological boondoggle".

     He says:- "The boss decides what tasks must be done....and asks the systems analyst to prepare the program. The rest of the workforce picks up the garbage which is left over at the edge of the programmed tasks....you will either like or dislike the picture depending on whether your present position makes it likely that you will be a boss/systems analyst or a garbage collector".

     However such dissenters were in a minority. There appeared to be some evidence to support the optimism of the Fortune article.

The DTI tests

     Some undramatic truths emerged when a programme for testing office installations under working conditions was put in hand by the UK Department of Trade and Industry (DTI) in 1981 (Anon, 1985. Pye, 1986). Twenty test sites in the offices of Central Government, Nationalised Industries, and Local Authorities were equipped. Site annual costs varied between £6000 and £10,000 per terminal.

     The programme concluded in 1985 having cost about £5.5M. This was a bold move - it provided working demonstrations of what could be done and gave users and equipment suppliers much needed experience. Implementation and evaluation was conducted by a consultancy group, and a report for the DTI was published in 1986.

     "Case Handling" work - that is the handling of multiple records for single cases such as an insurance policy or an employee - was done at six sites. Half of the sites concentrated on Text Production processes. Management Support applications were run at three primary sites, and eight other sites ran them as secondary applications.

The Case Handling sites were a disappointment "reflecting largely on the state of the Office Automation Industry in 1982". Text production included text preparation, telecommunication, and storage and retrieval. Although equipment and supplier's support ranged from very good to very bad and telecom software and equipment compatibility was a problem, the trial was considered valuable and all groups wanted to continue working with the support of Information Technology.

Management Support with information storage and retrieval facilities was not successful although it was re-oriented away from senior executives. The requirements for easily accessed comprehensive information were not realised.

The conclusions seemed to be that the trials generated a lot of interest and raised the level of awareness. They also showed that apart from the word processing area, most of the benefits advertised by the suppliers and their supporting core of magazine authors were, as suspected, pure hype. This hype has continued unabated ever since.

Very little happened in these extensive trials to indicate whether the executive's day was likely to be changed by IT - nothing got off the ground in this area. Although it appeared as if there were plenty of ready-to-use systems, with hindsight we can see that the trials were premature. More has happened in the last five years than in the previous twenty. For example the huge spate of business software which followed the launch of the IBM PC in the UK in 1983 did not feature in the trials.

Re-assessment

It's interesting to check the views of the "experts" from the earlier days to the present. A representative collection includes Edwards (1978, Bell Labs), Lochovsky (1983, Computer Systems Research Group, University of Toronto), Watanabe (1987, Nippon Electric), Bernier (1988, Peat Marwick), Strassman (1988, Independent Consultant), Computer Weekly contributions Harvey (1989) Rozen (1989) Meikeljohn (1989) and Ernest-Jones (1989), Wilson (1989, University of Sheffield), and Dantzig (1990, Booz Allen & Hamilton).

Edwards' remarks are based on the use of Englebart's NLS system developed at Stanford - a precursor of Hypermedia and very advanced for its time. The conclusions are about the "The portability of offices... remote management ...reduction of clerical positions, private secretaries, and middle managers as productivity increases".

Lochovsky prophesies "32 bit workstations ubiquitous in the office by 1990", with advances in natural language expert systems etc.; "a change in the whole nature of work as we know it in the office" with secretaries "becoming layout artists and format experts".

Watanabe sounds like an up-dated Lochovsky. He is looking into the future later, armed with an extra four years of galloping technology. Every information worker will have a desktop workstation, "multimedia" instead of 32 bit and "Networking among humans and resources" will include "the Intelligent Distributed Conference as a new general format for performing office work". This is a small sample of the literature, but fairly typical of the "ongoing confidence in technology" school.

Sufficient time has now elapsed for the "assessment of results" people to get to work. Disillusionment followed the DTI experiment in 1986. Since then, work on the assessment of results seems to have been stepped up.

Bernier, with reference to what he still refers to as "office automation", mildly suggests that "given the large national investment in this technology with its potential impact on the economy (notably in trade deficits) and on office employee's working lives, it seems important to provide more convincing tests of the office automation/productivity improvement hypothesis".

He goes on to describe a survey of the views of 58 managers in 11 organisations employing from 98 up to 50,000 people. A major problem was how to measure inputs and outputs and so productivity. Bernier concludes that "there is much more work to be done before the hypothesis that office technologies can improve productivity can actually be tested".

Strassman goes much further than Bernier and states that "there is absolutely no correlation between the level of investment in information technology and performance...the old input/output methods are not relevant". When boards ask for better justification, systems people and vendors reply "don't ask why, it's value is strategic".

From experience as chief information executive at General Foods, Kraft, and Xerox products, and later as a consultant, Strassman has come up with "Management's value added contribution" (which should increase with effective IT) as a measure, on the assumption that management, not capital, is the vital input.

The UK magazine "Computer Weekly" is not typical of the genre - it often takes a Strassman-like view of events. Typical story lines are "Disaster Story Part Two (Harvey 1989) in which the question "Will Executive Information Systems be a re-run of the Management Information Systems disaster story?" is asked. "What a waste of money in the City" (Rozen,1989) tells the story of design flaws and computer incompatibility problems involving delays costing "hundreds of millions of dollars".

"The measure of IT's true value" (Meiklejohn, 1989) is about the response to the request "raise your hand if you have any kind of formal procedures to measure the performance of your department" asked at a gathering of 90 senior UK IT managers. Three hands went up.

Computer Weekly also ran a two part feature in 1989 (Ernest-Jones 1989) about the returns on computer system investment. It consists of a series of quotes provided by representatives of IT-using companies, presumably in response to questions by an interviewer. This produced a very mixed response.

The main concern seems to be to justify the soaring costs of IT. An information executive at AT&T - IT budget over one billion dollars - said that measurements were the biggest IT issue for board directors and the biggest single failure of the industry. However Allied Dunbar, who armed 1500 salesmen with PCs for providing clients with on-the-spot assessments, consider that "hard cash returns have far outstripped investment".

Wilson received the support of Arthur Anderson when conducting a survey of the Information Technology Strategy of Times 500 companies in the

UK. The barriers to the formation of a strategy are stated to be (first five in order of importance) "Measuring Benefits, Nature of Business, Difficulty of Recruiting, Political Conflicts, and Existing IT Investment".

Wilson reports that out of the companies which had a strategy, 14% of respondents claimed that their IT strategy was "highly successful", and 59% said "reasonably successful".

He concludes:- "This study suggests that the picture may not be as black as others have painted. Certainly the survey reported here has gained response from more companies than has typically been the case and a certain degree of confidence can be expressed in the findings. At the very least it can be said the idea of information systems strategies is recognized by a good proportion of the companies in the Times 500 group, and has really taken hold in the financial services sector".

Finally, Dantzig reports mixed results in the US. "Properly applied, automation can and frequently does provide business answers... yet many managers that we have talked with recently express frustration with their own firm's progress in the use of information systems".

The rest of the piece is taken up with information about shortcomings, not about benefits. For example Dantzig recounts the remarks of a Vice President of a bank :- "Convinced that enhanced information system could both reduce expenses and serve as an additional source of revenue I initiated a large scale systems project... to bring in-house the processing for some 95,000 MasterCard customers... saving some $2M annually in bureau charges".

"A year and a half later... the project had slipped by four months. We subsequently learned that our company's long range plans focused almost entirely on non-consumer product areas. Our system development efforts provided very little in support of these goals. We had wasted the efforts of most of our development staff for close to 18 months and thrown away over $1M".

Dantzig's conclusions "...that limited awareness of Information System potential, technology-fostered language barriers, and the disjointedness of Information Systems within organisations have effectively blocked the integration of Systems into mainstream business activities" sound convincing.

Curiously enough, one helpful step which might prevent this kind of thing (which comes up time and time again) happening, would be to appoint an engineer/businessman as a main board director. If no such candidate is available it is the company's fault for not having the foresight to groom an engineer or a businessman to fulfill this role.

Assisting Manager's Decision Making and Saving his Time - the Target of the Equipment Manufacturers

There is no doubt that the equipment suppliers and the hyped-up brigade of magazine writers have the 5000-or-more-employee companies in mind when they talk about the "Electronic Office". So do the academics and others who pour scorn on the idea mainly for reasons to do with human conservatism and man-machine interaction problems.

The people in these companies who are a special target are managers/executives. The cost of their time saved is high so the potential savings are high. A company with 5000 or more employees is likely to have a substantial number of these people and the company's resources should be large enough to buy expensive systems if the systems can be shown to save time or raise the quality of decisions.

But most companies are not in this category.

According to the "FT top 500", the market capital of the 500th company (in Western Europe) is $536M, or say £300M, and the average number of employees for the bottom 20 is 9200 - in other words each of the top 500 employ at least 9200 people on average.

In a telecoms survey of the 17 major European countries by a consortium of five consultancy teams for the European Commission it was estimated that there were about 9000 organisations with more than 1000 employees, 52,000 between 200 and 1000, and 245,000 employing between 50 and 200. We don't know how many 1 to 50 concerns there are but it must be at least half a million.

Effects of information laissez-faire

Anthony Hopwood (1983) of the London Graduate School of Business Studies provides an example of the danger of failing to investigate the organisational impact of "unofficial" information.

The management of a British company which had survived a turbulent period with difficulty was about to disburse two thirds of its head office staff to a suburban site, with an expansion of its existing computer based management information system.

The move was abandoned following the examination of information flow in the company by a consultant. He found that the company had survived the crisis which had hit the industry primarily because of the close proximity of key members. Information was transmitted and acted upon very quickly - a role which had not been recognised in the plan for removal.

Michel Crozier (1983) recounts how an experimental computer-based system, commissioned by management, worked well on an experimental basis in a company. In production it was a complete failure "not because technical flaws emerged, but because there was an unexpected problem related to the social system of the plant. The computer was a kind of time and motion study machine which regulated production of paid workers. The problem was that it interfered with previous informal secretive arrangements which had helped both managers and workers".

A tacit agreement between foremen and employees had allowed the time worked figures to be falsified.

"Workers received more than the agreed rate which they felt was commensurate with the relative importance of the plant and the bargaining power of their union. The transparency introduced by the computer in the information gathering and processing routines meant that this arrangement could no longer be continued.

The subsequent analysis proved that the whole supervisory system at the plant had relied on the arbitrary leeway gained by the supervisors through tolerating the "cheating" by the workers. The wheels of the entire endeavour were oiled because the secret arrangement enabled all parties to have a margin for negotiation or the potential for making many other subordinate arrangements. Supervisors could use their bargaining power to obtain the co-operation of workers and their willingness to adjust quickly to crisis situations.

Conversely, shop stewards were able to maintain a strong influence on the workers because they would seem to be their natural partners in the constant bargaining with the supervisors. The advantages gained by the secret agreement meant that none of the parties wanted to accept the obvious solution, which would have been to adjust the rates of pay so that they could use the actual hours worked to achieve the required level of wages".

The information management concept

Is Information a resource in its own right requiring separate management? If it is, and because no part of an organisation can function without information, the acceptance of this idea means that an "outsider" - the new Information Manager - may have to interact with the Managers of all departments, probably including Production, R&D etc.

Terms such as "Information Management", "Competitive Advantage", and "Resource Management" started to appear in about 1977, and increased rapidly in the eighties. According to Broadbent (1988) there were 5 articles about these topics during 1977-1981 in Harvard Business Review and Sloan Management Review, but 25 during 1982-1986.

The idea of information management as a separate function in its own right seems to have originated in the seventies.

Woody Horton (1974) was one of the first to discuss the subject in detail. In talking about the need to manage both information and information tools he coined the term "Information Resources Management", suggesting that information should be a managed entity like other "human, physical, financial, and natural resources". William King was another leader who discussed similar idea from about 1975 onwards, particularly in King (1978).

An article full of pithy comment appeared in 1981 by Keen of the Sloan School of Management (1981). He chose to publish it in Communications of the ACM. In discussing long term changes in information organization he assembled a bibliography of 77 references, the earliest written in 1958.

"The point is not that managers are stupid or information systems irrelevant" says Keen, "but that decision making is multifaceted, emotive, conservative, and only partly cognitive. Formalized information technologies are not as self-evidently beneficial as technicians presume. Many descriptive models of decision making imply that "better" information will have virtually no impact".

Keen makes the following points about IT:-

1. Change must be self-motivated and based on a "felt need" with a contract between implementor and user built on mutual credibility and committment.

2. The difficulty of institutionalizing a system and embedding it in its organizational context so that it will stay alive when the designer/consultant leaves the scene.

3. The problem of operationalizing goals and identifying criteria for success

The bit I particularly like is Keen's political analysis:-

"Programs that have unclear goals or ambiguous specifications and rely on continuing high levels of competence and coordination are easy targets for skilled game players". Having described the predictable moves of players who Keen christens "Tenacity, Odd Man Out, and "Up For Grabs", he continues:-

"All these moves are found in information systems development. There is an additional maneuver (evidently the US way of spelling this word - Ed.) employed wherever computers are found - the Reputation Game. Here a manager gets a reputation as a bold innovator by sponsoring a new system - the closer to the state of the art the better, since this increases his visibility and creates excitement".

"The Reputation Gamer will have been transferred to a new position by the time the project collapses and can then ruefully say "when I was in charge of things....". The short tenure of upwardly mobile managers and their need to produce fast results encourages this move, which is only possible however when the goals of the project are not made operational or specific commitments made to deliver phased outputs".

"The simple, central argument presented here is that information systems development is political, as well as, sometimes far more than, technical in nature".

In 1982 McKenney and McFarlan wrote the first of several articles in the Harvard Business Review drawing attention to the need to co-ordinate "islands of information" - office automation, telecommunications, and data processing. A year later the subject had attracted enough interest for a state of the art review to be published (Yadav, 1983).

The convoluted example of the worker/supervisor agreement described earlier is a rather extreme case of arrangements which often exist in industry. Such understandings, coupled with general conservatism and the rather bad reputation of computerisation in general, may be a severe obstacle when attempting to canvas support from all parties for the introduction of centralised information management.

In regard to managers, "Computerised Information" often did not command support when the idea was first mooted. According to an article in the Harvard Business Review:- "If a manager does not want to use a personal computer his or her performance will not be adversely affected. This conclusion is based on the following observations.

1. The computer has not added to the important information required by top managers.

2. The important information required by top managers can best be supplied by staff personnel. It is not necessary for a manager to query a computer directly.

3. Computers with the same characteristics as the personal computer have been available to top managers of large and medium sized businesses for over fifteen years. If few top managers have been using these computers there is a considerable question about their utility".

Competitive Advantage

In a book containing the above words in its title, Ken Edwards (ICI, 1988) discusses the need to analyse an organisation's business objectives before deciding how IT can be used in support. Long interviews with senior managers, followed by extensive discussion and analysis are the first requirements. "From this are determined the factors upon which the achievement of objectives are critically dependent". Questions must then be answered about the Critical Success Factors that should be supported by an IT system and what type of business benefit it would bring.

Pointing out that successful implementation is likely to induce a reaction from competitors, Edwards suggests that these analytic activities must be a way of life - "an essential element of the resources that go in to making up a strategic plan".

Discussing "Strategic Value Analysis" Curtice (1988, Arthur D. Little) says "The key concept of SVA is that high-level strategic business objectives should help work done at lower organizational levels and identify specific Information system opportunities that support the objectives at a lower levels."

Bales of McKinsey (1988) thinks that "IT must be tightly integrated into a company's business strategy ....in certain businesses opportunities may exist to create structural competitive advantages with IT. Merrill Lynch's Cash Management Account and American Airlines SABRE reservation system are perhaps the best known of examples."

Palmer describes TRACS, CARS, and TOPS, acronyms for successive holiday reservation systems introduced by the Thomson Travel Group (1988). This is "a classic case study in the application of IT for competitive advantage ...the TOP network currently embodies 1500 lines and 42 locations. "The spectacular success with the travel trade forced other operators to develop TOP look-alike systems to the extent that these are now ubiquitous".

Palmer quotes a MORI survey in which it was found that Thomson's system is vastly superior to its competitors in speed of access and operation.

Note that Bales's and Palmer's systems are examples of tangible transactional systems which seem to have a better chance of success than "Office Information Technology".

Information Management, Information Technology, and people

The question of appointing an Information Manager, ultimately to manage all information within an organisation - an Information Overlord - is discussed in a book published in 1985 (Cronin).

In 1988 it seemed as if this might be happening because a display advertisement for "A Director of Information Systems and Telecommunications" appeared in the national press offering up to £100,000 for the job. The applicant's qualifications should include good human communication and strong management skills, systems policy and planning experience, and a technical background in IBM systems and telecommunications.

In fact the emphasis in the advertisement was on the technology. The word "information" was superfluous as the system mentioned could hardly be handling anything else. The advertiser was probably looking for a Director of Data Processing and Telecommunications which is quite different from a Director of Information.

In Cronin (1985), Martin White points out that the UK Cabinet Office 1983 ITAP report **Making a Business of Information** which emanated from an advisory panel (ITAP) "made a very good attempt at a difficult subject ....but the government failed to grasp the essential difference between technology in the service of information and information technology". Peter Drucker's terse comment made in the seventies amounts to the same thing: "All great ideas ultimately degenerate into hardware".

Lewis (1986) commented on a part of the ITAP report referring to the undervaluing of information services:- "It was also noted that both government and the information industries are fragmented in their approach to information and that both sides should take steps to bring their diverse interests together. Perhaps its main contribution was the introduction of the concept of "tradeable information" meaning information services or products which are potentially saleable and which according to current thinking should therefore be sold".

Lewis continues by expressing disappointment about the lack of government reaction to this report, particularly because "the panel felt that the uptake of information technology would be stimulated if some efforts were made to promote the development of the **information** which the technology was designed to process.

Lewis was director of Aslib, which changed its name from "Association of Special Libraries" to "The Association for Information Management" more closely to reflect its activities.

Peter Vickers (in Cronin, 1988) considers that "Management of information is not concerned simply with documents, messages, and data, but with the entire apparatus of information handling, which in most organisations today is in a state of anarchy. Such information-handling skills as do exist are scattered among information scientists, librarians, data processing personnel, systems designers, statisticians and records managers working in a variety of different departments....information management means bringing some order to the chaos."

The difficulties of implementing information management are outlined by Bob Wiggins (in Cronin, 1988), appointed Information Resources Manager at BP headquarters in 1984, but now at Scicon, in a piece about "The evolving information manager". Most of the other authors enthusiastically proclaim the benefits of appointing a Manager of Information Resources. Wiggins anticipates the problems.

The co-ordination of information activities means nosing about in other people's empires. Wiggins puts it "The need to satisfy local requirements often conflicts with corporate concerns for information". He advocates planning and co-ordinating activities by the Manager of a small Information Resources Unit which "should not become involved in the provision or detailed running of specific information services".

After talking about unnecessary duplication and the introduction of Standards he continues "considerable corporate and personal tensions are arising as organisations come to develop such an approach". This has the ring of reality about it and may well be one of the reasons why the appointment of an "Information Overlord" is a rarity.

The question of the appointment of a Chief Information Officer (CIO) received the attention of Coopers & Lybrand and is debated by Carlyle (1988). "Unfortunately the philosophical foundation for the chief information officer's title - unifying and guiding the entire corporation's information technology - bears little resemblance to the realities of the job", says Carlyle. Note, once again, that the topic of the information itself is seen as too boring to mention.

Supposedly CIOs should be "corporate eagles, using the view from their eyries to plot long term strategies that unite the business and technology sides of the house ....the CIO must be part of the inner circle of top officers to have any influence at all". But it turns out that "he or she has no direct control over any of the line organizations ...the pervasive quality of the job, guiding the flow of information throughout the corporation, had made other managers nervous ....in several cases the title created such animosity that its bearers gave it up happily; it turned them into targets". "It can take 10 years for a new piece of technology to bear fruit. Giving anything the label "technical research" or "long term" is the kiss of death in a cost-conscious environment".

It seems to me that there are several other factors contributing to the advance of IT without a commensurate advance in unified information management and information handling. The fact remains that in spite of anti-hype reaction and justifiable scepticism, IT continues to make progress. It is making even faster progress in the domestic field although "many domestic machines are created by gadget-mad engineers who forget to bear the ordinary consumer in mind" (Myerson, 1989).

The author continues "people demand enhanced super-dooper features on their domestic devices but cannot cope with the inevitable complications of using them .....men buy equipment for reasons of personal prestige and adornment .... products could be designed to look like children's toys but that would not serve the purpose of pampering the male ego".

In short, although the need for an activity to have the right **image** smacks of superficial media gloss and sales hype, the fact is that IT has it, while Information Science and Library Science ideas and personalities do not. IT advances, library budgets are cut. Absurd it may be, but Folders, Filing Cabinets and Books are out, computers are in.

Insofar as "information" has any image at all McDonald (1989), having concluded that records management and data management are the same thing, suggests that the only difference is one of perception. "Records management seems to bring to mind the image of underpaid clerks looking after paper records in file folders, while data management seems to bring to mind highly paid computer systems specialists or administrators planning and designing complex computerized databases". Perhaps the IS/LS image really does need some attention.

Alan Cane (1989), quotes some findings of a Brussels consultancy group OTR who analysed 60 typical analysts and programmers from 12 companies. Information service managers are "...poor communicators unable to sustain an effective dialogue either with senior management or their own staff. There is very little that can be done to improve this ...IS staff are lacking in influence and dominance ....most information technology specialists have poor knowledge of the business their company is in".

Margaret Slater (1987) comes to a more moderate but very similar conclusion. Her article is about the very topic of the IS/LS image. She plaintively asks "Our long-standing skills centred round information handling ought surely to merit us some place in the sunrise rather than the sunset industries?"

However "The generally low status and unimpressive image of librarians (as cited at a symposium) was also believed to lead to usage as a last resort and lack of faith in the library's ability to help ...not only do librarians suffer from an undesirable image of the buns, beads, and glasses variety, they also suffer from an anaemic, low profile, shallow image ...that can lead to virtual invisibility".

Unfortunately Slater makes few suggestions for image alteration. On the contrary the direct evidence she has unearthed includes careers advisers advice "If you want to end up as managing director don't enter library-information work".

A personal opinion cannot count for much against this weight of evidence but I don't get a "buns, beads, and glasses" image. Many of the queries addressed to librarians are of the "can you tell me where Cryogenics is kept?" variety which presents little more than an opportunity to be pleasant. However ask a question like "I'm trying to find out something about the design of chairs, and posture generally, in the context of comfort and health at work" and you will probably get a lot of help.

The reward for playing detective to put someone on the right track is a sense of achievement and pleasure in gratitude received. In any walk of life an interesting question stimulates an interesting answer. Whether the career structure in libraries enables the ambitious to get to the top is another matter.

Management politics

Should the Information Manager simply be brought in to rationalise the mechanics of information - that is to organise the equipment, telecom- munications, etc? This line was taken by Dickinson (1980) at Exxon. The Information Manager was given corporate responsibility for DP, office technology, and telecommunications.

The new manager carried out studies and provided consulting services worldwide including functional surveillance of new technology, coordination and information dissemination. He addressed problems of incompatibilities,

considered standards, developed simple transportable electronic filing
packages, and evaluated electronic mail services.

Do the properties of information make it amenable to unified
management, or are the different kinds of information handled in the
separate departments of an organistion better handled within those
departments?

There have been some cross-department trends such as the provision
of Management Information Systems, the setting up of Data Processing
Departments, and suggestions of a wider role for Information Officers -
hitherto a library based activity.

Levitan (1982) poses this question in the electronic office
context:- "The rapidly improving cost/performance ratio of computer hardware
and the proliferation of available technologies, especially those under the
umbrella of "office automation" require an enlightened management to connect
technology budgets to the values and objectives of the organization".

Management should "organize technical resources to fit the
objectives of a corporation...focus on people as well as technology for
improving services.... ...emphasize the team approach and lateral
relations...develop information services more in tune with business
needs...recognize the importance of training".

Levitan, who works for a company providing Information Resource
Management (IRM) services continues:- " IRM involves the administration of
all corporate information, of all manual and automated data, and of all
methods used for the communication, manipulation, and presentation of
information used. What does the balance sheet look like for IRM? Is it a
substantive area of management or just another slogan? On the plus side is
the fact that more than 85% of the references that support this view express
the belief that IRM is a substantive area. But IRM will not happen unless
senior management wants it to happen".

It should be beneficial to provide unified management of the means -
computers, microcomputers, office equipment and communications. This should
result in buying economies and equipment compatibility. Most departments in
an organisation would find that acceptable and would soon see the benefits.

However when it comes to the wholesale adoption of office
systems,local networks, shared resources, and centralised filing, small
departmental empires will crumble and the new Information Overlord is
unlikely to be received with rapture. Should the Information Manager be
involved with the information itself as recommended by Levitan? Could he do
the job properly without such involvement?

It seems unlikely that the Information Manager could successfully
fufill his role unless he gets involved with the requirements of different
classes of user and this must also cover the information itself. He may
need to have rather wider responsibilities that merely those of an
integrated technology implementor, and that will make it doubly difficult
for him to obtain cooperation. He will need very strong backing from top
management.

Rockart (1984) forcefully exhorts top management to become
involved:- "It is time for top management to get off the sidelines.

Recognising that information is a strategic resource implies a clear need to link information systems to business strategy and especially to ensure that business strategy is developed in the context of the new IT environment. In short, senior executives are feeling the need to become informed, energized, and engaged in information systems"

Rockart's recipe for management involvement contains a three stage process. First should come a consideration of strategy objectives culminating in a "focusing workshop"; next complete familiarisation and evaluation concluding with a "decisions scenarios workshop: then comes the prototype design, systems development, and evaluation and institutionalization.

Information Management issues today

Information on paper has increased with the increase in applications of Information Technology. The notion of the "paperless office" gradually died as this became evident, but it may quite possibly be revived. The advent of Electronic Data Information Exchange which handles purchase orders, shipping documents etc., an area responsible for the generation of huge amounts of paper, is one reason.

Another is the arrival of inexpensive devices for getting high quality images of information on paper into digital format. Several very large information storage and retrieval systems are now on the market for business use. This area was covered in Chapter 11. Arthur Andersen identify eight processes in Technical Information Management as used in their ATOL systems integration service (Anon, 1988) :-

Information Capture	Information Configuration
Information Interpretation	Information Storage & Retrieval
Information Creation and Review	Information-driven Processes
Information Management	Information Distribution

ATOL is targetted at organisations that have to process massive volumes of paperwork. A complete complex of equipment, which is working at their London office, commits Text, Graphics, Images, and Voice data to an Integrated computerized information system.

As judged by the numerous publications about the topic, major information management topics and activities today may be listed in a way which is more abstract and yet more specific. It includes:-

1. The variety of successful well managed Information Systems.

2. Value/productivity gains from Information Technology (IT).

3. Competitive advantage conferred by IT; strategic potential.

4. IT and operations management, but not information management.

5. Information Managers and Information Overlords.

6. Managers lack of understanding of IT. Will they use it?

7. Executive Information Systems (EIS).

The interest seems to centre on topics divisible into these seven groups with blurred edges. The kinds of publication in which the topic is discussed tends to support the idea that Information Technology per se, and the useful application of it are separate subjects.

What I don't see is a strong connection between Information/Library Science which is the concern of information organisers/disseminators, and Information Technology, the concern of hardware and software salesmen, managers who do not wish to appear fossilised, and unsure users. Evidently Information on paper, in folders, and in filing cabinets is different in some way from Information Technology Information.

Successful Systems

Regarding the first item on the above list, it is quite easy to find a number of manifestly successful applications where the dilemmas implied in other items on the list seem to be non-existent. Among these are Bank IT, as in the SWIFT inter-bank fund transfer system (in spite of its inadequacy), Credit Card, and Automatic Teller Machine networks, Building Society IT Electronic Data Interchange (EDI), Travel Agents holiday booking systems, Airline ticket reservation (SITA), Money Market Information Systems and so on.

These successes are all about **Transactional Tangible Information** usually associated with a **Specific Services** where the **Measurable Financial Advantage** of the application of IT can be convincingly demonstrated.

Most of the remaining items on the list - about **IT in Organisational and Management processes, and for the supply of Management Information, where the benefits are much harder to quantify,** have been discussed in this Chapter.
Something remains to be said about item 6, and rather more about item 7.

Manager's understanding of IT

If someone asks you what you do and you say you are engaged in "Information Technology", reactions vary from polite indifference to thinly veiled animosity. It seems to be regarded as a form of technical pollution. Worse still you are likely to be considered as being too clever by half.

So far as familiarisation with IT systems is concerned, only frequent use will eliminate the need for a course on it each time you want to use it again.

It's not surprising, therefore, to read that "Many managers have a guilty secret which they go to great lengths to hide from their subordinates. They do not really understand how their company's computer system works" (Skapinker 1988).

In a survey by the British Institute of Management aimed at general managers and completed by 750 BIM members, although more than half used a computer at least once a week, and over 40% every day, half said they had an inadequate knowledge of how to use it :-

"The unpalatable truth is that few organisations plan or rigorously manage their IT training and educational activities. As a result these activities are characterised by a failure to set goals and monitor results, little concept of value for money, and a focus on immediate operational needs".

Tandem computers commissioned an IT survey of manager's views by a market research company. the results were published in Anon (1988). The survey covered 42 of the top companies in the UK in a range of different activities. According to this survey "Information Technology is now seen as a strategic business weapon". However managerial reactions are mixed.

"Managers are frightened and feel threatened unless introduced to IT with care ....age is a significant factor, younger managers being much more receptive ....middle managers were identified as low points in terms of acceptance ....many chief executives were identified as computer illiterates although this was not seen as a problem provided that they appreciated the value and use of IT".

Executive/Management information systems

One of the reasons why the new name "Executive Information Systems" was introduced is because of the disastrous history of "Management Information Systems" and "Decision Support Systems".

A tremendous amount has been written about Management or Executive, Decision, Information, or Support Systems. In an MIS review for ARIST, Weiss (1970) had to consider 1600 documents. One of the earliest articles in which computers were considered for these functions was published by Rowe (1962).

As can be seen from the quotations at the beginning of this Chapter spanning a 20-year period, both expectations and realities generate the same divergent opinions whether it be 1968 or 1988.

Some of the remarks quoted by Weiss still seem to be applicable. "While we all have an intuitive idea about what is meant by Management Information System, formulating a precise and satisfactory definition is quite another matter". Moreover the "four perspectives" identified by Weiss - functional internal and external information, planning and control decision-making, scheduled or on-demand exception reporting, and database manipulation - still seem to be in evidence today.

Weiss continues "To some extent the difficulties that so many organisations have been having with computer-centred management information systems can be attributed to gaps in our understanding of the decision-making process itself". Another difficulty, common to all information systems, is the problem of cost-justifying the intangible.

Today the phrase which seems to have stuck is "Executive Information Systems" (EIS), which I shall use from now on. The software costs and implementation time/cost of EIS make them expensive. The requirements for installing EIS are the faith and the clout of the potential users. The intangibility of the benefits make it difficult to justify implementation in hard commercial terms.

Early work seems to have been concentrated upon management decision making processes. It provided academics with the opportunity to produce learned papers about mathematical modelling and gave them something to do with their computers. The field got a bad name when managers tried to use the systems for business purposes because the models used by system designers did not realistically simulate human decision making processes.

This kind of work has continued and has been expanded to some degree by the lure and glamour of Artificial Intelligence (AI). The success, or rather the lack of success - as at 1986 and still today - of applying AI to the problem has been well covered by Sutherland (1986).

"The degree of analytical challenge devolving on decision functionaries attempting to manage real-world organizations or processes" says Sutherland "is generally a consequence of two factors: 1. The degree of complexity associated with the environment in which the organization is resident, and 2. The level of the managerial hierarchy at which some functionary is operating".

Because of the current interest in AI it is worth quoting Sutherland's conclusions while enduring his rhetoric and alliteration :-

"The net effect (of AI developments) is a portrait of human intelligence that is little more than a thinly disguised allegory for the procedural predilections of contemporary analytical philosophers or theoretical mathematicians... thus as currently formulated, neither expert systems nor discovery constructs may be said to have any fundamentally unique contribution to make to information/decision system technology".

But "If somewhat redirected, the AI research and development agenda might indeed be extended to next generation systems...etc". So there is still some hope.

Today's EIS have moved in a rather different direction, and have been able to do so because of developments in computer power, business software, and graphic displays. Current trends seem to be as follows:-

1. Providing special software for the selective retrieval of data available from an organisation's mainframe computer, and/or from external information sources.

2. Arranging for the software to provide access to critical data sources via an interface directly useable by executives, rather than by information specialists, with "key indicator" information displayed in well designed colour graphic form.

3. Exploiting financial modelling usually of the multiple spread-sheet type, and the provision of calculations controlled by rules which may be switched by the user.

4. Providing exception reporting - i.e. providing information about key data when it varies by more than some pre-determined amount.

In an earlier article Moad (1988) reviews progress in the US where it is estimated that over 1000 EIS are now operating. EIS is said to be a challenge to information systems people in the company who are asked to get an EIS working quickly once the top people in the company have decided.

At the same time "a host of political problems arise when top executives suddenly get direct access to data that had previously been the proprietary domain of one department or another".

With regard to cost justification, most executives just don't attempt it, says Moad. "The payoffs from EIS's are different from other types of information systems in that they are often less tangible, less quantifiable ...with an EIS you're talking about providing top executives with better information, faster ....the real payoff is in giving an executive quick access to reliable information that can be used in new combinations and may lead to new ways of thinking and better decisions".

The principal suppliers of EIS in the UK are Comshare, Metapraxis using a UK-designed system, and Thorn-EMI. Prices depend on the need for members of the supplier's staff to organise and start up the system, and which modules are selected. It is unlikely that the installation/run charge will be less than £50,000, and there may be annual licence payments as well.

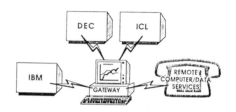

Access to multiple incompatible sources via a gateway

With Comshare's Commander system, which from July 1988 onwards was also marketed by IBM, the major components are the Executive Workstation, the mainframe-resident Workstation Manager software which controls the flow of data to workstations, the Information Integration software which extracts and merges data from a variety of sources, Application Packaging software tools, and the Execu-View interface/ modelling package.

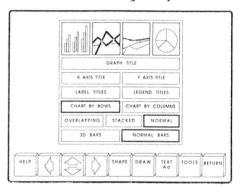

Screen of Comshare's workstation in "builder's tool" mode

Two interesting features are shown in the attached figures. The system provides data extraction from incompatible sources through a gateway - for instance from IBM machines with VM/CMS or MVS/TSO , DEC VAX's, or ICL machines with VME. The screen shows access to "builder's tools", provided for supporting staff who will tailor the system to local requirements.

Metapraxis provide similar facilities with their Resolve system but arrange it round an IBM PC/AT-or-clone type computer. The software for this "workstation" occupies 1.5 Mbytes of hard disk and another 5 Mbytes is required for site data. Data is exchanged automatically with a mainframe computer as needed. The company claims that its system is used in the boardrooms of BAE, BP, BT, Hanson, Glaxo, Prudential, Sears and Whitbread.

Thorn-EMI provide a different emphasis with their FCS-PILOT EIS system, although again the facilities provided are similar. The system runs on a DEC VAX or an IBM 9370 machine. According to David Friend of Pilot Executive Software, the US company for whom Thorn-EMI handle the system in Europe, "spreadsheets have been a great boon to analysts but a great disappointment to executives.

The people we think of as decision makers are not the people who use Decision Support Tools. Decision making - at least the kind that requires modelling and "what if" scenarios - is an infrequent activity far overshadowed by decision implementation. Management needs a feedback mechanism to tell them what is working and what is not. This kind of information has nothing to do with spreadsheets".

Some results have been reported about these systems (Harvey 1989). In a survey of 19 EIS installations, the finance director was the initiator and project controller. The three major suppliers have now been joined by a number of others who offer mainly PC-based systems.

Each takes a different view of what they think directors need to know and so offer different solutions. One thinks that news and events from the outside world should be available, others provide planning and modelling facilities, and yet others concentrate on key indicator presentation with limited amounts of data.

References

Anon.
Department of Trade & Industry, London.
Bulletin of office automation pilot projects. Number 7. May 1985.
Anon.
Arthur Andersen, 2 Arundel St., London. 1988.
Simplification through integration: ATOL centre.
Anon.
Countrywide Publications for Tandem Computers, Stockley Park,
Uxbridge, England. 1988.
Corporate trends in information technology - a high level
survey on trends and implications of systems in British
industry and commerce.
Bales, Carter F.
Datamation, 71-82, October 1st 1988.
The myths and realities of competitive advantage.
Bernier, Michel, et al.
Canadian Psychology 29(1), 116-125, 1988.
Productivity improvement and office automation:
a survey of managers.
Broadbent, Marianne, and Koenig, M.E.D.
In Annual Review of Information Science and Technology,
Volume 23, 1988. Martha E. Williams (Ed). Elsevier 1988.
Chapter 9. Information & information technology management.
Cane, Alan.
Financial Times, February 27th 1989, page 15.
Why computer babble is counter-productive.
Carlyle, Ralph E.
Datamation, 50-56, August 1st 1988.
CIO: misfit or misnomer?
Cronin, B.(Ed).
Aslib, London. 1985.
Information management: from strategies to action.
Crozier, Michael.
In Otway, H.J; Peltu, Malcolm. (Eds) Francis Pinter, London, 1983.
New office technology: human and organisational aspects.
Implications for the organisation.

526

Curtice, Robert M.
        Information Strategy, 16-24, Summer 1988.
                A formula that equates IS and prosperity
Dantzig, David F.
        Journal of Systems Managemnet 41(2), 32-37, February 1990.
                Untangling information systems.
Dickinson, Robert M.
        Industrial Engineering 50-55, July 1980.
                Exxon. How a major corporation is coping with the
                pressures of an office automation program.
Driscoll, James W.
        In Landau, Robert: Bair, James R.: Siegman, Jean H. (Eds). Ablex
        Publishing Corp., Norwood, N.J. 07648, USA. 1982. Emerging Office
        Systems. Page 259.
                Office automation: the dynamics of a technological
                boondoggle.
Edwards, Gwen C.
        Telecommunications Policy 2(2), 128-136, 1978.
                Organizational impacts of office automation.
Edwards, Ken.
        In Information Management & Competitive Success, Aslib,
        1988. (John Whitehead, Ed). pps 153-158.
                Introducing new technology: the management need
                to get IT right.
Ernest-Jones, Terry.
        Computer Weekly, pps 20-21,28. February 16th and 23rd 1989.
                Does your system give value for money? Productivity
                and the business PC.
Harvey, David.
        Computer Weekly, 20-21, April 20th 1989.
                Systems that suit the boardroom barons.
Harvey, David.
        Computer Weekly, page 2, May 25th 1989.
                Disaster story part two.
Higgins, J.C. and R. Finn.
        Omega, 5(5), 557-566, 1977.
                The chief executive and his information system.
Hopwood, Anthony G.
        In Otway, H.J; Peltu, Malcolm. (Eds) Francis Pinter, London, 1983.
        New office technology: human and organisational aspects. Page 37.
                Evaluating the real benefits.
Horton, Forest W.
        Association for Systems Management, Cleveland OH. 1974.
                How to harness information sources: a systems approach.
Keen, Peter G.W.
        Comm. ACM 24(1), 24-33, January 1981.
                Information systems and organizational change.
King, William R., and Cleland D.I.
        Van Nostrand Rheinold. New York. 1978.
                Strategic planning and Policy.
Levitan, Karen B,
        In Williams. Martha E. (Ed). Annual review of information science
        and technology. Volume 17. Knowledge Industries, White Plains NY.
        1982. Chapter 8. Page 227.
                Information Resources Management.

Lewis, D.A., and Martyn, J.
        Aslib Proceedings 38(1), 25-34, 1986.
                An appraisal of national information policy in the United
                Kingdom.
Lochovsky, Fred H.
        Proc. IEEE 71(4), 512-518, April 1983.
                Improving office productivity: a technology perspective.
McDonald, John.
        Records Management J. 1(1), 4-11, 1989.
                Records management and data management.
McKenny, James L., McFarlan F., et al.
        Harvard Business Rev., 6C(5), 109-119, 1982.
                The information archipelago: maps and bridges.
Meiklejohn, Ian.
        Computer Weekly, page 2, April 27th 1989,
                The measure of IT's true value.
Moad, Jeff.
        Datamation, 43-52, May 15th, 1988.
                The latest challenge for IS - the executive suite.
Myerson, Jeremy.
        The Daily Telegraph, page 15, July 3rd 1989.
                High-tech havoc in the home.
Palmer, Colin.
        Long Range Planning, 21(6), 26-29, 1988.
                Using IT for competitive advantage at Thompson Holidays.
Pye, Roger, Jim Bates et al.
        Report by KMG Thomson McClintock for the Dept. of Trade & Industry.
        1986.
                Profiting from Information Technology Vol. A: The way
                forward. Vol B: Final evaluation results.
Rockart, John F.
        Sloan Management Rev. 3-16, Summer 1984.
                Engaging top management in information technology.
Rowe, Alan J.
        Management International Review, 2, 9-22, Jan-Feb 1962.
                Assessing the artificial intelligence contribution to
                decision technology.
Rozen, John.
        Computer Weekly, March 2nd, 1989.
                What a waste of money in the City.
Skapinker, Michael.
        Financial Times, page 15, September 12th, 1988.
                The managers operating behind a culture of bluff.
Slater, Margaret.
        J. Information Science 13, 335-342, 1987.
                Careers and the occupational image.
Strassman, Paul. (Interviewed by David Harvey).
        Computer Weekly, 22-23, September 29th, 1988.
                Is your gamble on technology paying off?
Watababe, Hitoshi.
        IEEE Communications Magazine 25(12), 74-80, 1987.
                Integrated office systems: 1995 and beyond.
Weiss, Stanley D.
        In Annual Review of Information Science and Technology (Carlos
        Cuadra Ed). Volume 5, Encylopaedia Britannica, Chicago, 1970.
                Chapter 11. Management information systems.

528

Wiggins, R.E.
        J. Info. Sci. 12(1986), 293-299, 1986.
                Information management - a BP approach.
Wilson, T.D.
        International Journal of Information Mannagement 9, 245-258, 1989.
                The implementation of information system strategies in UK
                companies: aims and barriers to success.
Yadav, S.B.
        Database 14(3), 3-20, 1983.
                Determining an organisation's information require-
                ments: a state of the art review.
Zisman, Michael D.
        Sloan Management Review, 1-16, Spring 1978.
                Office automation. Revolution or evolution?

CHAPTER 21. OFFICE SYSTEMS PART 1:
INTRODUCTION, SYSTEMS, & WORD PROCESSING

> Communicative interactions are not "about" anything be-
> cause their stuff already inheres in the mind waiting to be
> brought up by a configuring pattern that we call messages
>   Marshall McLuhan

Introduction

Turoff and Hiltz (1980), when trying out different kinds of computer software, understood the problems of designing acceptable useable systems and sarcastically observed :- "Everyone knows how to transform a 1970 model office. Hire an interior decorator, knock down some walls, and hang up a lot of plants to make it **look** like pictures of the office of the future. ....order a few more computers and add the latest fillip - an electronic mail system. However none of this should touch top management - they should be left in their private corner offices dictating to their private secretaries and never clouding their brains by interacting with a computer in any way".

How do I contact those people who don't have an electronic mailbox?

FROM A PACIFIC TELESIS LEAFLET DESCRIBING
THEIR ELECTRONIC MAIL SYSTEM

With the decline in Manufacturing and Agriculture and growth of the Service Industries we can say with some certainty that these days most people work in an office of some kind. Even quite small offices may possess a photocopier, a facsimile machine, and a word-processing typewriter, or a microcomputer and printer with word processing software.

Some quite small offices have taken in the next stage as well - the use of a computer with software for other control and administration purposes. I know a small farmer who uses a microcomputer in the room in his farmhouse which does duty as an office for record keeping and processing - for example for milk yields.

I also know the owner of a metal plating business who employs six people and uses a computer system for his chemical delivery schedules, customer's plating specifications, control of plated items in and out, accounts, invoicing, and correspondence.

As a company grows bigger we can expect to find more microcomputers being used for Spreadsheets and Databases. Communicating word-processors may be used, and perhaps there will be a small PBX with a telephone operator. The accounts department will probably possess a dedicated small computer.

For specialised and larger organisations software packages are now available for almost every kind of business activity to run on microcomputers, minicomputers, or mainframes. There are packages for property management, cartography, pensions, project management, job costing, production management, econometrics, training - the list is endless.

At some stage may come the first realisation that something different is happening. Word Processors require people with special training, but communicating word processors imply a sufficient volume of work to justify resource sharing which means that "Office Systems" are here. Someone has got to organise the resources - for instance shared filing systems. The step from your own paper files in a cabinet to machine-stored files is a substantial one.

Further moves into Office Information Technology will mean substantial expenditure, specialist management, and staff who must be carried along with new interconnected systems. Unless new things are introduced gradually, explanations are given, and skills are rewarded, employees may become less than co-operative.

It is about this wider area that so much has been published and in which so many mistakes have been made as already discussed in Chapter 20. A review of the history and technology of office automation up to 1988 was published by Martin (1988).

Improved working conditions?

Olsen (1982) thinks that the location and temporal definition of work may be altered; people will work at home and enjoy increased flexibility and savings in commuting time; managers will monitor and control employees remotely. (This was how Orwell's "Inner Party" managed its affairs).

Giuliano (1982) suggests that office work can be divided into three evolutionary stages. First came the pre-industrial small office with little attention being paid to work flow or productivity. It was a friendly place with most people doing their own thing. Next came the "industrial" office - a much larger affair embodying work simplification and time and motion study not unlike a mass production line.

In the third stage "The company can expect dramatic savings in personnel costs. Staff reductions of as much as 50% have been common in departments making the change-over to a work station system. Those employees who remain benefit from a marked improvement in the quality of their working life". Giuliano also dwells on the developing "virtual office" - that is an office which is anywhere that the remotely connected worker happens to be.

A better life for secretaries?

Niels Bjorn-Andersen (1983) identifies three possibilities for the traditional secretarial role in "the changing roles of secretaries and clerks". If technology takes over routine tasks the secretary might become the "office wife" providing general support, passing on gossip etc. But "changing social attitudes and the elimination of the legitimacy of using a secretary as a status symbol means that the office-wife role is unlikely to grow significantly".

More likely the secretary will become a "girl Friday" taking on responsibilities such as information retrieval, telephoning and other PA activities. However the big jump is to the "manager's co-worker" - for example at Copenhagen Business School some secretaries do tasks like administering student's duties, negotiating with publishers over books and papers, and do some teaching. Lecturers actually write their own letters.

Productivity

Keen (1982) stresses the need for a definition of office productivity. He cites plans made by 25 American organisations with a commitment to technology, the main objective being an increase in the productivity of white collar workers. In only five cases were methods for measuring productivity suggested, although in all cases things like return on investment, application priorities etc., depend on having clear productivity criteria.

"Specialists involved in applying computer-based systems thrive on words that rarely get defined such as "productivity", "user involvement", and "top management commitment". They are used almost as magic spells, as if to use the labels is to create reality. These are of little value unless "productivity is translated into something concrete and meaningful".

Keen lists six basic resources: hardware; software; technical development staff; project control staff and methods; support staff; business planners. "A key element is handling the culture gap between users and designers. This requires participation of hybrid individuals who are fluent about the technology and literate about its applications. Studies of successful computerised systems show the importance of skilled hybrids - facilitators, change agents, educators, and consultants.

He continues:- "The studies of unsuccessful efforts attribute the negative consequences of a technocentric design focus or user departments which have no way to support the user and bridge the culture gap". In discussing the question of leadership and authority Keen says that "the leader must be an innovator, able to focus on problem solving, having a high credibility which allows risks to be taken and a degree of pragmatism which prevents extreme risks.

BE SELF JUSTIFYING. Be seen to contribute to productivity.

MAKE SOMEONE HAPPY by solving someone's problems or creating opportunities.

BE PHASEABLE with short phases and firm delivery dates.

TEACH designers and users.

DON'T PUT AT RISK morale, stability, and efficiency.

TABLE 21.1. KEY FACTORS IN INTRODUCING OFFICE SYSTEMS

Innovators are different to ideas people - they focus their energies on results, and show a readiness to seek out new ideas and know how to use ideas people". Keen's ideas about tackling office automation are shown in Table 21.1.

Chen (1982) criticises the omission of the evaluation of intangible benefits. It's hard to believe that any serious study could be carried out without this kind of evaluation, which, he might have added, is very hard to carry out. The quantification of intangibles is notoriously difficult.

Time saved can, of course, be costed, but it is difficult to bring credibility to estimates of the amount of time that might be saved.

Modelling Office Systems

An excellent review of the modelling work then in progress was published in 1980 by Ellis. In it a description of the ancestry of the Xerox Star - the "Officetalk" software, first implemented on the Alto computer - is given, with the Star not mentioned by name, presumably for commercial reasons. Information flow and processing considered as a tree structure with nodes at which activities are performed has also been discussed by Smith (1980) of Xerox.

Ellis comments:- "The problem of retaining social contact among workers is yet unsolved; the trend toward automation works against the goal of maintaining a social structure... there is a danger that informal conversation will be destroyed... with the possible exception of some word processing centres, most current automated office centres have not developed to the point where they have endangered channels of social conversation...the next steps in automation will probably require more effort toward maintaining informal communication channels".

Ellis published a further review in 1984 summarising the work at the Xerox Palo Alto Research Centre (PARC) with Information Control Nets covering information flow, electronic mail, and organisational needs. PARC was one of the leaders, if not **the** leader, in this field, so this article, containing a good bibliography, is well worth reading.

The SCOOP system has been described by Zisman (MIT 1978). It uses augmented Petri Nets - a formalised model for depicting information flow in an office, as discussed earlier by Peterson (1977). Zisman's comments about what he calls "automating goal producing functions" - the testing stage of which were at least 5 to 10 years away (from 1978) in his opinion - are worth quoting at length.

"It is the manager of an organization who has a notion of process. From a very simplistic viewpoint, the devices in the office are resources of the secretary, and the secretary is a resource of the manager. By mechanising devices we are addressing the resources of the secretary, but, by and large, not those of the manager.

However, when we attack office processes we are automating office functions, not office tasks, and are addressing problems of the manager. We are not suggesting that secretaries will be replaced, but we do suggest that some of the more structured, routine, and mundane responsibilities of the secretary and manager will be (almost) completely automated at this stage, thus making this group of workers available for more productive activities.

Zisman expresses the hope that as workers are relieved of mundane and routine functions which are turned over to computer control, there will be less employee alienation and quicker acceptance of the technology.

Although Zisman delves into behavioural matters to some degree, not a word is written about the possible unemployment consequences. Like most automation practitioners he cuts off at this point, and his remarks about "job enlargement" may indicate that he thinks unemployment is unlikely. He seems to believe that a smooth evolutionary transition will occur.

An IBM office model for automatically managing an operation such as accounts receivable has been described by Hammer. As machine readable forms pass through stages of processing, information from input "documents" is absorbed, e.g. receipt for goods, and other "documents" such as invoices are generated at the output. Similar work has been described by de Sousa (1980) where "print" and "control" data streams embody information about documents which may be processed and distributed.

Work has been in progress at IBM since about 1974 on a high level management language, now an IBM product, called "Query by example" (Zloof 1977 and 1980). The objective is to enable a user directly to express the equivalent of a lengthy program in order to manipulate data without having to acquire the skills of a programmer. Options are selected from menus which set up the program parameters.

Information may be mapped from one form to another or on to other objects such as letters - for example a name and address can be mapped from a form on to a letter in the correct position. The system enables a variety of objects such as charts, letters and facsmile documents to be created, edited, and communicated to others.

Another model called POISE has been described by David Croft (1984) and implemented at the University of Massachusetts. It uses a so-called intelligent interface for handling several kinds of information. For example the "Procedure Library" contains form filling procedures.

When a user enters certain details he is referred to the "Semantic Database" containing forms for completion. The objective, as in other similar systems, is to force formalisation amenable to computer manipulation. POISE also includes components for formalising procedure specifications and planning.

All this modelling work mainly based on improving the flow of office procedures does not seem to have reached the stage of actually improving work flow. Most of the improvements have come from making office tasks easier or by providing better means for communication.

Today's big office systems.

A number of very big organisations have invested large sums in big systems more as an Act of Faith than as the result of the analysis of potential quantifiable benefits. They have the resources to install the systems, to introduce those facilities likely to provide benefits, and then try them out on their staff.

Better, less expensive, long distance telecommunications and the successful and much wider use of Local Area Networks (LANs - first operating nearly 2C years ago), have been important factors. Glaxo, for example, operate the system shown in Figure 21.1. Part of the network serving only one division of the company, not the whole company, is shown.

The services consist of a number of terminals or workstations connected to a fibreoptic LAN. A workstation is a souped-up terminal usually with considerable built-in processing power.

Nearby sites with terminals are connected to the same network

534

through multiplexed cables. A "mux" at each end of a wideband cable enables
a number of communication channels to work through a single cable without
mutual interference. Heavy traffic to more distant sites is multiplexed
through high-capacity British Telecom Megastream links as shown in the upper
part of the figure.

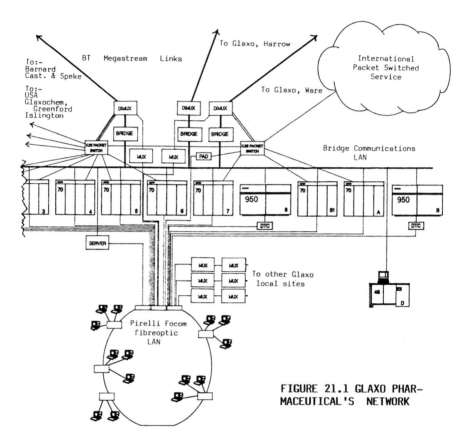

FIGURE 21.1 GLAXO PHAR-
MACEUTICAL'S NETWORK

Telecommunications are also provided using packet-switched circuits.
Packet switching provides certain economies and engineering advantages but
data handling has to conform to internationally agreed protocols (rules)
managed by computer controlled devices labelled "X25" in the figure - the
standardised interchange.

The system embodies a series of controlling Hewlett Packard small
computers shown across the middle of the figure, themselves inter-connected
through a separate LAN.

Systems in design and general offices today

Super-computers such as those made by Cray and the largest IBM
machines are able to work at speeds around 50 million floating point
calculations per second (MFLOPS). Workstations of similar power are now

available capable of performing the kinds of operation required for the construction and display of sophisticated engineering and design graphics.

The Ardent Titan workstation contains a number of processors operating in parallel, interconnected by busses running at 256 Mbytes/second. Large data files are stored in "stripes" across disks; a large file can be read into memory in one access. The workstation can run at 60 MFLOPS. Developments in technology have provided so much local power that access to a mainframe may be unnecessary. Power undreamt of a few years ago and unuseable at a distance because of the cost of the telecoms required to deliver it may now be situated at your desk.

The kind of office services available with appropriate hardware, software, and communications not unlike those at Glaxo, have been described by Dutton (1986, Mond division of ICI).

Application	First discussed	First introduced	Routinely available	Time span (Years)
Turnkey library systems	1980	1985	1986	6
Local area networks	1979	1981	1986	7
Facsimile		1978	1984	6*
Online search, internal databases	1972	1976	1984	12
End-user online search	1979	1983	1985	6
Viewdata	1978	1981	1984	6
Current awareness profiles	1965	1968	1971	6
Inter-communicating word processors (international)	1978	1981	1986	8
Mini microcomputers for text systems		1979	1984	5*

* The time span only covers the period from when the application was first introduced until it was routinely available, since a date for when the application was first discussed cannot realistically be given.

TABLE 21.2. ICI'S OFFICE SYSTEM DEVELOPMENT

A range of services are provided – for commercial activities they include word processing/filing, messaging, telexing, spreadsheets (to be discussed later), and database searching. Implementation, costing about £500,000 (late seventies and early eighties), was evolutionary, not revolutionary, as may be seen from Table 21.2 (after Dutton).

As a result of the Mond experience ICI installed a comprehensive system at their London headquarters (Figure 21.2).

In spite of all the office modelling and production flow work that went on up until the eighties, "office automation" today usually boils down to a set of more or less integrated software packages handling separate popular office tasks.

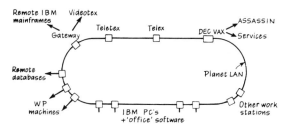

FIGURE 21.2. ICI'S HEAD OFFICE SYSTEM

The three major suppliers are IBM, Digital Equipment Corporation (DEC) and Hewlett Packard who offer OfficeVision, All-in-1, and NewWave respectively.

IBM OfficeVision is intended to replace older office products and will run on IBM personal computers, minicomputers, and mainframes. It includes Diary, in-house messaging, Screenmail - an electronic mail and database Netview managed network - as well as telecoms over token-ring LANs.

DEC's All-in-1 Phase 2 includes similar office packages and will run on VAX minicomputers MS-DOS, UNIX, OS/2 and Apple Macintoshes. (Figure 21.3)

Hewlett Packard's New Wave for PCs includes desk manager, electronic mail and database services with directory management and PC X25 links. It runs on HP's MPE operating system, MS-DOS, or UNIX. It includes "compound object management" for dealing with multimedia (Figure 21.4).

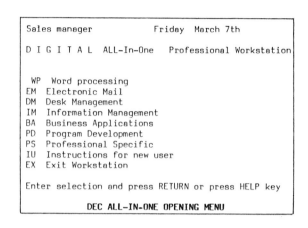

```
Sales manager                    Friday  March 7th

D I G I T A L   ALL-In-One    Professional Workstation


  WP   Word processing
  EM   Electronic Mail
  DM   Desk Management
  IM   Information Management
  BA   Business Applications
  PD   Program Development
  PS   Professional Specific
  IU   Instructions for new user
  EX   Exit Workstation

Enter selection and press RETURN or press HELP key

          DEC ALL-IN-ONE OPENING MENU
```

FIGURE 21.3

ODA (Office Document Architecture) is a set of standards "for structuring and encoding documents so that they can be interchanged between

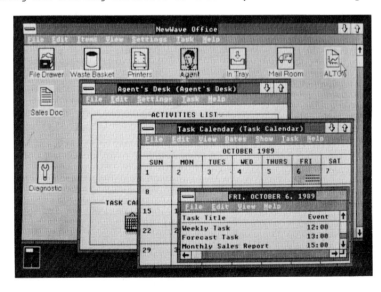

FIGURE 21.4. SCREEN FROM HEWLETT PACKARD'S NEW-WAVE OFFICE SYSTEM

dissimilar systems, viewed as intended by the document originator, or processed by other users. ODA is a joint effort of ISO and CCITT" (Ansen, 1989). For a very good introduction to ODA see Brown (1990).

It's easy to convey personal information in a letter, or to send elaborate information in a report, to someone in, say, New York, knowing that they will see it exactly as you intended - you simply post it to them. But such is the diversity of computers and data processing equipment and its interconnections, that an exchange of data to be reproduced as a document on a receiving machine is uncertain or may be impossible - unless it is between machines of the same type from the same manufacturer.

The OSI model, as explained in Chapter 7, defines and shows the relationship between the different parts of a system needed to compile, send, and reproduce a document or message from one machine to another (remote) machine, so that the document reproduced by the remote machine is presented just as the sender intended. The model identifies the successive modules/processes through which the outgoing data must pass before passing along a communications channel as code, to be subjected at the incoming end by the same processes in reverse.

The process of interest here corresponds to that part of the model known as the "Application Layer" - the first in the outgoing and the last in the incoming sequence of processes, and the one whereby humans interact with their machines - in this case the sending and receiving of documents - known as "Office Document Architecture" (ODA). The standard covering this process is ISO 8613 which became an International Standard in December 1987. The several hundred pages of the standard are immensely detailed.

A small number of OSI compatible applications are getting near to launching because they are driven by commercial imperatives. Examples are X400 electronic mail/file transfer systems and the MAP/TOP manufacturing and drawing office protocols. ODA is considered to be a "good thing" but its progress is leisurely. Its impact is unlikely to be directly felt for some years, but indirectly its effect is being felt now because new additions and improvements in document handling systems are increasingly OSI compatible in order to avoid their demise when OSI implementation becomes widespread.

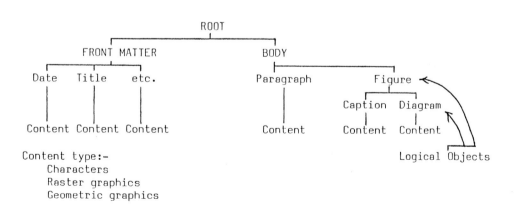

FIGURE 21.5. LOGICAL STRUCTURE OF REVISABLE DOCUMENT

538

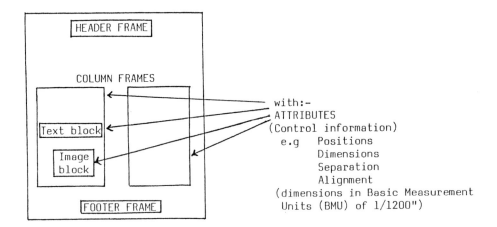

FIGURE 21.6. LAYOUT OF FORMATTED DOCUMENT

In the ISO 8613 standard, provision is made for describing a document in revisable (processable) form, with or without details about the style of its layout, or in formatted form - a "final" version - which is not intended to be edited.

A "Document Profile" is associated with this description which is a kind of surrogate providing information about the document's attributes such as date, author(s), abstract, keywords, security classification, and so on. To describe the document in revisable form, it must follow, for example in the case of a report, the kind of logical structure shown in Figure 21.5.

By applying control data to the Logical Objects in sequence, a formatted document may be produced containing objects such as pages, frames, and blocks, with page layouts - for example as in Figure 21.6.

Figure 21.7 shows the items which would need to be specified for a particular page containing a single column of text wrapped round a left aligned picture.

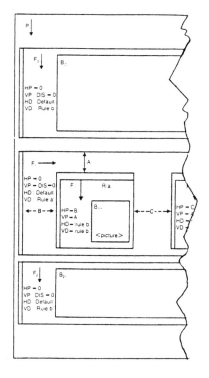

FIGURE 21.7. AN ODA-SPECIFIED PAGE

Trying to standardise document exchange and format   2. SGML

Another standard associated with ISO 8613 is coming into use - ISO 8879 covering SGML (Standard Generalised Markup Language) - a language which can be used to tag generically the parts of a document structured to the requirements of ISO 8613.

SGML incorporates document exchange standards from the viewpoint of publishers and printers. Unsurprisingly their viewpoint differs from the office systems and telecommunications people who are behind ODA. As is usual in standardisation politics, a compromise is "enacted" to accommodate the dominant teams of players. A much more desirable single standard is not enacted.

SGML embodies tags like "paragraph", "column", "table", "main body", "preface", "reference section" etc. Such tags have got to be inserted by someone, for example authors if they consider there is a payoff for their extra time - to be interpreted by a typesetting machine. They could also be used for selectively retrieving parts of the document for repackaging.

With SGML the beginning and end of logical units in a document (See Brown, 1989) are tagged. It takes the idea of formatting codes, as used in WP software, much further and instead of there being as many different codes as there are WP packages, SGML is a standard comprehensive markup code. It is an ISO standard and fits into the OSI model (see Chapter 7)

Brian (1988) says that "SGML is the internationally recognized standard for identifying text, enabling the different parts of the text's structure to be identified and described so that each part can be handled and accessed as appropriate....the work that has gone into it is colossal and complex, but the demands on the user are relatively simple and straightforward'.

We must take this enthusiasm with a grain of salt because if the "user" is an average author, the demands on him or her are not simple and straighforward. Learning and applying them is time consuming.

Brian classifies different types of documents, explains their structure, and then describes how the different parts may be tagged with SGML codes. He says "If inter-machine communication of electronically prepared information is to be possible on a world-wide basis, it is essential that a standard method of defining document structures be adopted by authors".

The people who attended an SGML conference in Ottawa in May 1988 were either from software companies, computer companies, large publishers, universities, or government departments. The list included Queen's University, Kingston, Ontario, Softquad, AITRC Columbus, Chemical Abstracts, Hewlett Packard, Xerox, and the Swedish Defence Dept. It seems that authors using SGML are likely to be Corporate Authors.

Many authors use word processing machines. Corporate Authors possibly excepted, they are reasonably content (having gone through a lengthy WP system learning period) to see their text represented on the screen laid out as intended, with margins, justification, headings, paragraphs, etc., more or less to their satisfaction.

The manuscript then goes to the publisher as camera-ready copy. If the publisher decides to accept a disk, the author does not have to mark up anything to preserve his format - the publisher's machine reads the embedded codes placed there automatically by the author's WP software as he sets out his text - assuming that the publisher has in his WP software collection the package which is compatible with the author's software.

Some Corporate Authors - for instance those who produce complex government publications - are now required to use SGML. One day magazine and book publisher may insist on discs marked up with SGML, having become fed up with the incompatibilities and limitations of WP codes. Until that time it's hard to understand why authors should want to learn SGML.

The purveyors of software for SGML authors take a different view. Thus Sobemap, a Belgian supplier, say "Building on the excitement and market education associated with desktop publishing, SoftQuad Author/Editor (their software price is $715, plus $995 for the "Rules Builder")... is built on the principle that a user can be most productive by taking advantage of the structure that every document has".

The user can "compose an outline of a document as the first step in the creative process ... work with others to create composite documents ....etc. etc." Five day SGML tutorials are offered to show them how to do it.

So for the time being authors have a choice. They may continue independently with their steam-driven WP software, or they may take on a number of the functions currently assumed by the publisher. Authors will wish to know how they may benefit should they adopt SGML.

Word Processing

Word Processing (WP) machines are used in medium/large organisations as a replacement for typewriters in typing pools. WP facilities almost as good as those provided on dedicated machines in the form of a microcomputer with WP software are in widespread use.

Word processing has come a long way since dedicated WP equipment started to be used in the sixties. In the seventies enthusiasm for WP systems became the basis for general euphoria about the office of the future. The success of word processing was extrapolated into utopian "office automation" scenarios.

The general thesis was that the nature of office work was going to be completely altered. The future for office workers was hypothesised in detail, not only in the tabloids but in the up-market technical journals as well.

A peculiar, cautious, non sequitur appeared in the **Communications of the ACM**. The whole nature of future work having been questioned in the article, this profound statement followed:- "Proposition 1: Automated office systems, especially text processing functions, can improve the quality of written documents produced".

Imagination was allowed to run riot even in the journal **Telecommunications Policy**. "By half past nine, Jim had handled virtually all his administrative tasks" - but not in his office. He had simply "moved out to his patio with the terminal".

Being totally automated Jim accomplished some remarkable feats by 9.30 a.m., including "taking copies of his subordinates' status reports, editing them into summary form, combining pieces of related projects and adding his overview. He then took one of his analyst's status reports, annotated it, provided further definition of the project, and returned it through the mails system".

At about the time that this was written, and strictly on this planet, the UK Central Computer & Telecommunications Agency came out with a report (Anon 1980) on a large scale trial of word processors. They paid up to £9000 for the machines - about £14,000 at today's prices. They concluded that "there were undoubted benefits to be derived from the selective use of WPs", but were careful not to be too enthusiastic, perhaps in case they had to spend more money.

Soon after this, falling prices and greater enthusiasms brought about a market boom. Sales of dedicated WP machines started to decline in 1985. Wordplex, a leading WP machine supplier, recognising the trend, decided to go in for computers and office systems at the beginning of 1984. However they continued to sell WP machines arguing that the special features required for efficient use could not so readily be incorporated into multi-purpose machines.

In 1986 the UK market for dedicated machines dropped by 25% to about £70M but microcomputer WP had boomed. By late 1987 the Amstrad PC selling at about £500 in the UK was being widely used for WP and so were many other micros. Amstrad's World sales reached over 750,000 microcomputers worth £375M.

By 1989 a reaction had set in. The title and sub-title of a Byte article summarise it well; "Is Bigger Better" and "Recent upgrades raise the question: when do bells and whistles overwhelm a product and its users?" The writer expresses his feelings about another WP package, "Moore II". "It has become so powerful and so enormous that you can spend weeks trying to figure out everything it can do".

Dedicated WP machines were eroded at the "bottom end" by electronic typewriters which included some WP functions. Word processing software is often provided for micros as part of combination packs with spreadsheet, communications and other items. The low incremental cost of adding WP in this way is yet another advantage. The special design features justifying the limited ongoing manufacture of dedicated WP machines have become almost unnecessary with the arrival of comprehensive software for micros.

In a recent survey, Wordstar 3.0 turned out to be the preferred machine, followed by Microsoft Word version 4.0, Multimate, Displaywrite 4, and Word Perfect. The US market for WP software is currently worth about $1 Billion annually.

In September 1990 Eglowstein et al reviewed 15 of the latest WYSIWYG WP packages for IBM PCs and Macintoshes. Their preference was for Ami Professional and Word For Windows for DOS PCs. They found it harder to make a choice of WP for The Mac, but decided on MindWrite or Nisus. But "If you are incorporating a Mac into a DOS Word Perfect shop, why not use the real thing? Word Perfect for the Mac is a superbly crafted product... If you are starting a mixed environment Word might be better than Word Perfect because the Windows and Mac versions are much closer in feel".

Operational aspects

Two very important factors are ease of use and flexibility - including the ease of switching between standard functions, using text/graphics combinations, and inter-connecting with other machines. A buyer might reasonably expect very comprehensive facilities from a dedicated WP machine, with great attention accorded to instructional and design details in order to make the facilities easy to use.

Such attention might be expected from microcomputer WP software by now but alas, such expectations are likely to be misplaced. The cut-throat competition between microcomputer software suopliers is accompanied by minimum attention to ease of use and good instruction books.

Inter-connected word processing machines or micros with WP software which possess or have access to sufficient storage, and incorporate file retrieval facilities, provide the means for document delivery, usually within one organisation on one or more sites. WP manufacturers call them "shared logic" systems if the workstations depend on certain functions performed by a central minicomputer, but "shared facility" if the workstations, normally connected to a central machine, can function autonomously if the central system breaks down. The usual software, equipment, and protocol problems mentioned elsewhere will usually arise if machines made by different manufacturers are inter-connected.

IBM WP MACHINE WITH CHINESE KEYBOARD

The effectiveness of WP for document composition

Patricia Wright (1987) refers to the work of Pullinger (1984) and Gould (1984). Mentioning Gould's comments on finding that WP-composed letters took 50% longer than written ones, she says: "one possible reason is that the first draft of the computer text may have received more revisions by authors, although the reason for this increase is not clear".

One of the reason for revisions and the increase in the WP author's time to type short business letters is that even if the keyboard is on your desk, it takes time to get the system up, take on board the format for a letter, back-up the completed letter in storage if you want to ensure that it won't be lost, and then print it.

But the preparational-time overhead per letter becomes small when a number of letters must be typed, some need changes, and addresses are stored in a merge-phrase file. The addressees details at the head of each letter and on the envelope may be positioned in one operation with no re-typing. No crossings-out or re-writes are needed in the event of a change.

Letter writing time is further reduced because the author's typing speed will certainly become faster than his writing speed with practice. Letters must still be printed, and so must a stick-on strip of envelope address labels. In spite of the extra time taken by these operations, total time will still be reduced.

For most kinds of work, the direct and consequential time and effort expended when using a word-processing machine for making **changes** - a very important factor - must be much **less** than when writing, dictating, or non-WP typewriting. It is true that with WP it is tempting to make unnecessary changes - the freedom of being able to make a change of any magnitude, free from time-wasting repercussions on subsequent pages, makes it hard to resist. But there are real benefits - for instance when a whole section of a paper is out of order it can be re-positioned bodily in seconds.

WP versus DTP

The dividing line between WP and Desktop Publishing has become blurred. Sophisticated WP software is available taking full advantage of the more powerful microcomputers with large memories now on the market.

For example Vuman specialise in WP software for multi-lingual and technical reports. Complex mathematical formulae may be produced. The latest version of Wordstar - the 2000 Plus package version 3.0 - will drive Postscript printers, provides a What You See Is What You Get (WYSIWYG) preview, will import art graphics, and handles line drawings. 512K of memory is needed and the software must be loaded from 21 5.25" floppy disks.

Current equipment and software

Current WP software offers more power, more speed and added facilities. Three generations of machines, operating systems, and WP software are compared in Figure 21.8 - A Sol microcomputer with Word Wizard (1978), a Vectorgraphic 4/30 with Memorite (1982), and a PS/2 with Word Perfect 5.0 (1989), The price of the PS/2 system complete with all the software shown in the figure is about one quarter that of the Vectorgraphic in real terms.

The Memorite software designed around 1980, is far more compact and less complex than its successor in this example - Word Perfect 5.0. All the major facilities needed are there in Memorite, including a very good speller.

Some are better. For example although Word Perfect has all kinds of options for text deletion, the most useful in Memorite is "delete up to...". You press one key and then type a symbol or word. On pressing "Return" the text between the cursor and the symbol or word are deleted and the gap is closed up. This is not provided on Word Perfect.

What you get in Word Perfect is a six times increase in software size and about the same increase in complexity for a wide range of "benefits" - some bells and whistles, some fringe benefits, and some valuable benefits. You also get a speed increase which in many instances is greater than the raw speed ratio increase might lead you to expect.

The product of processor speed and word length for the PS/2 is about 3.2 times that of the Vector; this provides a rough indication of expectations. In fact differences in file organisation wait states and disc accesses probably trebles that difference. Accordingly the user's waiting time when copying files, printing, etc., is often reduced by ten times with Word Perfect.

MACHINE	Processor Technology Sol computer	Vectorgraphic 4/30 computer	IBM PS/2 30-021 computer
WP SOFTWARE	Word Wizard	Memorite	Word Perfect 5.0
PROCESSOR	8080 8-bit 2MHz	Z80B 8-bit 5MHz	8086 16-bit 8MHz
OPERATING SYS.	CP/M 80	CP/M 80	DOS 4.0
MEMORY	64 K	128 K	640 K
DISCS	2 x 250 K	680 K + 5 M	680 K + 20 M
PRINTER	Diablo daisywheel	Diablo daisywheel	Epson 24-pin matrix
WP, DATABASE, OP.SYS. SIZE	350 K	800 K	7.2 M

FIGURE 21.8. COMPARISON OF WP SYSTEMS

Word Perfect benefits include:-

1.   The provision of utilities enabling sequences of operations to be carried out automatically instead of step by step.

2.   Entirely new useful features.

3.   Features providing improvements in the appearance of pages.

4.   Certain attributes normally only found in a Desktop Publishing System.

A user's expectations in view of the complexity increase of today's systems would be a corresponding increase in the amount and clarity of explanatory material. Unfortunately most of the material supplied with the computer, the operating system software, and the WP software shows that little attention has been paid to the most elementary instructional and indexing principles. The manuals have obviously not been tried out on a consumer before publication.

The manual supplied with the PS/2 contains no specification, and no list of functions, block diagram, general overview, performance data, memory size, or disk capacity. Nothing is said about the screen resolution or image facilities.

Word Perfect software has been well reviewed. Its predecessor was a close second to Samna when reviewed in 1987. When Word Perfect 5.0 first came out it was awarded joint first place in a brief review and comparison with others.

In April 1989, Word Perfect 5.0 was compared with Microsoft Word 5.0, Manuscript, Wordstar, Total Word, and Samna Word IV. In the reviewer's opinion "For general purpose word processing Word Perfect is hard to beat. Although it is rivalled in some respects by Wordstar, Total Word, and Samna Word IV, I find it more impressive than any of these".

The type of printer used makes a considerable difference to the appearance of a document and the potential for embellishments. 24-pin dot-matrix printers provide adequate performance and print quality for most purposes. Several different fonts are usually available up to about 12 point but graphics are limited and it is not possible to use software-controlled graphically constructed fonts.

A simple compact summary and guide to WP has been produced by Barnard (1989). It contains only 28 pages but succeeds in covering choice and costs, outputting to a phototypesetter, and preparing camera-ready copy.

Subjective impressions

Your feelings about a new system will depend on previous experience. I purchased a PS/2 machine with DOS 4.0, Word Perfect 5.0, and a 24-pin Epson printer. If I had never used a WP system this system would seem to be fantastic.

The supposed benefits of the system have already been described but what matters is whether these benefits turn out to be valuable in practice. My impressions are as follows:-

Considerable advances in operational speed with some very useful advanced new facilities; a huge increase in complexity.

Useless instruction manuals with bad indexes and no idea of logical arrangement.

Quite good advice, and very patient people at the end of "hot lines" to provide more information (free) about hardware or software. Unfortunately the lines are almost permanently engaged - a natural consequence of bad manuals.

Enormous increase needed in storage capacity partly because of the "new features at all costs" syndrome, and particularly because of graphics facilities.

Occasional examples of the need for a series of key strokes to execute the same operation that could be executed by two keystrokes on older systems.

No advances in regard to the man-machine interface.

The increase in speed is particularly noticeable in the reduced response time and in a much shorter time when waiting for a page to be printed. The time taken to print a page depends on content. Detailed graphics slow it up quite a bit. An A4 size page of characters takes 60-70 seconds from the moment of pressing the "print" key. Other functions such as disk copying or file retrieval are much faster than older systems.

In addition to including all the usual features of a good WP package Word Perfect 5.0 includes a number of extras and provides some of the facilities available in down-market DTP systems such as Fleet Street Editor or Finesse.

546

Fonts and styles

The availability of different fonts such as Roman and Sans Serif, in different styles such as condensed, outline, or italic, changeable at will from the keyboard, gives a document a better appearance. Proportional spacing also improves the look of a document.

If a dot-matrix printer is controlled to print "draft" it will print acceptable characters but with a visible dot structure, much faster than when it is in the "letter quality" (LQ) mode. An Epson LQ-100 24-pin dot-matrix printer, used in "Letter Quality" mode, took 67 seconds to print a particular page. It took 22 seconds to do the same page in "draft".

During the last few years improved dot-matrix printers have led to the gradual demise of the daisy-wheel printer - one of the least expensive ways of printing solid type. Such printers are inflexible because although they produce good quality characters, most only allow one font in normal or "bold" type. To change fonts you have to switch off and change to another wheel so the production of a document in several fonts is not really practicable.

Laser printers cost several times as much as 24-pin dot matrix (DM) printers so at what point does DM printing have to defer to laser? The answer is when the user decides that better quality and higher speed is needed, particularly and perhaps essentially, if he/she wants to print halftone illustrations.

In Word Perfect 5.0, fonts may be changed in the course of composing a document by pressing "CTRL/F8" (that is the ctrl key and a purpose-defined key together), consulting a font menu, selecting a font, and returning to the text. The selected font continues until further notice. Here are some examples:-

Work is the curse of the drinking classes
Work is the curse of the drinking classes
Work is the curse of the drinking classes
Work is the curse of the drinking classes
Work is the curse of the drinking classes
Work   is   the   curse   of   the
Work is the curse of the drinking classes
Work is the curse of the drinking classes
Work is the curse of the drinking classes
Work is the curse of the drinking classes
WORK IS THE CURSE OF THE

FIGURE 21.9 EXAMPLES OF STYLES AND FONTS

The styles/fonts shown in Figure 21.9 are Superscript, Outline, Shadow, Redline, Strikeout, Roman 5 characters per inch (cpi), Roman 12 point condensed proportionally spaced, Roman italic 20 cpi, Sans Serif 12 pt condensed proportionally spaced, Sans Serif 12 pt double underlined, and Roman 12 pt caps proportionally spaced double-wide bold, respectively.

These are fonts available with a particular dot-matrix printer. A much greater range is available with software generating "graphic fonts" provided the printer (for example a laser printer) can reproduce them.

The fonts available depend on the resident WP software and on the relationship between the WP software and the resident software installed in the printer's memory. A "driver" of the right kind must be included at the output end of the microcomputer. A driver is a software module specific to the printer. If the type of printer is changed, the micro has to be re-loaded with the correct driver. Usually the WP software will include drivers for many popular printers so this is just a matter of designation from a menu.

View document "WYSIWYG" feature

With Word Perfect 5.0 time you can see the complete page, black on a paper-white background, exactly as it will be printed with the vertical dimension just filling the screen, by pressing two keys and waiting a few seconds. This means that with A4 size you can easily see what the general layout looks like. Individual characters are distinguishable, but not quite readable.

However by using the "100%" or "200%" options, portions of the page can be made easily readable. Different fonts and graphics, which you can't see on the normal screen, are reproduced so you can check all aspects before printing a page.

This is a very useful feature and until recently was exceptional, but it is already out of date. The latest version of Word Perfect and other competitive WP software provide "online WYSIWYG" so that you get a continuous view of the final result.

Auto-referencing

Getting parts of the text keyed to references, and maintaining the references themselves as composition proceeds can be time consuming. The main problem is dealing with a new reference which needs to be inserted, for whatever reason, somewhere in some text which already contains, say, 20 superscript numbers keyed to full references at the end.

If the new reference comes between, say, numbers 10 and 11, it becomes the new 11, so that all subsequent numbers in the text must be found and changed. Then the reference itself must be typed and pushed into the list at the end; all later references have to be re-numbered.

With Word Perfect 5.0 the process is very simple. When a new reference is needed you leave a space for the number, press a key, and the screen becomes blank except for a number. Its value is determined by where the cursor was left in the text. If the preceding number was 10 the number displayed will be 11. You then type the details of reference 11 and when finished, press a key. The display switches back to where you left the cursor in the text, where a superscript 11 has been inserted. All the remaining numbers in the text have been increased by one.

After the new reference 11 is typed and the display switched back to the text, the complete citation is also automatically inserted into the right place in the list of references at the end of the document. All later reference numbers are incremented by one.

Graphics

A PS/2 30-021 comes with MGCA graphics, although nowhere in what are laughingly called instruction Books which come with the machine is a specification given of what you get. Most people won't know that a question about this topic needs to be asked before purchase. My dealer didn't know, and of course he could not find out whether it would handle graphics by looking it up in the manual.

The need for a graphics facility has been over-hyped by the DTP industry. You can do quite well if you want to include graphics by leaving a space in your camera-ready manuscript and pasting in hard copy. If the pasted-in item is well printed it will usually come out looking better than anything which has been reproduced from a computer graphics data file.

But it's a matter of opinion whether graphics is a fascinating time-wasting toy, something which adds real, if intangible, value to your composition, or something which must be included if a professional appearance is essential.

The Word Perfect reference manual says "The Graphics feature allows you to incorporate pictures or images from many different sources into your document. The capability to mix text and graphics together in the same document makes it easy to produce newsletters, instructional materials, and other documents where figures, diagrams, logos, and/or pictures are needed".

The procedure is to create a box of a specified size, position it on the page, and then retrieve a previously created file describing graphics or text into it. The box may be captioned or its contents edited. A caption, typed separately, may be positioned automatically inside or outside the box. When retrieved into a box of whatever size, the image is automatically shrunk to fit.

Another graphics aid is the "draw lines" feature, using the arrowed keys, with Word Perfect's "line draw" feature - quite useful for business graphics, organisational diagrams, etc.

The graphics you can actually print are simple but adequate for many purposes if you are using a 24-pin dot-matrix printer, but a laser printer must be used if a large choice of graphics are required.

DOS 4.0

The PS/2's operating system is Microsoft's well known PC-DOS - a version of MS-DOS written specifically for the IBM PC. The difference between the two lies in certain variations between their Basic Input-Output System (BIOS) sections. Single-user 16 bit MS-DOS was designed to be as compatible as possible with the widely used 8 bit CP/M 80, and there are many similarities, but also many additional features. The current version of PC-DOS, now usually simply called DOS, is DOS 4.0 and that has still more features.

The major difference that ex-CP/M users will find between CP/M and DOS are the file organisations - DOS files are arranged in a hierarchical "tree" structure, CP/M files are not. This allows for files to be grouped together under several master directories. A file is located by its disc and by its "path" through the tree, described in a specific manner.

In practice a Word Perfect 5.0 user sees very little of DOS, except when formatting diskettes, checking the tree arrangement, or changing housekeeping functions such as AUTOEXEC.BAT (a pain). Although it is DOS which is executing a range of housekeeping functions such as copying, filing, and printing, Word Perfect translates Word Perfect commands, or choices from its menus, into DOS commands. A user, having retrieved his or her directory on to the screen, can carry out almost all WP operations starting from the main menu shown on the screen beneath his own file directory.

Complexity, learning, and payoff

The facilities, commands, and general complexity of DOS 4.0/Word Perfect 5.0 are of a different order to early CP/M based systems. The special function keys F1 to F12 are often operated together with two other keys, and colour coded labelling is used on the keyboard. The "Quick Reference" guide provided lists 250 different commands.

The hard disk has a capacity of 21.3 Mbytes, and I now have nearly 7 Mbytes of data stored on it in 348 files. Of these, 22 are user's files in about 400 Kbytes of storage so the remaining 6.6 Mbytes of data are DOS and Word Perfect software plus a small amount for the mouse (not in use). With my old Vectorgraphic/Memorite CP/M system, current user files and software, database for indexing and locating reprints, tearsheets, reports, etc., about two thirds of a 5 Mbyte disc are occupied. This comparison gives an idea of the massive increase in the size and complexity of current software packages.

A special effort to introduce the user to the general arrangement and philosophy, a hardware and software specification showing limits, constraints etc., and really good instruction manuals might be expected in view of this considerable complexity. Particularly good indexes providing everyday synonyms for computer-jargon headings and other words used in the manual might also be expected.

Other necessary measures come to mind. Quite a small number of commands are used far more frequently than most others. A "high frequency" reference list for those commands is a must. Of course the instruction manuals will have been tried out on typical users and modified until the users found them acceptable. In fact nothing suggests that the suppliers gave these matters the slightest attention.

The references for this chapter will be found combined with those of Office Systems Part 2 (Chapter 22).

CHAPTER 22. OFFICE SYSTEMS PART 2: SERVICES AND EFFECTIVENESS.

Electronic Mail 1. Introduction

The phrase "Electronic Mail" is widely used to cover almost any electronic message system. "Message" as used here means "a unit of information transfer of any length", not, as in everyday language, "a brief communication usually from one person to another". Thus Facsimile, Telex, Teletext, and some kinds of Videotex services are sometimes referred to as "electronic mail" services.

The narrower definition, applicable here, is "a system consisting of a managed data network interconnecting subscriber's computers (often just terminals or microcomputers) with a store-and-forward computer which manages subscriber's mailboxes. A subscriber wishing to send a message despatches it to the addressee's mailbox. The addressee periodically checks his mailbox and downloads his messages".

The network may be managed by an EM company, or it may be owned by, say, two large users who have sufficient traffic to justify a direct connection between their computers for message transfers. But for most users, the economies of a multiple-user shared system managed by a third party EM company make it the preferred choice.

In 1977 the prestigious journal Science - usually dedicated to advances in biochemistry, molecular biology etc., saw fit to publish a review article entitled "Electronic Mail" (Potter, 1977) - see Figure 22.1

Potter says that "The concept of organised mail is believed to have emerged in about 4000 BC in the Persian Empire. Queen Elizabeth I issued a proclamation in 1591 which prohibited carrying of mail except by messengers authorised by the Master of the Posts. In America, the first postal system was authorised by the colonial legislature of Massachusetts in 1639".

Potter, a Xerox man, sees few problems ahead - "the evolution is inevitable" although "since the sociopolitics and economics are complex, it is beyond the intent of this article to address the question of who should own or operate the electronic mail system". It is interesting that he thought that EM would be developed as an integrated system; having mentioned the Post Office he finds it obligatory to back away from the contentious problems of the ownership of publicly available systems.

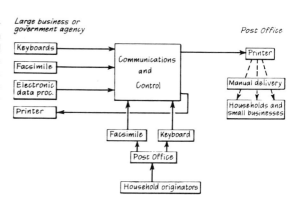

FIGURE 22.1. POTTER'S EM SYSTEM

As usual the politics turned out to be more important than the technology.

In the nineteen seventies the United States Post Office believed that it might be able to reverse its problems of rising costs and diminishing traffic by instituting an electronic mail system. There was considerable controversy as the deregulation of communication services was then under discussion. A number of private companies had already started up EM services.

In 1979, those companies, with allies in the Carter administration forced the USPS to think again. They obtained a ruling from the Federal Communications Commission (FCC) to stop the introduction of the USPS' ECOM (Electronic Computer Originated Mail service) system.

This service would enable large mailers such as insurance and credit card companies to connect to a USPS system which would receive data electrically and change it into hard copy for delivery using the existing mail distribution system. The USPS found itself involved in a battle against Washington and business interests.

Following this manoeuvring, a considerably revised form of ECOM was implemented. In February 1980 the USPS proposed that common carriers, with standards imposed upon them, would accept customers input, and would connect to USPS printing centres for onward conventional mail distribution. Apparently the FCC did not intervene.

Communication common carriers could also collect electronic messages as a service to lower volume mailers and re-package and sort them for transmission to post offices with ECOM printing equipment. By then the incentives had become considerable; the number of mailed items per day had grown to about 147 million in the US. (By comparison it was about 25 million in West Germany, 24 million in the UK, and 23.6 million in France).

Two day service was guaranteed at a cost of 26 cents for the first page (1200 character average) and 5 cents for the second, with a $50 annual fee. Common carriers, operating mainly for a number of lower volume users, were required to add a 10 cents surcharge. It was thought that ECOM could be successful, even with the specified limited objectives. Existing quite successful EM services such as GTE/Telenet, Dialcom, Compuserve etc., could connect to ECOM and help to make it successful.

In 1984 ECOM was virtually ended. It was never widely used and attempts made by the USPS to sell it to a private operator failed.

An article appeared in the Financial Times, September 14th, 1987 entitled "Electronic mail - the unfulfilled promise". The thrust of the article was that while inter-company EM systems were thriving, intra-company EM "....as a replacement for the postal services is virtually non-existent".

The article contains the statement that "David Chilvers believes that the success of public e-mail is dependent upon a critical mass of users". I am sure that Chilvers (whoever he may be) cannot really have delivered such a comment **ex cathedra**, as implied in this article. For most people this has been obvious for years.

The critical mass of users will not exist until a subscriber can send a message to any other subscriber on one of the numerous different existing EM networks. An international effort to standardise is in hand.

Electronic Mail 2. Standards & Services

The CCITT is a Geneva-based rule-making and discussion forum for the PTTs, with other interested parties in the telecommunications scene participating. In 1980 Discussion Group SG VII was formed to deal with one major topic - message handling.

In 1984 the CCITT passed its recommendation X400 Message Handling Standards. The Standards comprise rules to enable users to compose and send messages to others across a variety of systems and telecom links. It fits in to the "Master OSI Model" which accommodates all kinds of systems and links as already discussed.

The important parts of X400 for EM are the "User Agent" (UA, for instance software running on a PC) dealing with message formats and the rules for them, and the "Message Transfer Agent" (MTA, store and forward software in the same machine, or in a separate machine working for a number of UAs) which looks at the address and forwards the message to another MTA on the network.

The users name and address, must be registered in a special way with the local MTA. The body of a message can contain different types of data such as ASCII code, facsimile, spreadsheet file, etc.

British Telecom Gold, having taken over the US Dialcom network, is a world leader with about 500,000 mailboxes world-wide for its Gold service. For within-UK service it costs £50 to join and then 16p per A4 page. Later, BT Gold 400 was introduced for world service to subscribers (in theory) on all networks - variously estimated as between two and five million. The estimated numbers of mailboxes (source BIS Macintosh 1990) are shown in Table 22.1

It costs £1000 to join, about £5000 to obtain the X400 software for your computer, and 20p per A4 page - obviously a service for the user who sends so many messages that the initial costs become small per message.

The current problems are as follows. There is an optional incomplete online directory of Gold UK subscribers, but no printed directory. There is no directory of any kind to Gold overseas subscribers. CCITT agreement on the standardising of address formats was delayed, but it was agreed in 1989. Agreement was also reached on another standard, X500, for online directories. Access to the critical mass of subscribers via Telecom Gold 400 awaits the implementation of X400 and standardised address formats by all other EM networks.

Mailboxes per thousand of working population

	1988	1993
US	81	394
Canada	71	346
Sweden	29	70
UK	19	129
France	6	30
W.Ger.	2	41
Italy	2	11

TABLE 22.1. PUBLIC AND PRIVATE MAILBOXES

In May 1990 BT announced that it was introducing X500 directory software called Cohort 500. It should enable large organisations to set up proper directories for use by staff. The X500 software will run on various types of computer and this software and other offerings like it should eventually enable messages to be passed to addressees via separately owned interconnected X400 networks.

The big question for potential subscribers to BT Gold 500 therefore is what are the benefits now, and how quickly will subscribers to other EM networks become as easily accessible as other UK Gold subscribers are now?

However Gold lists a large number of business information and news services gatewayed to its network which can be logged-on from a menu. They include the FT's Profile, Infomat, ICC notes and stockbroker reports, Jordans, Kompass, ICC and others (Anon 1990).

Electronic mail is somewhat inconvenient for the usual man-machine interface reasons. Its benefits have been well touted. They include inter-company speed, the elimination of "telephone tag", and the elimination of memo copying, circulation, and filing. Total costs per message versus the UK Royal Mail are hard to estimate.

Apart from general purpose EM networks, private EM systems receive heavy useage within large companies. In a brief review of current activity, Spencer (1990) reports that IBM has the world's largest system with "about 350,000 employees of IBM throughout the world able to communicate with each other using electronic mail". Another very large company, Shell, "has been using e-mail throughout its organisation for the last five years".

The useage of electronic mail by the information departments of large organisations is of particular interest here. Glausiusz and Yates-Mercer (1990) obtained a response from 33 out of 48 information departments claiming to use e-mail. Most used their own service but of the 11 who used a bureau service, 8 used Telecom Gold. 70%-80% of these departments sent e-mail messages to other departments of the company, to information users, between UK sites, or between sites abroad. 21% sent e-mail to other companies in the UK, and 9% to companies abroad.

Of the users who sent messages to the information services, 64% of useage was for information requests, 30% photocopy requests, and 27% for interlibrary loans.

Most services said that e-mail was not used as a substitute for other forms of communication, nor had it reduced paperwork. Rather had it resulted in "improved communication". "The most significant impact was on communication with overseas sites".

A number of disadvantages were mentioned:-

* No way of knowing that a message had been received and read.

* Need to check mailboxes frequently (no envelope or bell).

* Number of users was below critical mass.

* Less impact than facsimile.

The authors expected that information scientists well versed in IT and its applications would have "welcomed the advent of e-mail and created innovative ways of using it... but in the majority this is not true... A surprisingly small number of information services in large organisations have and use e-mail, and of those that do, most use it for relatively routine and administrative activities".

Voice Messaging

Voice messaging is a kind of developed telephone recording-answering system. It is alleged (as at 1990) to enjoy a market of $280M and to have an enormous potential. It is a kind of voice equivalent to E-mail - a user speaks a message to a telephone number representing a "mailbox". The owner of the mailbox can telephone the number and using an appropriate access code listen to messages left for him or her.

The principal differences between voice-messaging systems and telephone answering systems are in benefits, scale, and facilities. The idea is that office staff are freed for taking, handling, and assuming the responsibility for delivering messages. A PC-based system can deal with up to about 500 voice mailboxes, and a special dedicated system for a larger number of some thousands.

Additional facilities may include routing options or the delivery of a single message to multiple destinations, pageing, logging etc. Modern systems usually compress and digitize voice before storage where older systems used clumsier tape recordings. Standardisation should assist voice-messaging and according to McClelland (1990) a standard called Audio Messaging Interchange Specification (AMIS) is gaining ground in the US.

Mailboxes per 1000 working people

	Private 1988	Private 1993	Public 1988	Public 1993
US	.07	4	7	95
UK	.7	6	1	12
Jap.	.3	2	.07	3
W. Ger.	.07	1	–	1
France	–	–	2	14
Italy	.1	1	.1	2

TABLE 22.2. VOICE MESSAGING

The number of voice mail boxes per thousand of population are estimated by BIS Mackintosh (1990) to be as shown in Table 22.2 for those countries where data is available.

Electronic Data Interchange (EDI)

EDI is a specialised form of EM for the purpose of the exchange of business data between trading partners such as Orders, Invoices, Bills of Lading, and other stereotype business "forms" such as delivery notes, credit notes and so forth. The "specialised" part lies in defining the data elements which make up any complete document, and arranging for special software to shift data elements between documents - for instance to provide the necessary correlation between elements in a purchaser's order record, and a seller's sales record.

Contrary to expectations, Electronic or Automated Office Systems have usually resulted in the generation of more paperwork, not less. EDI may well be the exception.

With regard to the potential of EDI for import/export documents, the EC put it like this (Anon, 1987):- "if 700 customs documents are to be replaced by a single administrative document in the community of 1992, the document will have to be electronic".

EDI systems have been operating in a limited way in the United States for some years. Gradual de-regulation of the use of communication channels accelerated the process. In Europe a few EDI systems have been running on private networks, but until recently the strict embargo, still in force in many countries, on the provision of services by third parties on lines leased from the PTT's - the only telecom links available - prevented commercial expansion.

Another reason for the popularity of EDI is the "just in time" philosophy adopted by many manufacturers, particularly car manufacturers. The speeding up of order/supply operations means that provided EDI reliably fulfills its potential, stocks may be run down almost to the point where parts are delivered from the supplier to the production line.

The major private EDI-type networks, and still by far the largest, are the now overloaded SWIFT network, operated by the banks, and SITA the airline's reservation network. SITA, the world's largest, was established in 1949 with a 50 baud link between Paris and Nice. By 1986 it was handling eleven billion messages a year with the major nodes in London, Hong Kong, and New York over an international 19,200 and 56,000 bps network.

There are now believed to be about 8000 companies in the US already engaged in EDI. The break-up of AT&T provoked a boom and EDI operators mainly adopted a standard called ANSI X12. Other standards are in use by the grocer and transport groups. By early 1988 there were nearly 4000 users and the business was worth $200M. Big companies such as Ford and General Motors may make it mandatory for their suppliers to be on EDI. The US EDI market is expected to reach nearly $2 billion in four year's time according to one forecast.

The US EDI operators, such as EDI-Express, Geisco, McDonnell Douglas, Sterling, and Control Data were forced, primarily by pressure from users, to inter-connect. Users now receive a single bill for service involving two operators. EM services, still mainly intra- rather than inter-company, do not, as yet, have the same interconnection incentives.

Retailers in the UK became interested in the late seventies, and in 1979 an organisation called the Article Number Association (ANA) started to develop a message format called the Trading Data Communications Standard (TRADACOMS). Much of it was adopted in the United Nations Trade Data Interchange system (UNTDA). Meanwhile ODETTE, a scheme for the European Motor Industry, and DISH, for the UK shipping industry, were developing their own standards. TRADANET is used world-wide for import/export documents.

Following de-regulation in the UK, a number of Value Added Network (VAN) licences have been issued to third parties who can now offer services using lines leased from BT or Mercury, releasing a pent-up demand. Geisco (US General Electric), ICL, IBM, AT&T Istel, International Network Services, and BT Tymnet are jockeying for position. The organizer of IBM's system, Fred Metzgen, left in August 1988 to start a consultancy service, EDI Matrix.

A new company International Network Services (INS), jointly owned by Geisco and ICL runs TRADANET, used by many large organisations such as IPC, Tesco, Marks & Spencer and BP. British Coal, a pioneer with its own network, transferred its operations to Istel. In August 1988, 40 large UK construction companies co-operated to start EDI trials. Between 700 and 2500 companies (according to which report you read) are now using EDI in the UK, while the rest of Europe lags a long way behind with about 2000 users.

Istel is used by the Motor Manufacturers and Traders and shares much of the UK EDI business with INS. IBM is some way behind. In June 1988 INS and ISTEL stated that they would link their networks, so they are now handling most of the UK's EDI transactions. The co-operation will link ISTEL users with US users through INS's Geisco US network.

An even bigger extension of UK EDI was reported in the press in July 1988 which would result in the creation of a critical mass of users - so large that many traders would be almost forced to join. It was stated that trials were about to start which would connect nearly 40,000 users on the Banks Automated Clearing System and INS. In November 1988 I was told that this was held up for "technical and political reasons".

In February 1990, 21 national Post Offices from Canada, Western Europe, Japan, United States, and Australia set up a cooperative EDI venture called Unipost. A European pilot project was expected in 1990.

Marks & Spencer has organised over 90% of its clothing suppliers on EDI, and ICI runs a private EDI network over leased lines to the US and Europe. ICI also uses the major European commercial services. True to form in the telecoms/computer industry, all the ingredients were in place for a first class non-standardised shambles.

In 1989 IBM announced a series of products called Expedite Data Interchange designed to pick out designated non-standard messages and convert them to EDI standard formats - US X.12 and ODETTE (car manufacturing). Conversion is available for AS/400, MVS, System 38, System 36 and PS/2.

Before everyone has had time to completely adopt entrenched positions, the United Nations Joint Task Force (JEDI) with strong support from the CEC (with visions of 1992) and countries outside Europe, is developing a hybrid called the Electronic Data Interchange for Administration Commerce and Transport (EDIFACT). The EDIFACT board held its inaugural meeting in Brussels on June 7th 1988. The ANA will be co-operating with its bar-code product numbering system now widely used in the food industry.

The main problem is still standardisation, but the EDIFACT standard is undoubtedly gaining ground. EDIFACT takes account of end-to-end communications and its component parts fit the OSI model.

EDIFACT processes follow recommended standards for its major component parts - Data Elements, Segments of related Data Elements, Codes, Syntax (structural rules), and Messages (Anon 1990). EDIFACT's major "competitors" are the Article Numbering Association's system used in an EDI scheme called TRADACOM and the American National Standards Institute standard, X.12.

In 1990 the CEC (Anon 1990) announced a two year project called TEDIS to co-ordinate various European EDI projects. Meanwhile the Conference of European Posts and Telegraphs (CEPT) - a rather secretive club with European PTTs as its members - formed a committee to consider the formation of something called Managed Data Network Services (MDNS).

The PTTs will transform their present grudging provision of leased

lines into an effective mix of channels and services. It could eliminate
the need for company telecommunication managers and digest EDI at one gulp.
If it ever happens that would indeed be a dramatic change.The EDI companies
do not seem to be disturbed by the prospect.

For a short review of current developments in EDI see McClelland
(1990). For a more detailed analysis of the value of EDI, Benjamin et al
(1990) focus on gaining competitive advantage.

They say:- "Until now EDI has been viewed largely as a strategic
issue whose major implementation challenge was to overcome the technical
problems of electronic links between firms. This however is an
over simplification of what the technology means to organisations and what
must be done to use it effectively".

"The most significant most overlooked factor in determining the
effective use of EDI is the organisation's ability to manage the changes in
structure and work processes that must attend the implementation of the
technology".

Spreadsheets

A spreadsheet calculator called Visicalc, developed by Dan Bricklin
of Software Arts Inc., appeared in 1978 for the Apple II. Each boosted the
sales of the other. Visicalc remained the leader until 1983 when the IBM PC
appeared and so did Lotus 1-2-3 (Spreadsheet - Database Management -
Business Graphics).

The Lotus package fully utilised the instruction set of the 8088 CPU
used in the IBM; it ran a much larger spreadsheet (2048 rows x 256 columns)
faster, using 500 Kbytes of memory instead of 64K as previously used. Lotus
expected their first year's sales to be about $3M. In the event they turned
out to be $53M and, like Visicalc before it, this boosted sales of the
hardware - the IBM PC. 1-2-3 did not use software translation based on the
earlier CP/M operating system as did many of the early PC packages. It was
written directly for the PC's 16 bit operating system. Many other
spreadsheet packages are now available.

A Spreadsheet consists of a grid of cells displayed on the screen of
a CRT. Data entered in any cell may be related to data in other cells
according to a chosen formula. One of the simplest and most frequently used
relationships is "Z1 = A1 + B1 + C1......+ Y1, where the software arranges
that data in a bottom cell, Z1, is the sum of the data in the column cells
A1...Y1 above it. If the data in, say, cell K1 is changed, Z1 immediately
shows a new figure for the summed data.

After entering data, usually on a prepared form rather than simply
in columns and rows, an alteration in one cell, made by a cursor "point and
enter" action, will generate appropriate figures in other cells. If, say,
salary increases were made in March on the financial model in Figure 22.2,
consequential changes would be made in all other appropriate places - for
instance to net income in March and later months.

A review of 15 current generation spreadsheets was provided by Apiki
et al in 1990. A major improvement is the 3-D provision for connecting
spreadsheet layers - as if you were able to choose a page from a ledger and
access data from any other page in the same position below it. Prices

ranged from $595 for Lotus 1-2-3 3.0, to ProQube 1.03 at $99. A major difference between these extremes is size - Lotus can handle a 8192 x 256 x 256 layers and 256 files in memory, ProQube 512 x 512 x 512 layers and 1 file in memory.

Much more complex mathematical relationships may be used and spreadsheets are particularly useful for posing "what if" questions to accounting data ("financial modelling"). Typically a screen cursor controlled by a mouse (the cursor's movement corresponds to the movement of a hand-held carriage - the mouse - moved over a flat surface) is moved to a space reserved for an appropriate formula, and the formula is entered.

Assets	Jan	Feb	Mar	Apr	May	June
Acct.s Receivable	1000.00	1050.00	1102.50	1157.63	1215.51	1276.28
Inventory	300.00	500.00	525.00	551.25	578.81	607.75
Other Assets	250.00	262.50	275.63	289.41	303.88	319.07
Total Assets	1550.00	1812.50	1903.13	1998.28	2098.20	2203.11
Liabilities						
Acct.s Payable	1000.00	916.67	840.28	770.25	706.07	647.23
Accrued Storage Cost	50.00	50.00	50.00	50.00	50.00	50.00
Accrued Salary	100.00	105.00	110.25	115.76	121.55	127.63
Accrued Other	50.00	52.50	55.13	57.88	60.78	63.81
Total Liabilities	1200.00	1124.17	1055.65	993.90	938.39	888.67
Earnings before tax	350.00	688.33	847.47	1004.38	1159.80	1314.43
Dept. Allowance	100.00	100.00	100.00	100.00	100.00	100.00
Taxable Income	250.00	588.33	747.47	904.38	1059.80	1214.43
Taxes	75.00	176.50	224.24	271.31	317.94	364.33
Net Income	175.00	411.83	523.23	633.07	741.86	850.10

FIGURE 22.2 SPREADSHEET EXAMPLE

Databases and Database Management Systems

We are concerned here with office databases, not those containing information which are searchable online - for example via Dialog. Office databases may be self-contained on microcomputers, or in large offices they may be one of the services made available to staff over a micro/terminal - mainframe link.

A database is a computerized filing system. In files based on paper, items are ordered by a single attribute - thus to find Bloggs in a card file about employees you thumb through the B's. If you want to find out how many employees earn more than £20,000 a year you must look at all the cards.

Three kinds of computerized systems are in general use known as **File Management Systems (FMS)**, **Hierarchical Filing Systems (HFS)**, and **Relational Database Systems (RDS)**.

An FMS such as the Lotus 1-2-3 add-on Data Manager, or Scimate, are well suited to office use. Scimate enables fast searches to be made of text in records, each describing numbered shelved documents - reports, cuttings, books, etc. The displayed "hit" records provide enough information to decide whether to get the document from the shelf.

For branching "family-tree-like" applications HFS or RDS are needed. For example the paint stored in warehouse bays could be supplied by different Manufacturers who make paint of different Types in a range of Colours. The connections in an HFS enable a response to be obtained from questions like "Which bin contains Dulux high-gloss primrose paint?" But for the system to respond to questions like "Which bins contain high-gloss paint?", additional "many to many" multiple links and pointers must be added "across the family tree".

An RDS system performs like a hierarchical "many to many" linked file but does it in a more elegant and simpler way. It is arranged as a series of spread-sheet-like grids with attributes in the cells. This enables logical operations to be performed, the most important of which is perhaps "join" - meaning "join tables together to form a new table".

The rules and operations for relational databases were formulated by Ted Codd (1970) in a classic paper. Later a language called the Structured English Query Language (SQL or "Sequel") was developed at IBM (Anon 1988). There is some argument about whether the claim made by some suppliers that their database software is "relational" really is relational.

Following the appearance of the management system in Lotus 1-2-3 a number of database software packages suitable for office use appeared. The Ashton Tate db series are probably the best known. What is not known is whether they are widely used in offices. Effectiveness will depend on the paper-to-computer changeover organising effort and transition time, ease of use, and whether individuals or specialised staff (for instance the information/library staff) do it.

Once done, details about each new item must be entered with due regard for the fact that the data is now intangible - the clues available in a paper-base system are no longer available - and must be easily retrievable.

Computer Conferencing and Teleconferencing

These activities were introduced both with the intention of offering economies over the conventional way of doing things, and to add a new dimension. An additional dimension, naturally never mentioned, is to enable people to participate in a game which many enjoy - messing about with new technology. If somebody else is paying for it the enjoyment is enhanced.

Computer conferencing is of two kinds classifiable (inadequately) as serious and light-hearted. Goldmark (1976) tried out serious computer conferencing as a means of reducing travelling, accommodation etc., but the best known early work was done by Turoff and Hiltz (1980) as part of their Electronic Information Exchange System (EIES) at the New Jersey Institute of Technology, starting around 1972. Similar work followed at Loughborough as part of the Blend project in the eighties (1984).

According to Hiltz (1978) "Within the next decade, however, it will begin to be used more and more as a communications medium which takes the place of many expensive and time consuming face-to-face meetings in business, government, and among the invisible colleges of scientific specialists in academe".

Some reasons why this has not happened have been given by Short (1976) anticipating the absence of "the coffee and biscuits" syndrome with videoconferencing using a TV link. Similar considerations apply for computer conferencing:-

"We had arranged for coffee or tea to be served and he didn't have any. We sat there drinking our coffee and passing the biscuits round while he looked increasingly glum... the omission of social chat may have deleterious consequences....the busy executive...may feel it advantageous to put in an appearance....chatting with subordinates". Some would say that this function, plus the handing out of praise and occasional brickbats, is an **essential** function of the busy executive.

Travelling time and expense may be saved, but there may be social losses:- "in the case of very large conferences it is not uncommon for a company to pay the expenses of its employees to travel and stay at a hotel to be wined and dined and generally to mix business with pleasure".

The second, more light-hearted type of computer conferencing is a less formal and more widespread activity of a rather different kind which is outside the "office system" area. It consists of special interest groups running mailbox-type operations such as "Car & Driver", "Bulletin Boards" etc., for the exchange of information between computer enthusiasts, and general purpose information services such as "The Source", "Prodigy" and others. Prodigy, a new venture, is charged at $10 per month for unlimited access. It is financed by intrusive advertising.

Teleconferencing or Videoconferencing enjoys limited success because there are several constraints. Special studios taking account of psychological factors are needed. Wideband connections as provided by BT's Satstream and Megastream may be required, although ways have been found for the 7 MHz bandwidth required for motion video to be substantially reduced according to circumstances down to below 100 KHz. At the bare minimum of around 64 Kbps, interaction is limited, but with special coding and compression schemes the performance of 300-400 Kbps systems is adequate for many purposes.

Rentable facilities are available for teleconferencing in the UK by BT Videoconferencing and Maxwell Satellite Communications, and in the US by Videoconferencing Sytems Inc., and others. Maxwell charge £1500 an hour for a 12 person videoconference with the US east coast. BT charges about £200 an hour for its 6-people London to Manchester service, but all do not have two-way video communication.

Effectiveness of Office Information Technology

It seems appropriate to end the three related chapters 20, 21, and 22, with a review of Effectiveness. There will be some overlap with Chapter 20 although the emphasis there was on the management of information per se.

As the "end product" of Information Technology is Information - a most intangible substance - it is not surprising that the assessment of the results of introducing IT into an organisation is difficult and the amount of IT investment needed is controversial.

At the top end of a list of items competing for a slice of the investment cake are things like a robot painting machine where the capital cost, amortisation, and reduction of production costs compared with present methods is relatively easy to calculate. IT is likely to be near the bottom of the "justifiable need for investment scale".

The 1990 Price Waterhouse edition of a series of annual reviews (Martin 1989, Martin 1990, Grindley 1991) was compiled with the aid of over 3000 "IT executives of organisations of all sizes and from all major industry sectors" and in conjunction with seven international publications.

The opinion panel described in the 1991 edition "consists of the data processing managers of 750 computer using companies in the UK with five or more staff in their data processing departments and is about a 15% sample of such installations". A typical response was 118 from companies with up to 500 employees, 254 from those from 500-5000, and 105 from above 5000, totalling 477 responses out of a potential of 750.

The publications are very well done and contain a large amount of useful information. They deserve our close attention. But there is a considerable difference in the composition of the 1990 international opinion panel and the 1991 UK opinion panel. This suggests that Price Waterhouse are unsure about from whom they should seek opinions. They have moved in the direction of asking "UK IT Directors". In a joint venture with the Financial Times they received opinions in 1990 from 100 IT directors in the UK's top 500 companies.

If they are unsure they have good reason to be. Data processing departments are not the best places to seek opinions. They may well be striving to preserve their identity in a situation where, so far as "Company IT" is concerned, they have been overtaken by events in the rest of the company.

IT Directors are rare birds, however welcome their appointment may be, confined to the very largest companies. "The question of whether to put an IT director on the main board is being hotly debated" say Price Waterhouse. "So far, very few from the traditional dp department have reached the rarified air of the boardroom". It seems odd that the dp department should be singled out as the only source of directors. There must be other, quite probably better, sources.

IT Philosophy

There seem to be several philosophies about Office IT effectiveness:-

1. Since the results of Office IT are extremely hard to quantify its introduction should be treated as an Act of Faith

In a recent article in the Financial Times (Cane 1990) it is suggested that:- "While all large companies are spending lavishly on IT and intend to carry on spending at the same or an increased rate, very few seem to believe that they get value for money out of their investment".

"One answer is that companies spend money on IT almost as an act of faith because they have no way of measuring its effectiveness. Investing in IT is like driving down a one-way street... once the direction has been set there is no turning back. The company has lost control of the direction and is forced to continue down the same road propelled by the momentum of previous IT investments".

The most important issue according to Grindley (1991) is "Integrating IT with corporate methods". From having been 3rd it has risen to being the most important (40% mention by the opinion panel in 1990). This philosophy is also really an "Act of Faith":- "IT executive has action man written all over it. Replace Executive with Director and whether you have the person to integrate IT with Corporate Objectives or not, you certainly have his title" says Martin.

2. Office IT provides a competitive advantage so it must be exploited.

Sir John Harvey-Jones, ex-chairman of ICI seems to belong to this school of thought. According to Cane (1990) he is a disciple of Professor

Scott-Morton (MIT) director of the study "Management in the 1990s" which "has opened up many of the complex relationships which determine whether a company can seize competitive advantage through IT.

He shares Scott-Morton's conviction that a continuous reappraisal of strategy is essential. "I do not believe that we can get sustainable competitive advantage through IT. You cannot make that one jump that keeps you ahead. But unless your IT is competitive then you are in a desperate situation" concludes Harvey-Jones.

3. **You cannot tell whether or not your Office IT is effective unless you can measure the results. Therefore you must devise a method of measurement.**

A paragraph in Grindley (1991) sums up the problem very well :-

"Government procurement policy is that IT investment must be justified by benefits. But with the advent of server/workstation architecture and the core/applications systems development model, the nature of the benefits is changing. When it comes to the expensive business of laying down the core however, procurement is divorced from applications. Justifying the server, the network, the shared database, what might be called the infrastructure platform, this is a whole new ball-game".

"Any attempt to apportion the infrastructure among the applications is on a hiding to nothing. The fact that any apportionement is completely arbitrary, although damning, is not the main problem. The fact is, as with most infrastructures, most of the applications won't have been thought of".

Another way of dealing with costs is with a chargeback system. "Chargeback systems have become one of today's panaceas" (Grindley 1991). "Reconstitute the IT department as IT Ltd., with its own revenue stream, and its profits can demonstrably lay the spectre of "value for money" for ever". But "...as one Chief Executive complained, charging the user fobs off the problem of value of IT money on to the operating areas of the company, instead of it resting on the heads of the strategy planners where it belongs".

Interestingly enough "cost containment" (Grindley 1991) although a major issue, is only the fourth most important, receiving a steady 12% mention over the years 1988 to 1990 in opinion surveys. "Meeting project deadlines", which also often means adhering to budgets, is considered to be more important, but less important than it was - a 50% mention in 1987 (the most important issue), declining to 30% in 1990 (second after "integrating IT with corporate methods").

Framel's ideas (Framel 1990) about managing IT costs as assets fall short of quantitative evaluation but make a good deal of sense - particularly when deciding "what to manage" as shown in Table 22.3 (next page).

Instead of identifying IT in terms of broad activities Framel identifies smaller component parts, allowing for the fact that "each organization is unique... information management is organization specific - a process that is tailored to fit the environment and specific needs of that unique organization".

Traditional categories

Data Processing	Data Communications	User Coordination
Data Architecture	Forms & Forms Control	Systems Development
Graphics	Education & Training	Security

Information Asset Management categories

Data Processing	Data Communications	User Coordination
Data Architecture	Forms & Forms Control	Voice Communications
Libraries	Decision Support Systems	Methods & Procedures
Publishing (e.g. DTP)	Systems Development	Graphics
Education & Training	Security	Office Systems
Reproduction	Records	Planning
Policies & Guidelines	Electronic Mail	

TABLE 22.3. FRAMEL'S ASSET CATEGORIES

The key areas in for the establishment of successful Information Assets Management (IAM) are:-

* Management Direction. Executives and managers must be personally involved.
* Integrated Planning. Direct correlation between goals and spending.
* Matching Needs & Technology. Technology assets must be needs/ opportunity driven.
* Expenditure Prioritization. Key stakeholders decide on priorities and are held accountable for effective expenditure.
* Involving Users. Users assume major role in project definition and implementation.
* Cost Effectiveness. All projects must receive cost effectiveness analysis before approval with cost analysis control methods established when operational.

4. **The amount that companies spend on IT is fairly well known. If my company spends about the same as other companies of a similar size then I've got it about right.**

Grindley (1991) provides some information. IT budgets by total number of employees was/will be as follows in the UK:-

	£,s (M per installation)		
			Forecast
Employees	1988	1989	1990
Up to 1000	.72	1.2	1.5
1000-10,000	4.0	3.6	4.1
Over 10,000	4.9	5.5	6.4

Some information is also provided by Ramsden & Ramsden (1990). 52%

of the 373 respondents to a questionnaire sent to Aslib members had IT budgets of "over £18,000". The publication contains a great deal of other interesting information about IT activities but it is a pity that no idea of the size of these organisations is provided. All we can learn is that the fact that half spend less than £18,000 must mean that half the members have very small information departments.

REFERENCES

Adie, Chris.
   PC User 11, 63-68, April 24th 1990.
      Email model.
Anon
   Report. Central Computer & Telecommunications Agency, Millbank, London.
   November 1980.
      A report of trials of stand-alone word processors in UK
      government typing pools 1979/80.
Anon.
   Wharton Publishing, 12 Eton St., Richmond, Surrey, England. 1984.
      The international office automation guide.
Anon.
   PC Magazine, 52-68, July 1988.
      SQL Databases: Data sans frontières.
Anon.
   CEC, Section DG XIII-D4, Brussels, Belgium. 1990.
      TEDIS - Trade Electronic Data Interchange Systems.
Anon.
   Dialcom booklet. British Telecom. London 1991.
      Gold 400.
Ansen, Debra.
   AT&T Technical Journal, 33-44, July/August 1989.
      Document architecture standards evolution.
Apiki, Steve; Diehl, Stanford; and Eglowstein, Howard.
   Byte 15(2) 148-165, February 1990.
      Not just numbers anymore.
Barnard, Michael.
   Blueprint Publishing. London. 1989.
      Making electronic manuscripts.
Benjamin, Robert I., de Long, David W., and Morton, M.S.S.
   Long Range Planning 23(1), 29-40, 1990.
      Electronic Data Interchange: how much competitive advantage?
Bjorn-Andersen, Nils.
   In Otway H.J., and Peltu, M. (Eds) (1983). New office technology: human
   and organisational aspects. Francis Pinter. London, 1983.
      The changing role of secretaries and clerks.
Brown, Heather.
   The Computer Journal 32(6), 505-516, 1989.
      Standards for structured documents.
Brown, Heather.
   In Rosenberg & Sherman (Eds). Springer-Verlag. 1990. Chapter 3.
      Using ODA for multimedia document format translation.
Caine, Alan.
   Financial Times, London. January 19th, 1990.
      A hostage to IT's fortune.
Caine, Alan.
   Financial Times, London. September 25th 1990.
      IT investment a one-way street.

Chen, Peter P.
    In Landau, Ronert; Bair, James H. et al (Eds). Emerging Office Systems
    Ablex Publishing, New Jersey. 1982. 223-230
        Problems and fundamental issues in cost benefit analysis of office
        automation systems.
Codd, Edgar F.
    Comm. ACM 13(6), June 1970.
        A relational model of data for large shared databanks.
Croft, W. Bruce; Lefkowitz, Lawrence S.
    ACM Trans. Office Info. 2(3), 197-212, July 1984.
        Task support in an office system.
de Sousa, M.R.
    IBM System Journal 20(1), 4-22, 1981.
        Electronic information exchange in an office environment.
Dutton, B.G.
    Aslib Proc., 38(11/12), 399-410, Nov/Dec 1986.
        Introducing Information Technology: experiences of a large
        industrial unit.
Ellis, Clarence A.; Nutt, Garry J.
    Computing Surveys 12(1), 27-60, March 1980.
        Office information systems and computer science.
Framel, John E.
    J. Systems Management 41(2), 12-19, February 1990.
        Managing information costs and technologies as assets.
Giuliano, Vincent E.
    Scientific American 247(3), 149-164, 1982.
        The mechanisation of office work.
Glausiusz, Josie A., and Yates-Mercer, Penelope A.
    J. Information Science 16(4), 249-256, 1990.
        Some impacts of electronic mail on information services.
Goldmark, Peter C., and B. Kraig.
    Report, Goldmark Communications, Stamford. November 19th 1976.
        Communications for Survival.
Gould, J.D.
    Human Factors 26, 391-406, 1984.
        Revising documents with text editors, handwriting and recognition
        systems.
Grindley, Kit (Ed).
    Price Waterhouse. London. 1991.
        Information technology review 1990/1991.
Guest, David.
    Datacom, 38-46, February 1990.
        EDI: it's not that simple.
Keen, Peter G.W.
    In Otway H.J., Peltu, Malcolm (Eds). New Office Technology. Francis
    Pinter. London. 1983.
        Strategic planning for the new system.
Martin, Brian (Ed).
    Price Waterhouse. London. 1989.
        Information technology review 1989/1990.
Martin, Brian (Ed).
    Price Waterhouse. London. 1990.
        International information technology review 1990.

Martin, Thomas.
  In Williams, M.E., (Ed). Annual Review of Information Science &
  Technology, Volume 23, 1988. Elsevier, Amsterdam 1988. Chapter 8.
    Office automation.
McClelland, Stephen.
  Telecommunications, 75-80, February 1990.
    Voice messaging gets a favourable hearing.
McClelland, Stephen.
  Telecommunications, 88-90, October 1990.
    EDI: an overview.
Olsen, Margarethe H; Lucas, Henry C.
  Comm. ACM 25(11), 838-847, November 1982.
    The impact of office automation on the organisation; some implications
    for research and practice.
Peterson, J.C.
  Computing Surveys 9(3), 223-252, September 1977.
    Petri Nets.
Potter, Robert J.
  Science 195(4283), 1160-1164, May 1977.
    Electronic mail.
Pullinger, D.J.
  Visible Language 23, 171-185, 1984.
    Design and presentation of computer human factors journal on the
    BLEND system.
Pye, Roger, Jim Bates and Laura Heath.
  Profiting from Office Automation. Report by KMG Thomson McLintock for
  the Department of Trade and Industry. 1986.
    Vol. A. The way forward. Vol. B. Final evaluation results.
Ramsden, Hilary and Ramsden, Stephen.
  Aslib Information Technology Survey 1990. Aslib, London.
    The use of information technology by information services.
Short, John, Ederyn Williams and Bruce Christie.
  John Wiley 1976.
    The social psychology of telecommunications.
Spencer, Peter.
  The Daily Telegraph, London. December 10th 1989.
    Where E-mail scores over the post.
Turoff, Murray and Roxanne Hiltz.
  Digest of the AFIPS Office Automation Conference, Atlanta, Georgia,
  May 1980.
    Structuring communications for the office of the future.
Wright, Patricia.
  In B.K.Brittan (Ed). Executive control processes in reading. Lawrence
  Erlbaum, New Jersey, 1987. 23-55.
    Reading and writing for electronic journals.
Zisman, Michael D.
  Sloan Management Review, 1-16, Spring 1978.
    Office automation. Revolution or evolution?
Zloof, Moshe M.
  IBM Syst. J. 16(4), 324-343, 1977.
    Query by example: a data base language.
Zloof, Moshe M.
  IBM Research Report RC8091 (No.35086) Jan 24th 1980. IBM Watson
  Research Centre, Yorktown Heights, NY 10598, USA.
    A language for office and business automation.

CHAPTER 23. INFORMATION TECHNOLOGY IN BANKING, RETAILING, AND PUBLISHING

BANKING AND RETAILING

Electronic Funds Transfer (EFT)

We do not hear a great deal from the two kinds of organisations who are deeply involved in the new technology and who pioneered large telecommunication networks. They are airlines and banks.

Banks were among the earliest pioneers of big network with the Swift system which started in 1977. It interconnected banks in 15 countries including the U.S., Canada, and major European countries. Later the whole of Western Europe became connected and the system was extended into Eastern Europe, South America, The Middle East, Africa and Asia.

Swift has about two thousand member banks in 46 countries, with 1200 actual banking locations. The system handled over 350,000 transactions per day but in the late eighties this increased to 1.3M.

By 1986 the system was becoming overloaded. The costs of an improved network, Swift2, escalated to £80M from the original $28M estimate. It is based on Unisys mainframes and an X25 Northern Telecom network (Black 1990). The long term objective is to include EDI (Electronic Data Interchange) services to Edifact standards (See Chapter 22).

In the UK, a number of clearing banks are interconnected by the CHAPS EFT network for the direct transfer of amounts exceeding £10,000. For example the contract formalities and funds transfer for a house purchase could be a same-day transaction replacing the notoriously slow procedures which usually apply.

These banks each operate a Tandem backed-up computer gatewayed to PSS with "a closed user group" arrangement, fully protected by encrypted communications. Other smaller banks and corporate customers can arrange to use certain facilities by arrangement with the clearing banks.

In late 1989 a fault in CHAPS software caused £2 billion to be paid out to various companies twice. The bank in question discovered the error within an hour and most was recovered "as a result of the goodwill of the close-knit banking community and its customers".

The automation of cheque clearance processes has received an on-going effort culminating in a standard to extend the usefulness of schemes like the well known E-13B standard for machine readable characters on cheques. Inter -Bank Standard 3, part 2, caters for banks using Optical Character Recognition schemes (OCR) for clearance as well as those using E-13B.

The mind boggles at the consequences of the instant transfer of all funds electronically. The implications of releasing the enormous sums of money at present more or less in limbo during the cheque clearance process are enormous.

Building Society EFT

Most building societies in the UK use terminals online to a central computer to handle withdrawals and receipts and to up-date customer's ("member's") passbooks. The societies added Automatic Teller Machines (ATMs) for cash dispensation, forming two main groups each using common facilities - Matrix and Link, the latter including banks and other financial institutions. Any customer of a society in a group can use an ATM belonging to any other society in that group.

British Telecom announced in June 1989 that they would be running the LINK ATM network, expected to expand so that customers of 38 banks and building societies could use 4200 ATMs. The main switch on the LINK network would also connect to the PLUS SYSTEM network in Denver, Colorado, which services 26,000 ATMs in other countries.

The 1988 Financial Services Act opened up competition between banks, building societies, estate agents, solicitors and brokers for mortgage and other services. Customers provide considerable details about themselves when opening a mortgage, and that data may be used to enable an organisation to offer other services to a potential customer. The Act also provides protection for customers, strictly applied to ensure that they are given the best and most relevant information.

McLeod (1988) quotes the chief executive of the West of England building society who operate their own system using ISC Pinnacle Plus software. "Like most building societies we want to provide a one-stop financial services shop", he says.

Retail EFT: EFTPOS

Apart from inter-bank transactions and cheque clearance there is another trend of even greater significance - the move towards the "cashless society", starting with EFT between retailers and banks. Foster (1986) thinks that if EFT is introduced at the point of sale and if all cheque transactions are replaced by EFT debit card transactions eliminating vouchers, then retailers could expect a 50% saving in payment time and almost 20% in costs.

This analysis assumes there will be no shift away from cash transactions. It would be interesting to know whether an allowance for "running-in investment time" is included in this calculation. There is bound to be a fairly long expensive period during which a complete system is being operated on behalf of a small growing number of retailers and their customers.

EFTPOS (Electronic Funds Transfer at Point Of Sale) means that a buyer inserts a card at the check-out desk in a shop to pay for goods purchased by immediate funds transfer from his or her bank account to the shop's. The transaction proceeds via a telephone line connection.

Bar-codes - small lines and spaces marked on the packing of all goods - are an essential feature of EFTPOS. The checkout operator need no longer read and enter prices into the till. Each item is passed across a glass plate so that a laser beneath it can read the codes and send the data to a computer. The data is returned, appropriately formatted, to a printer alongside the till for printing a customer receipt list.

A more recent technique is a Radio Frequency (RF) tag which can be read more easily at a checkout point since it is freer from obstructions than a bar code read by a laser light beam.

Bar-code technique became widely used in the US and the rest of the world lagged until about 1985. After that, large investments were made in other countries. By 1988 Sainsburys, a UK supermarket chain, had installed systems in over 90% of its shops. According to Ryder (1990) the market for bar-code and other kinds of automatic identification products was worth nearly £2.5 billion in 1990.

Cutler and Rowe (1990) have discussed the pros and cons of the system. Customers benefit by getting an itemised receipt and lower error rate. Stores benefit by being able to change prices automatically making it easier to confirm to the Trade Descriptions Act - they can be prosecuted for over-charging so it behoves to charge the correct current price.. System security is better and so (potentially) is stock control.

However the effects of a breakdown may be disruptive. Fears of unemployment seemed to be unjustified; the main effect on staffing was a change of job. But the installation of bar-code tills may result in a reduction in costs because of deskilling and reduced wages:- "Shopfloor workers from all departments are now scheduled to pick goods or sit on scanning terminals for certain periods each week. The work of many has been effectively deskilled in that former multi-purpose shopfloor workers are increasingly turned into low grade packers".

It is suggested that "sleight of hand" price changing may occur:- "With pricing, scanning unquestionably passes power to the company and away from the customer". Sales data and stocktaking is no better than before because shortcomings in this area lie outside the EFTPOS system.

Banks and retailers stand to benefit from EFTPOS because of reductions in paperwork handling compared with, say, credit card payment, as mentioned above. The customer benefit is the price reduction on goods which will occur because of this cheaper more efficient method of payment - but don't take this remark too seriously. The first thing that customers will lose is the credit part of the credit card.

The idea of total EFT based on terminals in shops is a big collaborative venture not so much concerning people as technology. It will certainly require the involvement of many planners, and once installed there will be some changes in the work of the person running each point of sale station. Presumably there will still be a need for about the same staff/customer ratio to handle the checking, totalling, and registering of purchased goods.

Clearing banks, and more recently smaller banks, have been discussing ways of launching a nationwide system in the UK for some years. A pilot scheme scheduled for use in Southampton early in 1983 was shelved on the grounds of too high an initial cost. It's the usual problem of financing until a critical mass is reached. It won't be long before something happens. Various bits of new technology keep appearing: taken together they will make the whole thing possible.

It was thought that Britain would be the first country to embark on a system of this kind on any scale. British Telecom, the clearing banks, and IBM were ready to start. The Banks were prepared to make the equipment investment if the government agreed to the go-ahead in this politically sensitive operation.

In September 1989 the trial of a national system called Switch was initiated by a group called EFTPOS UK consisting of 13 banks and building societies. Technically it was a success but it was opposed by retailers for being too expensive and designed primarily to benefit banks. It was abandoned apparently because of lack of standards and increased competition between banks which made agreements less likely.

A major problem was disagreement about a prime requirement - the acceptance of different cards used in different entrenched systems by a single terminal. "Whether the issue of EFTPOS standards can be resolved remains to be seen... with co-operation between banks in short supply, it could be a long time before the turmoil disappears" (Mill 1990).

However there is nothing to prevent bilateral arrangements. For example in 1989 Lloyds Bank announced a four year EFTPOS contract with B&Q, a do-it-yourself chain of stores. 2000 terminals will be installed in the stores. Processing and authorisation data will be transported over the bank's and the retailer's own lines and handled by their own computers.

Smart Cards

Another parallel development in banking and retailing is the so-called "Smart Card" - that is a credit card carrying a passive magnetic strip for wiping credit or debit data on or off when inserted in a machine, or containing a microprocessor for more sophisticated operations. One advantage is that the micro-card is said to be very secure.

Smart cards could be used for cashless shopping. French Companies are the leaders in the field and are hoping to establish a de facto standard. US banks have ordered cards from France for experimental purposes. The first major application in France is for pay-telephones - 200,000 cards were initially ordered from Bull.

"Plastic Cards" were the subject of a comprehensive review at the end of 1989 (Barchard 1989).

Banking services - banks of the future

Until quite recently new High Street Banks keep appearing in the UK, for the time being the need for a row of people behind the counter remained whatever is going on behind the scenes. Current activity in the further development of cash dispensing and other systems may change that. For example Barclay's have introduced, on an experimental basis, the counter equivalent but much cheaper version of the ATM (Automatic Teller Machine), now to be found outside many banks.

The customer, using her PIN (Personal Identification Number) keys the amount required; the teller on the opposite side of the counter observes the operation and hands over the cash. The point is that the customer is doing all the bank's associated "paperwork" while keying.

However a large investment is being made by all major banks in connecting the machine outside the bank to a communications network enabling it to do much more than simply identify a customer, pay out cash, and debit his account. In the US nearly 50,000 ATM's have been installed compared to a few thousand six years ago. In January 1985 21 UK banks and Building Societies started to connect ATMs to the LINK network and planned to extend into airports, shopping centres, and to connect to foreign networks (See page 568).

In February 1985 NCR announced an ATM incorporating cash withdrawal and deposit facilities, loans, insurance, buying and selling shares, and providing investment and other advice via an interactive videodisk machine and display tube. The machine is of modular construction so that semi custom-built variations can be supplied according to the requirements of any bank. Typical price is £23,000.

Home banking

New developments in "Home Banking Systems" are announced almost daily, but the mix of resources needed seems to be inhibiting take-off as with point of scale schemes. In the UK the best known is probably the Nottingham Building Society/Prestel system called Homelink. In addition to account management, such as switching cash into a deposit account to minimise interest loss, bill paying, statement check etc., Homelink has provided other services to make the whole idea more interesting.

The services include regular auctions with bids accepted from terminals for goods, buying goods for delivery at home, flights and holiday arrangements, etc. Homelink has been followed by similar services - Midland Bank in 1984, and Bank of Scotland in 1985. Since the Knoxville experiment in the US, several banks including Chemical Bank and Bank of America offer home banking services.

Compuserve operates one of the largest services in the US for which software for all major personal computers is available. Banks in many parts of the US allow Compuserve to be used for bill payments, and Compuserve now offers hundreds of different services. Evening connect rates (September 1984) were $6 per hour.

In 1990 Compuserve claimed 625,000 members in 24 countries "the world's largest information service for personal computers". Compuserve is accessible in Europe via nodes on various networks - Istel, Transpac, and CSC at $12.50 per connect hour (Anon 1990), plus communication surcharges of $9.50, $9.50, and $20.50 respectively.

In the Compuserve Almanac (Anon 1989) under "Banking", Compuserve describes its Home Banking service as "delivering banking services directly to you through your personal computer terminal... 24 hours a day... allowing you to view your account balances, pay bills, and transfer funds... some have the ability to correspond with your banker via electronic mail... check the online description of the banks you are considering for their services and interest rates".

It seems likely that labour-intensive banks will attempt to mechanise all banking transactions and they will be handled by machines outside the bank or in special within-bank areas. Most of a much reduced labour force will be working behind the scenes or in a comfortable personal service area providing consultation and advice.

Communications: security

Hebditch considered (1982) that if communication costs are going to increase over the next ten years to meet the high convergent costs of digital technology, then it is going to be increasingly important to design systems to minimise dependency on telecommunications. "The less data you transmit the less bandwidth you require and the less cost you will incur.... further reinforcing the trend towards distributed processing".

"The localisation of computer power will make it increasingly feasible to employ office automation procedures well established in the commercial sector e.g. word processing, electronic mail etc., to be employed by banks without putting additional and unwelcome pressure on the communications network".

That may have become true for within-bank office procedures. But for fund transfer systems telecommunications is essential.

The phrase "as safe as the Bank of England" is a reminder of the major concern of banks with all aspects of security, particularly in telecommunication links. D.W.Davies (1982) clearly explains the general principles and degrees of security obtainable with different arrangements for the transmission of data, starting with a description of the "RSA" method (the initial letter of the names of its three MIT inventors in 1978).

In this method the sender computes a number called the "Authenticator" derived from the content of the whole message, using a secret key. The recipient possesses a secret key and also computes the Authenticator, comparing it with the sender's which is included with the message. Fairly large keys are needed and Davis recommends 512 bits for the RSA system.

"The best known method (for breaking) would then occupy 200 million years". The computation in RSA is of course done automatically and quite quickly. A chip designed for the purpose can do it in about one second, but this has since been improved to 20 milliseconds.

Other security requirements

Davies continues with a description of security considerations in cash dispensers with reference to the personal identification number (Pin) and discusses "Electronic Cheques" - that is information about money which is telecommunicated accompanied by a secret key. For example the Chase Manhattan Bank has developed a microprocessor "data authentication" device to be used in telephone line transmission of funds data from remote terminals. It greatly reduces the possibility of transmission errors and fraud by an automatic exchange of keys between the remote terminal and the host computer.

Personal identification is of course an essential factor in cash transfer, the time honoured method being a signature on a cheque. The whole edifice behind cheque schemes can still be retained, if a human teller is no longer present, by the use of automatic recognition systems. Developments in pattern recognition enable the unique information describing a particular fingerprint to be encoded in 200 bytes. A system called "Finger-matrix" has been developed in the US for use alongside keyboards.

The customer places the index finger on a pressure plate, and the machine scans the image comparing the resultant code with codes held in a central store. Signature verifying devices are available working on a similar principle, although the matching of the pattern derived from a scanned signature with one held in a central store is said to be less reliable than the fingerprint system.

ELECTRONIC PUBLISHING

> Reading maketh a full man, conference
> a ready man, and writing an exact man.
> Francis Bacon.

Introduction

As Humpty-Dumpty would have said, had he been consulted, "Electronic Publishing means just what a person intends it to mean, neither more nor less".

Claude Bishop (1985), a scientific journal editor, said "if by electronic publishing we mean the application of electronic processing technologies in the production of hard-copy journals, then it is already with us".

"But the next stage is much more nebulous... The important fact is that the working documents of scientists are hard copies of papers that can be read, scanned, flipped, carried around from desk to lab to home, and spread out on a working surface for comparison, annotation, and cross-referencing. None of this can be done with a video display unit and therefore exclusively electronic journals can expect to encounter the same customer resistance as microfiche".

For three equipment vendors, combining their offerings also in 1985, it meant a new system - "A full electronic publishing package". It consisted of an Imagitex image scanner, an Interleaf composition system for integrating text and graphics, and a Monotype raster image processor producing high resolution printed output on paper or film.

In Mastroddi (1986) - covering a number of CEC sponsored and other projects - the electronic publishing spectrum is further widened to include such diverse topics as the Japanese Hi-Ovis experiment for domestic consumers, tele-editing and refereeing, Minitel, and CD-ROMs.

Lee et al (1988) think that electronic publishing includes bibliographic databases, referral databases (covering non-published or non-print sources), text databases, and numeric databases. The major change they identify is "the shift from online access to optical disc technology... which may have a favourable effect on neglected information services. Many pages can be stored on CD-ROM and users of CD-ROM pay no separate search fees or connect-time charges".

Lee et al stress the problem of command languages and emphasise the potential importance of expert systems. There is "...a larger movement, proceeding irregularly, towards a greater degree of integration of access to various information products and services..." but "...they are still far from achieving the broader objectives of a common command language and other mechanisms for making the techniques of database query transparent to the user".

Moving on to 1989, for Gabriel (Gabriel 1989), a university librarian, "Electronic publishing is a subject so kaleidoscopic it refuses to submit to a simple definition encompassing as it does computerised typesetting, videotex, electronic mail and journals and books, CD-ROM, facsimile, personal computers, online databases, and the manifold operations commonly represented by the generic term "desktop publishing".

Fischer and Feder (1990) provide a survey of "The electronic information industry". They consider the "industry" to be providers of information from databases online via a telecoms link and from magnetic media - tape, smart cards, floppy disc, and CD-ROM. In 1989 (Source: Link Resources), the revenue earned in Europe and the US from delivery via these media was as shown in Table 23.1.

Media	Revenue 1989 $M
Dial-up	3900
Leased line	2800
Tape	687
CD-ROM	352
Fax and misc.	339
Floppy disc	307
Broadcast	307

TABLE 23.1
Electronic
Publishing media

For the purposes of this book, electronic publishing is the computer-aided inputting, production, or processing of printed or never-to-be-in-print "information", or the distribution of information, reproduced and often read using an electronic system.

Can an organisation be in "The electronic information industry" and not be an "electronic publisher"? What constitutes "electronic publication?".

Whatever the definition, Kist (1987), in his wide ranging survey of the subject, suggests that a quotation by Brinberg in **Publishers Weekly** provides a compelling reason for on-going commercial interest in EP:- "The greatest risk is to stay out of the game".

Computer aided production

In 1991 information technology intrudes into the production of printed material at every stage. As it encroached on traditional printing methods it achieved notoriety because of friction generated between employees and management as old crafts were rendered obsolete and the old camaraderie engendered by tough working conditions gradually disappeared.

Areas which have been transformed include information inputting, sorting and layout, composition, and reproduction . Keying directly into a computer with disk storage is a different proposition from typing on to paper. The software can include a variety of aids to reduce the work chore, in addition to normal Word Processing aids.

As an example of computer-aided input processing, at the Institute for Scientific Information, Philadelphia, information about hundreds of thousands of printed-page scientific articles with their references are input annually. When an operator inputs a reference to an earlier article, there is a high probability that the article will already be in the system. As soon as the operator has typed the small number of characters needed to uniquely identify the reference, the item is automatically looked up and the complete reference is displayed for checking and automatically input, thereby saving a great deal of keying time.

Developments in photo-typesetting have revolutionised printing, particularly for very large runs of frequently repeated publications such as telephone directories. These machines work at very high speeds from computer tape or disc. Their precursor was the 1966 Digiset where the page image was reproduced on a CRT, replacing the old photographic master.

Author directly-generated printing

This subject was discussed by Holloway in a most useful 1985 publication. Many authors type into a WP machine or microcomputer and print camera-ready copy or despatch a disk to a publisher. However this information cannot be directly used by a phototypesetting machine unless the disk can be read by the particular machine owned by the publisher. Furthermore a phototypesetter requires codes embedded in the copy to tell it what to do e.g. end line, change type face, etc, and it must strip out those codes before printing.

The codes must be inserted in the text, or tags must be inserted to be converted into instructions for the phototypesetter. Different machines require different codes so there is a standardisation problem. Holloway (1985) described the more or less inconvenient ways of getting the codes inserted.

The arrival of "what you see is what you print" microcomputers such as a Macintosh with a Laserwriter printer enables good camera-ready copy with different fonts and graphics to be produced. With Apple's PostScript software running on a Macintosh, codes are included in the text enabling it to be directly read and printed by a Linotron 101 typesetter. This system removes some of the encoding hassle for the author because most of the codes are generated automatically and inserted by the software. For instance when the author changes a font or underlines the software inserts a code.

To try and break the whole problem Xerox, in conjunction with a number of computer companies (excluding IBM) attempted to introduce its Interpress page descriptor language as a standard. It did not succeed. When software becomes available for a number of WP machines/microcomputers, readable by a number of phototypesetting machines, then the author type-to-publish revolution will have arrived.

Attempts to do just this by SGML or ODA code standardisation, currently requiring a good deal of extra work from an author, are described in Chapter 21.

The Electronic Publishing Industry

Commercial publishers are experimenting with electronic publications which bear some resemblance to those in print, aimed at people who are already using terminal/communication facilities because they are engaged in "electronic" information-seeking or other activities requiring a terminal. Some or all of these people are the ready-made potential customer base.

Other publishers, often with large conventional publishing interests, already generate text and graphics in machine readable form as part of their printed product production processes. These publishers are also experimenting with electronic forms of publication for the general public particularly the business community. They are accumulating experience and testing the ground ready to participate in the expected growth, and to be ready to shift from their printed product base as and when it starts to be undermined.

Gurnsey (1982) provides a lot of information in a most useful compact publication. US publishing revenues exceeded $33 billion in 1980. Deregulation has enabled publishing to become a multi-media industry. For example only a third of Time Inc's $3 billion comes from print, compared with 90% for Berteleman, Europe's biggest publisher, with a similar revenue. Data is provided in appendices showing how widely diversified some of the larger US publishers have become.

The companies which receive special mention for having moved into electronic publishing are Dow Jones, Standard & Poors and VNU/Arete. The ten major companies in Europe and the US whose main business is conventional publishing and who are, no doubt, watching every move made by others into electronic publishing are shown on the right in order of revenue.

Bertelsman/Grunner & Jahr	Ger.
Times Inc.	US
Times Mirror	US
S.Pearson/Pears.-Longman	UK
Axel Springer Verlag	Ger.
Gannett Inc.	US
Knight Ridder Newspapers	US
Thomson Organisation	UK
McGraw Hill	US
Associated Newspapers	UK

Gurnsey suggests that "The key to success in electronic publishing is probably a vertically integrated corporate structure, a good revenue base from which to fund capital investment, a clear indication of the needs of users, and the ability to react quickly and positively to new technological and marketing opportunities".

The answer to the publisher's dilemma - should he jump in a particular direction or wait and see for a bit - is probably evident from the present actions of publishers who are probing new areas cautiously. Gurnsey concludes that electronic publishing is in a mess:- "...a long way from user acceptance" and "suffering from a plethora of misinformation and false claims".

Fringe activities

This is a question of definition. The label "electronic publishing" is sometimes used to cover what I call fringe activities because many publishers are involved in, or have diversified into, the Entertainment Industry, or because entertainment and information are lumped together. For example Gurnsey includes the 100 television stations (I'm sure that figure is a gross under-estimate), 4370 cable operators, and nearly 10,000 radio stations in the US as part of the electronic publishing infrastructure. This leads to the idea of dominant national information providers - CBS, NBC, and ABC - and a number of local information providers. Another example is the 200 private TV stations in Italy.

The Electronic Scientific Journal

There is some anxiety about the survival of the scientific journal, particularly the small specialised journal, which has evolved from two publications which first appeared in the 17th century, the Philosophical Transactions and the Journal des Scavans.

The electronic journal idea is usually attributed to Senders. In 1976 he suggested that printed scientific journals might become extinct because of increasing costs, falling subscriptions, and general problems of distribution and finding the information published in them. His feeling was not so much that electronic substitutes were desirable but that economic pressures would force their birth. He suggested a plausible scenario and the idea sparked off much new technology whizz-kiddery.

A whole page advertisement appeared in the New York Times of May 21st 1979 about the "Alpex 900 Information Network". It contained the headline, in 144 point type, "Publishers: your information network is ready". According to the blurb, a publisher types copy into a special terminal from which it is transferred to the Alpex data centre. A subscriber to the service "places a phone call and sees the information displayed on his own TV set". The service "fulfills publisher's urgent needs for a fast and economical method of electronic transmission to subscribers".

That seems to have been the first and last appearance of the idea. Perhaps the cost of the whole page ad. was just too much.

Commencing in 1973 The National Science Foundation (NSF) funded Westat Inc., and Aspen systems to study the feasibility of an Editorial Processing Centre (EPC - Berul, 1974)). Later it also funded SRI International, who considered the role of an EPC in a complete electronic scientific information system.

An EPC is a system designed for use co-operatively by small/medium size publishers and authors, editors, and referees, (particularly for scientific journals) who would exchange "electronic manuscripts" which would be published in "electronic" or conventional journals. It would also connect to a network for disseminating information derived from the EPC database.

There was a lot of discussion about this idea at the time. Costing was done showing that it was economically feasible for a group of small publishers. It seemed to be a way out of the higher-cost declining-subscription problems being experienced by many of the smaller scientific journal publishers, offering both computer-aided publication with paper end-products, with provision, in due course, for electronically displayed information. Having financed the venture, the NSF withdrew saying, in effect, "there you are lads, it works, now get together and try it". There were no takers.

The next attempt was the Electronic Information Exchange System (EIES), based on a computer at the New Jersey Institute of Technology, with MIT also involved, and participants with their terminals interconnected via Telenet (Turoff 1978)). This was a large scale experiment in computer conferencing but also included two actual electronic journals - **Chimo** and **The Mental Workload.**

In a later article about this system, (Guillaume 1980), it seemed that it had not been very successful. At the end of the evaluation period "only one paper had been submitted to the electronic journal, a single author production. Conference activity was still dominated by a select few, many participants ceasing completely to contribute. Maintenance functions were missing and task functions were still ineffectively carried out".

The British Post Office helped to put a blight on the system by ruling that the use of Telenet by third parties infringed its monopoly. The third parties were the substantial UK contingent of contributors and editors proposed for the Mental Workload. In the event they contributed nothing.

Hiltz (1986) co-worker with Turoff took the view that there is much more to be learnt and would probably disagree with the more limited view expressed by Guillaume about just one part of the experiment. Teleconferencing or Computer Conferencing, as discussed by Hiltz, is a near relative of the Electronic Journal since it has been used to place scientists engaged in a similar research area in ongoing contact with each other.

Freeman (1984) also thought that this idea had some way to go. An experiment which started in 1978 involved a number of social scientists interested in social networks. The conclusions are not very definite - indeed "perhaps the most important conclusion is that there are no true conclusions". However the computer conference, it was felt, had a considerable impact.

Nothing daunted, the UK universities of Loughborough and Birmingham, supported by the British Library, decided to have another go, building on the EIES experience. Once again it seemed that the economic problems of the scientific journal system were the driving force. The BLEND experiment, described by Shackel and Pullinger (1983), explored various forms of communication between scientists using terminals connected to a DEC 20 central computer.

"It was said that "Even if electronic journals are obviously efficient for transmitting information, there remains the possibility that users none the less do not like this medium of communication. Therefore questionnaires, interviews..etc...will be used to establish measures of acceptability".

After four years two issues of a journal called **Computer Human Factors** each containing four papers, editorials, and discussions, a "Poster Paper" journal contain 21 papers, and a journal called **References, Abstracts, and Annotations Journal** containing abstracts from seven journals and a general bibliography, were published.

Wilson (1984) describes the joint authorship of a paper by five "distributed authors" using the BLEND facilities. In particular he discusses the possibility of "active mailboxes" wherein certain secretarial functions could be performed on incoming messages/documents received in one mailbox from a number of different people.

However later observations by Oakeshott (1985) were gloomy. There were not sufficient incentives in the form of results nor enough motivation to contribute, online networks slowed down processes, and the technology was generally inconvenient.

The great problem in such experiments is to simulate real world conditions, in particular to get to the "critical mass" point - rather like an electronic mail system which cannot attract new subscribers because the people to whom you want to send messages don't subscribe. Authors won't be motivated to contribute to a journal with few readers.

Back in 1975 Garfield suggested that:- "For at least the next decade, I believe the printed journal will continue to be the main form of scientific publication. Besides the reluctance of scientists in general to give up things which are familiar and comfortable, present publishers, advertisers, printers, and editors have a vested interest in maintaining printed journals".

12 years later Freeman's conclusions (Freeman 1987) about electronic journals were:- "It seems unlikely that the electronic journal will soon replace the traditional journal format which has served us so well for these many decades. Rather, more likely it will carve out its own niche by providing those kind of services unique to the electronic medium - services which emphasise interactive capabilities with databases and other colleagues, the communication of brief and highly current information, as well as the handling of large blocks of statistical information so valuable to the scientific community".

Scientific journals and the sociology of science.

The main objective of experimental electronic journals is the efficient dissemination of information. Information dissemination is only one of the functions of printed journals and these other functions are likely to contribute to their endurance.

They include the benefit provided for the author in building up his reputation both at the time of publication - particularly in establishing his priority for a new discovery - and in knowing that his collected works are solidly accessible today and for future generations through the reference library process.

For the reader, they include the benefit of being able to assimilate information provided by knowledgeable people in their field, and of reading the editorials, the letters, the news items, the book reviews, the advertisements, and the situations vacant - a comprehensive blend of professional information requirements.

The importance of the printed journal in the efforts of Watson & Crick (Watson 1968) to stay ahead of Pauling is clearly evident from Watson's account of their discovery.

"It seemed almost unbelievable that the DNA structure was solved, that the answer was incredibly exciting and that our names would be associated with the double helix as Pauling's was with the alpha helix". Just prior to publication Watson expresses his delight that Pauling was "still way off base", but Watson cleared the decks for publication just in case. In fact Pauling was hot on the same track.

Francis Crick and Watson "stood over her (his sister) as she typed the article. On Tuesday it was sent up to Bragg's office, and on Wednesday April 2nd, it went off to the editors of Nature". It was published in that same month (1953). This rapid action was taken in order to establish the earliest possible publication date by submission to a prestigious fast-publishing weekly journal, via an influential scientist (Bragg). Watson & Crick later received the Nobel prize.

Electronic Books

The "Death of Print" has been forecast for many years and today the forecasters are as busy as ever. The idea is phrased in dramatic terms:- "The 500-year era of print is drawing to its close" says Dr. Frank Lukey, future product manager of Silver Platter, CD-ROM supplier. "In only 5-10 years a range of electronic books will be available of which the most common will be the portable book which will really sell the idea".

Some years ago a device called the Izon micrographics reader was developed, supposedly to sell for about $100. It used an optical compression system with a form of Fresnel lense housed in a book-size box, with the expectation of breaking the portability barrier imposed by normal microfiche readers. It disappeared without a trace.

But the "electronic book" is not dead. A new version was proposed, based on VLSI (Very Large Scale Integrated) circuits according to Murray (1981). It would be book-size with a flat screen display, the words being encoded as 12 bit numbers stored, together with coarse graphics, in a memory of about 14 Mbytes.

The method of compression would enable the text of a novel to be stored. "Books" would come in small plug-in memories, and an on-board microprocessor would handle decoding and presentation. The device would include a keyboard and string-searching capabilities for "publications" requiring that facility. It is suggested that the electronic book would "alter the nature of libraries, increase the efficiency of the scientific, legal, and medical professions, minimise information access time in industry, and modify the operation of the educational system".

But well before Murray's ideas, Alan Kay's Dynabook aroused great interest when first suggested in 1968, and it still does (Ryan 1991). Kay actually started designing the machine when he was at PARC but:- "as it turned out Xerox sort of punked out midway in the thing. All we did was invent workstations and Macintoshes, and stuff like that".

"In the Dynabook form the computer of the future is a notebook with a million pixel screen, eight processors, and both wireless and cabled networking". But it will move beyond "McLuhan's notion that the printed book created the individual... if you tie interest in simulations with pervasive networking and ask what impact that is going to have on culture as a whole, I would say that it creates sceptical man".

"When you have something on your person at all times that is as innocuous as pencil and paper, that is continuously connected to the information utilities of our culture, and that you can use to play what-if games based on the information, there's going to be far less you have to take on faith".

A dictionary is the kind of book amenable to the "electronic" treatment because "new editions" can be "published" simply by issuing a disc. It is likely that software, already developed for dictionary production, can be adapted for user look-up.

Such is the case with the Oxford English Dictionary. Software and a database comprising the computerised 16 volume OED edition were developed at the University of Waterloo, Ontario, Canada (Giguere 1989). A supplement was combined with it in the UK, and a new 20 volume edition was published.

It is planned to introduce an electronically searchable edition of the 540 Mbyte dictionary in the early nineties.

Electronics versus print on paper

Inefficient as the paper journal maybe, the fact is that at the display-human interface the print-human match is far better than the machine-human match, both in information transfer and behavioural terms. For general browsing, book reading, scanning news items, appreciating pictures or drawings, and being generally entertained, print on paper is superior.

It can be written on, carried about, and digested in aeroplanes, on trains, or in the bath. It looks nice on shelves, and makes a very acceptable gift. In newspaper form it continues to be useful at its death. It is widely used for wrapping up fish and chips.

Referring specifically to books, "there is simply no experience in life that matches silent reading....readers make everything happen just the way they want it to. The actions, scenes, and voices in a book come to life entirely in the reader's mind" says Jennings (1983). "Sometimes when I can't go to sleep I see the family of the future. Dressed in three-tone shorts and shirts of disposable papersilk they sit before the television wall of their apartment; only their eyes are moving. After I've looked for a while I always see - otherwise I'd die - a pigheaded soul in the corner with a book; only his eyes are moving but in them there is a different look".

Unquestionably the economic pressures have got to be very strong to dent the print-human relationship. Quite apart from the aesthetics and other pleasant or convenient aspects of print, electronic information distribution on any scale awaits the placement of a communications and terminal infrastructure with a customer base of critical mass. The prospect of profits in consequence of mounting the nth service at relatively low cost will provide the incentive for further expansion as discussed elsewhere in this book.

But the advantages of print diminish and may be superseded when searching for and retrieving a specific chunk of information, knowing that when found it will be completely up to date. This is when easily up-dated information on a machine comes into its own and this is the area where innovations are appearing. Online encyclopaedias, stock exchange prices, airline schedules, and news items are examples.

After the item has been located, it is convenient to be able to read it on the self-same machine. Machines can display most kinds of information likely to be needed in this situation. That convenience must be balanced against adequacy of presentation. For some items it still may be necessary to introduce the inconvenience of referring the user to a place where the wanted information can be seen in print - i.e a library.

This requirement will gradually disappear as electronic input, storage, and reproduction and display techniques, improve and costs decrease. The current practice of providing an information surrogate when the amount of information is too expensive to store and transmit will also gradually disappear to be replaced by the complete text.

REFERENCES

Anon.
  Proceedings of the Electronic Banking Conference, London, October, 1982. Published by Oyez Scientific and Technical Services Ltd., Bath House, 56 Holborn Viaduct, London, EC1A 2EX, England.
Anon.
  Financial Times, October 22nd 1984.
    FT Survey: computers in banking.
Anon.
  Compuserve, PO Box 20212, Columbus, Ohio. 1989.
    Compuserve Almanac (Fifth Edition).
Anon.
  Leaflet from Compuserve, PO Box 676, Bristol, UK. 1990.
    Compuserve Forum.
Barchard, David.
  The Financial Times: survey, December 6th 1989.
    Plastic cards.
Berul, Lawrence W; Krevitt, Beth I.
  In Zunde, Pranas (Ed). Proc 37th ASIS meeting, Atlanta, Ga.,USA. October 1974. Published by American Society for Information Science, Washington DC. Pps 98-102.
    Innovative editorial procedure: the Editorial Processing Center concept.
Bishop, Claude T.
  Quarterly Rev. Biol. 60(1), 43-52, March 1985.
    Electronic publishing: to be or not to be.
Cutler, Kristie, and Rowe, Christopher.
  Behaviour & Information Technology 9(2), 157-169, 1990.
    Scanning in the supermarket: for better or worse? A case study in introducing electronic point of sale.
Davies, D.W.
  In Anon. Banking Conf. 1982.
    The potential of public key ciphers and signatures in banking.
Fischer, Margaret T., and Feder, Judith.
  In Raitt, David I. (Ed). Proceedings of the 14th International Online Information Meeting, London. December 1990. Learned Information (Europe), Oxford & New Jersey. Pps 515-526.
    The electronic information industry and forecast: in Europe, North America and Japan.
Foster, Eric.
  In Cawkell, A.E. (Ed). Handbook of information technology and office systems. North Holland. 1986. Chapter 50.
    New developments in banking technology and retail cash transfer systems.
Freeman, Linton C.
  Social Networks 6, 201-221, 1984.
    The impact of computer based communication on the social structure of an emerging scientific specialty.
Gabriel, Michael R.
  JAI Press, Greenwich, Connecticut, 1989.
    A guide to the literature of electronic publishing.

Garfield, Eugene.
   Sci-Tech News 29(2), 42-44, April 1975.
      Is there a future for the scientific journal?
Giguere, Eric.
   Byte 14(12), 371-374, December 1989.
      Electronic Oxford.
Guillaume, Jeanne.
   Can. J. Info.Sci. 5, 21-29, 1980.
      Computer conferencing and the development of an electronic journal.
Gurnsey, John.
   Learned Information, Oxford, 1982.
      Electronic document delivery. III: electronic publishing trends in
      Europe and the United States.
Hebditch, David.
   In Anon. Banking Conf. 1982
      Impact of network technologies on banking automation.
Hiltz, Starr Roxanne.
   In Cawkell, A.E. (Ed). Handbook of information technology and office
   systems. North Holland. 1986. Chapter 46.
      Recent developments in teleconferencing and related technology.
Holloway, Henry L.
   Elsevier, Oxford, EIB Report no.7., for Primary Communications Centre,
   Univ. of Leicester, England, 1985.
      Author-generated phototypesetting: author-publisher printer links.
Jennings, Laura.
   The Futurist 17(2), 5-11, April 1983.
      Why books will survive.
Kist, Joost.
   Croom Helm, Beckenham, England. 1987.
      Electronic Publishing.
Lee, Joel M., Whitely,W.P., et al.
   Library Trends 673-693, Spring 1988.
      Electronic publishing in library and information science.
Mastroddi, Franco (Ed.).
   Kogan Page. London. 1987.
      Electronic publishing: the new way to communicate.
McLeod, Marcia.
   Which Computer? 64-68, December 1988.
      Building societies.
Mill, Jenny.
   Computer Weekly, 38-39, April 5th 1990.
      Pushing in at the checkout.
Murray, John M., Klingenstein, Kenneth J.
   IEEE Trans. Indust. Electronics IE-29(1), 82-91, February 1981.
      The architecture of an electronic book.
Oakeshott, P.
   Scholarly Publishing 17(1), 25-36, 1985.
      The BLEND experiment in electronic publishing.
Read, Charles N.
   Long Range Planning 16(4), 21-30, August 1983.
      Information technology in banking.
Ryan, Bob.
   Byte 16(2), 203-208, February 1991.
      Dynabook revisited with Alan Kay.
Ryder, Don.
   The Financial Times; survey, Automatic Identification. May 23rd 1990.
      Europe market nears $2.5 billion.

Senders, John.
  Amer.Sociol. 11, 160-164, August 1976.
    The scientific journal of the future.
Shackel, Brian; Pullinger D.J et al.
  The Computer Journal, 26(3), 247-254, 1983.
    The Blend-Linc project on "electronic journals" after two years.
Turoff, Murray;
  Bull. Amer.Soc. Info. Sci 41(1),9-10, 1978.
     The EIES experience.
Watson, James D.
  Weidenfeld & Nicholson (1968).
    The double helix.
White, Nick.
  Data Processing 26(3), 29-32, April 1984.
    Network management of integrated banking systems.
Whitby, Oliver.
  J. Research Communic. Studies 2(1979/80), 9-23.
    Computer architecture for external editorial processing.
Wilson, P.A; Maude, T.I. et al.
  In Smith, H.T. (Ed), Computer Based Message Services, North Holland, 1984.
  Pages 137-165.
    The active mailbox - your online secretary.

CHAPTER 24. DESKTOP PUBLISHING

Experience is the name everyone gives to their mistakes
Oscar Wilde

This chapter will contain only supplementary information about DTP
hardware. The reader is referred to earlier chapters about hardware,
particularly to Chapter 4 (Input and Output Technology)

Moving from Word Processing to Desktop Publishing

People who customarily use a word processing system - these days a
very large number of people - may well feel that it's time to move beyond
the "typewriter look". The appearance of a document produced on a DTP
system can look almost as good as one produced by a professional print-shop.

This can be done either by obtaining an improved WP system or by
obtaining or adding a DTP system to an existing WP system. The dividing
line between a WP system and a DTP system is blurred. Some WP systems can
now perform many functions which were formerly the preserve of DTP.

Considerations of purchase price and the required degree of
improvement are important but there are at least two other matters to
consider as well when new equipment or software are to be purchased -
installing/learning time (ILT) and file conversion.

If the required degree of improvement can be obtained by up-grading
an existing WP system and buying a better printer, then ILT may be
relatively painless and short. If a DTP system is to be purchased requiring
new equipment and new software ILT will be painful and lengthy.

Pain and time wasting depend on the occupational environment; the
user may be a self-employed non-technical person, or, at the other extreme,
may be an employee within a large organisation employing staff who provide
technical and operational back-up and training to anyone in need of it.

It is quite likely that the user may have files which must be
useable on the new equipment - for example for the ongoing up-dating and use
of a database. If they won't run on the new machine simply by transferring
discs, file conversion may be necessary. The worst case will be a move to
different equipment with completely different operating system and
application software.

This book is being composed on a satisfactory WP system with a
daisywheel printer, although the writer also possesses a much improved
system. Quite a lot of work was done on the book before the new system
arrived, but it was not considered feasible to convert the existing files to
run on it . The cost/time factor of file conversion to a different operating
system with different embedded WP codes made it prohibitively expensive.

An alternative approach to evade file conversion problems is to run
an old and a new systems in parallel. Start new publications on the new
system and because the life of much information is short, the old system
will gradually fall out of use. Unfortunately a few old files will endure

and the required life of the old system will be hard to calculate.

Meanwhile you may opt to pay for two maintenance contracts. If attendance within 24 hours is required this is not cheap. Faults on the old system are likely to become more frequent.

Having completed the move to the new system one way or another, is there a finite payback time and what is it? If you continue to do the same kind of things but everything works faster and more efficiently the same tasks will be completed more quickly.

Moreover you may be able to work differently. For example when several people with stand-alone systems are involved there should be considerable benefits when it's time for a change by buying machines with multi-tasking software and shared major resources such as storage and laser printers.

A major objective of any change is to produce work of better quality. The appearance of a page can be greatly improved to something that looks much more professional. You and others may very pleased with the result but will there be a tangible financial return - for instance if you work on a payment by results basis will the improved results mean more work for more money?

It is difficult to come up with a quantifiable argument in support of a change and I will not tax your patience with specific cases since no two cases are the same. However the above remarks may focus your thoughts on a number of aspects requiring consideration.

Introduction to Desktop Publishing

For the purposes of this article Desktop Publishing (DTP) means preparing on-paper camera-ready pages, or pages on disk ready for loading into a typesetting machine.

A DTP production can be just a single stand-alone page, for example a notice-board announcement or a set of co-ordinated pages, such as a report, or a much larger set of pages, such as a book.

Page make-up data may consist of header lines in a bold large font chosen from a large selection of fonts, and columns of text interspersed with ruled dividing lines and possibly surrounded by a border. The text may include ruled boxes containing text in the same or a different font, or figures with captions. There may be some tables or line drawings with or without embedded text, or halftone illustrations occupying a small part or the whole of a page. A variety of artistic effects may be included.

As DTP grew, the difference between Word Processing (WP) and DTP remained quite clear until about 1986. WP machines were for text manipulation - many functions were "typewriter enhancements". A change of font usually meant a change in the printing head. With the same head the type could be normal or "bold" obtained by over-striking. Graphics were primitive.

In the last two years WP software has moved steadily up-market with added DTP functions. Recent WP packages may fulfill many people's "DTP requirements". As far back as 1988 a book called "Word Perfect 5: Desktop in Style" (Will-Harris 1988) was published.

This 500 page book was written and edited with a WP package - WordPerfect 5.0. The body text is set in Bitstream Fontware's Goudy Old Style accompanied by a variety of headings and embellishments. To produce the desired effect the author used equipment normally associated with DTP - for example an HP Scanjet scanner, a high resolution Genius full page monitor and a QMS-PS 810 Postscript printer for proofs.

One of the virtues of this book is that a number of pages with every detail about how they were composed are provided. A large number of additional examples are included showing how WordPerfect codes are used in each example.

Figure 24.1 is a page from the book created by its author as an example of what can be done.

PC Paintbrush software was used to make the header and footer, and the HP scanner with GEM scan software for the house, scanned from an old magazine. It was printed with an HP Laserjet II printer.

Another, more mundane book, has been written about Word Perfect by La Pier (1990). It explains the purpose of most of the keys/commands, but does not venture into DTP aspects. But it contains some good advice:-

"If two grant applications are submitted to a foundation and one is slick, neat, and attractive, while the other is obviously corrected with white-out, not formatted at

FIGURE 24.1. BOOK PAGE FORMED WITH WORD PERFECT

all, and unattractive, it is quite clear which application is seriously considered regardless of the content. The reader doesn't get to the content: the first impression is the one which has the greatest impact and gives the greatest credibility to the document".

Although the gap between WP and DTP "page-formatting software" (PFS) packages is being narrowed, the latter includes additional facilities for page composition. DTP comes into its own for sets of co-ordinated pages because matters such as automatic page-to-page overflow of contents, style continuity, page numbering and indexing etc., are automatically handled.

Aldus' Pagemaker and Xerox's Ventura soon emerged as the leaders. Data for pages can be drawn from WP-created text files, arranged in columns with ruled dividing lines surrounded by a border, printed in fonts chosen from a large selection, and surmounted by large headline or outline "art" characters.

Ruled boxes containing text in the same or a different font, or figures with captions, may be inset. There may be tables or line drawings with or without embedded text, or halftone illustrations occupying a small part or the whole of a page.

Further embellishments continually appear. Text flows automatically round boxes (Figure 24.2) and overflows smoothly on to later pages. Graphics may be croppped & changed in shape or size (scaled) to exactly fit into a space. Typography may be chosen, layouts designed and sufficient white space included to make each page look interesting and aesthetically pleasing. Colour is now feasible.

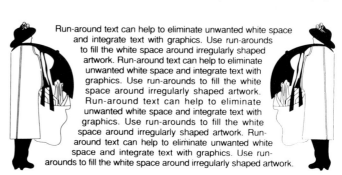

Run-around text can help to eliminate unwanted white space and integrate text with graphics. Use run-arounds to fill the white space around irregularly shaped artwork. Run-around text can help to eliminate unwanted white space and integrate text with graphics. Use run-arounds to fill the white space around irregularly shaped artwork. Run-around text can help to eliminate unwanted white space and integrate text with graphics. Use run-arounds to fill the white space around irregularly shaped artwork. Run-around text can help to eliminate unwanted white space and integrate text with graphics. Use run-arounds to fill the white space around irregularly shaped artwork.

FIGURE 24.2. TEXT FLOWS AUTOMATICALLY ROUND GRAPHICS

This idyllic page will not be realised unless the system is under the control of a capable experienced operator. In an article in an IEEE journal, critical of the hype surrounding DTP, the author rightly said "DP machines and fancy fonts alone do not an artist make". However the appearance of a page, formerly produced by professional publishing house, created with a system costing £5000 to £10,000 in the hands of an experienced person should be acceptable for most purposes.

History

The history of microcomputer development was covered in Chapter 18. There may be a small amount of duplication in this potted history of DTP.

The ancestor of present systems was undoubtedly the Xerox Star machine and its Smalltalk software - first demonstrated at the Palo Alto Research Centre (PARC) in 1978 with pages generated on a laser printer. The concept was ahead of its time and a further five years elapsed before there was any inkling of what was coming next. Many of the ideas in the Star were incorporated in the Apple Lisa machine with its daisywheel printer, which the company offered for around $12,000 in January 1983.

This machine embodied the 5 Mhz Motorola 68000 processor, with its 32 bit internal and 16 bit external busses. The processor became available in 1979 - the year in which the Lisa project first started. Apple developed a memory management system for relocating large blocks of code in memory, controllable by the 68000.

There were 2.5 Mbytes of software - far more than was usual at the time - comprising what Apple called the "Desktop Manager System". This system included a "point and select" cursor controller called a Mouse which bypassed the need to learn character-by-character commands.

Overlapping pages called "Windows" on which temporarily suspended tasks were visible, appeared on the CRT screen, and a 720 x 364 pixel bit-mapped display was used - much better than was then available on other microcomputers. A new word was coined for it - WYSIWYG - What You See Is What You Get (on the printer).

The potential of the Word Processing and graphics software called LisaWrite and LisaDraw respectively, was not immediately obvious, and people were not prepared to pay the high asking price. In spite of price slashing, Apple's profits plunged from $19M to $6M in the last quarter of 1983 - a result to which Lisa must have contributed. By December 1984 Lisa's price was down to $8000.

Apple brought in John Sculley from Pepsi-Cola in May 1983 at a $2M annual salary to back up design geniuses Steve Wozniak and Steve Jobs with commercial clout. In May 1984 Apple announced the Macintosh at $3000 with printer and several versions of Lisa2 at prices between $3500 and $5500 (without printer). The Mac, based on Lisa, was well received although it suffered from a limited 128K memory and s single disk drive.

In August 1984 Hewlett Packard introduced the Laserjet printer with a 300 pels/inch resolution at a price of $3495, less than one third of the price of anything similar, thanks to the Japanese Canon LBP-CX laser engine.

In September it became known that Apple was developing its own laser printer, and it introduced the "Laserwriter" in 1985 at nearly double the price of the Laserjet. However this printer has an on-board powerful processor to handle high quality reproduction. By 1986 laser printers had become almost mandatory for DTP. Images are represented by dots usually reproduced at a density of 300 per inch.

Meanwhile software companies, noting the potential of Apple's Desktop Manager, started offering compatible page formatting software - that is they supplemented existing Apple Mac facilities with application software specifically to enable a user to recall files representing text, graphics, etc., to arrange them on a displayed representation of a printed page, and then to print the page on the laser printer.

The idea of actually generating complete publications in this manner was given an impetus in a 1985 article by Terry Ulick in his own publication **Professional & Corporate Publishing** suggesting that the cost of typesetting for promotional literature could be enormously reduced if page-making was carried out in-house using a Macintosh system. The response was so great that Ulick discontinued his publication and launched "Personal Publishing" - a magazine dedicated to DTP, whose pages were prepared on the Mac. Ulick's first promotional leaflet brought in 10,000 subscriptions.

Later Apple introduced the Mac Plus with larger memory, and in 1987 the Mac SE at around $3000 and the Mac II. Mac II embodies six slots for plug-in boards to expand its facilities and a 15Mhz 68020 processor, with a 68881 co-processor to speed up operations. It includes good facilities for handling colour. Using the Dhrystone benchmark (usually considered to be one of the best for comparing machine performance) Mac II measures at about four times faster than the Plus or the SE.

The ubiquity of the IBM PC, and later the more powerful PC/AT and its various less expensive clones, constituting a hardware base very much larger than the Mac series, soon made it a target for DTP software developers. Retailers followed by offering PC based DTP systems of great flexibility since a large number of micro/software/printer combinations could be interconnected and sold at attractive prices.

Current progress and growth

The most recent development is the introduction of new versions of existing WP packages, or completely new packages which contain added functions, but usually short of page layout facilities, hitherto found only in DTP systems.

Increasing chip power, the falling cost of microcomputers, the development of better inexpensive printers, and the success of DTP encouraged the WP software people to move up-market. They correctly foresaw that there was an intermediate market for software which could greatly improve the appearance of in-house paperwork, reports etc., and that it could be produced without DTP frills at a considerably lower price.

According to Romtec (Maidenhead UK) 43% of DTP systems ever purchased were bought in 1988 with Macintoshes accounting for 53% of DTP machines, the first choice for small companies. PCs accounted for 39% with a substantial proportion used in large organisations. Pagemaker was the software leader with 41% of all installations, Ventura 20%, Quark Express 10%.

In 1992, the European DTP market will bottom out according to a 1990 forecast from Frost & Sullivan. UK revenues at $384M in 1988 will have risen to $737M by 1994 inclusive of all hardware and software, an increase of 18,400 installations. In Europe the corresponding revenues will be from $1.8 to $3.9 billion, an increase of 97,000 installations.

Typography and page layouts.

A great deal of thought has been put into the design of fonts and many fonts are registered designs. The famous typographer Stanley Morison said that "Typography...is the art of so arranging letters, distributing the space and controlling the type as to aid to the maximum the reader's comprehension of text". Professional page-makeup people would argue that the typographical compilation of a page can only be properly done by a professional.

The Apple Macintosh deservedly gets the credit for providing the first and best vehicle for DTP. One of several important reasons for this is that for the Mac, everything is a graphic. A bit-map graphically-constructed library of type faces and type sizes are stored in its library. A printed character of whatever kind approximately resembles a displayed character so in this respect it really is nearly WYSIWYG.

Terms likely to be encountered in DTP page design with some examples of   use are shown in Figure 24.3 Note the following numbered features :-

1) Line lengths adjusted by equal width interword spacing, not inter-character spacing.
2) Space between baselines ("leading") is made point size plus two points.
3) "Baseline" is an imaginary line along the base of non-descending letters.
4) Automatically justified lines hyphenated at optimum break-points.
5) No-aliasing (false contours or "jaggies").
6) Different fonts on the the same page.
7) Font of a particular weight (bold).
8) Style of font (italics).
9) No Orphans or Widows.
1C) Multiple-columns
11) Auto-kerning
12) Proportional spacing
13) Ascender
14) Descender
15) Glyph

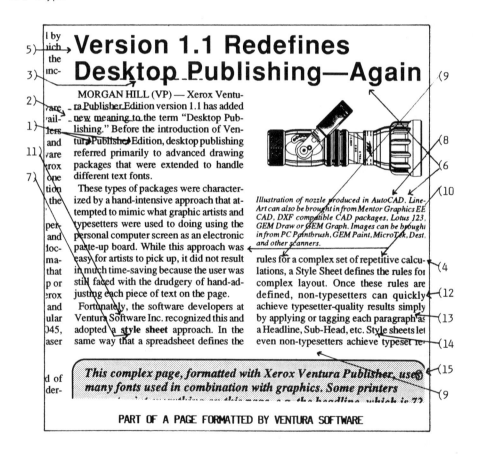

FIGURE 24.3. TYPOGRAPHY

A brief mention to "vector drawing" was made in Chapter 5 with reference to the generation of images with "outlines" - lines formed from individual pixels. This was also mentioned in the section in that chapter about Postcript.

More specific descriptions than the general term "vector" - meaning a variable quantity having magnitude and direction - are needed for a discussion about fonts. Digitized fonts may be bit-map, outline, or stroke. With **bit-map fonts**, in which the shape of a character is defined by a pixel pattern, each character can be individually changed or "edited" by a user.

An **outline** font is computed from a mathematical specification so once specified,characters may easily be rotated, altered in shape, or scaled to provide a huge range of different sizes. However unless a large amount of computing power is available, the rate of formation of a character is relatively slow. The best known application of outline (vector) fonts is in the Postscript system described in part 2 of chapter 5.

Stroke fonts are constructed by assembling straight or curved lines of pixels. The thickness depends on the number of pixels at right angles to the direction of the stroke. Computation is needed but much less than for outlines. Consequently formation is faster, but the range of available fonts is considerably smaller unless excessively complicated designs are included.

For more details see Collins (1989). Some details about fonts and point sizes are provided in Figure 24.4. More will be said about them in later sections of this chapter about displays, printers, and the appearance of pages.

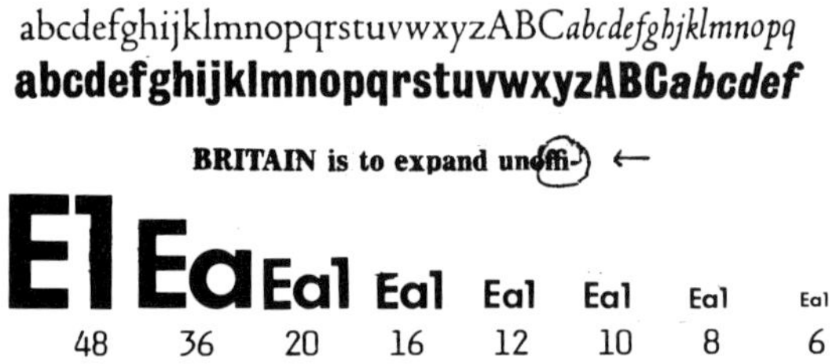

FIGURE 24.4. FONTS AND POINT SIZES

The word "Type" refers to the individual lead slugs bearing a letter in relief used in traditional typesetting, but the word is also used to refer to the collective printed result e.g. a page of type.

A Font consists of Glyphs (the letters which are members of a font) of the same design. A large number of fonts have been designed and named e.g. Times, Times italic, Gill Sans, and Helvetica. The lower part of letters like "gpqy" are known as "descenders", the upper part of "bdfh" as "ascenders". Fonts are sized in Points - 1 point is 1/72 inches or 0.353mm. Printers also use measurements in **Picas**, 1 pica = 12 points, **Ems**, a measurement of type width named after "m", the widest letter, which also equals 12 points, and **Ens** which are half an Em.

With most computer printers, fonts can be varied into different "type styles". For example the motion of the printing head can be controlled to produce stretched or condensed glyphs which really deserve to be called by different font names.

The "Baseline" is an imaginary line drawn along the bottom of non-descending characters. In order for the ascenders and descenders of successive lines of type to clear each other the distance between baselines is normally set at the point size plus one or two points. The intervening space is called "Leading" after the thin lead strip used in traditional typesetting.

An Orphan is the first line of a paragraph on the next page appearing on its own at the bottom of the preceding page. A Widow is the last line of a paragraph on the preceding page appearing on its own at the top of the following page. Kerning is the overlapping of glyphs and is considered to produce a more pleasing effect.

A Ligature is another artifact considered to look better. It is a composite glyph designed from normally separate glyphs usually "f's", "l's" or "i's" such as the glyph formed by "ffi" in the word "efficient". Proportional spacing means that glyphs are allocated spaces according to their size. Examples of ligatures, kerning and proportional spacing are shown in Figures 24.3 and 24.4.

Fonts are taken very seriously by DTP suppliers. Apple's graphically constructed font, Adobe's Postscript fonts, Illustrator software, and laser printers provided a quality approaching type-set fonts.

In 1990 both Apple and Adobe decided to step up font competition. Apple got round Adobe's monopoly of scaleable outline fonts and announced in 1990 that their much improved "Royal" font standard would be included with their new System 7.0. software. They also reached agreement with Microsoft who said they would include Royal with IBM's OS/2 software.

Adobe responded with an inexpensive utility called Adobe Type Manager (ATM) with code specific to Apple processors. It will generate smooth screen bit-mapped fonts closely resembling the Postscript font in appearance and size - a great improvement on the existing system which displays whichever existing bit-mapped font is nearest to the printed font selected.

It also improves the reproduction quality of non-Postscript Apple, Hewlett Packard, and other printers, which will then provide fonts of Postscript quality. For more information see Whitby (1990).

Colour

Colour theory, scanners, systems, printers, and colour separations were discussed in Chapter 5. Although handling the number of bits in a page of colour in a reasonable period of time remain a problem, inputting and processing colour data in a powerful microcomputer is reasonably satisfactory. Displaying or printing is less so.

Output processing for colour CRTs, and the CRTs themselves, have improved enormously, but using a CRT to assess the likely quality of a colour print is not very satisfactory. The quality of a colour print is a matter of subjective assessment, but the consensus seems to be that good colour reproduction can only be obtained through the colour separation route.

The Apple MacIntosh II is a favourite micromputer for colour. It has encouraged the introduction of special processing software.

For example it is claimed that Photomac (from Data Translation at Marlborough, MA at $695)) software is designed for serious colour printing. It accepts 24-bit colour input and provides the means for design alteration and retouching with the objective of saving files in Postscript for the production of colour separations.

Colours can be modified by changing Red-Green-Blue proportions or by varying liminance, hue, and saturation. Retouching can be carried out with the electronic equivalent of an airbrush or paintbrush.

However Chris Lynn from Crosfield Electronics, a major supplier of sophisticated colour printing equipment, is quoted as saying:-

"The reprographics technician needs to understand chokes and spreads, undercolour removal, tone correction, unsharp masking, dot gain and all the other facets of the complex process of providing the quality of colour print which the customer has become educated to expect. Nobody has yet encapsulated these skills in colour desktop publishing systems".

DTP equipment and software 1. Introduction

Until quite recently, IBM/clone PC-based DTP systems were less expensive than Mac-based systems - the availability of much less expensive laser printers, now a highly competitive market, was responsible for some of the difference. The recent introduction of a range of considerably less expensive Macs by Apple have narrowed the difference.

Many people think that Mac-based systems, representing a planned integrated approach to DTP, have a performance and useability edge over PC-based systems. Apple have had the time to smooth out the rough edges. IBM introduced its own complete DTP system in the UK in September 1987.

Descriptions of DTP equipment, software functions, and performance capabilities are often optimistically framed and hard to understand. New software offering fancy features keeps appearing. It is often of an "add-on" nature and is dependent on the user already possessing compatible supporting software without which it will not work.

Systems are tending to become a hotch-potch of overlapping functions requiring many more steps to get a result compared with a single unified design. The field has grown from almost nothing in 1986 to what the sales-driven DTP publications proclaim is easily the fastest growing microcomputer application and already one of the largest. Perhaps this proclamation is true.

It is hard to keep up to date and difficult to decide which dealers are solidly based, employ salesman who understand what they are selling, and will assist you in installation. Instruction manuals can be a disaster.

DTP equipment and software 2. Data sources and scanners

Data in the files stored in a DTP microcomputer, to be used in page construction, may have come from a variety of sources such as data from image scanners, or from Optical Character Recognition (OCR) software. Other sources include "frame grabbers" to capture one frame of picture data from a TV receiver or a TV camera, a telecoms channel, or a keyboard used with Word Processing software to create text.

Data may also be stored in files associated with special purpose software, in place in the same machine - for instance database or spreadsheet software.

Compression, described in detail in Chapter 5, is an important function in DTP particularly the compression of image data. Most scanners come with compression/decompression software.

It is certainly convenient to have everything needed already stored and ready to be retrieved in the DTP computer so that completely formatted pages may be created without shifting out of it. But it should be remembered that for camera-ready pages, pasting original graphics or illustrations into spaces left in the text has one advantage. The original is directly photographed for plate making and suffers very little degradation. Graphics and illustrations which have been digitized, recalled from files, and fitted into pages are likely to be of lower quality.

An important additional but optional element in a DTP outfit comprising the microcomputer, DTP software, printer, is a scanner - the most popular embodying CCD strip sensors and working at 300 pels/inch (See Chapter 5). Pages are fed in singly through rollers or laid on the surface of a glass plate for scanning. Most come with software for re-arranging the pixel distribution derived from halftone pictures so that a halftone effect is produced when the image is laser-printed.

As an alternative to treating text as a "bit map" in the same way as an image, some scanners include Optical Character Recognition (OCR) software which generates ASCII code enabling later character by character editing. Compression and de-compression software to enable more data to be stored in a smaller space usually comes with the scanner.

DTP equipment and software 3. Displays, Printers, and page appearance.

Printers of all kinds are described in Chapter 5 but some matters specific to DTP need elaboration.

The up-market moves of dot matrix printer manufacturers have assisted the WP suppliers; at the upper end, prices overlap with laser printers at around £1000 although for "Improved WP" a printer which costs far less than any laser printer will do very well.

A 24 pin dot-matrix printer can print at around 360 x 360 dots per inch. These machines are no longer set up by fiddling about with banks of miniature DIP switches - all the data they need for an author's control purposes, font generation etc., is usually held in their own EPROM memories controllable by the parent micro.

The printing head of the £300-plus present generation of dot-matrix printers consists of 24 pattern-forming needles each of which may shoot out against the ink ribbon (which is more expensive than normal ribbons) up to one thousand times per second. The printer requires a motor to step the head across the paper with great accuracy - yet another example of the mass-produced low-cost high-precision engineering at which the Japanese excel. However these printers are relatively noisy.

The large number of high-speed needles enables this type of printer to print solid "Near Letter Quality (NLQ)" type - as opposed to "dotted" ("draft") type - much faster. For example the Epson LQ-500 (£395) prints letter quality at 50 Characters Per Second (cps), draft at 150 cps. It can also reproduce graphics at 360 x 180 dots per inch since each needle is individually addressable. It embodies 10 10-to-12 point fonts/type styles. As you go up the Epson range the speed and the number of fonts increases. Plug-in font cartridges are available to extend the range.

These printers of course have to be controlled by WP software. The WP software must include a "driver" - a software module acting as an interface which knows what to send to a particular printer when it receives data from the WP system.

We are used to the very high quality and pleasing appearance of well printed pages. Is it possible to obtain comparable quality out of a DTP system? Is WYSIWYG - "What You See (on the display) Is What You Get (on the printed output)" true?

The reproduction of fine detail in dot-structure systems requires a lot of dots - say 300 per inch. What will the detail look like on Cathode Ray Tube Displays which are nearly always specified as reproducing p x q pels? This question was considered at length in Chapter 5.

The best generally available "19 inch screen monitors" (meaning 19" diagonally), capable of reproducing an A4 page full size, typically display 1280 (vert.) x 1024 (horiz.) pixels and cost around £2500. The useable screen area is about 13.5 x 10.8 inches, which works out at about 95 dots per inch. Today's Apple machines have the same screen as their ancestor, Lisa, introduced in 1983 with a 72 dots/inch screen - considered at the time to be astounding.

24 pin dot matrix printers and the laser printers normally used for DTP can print at 300 dots/inch. They will reproduce text or bilevel graphics received from a "bit-mapped" file - a bit by bit representation of a page via DTP software such as Pagemaker or Ventura. The data in the file, usually at 300 dots/inch, will have come as text or graphics created beforehand. There will be a one-to-one page-pel to printed-dot relationship. Postscript printers will do better still - they are not tied to bit-map resolution.

You may be able to get by with the screen supplied with the microcomputer but this will usually provide a "well-below-WYSIWYG" check on what will be printed on a laser printer and miles below what will be printed if you send your disks to a Linotron-equipped printing shop.

In other words this is WYSILTYG - What You See Is Less Than You Get. Even if the CRT presents the page full-size on a £2500 monitor, the resolution will be much inferior to the printed version. However the screen pre-view of the page is likely to be good enough for the viewer to judge fairly well how the printed version will look.

DTP systems, of course, normally arrive with much smaller monitors. The big monitor is an expensive extra but for a well-used page-formatting system the much better presentation may be well worth the extra cost.

As DTP operations are often carried out using a display which is not WYSIWYG, many systems include a function called "Greeking" - a small representation of the page layout as shown in Figure 24.5 - to provide a quick impression of what the whole page layout looks like. That helps, but assuming that A4 pages will be printed, CRTs supplied with micros are seldom large enough to display the page full size. You have to look first at one half, then at the other. A 19" monitor such as the Taxan Viking, which can display the whole page, provides a full-size preview so that those small adjustments which make all the difference can be fully appreciated. For those who want to be able to really see what the page looks like before it is printed, it's well worth having.

FIGURE 24.5. A "GREEKED" PAGE

An example of halftone printing is shown in Figure 24.6, printed on a Lasermaster RX 300 dots/inch printer, having been scanned into a micro-microcomputer from a Canon IX-12 300 dots/inch scanner. This is about as good a compromise as can be expected between tonal reproduction and detail resolution when using relatively inexpensive 300 dots per inch equipment and standard software.

Figure 24.7, scanned and printed using 600 dots/inch equipment costing a great deal more money, shows improved

FIGURE 24.6 LASER PRINTED "DITHERED" HALFTONES

tonal gradations. Figs 24.6 and 24.7 are not to the same scale so that the actual number of dots per area do not represent the real difference between the two systems. Note the poorer quality of the first by examining the water to the right of the mooring post in Figure 24.6 under a magnifying glass and compare with the tonal transitions in the area around the eyes in Figure 24.7.

FIGURE 24.7.

600 DPI LASER
"DITHERED"
HALFTONES

Dot-matrix printer quality and fonts

In a Byte review (Stewart 1987) it was concluded that "No printing technology on the horizon can compete with dot matrix impact technology as a low cost yet versatile system of printing. Dot matrix printers have put daisy-wheel (this book is printed with a daisy-wheel printer) quality under siege and they can even make a respectable attempt at laser printer production". This statement is probably still true.

Dot matrix printers usually come with several "resident" fonts not exceeding 12 points in size. Variations in style are usually provided and rather misleadingly quite a range of spreads such as "6 characters per inch" (cpi), 8 cpi, 10 cpi,. etc. The characters in these ranges are all the same size - "6 cpi" does not mean larger characters; they are simply more spread out.

In order to provide larger fonts it is necessary to "construct" each character as a graphic, designed as a smooth outline filled with pixels to provide a satisfactory appearance without jagged edges. This requires much more memory than is provided with dot-matrix printers, and special software.

Until quite recently this could not be done with these printers but special software is now available which emulates a Hewlett Packard Laserjet and which can be used with Laserjet-compatible downloadable software-constructed fonts which are available from several suppliers. When a microcomputer is loaded with downloadable fonts, a Laserjet driver, and a software package called Lasertwin (from Metro Software, Henley-on-Thames, UK), it will produce Laserjet-like graphics from a dot-matrix printer.

The larger the font or the more complex the graphic the longer the printing time will be, but if large font is used just for headers etc., the slow-down is acceptable. The result of printing large sizes using this software and a 24-pin dot-matrix printer is shown in Figure 24.8

HENLEY BADMINTON CLUB

GETS LOCAL SUPPORT

FIGURE 24.8. DOWNLOADED SOFTWARE FONT FROM A 24-PIN DOT-MATRIX PRINTER

The fonts and symbols shown in Figure 24.9 can be printed on a dot matrix printer if the driving microcomputer (using PC-DOS, MS-DOS, or CP/M operating systems) is loaded with **Fancy Font** software. The examples shown come from the range of fonts supplied in 8 to 24 points together with a collection of 1500 mathematical, foreign and other symbols.

Using WordPerfect 5.0, or the more recent version 5.1 with certain new features, you can select either one of the printer-resident fonts or one of the "download-able fonts" available from the software and stored as dot patterns. This package is fairly convenient from an author's viewpoint. To change fonts for a word, line, or paragraph just typed, you specify the text by a simple marking procedure, and press a key to call-up a fonts option menu. Having selected a font you return to the text display. The selected area will be printed in the chosen

FIGURE 24.9. FANCY SYMBOLS AND FONTS

font, line lengths will be automatically adjusted, and the system will then return to the original font. Wordperfect is also able to "import" graphics resident in certain other software packages.

A number of examples of page creation will be provided later in this chapter. As mentioned above a large, high resolution monitor makes it easier for the user to visualise what the printed version will look like - nearer to true WYSIWYG. Figure 24.10 shows a Taxan monitor, with a 19" (diagonal) screen in use.

With higher priced equipment, pages could be "improved" depending on the capabilities of the printer, the WP software, and any other software packages added such as Fancy Font or graphic drawing packages.

600

At the top
end of the DTP
potential we come
to fully fledged
page - formatting
software running
on perhaps an
Apple Macintosh II
with a scanner and
laser printer.

"Zoom" facility

The "zoom"
facility included
in many software
packages gets
round the screen
resolution limit-
ations for certain
kinds of applicat-
ion. Figure 24.11
(printed following
operations conduc-
ted with an Apple
Macintosh) shows
part of a "page"
from a software
package containing
ready-made images.

FIGURE 24.10. DTP WITH A TAXAN 19" MONITOR

In the centre
an image of the car has been selected and enlarged by zooming and a word has
been clumsily written on one headlamp by mouse movements. The image has
then been reduced and boxed under DTP program control for inclusion on a
page, as shown on the right. This facility enables detail "pixel editing"
to be carried out in a way which would be impossible under normal screen
viewing conditions.

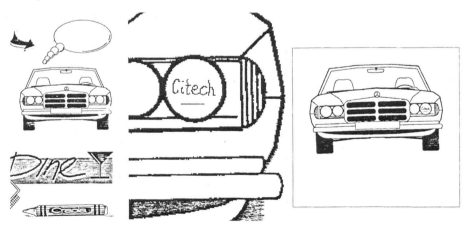

FIGURE 24.11. USING THE ZOOM FACILITY

For better freehand drawing, other software is available. For example freehand drawings created with the Electric Studio Light Pen (used against the screen), provide a far better degree of control than is possible with the clumsier mouse-cursor combination.

Page Formatting Desktop Publishing Software, and the Operating Environment

DTP software (DTPS) - the heart of a DTP system - presents an area on the screen representing a page, into which the page ingredients - stored files of text, graphics etc., or created-as-you-go material - may be fitted. A range of electronic paste-up and scaling facilities with choice of fonts are provided to allow pages to be individually styled. The display is controlled by the machine's operating system in association with the DTPS.

Line drawings such as pie charts or boxed diagrams may be included, with halftone illustrations and graphics of different sizes captioned and embedded in wrap-around text, or columnised in fonts chosen from a large range.

---

* Pages prepared by "electronic paste-up".
* Selection of ready-made master page/template designs
* On-page text integration with graphics
* Text wraps round regular or irregular graphics
* Text threads and flows from page to page
* Font may be changed at any point
* Automatic hyphenation
* Tools for drawings
* Graphics re-sizing and re-positioning
* Automatic kerning
* Provision for colour

	Interleaf	Ventura	Pagemaker	Quark Xpress
Supplier (in the UK)	IBM	Rank-Xerox	Aldus	Computers Unlimited
Approx Price £s	720	795	695	695
D=DOS, MC=Mac, OS=OS/2	DOS OS	DOS OS	MS MC OS	MC
Environment	Own	Gem, Windows	Windows	Apple
Memory needed	2 Mb	640K, 3 MB	640K	1 Mb
Print. Sup't. L=Laserjet P=Postscript	P	P	L P	L P

TABLE 24.1. MAJOR DTP SOFTWARE (CURRENT VERSIONS)

There is now a large choice of DTPS and even if an application is clearly defined and well understood it may not be easy to decide from specifications and prices which package is likely to be most suitable. Demonstrations are essential.

The major systems listed in Table 24.1 include all the features or enable all the operations listed at the beginning to be carried out.

Pagemaker easily led in 1986 but version 3.5, introduced at the end of 1989 did not cater for multiple files nor standard WP features such as a speller, search and replace, etc.

Pagemaker 4.0, recently introduced, overcomes many of these limitations (Jones 1990) and now includes a multilingual spelling checker, improved typographic control, fonts from 4 to 650 points, form rotation, a new indexing system, etc.

Features missing form Pagemaker 3.5 were included in the first version of **Quark Express** in 1987, considered to be one of the easiest systems to learn. Disadvantages of Quark Express include the adjustments needed for run-around text, the cumbersome method of creating drop capitals (capital letters extending downwards over several lines), and the limited manipulation provided for graphics. Quark Express is considered to be too limited for professional publishers, but fine for others.

Ventura is the prime choice for page layout, but only very simple facilities are provided for text or graphics so that other software will usually be required as well. Brown has written a useful article (Brown 1989) about dealing with a number of Ventura problems and also about getting the most out of it. Ventura is considered to be one of the best packages for general purposes and for large structured documents. A new version running with Windows 3.0 and DOS 3.01 was introduced in 1990.

Interleaf is a very large comprehensive package aimed at corporate users. It is especially suitable for very long documents or books.

Quark Express provides for almost complete freedom of layout with very good typographical control - type sizes can be altered in .25 point increments and leading in .001 point steps. It is good for colour and widely used by professional publishers.

To check the performance of these packages it would be necessary to use them to create several different kinds of pages and complete documents. I have not been through the time consuming process of learning how to use them well enough to provide a critical review. Most of the published reports are obviously the result of superficial testing.

Another difficulty is that new versions of the software, produced quite frequently in consequence of the intense competition, may make comparisons out of date. Factual information provided here covers the latest versions. Other information comes from my own limited experience together with a consensus from others who have used earlier versions.

Pagemaker seems to be satisfactory for single pages and relatively small documents. The Pagemaker-Macintosh combination is arguably the best integrated package, but it does not include facilities for reports, book chapters, and indexing.

DTP software does not, of course, take care of the many computer housekeeping functions (control of memory, disk, inputs and outputs, etc). These are performed by the operating system. Nor does it necessarily include software for handling imported files or facilities to enable the user to create or to change page material with menu-aided window displays.

The "Operating Environment" software usually deals with these requirements. Examples include HP Windows, Microsoft Windows, PC Paint and MacPaint. The other major software which most people will require will be resident Word Processing software, or the facility to import text from one or more WP software packages, via floppy disk.

Illustrator software, from Adobe who also designed Postscript and is used in conjunction with it, takes these operations a stage further in several respects and deserves a special mention. It provides for more elaborate creative graphics.

Selection of the "curve" symbol may be followed by pulling out a tangential "handle" at any point by pointing and moving the mouse cursor. By dragging the handle with the mouse the curve may be changed into almost any curved form - for example into a sinusoidal waveform.

The position of an image may be changed by dragging it with the mouse - the cursor changes into two crosshairs intersecting at the bottom left and the image may be moved bodily to any location on the screen. All, or that part of the image now lying above and to the right of the crosshairs, will appear in that position on the printed page.

Illustrator can be used as an aid for the professional artist. For example it will provide a faint displayed image, of, say, a scanned-in sketch so that the user can trace over it in bolder lines either to produce a modified sketch or to augment, in-fill it, or change details. Alternatively it may be used to ease the creation of an own-drawing. In Figure 24.12 the left hand photograph is ready to be scanned-in to a Mac as a "foundation". The right hand image shows part of it after "editing" using Illustrator's facilities and printing with a Postscript typesetter.

FIGURE 24.12. "EDITING" AN IMAGE USING ADOBE ILLUSTRATOR

Adobe introduced utility software called Adobe Type Manager in 1990 to provide better fonts on a Macintosh (see earlier section "Typography".

Putting a DTP system together

The minimum requirements are a suitable microcomputer with a non-Postscript laser printer, with a DTP package and the appropriate operating system. Such a system, falling short of many requirements, would cost about £5000.

An **Apple MacIntosh** based system with Pagemaker is itemised here (Thames Valley Microcomputers quotation) as an example of a comprehensive system for all-round use, and one which is properly integrated, reasonably easy to learn, and widely used. It includes :-

Item	Price £'s	
Apple Macintosh SE with 1Mbyte memory, 800 Kbyte floppy disk and 20 Mbyte hard disk drives.	2895	
Microtek 300 dots/inch scanner with Versascan scanning control software.	2100	*
Apple Laserwriter Plus with Postscript	4495	
Megastream 1024 x 1024 pels 19" monitor with plug-in board and software	1795	*
Pagemaker version 3.0 includes software for working with scanners which generate TIFF or MacPaint file formats	495	
McWrite WP software	95	
McPaint bit-mapped drawing software Enables pixel by pixel editing on images imported from scanners and provides a selection of halftone algorithms	95	*
McDraw software	95	*
Cricket Graph business and other graphic software	175	*
	12240	

By dropping the scanner, external monitor, and non-essential software (all marked *) the price for a less comprehensive outfit becomes £7980.

Three other system examples follow:-

IBM Personal Publishing System

System 2/30-021 or PC/AT with 640K memory 1.2 Mbyte floppy and 30 Mbyte hard disk drives and MS DOS operating system	4000
4216 personal pageprinter (laser) with adaptor card, application program and Postscript	3370
Pagemaker version 3.0	606
Microsoft windows operating environment	77
	8053

Canon Express

Canon A-22EX with 640K memory, 2 Mbytes extended
memory, floppy disk and 40 Mbyte hard disk drive
Canon IX-12 scanner
Canon Laser beam Printer
Software: DOS, Canon Pagemaker-type DTP
software, WP software, scanning control
and printer software

Complete bundled price   **8950**

SMM Vectra

Vectra ES/12 model 20 with 640K memory, and 1.2
Mbyte and 20 Mbyte hard disk drives with mouse
and MS DOS   3609
Hewlett Packard (HP) Scanjet scanner with software   1831
HP Laserjet series 2   2650
Pagemaker   689
HP Windows operating environment   119
                                                                  8898

Note that Pagemaker 3.0 is listed – somewhat less expensive than
4.0. These prices are of the right order but there are frequent changes.

Applications

The illustrations in the operational sequence which follows were
provided by Taxan using the following equipment and software at their
Bracknell offices:-

Hewlett Packard (HP) Vectra microcomputer model QB 4/16, a machine with
   an 80386 16 MHz processor, 2 Mbytes of memory and a 40 Mbyte hard disk
   running on MS-DOS 3.3.
HP Scanjet 300 dots/inch scanner with Versascan controlling software.
HP Laserjet series 2, 300 dots/inch printer with plug-in board,
   Jetscript page description language (licensed Postscript) and Laserjet
   driver.
Aldus Pagemaker 3.0 DTP software with Microsoft Windows 2.
Taxan Viking 19" display monitor controlled by a plug-in board.

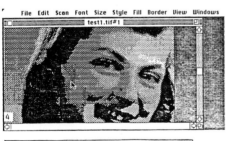

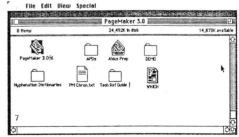

FIGURE 24.13. SUCCESSIVE OPERATIONS USING PAGEMAKER

TAXAN ARE A MARKET LEADER IN PERIPHERAL PRODUCTS

There's no secret to our success. It stems from our skill in providing effective solutions to the problems facing today's and tomorrow's computer users. It stems from our dedication and expertise in the development and application of the latest proven technology. Simply stated Taxan provides the highest quality products at the most affordable prices. In answering today's needs, our designers are anticipating future demands as well. We can do this because Taxan sells on a worldwide scale, backed by the industrial strength of Kaga Electronics, a major Japanese electronics company with an international reputation for research and development. We know that in today's information orientated society, technical innovation and the broadening of applications are the two major challenges that must be faced by any company establishing a respected position within the computer industry. This fundamental understanding shapes and motivates the activities of Taxan (UK) Ltd.

VIKING GREY SCALE
Display System
For the Apple Macintosh II

The Viking Grey Scale Display System for the Apple Macintosh II consists of a 19" ultra high resolution analogue monochrome monitor which is connected to an extremely powerful video controller card. It is ideal for applications requiring photorealistic images with precise text and line detail.

FEATURES

◆ For use with Apple Macintosh II.

◆ Non-glare anti-reflection coated screen (OCLI panel) improves contrast and reduces glare without loss of resolution.

◆ A video bandwidth of more than 64 MHz assures super sharp text band graphics.

◆ A non-interlace display resolution of 1024 x 768 pixel refreshed at 60 Hz provides true 72 DPI resolution for actual size WYSIWYG screen displays.

◆ Supports 1, 2, 4 or 8 bit software for greater flexibility.

Compact design large screen system for maximum operator comfort.

A purpose built optional tilt/swivel stand (KTSV1) is available to provide the optimum viewing positions.

FIGURE 24.14. A LASER-PRINTED PAGEMAKER PAGE.

When formatting a page the usual procedure would be to type the text using WP software and store it in a file. In this case we used an existing stored text file created earlier.

When a DTP system is demonstrated to a potential buyer by a skilled operator who rapidly juggles with menus using the mouse it's impossible to tell whether the system is going to be convenient to use or easy to learn.

With the system illustrated in Figure 24.13 (showing "screen dumps" from a demonstration created earlier on a different computer) & assuming that all the equipment and software has **previously been made to work properly**, the procedure is fairly simple. The above phrase in bold is all important. If at all possible you should see the whole system demonstrated with all the software you intend to buy working together before you buy it.

Part of a scanned-in page is being cropped, and clicking with the mouse on the "Write Now" icon will store the edited version. In the top right screen part of the text file to be used in Pagemaker 3.0 is shown. That software will be loaded by clicking on the Pagemaker ikon shown on the menu following.

The result is the simple page design, obviously needing some further work done on it, shown in Figure 24.14. The illustration provides an idea of the sort of quality to be expected from a laser printer.

Recent progress

Desktop publishing operations have been widely reported and up-market DTP has extended into the professional printing area (Langdale 1990). For example the London **Evening Standard** has invested £1.6M in a network of 75 Macs and Pcs with 8 file servers, six scanners, 20 Mac display booking terminals with 20 more for display and makeups. One result has been a decrease in required staffing from 100 to 18.

The **European** uses Scitex Visionary/Quark Express software on Macs for colour with 8 Gbytes of storage and its 40 reports use Mac SE20s with 4 600 Mbyte disc drives. An Ethernet network is used for inter-connection.

In the library/information area Edkins (1990) has described work in the library with a Mac II, scanner, laser printer, and colour monitor - total purchasing price £8480 - at an agricultural research station for form design, production of notices and labels, display boards for exhibits and a weekly publication called "Library List".

Peter Stubley (1989) briefly discusses the use of scanners for importing graphics and comments about incompatibility problems. Stubley also describes Macintosh DTP in an article in Program (1988) . D.R.K.Brownrigg (1989) provides a short useful review entitled "Graphics with small systems".

Steve Smith's group use DTP at Surrey County Library Headquarters, Dorking, England with two Apple Macintoshes - an SE and a II, a scanner and a Dataproducts LZR 2665 laser printer. The LZR is expensive by DTP standards, but it can churn out copies at 26 pages a minute. Smith uses it directly for print runs - and Dorking supply printed material to many other libraries in the county. He chose the Quark Express ,   Cricket Draw, and

Whifflet Computer Centre

COMPUTER NEWS

November 1988   **Issue No. 9**

WELCOME

Welcome back to this new look Computer News. In this edition there are articles about an Open Day the Computer Centre is holding in Airdrie Library; news of a new Desktop Publishing Pack stolen games; an our regular rundown of the most used leisur games in the Computer Centr

READ ON!

Computer Cer
OPEN DAY

On Monday 28th November the Computer Centre v be closed to enable to hold an open da Airdrie Library.

This open day will be a chance for the people of Airdrie to view the facilities we have on offer. It will also give us the chance to find out if we are meeting the computing needs of community groups and businesses in the area.

STOLEN GAMES

Over the past few months some computer games were taken from the Centre. This only deprives other users of their use. We therefore ask everyone to ensure that any

FIGURE 24.16
LIBRARY DTP-
MONKLANDS
(Left)

FIGURE 24.15
LIBRARY DTP-
SURREY
(Below)

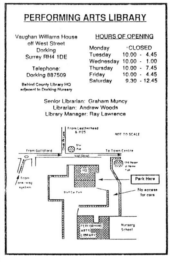

PERFORMING ARTS LIBRARY

Vaughan Williams House
off West Street
Dorking
Surrey RH4 1DE

Telephone:
Dorking 887509

Behind County Library HQ
adjacent to Dorking Nursery

HOURS OF OPENING

Monday	CLOSED
Tuesday	10.00 - 4.45
Wednesday	10.00 - 1.00
Thursday	10.00 - 7.45
Friday	10.00 - 4.45
Saturday	9.30 - 12.45

Senior Librarian: Graham Muncy
Librarian: Andrew Woods
Library Manager: Ray Lawrence

SURREY

Performing Arts Library

LIBRARIES

Superpaint graphics packages. Since the staff carry out all operations from text input, page formatting, design, to printing, they are not subject to external delays - for instance from a Linotron printshop. Some examples of the kind of work they do are shown in Figure 24.15.

Mr J.Fox, Chief Librarian at Monklands library services, Coatbridge, Scotland, pursuaded The Scottish Office to fund a DTP service which is run by Colin Smith, not only for the library, but also for use by the public. Smith works as a computer instructor for community services. A member of the public can receive instruction on the DTP equipment for a small fee, and subsequently prepare and print pages free.

This enterprising effort has been mounted for an equipment expenditure of about £1400. An Amstrad PC1640 with Newsmaster II DTP software and a 9-pin dot matrix MSP-15E printer is used. It must be one of the least expensive DTP systems available. A page of their work is shown in Figure 24.16. Note the slightly ragged appearance of some of the characters. This will probably not be noticed by most people.

**FIGURE 24.18
INTERLEAF SYST.**
Completed page
(Right)

**FIGURE 24.17
INTERLEAF SYST.**
Scaling and
fitting
(below)

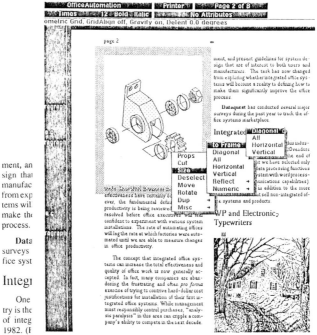

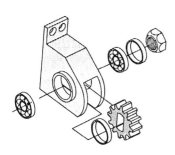

ment, an
sign that
manufac
from exp
tems wil
make the
process.

Data
surveys
fice syst

Integi

One
try is the
of integ
1982. (F systems that have data processing functions co-resident on the system with word processing and data communications capabilities). These vendors are in addition to the more than 200 vendors that sell non-integrated office systems and products.

WP and Electronic Typewriters

made. Individual increases in efficiency and effectiveness have certainly occurred. However, the fundamental definition of office productivity is being reviewed, and must be resolved before office executives will feel confident to experiment with various system installations. The rate of automating offices will lag the rate at which factories were automated until we are able to measure changes in office productivity.

The concept that integrated office systems can increase the total effectiveness and quality of office work is now generally accepted. In fact, many companies are abandoning the frustrating and often *pro forma* exercise ˙ ᶠ trying to contrive hard-dollar cost ju˙ ͏ ᵗ ᶠᵒʳ˙ ᵘˡᵃᵗⁱᶜ ᵇᵉⁱʳ fᵘ in-
ᵗ ᵃᵣ

Turning to specific examples of the special features of DTP systems, The Interleaf DTP software provides numerous facilities, one of which is shown in Figures 24.17 and 24.18.

In Figure 24.17 it is required that the figure within the border which has been moved on to a 2-column page should be fitted into a chosen position. The selected lines on the three menus shown overlaying the page are commands to alter the **size** of the bordered image to fit the page **frame** while maintaining its **diagonal** proportions - i.e. stretching it either vertically of horizontally is not allowed.

As the consequence of these commands the edited page takes the form shown in Figure 24.18.

Interleaf is a comprehensive system requiring 25 MBytes of disc just for its sub-directories. It includes a large "clip-art" file of designs. Any part of a design displayed on the screen may be selected and "pasted-in"

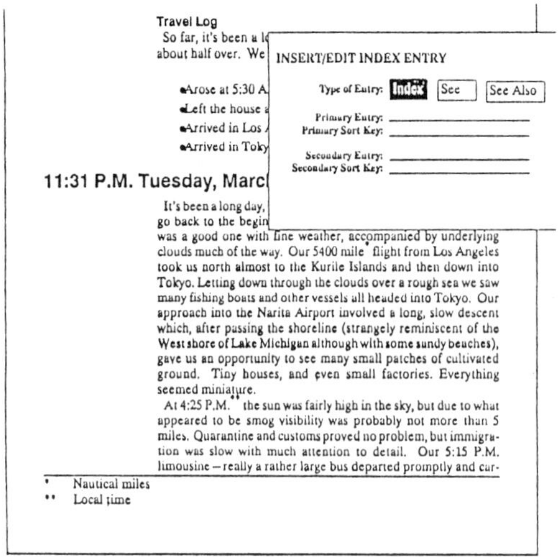

Travel Log
So far, it's been a l[...]
about half over. We[...]

INSERT/EDIT INDEX ENTRY

Type of Entry: **Index** | See | See Also

Primary Entry: _____
Primary Sort Key: _____

Secondary Entry: _____
Secondary Sort Key: _____

◆Arose at 5:30 A[...]
◆Left the house [...]
◆Arrived in Los [...]
◆Arrived in Tok[...]

11:31 P.M. Tuesday, Marc[...]

It's been a long day,
go back to the begin[...]
was a good one with fine weather, accompanied by underlying
clouds much of the way. Our 5400 mile* flight from Los Angeles
took us north almost to the Kurile Islands and then down into
Tokyo. Letting down through the clouds over a rough sea we saw
many fishing boats and other vessels all headed into Tokyo. Our
approach into the Narita Airport involved a long, slow descent
which, after passing the shoreline (strangely reminiscent of the
West shore of Lake Michigan although with some sandy beaches),
gave us an opportunity to see many small patches of cultivated
ground. Tiny houses, and even small factories. Everything
seemed miniature.
    At 4:25 P.M.** the sun was fairly high in the sky, but due to what
appeared to be smog visibility was probably not more than 5
miles. Quarantine and customs proved no problem, but immigration was slow with much attention to detail. Our 5:15 P.M.
limousine — really a rather large bus departed promptly and cur-

* Nautical miles
** Local time

INDEX

Table counter, 5-91 - 5-92
Tags, 5-89, 7-6
Center
    See Alignment
Centimeter, 5-72
Chapter
    Defined, I-2
    See all files associated with, 5-160
Chapter counter, 5-2, 5-46 - 5-47
Chapter file
    Difference from text file, 4-21
Character formatting
    See Style sheet
Character space
    Changing, 4-16
Characters
    See Alt key
    See Foreign character
Clear menu, 3-16
Clipboard
    Defined, I-2
    Frame, 5-26
    Graphic, 5-27
    Text, 5-25
Color, 3-20
Column balance, 5-78
    Columns don't balance exactly, 5-80
Column break, 5-113 - 5-114
Column guides, 5-151
    Underlying page used as grid, 7-8
Column rules, 5-93
Column snap, 5-154, 6-7
Columns, 5-73 - 5-76
    Different left/right page, 5-76
    Equal, 5-74
    See also Margins & Columns
    Unequal, 5-75
CONFIG.SYS, 2-6
Contents of package, 1-2

**FIGURE 24.19
INDEXING WITH VENTURA**

to a position in a document in the manner just described. Interleaf includes its own comprehensive WP software so text need not first be prepared using other software although text can be imported from many other packages as needed.

Another example of a special facility is the index module included in Ventura to assist in the indexing of a book or report. 150 Kbytes of text can be formed into a chapter, with a total not exceeding 64 chapters with Ventura, and more in later versions.

Indexing is an essential chore. Many publications including books and all reports are enhanced by a good index and this module greatly reduces that chore.

To index a multi-chaptered text, each page can be overlaid with a form ready for the insertion of the first term as shown in Figure 24.19. Provision is made for Primary and Secondary entries which appear as shown in the second illustration when printed.

When all chapters are completed, a second type of form - the "generate index" form - can be made to appear with provision for adjusting the styling of the index.

Most authors who compile their own indexes will welcome this helpful aid which does of course sort and lay out the index as shown - an operation which will save a very great deal of time. What the module does not do is bring to the index the knowledge of the professional indexer who anticipates with his knowledge of classification and the use of synonyms where a searcher is likely to look.

One of the occasions where the services of such a person are needed perhaps more than on any other is during the preparation of an instruction manual. This applies particularly to those foreign language (computerese) disasters supplied with software for ordinary people. The next time the screen freezes in your system, try and find the appropriate heading in the index. In fact you need not bother, it's most unlikely that there will be one.

Specialised software requires special features. Mathtype, available

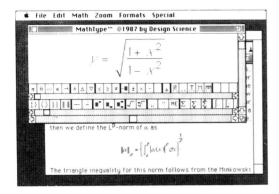

in the UK from Heyden & Son, London, is a mathematical equation editor for use on Macintish microcomputers. Composing equation formats with WP or DTP software packages is difficult and is usually attempted with Mac-Draw or by drawing them in later.

Part of the composition sequence for the equation shown at the top in Figure 24.20 is illustrated in the screens which follow. The explanation is self evident.

Finally, special operations with a sophisticated package called Design Studio from Letraset is shown in Figure 24.21.

The objective is to remove part of an illustration on one side of an irregular edge, and arrange for text to run around the edge on the removed-part side.

The edge in question is the diagonal irregular line formed by the body of the leaning girl. The procedure is to select the "polygon tool" and trace the edge with the mouse/cursor, clicking each time you change direction. Only straight lines may be drawn but they can be extremely short. The first attempt is shown at the top of the second picture.

The drawn edge may be edited by viewing the clicked points and dragging points with the mouse (bottom half picture).

The next step is to select "text block" tool and enclose the area to be blocked by drawing a vertical and horizontal line (visible in the third picture). By selecting the "I-beam" tool

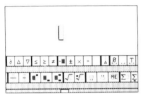

Step 1: The dotted box is an empty slot ready to accept input from the keyboard. The L-shaped insertion point shows where text will appear. First we type "y=".

Step 2: We now need a square-root (radical) sign. We enter this by clicking on the $\sqrt{}$ icon in the Template Drawer or by typing ⌘R. Note that all spacing is done automatically.

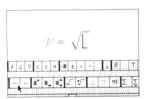

Step 3: The square-root has been inserted with a new empty slot containing the insertion point. We can now insert a fraction template by clicking on the icon or by typing ⌘F.

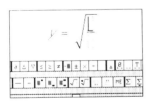

Step 4: The fraction has been inserted. Note how the square-root has expanded automatically to accomodate the fraction. We now type "1+x" into the numerator.

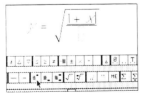

Step 5: The square-root has expanded, the denominator centered, and spacing added around the "+". All done automatically. Now we click on the icon or type ⌘H to add a superscript.

FIGURE 24.20. FORMING AN EQUATION WITH MATHTYPE

612

and clicking with the mouse inside the blocked area, the blocked-out area
will be made ready to receive text. A text file may be chosen and by
clicking on "get text" the text file will appear on the right with the left
hand margin of each line following the contours of the ragged edge.

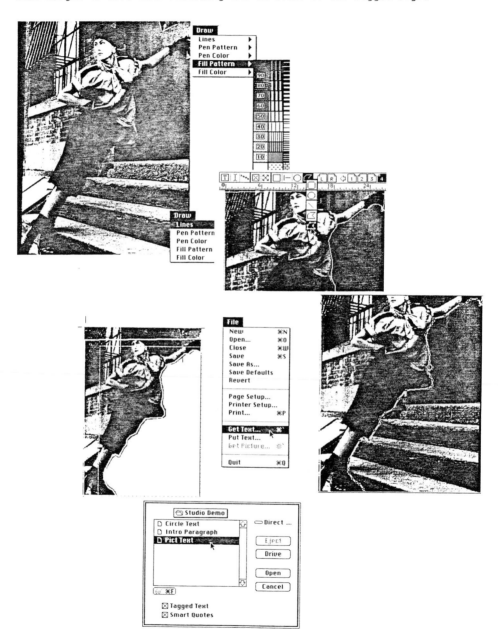

FIGURE 24.21. RUNNING TEXT ROUND A BLOCKED-OUT DRAWN AREA

REFERENCES

Anon.
  Personal Computer World Supplement, February 1988.
    Linking up to a typesetter.
Barbe, D.F.
  Proc. Soc. Photo-optical Instrumentation Engineers (SPIE) Vol
  762, 1987, Electro-optical imaging systems integration. Pps
  20-34.
    State of the art in visible spectrum solid state
    imagers.
Brown, Edward.
  Tech PC User, 28-35, April 1989.
    Make the most of Ventura.
Brownrigg, David.
  In SCIL '89 International. Proceedings of the third annual conf-
  erence on small computers in libraries. London February 1989.
  Meckler, Westport and London. 1989.   70-79.
    Graphics with small systems.
Collins, John.
  Byte 14(11), 403-408, November 1989.
    The ABCs of digital type.
Edkins, Jennifer.
  Program 24(2), 155-168, April 1990.
    Library applications of desktop publishing in practice:
    a tool and a resource.
Firth, R.R., et al.
  J.Imaging Technol., 14(3), 78-89, June 1988.
    A continuous tone laser color printer.
Goertzel, Gerald, & Thompson G.R.
  IBM J. Res.& Devel. 31(1), 1987.
    Digital halftoning on the IBM 4250 printer.
Hartley, James.
  Educational Communication and Technology Journal 35(1), 3-17, 1987.
    Designing electronic text: the role of print-based
    research. (Review article with 102 references).
Jones, Graham
  Desktop Publishing Today, 33-34, October 1988.
    Enhanced words. (Short reviews of six WP packages).
Jones, Graham.
  Desktop Publishing Today, 16-18, March 1990.
    On the make.
Landale, Tony.
  Desktop Publishing Today, 26-30, March 1990.
    Setting standards.
La Pier, Cynthia B.
  Meckler. Westport and London. 1990.
    The librarian's guide to WordPerfect 5.0.
Liskin, Miriam.
  Personal Computing, 43-52, March 1987.
    Mastering printer drivers.
Mikami, Tomohisa et al.
  Fujitsu Sci. Tech. J., 24(2), 166-175, June 1988.
    Full colour image printer.

614

Mokhof, Nicolas.
  Electronic Design, 75-82, October 29th 1987.
    Printing images at 300 dots/inch; laser printers come
    into their own.
Perry, Tekla S.
  IEEE Spectrum, 25(5), 42-46, May 1988.
    Postscript prints anything: a case history.
Stewart, George A., and Jane Tazelaar.
  Byte, 12(4),203-217, April 1987.
    State of the art in dot matrix impact printers.
Stibic, von Vlado.
  Nachr.f.Dokum. 36(4/5), 172-178, 1985.
    Printed versus displayed information. (In English).
Stoffel, J.C. & Moreland J.F.
  IEEE Trans Communic. COM-29 (12), 1898-1925, December 1981.
    A survey of electronic techniques for pictorial image
    reproduction. (Ed. - The classic paper on the subject)
Stubley, Peter.
  Program 22(3), 247-261, July 1988.
    Desktop publishing on the Macintosh; six questions
    answered for librarians.
Stubley, Peter.
  In SCIL '89 International. Proceedings of the third annual conf-
  erence on small computers in libraries. London February 1989.
  Meckler, Westport and London. 1989. 66-69.
    Desktop publishing packages.
Takeuchi, Ryozo, et al.
  J. Imaging Technol. 14(3), 68-72, June 1988.
    Color image scanner with an RGB linear image sensor.
Townsend, Kevin J.
  Elsevier Advanced Technology Publications, Oxford, 1988.
    Desktop publishing; technology and markets.
Wang, Chih.
  The Electronic Library, 5(2), 89-92, April 1987.
    Electronic publishing and its impact on print publishing
    and other selected library materials: a review, proposal,
    and design for further research. (46 references).
Whitby, Max.
  Desktop Publishing, 20-23, February 1990.
    New year's resolution.
Wilkins, A.J. and M.I.Nimmo-Smith.
  Ergonomics 30(12), 1705-1720, 1987.
    The clarity and comfort of printed text.
Will-Harris, Daniel.
  Peachbit Press, Berkeley, Ca. 1988.
    WordPerfect 5.0: desktop publishing in style.
Witten, Ian H.
  Int.J.Man-Machine Studies 23, 623-697, 1985.
    Elements of computer typography.
    (Excellent on fundamentals)

CHAPTER 25. CABLE SYSTEMS AND MARKETS

Introduction

A cable network has two great advantages - information can be moved in both directions (unlike broadcast television which has wide bandwidth but not the two way facility), and the bandwidth is wide (unlike the telephone system which has the two way facility but not the bandwidth).

Current general interest in cable systems is centred on home television entertainment based mainly on experience in the United States. However once cable connections are made to large numbers of premises of any kind, a highway for the flow of any kind of data is in place. Its uses will depend on market considerations and the regulatory climate.

The feasibility of cable information networks and associated devices, like many other systems, is based upon the availability of reliable, compact, cheap semiconductor storage and processing electronics, now a fait accompli.

The prospects for the adoption of cable instead of, or in conjunction with, broadcast television, depend on one or more of the following factors:-

1. Existence of satisfactory broadcast reception conditions.

2. Demand for the variety of entertainment provided by more channels at given charges.

3. Incentives and capital available for distribution and programme providers.

4. Development of lower cost distribution technology.

5. Regulatory intervention.

6. Competition from DBS television programmes and from information providers who are already broadcasting relayed data from satellites direct to small receivers in businesses and homes.

Quite a number of cable systems exist for reason 1 - a community is too far from TV stations for satisfactory reception, or it is situated in an area of bad reception caused by tall buildings, hills, etc.

For example well over 2 million people subscribe in Switzerland out of a population of 6.5 million. About 20 million households in Europe are connected to cable (1985 figures); many stations are licensed to carry existing TV programmes only. In the UK about 250,000 households were connected in the mid-eighties.

In 1970 a very rosy future was forecast for cable TV in the US. 80% penetration of US households was forecast by 1980. The forecasters were unable to foresee that only the incentive of more or less unrestricted programme franchises would generate the necessary financial support.

Cable took off in the US because the opportunists stepped in when the FCC first removed some programme controls in 1975 and because of a combination of factors occurring from 1980 onwards to be described later.

THE TECHNOLOGY

Schemes for implementing cable systems are shown, shorn of all details in Figure 25.1, The distributing station comprises the means of inputting information, typically television pictures, into a number of channels. In this case four kinds of input are shown each having a bandwidth of 8 MHz for good quality colour. This is called the "head end" of the system which sends data "downstream" to subscribers.

The programmes could come from TV studios, telecine machines – that is machines capable of running 35mm film and converting it to TV images – or from a remote source, the satellite transmitter RT in the figure and the satellite-receiver link SL1. The head end station distributes the programmes to its local audience.

The four television programmes, separated by appropriate guard bands of relatively narrow bandwidth, are combined in the device C> and distributed via a trunk line with repeaters, R, to boost the signals at suitable intervals. The trunk line may be wideband coaxial cable or fibreoptic cable. If the latter, the device EOC (electro-optical convertor) will be required.

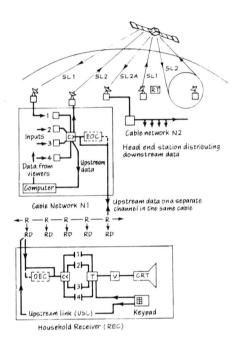

FIGURE 25.1. CABLE NETWORK

Local distribution lines, RD, are tapped off to feed groups of subscribers from repeater/distribution points R. The distribution network may be part co-axial and part fibreoptic as dictated by traffic and economic considerations. Its bandwidth must be adequate to accommodate the combined bandwidth of the individual channels plus guardbands - 300 MHz or more is needed to accommodate 24 or more TV channels.

A receiver, REC, is fed from the local cable passing along the street. If fibreoptic transmission is used it will incorporate an opto-electric convertor, OEC. For transmission through the network, incoming signals will be fed directly to C<, a device performing the inverse function to >C at the transmitter.

At the receiver the frequencies used for distribution are shifted to come within the range of the frequencies received in standard TV receivers (shown as 1,2,3,4 with the tuner T). The tuned signal is passed to the CRT via video circuits V. If optical fibres F1, F2, are used, channel switching can be arranged with an electro-mechanical switch which moves the face of the common receiving fibre against the face of either F1 or F2.

Another method of distribution is shown in Figure 25.1. This is a Direct Broadcast Satellite (DBS) not a cable system - probably cable's major competing technology. The sending station can broadcast information direct to individual receiving stations using its own transmitting dish for up-down signals via a transponder on the satellite.

The signals are re-transmitted by the transponder to an area on the earth's surface wherein lie the cable company's subscribers, via the link SL2. Alternatively signals could be relayed to another area distribution station and into the cable network, N2, via path SL2A.

Interactive facilities

The basic interactive facilities shown in the figure include the keypad attached to the receiver which may be used to transmit signals "upstream" to the distribution station via the link LSC. A computer at the distribution station receives the up-stream signals for processing.

The problem of organising interactive facilities has been well recognised and was described by Kay (1976) during the pioneering work sponsored by the National Science Foundation. Seven grants were awarded in 1974 for experimental systems to deliver social and administrative services via interactive cable television.

If n users can transmit signals of some kind upstream simultaneously, the channel bandwidth, w, must be at least w x n. There could also be a requirement for TV pictures to be generated by a subscriber and sent back to the head end - as in video conferencing. In that case a full TV bandwidth will be required on the return link.

Alternatively subscriber data transmission may be no more than a need to distinguish between 1 out of b buttons, as in the US Qube system. By 1979 this system had been running for some time in Columbus, Ohio, with 29,000 of its subscribers able to communicate over the cable by depressing one of five buttons.

Say 8 buttons are fitted (requiring a 3 bit code), and a communication rate of 3 bits per second is required - i.e there is provision for one out 8 choices to be made at a maximum rate of one per second. The theoretical bandwidth needed would only be 1.5Hz so the total bandwidth required by 29,000 subscribers would only be 43.5 KHz.

In practice all the subscriber circuits could be packed into one channel as individual frequency bands with intervening guard bands so one 100 KHz channel would, in theory, suffice. In the Qube system, an announcer said to viewers "if you use Gnasher cleaner for your dentures (or words to that effect) press button 1; if you've never heard of it press 2".

An arrangement such as that just described is adequate for such purposes. The computer at the head end simply counts the yes/no responses and expresses them to the announcer as, say, percentages of total responses. Whether such a restricted system has a future is another matter.

If subscribers were to be provided with full alpha-numeric keyboards, each would need a bandwidth of, say, 150 Hz permitting rates of 300 bps or around 30 char/sec. That would require one hundred times the bandwidth of Qube - say 1G MHz - consuming a substantial fraction of the available bandwidth.

A flexible cable system (or perhaps I should say a cable system with flexible facilities) could provide some mix of economically feasible facilities for subscribers with different needs. It might provide for some subscribers with non-interactive, some with low-speed interactive, and some with higher speed interactive facilities at different prices. It might embody a channel for teleconferences available by special arrangement.

Another technique, called "narrowcasting" provides computer control of the channel viewed by individual subscribers from the head-end. This can be used for the selective addressing of programmes or advertising to homes, schools, businesses etc., according to some pre-arranged pattern.

Cable configurations with up-stream facilities

In Figure 25.1 a low bandwidth return path is shown because repeaters (wideband amplifiers)in the normal **tree-and-branch** distribution arrangement are usually only fitted for downstream signals. Most US systems are of this type, although more recent US tree and branch systems have an upstream channel with its own repeaters having a bandwidth of up to 30MHz.

In some systems, subscribers are "polled" to see if they have any messages. This means that the head-end computer periodically interrogates all subscribers - and there might be 1C0,00C of them - to see if they have anything stored ready to transmit and if so, gets it transmitted back to the head end. Such an operation may take up to 10 seconds per complete cycle so it's really suitable only for low data rate systems like the Qube. Bandwidth has been traded for time.

However **multi-star switched systems** are now working which deal with the bandwidth problem in a different way. One such system has been developed at British Telecom's research establishment at Martlesham Heath (Fox 1983). It consists of a distribution station at the centre of a web-like network with a number of trunk connections radiating out to Wideband Flexibility Points (WFP). These WFP's in turn radiate local connections to individual subscribers.

The system may be all coax, or fibreoptic for the trunk connections and coax from WFP's to subscribers. With fibres, long distances without repeaters are possible. WFP to subscriber connections are short and don't need repeaters for coax. Consequently a direct wideband path is available between subscriber and head end. If there are any long distance paths then wideband down and up repeaters are fitted.

Typically a system will consist of some tens or even hundreds of wideband trunks with each WFP connecting to up to 300 subscribers by 100 Mhz lines for up or down stream data. Services can consist of TV, radio, and data transmission channels.

At least three TV programmes could be viewed by a subscribing establishment on three different receivers. Channel selection would be by a microprocessor-controlled video switch at a WFP. Each subscriber has a low speed data link for controlling his switch.

Alternatively a subscriber could use one channel for an up-stream video link (e.g.for video conferencing) the other two being used for reception. An up-stream connection could be routed into British Telecom's System-X digital communications system, which is gradually permeating through the country, at the head end. In this case it is likely that the subscriber will wish to originate data at 64 Kbps or 2 Mbps.

In Britain it was hoped that cable operators would install systems of this kind at the outset, because if tree and branch systems were installed, operators would be locked in to a system without the potential for advanced services which may well soon be needed. On the other hand complete fibreoptic systems are more expensive at present.

Current developments: distribution paths

In common with other information systems, cable technology has benefitted by a host of technical developments resulting in the production of low cost complex transmission and processing electronic devices whose dimensions and prices decrease every year.

Communications developments include wider bandwidth at lower cost by improvements in the design of coaxial cable, the development of fibreoptic systems with yet wider bandwidth, and the availability of wideband transponders for relaying television signals from satellites.

A satellite transponder typically has a bandwidth of 500 MHz and can handle 12 television channels with either horizontal or vertical polarisation, or 24 if it has both. Polarisation simply means the generation of a single-plane electric field. The bandwidth can be doubled if two signals are transmitted with their planes at right angles, each being receivable without mutual interference by an appropriately polarised receiving aerial/antenna.

It may be as well to clearly differentiate between the systems shown in Figure 25.1. Television signals are at present conveyed by :-

1. Broadcasting on different channels "over the air". At a receiver a channel is selected by switching to the tuned circuit for the desired channel.

2. Wideband or fibreoptic cable, where the energy is contained within the cable and, unlike over-the-air broadcasting, does not occupy scarce bandwidth or interfere with other broadcasts. A single wide-band cable can contain a number of channels in different frequency bands selected by switching to different tuned circuits at the receiver.

3. Relaying signals from one transmitter to a distant receiver via a satellite or by a succession of hops from one terrestrial micro-wave tower to another. Thus one studio/transmission facility can relay television signals to one or more earth receiving stations, via satellite, and each station can feed a number of subscribers via cable.

4. Direct Broadcast Satellite (DBS).

Because satellite signals can be sent/received in a narrow beam, somewhat in the manner of a searchlight, interference can be much lower than with conventional broadcasting. Signal power outside the beam is negligible. Incidentally American viewers have a partic- ular incentive to subscribe to cable systems. The NTSC (unoffic- ially known as Never The Same Colour) 525 line system is very susceptible to phase errors caused by multiple reflections. Recep- tion with poor colour is experienced in cities with high buildings. European systems are much less susceptible and have better definition.

Information markets

Electronic information services for the biggest mass market - the home - is much more than simply modified TV receivers, home computers, etc. The concept involves "Readiness Potential and an Enabling Infrastructure". This fact was well recognised by Paul Barran (an ARPA pioneer) back in 1975 when he reviewed the cable TV situation.

If his article (Barran 1975) was re-published with minor changes, it would be as relevant today as it was then. Even as late as 1978 expansion was unexpectedly slow. By that date cable had made little progress into the "Top 100" market; less than 10% of households therein were cable subscribers.

The scope of Barran's article did not include regulation; his assessment of other problems was as follows-

People at home will only pay very small sums for information. A suitable terminal must do almost everything for everybody but it must be cheap - really cheap. To reduce fixed costs to acceptable levels, uniform standards are required. A good system must have self-instructing capabilities, self-indexing capability, and commonality of input formats. The overwhelming use of this terminal will be for watching the nth rerun of "I love Lucy" (then a highly popular TV programme).

The program selection of PORT (Plain Ordinary Rotten Television) should not be complicated by the addition of new services - a comment reminiscent of the continuing overwhelming use of POTS (Plain Old Telephone Service) for information transmission.

The 525 line TV standard has insufficient resolution if the designer tries to squeeze in more than 40 characters or 20 lines. It is more likely that each individual service will be provided by separate national or international companies.

Local franchised systems will be a common carrier for others. There must be a measure of confidence in reliability, freedom from eavesdropping, freedom from error, and freedom from malicious mischief (a correct forecast of "hackers", then unknown).

For 1975 this was a penetrating analysis. Barran said:- "Those companies that might logically be providing leadership have been sitting back and waiting. Everyone is waiting for something to happen and nothing ever does... some strong external force is needed to change the dynamics of the game." This was not to happen for another five years.

New kinds of services

The special qualities of cable seem well suited for other kinds of non-TV services for which the technology exists, such as videotex services. In telephone line videotex the bandwidth for user-generated data is adequate for most applications, but it imposes limits on certain kinds of downstream data.

As discussed in Chapter 26, broadcast-television teletext usually shares a channel with entertainment TV. There is sufficient space only for cyclic magazines with the maximum number of pages limited by the acceptable waiting time between page selection and "frame grabbing". But a cable system may embody a sufficient number of wideband channels for one channel to be dedicated entirely to a teletext service with a large number of pages, and another channel for special control services.

For an installation charge of $800 and a monthly charge of $16, Qube provided special services for 5000 homes including home security, fire protection, and emergencies. The system consists of transducers in the home to change physical into electrical changes, data transmission facilities, and a fraction of the cable bandwidth to carry the data back to a computer at the head end. The computer sends the information to the appropriate place for action - for instance information from smoke detectors goes to the fire department.

In due course services may be introduced by public utilities for meter or gas consumption measurement and billing, energy control, etc.

The Threat - Direct Broadcast Satellites (DBS)

The fourth method of those listed in the previous paragraph, the subject for much speculation, is direct transmission via a satellite transponder which receives the signal from an earth transmitter aimed at it, and re-transmits the signal via another aerial aimed at a specific area on the earth's surface. Within that area, subscribers have rooftop dishes aimed at the satellite.

The satellite-to-receivers beam may be deliberately broadened to cover a wider area so precautions must be taken to stop mutual interference which could be caused by the overlapping "footprints" of other satellites working at the same frequencies.

In due course, systems involving satellite links could incorporate two-way facilities. A low-speed link, say by telephone line back to the head-end - a rather clumsy arrangement - as an alternative.

DBS systems arouse particular interest because no terrestrial links are needed. The vested interests in control of those links are bypassed unless those same interests are also enpowered to control satellite transmissions as part of the regulatory policy. DBS subscribers will require a sensitive receiver with an accurately pointed dish, double frequency conversion receivers and special decoding circuits.

By 1984 there were already 40,000 TeleVision Receive Only (TVRO) stations in the US. These were used by technology buffs or stunt-conscious people exploiting the POOOJ (Put One Over On the Jones) syndrome. These people can pick up a variety of programmes, for which they pay nothing, depending upon the "footprints" of the satellites within which they lie.

Cable - at least for TV entertainment - may find itself in fierce competition with DBS. By the late eighties DBS receiver prices had dropped to a level within the means of many people. But receiver prices are only one of a complex set of circumstances which lead to the dominance of a particular system - as discussed in several parts of this book.

In the US in June 1980 the FCC accepted an application to start a DBS service at 12GHz for people with one metre rooftop dishes and the necessary equipment. In 1981 it considered three more contenders, appreciating the lead time needed for frequency allocations and other preparations.

Early in 1982 British Aerospace announced its intention to launch a DBS in 1986. The BBC would use two of the five channels available in the UK under international allocations of the spectrum. Coincidentally better colour television systems will be considered. The present PAL system is a compromise attempt to get a lot of information into the narrowest possible bandwidth. Much has happened since the early eighties and DBS in Europe is now commonplace - as described in Chapter 9.

George Valentine of Rank Trident (UK) asked in 1983 "Satellites and cable - will they mix?" and then debunked this combination:- "DBS system operators have succeeded in creating symbiotic relationships with cable service operators whereby DBS home services provide additional channels... but they don't. There is no significant DBS in the world at present".

"It won't be operating in the US before 1986 at the earliest. The British government probably created confusion by publishing a discussion paper called "Direct broadcast by satellite" when the paper ought to have been called "The use of satellites for the distribution of television signals".

But then IT forecasting is notoriously inaccurate.

DEVELOPMENT OF CABLE TV IN THE USA

A study of events in the USA leading to the state of cable TV in that country - around 25 million subscribers in 1984 - reveals a fascinating struggle between conflicting forces. Many of these forces have parallels in other countries - high cost of entry, the "chicken and egg" situation (without a network there can be no services, without revenues there can be no network), technological readiness, and the regulatory situation.

One influence, unique to the US, is the first amendment to the Constitution about the freedom of the press - and its extension to cover other media.

In 1958 the existence of cable systems, albeit in a small way, prompted an enquiry by the Federal Communications Commission (FCC), but the FCC concluded that there was no need to control programme content. It did, however, control the issue of licences to microwave TV relay systems at that time. A little later a request for a licence at Riverton, Wyoming, was refused because the FCC considered that programme duplication by the proposed cable relay station would result in the demise of the local TV station.

This decision, affirmed on appeal in **Carter Mountain Transmission Corp. vs FCC,** became the foundation of the FCC's regulatory role. Circumstances had forced a change of attitude.

In 1965 the FCC asserted wide jurisdiction over all cable systems. It established "mandatory carriage" in which a cable system, channel capacity permitting, had to carry the programmes from the local TV stations covering the same area. It also established the "non-duplication concept", prohibiting the cable operator from generating duplicatory local programmes.

The notion of the "top 100 markets" for television broadcasting was introduced at this time - covering the TV broadcasting stations providing for over 80% of the US population. Cable TV might compete with these stations by "importing" distant signals (having made no payment for the programmes) and distributing them locally. It was thought that this might undermine the foundations of US broadcast TV, and it was the FCC rule prohibiting such importation which slowed up cable development.

1968 saw the publication of the Friendly Report advocating cable in cities, particularly in New York. The report contained comments about the "communications revolution" giving widespread publicity to its potential. Later in the year a Presidential report (the Rostow report) defined the place of cable in national telecommunications policy. In particular it emphasised the need for regulation with the words "policy should guard against excessive concentration in the control of communications media".

These reports, "blue sky" treatment by the press, and the advance of technology in general, fostered the belief that cable TV would take off. It was forecast that 70% of the US population would be receiving cable TV by 1980. In fact nothing like this happened **until** 1980 when there was a change of climate.

WHY THE CLIMATE CHANGED IN 1980

1. De-regulation

By the late seventies demand started to pick up in the big US market composed of people with a propensity to spend some of their relatively large amount of disposable income on a wider selection of entertainment.

Expansion in the US was boosted by less regulatory intervention and improved distribution technology. Today a large choice of programmes are available as a mixed bag of cheap basic services supplied when cable is installed, as services sponsored by advertisers, and as pay as you go services.

For many years the FCC had been concerned with the situation in broadcasting where bandwidth is a scarce commodity. The Supreme Court, with the First Amendment in mind, upheld FCC action in Red Lion Broadcasting vs FCC (1969). It was considered that viewers and listeners should have access to "an uninhibited marketplace of ideas" and that it was right for the FCC to pursue a licensing policy which encouraged diversity.

In cable television, bandwidth is not a scarce commodity. In the absence of evidence showing a strong demand for better access (for public, educational, or local government programs, as already provided for in earlier FCC rules) there would seem to be a case for the same liberal regulatory conditions as apply to newspapers (A number of experiments on the benefits of cable TV for programmes catering for communal requirements and social needs, sponsored by the National Science Foundation, had been abandoned).

This was the view taken by circuit court in a famous case, **Home Box Office vs FCC** (1977) followed by **Midwest Video Corp. vs FCC** (1978), upheld in the Supreme Court. The FCC's cable access requirements were defeated. More than this, the FCC had to set aside requirements for the provision of two way facilities and also the rule for a minimum of 20 channels in systems with 3500 or more subscribers. These were a part of its "access" requirement mentioned above.

Questions like what is two way capacity?, what is two way service?, and what operational requirements should there be if this aspect should be a consideration in franchising, were discussed.

In 1980, with satellite relays becoming an attractive way of linking up cable distribution systems in different parts of the country, the FCC removed restrictions on the reception and re-transmission of distant signals. The reason why such relays became available was that the Nixon administration reversed the Johnson policy by allowing the operation of commercial satellites in a so-called "open skies" policy within the US.

In this new competitive situation with the consequent diversity of choice, the need for regulatory intervention diminishes since the requirements of the First Amendment are satisfied.

Some tidying up remained to be done but these events removed a number of the restrictions responsible for the slow growth of cable TV. They were strongly influenced by the existence of the First Amendment, and to that extent the scenario is unique. However the way in which cable TV subsequently developed in the US contained some precedents of interest to other countries where cable TV was at an earlier stage of its development.

2. Technical Developments

Rapid advances in telecommunications, particularly satellite relays, made many of the earlier regulatory conditions obsolete or irrelevant.

3. Commercial incentives

Home Box Office initiated pay TV in 1972 but growth was slow until 1976 when about 800,000 subscribers viewed programmes on 250 systems - 7% of all cable systems. Later, the combined effect of the events already described resulted in the take off of cable systems. By 1980 pay TV on 2000 systems was viewed by 7.5 million subscribers - about half the total number.

By 1982 the total number of cable TV subscribers was estimated to be 25 million and growing rapidly. Apparently the US viewing public had an insatiable appetite for movies - the supply being led by Home Box Office, followed by Showtime.

Since 1975, US expansion has been based on the public's propensity to pay for old or blue movies; a relatively small number of "quality" programmes have also been provided.

Anything went. On Manhattan cable, Ugly George's claim to fame was that he asked women to undress in the street, and occasionally one obliged. The Rainbow channel advised:- "send the kids to bed and turn on the Escapade channel to see Naughty Nymphs, Hot T-Shirts" etc.

At the other end of the cultural spectrum the Rockefeller Centre (Radio City) announced a joint venture with RCA "to offer high quality entertainment". In May 1981 they reached agreement with BBC enterprises to provide up to 40% of the programmes.

However CBS programmes, concentrating on "cultural" material, closed down in September 1982, having been unable to attract the advertising revenue needed for its survival.

The movie industry tried to move in in a big way in 1980 when Getty Oil formed a joint venture - Premiere - with Columbia, Paramount, Universal and 20th Century Fox to provide up to 15 films a month. The venture was stopped by the Justice department, on the grounds of violation of the anti-trust laws.

Finance

There are two methods of financing. Cable TV companies offer "basic channel" fare for a fixed monthly charge which includes the cable fee and some programmes. The cable company, which may have paid a large sum for the area franchise from the local town or city authority, also obtains revenue from paid advertising.

A viewer can pay extra for first-run films, sport, or star entertainment supplied to the cable company by programme distributors with the added attraction of the absence of advertising. This revenue is split between the distributor and the cable company.

Cable TV in the US ran into difficult times in 1982 with the industry heavily in debt although it was felt that survivors would be reaping rewards in the second half of the decade. The cost per mile for new franchise equipment was $52,000. With about 75 subscribers per mile this meant an investment of $700 per subscriber, the required revenue per month then working out at about $29.

Direct Broadcast Satellite (DBS) TV became a possible threat. Full time employment in the industry 1981 was quoted at 51,000 but it is not clear what comprised "the industry".

If this figure represented jobs in all parts of the industry, the cable job potential for countries like the UK would not be large. Home Box Office was believed to be one of the only pay TV companies making any money and advertising revenue from cable TV was disappointing. It was $129M in 1981 compared with nearly $13 Billion for the three national TV networks.

Recent developments

New technical developments in the US are now mainly in DBS. Roof top antennas of around 1 metre diameter receive the satellite 12 GHz 500 MHz bandwidth downlink, and an attached convertor changes the signals to a 500 MHz band centred at 1 Ghz. This enables a longer cable to be used between the antenna and the receiver.

The development of cheap low noise amplifiers at these frequencies and advances in electronics generally enables the antenna and a receiver with addressable scrambling equipment for 24 channels to be produced for about $600.

New services continued to appear on cable and the second half of the eighties was much more promising. Compucard currently operate a service via The Source, Dow Jones, and other systems in the US and in Europe, enabling customers to "go shopping" by checking alternatives from a "catalogue" database, order and pay using a credit card number, and then have the goods delivered.

In 1974 there were 8.5 million subscribers served by 3100 different systems, in 1982 there were 25 million subscribers served by 4100 systems, and by 1988 there were an estimated 44 million subscribers.

By now cable networks are connected to well over half of all US households. Nearly all are "delivery only" systems, earlier FCC regulatory attempts to ensure that cable operators installed systems capable of two-way service having been abandoned. Many are provided by small local operators, often "networked" by satellite - that is programmes are distributed from a central provider by satellite up-down link to the local cable service who distribute to households.

Cable is used almost entirely to provide multi-channel TV entertainment. If the average cable TV expenditure of those connected was only $15 a month in 1986, revenues (excluding advertising) were nearly $8000M - probably a conservative estimate. Current revenue (1991) is about $14,000M.

According to Danczak (1989) it takes about 2 years to complete cable laying for a franchise at a cost of about $30,000 per mile. The cost per subscriber is about $1500.

In 1990, US telecom companies sought to lift the ban imposed in the 1984 Cable Act on their entry to cable TV. But consideration before Congress of two Bills, supported by the Bush administration, were deferred until next year. US telecom companies have been very active in buying in to UK franchises in the expectation of cable de-regulation to allow its use for general telecoms (See UK section below).

CABLE DEVELOPMENTS IN OTHER COUNTRIES

Europe

About 27% of Europe's 125m households are expected to be cabled by 1992 (best case) with $4.7 billion revenue, and 16% (worst case) with $2.6 billion. 20M people in Europe were connected to some kind of cable TV system in 1984, usually "first generation", licensed to transmit only existing TV programmes, although many experiments are in progress.

Canada

In Saskatchewan, Canada, a fairly large fibreoptic network already exists. Some 400 miles of it existed in 1981 with a link between Regina and Yorkton. Another 700 miles were added in 1982. The trunk cable is fibreoptic, with coaxial links to houses. Installation cost per household was about $700. The system lost money but was expected to break even in the late 80s.

By the late eighties Canada had a higher number of cable subscriptions per capita than the US. The scale of operations was typified by the purchase in December 1987 by a cable consortium, of SCI Holdings - a cable TV company with nearly 1.5 million subscribers in debt to the tune of $2,000M - for a price of $2,000M.

By 1990 a major supplier of cable services, Cancom, delivered signals to nearly 2000 cable companies via satellite (Simon 1990). Provided they install Cancom decoders at the head-end of their systems, these companies can then deliver TV to customers over their cable systems. The head-end has decreased in price from C$50,000 to a 1990 price of C$18,000.

France

In France an interactive wideband 15 channel fibreoptic system was scheduled to be working in 1500 homes in 1983. In 1982 a scheme was announced for 20,000 homes to be wired in, commencing in 1983 for one basic service providing ultimately 60 channels, with additional telephone, videotex, and home security services. The first phase (83-85) was expected to cost 6 billion francs, 2.5 billion born by the government, 1.5 billion by local authorities, and 2 billion provided by the programme industry. Nothing was stated about subscriber charges or revenues.

Germany

Several pilot programmes were proposed in West Germany for Ludwigshafen, Munich, Berlin and Dortmund. The Dortmund project was institutionally modelled on the IBA in Britain. The service was scheduled to pass 150,000 homes and provide 11 channels by the end of 1985. 50 companies expressed interest in providing programmes. 35M Dm for the four German pilot schemes covering a three year period was provided by fees from householders.

Japan

The Japanese Hi-Ovis (at Higashi Ikoma) and CCIS (at Tama) projects received wide publicity. The systems consisted of distribution via cables each containing 38 optical fibres to subscribers, with one sending and one receiving fibre per subscriber. The scheme was government financed to the tune of around $20M, but ultimately cost about $150M. It covered far fewer subscribers (500 households) than originally intended but the services were elaborate with wideband downstream and upstream paths.

Upstream TV signals were generated from homes using TV cameras. The basic services were TV re-transmissions, locally generated TV services, video-by-request programmes, and still picture information services.

A hard copy "memo" service was available for users with dot-matrix printers to receive local news, public notices, notices from members of the community, etc. A newspaper was even transmitted by a facsimile machine in Tokyo via a microwave link to the head end which could be received by appropriate equipment hooked on to the cable.

The system had several limitations and while "some considerations on the future development of the electronic media can be made... some further development seems necessary". The prospects for such systems in Japan seem vague:- "It was a dream system ten years ago and the experiment is shortening the gap between dream and reality" (Kawahata 1987).

Netherlands

Cees Wolzak of VNU describes how cable is run in his country without mincing words. VNU is a large publisher heavily involved in "electronic publishing". In the mid-eighties it employed 7500 people with annual sales of $550M. "You may have seen our cable magazine from Zaltbommel and you may be thinking that the Netherlands is a paradise for publishers who want to get moving with the electronic media.

Forget it! When it comes to electronic or video publishing in the Netherlands there are only two rules. Rule 1. Everything is forbidden. Rule 2. Nothing is allowed. It would take me all day to explain why and my blood pressure can't stand the strain. My plea to the politicians is simply this - we are willing to take the risks in the cable TV marketplace - please give us the chance to take them!"

I have not seen any official rebuttal of these remarks. Restrictive Dutch cable may be. The fact remains that the country has the most comprehensive cable network in Europe.

Switzerland

In Switzerland some 2M people subscribed to cable TV by the mid-eighties - popular because of bad reception of ordinary TV in a mountainous country. About 20,000 people receive a "TV newspaper", operated by two local newspapers in the town of Baden, with the co-operation of the Autophon cable network. Regional and local news is supplied. However it is believed that the "newspaper" is not very popular.

UK: 1. Early systems

In this section the history and political and organisational progress of cable in the UK is reviewed. Recent substantial changes in the general de-regulation of UK telecoms, some of which bear on cable, are discussed in Chapter 29.

About 2.5M homes subscribe to "first generation" cable TV in Britain, with a further 2M within connection range. These networks are mainly to relay existing television programmes from a receiver at a high point to homes which otherwise would be experiencing poor reception. The limited facilities available on these systems, dispersed around the country, are of no use for forming the core of a "second generation network".

In 1980 it was expected that a number of companies including

Rediffusion, British Relay, Radio Rentals and others would be applying for licences to operate experimental pay TV cable networks at several centres including Reading, Hull, Swindon, Rochester, and Northampton. It was expected that 250,000 homes might be connected in the next year or two. There would be no advertising, and a mix of films, sport, and other entertainment would be offered. Subscriptions were expected to be £5-£7 a month.

In the event something like that happened. For example Philips Cablevision operated a system in Northampton, capable of delivering 30 channels in a 300 MHz bandwidth. In practice 7 channels were delivered to 12,000 homes, providing normal UK TV programmes, but for an extra subscription a decoder box could be fitted at a receiver for a viewer to receive films transmitted from the local cable station. Programmes were the responsibility of a separate company, Select TV.

Philips also operated a microwave link for supplying programmes to Milton Keynes, one of Britain's "New Towns", where British Telecomm operated a small "wired home" experiment. At Milton Keynes a number of homes received these programmes and Prestel via optical fibre connections.

There were probably about 200,000 people around the country connected to these "second generation" networks (but not by fibres, so far as is known, except at Milton Keynes). It appeared as if the small nucleus of a national system, operationally resembling the US system in some respects, existed.

UK: 2. The Big Push

In July 1981 the Conservative government decided to launch a major Information Technology intitiative, believing that the country needed a push into a new industry with a big employment and export potential. The Prime Minister, Margaret Thatcher, appointed a six man team of information technology (IT) advisers - four from industry, one from inter-bank research and one from a university computer centre. An assessment of the cable system potential became one of their priorities.

The government was looking for a network with a potential for non-entertainment services such as online databases, electronic publishing, security, utility, and environmental control systems, EFT, reservations and shopping, electronic mail, education and general business use, together with the creation of a supporting and exporting information industry. But they thought that the most likely near-future utilisation and funding, assuming no government funding, would come from the Entertainment Industry.

The IT group made major recommendations to the government in a report from the Cabinet Office, dated February 1982, including a go-ahead for Direct Broadcast Satellites, (Anon 1982).

The Cabinet report received wide comment. A trade newspaper, Computer Weekly, said "Let's back the visionaries" but New Scientist, a widely read magazine said "Plans to wire up Britain are unlikely to go ahead...they threaten vested interests and are technically inept". The leader of the Engineering Union said "it could be an expensive mistake".

Peter Jay, Channel 4 TV-AM chairman, was reported to have compared the birth of cable to the renaissance, but Colin Shaw, Independent

Broadcasting Authority (IBA) programme director, thought that cable people were "smilers with knives pretending they are producing the renaissance". Roy Hattersley, Labour MP, thought that cable could "deny viewers programmes they presently enjoy" and Philip Whitehead, also Labour, thought it contained elements of economic nonsense.

A well known oracle of the Arts, Melvin Bragg, emphasised the two-culture problem by giving us a clear definition in the Sunday Times:- "Only a small percentage of people know what cable is. It is, quite simply, a piece of wire". He followed this technical exposition with a clear view of the future:- "It's goodbye to Auntie (the BBC)".

"Over the past 60 years the UK has had a broadcasting system based on two major elements: what the producers thought was good and what the audience liked best. The resulting consensus has been envied world wide... will Auntie be replaced by liberators or barbarians?"

British Telecomm said (in effect) "We are the best people to do it". But the role of British Telecomm was not made clear. Somebody said that the report was rather like a preview of the Pope's visit without a mention of the catholic church, although the report did say that it thought BT should have a competitive but not dominant role. Many people thought that one lot of people digging up the roads was sufficient. BT has the right (wayleaves)to dig holes. In many places it would not need to dig any extra ones.

The objectives of the government initiative were to lift restrictions on cable systems, to promote the complimentary development of DBS and cable, and to generate economic activity in information technology.

The Cabinet Report thought that the direct market for equipment and services would be £3000M or more. This, together with the possibilities for the sale of UK programmes, which already enjoyed a high reputation, made it essential for a UK technological lead to be established.

The report suggested that fibreoptic cable would probably be used for trunk lines and co-ax for local links. It considered that the return on capital would be sufficient to encourage private investment, so there would be no need for public funding; cable would not place as heavy a burden of investment on consumers as would an equivalent DBS system.

Programme costs for all the UK broadcasting at the time was around £1000M annually, providing some idea of the costs of programmes for cable. The IT report thought that all this would generate considerable economic activity and new employment.

UK: 3. The Hunt Report

The Cabinet IT group was immediately succeeded by a second group under Lord Hunt which reported on September 1982, and released its report on October 12th (Hunt 1982).

The Hunt report included the following recommendations:-

* Four functionaries - The provider,the operator, the programme or service provider, and the programme maker, the key figure being the operator.

* Competitive franchising with a 1C year term and local participation for not more than 500,000 homes per franchise, with no restrictions on number of channels, prices charged, programme content (except decency standards) or use of out-of-area or foreign programmes. Revenues from basic subscription, extra programmes and advertising, but no Pay-per-item TV or exclusivity for popular events.

* No ownership by companies or political, religious, or foreign bodies. Cable companies must carry the programmes of the four broadcast TV channels.

* New supervisory authority and no national common carrier network. Complimentary service from Direct Broadcast Satellite (DBS) from the five channels available to the UK.

At the techical level the hope probably was that Britain would be able to leapfrog into fibreoptic distribution. If it did not it could be installing an obsolescent system based on conventional cables.

UK: 4. Reaction to the Hunt Report

The British media overwhelmingly selected the possible effects on programme content as the most interesting aspect of the report. A BBC spokesman is reported to have said that cable operators would be free to offer either "wall to wall Dallas" or "wall to wall Starsky & Hutch" (according to whether you read the Telegraph or the Financial Times).

The Daily Telegraph carried a headline claiming "Cable TV may cost viewers £20 a month" (rental). In the same piece it reported that Richard Dennis of Rediffusion was claiming a cost of between £5 and £6 a month. It considered that the report was a traditional British fudge. While feeling that the UK has from time to time a standard of television programmes the world envies it asks why any organisation should claim a monopoly for fathoming a consumer's obscure needs.

The Financial Times said that the report was "a fiendishly clever web of British compromise" - evidently a distinct improvement on "British fudge". The FT's financial columnist thought that "the package is just what the budding industry wanted...only one major criticism levelled at the report.. the franchise period should be more than 8 years to allow a longer period for investment write-off period".

The Independent Broadcasting Authority (IBA) thought it was much worse than a fudge - "an Exocet sent into the sides of the BBC and ITV (Independent Television)". Lord Thomson, IBA Chairman, suggested in his own newspaper, the Sunday Times, that the report was "Pie in the sky"... We do not believe that Britain should be floated into the brave new world of push-button shopping and banking on an unregulated flood of cheap imported entertainment and soft porn films".

UK: 5. Technical standards

Another committee under Dr Edward Eden was required to make technical recommendations by March 1st 1983. The committee is said to have considered that this speed was "unprecedented".

There was certainly some danger that an obsolescing technology might be standardised in consequence of a decision made too early. On the other hand with a rapidly advancing technology there is always something better round the corner; at what point do you say "stop - we'll settle for this"?

If the UK was to have an inter-connectable wideband network it was probably felt necessary to set the standard to avoid a drift into the general chaos which characterises other telecom networks.

The technical recommendations were eventually published in Cmnd 8866, an April 1983 "White Paper" (Anon 1983). They were weakly reasonable. switched-star networks were "encouraged" by offering 20 year licences when they were used, but only 12 years would be offered for tree and branch licences; the ducts used must allow for later conversion to star. Switches were already available - BT had a switch for 300 users and Plessey had proposed a 1500 user switch.

UK: 6. Developments from 1983 to 1985

1983 was a year of hope and negotiations. Among companies expected to benefit were Racal (who proposed to move into distribution), Philips, BICC, and British Telecom, with Thorn EMI and Granada picking up a good deal of the programme distribution.

In 1984 considerations of the risks involved soon caused a flurry of activity. There were several closures and the realisation of costs and the need for long-term large investment dawned.

Eleven of the proposed twelve franchises, limited to 100,000 homes each, were granted in cities around the country. But in 1984 a series of pessimistic announcements and reports appeared about costs.

In one report (McKinsey April 1984) it was suggested that the franchises as then contemplated would never make a profit. The whole idea that launching of the UK network should be based on entertainment only was questioned. The network should be treated as a data highway and inter-business communications plus entertainment should enable franchises to break even in the 1990s.

Other discouraging events were the abolishing of first year capital allowances which would have been helpful to the franchisees and the possibility that competition from DBS would come sooner than had been thought.

It was becoming realised that the government's attempts to impose programme control, influenced on the one hand by the anti-porn/violence lobby, and on the other by its desire to protect the BBC and ITA quality programs, might leave the cable companies with an unappealing programme mix.

It was also felt that the limitation of 100,000 homes per franchise might be too small for profitability and that technical standards had been set too high.

The Plessey/Scientific Atlanta company, developing video switches for cable, shut down. Rediffusion, BET and Visionhire moved out of cable and Robert Maxwell bought Rediffusion Cablevision. The franchisees were experiencing financial and marketing problems. In contrast to the flood of applicants for the first round, only one application per franchise was received in the second round of franchising completed in May 1985. The cost of cabling an area of 100,000 homes was now estimated at around £30M. This round was managed by the new Cable Authority, appointed in January.

In 1985, prices averaged about £18 per month for up to 20 channels. The pay-TV service SelectTv ceased operations. The Cable Authority backed Multi-Microwave Distribution Systems - the local low-power microwave broadcasting of programmes direct to homes - reducing by several years the time taken to wire up customers in a franchise.

UK: 7. 1985 onwards; a change of sentiment

Some good news started to appear in 1985. In March it was claimed that in areas taking cable more people watched cable programmes than the BBC. The most popular programmes on Cablevision were Movie Channel, Music Box (pop) and Sky (general entertainment). Over one million homes were passed by the first eleven franchisees and over half a million by the second five. It was planned to advertise for franchises in five new areas every four months.

The first new multi-channel franchise to become operational was Swindon, but the initial demand from homes passed was disappointing. Charges for the 13 standard channels were reduced to £5.95 per month. The demand from other areas was also disappointing. But the first subscribers at Swindon were delighted by the wide choice offered and it was hoped that their enthusiasm would be contagious.

Optimism was increased by more profitable results in the US with 1987 advertising revenues increasing to $1,000M.

About a quarter of a million homes were connected by the end of 1988 supplied by 10 franchise operators. However a number of other licensed franchisees did not start operations. The 1981 government expectations that cable would provide an entertainment-led route into wideband information services had not materialised.

But other opportunities materialised at a rate comparable with the pace of de-regulation and expected de-regulation. The gradual thaw encouraged UK cable operators to try out quite different kinds of service. In 1987 Windsor cable television announced a connection to Mercury for a pilot telephone scheme competing with BT. Windsor covers the Slough Trading Estate - one of the largest and most successful factory areas in the country. Windsor expected gross revenues of £50 per line per month; by 1989 it was reported that they were receiving £135.

A number of American companies invested in UK cable, particularly telephone companies, believing that cable would eventually lead them to participation in UK general telecoms. In their own country they are not allowed to become cable operators. The UK not only holds out the prospect of new revenue, but also the chance to accumulate experience in case similar de-regulation occurs in the US.

In February 1988 the US securities group Prudential Bache invested $100M in City Centre Cable which had won a West London franchise. There was some interest in cable for home utility services. Tenders were invited for the largest franchise yet - 400,000 homes in the West Midlands.

In 1989 Pacific Telesis invested in East London Telecommunications, a franchise in the developing docklands area and installed its first telephone lines. Pacific Telesis are also investing in the Redbridge area and the Waltham Forest franchises. US West became a shareholder in Windsor television who by 1989 had installed over 500 business lines. US West in conjunction with United Cable also invested in the Croydon franchise.

In 1990, 26 new franchises, including such plums as Oxford and Liverpool were offered by the government, and the ban on foreign ownership was lifted, bringing the total number of franchises awarded to 41, passing nearly 5 million homes. The 1990 franchises were not required to include channels transmitting programmes from the BBC and BSB (now defunct). A further 31 advertised franchises will bring the total number of homes passed to over 9 million.

It was also reported in 1990 that East London Telecoms, West Side Cable, Cable Camden, and Westminster Cable, three partly owned by US companies, were intending to form a consortium with London-wide operations.

UK: 8. The UK telecoms review

The review, published on November 13th 1990 (Anon 1990), proposes further de-regulatory measures in a climate where already "No other country in the world offers such competition in the local network", particularly in regard to the role of cable where "the UK cable industry - dominated by US Bell companies and cable companies - is perhaps the biggest beneficiary (Hayes 1990).

"Equal Access" means providing the means for a subscriber to use a prefix code in order to freely select one of several telecom companies for telephone services including local services, via the "local loop". A few cable companies are doing this now, but they have to arrange to be switched to a customer by BT or Mercury because these companies are the only ones able to use the local loop - the line from a subscriber's premises to a telephone exchange.

For this proposal to have any real impact, cable companies will have to inter-connect with each other and have freer access to the local loop. There would then be a real competitive alternative which should result in price reductions, compared with the much more limited existing BT/Mercury duopoly.

It is expected that in return for being allowed such access the cable companies will have to assume some kind of universal service obligation - that is they will not be allowed simply to cream off the business traffic.

British Telecom is expected to try and get permission to provide entertainment over its network before 1997 - the earliest date under the new proposals, and meanwhile to get out of cable altogether as a bargaining point.

BT have also argued that they do not object to US Belcos being able to enter UK cable with their "pockets stuffed with cash from their largely monopolistic US telecom operations" but do object to the absence of reciprocal measures. Lord Sharp, formerly chairman of Cable & Wireless, is quoted as saying:- "The US governmment should reflect on the asymmetry of the Belcos exploiting their local monoply positions to cross-subsidise market entries overseas". (The 1984 US Communications Act limits foreign ownership of US telecom companies to 20% and bans foreign management).

UK: 9. Futures

Unfortunately government push instead of market pull is probably needed if the country wants to establish a new kind of information industry instead of being a follower and importer. This is unfortunate - second best to a market driven approach. Inevitably people point to an earlier advance by dictat - Prestel - which seemed to be a very good idea, but was unwisely marketed.

The UK has neither the resources, the entrepreneurial access to finance, or a sufficiently developed market place to enable Information Infrastructures to "just grow" at a reasonable speed. The UK government got the general approach right - first, vigorously raise the issue, then get the debating over at a rate compatible with the 1980s rather than with the Edwardians, then pass the enabling legislation with minimum delay.

As Veljanovski (1984) points out, cable is risky, technology changes are hard to predict and the market is uncertain. "The uncertain nature of cable expansion and the complexities of its output make any attempt to subject the industry to detailed regulation counter-productive".

But perhaps de-regulation on a scale not contemplated in the early eighties with network expansion driven by telecom expectations will provide a highway upon which information services will ride.

According to Thynne (1989) the majority of British homes should be able to receive up to 50 TV channels and 20 radio stations via cable by the end of the nineties. Thynne quotes Tony Currie of the Cable Authority:- "It will also mean the end of the satellite dish".

Cable is being used at present to transport entertainment programmes. So far, telephone communications are being added only in a small way, and information services not at all. However in 1990 Southwestern Bell, once part of AT&T, was reported to be considering the provision of information services from sources outside its franchise (Evagora 1990). Southwestern Bell controls Oyston Cable - owner of the Preston and Liverpool franchises.

The "takeover" by US companies received considerable attention in 1990 (Bradshaw, Snoddy, Gribben, 1990). It was reported in the Daily Telegraph (Gribben) that "American Companies will end up as the biggest shareholders and investors because British firms failed to provide sufficient interest. They will supply more than 90% of the £4.5 Billion being spent to expand the network the Cable Authority said yesterday after announcing the award of the last batch of 135 franchises to cable Britain".

REFERENCES

Anon.
   Cabinet office: IT advisory panel. HMSO, London, February 1982.
     Report on cable systems.

636

Anon
  Cmnd 8866 ("White Paper"). HMSO April 1983.
    The development of cable systems and services.
Anon.
  IEEE Spectrum, 21(9), 57-62, Septemeber 1984.
    Direct broadcast satellites: television stations in orbit.
Anon.
  HMSO November 1990.
    Competition and choice: telecommunications policy for the 199Ca.
Barran, Paul.
  IEEE TRans. Com. 23(1), 178-184, January 1975.
    Broadband interactive communication services to the home.
    Part 2: impasse.
Bradshaw, Della.
  The Financial Times, September 27th 1990.
    A struggle to be at your service.
Clement-Jones, Tim.
  Telecommunications Policy, 7, 204-214, September 1983.
    Cable and stallite TV in the UK and Europe: the emerging legal issues.
Danczak, Jenny.
  British Library Research Paper No. 59. British Library Publications
  Unit, Boston Spa, England. 1989.
    Cable and satellite: the potential for the information market.
Estrin, Deborah L; Sirbu, Marvin A.
  J.Telecom. Networks 103-115, 1984.
    Cable television networks as an alternative to the local loop.
Evagora, Andreas.
  Communications Week International, May 21st, 1990.
    Bell considers new approach.
Fox, J.R
  Report 374-16 BT Research Labs, Martlesham Heath, Ipswich IP5 7RE,
  England. 1983.
    Fibre optics in a multi-star wideband local network.
Gribben, Roland.
  The Daily Telegraph, July 11th 1990.
    US control of cable networks likely.
Hatamian, M; Bowen, E.G.
  AT&T Tech J. 64(2), 347-367, February 1985.
    Homenet: a broadband voice-data-video network on CATV systems.
Hayes, Dawn.
  Communications Week International, November 26th 1990.
      Users hopeful yet cautious.
Hunt of Tanworth, Lord (Chairman).
  The Home Office. Cmnd 8679, October, 1982. Published by HMSO, 49, High
  Holborn, London WC1V 6HM.
    Report of enquiry into cable expansion and broadcasting policy.
Kawahata, M. and Miyabe J.
  In Mastroddi, Franco (Ed.). Electronic publishing: the new way to
  communicate. Kogan Page (for the CEC). London 1987. 29-37.
    Social impacts of new electronic publishing media - some findings of
    the Hi-Ovis experiment.
Kay, Peg and Gerendasy, Stanley.
  NSF Report NSF/RA-760161, National Science Foundation, Washington, 1976.
    Social services and cable TV.
Litman, Barry and Eun, Susanna.
  Telecommunications Policy 5(2), 121-135, June 1981.
    The emerging oligopy of pay TV in the USA.

McCron, R,.
   J.Educ.Television 10(1), 7-18, 1984.
      New technologies, new opportunities? The potential of cable in
      educational and social action broadcasting.
Page, John R.U.
   In Proc. 6th Online Information meeting, London. Learned Information,
   Oxford. 1982. Pps 155-160.
      Broadcast satellites in association with other broadband techniques for
      innovative methods of information distribution.
Simon, Bernard.
   The Financial Times, September 28th, 1990.
      The signal reaches out.
Snoddy, Raymond.
   The Financial Times, July 11th 1990.
      US companies ahead in cable goldrush.
Thynne, Jane.
   The Daily Telegraph, December 27th 1989.
      Boom in cable TV may leave satellite dishes washed up.
Veljanovski, Cento.
   Telecommunications Policy, 8, 290-306, December 1984.
      Regulatory options for cable TV in the UK.

CHAPTER 26. TELEVISION-BASED INFORMATION SYSTEMS: VIDEOTEX AND HIGH DEFINITION TELEVISION (HDTV)

VIDEOTEX

Videotex is a generic name covering systems for disseminating information electronically for display on terminals or modified TV receivers. Viewers are provided with easily understood control procedures. The original systems were called Teletext and Viewdata.

Videotex got off to a bad start - some would say that it has never achieved its promise - but if all the systems which come under the Videotex label today are considered, that is too sweeping a statement.

According to Noll (1985):- "After two years of initial commercial operation, well over $50 million in development and other expenses, hundreds of information providers, and a content of nearly 200,000 frames of information. Prestel (the pioneer, originally called Viewdata - Ed) achieved penetration in only a little more than 1000 British homes".

Although the total number of Prestel terminals, including business and residential use, had increased to about 13,000 by the end of 1981, this was called a pathetic performance when measured against a forecast made by the British Post Office in 1978 of 1 million users by the end of 1981".

"... but the success of teletext is equally baffling. As of mid-1981 there were about 160,000 teletext-equipped TV sets in use in England. By mid-1984 this number had grown to more than one million".

Contrasting reports about videotex abound. Some clues to what might be claimed to be a considerable success are contained in the following extract (Kusekoski 1989) :-

"With videotex an "Electronic document" can be updated or taken out of circulation instantly, reducing the risk of bad business decisions based on incorrect information... With videotex, accounting features determine what information is being used and by whom. Under utilized information can be eliminated from the system".

"Corporate videotex is making one of its greatest contributions in helping the Digital (i.e. the computer company DEC - Ed.) sales organization to compete in today's dynamic market place). In the past, sales representatives have found searching through a large variety of printed and online sources for the information they need, to be a time-consuming and frustrating experience.

Users of (DEC's) ACCESS have indicated that they can now retrieve information ... from 16 different databases ranging from numeric data to produce information and external market intelligence... in about one fifth of the time previously required".

Teletext

It is sometimes overlooked that the methods by which data and graphics were to be transmitted and displayed by the page on modified domestic TV receivers were worked out by the BBC, the Independent Broadcasting Authority (IBA), and the British Radio Equipment Manufacturers

Association. No representatives from the Post Office (the part which is now British Telecom) appear among the names of the "Combined Working Group" on their report (Anon 1974).

Their objective was to provide a broadcast information service by transmitting pages for display on a modified TV receiver consisting of 24 rows of 40 alpha-numeric characters (in ISO-7 ASCII code) or six-element graphic "characters", in 8 different colours, requiring 45 bytes per row including control data.

This coded data would be transmitted at a speed of just under 7 Mbps in a time interval corresponding to two lines of each television field (spare lines unoccupied by TV picture data). As fields are repeated 50 times a second this amounts to about 4 complete teletext pages every second.

Modified TV receivers would contain a decoder, and a store for one page of data. The stored data would be continuously scanned and displayed on the TV tube.

If a repeating "magazine" of 100 pages is broadcast, the net effect is that a database sweeps past every TV receiver every 25 seconds (approx). Each page is identified by a key enabling any viewer to capture and store it by setting his receiver to that key. The average waiting time for a selected page would be about 12.5 seconds.

In a PAL 625 line TV frame (PAL is a TV standard used in many countries including the UK) there are actually 16 spare lines unoccupied by television entertainment signals. Since 1980, some of these have been used to carry teletext signals enabling extra pages of information to be added without increasing the "page capture" waiting time. For example the BBC now uses 7 of the spare lines and IBA 10. Other lines have been reserved to carry data for enhanced services as described in the "Standards" section below.

Viewdata

Samuel Fedida, head of the Post Office R18 research division, presented some ideas about a scheme called "Viewdata" (later re-named "Prestel") comparing it with teletext as an information source (Fedida 1976), later providing a technical description (Fedida 1977), and then describing an arrangement of networks for national or global coverage (Fedida 1978).

Viewdata as first set-out is a scheme where a central computer is dialled up via the Public Switched Telephone Network (PSTN) from a terminal. Pages requested from the viewdata database are downloaded to the terminal. The "terminal" is normally a teletext/TV receiver. Viewdata embodies the same coding/store/display scheme as teletext so much of the receiving system is common to both.

For viewdata (with a small "v" because it has since become the generic name for a particular kind of videotex system) there is an additional modification comprising a "keypad" and a connection to the viewer's telephone line via a modem, so transmission technology is quite different to teletext's "line bursts".

Although it is possible to send data much faster over the PSTN today, Prestel delivers data at the rather slow rate of 1200 bits per second. Thus once a page, comprising about 10 Kbits has been requested and found by the Prestel computer, it takes about 8 seconds to become fully displayed. Request data sent by a user goes at 75 bps which is adequate for most purposes.

Retrieval is eased by providing a tree-like index to the pages, of which there may be a very large number. The user is first presented with, say, a choice of 10 major subject areas. Upon choosing one, he or she is presented with a second display of ten sub-divisions of that subject and so on.

If there are 100,000 pages in the database, 4 successive index-selection page displays would lead to a display of a record page containing the wanted information. Alternatively if the number of the wanted page is known at the outset, its number may be directly keyed.

In the case of the Scitel example shown in Figure 26.1, keying number 86 retrieves the starting index page, 2 retrieves index page 862, "Advances in Science", 3 retrieves index page 8623 "Social Sciences" and that page offers choices of information pages such as 86230 "Social Studies" as shown at the bottom of the Figure.

If you don't know the page number, this procedure may be simple but it's cumbersome. Keyword access was introduced in 1987. A keyword provides access to broad "headings" - e.g. "trains". There is no boolean facility such as "trains AND Plymouth AND Sunday".

Because all keywords are broad terms they are, in effect, an "index to an index". They switch you to narrowly indexed pages at lower levels in the selection hierarchy, not direct to information pages. An attempt is made to deal with synonyms by Prestel staff who note word useage. Thus if "railway" was used frequently, arrangements would be made for that word to trigger a display of a "railway choices" page.

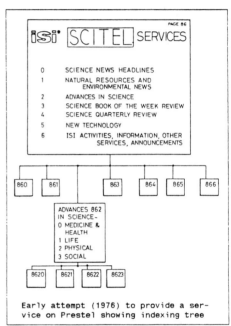

Early attempt (1976) to provide a service on Prestel showing indexing tree

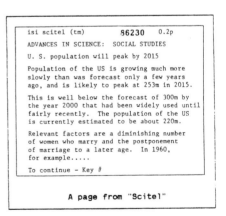

A page from "Scitel"

FIGURE 26.1. PRESTEL INDEXING

Prestel is connected to other databases by a "gateway" - that is Prestel can route a caller to another system via a telecoms link where there may be additional search or processing facilities. If you are gatewayed to an associated service, you may be able to use these facilities. For instance if you access the Educational Service to find out, say, what turboencabulator courses are available, the Educational Service system will process its current data and tell you what there is.

Activities in other countries

A 16 bit system developed in France called Antiope was developed soon after viewdata (Prestel) was launched. The extra bits enable special characters and better graphics to be displayed at the expense of more storage at the receiver - at that time rather expensive.

The Japanese developed a system which they called Captain using a system of graphic sub-blocks to enable Kanji/Hiragana characters to be constructed. It required quite a large store at the receiver.

The Canadians decided that considerably better graphics were required. Their system was an early simpler implementation of the ideas later developed for Postscript (Chapter 5). 8-bit codes are used to transmit picture description instruction co-ordinates to a microprocessor at the receiver which constructs graphics out of lines, polygons, arcs, etc. In the US, AT&T introduced a system based on Telidon called North American Presentation Level Protocol Syntax (NALPS) which provides a choice of 16 colours among other things (Ninke 1985). It was ratified as a US standard in 1985.

A number of other countries for example West Germany with "Bildschirmtext" followed, mostly using the Prestel system, but there was an extraordinary row about the alternative systems. The British had hoped to establish a Prestel-based standard, no doubt with an eye on the export market, and there was an acrimonious exchange in the 1981 technical press in which K.E. Clarke (UK) remarked "The debate on Viewdata is the most bitter controversy about communications standards since the arguments about colour television 20 years ago".

Standards

The British had tried to bring in a standard for a pioneering invention in an area of rapid technical developments too soon. The idea was to get international agreement quickly with a simple mass-produced circuit board that could be fitted cheaply to TVs.

Eventually a compromise was reached, typical of standards politics, in which everybody was able to do their own thing. The CCITT 1980 recommendation S.100 proposed four different options "alphamosaic characters, geometric systems, Dynamically Redefinable Character Sets (DRCS), and photographic representation".

In 1985 a "World System Teletext Specification" called CEPT 5 was agreed (Anon. DTI 1985), listing five "presentation levels":-

Level 1: 1976 specification with some enhancements.

Level 2:   8 different character sets, 32 colours, no need for
space before changing colour, extra characters, smoother mosaics,
and other improvements.

Level 3:   Method of implementing DRCS (anticipating Postscript)

Level 4:   Alpha-geometric display facilities.

Level 5:   Alpha-photographic display facilities.

To implement the new levels the receiver must contain a controlling
microcomputer and additional storage.

The way the arrangements are implemented is as follows. The 45 byte
row comprising data to describe 40 displayed characters and control data is
now called a "packet"; it includes bits specifying a packet number from
0-32. Packets 0-23 carry the original 24 rows and are read by standard
receiver decoders. Packets 25 to 31, one per spare TV line, are designated
to carry data covering a whole range of functions for the new "presentation"
levels. For example one of the packets is concerned with languages.

The standard Prestel-type alpha-mosaic character set called T/TE
06-01 was adopted in 1981, and became used throughout Europe. The set
contains space for a few special "national option" characters so character
sets are slightly different - e.g. the French set includes accented
characters, the German an umlaut and so on.

The new arrangements allow for any of the national option characters
to be re-defined, instead of being incorporated as a fixed set. They also
allow for completely different character sets - e.g. Greek, Arabic,
Cyrillic, etc., to be designated. This would enable more than one language
to be included on the same page - for example foreign names, quotations etc.

In fact the above "world specification" is not a world specification
at all. The North American standard, based on the Canadian telidon, was
devised by AT&T outside the CCITT/CEPT.

Public videotex: technology and payback

Raymond takes rather a caustic swipe at videotex technology
rationale (Raymond 1989). "The need to attract a large market in a very
short time and the desire to keep costs low led to strategies that maximally
employed existing services and hardware. This meant that the systems were
determined both by the lowest common denominator in existing equipment and
fuzzy predictions for technological development in the near term".

"The most effective amortization would result if the system was
completely homogeneous, both geographically and temporally. As a result
videotex promotors attempted to design systems which were consistent over
national and international boundaries, and to be both upward and downward
compatible with future systems. These concerns led to a protracted squabble
about encoding systems, and the various tradeoffs which they represented, in
a futile attempt to arrive at a single permanent standard".

Unfortunately the result was the worst of all worlds. A person
familiar with current processing, transmission, and display technology,

would, on looking at a videotex screen for the first time, be struck by the dated rather crude performance.

"Homogeneity" sounds like a reasonable view, but the policy implemented in the UK and in France amounted to "We think that this system is good for you and so we will provide it and pay the implementation and launching costs". Such magnanimity usually requires government backing.

In France, little was said about actual costs. The price charged for receivers is very low and the result has been the widespread use of Minitel videotex terminals. This policy amounts to arguing that market forces will be insufficient to bring about the long term intangible benefits of an effective videotex infrastructure; it should be considered as a public good.

But if large sums are to be spent without easily quantifiable returns a government should ideally first make a compelling case for spending more from the taxpayer's finite purse. There is no project so important that the sky's the limit. The channel tunnel has run into a lot of justifiable flak and it highlights the control problems inherent in government-driven rather then market-driven policy. If you are the implementing authority, once you have got beyond a certain point you don't withdraw even when expenditure becomes far more than was anticipated. You just lean heavily on the government.

If the French authorities had been able to foresee Minitel's successful outcome perhaps they would have provided some information about its real costs. Unfortunately they allowed themselves to be found out by the public watchdog Cour des Comptes. Teletel cost FF 530M in 1988 and will still be losing FF 400M in 1995 according to this organisation so the project has allowed itself to be unnecessarily blighted.

However Teletel is thrusting ahead regardless. Having achieved a reported 5 million subscribers in France it arranged a joint venture in 1989 with Infonet which will provide an "information exchange" by enabling subscribers on the US Infonet network to access the Minitel directory.

In late 1989 a company called Aldoda International announced that it would provide Minitel-emulating software for PCs and arrange a UK gateway to the Minitel network in France charging time at 7p per minute.

Public videotex 1. Prestel in the mid eighties

In spite of the prospects for all kinds of good things in the 1986 specifications, it seems that the large system operators, for example British Telecom, are not prepared to put good money after bad. They soldier on with what they have with piecemeal improvements. They have made a very large software investment and are lumbered with their own PSTN which was not designed for this type of service.

In 1986 it was stated that (Anon.1989) "Prestel... will progressively switch from its own outmoded network... to PSS, the UK packet switched networks... Multistream and other data services... working (up to) 2400/2400 full duplex". This sounds like some kind of a breakthrough.

But the statement is rather misleading and should be re-stated as follows "If you are already a PSS user with, say, X.25 (a protocol/interface) connections to a network node, you can make better use of Prestel by accessing it via PSS, taking advantage of PSS's lower transmission costs and lower error rates".

For some reason which escapes me, the maximum PSTN downleading speed is 1400 bps, but using PSS it is 2400 bps and upwards. However the potential benefit of PSS high speed operation, - for instance the almost instant display of a page at 9600 bps or faster - is not realised because the system is computer bound, not transmission link bound, so far as speed is concerned.

There have been some modest improvements. The constraints of the PSTN's bandwidth, the big investment in old software/hardware, and a loss-making service are considerable. But, you may say, Prestel started to run profitably in 1985 (Green-Armytage 1985). I find that hard to accept. Have R&D costs from about 1973 onwards been included and what was the lost opportunity cost (from discounted cash flow considerations)?

BT did some work on a system called "Photovideotex" to provide large high-resolution pictures, (Arbuthnot 1986). A BT glossy urged you to contact the marketing department, giving the impression that it was a here-and-now technology, and an article appeared (Scales 1986) saying "British Telecom's Photovideotex system is now in production... with the first major application expected to be up and running by April". It was not, and is not today.

Public videotex. 2. Success in sight?

New York Pulse, run by the New York Times, shut down in 1987, following the 1986 closure of Viewtron, run by Knight-Ridder, and the closure of Gateway run by the Times Mirror. Earlier Keycom, which planned a service for 700,000 subscribers in Chicago, attracted a few hundred customers after an expensive advertising campaign and closed less than a year later.

The US Belco Pacific Telesis planned to provide a videotex gateway to its system for users in San Francisco, but postponed the idea indefinitely in 1989 stating that there was insufficient evidence of demand for the service.

Some interesting comments have been made about Viewtron (Atwater 1985) of general interest to system planners. "The significant change in ratings of nine out of seventeen attributes after exposure to Viewtron demonstrates the futility of asking respondents about hypothetical services that they have never seen".

Once again this shows how difficult it is to conduct market research (assuming that any other videotex planners do any) where there are conceptualisation problems. Credible results can only be expected from surveys like stopping people in the High Street to get them to sniff at different soaps and state their preference.

However there has been a change. Public videotex appears to be in fashion again.

In mid-1988 Bell Canada said it proposed to spend $30M in mounting an experiment called "Alex" to provide videotex services to 20,000 subscribers in Montreal. The service will emulate Minitel but will use the NAPLPS standard for better graphics. The Belcos U.S. West and Nynex are both introducing videotex. U.S. West will be providing a videotex gateway to its network, having solved the software problems with the aid of the US Minitel subsidiary. Nynex is distributing services in association with Prodigy, the IBM/Sears Roebuck videotex venture.

Something of a coup was pulled off by BT in conjunction with Marconi who contracted in 1985 to provide a large all-purpose system for Singapore to be called Teleview. The policy is again to provide government funding to create an infrastructure (for households, business, and industry) but this time success seems likely.

The system is now coming into use and uses Prestel-type computers and software - but two important constraints have been lifted by providing adequate finance. Firstly, terminals will be microcomputers with high resolution displays able to store and process data in quantity. Secondly, the terminals will request data via telephone line but receive it via a dedicated TV channel. The speed/bandwidth of the channel provide the means for a fast, high resolution, service.

In the UK, Prestel is becoming modestly successful. BT is putting up with its technical limitations and concentrations on services such as connection to Telecom Gold, now the world's largest electronic mail system, providing business services, etc. The number of subscribers has risen to about 130,000. BT is said to have turned down plans to introduce free Minitel-type terminals, but Mercury is said to be considering ways of accessing Minitel.

The explanation of the French phenomenon, mentioned above, seems to lie in the right selection of conditions. A fairly large introduction in the form of a "substitute telephone directory" with free terminals was a good way to introduce laymen to computers. It reinforces the keeping-up-with-the Duponts syndrome; Jules acquires a certain cachet when he sees his friend struggling with a telephone book and is prompted to say "de quoi s'agit-t-il? Quelle hassle! Servez-vous de Minitel comme moi!

It must have encouraged useage to subsidise a subscriber's acquisition of Minitel so that it originally cost him nothing or almost nothing. Much of the available information cost little to retrieve. Prestel was expensive to acquire and expensive to run. Domestic users simply did not have that amount of disposable income for that kind of information.

Anderla (1991) points out that in 1985 conventional ASCII-code online systems accounted for over 90% of online transactions in France, and videotex 7%. By 1989 ASCII had dropped to 54% with Minitel videotex at 40% and CD-ROM at 6%. Anderla quotes Jacques Faule, confronted with a real puzzle like many French librarians:- "Although searching a large database e.g. Pascal via an ASCII host is three of four times more cost effective than using a Minitel terminal, it is Minitel which is gaining in popularity and market share while conventional online is being squeezed out".

The explanation seems to be "Minitel's lower connect time even though transactions are more time consuming, almost painless costs amalgamated with the telephone bill, and its user-friendly image". Considerable detail about Minitel users and services and about European videotex in general has been provided in Anon (1989).

In Italy, with optimistic projections about the market, plans are afoot to combine the so far rather feeble videotex attempts by Olivetti and the PTT STET, possibly including Fiat and IBM. There are said to be 100,000 terminals in use, but this may be an exaggeration. It is far from clear how plans to triple the number of terminals by the end of 1990 will be carried out. There are also plans to interconnect with France, U.K. and Germany.

The Dutch are having another go in spite of the collapse of earlier attempts - notably the end of the VNU (a major player in the information business) cable/telephone system. Holland has a very high cable penetration. The plan is to organise a hybrid service and 40 information providers have shown an interest.

The Japanese remain as enthusiastic as ever about Captain. Different protocols have been introduced to provide for a range of interactive service such as Home banking and shopping and electronic mail (Terayama 1989).

A new 16 bit colour system, Hi-Captain, has been developed (Shoji 1989) for use with ISDN 64 Kbps telecommunications and is said to be installed at a number of sites. It is to be followed by a multimedia database system with mixed-mode halftone reproduction (See Chapter 10) and Group 4 facsimile-type hard-copy printing.

Private Videotex

It is sometimes said that public videotex "failure is counterbalanced by private videotex's success". This may be an over-statement but having ticked over for some years, private videotex seems to have caught on in several fields. Digital Equipment Corporation operates one of the largest successful private videotex systems (Kusekoski 1989) as has already been mentioned.

Private videotex systems can be of several different kinds from an existing mainframe computer/terminals system with software which converts it into a vidoetex database host computer/ videotex terminals system, to a small minicomputer/microcomputer based system. A particular requirement may be for a publicly available service based on vandal-proof terminals.

There is no doubt that private videotex has achieved some success in the UK. In 1987 it was claimed that there was 100,000 terminals in use, and that equipment sales would be over £60M in that year. Perhaps the biggest success has been in the travel industry (Weinstein 1987). The major organisations using it for this purpose are Thomson, Intasum and Thomas Cook. Virtually all travel agent's shops use at least one videotex terminal.

A review of videotex for UK local community and other services was provided in 1988 (Forster 1988) and 1989 (Griffiths 1989). These services usually based on a library or library cooperative, seem to have come into quite widespread use in the UK. Some provide free local information services and/or a closed-user service, the users with their own terminals being members of a local commercial organisation which pays for use of the system.

There is one intriguing area in which experiments have been conducted for many years - home shopping. The behaviour of people, given a home-shopping scheme in a Prestel environment (technology is not discussed) has been described in Buckley (1990) and Fenn (1990).

One of the most comprehensive tests was also one of the earliest - the Japanese Hi-Ovis experiment (Kawahata 1986). The costs of this experimental scheme were about £100M and the services provided were free. The home shopping experiment included the selection of a wide range of goods, ordering, and payment. Purchased goods were delivered. The system used fibreoptic telecoms and two way visual communication using normal TV screens.

Not much "demand information" can be gained from this experiment in view of its cost and charges. However, say the authors, "In order to exploit the potential fully... HDTV or some other ways to improve the quality are needed. It is necessary to provide services of the still picture type with photographic quality". If this be correct, videotex home shopping is in for a hard time given that TV quality, or better, is needed.

The Prodigy videotex service being organised by Trintex, owned by Sears Roebuck and IBM, is probably the largest system running today. A former partner, CBS, pulled out. $10 per month will be charged for unlimited time, and most of the revenue is expected to come from on-screen advertising. Terminals will be IBM, Mac, or Apple PCs.

Prodigy was launched in 1989 and by November 1990 claimed that the number of online subscribers had increased to 460,000 from 50,000 in January 1989. It added to its own network in 1990 by linking up with BT Tymnet. In 1990 Nynex signed a distribution agreement with Prodigy to cover the north-eastern part of the US.

Prodigy is starting to resemble Compuserve. Online access to the **American Academic Encylopedia** and the **Mobil Travel Guide** is provided. Prodigy start-up software is included with IBM's PS/1, a low cost machine specifically designed for domestic use.

Home shopping is an attractive idea for the elderly and there have been some services of this kind in the UK. Since they are provided free they are dependent on finance from the local authority. Bradford ran such a system which was well received but closed because funds were cut off.

Conclusions

In the Raymond (1989) piece already mentioned criticising policy, the writer continues with a discussion about the acquisition of goods to increase status - an aspect of the keeping-up-with-the-Joneses syndrome. Videotex, he suggests, does nothing for your pecking order. As a low-cost boringly simple device it has no glamour.

Other reasons for "failure" are suggested (Grover 1989):- "Videotex advocates spent years debating the technical specifications for the system while virtually ignoring the question of whether the consumer even wanted the service. It was the technology that was marketed not the concept. The marketing thrust of most companies failed to stress what videotex would do for the consumer that could not be done otherwise".

From the foregoing review it is hard to decide whether videotex has been a failure or a success.

The reason for this difficulty is that both these words are subjective - success and failure are hard to define. Is Minitel a success for example? Another difficulty is that videotex is one of these portmanteau words covering very wide variations. Some applications are so different from others that it is unhelpful to lump them together.

Perhaps we may conclude that the jury is still out on public videotex while private videotex has been a modest success.

HIGH DEFINITION TELEVISION (HDTV)

Introduction

HDTV has applications in high quality text and image display for information systems, as well as for entertainment TV. It impacts semiconductors, display devices, and general consumer electronics. It will probably affect the entire 35mm film creative and distribution industry. One estimate pieces the market for HDTV domestic receivers alone at $40 billion by the year 2010. It may seem to be a fringe "information system" but its enormous potential importance earns it a section in this book.

According to Lippman (1990) "The by-products of HDTV contain the real gold. Our imaging systems are at the threshold of a transformation from simple analog devices to high speed digital image processors. The impact of research in TV systems has effects that range from new ways to process high-rate image data to techniques for scaling, representing, compressing, and displaying moving image data. This knowledge is useful at any resolution and in any system".

HDTV is one of the major service planned to be accommodated in the Integrated Broadband Communications Network (IBC) being developed under the CEC RACE programme. The telecommunications accommodation needed for HDTV might bring a wideband universal network into existence sooner than would otherwise be the case. On it could ride information services as was envisaged in the UK government's 1981 initiative for an entertainment-led wideband Cable network which never took off.

World television, pioneered in the UK with a 405 line system in 1936, did not get under way until well after the war. Three incompatible systems NTSC, PAL, and SECAM were developed mainly for political reasons and have become entrenched since 1953 - NTSC in North America, Japan, and parts of South America; SECAM in France, parts of South America and the communist bloc except China; PAL in the rest of the world.

These schemes provide inadequate performance in a number of respects because of the design economics resulting from the need to transmit a lot of data through systems in which inexpensive mass-produced receivers are the most important component.

The Japanese have been working on HDTV since the early seventies. At a meeting of the International Radio Consultative Committee at Geneva in November 1985, they proposed a world standard based on an 1125 line picture repeated at a 60 Hz rate, backed by the United States (PAL provides a 625 line 50 Hz picture). Any further action was, however, postponed for a year.

The enormity of this proposal took a little while to sink in. Japan dominates world consumer electronics. Now here they were with a proposal which if accepted would have amounted to "the surrender of the lucrative television revolution of the 1990s by the rest of the world to Japan without firing a shot" as one observer put it. At one stroke it would make existing TV obsolete, and provide the Japanese with the opportunity to provide replacement TV sets. The biggest consumer market of all, by far, would be theirs.

In view of the huge investment in existing TV systems this was too much for the Europeans who reacted sharply. The Americans also changed their minds about supporting the Japanese proposals. HDTV is one of the major systems which is expected to run on future broadband networks. During the next ten years very large investments are likely to be made in HDTV primarily for the purpose of domestic entertainment.

The major HDTV technical systems can only be briefly discussed in this chapter in order to leave room for the politics which are arguably more important. For a comprehensive review of the technical background, see Rzeszewski (1990). Another source of HDTV and Television information about all kinds of television equipment, general progress, description of the work being done at companies and institutions etc., is the SMPTE annual review, the latest in Anon 1990.

The Expected Improvements

Without going into too much technical detail (see Gaggioni 1987 for a good review of the problems), un-natural effects are produced in existing TV from colour artefacts such as "dot-crawl" and patterning of various kinds, from scanning artefacts such as flicker and low frequency patterns, and from bandwidth limitations which limit picture detail and produce a break-up of motion. The shape of the picture is also far from ideal.

High definition Television provides improved viewing approaching that of a cinema theatre. The number of lines are increased so that more detail becomes visible and the screen is made considerably wider.

In the Information Technology field, display resolution is usually specified in terms of so many "dots per inch". The best available monochrome cathode ray tube display has a resolution of about 300 dots in the eleven inches available vertically on its "19 inch" (measured diagonally) screen. However the price of such a tube rules it completely out of court for TV receivers. In any case colour is at present unavailable with this kind of resolution. The actual TV display size is about 13.5" wide and 11" high on a 19" tube.

In the television world, display performance is expressed in terms of the number of lines on the screen. On the CRT display just described, there would be slightly over 3000 lines, which is adequate for almost any viewing requirement (Infante 1985). Standard 35mm film has a resolution equivalent to well over 2000 lines, but, for various reasons, the net effective viewing resolution in a motion picture theatre is about 800 lines (Kaiser 1985).

Some idea of the effect of increasing the resolution/bandwidth may be assessed from the illustrations in Figure 26.2. These are photocopies of

650

colour photographs so have suffered in reproduction. Three enlargements of
the area within the rectangle in the main photograph are shown. The effect
on the resolution as the transmission bandwidth is increased is clear
although in the original colour photographs (these are photocopies) it is
very marked.

Note.
These illustrations are simulations of television-screen pictures
shown here by courtesy of Eastman Kodak. Photographs on 35 mm
film were scanned with a 2000 dots/inch flying spot scanner
and the digitised results were processed to simulate on the lower
left 500 lines with 3.78 MHz bandwidth, centre 1000 lines 17.6 MHz
bandwidth, right 1400 lines 74 MHz bandwidth.

To bring
an added note
of realism the
width of the
picture needs
to be wider
than it is on
a normal tel-
evision set.
According to
some research
carried out by
Philips at
Eindhoven, HD-
TV "will have
absolutely no
effect in many
living rooms
if not comb-
ined with an
increase in
picture width"
(Westerink 19-
89).

HDTV re-
search in Jap-
an (Hatada
1980) indic-
ates that
a horizontal
viewing an-
gle of about
30C° at a
viewing dis-
tance of three
times the
screen height
is required.
For long

FIGURE 26.2. EFFECT OF CHANGING THE BANDWIDTH

viewing periods or for watching rapid motion, the distance should be
increased to four times. The actual width used for HDTV depends on the
standard adopted, as discussed below.

The Japanese consider that the width:height ratio should be 5:3 and that under the viewing conditions just discussed, increasing resolution above 1125 lines would not produce an appreciable improvement.

For a technical discussion about the effects of resolution and picture size on quality see Barten (1989).

Events in Japan

A year after the postponement mentioned in the Introduction above, the Japanese again proposed that the system which they had invented for High Definition Television (HDTV) should become a world standard.

Needless to say, at this meeting - of the International Committee of Radiodiffusion (CCIR) at Dubrovnik held in May 1986 - resistance to the proposal had hardened.

The Japanese approach is to introduce an entirely new system which will displace existing TV, using a method for compressing the signals called Multiple Sub-Nyquist Sampling Encoding (MUSE). It was developed by a team under Takashi Fujio, Director General of the research laboratories of NHK, the Japan Broadcasting Corporation. Advances are so rapid that the MUSE receiver decoder which originally contained 200 chips and 50 printed circuit boards has been reduced to 96 chips and 2 printed circuit boards. No doubt further reductions are pending.

An associated system called Advanced Definition TV (ADTV) or Extended Definition Television (EDTV) for terrestrial broadcasting includes "Narrow MUSE" and a version of MUSE which is compatible with the existing NTSC system, possibly a contender for adoption in the US (Ono 1990).

In ADTV, HDTV data, including separated brightness and colour signals, ghost cancelling signals, and other processing data is broadcast in a separate 6 MHz channel. Existing receivers do not pick up this channel and reproduce a normal NTSC image. HDTV receivers pick up signals from the additional channel and reproduce a 16:9 picture shape.

NHK charge a $200,000 licence fee for information about the MUSE decoder. As at July 1990 only one US company, Texas Instruments, had paid for a licence.

In 1988, the international demonstration opportunity presented by the 1988 Seoul Olympics was taken up, and with each £40,000 1125 line 37-inch screen receiver, specially made and paid for by the PTT, NHK installed over 200 sets in public places.

Transmissions were started via the BS-2 satellite in June 1989, for one hour per day. Full HDTV service was planned for late 1990. Special receivers are required since HDTV cannot be received on any existing sets. Toshiba has developed a compatible video recorder capable of running for 3 hours.

The Japanese Ministry of International Trade & Industry (MITI) and NHK are organising the production of receivers from 9 different Japanese manufacturers. The target selling price is $4000. Sony has developed an HDTV camera, smaller than typical existing cameras, which they expect to be able to sell for $75,000.

Sony have also developed an HDTV videodisc player and, as at August 1989, had sold 40 of them at $25,000 each with discs which play for up to 15 minutes and cost $1600 each.

Two private organisations have been established to publicise HDTV. A company called Koudo Eizo does tests and research on technology while Nihon Hi Vision rents studio, transmitting, and receiving equipment.

In mid-1989 the Japanese introduced a simple alternative to HDTV called Clear Vision (they call HDTV Hi-Vision). In clear Vision the TV camera records on 1125 lines which studio equipment converts to 525 lines for transmission. A Clear Vision receiver contains a frame store which records each frame and displays it twice. Apparently this produces a remarkable improvement. New television sets with Clear Vision already sell for only £1600. A special reference pulse is broadcast with Clear Vision which is compared with a pulse generated in the receiver, enabling ghost images to be cancelled.

With this kind of committed effort and investment, plus the effort being put in on display devices described below, it is hard to see how anyone can catch the Japanese. Whatever standards are adopted in Europe and the US, the Japanese should get a substantial part of the business.

The European Reaction

The Japanese proposal united the European manufacturers and establishment as never before. Had it been accepted, and the system and the television receivers had been manufactured and marketed, then all the world's existing television systems and receivers would have become obsolete. The television market would probably have gone the way of cars, cameras, video recorders etc.,which have become totally Japanese dominated.

The European approach is to introduce HDTV in a series of steps which will not displace existing technology, and will not add significant costs to receivers at each step.

The Single European Act, signed in 1985 by the 12 member states, includes a requirement to strengthen the scientific and technological basis of European industry. Accordingly the Community has done some work on the adoption of a new broadcasting standard for satellite TV and the development of European HDTV technology. For TV transmitted via satellite, the new broadcasting standard will mean the end of the division of Europe into PAL and SECAM.

They will be replaced by MAC standards (see below) supposed to be introduced in late 1989/1990 in the TDF1, TVSAT2, BSB, and Olympus satellites. Signals from these satellites would be receivable on new MAC receivers and also on existing PAL and SECAM sets with the addition of a low cost converter.

The European reaction was organised jointly by the European Commission and 30 electronics companies led by Robert Bosch, West Germany; Philips, Netherlands; Thomson, France, and Thorn EMI, U.K. The EC provided additional funds under the Eureka programme.

The objective has been to develop an HDTV system to be proposed as a European, if not a world standard, at a CCIR meeting in 1990. In March 1989 the EC decided to increase their support of the U.K. and West German HDTV effort in the Eureka programme, providing up to 36% of the U.K.'s expenditure of about $20M in the years 1986 - 1990 and up to 50% of West Germany's spending of about $48M in the period 1984 - 1990.

In November 1989 the EEC states, under the aegis of the Commission, discussed the idea of a strategic alliance between HDTV equipment manufacturers, TV stations, and programme producers for television and the cinema - reminiscent of Japanese MITI strategies. In December the Commission convened a meeting to launch the European Economic Interest Group for HDTV - a meeting attended by representatives of consumers, manufacturers, programme producers, broadcasters and transmission authorities.

Dates around 1995 have been suggested for a start-up of HDTV broadcasting in Europe. The course which HDTV will follow during the next few years is uncertain. The political incentives to get on with it and the potential commercial gains are so high that it will certainly come, perhaps having a substantial impact on the telecommunication scene round about the year 2000.

Developments in the United States

The Americans do not yet appear to be mounting a very large HDTV effort, although it has been suggested that HDTV presents the last hope for their rapidly deteriorating consumer electronics industry.

Early in 1989 the Defence Advanced Research Projects Agency (DARPA) invited proposals for HDTV receiver displays and processors. It received 87 and selected 5 for funding out of its $30M allocated for the purpose.

In 1989, the American Electronics Association, representing a group of US electronics companies, said that a minimum of $1.3 billion of Federal aid would be needed to organise a competitive HDTV system.

In February 1989 AT&T and Zenith announced a $24M project to develop an HDTV receiver able to receive signals within the NTSC specified bandwidth of 6 MHz. Additional information is sent during the short intervals between successive frames. AT&T expects to develop Gallium Arsenide - a semiconductor technology capable of very fast switching - for signal processing.

In February 1991 it was announced that this digital system would be demonstrated in November 1991. A new compression algorithm will be used so that the signal can be sent through a 6 MHz television channel. The receiver will include a signal processor working at one thousand million operations per second for decoding and picture formatting.

Philips plans to build a $100M factory for making HDTV picture tubes in the U.S. They expect to produce tubes with screens of about 30" size.

In September 1988 the US Federal Communications Commission (FCC) stipulated that NTSC receivers must not be replaced; HDTV signals should be transmitted in such a way that NTSC sets could receive the programmes or they should be transmitted on a separate channel. In both cases the programmes would be seen on NTSC sets, but special sets would be needed to display them in HDTV form.

An HDTV bill was introduced in the House of Representatives in March 1989 to provide funding for an industry Consortium, probably to be defined by the American Electronics Association. Funding of $100M a year for a 5 year period was proposed, and tax incentives for R & D were also suggested.

The Alternative Standards

The Europeans and the Japanese now both have proposals for different international standards (Jurgen 1989). There are a number of proposals in the United States - a representative system is Advanced Compatible TV (ACTV), similar to the Japanese ACTV/EDTV, being tested at the Sarnoff Research Centre.

The main features dictating HDTV performance are the number of lines considered necessary for adequate resolution, the rate for repeating each complete picture frame in order to provide the illusion of a steady flicker-free picture, the frame width, and the bandwidth needed for the telecommunications channel. The characteristics of three major systems are shown in Table 26.1.

Systems	Picture shape (W H)	No. lines	Frames per sec.	Compression : Bandwidth (MHz) Before	After	Bit-rate if digit- ised (Mbps)
NHK HDTV	5:3	1125	60	30	8 (Muse)	2000 (appr)
HD-MAC	16:9	1250	50	25	12	
ACTV	16:9	1050	60	-	6 (Sep.ch.)	

TABLE 26.1. PROPOSED HDTV STANDARDS

The proposed European Standard developed under Eureka is derived from a scheme by the Independent Broadcasting Authority (IBA) for TV DBS satellite transmission in the U.K. called Multiplexed Analogue Component (MAC). The Eureka variation, HD-MAC, doubles the number of lines from 625 to 1250 and increases the width of the picture. Ordinary TV sets receiving the signals will reproduce a normal picture.

To transmit the signals a channel bandwidth of 25 MHz is required so a compression system is used to reduce the required bandwidth to 12 MHz - feasible for available satellite channels. The compression system works by digitising the picture with a computer which decides, on a frame to frame basis, which parts of the picture contain motion and which do not.

A fast data rate is needed for the difference signal required to supply new data about motion for each succeeding frame. A slow data rate suffices for describing stationary parts of the picture because there is no frame-to-frame change of information.

At the receiver the picture is produced by combining decoded data about stationary and moving parts. The HD-MAC system broadcasts at 625 lines accompanied by the necessary codes to double the number to 1250 and supply additional data. 625 lines are received so if the set is a conventional PAL 625 line TV, it cannot receive the doubling and other codes, so it reproduces a standard PAL picture. If it is an HDTV receiver with wide screen etc., it receives the extra data and a wide 1250 line picture is reproduced. In other words the system does not make existing receivers obsolete.

A Codec (Coder-Decoder) has been developed under the Eureka project (Molo 1990) for HDTV digital transmission with several commercial applications in mind:-

1. High quality links between television studios.

2. Outside point-to-point transmissions, videoconferencing, electronic distribution of films to cinemas.

3. Digital TV distribution via satellite in lieu of Analogue.

A version of HD-MAC called D2-MAC was to be adopted as the European Standard and used in the proposed British Satellite Broadcasting (BSB) service. BSB was taken over by Sky Television in 1990, committed to using PAL with its Astra satellite. EC rules dictate the use of D2-MAC which is needed for HDTV. Thomson have made a very large investment in D2-MAC systems.

The 1991 controversy is a battle between the here-and-now commercially feasible (Sky) and the need for paving the way for a more advanced future (EC). Some kind of compromise seems likely. One contender in such a compromise would probably be "Extended PAL" with a 16:9 screen, due to be demonstrated in August 1991, compatible with standard PAL. It may be better to use this system with fairly large CRTs and await the lighter, cheaper HDTV displays expected in the late nineties for digital HDTV. CRTs of a suitable size for currently proposed full HDTV would be expensive and extremely heavy (Loe 1990).

A TV colour signal of over 1000 lines requires a bandwidth of 25 MHz or more, compared with 6 MHz for conventional TV. To digitise HDTV - the way all signals will eventually be transported - a bit rate of around 2 Gbps may be required. To overcome difficulties associated with this rate there have been two lines of technical attack - firstly, compress the signals using certain digital techniques in the process, and secondly devise a system which is compatible with existing systems.

Developing Special Display Devices

It seems likely that whatever the outcome of existing controversies and differing proposals for Standards, the company which successfully develops and manufactures a flat panel display which measures at least 40" diagonally and produces a picture as bright as a conventional TV picture, will corner the market. It is very likely that the company will be Japanese.

In October 1988, MITI and 12 Japanese companies asked for $40M to help fund the development of a liquid crystal display with an area of one square metre. The Ministry of Posts and Telecoms together with four other companies has asked the Japan Key Technology Centre for $30M for a similar project. Recent progress has been described by Tannas (1989).

Plasma panel displays, which work by switching rows of very small elements which glow when energised, have been developed up to a 20" size but they are not bright enough. NHK hope to produce a 50" plasma panel for HDTV by 1992.

By 1989 MITI and the 12 company consortium had increased their commitment to $400M for the large liquid crystal display. Meanwhile improved large displays have been produced using three projection cathode ray tubes with 6" screens, one for each colour. A picture up to 5 ft. wide can be provided. Kawashima (1988) and others have described a receiver with a 50" rear project display and another receiver with a 180" projection display for use in theatres. Receivers using back projection on to a 40" screen are expected to sell for $3000 in the 1990s - about the same price as consumers paid for a colour television receiver in the United States in the 1950s.

HDTV and 35 mm Film

Film is, of course, a major information and educational media as well as being the media for "The Movies" - whether in cinemas or via television. Directly viewed pictures from 35mm film are of high quality; that quality is unlikely to survive its passage through the system when film is shown on TV.

Problems include the aspect-ratio of film (bits get cut off the sides on narrower TV screens), dealing with this difficulty before it gets on television by transferring from film to videotape centralising the action during the process, or having to use poorer quality 16mm film for distributing copies of about the right aspect ratio for TV.

If the public gets accustomed to the high quality of non-film HDTV, with digital wideband (wideband audio, that is) sound, and eventually with fully digitised picture transmission, the lower quality of material broadcast from film and shown on HDTV will become glaringly obvious.

The costs of making a film on 35mm stock, and considerations about making a profit from the showing of the film at the movies and from showing it on TV with acceptable quality, may bring about the radical change of making it on HDTV videotape in the first place. In the late 1990s perhaps cinemas will enjoy a short lived resurgence by showing Features from HDTV tape. It will be short-lived because the incentive of "getting out to see a big-screen movie" will diminish once you've got a high quality big screen at home.

Will "film entertainment" of the future be reduced to viewing videotape recordings on TV at home, 35mm film having become obsolete? Exactly how will the elaborate chain of creation and distribution in the existing film industry be affected? Will 35mm film still be used, but specifically re-designed for HDTV use or will it simply disappear?

HDTV Growth Rates and Markets

MITI estimates the market for HDTV at $6 Billion for hardware and $2 Billion for programming. Appreciable market penetration to typical consumers is expected in 1995. There is no doubt that the Japanese are making the same single-minded effort and are using the same strategies to capture the market that they have used so successfully in other fields. They are already considering the programme-supply aspect of HDTV by buying US companies in the entertainment business.

In a survey conducted by the IEEE in the US, 80% of technically oriented consumers said they would pay more for an HDTV receiver than for an ordinary television set. About half of these said they would pay 25% more, rather less than half said they would pay up to 75% more, and about 10% said they would pay more than 75% more. Half of this sample said they watched television less than 1 hour a day and the other half watched an average of about 4 hours. Their families watched television more than they did.

In a report from the U.S. Congressional Budget Office it was estimated that the market for HDTV in the US would reach $140 Billion during the next 20 years. The American Electronics Association believes that a successful entry into the HDTV market would bring 700,000 new jobs, and assure the security for thousands of existing jobs.

HDTV represents a significant market for semiconductors. Dataquest estimate that it would be worth $641M for European HD-MAC standard equipment alone. The American Electronics Association makes certain assumptions for start-up dates when assessing the HDTV chip market (Iverson 1989). If a system for enhanced definition TV starts broadcasting in 1993 in the US, the chip market for the appropriate receivers is estimated at about $450M by the year 2000. If HDTV broadcasting starts in 1996, the market would be about $100M by 2000, climbing to $700M by 2010.

Technical Futures

The foregoing discussion has been confined to the distribution of HDTV by satellite channels - Japanese and European satellites have been mentioned - one way of achieving widespread distribution of wideband data in a number of selectable channels for entertainment purposes.

But it is not the only way. There are several other aspects to be considered:-

1. The transmission of fully digitised television signals.

At present the quality of television suffers because of the passage of the TV signals through the chain of mainly analogue paths and continuing use of the basically analogue systems. One major reason for retaining this technique for some time is that the enormous installed investment, much of it made by consumers, can only be replaced slowly.

The benefits of digitisation in overcoming problems associated with noise and amplification. The comparative ease with which processing may be carried out on digital systems is well known.

2. HDTV digital signal transmission through Cable.

The transmission of HDTV digital signals over fibreoptic cable is being carried out in Japan. The data rate is 400 Megabits per second (Mbps) for a digitised HDTV signal which occupies a bandwidth of 20 MHz in analogue form. Various bit rates have been proposed in Germany and Japan at up to

2.24 Gigabits per second (Gbps) over main distribution cables and at up to 400 Mbps over subscriber lines. High-speed chips for switching such signals are being developed.

3. Cable and Public Networks as a media for HDTV.

Cable networks - that is wideband cable passing along a street to which household may be connected - has penetrated over half US households. Cable is used almost entirely to provide multi-channel TV entertainment. It is even more widely used in some European countries, particularly, Switzerland, Holland and Belgium.

The gradual regulatory thaw has encouraged UK Cable operators to try out quite different kinds of service. Thus in 1987 Windsor Cable arranged for a connection to Mercury and started a pilot telephone service aimed at local businesses.

Cable installations started with short runs of twisted pair wires which could carry a few TV channels, but most now use co-axial cable, capable of carrying many more. Co-ax will be replaced by fibreoptic cables in due course providing sufficient bandwidth for numerous channels, two way services, and HDTV.

Other Wideband Networks

Public telephone systems are gradually being changed into wideband networks. Inter-exchange channels are already digitised and wideband digital exchanges are being installed in many countries. The provision of subscriber-to-subscriber digitised speech and data services is constrained by the "local loop" wiring - the copper-pair between the local exchange and the customer which stands outside the major digitisation effort.

The Integrated Services Digital Network (ISDN) - requiring end-to-end digitisation - is being slowly introduced. In the UK it may take to "the end of the century" (Garbutt 1985). The next stage is to move towards the Broadband ISDN (B-ISDN) and the Integrated Broadband Communication Network (IBCN). Development work is proceeding under the RACE programme, set up by the DGXIII division of the EC in 1985 and backed by 1.1 billion ecu - about £700M. Over 300 PTTs, universities and companies are involved.

The term "Intelligent Network" was coined in the US for a post-ISDN development to "create services defined by customers, introduce standard interfaces to encourage a wide choice of suppliers of compatible equipment, and to create a flexible network architecture".

The CCITT will publish details about the objectives and provide a description for a European Intelligent Network in 1990 and expects to have interface specifications ready in 1991. Such a network would combine transmission and switching with data processing, and unify public, private, mobile, and VAN services. Integrated services for public and private use would be provided. Such a network would be all-digital and fibre with end to end network management.

In short, a "terrestrial" delivery systems is developing in parallel with satellites, and unless Cable operators can see a return on installing fibreoptic cable through to homes within the next few years, satellites may get their first, perhaps on some scale by the end of this decade. Delivery through a public wideband network is further away - perhaps around 2010, or later.

At some stage someone may realise that all these immense un-coordinated efforts to create public and private networks which may include separate entertainment-led wideband satellite and fibreoptic networks, are separate empires waiting to be interconnected to form a single universal network. It remains to be seen whether there will then be a period of painful political and technical convergence leading to a single connection for households, offices, businesses, etc., through which all communications to the outside world will flow.

The impact of all this on information services becomes evident when it is remembered that an efficiently compressed page of text, with a quarter-page 3CO dots/inch halftone photograph containing about 1.4 Mbits of data included in it, would take about 5 minutes to transmit over the Public Switched Telephone Network.

A communication channel capable of transporting HDTV signals could be multiplexed (split up) into 100 independent channels each capable of about 4 Megabits per second reducing the time to send the page to about 0.3 seconds, at what should be a very small fraction of today's prices.

REFERENCES

Anderla, Georges.
  Information World Review, page 10, January 1991.
    The Minitel challenge must make online hosts reassess.
Anon.
  Report published jointly by the BBC, IBA, and BREMA.
  London, October 1974 (The "White Book").
    Specification of standards for information transmission
    by digitally coded signals in the field blanking interval
    of 625 line television signals.
Anon.
  Report published by the Department of Trade & Industry
  DTI, London, 1985 (CEPT specifications).
    World system teletext technical specification (revised
    March, 1985).
Anon.
  Information Media & Technology 20(1), page 13, 1987.
    Prestel: new network - new features.
Anon.
  Information Market Observatory report 89/7, CEC Luxembourg 1989.
    The impact of videotex on the online market.
Anon.
  SMPTE Journal, 276-317, April 1990.
    Television.
Arbuthnot, Charles P., Hudson, G.P.
  IEEE Trans. Consumer Electronics CE 32 (3), 538-540, 1985.
    A low cost high performance picture display for photovideotex.
Atwater, Tony, Heater, C., et al.
  Journalism Quarterly, 62, 807-815, 1985.
    Foreshadowing the electronic publishing age: first
    exposures to viewtron.

660

Barten, Peter G.J.
  Proc. SID 30(2), 67-71, 1989.
    The effects of picture size and definition on perceived image quality.
Buckley, Paul, and Long, John.
  Behaviour & Information Technology 9(1), 47-61, 1990.
    Using videotex for shopping - a qualitative analysis.
Fedida, S.
  Post Office Research Department Report 564, Martlesham Heath,
  England, September 1976.
    Viewdata and Teletext as complimentary information
    systems.
Fedida, S.
  Wireless World 83 (1497) pps 32-36, 51-54, 65-69, 55-59
  February-May 1977, 84 (1508) pps 43-49, April 1978.
    Viewdata (in 5 parts).
Fedida, S.
  In Elton, M.C.J. et al (Eds). Evaluating new telecommunications
  services. Plenum Press, 1978. pages 531-567.
    Viewdata networks.
Fenn, P. Susan and Buckley, P.K.
  Behaviour & Information Technology 9(1), 63-80, 1990.
    Ordering goods with videotex, or just fill in the
    details.
Forster, W.A. et al
  Aslib Information 16(5), 116-129, May 1988.
    Videotex special section.
Gaggioni, H.P.
  IEEE Communications Magazine 25(11), 20-36, November 1987.
    The evolution of video technologies.
Garbutt, B.N.
  British Telecommunications Engineering 3, 300-303, January 1985.
    Digital restructuring of the British Telecom network.
Green-Armytage, J.
  Computer Weekly, August 1st, 1985.
    Prestel profits at six.
Griffiths, Ann Vernon., et al.
  Aslib Information 17(5), 123-127, May 1989.
    Videotex special section.
Grover, Varun, and Sabherwal, R.
  Journal of Systems Management, 31-37, June 1989.
    Poor Performance of videotex systems.
Hatada, T., Sakata, H.. and Kusaka, H.
  SMPTE J., 89, 650-659, August 1980.
    Psychophysical analysis of the sensation of reality
    induced by a visual wide-field display.
Infante, C.
  Proc. SID 26(1), 23-26, 1985.
    On the resolution of raster scanned CRT displays.
Iverson, Wesley R.
  Electronics, 70-75, March 1989.
    US gropes for unity on HDTV.
Jurgen, Ronald K.
  IEEE Spectrum 26(10), 26-30, October 1989.
    Chasing Japan in the HDTV race.

Kaiser, A., Mahler, H.W.
  SMPTE J., 654-659, June 1985.
    Resolution requirements for HDTV based on the
    performance of 35mm motion picture films for
    theatrical viewing.
Kawahata, M., and Miyabe J.
  In Mastroddi, Franco (Ed.). Electronic publishing; the new way
  to communicate. Kogan Page, London for the CEC. 1987.
    Social impacts of new electronic publishing media - some
    findings of the Hi-Ovis experiment.
Kawashima, Masahiro, Yamamoto, K., et al.
  IEEE Trans. Consumer Electronics 34(1), 88-109, February 1988.
    Display and projection devices for HDTV.
Kusekoski, Gene.
  MIS Quarterly, 446-456, December 1989.
    Corporate videotex: a strategic business information
    system.
Lippman, Andrew.
  Byte 15(13), 297-305, December 1990.
    HDTV sparks a digital revolution.
Loe, Simon.
  Electronic World News, page 3, December 10th 1990.
    Europe's HDTV in disarray.
Molo, Francesco.
  Telecommunications, 47-55, July 1990.
    Development trends in high definition television.
Ninke, William N.
  Proc. IEEE 73(4), 740-753, 1985.
    Design considerations of NAPLPS, the data syntax for
    videotex and teletext in North America.
Noll, Michael A.
  Information & Management 9, 99-109, 1985.
    Videotex: anatomy of failure.
Ono, Yozo.
  SMPTE Journal, 4-15, January 1990.
    HDTV and today's broadcasting world.
Raymond, Darell R.
  Canadian Journal of Information Science 14(1), 27-38, 1989.
    Why videotex is (still) a failure.
Rzeszewski, Theodore S.
  Proc. IEEE 78(5), 789-804, May 1990.
    A technical assessment of advanced television.
Scales, Ian.
  Communications Management, page 11, March 1986.
    Pictures on a screen.
Shoji, Kimiaki, Okamoto, S. et al.
  NTT Review 1(3), 49-56, September 1989.
    Great progress in new visual communication systems - Hi-Captain,
    VRS, C&DS.
Tannas, Lawrence E.
  IEEE Spectrum 26(10), 31-34, October 1989.
    HSRC displays in Japan; projection CRT systems.
Terayama, Yukio, Kozasa, S., et al.
  NTT Review 1(3), 31-37, September 1989.
    Transformation of the Captain system - rapidly adapting to individual
    needs.

662

Ungerer, Herbert.
  European Perspective Series. CEC Brussels 1988. Available from
  CEC Luxembourg. Page 156.
    Telecommunications in Europe.
Weinstein, Caroline.
  Communications Management, 17-22, May 1987.
    It's as easy as ABC.
Westerink, J., and Roufs, J.A.J.
  SMPTE J., 113-119, February 1989.
    Subjective image quality as a function of the viewing
    distance, resolution, and picture size.

CHAPTER 27. MICROFORM SYSTEMS

Introduction and history

The first patent for microfilm was granted in 1859. Microfilm was used during the Franco-Prussian war to send carrier pidgeon messages from besieged Paris in 1871. Little use of the technique was made until microfilming was carried out in libraries during the first world war to ensure the preservation of important material. Wider use came with the the the Kodak Recordak continuous microfilm recording camera developed in 1927. This camera was used in 1928 to photograph cheques. Microform images were viewed in a US court to identify endorsements in a fraud case in the following year.

In the 1930s an American, Eugene Power, realised that microfilming could be used to bring copies of documents in European libraries to US libraries. He founded University Microfilms, still thriving today, to do the job.

Atherton Seidell used film strips called Filmstats in a microform system in 1935 and in 1939 he microfilmed periodicals at the US Army Medical Library, later to become the National Library of Medicine. During the 1939-45 war, microfilming of air-letters was extensively carried out for weight-reduction purposes, but microforms did not become generally used until well after the war.

Micrographic Systems provide for the creation, processing, retrieval, and reproduction of small images for viewing. **Microforms** are photographs of images, often from printed pages, which have been reduced in size for easier storage. Special machines are available for page photography which usually operate on a step and repeat basis using either a flat bed or rotary method.

The Annual Review of Information Science and Technology prepared under the aegis of the American Society for Information Science includes chapters about basic techniques and technologies. A chapter about Microforms appeared in 1969, and in 1970, 1971, 1973, and 1976. In the 1969 review chapter, the writer concluded "Microform technology is not well. It is a field riddled with unsystematic disconnected collections of gimmicks masquerading as systems".

In the more recent (1976) review, the writer concluded "Microform has almost disappeared. The most important trend has been and will continue to be the interaction of microforms into larger information systems... the real growth will come from the "disappearance" of microforms by integration into systems where they are appropriate". He forecasted, possibly correctly, the greater use of COM, and incorrectly, its increasing use for document delivery in conjunction with online retrieval systems.

The decreasing frequency of the chapters and then their absence from 1977 onwards, and the decreasing number of references to microforms in the comprehensive index provided with each edition are evidence of microform's decline - at least in the areas covered by the Annual Review.

However the 1987 Review contains the statement (Lunin 1987):-
"There is also renewed interest in using microfiche for storage and retrieval of large quantities of images and videodisk technology. A

minicomputer that stores the microfilm address and descriptors and controls the retrieval of specific document images can be used to create and maintain the image database". But this "renewed interest" seems to be based on just one system.

In 1980, Bernard Williams, the leading UK microform authority, wrote a defensive article in the face of what he called "microchip jitters" (Williams 1980). He claims that the steady growth of about 20% per annum continues and that microforms have come into widespread use for the storage of business documents, providing several examples, and citing situations where microforms score -

1. For storage and retrieval of engineering drawings, maps, plans, and similar documents.
2. As a third mode of computer output complimenting paper and online access.
3. For publications where demand in printed format would make production uneconomic.
4. For utility publishing of parts lists, patents, theses, etc.

Williams admits that although viewing devices have improved they need to be better but considers that neither print nor microfilm will be easily displaced. However he anticipates inroads from videotex and videodisk.

The development of microform systems seem to have reached a plateau. They are not greatly different today to what they were ten years ago. Microforms seem to have found their niche where there is a requirement for the distribution of reference data which needs to be periodically up-dated at intervals greater than a day or two.

The up-dating costs are low; massive quantities of information on cheap fiche cards are simply replaced by massive quantities of information on new ones sent by post. People will put up with reading a few lines of references or component data on a viewer, knowing that it is up to date.

For page by page reading, microforms are sometimes used in libraries to provide access to a very large collection of documents or books. It may not be possible to justify the storage cost of print on paper for massive volumes in city centres for public useage when the demand is relatively small.

A cabinet of fiche and a viewer may be a cost-effective substitute if the once only filming and indexing cost can be justified; the filming job may, of course, already have been done elsewhere. Library clients, confronted by a situation where they can have access to a collection - for example of UK House of Commons proceedings (Hansard) - which otherwise could not be on site, have to use the microform viewers (unwillingly - see below).

In the introduction to a very good review article (Cox 1987), the author reviews many major microform projects in the library field. But almost without exception these projects were initiated before 1980; there is very little discussion about present or future projects.

Nevertheless Cox points to the continuing importance of microforms which :- "bring benefits to the users of academic libraries especially in the humanities and the social sciences. The use of microcopying to preserve the contents of books... subject to acidic decay has been with us for fifty years but is becoming yet more important".

The author discusses other aspects:- "Librarians have been virtually the only customers for micropublications yet they have had very little influence over the suppliers. Because they are in a completely different format from books, microforms have presented special problems in acquisition, cataloguing, and use".

"Despite early predictions, microphotography has not radically altered the nature of libraries and has not been generally used to save space. It is passing through a transitional phase because of the development of computers and other new equipment. Computer Output Microform catalogues are now commonly to be found in libraries".

Cox says, in passing:- "The market for scholarly reprints began to take off at the end of the 1950s. The continuing aversion of readers to microforms was in no small way responsible".

Blick (1984) discusses the standard library problem about what to do about the constant pressure for more shelf space for journal issues. He decided to subscribe to the fiche edition as well as to the hard copy of each journal, discarding the hard copies after 3-5 years. He provided manually operated readers for library users and a reader-printer for library staff for the supply of hard copy of old journals to users when requested.

Most journals can be purchased alternatively on fiche. The cost of hard copy and fiche editions for some typical journals are shown in Table 27.1 (after Blick). The net extra cost of this policy was 7.5% on to the primary journal budget excluding the reduced costs of inter-library loans and saved space. Positive fiche (i.e. black print on a white background) was preferred. Blick stresses the need to carry users with you when introducing fiche and states that not only will the library now have substantial back runs but it will not require additional space for ten years. The majority of users realised the need for the new policy and accepted it.

Journal	Hard copy	Fiche
Brit.J.Canc.	£ 85	£ 8.77*
Experientia	£122.15	£ 12.34*
J.Physiol.	£315	£ 40.26*
Bioch.Pharm.	£307.35	£146.34x
Tetrahedron	£460.98	£219.51x

* from University Microfilms
x from Pergamon Press

TABLE 27.1. JOURNAL COSTS

Public libraries use COM (see below) produced fiche for book catalogues, banks use microforms for current account balances, and garages use them for parts catalogues. Although Com/fiche systems in libraries will be around for some years yet, they will gradually be replaced by CD-ROM systems or terminals on-line to remote computer databases. Computer based on-line library catalogues are one out of many services available via the same terminal/telecoms facilities. Fiche-based business systems are unlikely to survive.

In mid-1984 a Kodak representative claimed that optical disks (ODs) would not displace microforms in the forseeable future. He pointed out that equipment was available for digitising microfilm so the advantages of digitisation did not lie exclusively with ODs.

Placing the UK cost of optical storage work stations then available at £50,000, which is far higher than microform equipment with the same capacity, he also compared OD costs at £200 for 10,000 A4 documents with a £5 roll of microfilm capable of storing 50,000 A4 documents. But the future came nearer more quickly than expected. Optical-disc based systems are being used instead (See Chapter 10).

COM and other computer assisted microform systems will continue to be used in Banking, Government, Insurance, and Utilities, for correspondence, accounts, correspondence, computer assisted graphics, and micro-facsimile, but will gradually be displaced by other systems.

MICROFORM TYPES

Film

Microforms may be produced as image frames on 35mm roll film typically 30 metres long, contained in a cassette or cartridge. The film can be run through a motorised viewing machine which may have facilities for frame selection using a code, such as a bar code, signifying indexing terms which were filmed with the image.

The machine stops at those frames containing terms selected from a keyboard and a frame is reproduced at a convenient size for viewing by means of a light source, optical system and viewing screen. Some machines provide for the printing of a copy of the image.

Fiche

Alternatively microforms may be produced in flat film format. With **Microfiche**, the most common, a number of images are stored on a piece of photographic film, typically as a 6 x 4 inch film card. A popular reduction size is x 42 with 208 frames per card. Size reductions have been used down to about x 140 providing 3200 frames per card (NCR PCMI ultra-fiche).

In a manually operated fiche-viewing machine the wanted fiche is roughly identified visually and the card, mounted on a movable carriage, is moved around beneath the viewing machine until the required frame is positioned for the projection of a magnified image, usually on a screen which is part of the machine.

Colour fiche

Colour fiche and colour fiche viewing equipment are available although not widely used. A x 24 reduction fiche at a processing cost of about 2 cents per frame is probably the most popular.

Computer Output Microfilm (COM)

The rate of production of microfiche can be increased by the Computer Output Microfilm (COM) technique in which images on a Cathode Ray Tube are successively microfilmed by a step and repeat camera at 250 frames per minute or more. The CRT is driven by a computer with software to control the generation of the images at high speed from data on tape.

Alternatively a film image may be created by a computer controlled laser beam writing on to thermally dry-processed film. COM fiche cards usually contain 270 images at x 48 reduction, or 208 at x 42. An eye-legible title is provided at the top of each card.

There are probably some thousands of COM users in Europe, and perhaps 20,000 or more in the US, the majority using COM bureaux production services. COM catalogues are fairly widely used in libraries where space saving and up-dating convenience may outweigh user resistance.

Computer Input Microfilm (CIM)

CIM is a term usually used to describe equipment which scans microfilm and converts the images to analogue or digital data to be telecommunicated for reconstruction remotely or stored for further processing. Compuscan, Digiscan, IBM and others manufacture equipment for this purpose.

RETRIEVAL SYSTEMS

In the late 60s and 70s, the microform world received the impact of convergence, integrated circuits, compact reliable electronics etc., and this led to the production of a number of automated viewing systems. Typically these systems consisted of an electrically operated magazine, "carousel" style, for holding a number of fiche cards, and a computer based indexing and retrieval system for selecting a fiche by means of a code associated with it. The fiche is then rapidly selected and projected from the computer-controlled carousel.

The computer, operator's terminal and fiche machine could be in the same room or on different sites with the machine accessible from several remote viewing CRT terminals. The selected image would be transmitted to a terminal CRT, television fashion, via a telecoms link.

One such machine, the Automated Microfiche Terminal, developed by GEC-Marconi, embodied a magazine housing 128 x 3500 fiche frames - a total of 448,000 A4 frames. The machine responded to a seven figure instruction which caused a particular frame on a particular fiche card to be positioned under the optical system within a few seconds.

A somewhat similar system was developed by Stabletron in the UK and marketed by Antone. The system comprised a carousel and an electronic image storage arrangement. A frame image selected by the computer-controlled carousel could be viewed remotely over a high resolution TV system beside terminal 1 while another frame was being selected by terminal 2.

With storage for several images the "store and hold" facility meant that the carousel was freed for on-going selection by any terminal while other viewers were gazing at their stored pictures, selected earlier. The system also embodied facilities for overlaying separately generated text on to fiche images.

A carousel manufactured by Image Systems (IS) became quite widely used in a number of automated systems. For example the Daily Mirror newspaper group used ten IS carousels controlled by a Univac computer for a morgue file. About 15 "Telefiche" systems, made by Planning Research Corp., were in use in the US in 1979. In this case characters from a fiche were

668

digitised, the fiche having been selected from a remote terminal. Data was sent along a telephone line to be displayed near the remote terminal.

Various combinations of microform image systems, computers, telecommunications systems etc., have since come into use in which the microform element has become one component in several converging IT systems.

Following an R&D programme said to have cost £5M, a company owned mainly by Combined Technologies Corporation (COMTECH) called Mnemos launched a new kind of system in 1982 and expected to commence UK deliveries in June 1984 from sub-contracted production carried out in the United States. The Mnemos 6000 work station consists of a keyboard, microcomputer 40 character digital display strip, optical disk drive, head, special disc, and a rear projection screen for viewing magnified microform images from the disc.

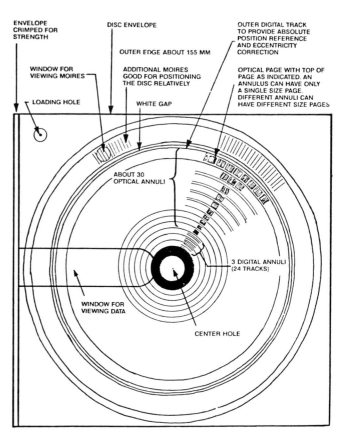

FIGURE 27.1. THE MNEMOS DISC

The flexible transparent disc, is housed in a jacket with a radial slot for optical access, looking rather like a large floppy disc, ready for loading into the work station (Figure 27.1). The outermost ring (annulus) on the disk contains moire fringes - visible as a "watered silk" pattern of lines - spaced with great accuracy. They are detected by a light beam projected through a hole in the disk cover. This provides a reference for very accurate disk positioning.

Glass master disks are prepared from customer taped data at Mnemos using a computer-controlled electron beam. Replicated plastic disks can be cheaply generated from them; Mnemos claim a fifty year life for these disks. Only Mnemos can make the master disks. A set of concentric rings in the middle area of the disk contain transparent microform frames recorded at x 88 reduction from which an image under the Reading Head (RH) may be projected on to an integral viewing screen.

The 6000 was aimed at organisations which needed to distribute large volumes of information for many users - in products such as parts catalogues, time-tables, engineering drawings, directories etc. It contained some innovative ideas but seems to have foundered; nothing has been heard of it since.

In 1984 Rank Xerox-Cintel announced the "Retriever" for retrieving film strips carrying 3000 frames per strip at a x 215 reduction. 300 or more strips were housed in a drum magazine. The required frame is selected from a keyboard and a CCD scanner converts the image to digital form which is then presented on a high resolution display.

The machine cost £50,000 with workstations at £10,000 each, and image photographic recording, to be carried out by Rank, was expected to cost about 3.5p per image. No further information has been received about this system.

Xerox in the US does not seem to have attempted to enter the microform market. In 1988/1989 it produced custom-built systems using non-microform storage for the US government, one of which replaced a microfiche system for engineering drawings.

VIEWING EQUIPMENT

Modern manual fiche viewers are compact and many produce clear images, provided the filmed images are properly recorded, but it is not easy to produce a really portable high quality viewer.

In 1972 an ingenious attempt was made to overcome the portability problem by Izon. The Izon book-size viewing machine used 500 tiny lenses spaced about one inch from an image on film reduced 25 times. The screen was 7" x 9" and the lense system eliminated the need for the usual long optical path which determines the minimum size of conventional viewers.

It was thought possible to mass produce the viewer and sell it for around $5. By 1978 $6M had been spent on R&D, and the selling price was expected to be $250 when mass produced. The machine has not been heard of since.

Cheap hand held viewers are available and briefcase size viewers were pioneered by Visidyne in the US with its rear projection 14 inch wide screen model. One of the most popular general purpose viewers was the German CUBE, later manufactured in the US. In the UK in the mid-eighties the Saul LG16 FCA at £235 for the basic model was a good general purpose machine.

Reader-printer 35mm roll film machines have been available for many years. The film is motor driven and is rapidly passed through the machine, stopping as instructed at a selected frame. Bar codes, sensed by the selection mechanism, are recorded along the edge of the film. The selected frame is magnified and projected for viewing and can be printed.

Affordable automatic fiche retrieval systems for general use (as opposed to the high capacity expensive machines already mentioned) have been available for some years. A portable microprocessor controlled machine made in Germany called FACTS sold in the UK as HYDRA for £2250 by Eurocom. This machine embodies a large screen, keyboard, and cassette-loading retrieval system.

A cassette will take 30 standard COM fiche cards so up to about 9000 frames can be stored. The normal method of use is to call up an index frame which provides a fiche number, and key that number to get the desired fiche. Retrieval time for any fiche is less than 4 seconds.

However the expected growth of automated systems or for that matter for all types of microform systems, has not taken place at anything like the rate of CRT-based image reproducing systems. On the face of it this is surprising because the aesthetics, convenience, portability, and text capacity of CRT systems leaves much to be desired.

Moreover the advantages of the printed page in respect of layout, captions, variety of fonts and information capacity are present in most fiche images, since they are usually reproductions of paper pages.

The reason may have something to do with people's familiarity with the CRT in another guise - the telly - a flashier (metaphorically) embodiment of a computer terminal - or the multi-function advantages of a terminal. You cannot manipulate text or blend information called from storage into the required format in a fiche system. A relatively low resolution CRT-based system is satisfactory for manipulating text, and text is more widely used than high resolution graphics. Fiche excels in the more limited application of the page by page reproduction of graphics.

ADVANTAGES OF MICROFORMS

Information can be stored on microform very cheaply. The comparative costs of media storage for 1 Mbyte (1979) were estimated as in Table 27.2. Since then disk storage has become cheaper but still leaving microform with a clear advantage. 1 Mbyte represents a page of text/graphics of fair quality. However even if the quality was improved for the reproduction of high quality graphics, the fiche cost would not increase much, always assuming that the costs of preparing the master fiche are defrayed over a number of copies.

	$
Microfiche	0.3
Floppy Disk	20
Mag.tape	5.2
8Mb diskpack	9.6

TABLE 27.2. COSTS OF STORAGE.

Huge amounts of information can be stored in a small space. Fiche is cheap to store, cheap to airmail, and rapidly produced. With optically viewed fiche the expense of high resolution and inherently wide bandwidth needed for comparable transmission and reproduction in electronic systems is absent.

However it is the complex mix of cost, convenience, competition and social and behavioural factors which determine whether a particular technology becomes widely adopted. It would seem that fiche could replace images on paper for many applications but has not done so.

Badly needed storage space could be released for other purposes in offices, libraries etc. I still possess a 2" x 2" fiche, used at one time as an advertisement by a fiche supplier, containing the 800,000 words of the Bible on 1245 pages - an area reduction of 62,500 times. At this reduction the contents of the British Museum library could be stored in a few filing cabinets.

You would think that a fiche cabinet surrounded by microform viewing machines would by now be commonplace in libraries and offices. This would result not only in space economy but also in many fringe benefits such as ease of handling, low cost of storage space, easier administrative control etc. The fact is that such a scenario is not commonplace.

DISADVANTAGES OF MICROFORMS

The reasons for the unpopularity of microforms compared to print on paper seem to be as follows:-

1. Some microform originals or some viewers produce fuzzy images. Some are hard   to use or cannot be viewed off-axis.

2. The wanted image may take time to find. Special attention must be paid to the overall speed of microform retrieval because unlike print on paper, images are not immediately visible. Perhaps the special need for good indexing does not receive the attention it deserves in some systems.

3. You cannot annotate or make marks on microforms.

4. Microforms are not portable. You cannot read them in the train or the loo (UK/US translation = john).

5. Cross referencing, scanning, browsing etc., is not so convenient. This indicates an even greater need for good indexing.

The unpopularity of microforms for users have prompted many articles. At a conference of the National Micrographics Association, the audience was asked to indicate personal possession of a microform viewer. Disastrously, only two hands went up. Gwyneth Pawsey, a librarian at the Rolls Royce research centre, published a report (Pawsey 1965) which gave the reasons for the limited use of US government reports supplied on fiche. It included some of the items in the above list. In 1991 the same comments still apply.

Current developments

In 1988 a spokesman for the UK company Microfilm Reprographics was reported as saying "this is a market with an enormous growth potential". The comment was made on the occasion of an offer of $18.6M for a US company, Computer Microfilm Corporation, engaged in similar activities. However Agfa-Gevaert, a major producer of film, consider that "electrical imaging may eventually take over from film".

Microforms were not even considered for archival storage in the "Knowledge Warehouse" project (Williamson 1988). In a discussion comparing the merits of different media for archival purposes, only tape, magnetic discs, and optical discs are mentioned.

While storage on CD-ROMs and WORMS must be making big dents in the microform market, hybrid systems are also being offered. For example in

Business Newsbank's service in which articles from 600 publications are indexed on CD-ROM, published every month, limitations in CD-ROM storage space are overcome by supplying about 6,500 full-text articles on ten fiche with each CD-ROM.

A comprehensive report about Document Image Processing systems for business purposes business was published recently (Hales 1990).

The report states:- "Micrographics systems are likely to remain preferable for many small or medium-sized document systems on economic grounds. There is a substantial installed base. It has been estimated that there are between four and five million microfilm readers world-wide and about 200,000 Computer Assisted Retrieval (CAR) systems, mostly in the USA.

There are many major document capture projects already under way, involving substantial investments, which will not be able to change storage media now". In a table of nine hardware suppliers provided in the report, three include microform storage. However microforms are used in only one of the ten "case history" large-organisation applications described.

Conclusions

One gets the impression that microforms are being carried forward by their own momentum and by the large investment surrounding installed systems. Reports about new developments or improved systems are few. Perhaps that same seldomly reported influence which pervades videotex also pervades microforms. These two areas are not glamorous headline material and are not perceived as items to cultivate in the pursuit of keeping up with the Jones's.

FURTHER READING

Blick,A.R; Ward S.M.
  Aslib Proc. 36(4), 165-176, April 1984.
    A microform policy to reduce the physical growth of industrial
    libraries.
Cox, Dennis.
  J. Documentation 43(4), 334-349, December 1987.
    The contribution of microphotography and reprints to the development
    of libraries.
Grimaldi, John E.
  J. Imaging Technology 10(4), 143-145, August 1984.
    How does one store color business graphics? - computer generated color
    microfiche.
Hales, Keith and Jeffcoate, Judith.
  Report Ovum Ltd., 7 Rathbone St., London. 1990.
    Document image processing: the commercial impact.
Lunin, Lois F.
  In Williams, Martha E. (Ed.). Annual Review of Information Science and
  Technology,. Volume, 22 1987. Elsevier, Amsterdam (for ASIS). Chapter 6.
    Electronic image information.
Pawsey, Gwyneth
  Report number RR(OH) 233, December 1965. Published by
  Rolls Royce Ltd., Advanced Research Dept, Old Hall,
  Littleover, Derby, England.

Spang, Lothar; Collier, Monica; Thompson, Donald D; Dwyer, James R; Boss,
   Richard..
      ASIS Bulletin, 7(1), 11-30, October 1980
      Special section on micrographics.
Williams, Bernard.
   Communication Technology Impact 2(7), October 1980, 1-6.
      Microfilm: a future in the age of the microchip.
Williamson, Robin.
   Report. Elsevier Science Publishers, Oxford. 1988.
      Electronic text archiving.

CHAPTER 28.   MULTIMEDIA AND HYPERTEXT

"When I use a word" Humpty-Dumpty said in rather a scornful tone "it means
just what I choose it to mean - neither more nor less". "The question is"
said Alice "whether you can make multimedia mean so many different things".
"The question is" said Humpty-Dumpty "which is to be master - that's all".
(With apologies to Lewis Carroll)

INTRODUCTION

If the meaning of a word may be discovered from its useage, then
"Multimedia" means "The processing of information derived from or presented
in several different media". "Hypermedia" seems to be used as a synonym for
both Hypertext and Multimedia but since "Hyper - " means "over or
excessive" perhaps it should be avoided.

The presentation of text with graphics, derived from several
different "media" such as WORMS, CD-ROMs, scanners etc., may reasonably be
labelled "multimedia". "Multimedia" also covers the presentation of
information with sound, animation, and motion video as well as with text and
graphics. In answering Humpty-Dumpty's question in Lewis Carroll's
mis-quotation (above) "who will be the master"? The second much broader
description will be the chosen meaning here.

Although hypertext arrived before multimedia and is far more widely
used it can be considered as a multimedia component. Hypertext started as
software for constructing a database of linked text fragments. It is used
more widely partly because of its earlier arrival and partly because text is
a primary form of human communication.

Many multimedia software packages ride on software developed for
hypertext, for the good reason that the next form of communication to be
included within a linked hypertext fragment was graphics. Accordingly
hypertext will come first in this chapter.

HYPERTEXT

Introduction

The word Hypertext was coined by Ted Nelson (Nelson 1981).
Marchioni (1988) writes:- "From the writer's point of view, hypertext
systems are the next generation of word processing. In addition to word
processing features like block moves, search and replace, and spell or style
checking, hypertext writing tools may support and extend the writing process
with telescoping outlines, posted notes that do not affect the main text,
electronic bookmarks, and browsing modes".

"From the reader's point of view, hypertext systems are a new
generation of database management. Full text is available from multiple
perspectives, for various purposes, and through different search strategies.
Thus hypertext databases are more malleable to the user than print or early
electronic text formats".

Hypertext is a fine toy for academics, encouraging a breakout from the idea that most information should be arranged linearly. Academics who love research and experimentation per se, love Hypertext and love writing articles about it. It is obviously a "Good Thing" but until quite recently people have not known quite what to do with it, or how it might be usefully applied. In an attempt to bring Hypertext down to earth some typical manifestations of it are described below:-

1. As a "free for all" tool for information creation, processing, or browsing, enabling "authors and readers.. to add annotations and original links. In effect the boundary between author and reader should largely disappear"(Yankelovitch 1985).

2. As an "electronic notebook/gallery" for storing sentences, paragraphs, odd notes, ideas, chapters, an index, imported press cuttings, illustrations and sketches, etc., in readiness for the composition of a literary work of some kind. Another example of this type of application is a "chunked" form of a normally linear publication as an aid to its construction and access to it by the use of links.

3. As a database system based on hypertext software, resembling a conventional database, containing numerous records in a file; it may be up-dated; wanted records may be retrieved by asking suitably posed questions. The file and question arrangements are controlled by a set of rules governing the file structure and the query language. The database is hypertext-based because its author wants to offer several useful features to users which are unavailable with conventional database software.

This is certainly not an exhaustive list of possible applications, but it is representative of the free for all, compositional, and information storage and retrieval aspects which have been widely discussed.

By 1987, hypertext activities had prompted an excellent review (Conklin 1987) For a good bibliography, see Nielsen (1987) in hypertext's very own journal.

There must be thousands of people using hypertex in some way because Apple's "Hypercard" hypertex software is supplied free with Apple Macintosh computers. Hypercard includes a fairly simply programming language called "Hypertalk" with which "Scripts" - a string of instructions mostly in plain English - may be written. Several books are available about Hypercard. I can recommend Apple's guide (Anon 1988) on the subject.

Hypercard General Arrangement

When the word "author" is used here it refers to a person who is creating or changing items in the system. A "user" is a person who is using an already designed system and does not normally change it. Of course a person may often be both an author and user of the same system.

Hypercard was preceded by and co-exists with a number of older systems which are broadly similar but not generally available. Some similar new systems are available competing with Hypercard - the huge customer base for IBM PCs and others running on the MS/DOS operating system made competition inevitable. For example HyperPad from Brightfill-Roberts sells at $100. However to understand Hypercard is to understand a good deal about

676

hypertex in general.

Hypercard's **Fields**, **Cards** and **Stacks** roughly correspond to database fields, records and files. A Card is Hypercard's smallest unit of information - the minimum amount of displayable information is one Card. Hypercard Fields of information are displayed on a 342 x 512 pixel size numbered Card - in other words a Mac screen-full. The field for editable text is displayed in a window, or a series of windows, which can occupy most of the screen. It can contain up to 30,000 characters and graphics in scrollable lines; the text is all in the same font selectable from a number of alternatives.

A "Find" command will search through all Cards in a Stack for a character string in a named Field. A Card actually overlays a **Background** which may be invisible if the Card completely overlays it. Usually a Background is visible and contains information common to a number of Cards, or to all the Cards in the Stack.

As a simple example, consider a Stack consisting of three Cards - an article, a glossary, and a references card. The three Cards might have the same Background consisting of a small rectangle at the top containing the author's name, a larger rectangle containing the title, and a considerably larger rectangle acting as a window for the text or the glossary, article, or index. The same operational facilities are available for a Background as for a Card. Backgrounds are numbered - in this example Background number 1 is being used with Cards 1,2 and 3.

A Background resembles a form in some respects. In the case above, the form consists of rectangular spaces for the author's name and title, and a large rectangular space for the text. An author is provided with facilities for "form" design - thus the size and location of the rectangles on the Background may be designed into a fixed position.

A Hypercard system may contain many or no "Information" Stacks, but it must contain a special Stack called the **Home Stack** used for "housekeeping" purposes. The first Card in the Home Stack is shown in Figure 28.1

A Card typically contains up to about 100 Kbytes of data plus its associated Script. Stack size may be up to 512 Mbytes. A whole Card is brought into memory and 2 Mbytes of RAM is recommended for the Mac plus a hard disk of, say, 20 Mbytes.

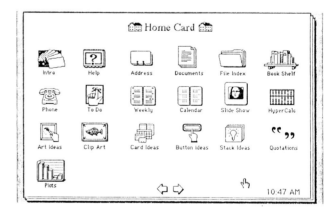

FIGURE 28.2. HYPERCARD "HOME" CARD

Hypercard Messages

Hypercard activities are initiated by **Messages** which may be commands such as "finds", or within-system descriptive messages such as "mouse is within button area" or "mouse up" when the mouse is clicked. A user can send a message which must include a Keyword, to the current Card, or to an Object by typing it into a special area called a **Message Box**.

Messages are sent to Buttons, Fields, Background, Stack, Home stack, and Hypercard in that order. Each object has an ID number. A stack must have a name, and other objects may be given names at the author's option.

Each of these six **Objects** has a **Handler** attached to it. A Handler comprises statements in the **Hypertalk** language collectively called a **Script**. The **Keyword** of a message in transit is matched against the Keyword of a Button's script - the first Object it meets. If there is no match it goes on to try a field, then Background for a Keyword match, and so on through the hierarchy. When a match is found with an Object a Script is executed.

Hypercard Buttons

One of the most interesting features in Hypercard is a **Button**. A Button is a small labelled rectangular area. When the cursor is directed over it with the mouse and the mouse is clicked, a Script is executed to perform some kind of action. A Button may be on the Background, in which case its action is the same whatever the overlaid Card, or it may be on a Card, in which case its action applies to that Card only.

One of the most useful actions, and perhaps the most important Hypercard "extra" not present on a conventional database, is the Button action which links to another Card in the same or in another Stack, causing it to be displayed.

Even more exotic features

Hypercard version 1.2, introduced in late 1988, included some improvements taking it into the multimedia area - for instance to use data from a CD-ROM drive connected to the Mac, including text, sound, and music data.

In 1990 Apple introduced Hypercard 2.0. The major improvements are the support of several windows - one of the windows can contain a Script display and editor - and a further move towards multimedia allowing colour or grey scale images to appear on cards.

Hypercard 2.0. still supplied free with Macs, comes on one 1.44 Mbyte disc with an instruction manual. Extras include help and support discs and a set of manuals.

Hypercard Authoring

The first two numbered pararaphs in the Introduction are "author" activities. Programs must be written - an idea which is unthinkable to the average user. The vast majority of people who sit in front of a computer are "users", not "authors". Certainly 90% of the people who use a microcomputer for its most popular application - word processing - have no "author" interest whatever. It's annoying enough having to learn how to use the thing. 80% of the people who use computers in business are in the same category. They have better things to do than learn how to write programs.

Hypercard alleviates this barrier somewhat. People who are a little more curious and a little more adventurous will find that a very much smaller amount of time is needed to make changes which considerably affect performance. Even to make quite radical changes no special programming training is needed - a "user" can also become an "author" without a commitment to an excessively long learning period.

For example Button linking can be changed quite easily, and that can entirely change Card inter-relationships and user routes. Such a change can be included by filling in a "button form" and carrying out a few mouse selection-and-clicking operations.

It takes more learning time than this to change the Hypertalk Script associated with an object. However Hypertalk consists of standard English phrases and keywords which makes any change relatively easy.

Hypertext applications 1.   Electronic journals re-born?

Hypercard seems to embody most of the facilities expected by people already using other hypertext systems. Academic work has been mainly conducted with other similar but earlier systems.

Conklin says in his article (1987):- "This article can only hint at the potential of hypertext. In fact one must work for a while for the collection of features to coalesce into a useful tool". Hypertext's hard-to-describe attributes make a product like Hypercard hard to sell as a software package. This was one reason why Bill Atkinson, who wrote Apple's MacPaint program, pursuaded Apple to give it away free with the Mac providing a further incentive for buying the machine.

Conklin continues "The database is a network of textual, and perhaps graphical nodes...which represent pointers to other nodes in the database... link icons cause the system to find the referenced node and immediately open a new window on the screen. The user can easily create new nodes and new links to new nodes, for annotation, comment, elaboration, etc. The database can be browsed by following links... by searching for a word string... or by navigating using a graphical browser" (Note that this user is in fact an author by my definition).

The most imaginative ideas came from the earlier experimenters. Nelson's "Xanadu" is an "evolving corpus continually expanding without fundamental changes". The long range goal of Xanadu is to bring about the revolutionary process of placing the entire world's literary corpus online.

R.H.Trigg, who later was a major contributor to the Xerox PARC NoteCards system, suggested in a 1983 thesis that "all paper writing, critiquing, and refereeing will be performed on online... New papers will be written using the network, often collaborated on by multiple authors, and submitted to online electronic journals".

But the fact is that print on paper and technical and scientific journals have evolved the way they have for good reasons (as discussed earlier in this book). Not least are certain aesthetic and sociological attributes which are impossible to emulate with machine-based systems. Well before Trigg wrote his remarks, lengthy "Computerising" experiments and pilot studies had been tried and found wanting. Editorial Processing Centers were a notable failure.

Electronic Journals were launched (for instance **Chimo** and **The Mental Workload**), and petered out. In 1980 Guillaume (1980) reported "only 1 paper had been submitted to the electronic journal, a single author production".

Meadows (1987) does not list any of these failures in a short piece about electronic journals. He prefers to switch attention to the widespread use by scientific authors of word processing machines and personal information systems. However this activity is far more limited than the electronic journal concept of the late seventies.

Nelson's Xanadu resembles the original electronic journal idea, is well financed, and is expected to emerge eventually as some kind of a product. It remains to be seen whether it turns out to be a flash in the pan for academic computer fanatics, or an intellectually stimulating concept with a great future.

Conklin devotes much attention to "The Power of Linking" between documents, references, successive pieces of text, tables, figures, etc. The idea of building linked directed graphs, he suggests, is similar to a semantic network wherein concepts represented as nodes and indexed by semantic contents tend to cluster together.

The problems of hypertext, which I shall examine in a moment, are "getting lost in space", and the "cognitive overhead" involved when creating, naming, and keeping track of links, and - when working as a user, not as an author - to maintain concentration while following different trails.

Hypertext Applications 2. An Aid to Composition

Conklin says "Authoring obviously has much to do with the structuring of ideas, order of presentation, and conceptual exploration. Few authors simply sit down and pour out a finished text, and not all editing is just "wordsmithing" and polishing. In a broad sense, authoring is the design of a document. The unit of this level of authoring is the idea or concept, and this level of work can be effectively supported by hypertext".

For the user, Conklin continues, "hypertex may also offer new possibilities for processing large or complex information sources... The essential advantage of non-linear text is the ability to order text in different ways depending on different viewpoints".

McKnight (1988) also offers some views on document construction, suggesting that hypertext may not be helpful for some kinds of literature but may be suited to others. Hypertex is said to free information from the linear form of the printed page, but that may not be necessary or desirable. The development of the theme in a detective novel or of the construction of mathematical theorems, for example, are necessarily linear.

However "The repair manual type of text... and the encyclopaedia with options to jump to a new node... are just two examples of placing information in the global structure of a hierarchy... which perhaps best suit particular kinds of document and task".

An example showing this type of application is shown in Figure 28.2. The publication from which it is abstracted is a user's instruction manual describing how to use a Hypercard-based system about an Interface Design called DRUID (Hardman 1989).

A card is provided for each sub-section in the section of the manual about DATA ENTRY. The user has elected to point to the "see also" reference 4.4-15. The system response is to highlight this item and display its title. Upon clicking on the SHOW button the card containing the selected item is displayed.

Note the PREV and NEXT buttons for the previous and next cards in the USER GUIDANCE section, and the RETURN button option for returning to the card previously selected - the DATA ENTRY card. McKnight continues with an example of how a journal might be structured with **Guide**. Certain user-advantages are claimed by sub-dividing an article into title and Author, Abstract, Introduction, Method, Results, Discussion, Conclusion, and References.

Guide originated at the University of Kent in 1982, was introduced by Office Workstations Ltd (OWL) well before Hypercard, and is used in the US, but OWL does not have the advantage of Apple's marketing clout and free supply.

"Readers prefer... a "note" link; selecting a citation causes a dropdown window containing the reference to appear... key terms in the abstract can be used as appropriate points in the body text; points in the conclusion can be linked back to the body text which leads to them. In this way, the reader can move through the text in a manner suited for the purpose of accessing it" says McKnight.

People who write about Hypercard, or for that matter about any activity which involves gazing at "electronic text", take little account of the body of literature which compares reading from a CRT screen with reading from print (as discussed elsewhere in this book). Much of this work is about subjective experiments using students who were obliged to read CRT or print for the purposes of the experiment.

Reading preferences, given a free choice and equal availability and cost of media, and a free choice of the location in which to do the reading have not been so thoroughly researched.

Hypertext Applications 3. The Hypertext database

As the author correctly says when describing a Hypertext database: "Very little is published about the good, or bad, aspects of a completed Hypertext". She goes on to talk about the use of the Glascow guide (Baird 1988). This scheme represents a considerable effort at the University of Strathclyde - after starting in November 1987 the team working on it grew to 21 people.

A number of Mac SE machines, scanner, laser printer, and Adobe illustrator graphics software have been used in this multi-user Apple-talk (Local Area Network) scheme organised by the University. (Apple-talk packet-switched protocol is designed for small networks using twisted pair

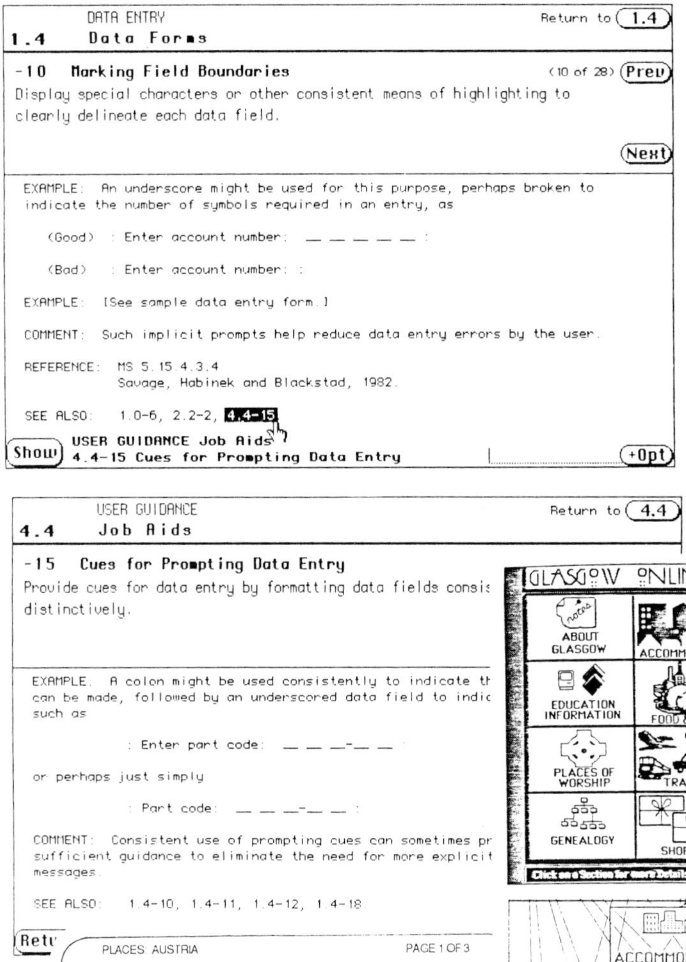

```
        DATA ENTRY                          Return to ( 1.4 )
1.4     Data Forms

-10   Marking Field Boundaries              (10 of 28) (Prev)
Display special characters or other consistent means of highlighting to
clearly delineate each data field.

                                                        (Next)

EXAMPLE:  An underscore might be used for this purpose, perhaps broken to
  indicate the number of symbols required in an entry, as

  (Good)  : Enter account number:  _ _ _ _ _ :

  (Bad)   : Enter account number: :

EXAMPLE:  [See sample data entry form.]

COMMENT:  Such implicit prompts help reduce data entry errors by the user.

REFERENCE:  MS 5.15.4.3.4
            Savage, Habinek and Blackstad, 1982.

SEE ALSO:  1.0-6, 2.2-2, 4.4-15
 (Show)   USER GUIDANCE Job Aids
          4.4-15 Cues for Prompting Data Entry          (+Opt)
```

FIG 28.2.

CARDS IN
THE MITRE
"DRUID"
SYSTEM

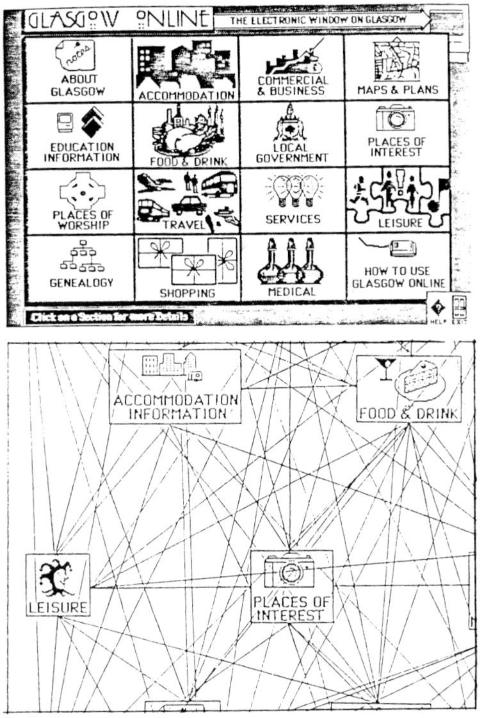

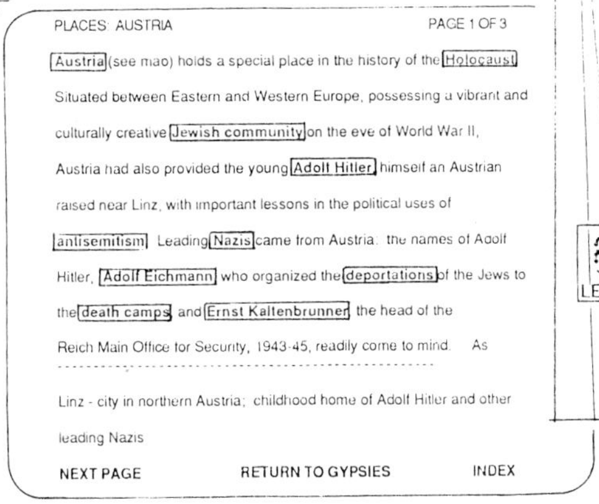

```
        USER GUIDANCE                       Return to ( 4.4 )
4.4     Job Aids

-15   Cues for Prompting Data Entry
Provide cues for data entry by formatting data fields consis
distinctively.

EXAMPLE.  A colon might be used consistently to indicate th
  can be made, followed by an underscored data field to indic
  such as

      : Enter part code:  _ _ _-_ _ :

or perhaps just simply

      : Part code:  _ _ _-_ _ :

COMMENT:  Consistent use of prompting cues can sometimes pr
  sufficient guidance to eliminate the need for more explicit
  messages.

SEE ALSO:  1.4-10, 1.4-11, 1.4-12, 1.4-18
(Retu
```

```
PLACES: AUSTRIA                      PAGE 1 OF 3

Austria (see map) holds a special place in the history of the Holocaust.

Situated between Eastern and Western Europe, possessing a vibrant and

culturally creative Jewish community on the eve of World War II,

Austria had also provided the young Adolf Hitler, himself an Austrian

raised near Linz, with important lessons in the political uses of

antisemitism. Leading Nazis came from Austria: the names of Adolf

Hitler, Adolf Eichmann who organized the deportations of the Jews to

the death camps, and Ernst Kaltenbrunner, the head of the

Reich Main Office for Security, 1943-45, readily come to mind.   As

Linz - city in northern Austria; childhood home of Adolf Hitler and other

leading Nazis

NEXT PAGE           RETURN TO GYPSIES          INDEX
```

FIGURE 28.4
HYPERTIES BROWSER

FIGURE 28.3
GLASGOW ONLINE GUIDE

inter-connections over a range of about 300 metres). Database development has been a research project but the end product is a regularly up-dated Hypercard system useable by the general public.

The illustration in Figure 28.3 shows the Home Card and a part of the hypercard network. For example, a user who looks at a card providing details of a particular category of hotel can jump to a map showing its location, and then either return to the first card, look at the previous and next cards in the "hotel section", or "press" any of the other buttons provided by the authors which are attempts to guess what a user might want to do next.

The Hyperties Browser (Figure 28.4) is a pre-Hypercard example of a hypertext database running on the IBM PC (Schneiderman 1966). The illustration shows a simple but effective idea to enable readers of an Encyclopaedia article about "The Holocaust" to jump to related topics.

A card for any highlighted topic will be displayed when a highlighted item is touched using a touch-screen display - in other words each item is a form of "Button".

Indexing re-visited. Navigating and Browsing

Hypertext indexing is the cause of much academic puffing and blowing, wishful think- ing confusion, and plain ignorance. Of course the word "indexing" is rarely used - "navigat- ion" escapes the fright- ful boredom engendered by that word. It seems extraordinary that there is so much confusion about the activities of "authors" and "users".

Yankelovich (1985) says:- "Ideally, auth- ors and readers should have the same set of integrated tools that allow them to browse through other material during the document preparation process and to add annotations and original links as they progress through an inf- ormation web. In effect the boundary between author & reader should largely disappear".

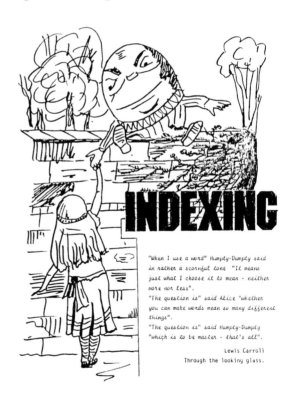

"When I use a word" Humpty-Dumpty said in rather a scornful tone "It means just what I choose it to mean - neither more nor less".
"The question is" said Alice "whether you can make words mean so many different things".
"The question is" said Humpty-Dumpty "which is to be master - that's all".

Lewis Carroll
Through the looking glass.

▲ **FIGURE 28.5. HUMPTY-DUMPTY AGAIN**

But in a non-ideal world, if the "user" is going to be a different person from the "author" this is, of course, a recipe for disaster. The author can have a lot of fun creating a network of Cards. Putting on his user's hat, he can delight in roaming through it on trails of his own making, wondering about the next serendipitous gem that will turn up. Anyone else who wants to extract anything from the system is at the mercy of the author's imagination. We are back with Humpty Dumpty - these immortal words cannot be repeated often enough so here they are again (Figure 28.5).

The problem was recognised early on with the Xerox PARC Notecards Hypertex system in which applications using Lisp - a language developed for Artificial Intelligence (AI) research - could be included in the system. This could be used to provide additional conceptual information; Notecards was, and maybe still is, quite widely used, but it is not known whether the use of AI is successfull.

The same problem has been addressed by Rada (1988) who discusses the idea of harnessing expert system techniques to the construction of an embedded conceptual net.

Questions about hermeneutics (interpretation) have been discussed by Doland (1989):- "the designer must decide what users need to know at each end of a hypertext link in order to make use of what they find there... how much interpretation must the designer-author attach... how can we maintain the balance of alternative knowledges within hypertext systems?... How is it possible within an educational environment to utilize a linked document without "fixing" interpretation"?

It is much more interesting to grapple with new ideas than resurrecting and polishing up some of the old ones, but the application of "old-fashioned" indexing techniques to Hypertext would do no harm at all.

This notion is implied by Frisse (1988). In this article "hierarchical data structures" - Cards arranged in a tree structure - are discussed, and so is "the controlled vocabulary, MESH, used by the National Library of Medicine".

The mysteries of librarianship and information science are revealed and summarised in one terse sentence:- "you must create a vocabulary so that each card is classified by at least one term, and you must have a relatively uniform distribution of classification terms among all Hypertext cards. Both criteria are difficult to achieve. Second, the contents of the cards using the indexing terms must be classified manually, a prohibitive expense for most authors".

This kind of plain, true, hype-free stuff is rare indeed in computer journals. The article continues with a description of Salton's weighted indexing term methods but ends on a gloomy note:- "it's difficult to use hypertext effectively... it's clear that many problems in the field are unresolved".

Other aspects and applications

Many articles have been published about various other aspects of hypertex.

Landow (1989) describes several hypertext systems created for courses in literary education. For example "Intertext" includes author biographies and brief essays "containing questions that refer students back to reading and ask them to apply their newly acquired information to an included sample portion of text, or encourage them to follow links to other files".

Utting (1989) discusses navigational aids in the form of various types of maps with strategies for dealing with very large maps containing as many as 2000 links. Complete global maps of this size are not feasible and ways of representing "path events" during searches are described so that they can be used for future reference.

Foss (1989) describes the use of "browsers" to support the process of pursuing and returning from digressions when using Hypertext systems. Again this consists of various ways of clarifying maps.

Begoray (1990) provides an introduction and review to "hypermedia". This term is used to describe "hypertext with graphics". It covers a number of design issues such as "granularity" - that is the extent to which information should be sub-divided into "nodes" containing "a discrete block of editable substance".

A table of systems and their originators is given, their purpose discussed, and a short review of each is provided. Several areas of application are identified - Information access, Authoring scope, Support for conventional writing, Support for argumentation, Author Collaboration, and as a Publishing medium.

A similar type of article, but considering "applications in planning" and therefore only covering systems in that area, has been published by Wiggins (1990).

The use of multimedia systems over networks is discussed by Ziegler (1990) and Bulick (1990). Ziegler is interested in multimedia conferencing. Voice delivery requires consideration of "regulated speech control" (only one person is allowed to talk at a time) and "unregulated" where all participants can speak simultaneously. This has implications in the handling of voice packets over networks. Little is said about video delivery.

Bulick considers the requirements in network-based multimedia information retrieval - a potentially important topic. This requires several problems to be solved and they probably will not be solved in the near future. They include the provision of networks with sufficient bandwidth, inexpensive user appliances (as cheap as personal computers), adoption of standards for compression, packaging and transport, and the provision of a corpus of multimedia information.

MULTIMEDIA

History up to the mid-eighties

Bush's article "As we may think" (Bush 1945) is widely quoted. Not so well known is a piece he contributed to a book 24 years later entitled "Memex revisited" (Bush 1969). In it he reminds us about the Memex machine described in his earlier article as "a sort of mechanized private file and library", and discusses its feasibility in the light of recent developments.

He talks about transistors and video recorders, and considers that Memex has become technically feasible, but thinks that progress will be slow for two reasons. First "... there is no profit in libraries. Government spends billions on space since it has glamor and hence public appeal. There is no glamor about libraries and the public do not understand that the welfare of their children depends far more upon effective libraries than it does on the collecting of a bucket of talcum powder from the moon".

Secondly, says Bush, "... is the task of selection. And here, in spite of great progress, we are still lame". In other words progress with automatic indexing has been slow - although he does consider that artificial intelligence (in his terms "a Memex learning from its experience"), has possibilities. With regard to personal computers, Bush says: "They will be delayed in coming principally by costs, and we know that costs will go down, how much and how rapidly none can tell".

Although Bush's second article was followed by extraordinary developments in technology and steadily falling costs, the situation in libraries has not changed very much, neither has the indexing situation. However systems something like a Memex are now in sight.

Early experiments with multi-media information were made by a team of MIT under Richard Bolt (Bolt 1977). The user sat in a special chair fitted with joystick controls in a room also containing a large screen on to which images were projected from the rear (Figure 28.6). The smaller display nearby was used "as a navigational aid for the user while piloting through data presented on the large screen". Stereo sound was included.

The group was particularly interested in pseudo-3D spatial presentation with auditory cues and wide bandwidth graphics, using material of the kind used in the Domesday project referred to later.

As about the same time, Arthur C. Clarke, who had forecast a communication satellite system with exceptional accuracy back in 1945, started to speculate about a different kind of multimedia system which was to appear many years later. He was considering the possibilities of a "shoebox size" encyclopaedia and communication system (Clarke 1977).

In 1981 Nelson set out some of his ideas about Xanadu as mentioned earlier (Nelson 1981) and added some further considerations some years later (Nelson 1986).

In 1983 Maekawa et al (Maekawa 1983) at the Department of Information Science, University of Tokyo, described the multimedia machine shown in Figure 28.7 which they claim as "now being implemented on an experimental system". The system was used to create "menu-driven I-trees" - a method of combining information drawn from different sources while observing a "windows" display in order to produce a multimedia document.

Maekawa describes a variety of hardware including a TI/990 minicomputer with a 100 Mbyte disc, several microcomputers, a high resolution graphics display, a TV camera, optical disc equipment etc. No printing facilities are described and little information is provided about software. The machine was "expected to increase productivity in the office of the future" but as far as I can tell it never did.

686

In July 1984 Dahmke (Dahmke 1984) followed a long article about an "electronic" Grolier's American Encyclopaedia with a perceptive note anticipating what might be needed when "digital television and audio become affordable (in five to seven years) and we'll be able to ... let personal computers store and retrieve video images or ... record digital TV images and retrieve, display, and process them on digital computers".

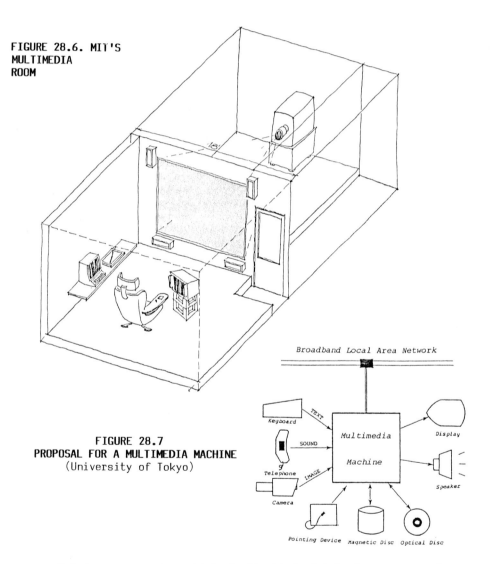

FIGURE 28.6. MIT'S MULTIMEDIA ROOM

FIGURE 28.7
PROPOSAL FOR A MULTIMEDIA MACHINE
(University of Tokyo)

Dahmke goes on to anticipate the kind of interfaces now used on the Mac/MediaMaker system (to be described) "in order to give the programmer tight control over the timing of the player and to control the video overlay circuit" - quite an accurate description of what was actually done five years later.

A few months after this, Weyer (Weyer 1985) described an encyclopaedia system which was far ahead of Grolier. Weyer realised that low cost computing power was becoming a reality. The future encyclopaedia should be "as comprehensive and detailed as the best current print encyclopedia".

However full advantage should be be taken of the possibilities of not just text and static pictures, but also video sequences, animation, simulations, music, and voice ... what the user sees would be custom-generated and based on the encyclopedia system's model of the user's interests, vocabulary, knowledge of specific subjects, and previous interactions with the system".

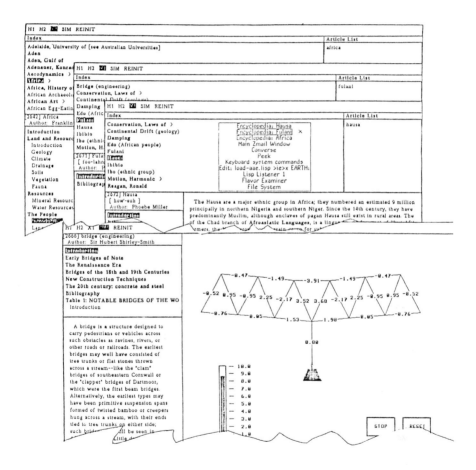

FIGURE 28.8.   WAYER'S ENCYLOPAEDIA

The proposed system would go beyond browsing and would employ four metaphors. A Model which is a representation of knowledge, A Tour, which is an information path through the model, a Filter which moderates detail, and a Guide which takes account of the user's profile and background knowledge.

688

Weyer provides an example of his intentions by showing Hypercard-like access to an entry, and interactive learning (Figure 28.8). In figure 28.8:- "after specifying a load on the bridge we see the effects of forces transmitted to various truss members ... The bridge article might lead us to the spectacular collapse of the Tacoma Narrows Bridge (footage of the collapse and a series of experiments are available on videodisc)".

FIGURE 28.9.   DOMESDAY PROJECT
(Each dot represents a data area)

By the mid-eighties a group in the UK had decided that technology/costs had moved on to the point where a nation-wide multimedia presentation system was feasible. The end product was the Domesday 12"double-sided Laservision disc database used on a Philips-made Laservision player, with controlling software, and an Acorn microcomputer, 14" colour monitor, and mouse.

The idea seems to have come from Peter Armstrong at the BBC and John Goddard of the Department of Geography, University of Newcastle (Goddard 1986). 1986 would be the 900th anniversary of William the First's survey of

Britain. The project was conceived as a latter-day Domesday survey and public educational project supported by several investors, the BBC's share being over £1M. The BBC's team consisted of 40 members, with four supporting teams at Universities. 14,000 Schools throughout the country assisted with data collection.

The National Disc, covering Culture, Economy, Society, and the Environment, includes 1500 articles and essays, census data, statistics, and "surrogate walks" supported by 20,000 photographs through houses, farms, the countryside, etc. The Community Disc consists of maps of the country with the means of zooming down to small local areas, 4 x 3 Km in size, starting from the national map. Local Information supported by text and photographs is available for most parts of the country as shown in Figure 28.9.

The Ecodisc about the environment was introduced in 1987, followed by Datamerge, for adding own data, Display for own "storybook" presentations, and later a disc about London.

The Domesday project is remarkable by any standards. When considering that it runs on an 8-bit computer with a 64K memory and a display resolution for 16 colours of only 160 x 256 pixels designed many years ago, the results are almost incredible. Unfortunately the technical brilliance of the system has been overshadowed by unrealistic budgets and bad marketing.

It was expected that 10,000 units would be sold at £1500 each. By late 1987 about 1000 had been sold at £3500 each. It is now sold by a company called Cimnetts at £1795, with suppliers BBC, Acorn, and Philips taking a loss.

Reference was made above to early work at the MIT Media Laboratory. In June 1989 the same laboratory provided a demonstration at the Hypertext II conference at York in support of a paper by Brondmo (1989). It was a documentary about the Charles river with text, graphics, digital sound, and motion video. The video came from a Laserdisc player with sections selected and duration-controlled from Hypercard software running on a Mac II.

Multimedia Philosophy, and prospects

The bones of the multimedia idea can be seen in the object-oriented scheme incorporated in the Star machine devised by the people of Xerox's Palo Alto research labs in the late seventies.

If a user is able to invoke the behaviour of an object on the screen which embodies certain properties of data, then the system may legitimately be called "object-oriented". The system interacts in a familiar, real world manner with the user, instead of imposing the mechanics of its hardware and software upon him.

In multimedia, extra dimensions of information are added to object-orientation so that the user employs all his or her senses (excluding, for the time being, small) in the exchange of information with the machine. The situation is made to seem quite like the familiar real world environment.

It's interesting to speculate about where this new degree of freedom may lead. Is multimedia just a flash in the pan hyped up by manufacturers to join VCR's, Camcorders, Desktop Publishing, DAT, and other gadgets with which we can apparently no longer do without, but which are running out of steam?

Alternatively is McLuhan's vision on the way to fulfilment? In one of his earlier books, Gutenberg Galaxy (1962), McLuhan suggested that communications media determine the nature of social organisation. New media provide humans with new psychological-structural equipment. Will the prediction of either a $17 billion market by 1994, or a $24 billion market, also predicted for that very same year, come true?

Lewis Mumford (1968) thought that:- "by centring attention on the printed word, people lost that balance between the sensuous and intellectual, between the concrete and the abstract... to exist was to exist in print: the rest of the world became more shadowy".

Mumford also thought that McLuhan was pressing forward in the interests of the military and commerce to a scenario where the "sole vestige of the world of concrete forms and ordered experience will be the sounds and images on the constantly present television screen or such abstract derivative information as can be transferred to the computer" (Carey, 1981).

Be that as it may, one thing is obvious and that is that the boundaries between Information, Entertainment, Education and Commerce are becoming even fuzzier. Will, for example, multimedia online databases greatly enhanced by graphics and sound appear with "a controlled pictorial index language whose terms are the descriptors of the significant structure in digital images" as confidently claimed by Bordogna et al (1990)? It is already being claimed that "Multimedia databases will radically change the way you look at and work with information" (Shetler, 1990).

Shetler's Binary Large Objects (BLOB) database may "present you with any combination of data fields, images, and text objects" and may contain "spreadsheets, graphs, fax, object-code modules, satellite data, voice patterns, or any digitised data... it could be very large - up to 2 gigabytes" ("Satellite data" is much the same as any other data but it sounds impressive). For online access you will have to await the arrival of SONET (optical) telecoms otherwise it will take a week for the stuff to arrive.

Why shouldn't the presentation of information about, say, houses for sale, be accompanied by the sight and smells of the neighbourhood? The enterprising Estate Agent who sends you an entertaining disc may be stealing a competitive advantage.

Why should't shareholders receive clips on videotape showing the products of their company in use, with the report (which would be much more interesting if its sections came up via hypertext links) which they receive annually from the chairman?

Indeed, why in the home of the late nineties shouldn't "the multimedia machine be a computerised entertainment centre combining the functions of today's audio and video systems, television set, games machine, and home computer?" (Cookson, 1990).

All these things may happen but there are quite a few constraints. In a recent review of Macromind Director in the October 1990 issue of Byte, the writer says "The Overview Module allows business people to create excellent presentations easily".

A related subject was recently discussed in a UK national newspaper (Virgo, 1990). "Organisations buying computer systems generally ignore the largest costs.. the cost of disruption and training is commonly up to double the cost of developing and testing the software which is itself double the cost of the hardware".

To cover the cost of the technical effort and expertise needed to acquire and use appropriate multimedia hardware and software, together with the time and the artistic and creative effort of providing a presentation, you should probably double the number again.

Complaints about understanding and learning about multimedia software, joining the huge volume of complaints about software in general, have already started to appear. Pournelle (1990) describes the agonies of "genlocking" and getting multi-frequency monitors to work properly. With regard to Instruction Manuals, Pournelle reports that his wife, a competent computer experimenter, found that in the manual for a Willow video board "there was not one single sentence in 12 pages of text that she understood".

But liberation is at hand to offset these constraints. Multimedia processing, particularly motion video processing, is severely constrained by processing power at the moment. That power could be available quite soon if people did not keep moving the goalposts. They are already on about real time graphics processing requiring about 20 Mips, and rendering to produce photographic realism which requires 300 Mips. To do what is being done now, faster, does not need this much power.

Graphics processing, which requires a dedicated computer within a computer, is advancing rapidly. IBM lapses into hype-language when enthusing about its new PS/2 90 and 95 machines which "thanks to dazzling XGA (Extended Graphics Array)... (provide) a new standard in high resolution quality, conjured up in the blink of any eye".

The other liberating factor is compression. Compression is about the only development which does not receive the hype it deserves (Cawkell 1990). Two groups - Joint Photographic Experts Group (JPEG) and Motion Pictures Experts Group (MPEG) have been working on standards. CCITT standard H.261 has been agreed and a Codec enabling videoconferencing to be carried on at bit rates of from 64 Kbps to 2 Mbps is already used by British Telecom.

The Multimedia "end-product" at the present time is usually a "multimedia presentation". Multimedia enhancements seem to add real value in educational and training, and it is in these areas where applications are appearing. Boring old, plain vanilla, business or information providers have not yet acquired the gizmos needed to add the necessary multimedia bezazz (to use some foreign but explicit words). But you don't try and justify the cost of intangibles like your new multimedia fun-image - it's an act of faith.

As usual, and in spite of these various uncertainties, there is no shortage of forecasts of an assured multimedia future.

According to a recent report (Anon 1989) the future of multimedia is rosy - the norm for all IT forecasts. The "$17 billion market in 1994" is just for PC multimedia. Its accuracy will probably be no worse than other forecasts - and multimedia is going to do everything for us including "providing entertainment, managing the environment, and ensuring security".

Gale (1990) is prepared to be quite specific about the future. In 1994 he foresees "18 multimedia applications, 22 market segments, and 14 end user platforms". The details are rather less specific - for instance "documentation" as an application, "consumer" as a market segment, and "computerised entertainment/information systems" as an end user platform".

"The major markets in 1994 (in current millions of dollars) will be Consumer 4337, Heavy Manufacturing 2211, Other 2103, Government 2055, Motion Pictures 1239, Education & Libraries 850, Computer and Information Services 450, and Retail Trades 352. Total $13,597 Million", Gale continues.

First generation hardware

The Apple Macintosh microcomputer, introduced in 1984, was noted mainly for its high resolution 512 x 384 pixel screen and excellent graphic user interface. It had an 8 MHz processor, 16/24 bit data path/bus, 400K floppy drive and 128K memory. But its integrated design and lack of slots for cards provided no scope for third party developers. The Mac II, which came out in 1987, has become the leading machine for multimedia applications. Its main features are:-

* 15.7 MHz 68020 processor with six NuBus slots for 96-pin cards and 68881 co-processor (4 to 40 times faster than the Mac Plus).
* 32 bit data path/bus.
* 1 to 8 Mbyte memory and up to 80 Mbyte internal hard disc.
* Video output card with colour lookup table. 32 bit colour.
  the Apple video card limits the potential to 8 bit pixels providing 256 colours from a 16.7 million colour palette on a 640 x 480
  pixel screen . Third party suppliers can provide cards giving
  a much larger choice of colours.
* Screen stretchable to spread over up to 6 monitors.
* Stereo sound with 4 synthesizers available.
* 2 Serial Ports, several bus connectors and an SCSI interface with
  pseudo-DMA or triple rate data transfer.
* Current price for a 2 Mbyte memory, 80 Mbyte disc, and 13"
  colour monitor version is about £6000 in the UK.

In 1990 Apple introduced the Mac IIfx with a 40 MHz 68030 processor and 68882 co-processor, cache memory, and 3 auxiliary processors. This makes the machine up to four times faster than the improved Mac II (the Mac IIx). The US price is about $12,000. Apple also introduced the 20 Million Instructions Per Second (MIPS) 8/24 GC display card, with a 30MHz RISC processor on board, providing 8 bit colour at 640 x 480 pixels, or 8 bit (256 level) grey scale at 1152 x 870 pixels. The price is about $2000.

A major reason why the Mac II has become the multimedia leader is the slots which open it up to third party suppliers. A huge range of add-on hardware and software has become available. Another reason is that in multimedia applications the "Mac is doing what it does best - providing a consistent user interface, seamless data exchange, and gorgeous 24-bit colour graphics" (quoting the remarks of a Mac enthusiast).

The Commodore Amiga microcomputer was noted for its colour before the Mac. It could also display video images from an external source synchronised to on-screen effects produced by its user ("Genlocking"). However for several years it has been eclipsed by Apple. In 1990 Commodore made a strong bid to catch up with a new machine - the Amiga 3000 - having a performance nearly matching the Mac II at half the price (£3160 with 2 Mbyte memory, 40 Mbyte drive, £3610 with 100 Mbyte drive).

The 3000 is a 32 bit machine with the same processors as the Mac IIfx - 68030 and 69991 co-processor - running at up to 25 MHz. The machine includes an enhancement of the Amiga special set of three controller chips which provide much of its multimedia capabilities. The "Agnes" chip is a graphics processor providing functions like fast drawing, filling, and moving blocks of pixels; "Denise" deals with computer and video resolution and scanning; "Paula" handles sound.

Memory is from 1 to 16 Mbytes, with internal hard disc up to 100 Mbytes. The screen displays 4 bit per pixel colour out of 4096 colours at 640 x 400 pixels. Four expansion card sockets are provided. A 200 pin socket is also fitted ready to accept a next generation 68040 processor. Ports are similar to the Apple II. In addition to its new Amiga version 2.0 operating system, the 3000 will also run Unix.

IBM announced its entry into the multimedia arena at the beginning of 1990 with its Audio Capture, Playback Adaptor, Video Capture Adapter/A, M-motion videocard or Videologic DVA 4000 card, and various other adaptors. There are two versions of these items - for PC XTs/ATs or for PS/2s.

Other manufacturers also supply first generation multimedia hardware but Apple followed by Amiga seem to be the leaders. It is to early to say at the time of writing what impact IBM will have on the scene.

At present the equipment needed to provide a fully fledged multimedia show is untidy and may be expensive. It may require a Mac II with additional boards, CD-ROM player, videodisc player, videotape player, external sound amplifier, and loudspeakers, with assorted software, interconnecting cables, and the space to accommodate it all. This is the penalty for using a cobbled-together rather than a purpose-designed solution.

However most of the units are mass-produced in a competitive market. Only if multimedia demand becomes large enough are we likely to see a purpose-designed "one-box" machine. The design would have to be very ingenious to compete with the flexibility of choice provided by the present multiple-boxes multiple-software arrangements.

First generation software; multimedia presentations

Much of the currently available multimedia software is "Mac-based multimedia software." Most of this section will be about Mac-based software with some mention of multimedia software for Amiga and IBM machines. It is with this "first generation software" that the realisation of most people's multimedia interests will be achieved today. Obviously a very close eye will need to be kept on second generation activities, particularly on DV-I, to be discussed later.

Mac multimedia systems are usually controlled by Hypercard,

described earlier. An explanation of some basic aspects of sound and video follow and some of the more interesting items of equipment and software and the way they are used will be discussed.

A large amount of software is available of two kinds - that which comes with virtually "ready to play" multimedia presentations, and that which is available for loading into a machine to assist in "authoring", that is for the creation of multimedia presentations. It exists now and its potential is only just starting to be exploited in contrast to second generation software (discussed later) which is only just starting to appear.

Hypercard control

Hypercard, or one of its more recent alternatives such as Supercard or Hyperdoc, is a suitable software package to control a presentation comprising text, sound, music, voice, graphics, pictures, animation or motion video. Equipment arrangements for a comprehensive presentation are shown in Figure 28.10.

Multimedia interest in Hypercard centres on access to third party software. A Command is a Message containing a keyword which will cause the script for an object containing that keyword to be executed. A Function in some kind of instruction. External Commands (XCMD) cause a "resource", or code module, written in Pascal or Assembly language, to be executed by a command message. An SCMD can be used to control Driver software associated with an external device such as a videodisc player.

A resource has to be written by a programmer but when Hypercard-compatible devices and software, or special purpose software is used this is not necessary because the software includes ready-made resource code and driver and the XCMD can be installed in a Hypercard stack. The user can then create a button, labelled appropriately, to execute a script containing the XCMD.

Adding Voice and Music

The Mac II contains a small loudspeaker and also includes a stereo output socket for connection to an external amplifier and loudspeakers. Sound quality and cost considerations are the same as those applying to domestic hi-fi equipment.

One way of adding sound to visual material is to use an Apple CD-SC drive, which plays CDs, or the audio tracks from CD-ROMs, in conjunction with Apple Hypercard CD Audio Toolkit. The toolkit provides XCMDs for a Hypercard stack to control the player by accurately selecting passages of speech or music from the disc.

This is not only convenient but it provides the great advantage that the stored music consumes no memory or disc storage in the micro. The CD-Audio Stack from Voyager (Santa Monica) automatically generate buttons for track selection purposes. Musical instruments and synthesizers are connected to computers via the standardised Musical Instrument Digital Interface (MIDI). Apple make a connector interface which plugs into a Mac serial port and provide the driver and software to manage incoming sound.

To digitize, the value (level) of the amplitude of the sound

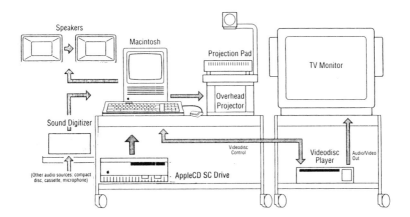

FIGURE 28.10. MULTIMEDIA EQUIPMENT ARRANGEMENT

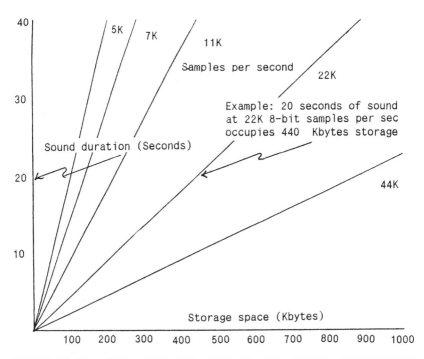

FIGURE 28.11. SOUND DURATION, SAMPLES, AND STORAGE REQUIREMENTS

waveform is periodically sampled. A 4 bit sample, providing 16 different
values, would provide poor quality since there is insufficient data to
properly reconstruct the waveform; 16 bits are needed to provide high
quality. If the sampling rate is too low, data between samples which should
be digitised will be lost and the high frequency response will suffer.
Sampling at 22,000 times per second with 8 bit (256 levels) per sample
produces digitized sound of quite good quality.

When sound is digitized, sound passages may be represented as "frozen waveforms" on the screen and all kinds of control and editing functions become possible. However the real, playable, sound, behind the screen representation of it, eats up computer storage space.

Figure 28.11 shows the sound playback duration for different digitizing conditions. If the sound amplifier and speakers are of high quality, and it is important to reproduce a piece of music with the highest quality, an increase of the rate to 44K 8-bit samples per second requires 1 Mbyte of storage for a 22.7 second recording.

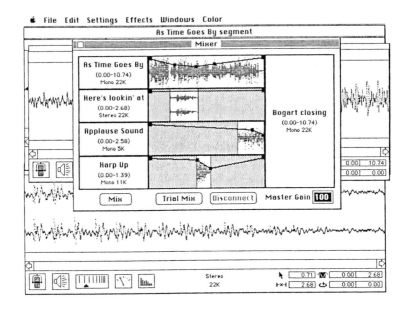

FIGURE 28.12. MIXING SOUND CHANNELS WITH "SOUND EDIT"

It is important to know about the constraints of storing digitized sound in RAM memory or on disk. The duration of a continuous passage of sound stored in memory is proportional to memory size. If the memory is too small and must be filled from disc during the passage, there will be a break in the sound unless special measures are taken.

The "special measures" are to add processing power with appropriate software to re-load memory almost instantaneously. This will require an extra card for the Mac with its own digital processor.

One of the best known sound devices is the Farallon (Emeryville, Ca) MacRecorder Sound System 2.0 outfit. A small electronic digitizing box plugs into the serial port of a Mac for voice, sound effects, or music input. Farallon's Hypersound software creates a stack with XCMD Commands to record or play sound. Sound Edit is an associated software package which provides a range of facilities including compression options, cut and paste sounds represented as frozen waveforms on the screen, mix sound channels, alter quality, and so on. Figure 28.12 shows the appearance of the screen when different sound channels are being mixed into a single channel.

Controlling and using pictures and Video

The major sources of still graphics or full colour illustrations are scanned items, or graphics and art of various kinds, either newly created or imported from other software. A Hypercard can contain graphics and illustrations in colour up to a size of 18" x 18", 1280 x 1280 pixels. if parts cannot be seen because the screen is too small, those parts may be scrolled on to the screen.

Animation - meaning usually relatively unsophisticated motion - may be created without excessive cost or effort. Greater realism requires more expense and professionalism. One way of making animation sequences is to create a picture, copy it on to second card, alter it slightly using Apple paint, copy the altered picture onto a third card, and so on.

Studio One from Electronic Arts (UK) offer Studio 1 software for animation control from Hypercard stacks with XCMD driver control for loading and playing sequences. It includes the automatic creation of intermediate frames of smooth animation between two different scenes.

Motion Video

The idea of capturing, processing, and outputting motion video on a microcomputer is relatively new and is surrounded by nasty technical complications.

Motion video, usually in either NTSC or European PAL analogue form, may be imported from TV receivers, cameras, videotape or videodiscs. Data is displayed on a CRT by smooth pixel-to-pixel changes of brightness and colour in direct proportion to the light reflected from the original objects. The NTSC system uses 525 scanning lines per frame repeating 60 times per second. PAL uses 625 lines repeating 50 times per second.

Both systems use interlaced scanning in which each frame is divided into two fields of alternate lines each repeated 30 (NTSC) or 25 (PAL) per second to reduce the flicker which would otherwise be noticeable.

In computer systems, images are represented as an array of picture elements (pixels). Until they are translated for display on the CRT, colours are represented by bit codes.

The consequences of these substantial differences between TV and computer representations of pictures are fivefold:-.

* Incoming data must be digitized for processing by the user.

* If not digitized it must be synchronised so that, combined with any internally generated data, it may be viewed as a stable display.

* Considerable processing power must be available to move very large numbers of bits if image changes produced by the user's processing and editing commands are to be viewed without delay.

* A monitor with appropriate resolution, scanning rate, and colour capabilities must be used for viewing the work.

* The presentation needs to be recorded for repeat performances.

The main motion video functions which can be handled using a Mac II with 4-8 Mbytes of RAM, at least 80 Mbytes of disc, a colour monitor, and a variety of third party plug-in boards and software are:-

* Import TV-standard NTSC or PAL motion video from a Hypercard-controlled videodisc player or a camera, and display it in real time in a window on the Mac's screen The Mac is not fast enough to allow full-screen colour motion video at TV resolution.

* Connect the monitor directly to the video source, such as a video-disc player, for the direct full-screen colour TV resolution dis-play of motion video, and control the videodisc from Hypercards, while presenting associated material on the Mac's screen.

* Overlay and synchronise ("Genlock") Mac text and graphics non-interlaced picture data, with the imported interlaced compos-ite TV signals (which contain all the synchronising and picture data within the signal). Record the composited pictures in NTSC or PAL format on VHS, or better still, S-VHS Videotape for presentation later.

* Use the tape containing recordings for mastering videodiscs if an interactive presentation is required. The random access seek time for Level 3 Laservision-type Constant Angular Velocity (CAV) videodisc players with Hypercard player control via an RS232 connec-tor, ranges from 3 seconds to 0.5 seconds for more expensive models.

* Replace video data in a given colour (the "key" colour) with a different set of video data if you want to add special effects.

* Capture and digitize video frame-by-frame with a "frame-grabber", and output frames with added animation frame-by-frame under Hyper-card control.

Figure 28.13 shows progress in preparing a presentation using the Overview window in Macromind Director (Macromind Inc., San Francisco), a software presentation program enabling most of the functions described above to be implemented. Event sequences including text, graphics, sound, transition effects, and animation are being controlled with the aid of selection ikons and a display of the complete sequence.

A separate good quality monitor is desirable for these operations and essential for some of them. Monitors, or more particularly the CRT's inside them, continue to improve. The currently most popular are probably the 14" and 17" (screen diagonal) 640 x 480 pixel (IBM VGA resolution) monitors. A colour tube costs about $300. By the time LCD display panels get to this stage, CRT's will probably have been improved to 1000 x 1000 pixels and will cost $150, so the CRT monitor will be around for some years yet.

The Mac II's normal 640 x 480 display is driven by a fixed speed scanning waveform generator. Suppliers offer adaptors to generate scanning speeds enabling, for example, 800 x 560 pixels or 1365 x 1024 pixels to be displayed on large monitors such the 37" Mitsubishi.

Auto-tracking monitors adjust their scanning rates automatically to synchronise. Typical ranges are 30-57 KHz horizontal and 40-75 Hz vertical. Monitors are available which will run on NTSC or PAL composite video signals, RGB analog, or RGB TTL. Armed with these alternatives the monitor should cope with almost any requirement.

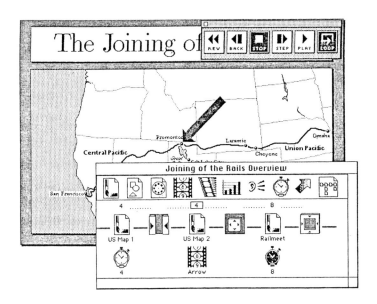

FIGURE 28.13.   PRESENTATION PREPARATION WITH MACROMIND DIRECTOR

Examples of presentation systems :-

IBM

IBM supplies two main software packages to be used in conjunction with PCs or PS/2s and the adaptors/cards described earlier. Audio Visual Connection (AVC) is the major package, suitable for corporate presentations, and Storyboard Live, which is a less comprehensive package.

AVC runs with DOS 4.0 or OS/2 and provides a wide range of facilities including:-

* Graphics superimposition over video and full motion video from cameras, recorders, or television sources.

* Digitization and storage of up to two stereo sound sources. MIDI input support.

* Control of video and audio functions and source selection of up to three video sources.

* Audio-Visual Authoring (AVA) with Scripting Language for tying audio and video sources together and for story authoring and editing.

* High resolution mode with 640 x 480 pixel display and 256 colours.

Storyboard Live also enables users to incorporate drawing, painting, animation, motion video, and voice and music. It sells in the UK for £395. Unlike AVC there is a memory limitation (no extended memory) which may limit some types of presentation.

Amiga

A package primarily designed for video special effects called the Video Toaster was introduced in 1991 by Newtek (Topeka, KS). It consists of software and a plug-in board for Amiga 2000 or 2500 machines with 5 Mbytes of memory, and sells for $1595 in the US..

It includes:-

* A switcher for providing cuts, fades, or wipes from up to 7 video
  input sources.

* Provision for special effects such as tumble, stretch, mosaic,
  roll, etc., on broadcast video in real time.

* Create animated videos in TV resolution and 16.8 million colours.

* Add titles using a chosen font with shadowing, scroll, crawl, etc.

* Create original art or paint on captured stills or broadcast TV
  frames, overlay graphics, create colour special effects etc.

An overview of "desktop video" with special reference to Amiga machines has been provided by Cook (1990).

Mac

The Mediamaker software package provides the means for devising comprehensive multimedia presentations. It was developed by the BBC Interactive Television Unit (ITU) - the same team that developed Domesday, from which they appear to have learned a marketing lesson.

Members of the ITU formed a company - The Multimedia Corporation - and Mediamaker is published on their behalf by Macromind (San Francisco). It is available for $495 from Macromind, and in the UK from Macromind's distributor, Computers Unlimited (London) for £575.

MediaMaker enables a 10 minute (or multiples of ten minutes) videotape presentation to be created by assembling still or moving data, with sound, in colour, drawn from a variety of sources. The source media may include Mac storage (for text or graphics), and various kinds of video tape or disc players. An Apple Mac SE or II, preferably with a 4 Mbyte memory for colour and hard disc is required.

The software includes multiple external device control, graphic and animation overlay, multiple windows, media segment editor, special user interface and record to videotape, media multiple track control, and so on.

A variety of cards and peripherals are required with the Mac depending on which parts of the software are to be used. They include a Mass Microsystems Quickimage, A ColorSpace card, a Videologic video overlay board for video in windows, and appropriate videotape output devices such as

TrueVision NuVista, RasterOPs Video Expander, etc.

Peripherals may include a Sony Video-8 tape recorder, a Panasonic S-VHS tape recorder, a Sony or Pioneer CD-ROM player and Videodisc player, an Apple CD-SC CD-ROM player for audio, and others.

A typical hardware collection would probably cost £10,000 - £15,000 in total.

Figure 28.14 shows the "Palette" - pictorial indexing tags (picons) - displayed on the upper half of the screen of the Mac's colour monitor. At the bottom is the assembly track - where the sequence of program items to which the picons point, are lined up and scheduled.

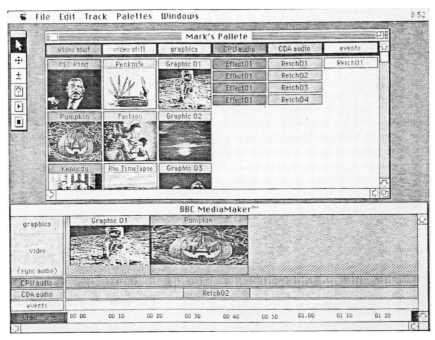

FIGURE 28.14. MEDIAMAKER – PALETTE AND ASSEMBLY TRACK

A picon may represent a still image such as graphics or an illustration, or an "indexing still" from a motion-video clip of given duration, with synchronised audio, sound effects, speech, background music, etc. A word or short phrase describing a picon appears above it. More picons, which are stored as Mac files, may be viewed by scrolling. The picon set which is immediately available will have been chosen and loaded from the "library" of items stored in the various source media, by the "producer" for composing a programme.

To assemble a programme, a picon from the palette is dragged with the mouse on to the MediaMaker assembly track. The track is calibrated in time. When dragged on to it, the picon's length is automatically expanded or shrunk so that its duration occupies a corresponding length of track. The next picon is selected in the same way. The track may be scrolled horizontally and will finally contain a succession of picons representing

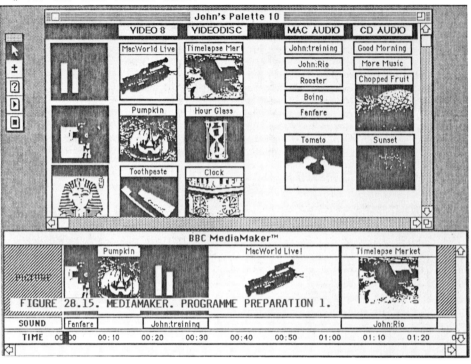

FIGURE 28.15. MEDIAMAKER. PROGRAMME PREPARATION 1.

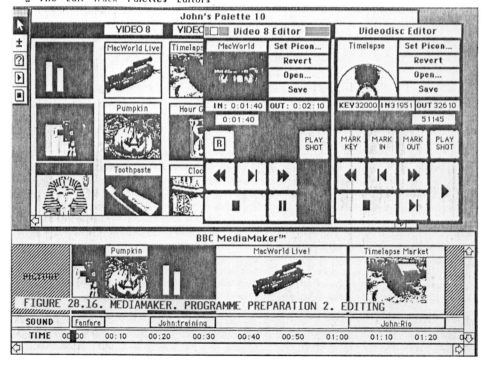

FIGURE 28.16. MEDIAMAKER. PROGRAMME PREPARATION 2. EDITING

the programme's content and duration. Adjustments may be made to the
time/length of a picon, resulting in a corresponding change in the duration
of an item should programme timing need to be altered.

Figure 20.15 is a "screen dump" print taken during operations. It
is of course in colour and as reproduced here in black and white some of the
images do not reproduce; for instance a title "Mac Graphics" appears over
the first column of picons, reproduced here as black. Figure 20.16 shows
the palette in the process of being edited.

A video-8 editor window and a videodisc editor window have been
called on to the screen, overlaying picons in the top right area. An
editing window includes the means for controlling the source media to play
the chosen item while it is viewed on a separate monitor. Part or all of it
may be chosen, and the duration of the part appears in the window. This
data is "attached" to the picon which is then displayed on the palette.

Data available from the Macintosh's disc is stored in the usual way
as a retrievable named file. A CD contains digitized stored audio, and a
CD-ROM digitized text, graphics etc. Methods for storing program items on
these media on indexed tracks from which they may be retrieved are well
known.

The Sony video-8 player is able to store indexed clips of motion
video which may be retrieved at high speed. The total playing time of the
tape is up to 90 minutes. The 30 seconds taken to completely rewind it
represents the longest possible time to locate a wanted item, but usually
the response time will be much shorter.

The retrieval process is controlled from the Mac by reference to the
tape's index stored on floppy disc. An on-disc keyword index is included.
This must be created and provided by whoever compiled the tape , to be made
available with the associated motion videotape when purchased. Tape
accessing is controlled by a counter and the system locates an item on the
tape with a timing accuracy of plus or minus 0.5 seconds.

In order to view the completed programme the MediaMaker software
calls up the indexed items from their respective sources. The sources
deliver them to a separate video tape recorder in the correct sequence and
duration. The program is played back and viewed on a separate monitor.

Special facilities are provided to ensure a smooth flow "at the
joints" between the parts which make up the complete presentation. One
problem is the elimination of the access-time gap which would otherwise
appear each time an item is recalled from the video-8 player. The present
rather crude solution is to edit out the gaps when recording the complete
presentation tape again on to a second tape.

Now for something completely different in the way of multimedia
presentations. A multimedia magazine appeared on floppy disc in February
1991 (Coghlan 1991). The 130 page Magazine called **PC Vision,** published in
Melbourne, Australia, will sell for A$3.95 (£1.60) and includes advertising.
It will include colour graphics and animation. "Page" turning commands will
be included.

The last word in multimedia presentation, as at spring 1991, is
"Virtual reality". A leaflet urging people to go to a conference about it

says:- "Over the next few years it will have a major impact in such key areas as education, industrial and professional training, entertainment and leisure, simulation, computer-aided design, telerobotics, scientific visualisation, military and security applications, and in creating a new generation of interfaces for users of large, complex, multimedia databases... virtual reality solves the man-machine interface problem by removing the interface".

Virtual reality consists of the user inside a special suit which includes sensor-gloves to follow finger and hand movements and in-front-of-the-eyes screens for viewing the virtual world created by the software. I haven't tried it yet but if the interface problems which have been with long-suffering computer users since Babbage are going to be solved "over the next few years" I must make more of an effort to show some interest.

Second Generation Hardware and Software

"Second Generation Hardware", as discussed here, means "purpose designed multimedia hardware" rather than hardware based on an established microcomputer. Little general experience has yet been accumulated with this hardware, nor with "Second Generation Software" with the possible exception of those organisations engaged in producing new titles to run on second generation machines.

Commodore CDTV

In August 1990 Commodore introduced the CDTV interactive graphics CD-ROM player/microcomputer and demonstrated the machine at the November Computer graphics show at Alexander Palace, London. CDTV disc preparation is much less expensive than preparing CD-I discs, and since Commodore expected 100 disc titles before the end of the year, the CDTV, capable of providing CD-I-like presentations, is intended to make its mark well before CD-I gets going.

The price with software is £699. The CDTV is a CD-ROM player and integral Amiga computer with a 68000 processor and a set of ports including RS232 serial and parallel, external drive, stereo out, video out, composite video out, MIDI interface for music, and the usual ports for desktop peripherals.

The potential of the CDTV for "authoring" except by suppliers of ready to use discs mainly for entertainment using conventional mastering processes, will become evident when more information is available about the software. The machine includes a 64 Kbyte card memory slot, but no floppy disc drive. The kind of activities which third party suppliers will pursue remains to be seen.

There are several CD-ROM points of interest with this machine. A proprietary compression system will be used of an unspecified performance pending agreement on compression standards. The importance of effective compression can hardly be over estimated. The capacity of CD-ROMs for the CDTV will be increased by using the six spare 8-bit control channels for graphics.

Another point of interest is the attention being paid by Amiga to sound quality. Potential CD-ROM sound quality is the same as potential CD sound quality. It seems not to be widely known that Compact Disc players do not necessarily reproduce the potentially excellent sound quality available from a disc. To digitize sound for recording purposes, 8-bit samples are generated by sampling the original analogue waveform at 44 KHz. However the process results in the acquisition of harmonic data which sounds unpleasant.

To get rid of them a technique called "oversampling and filtering" is used in CD and CD-ROM players. The scientific basis for it is doubtful, but the improvement is undoubted. Bit rates are increased and if the discerning purchaser knows how to ask the right questions and the vendor knows the answers (which he may not), he will hear about "8 x 2", "16 x 4" etc., players. The first figure denotes the number of bits per sample, and the second the pseudo-sampling ("oversampling") rate.

The best CD players, such as the Cambridge Audio CD3, embody "16 x 16" which means "16 bits with 16 times oversampling". Oversampling is used in the Amiga CDTV.

CD-ROM XA (Extended Architecture)

CD-ROM XA, announced by Philips, Sony, and Microsoft in September 1988, is a disc format which will provide some of the functions available on CD-I without departing much from established CD-ROM techniques. It will conform to the ISO 9660 standard.

The main advance towards multimedia with XA is a new standard text/graphics format for microcomputers independent of operating systems, and a coding system for sound as specified for CD-I, but with discs playable on both CD-ROM and CD-I players.

CD-I (Compact Disc Interactive)

CD-I players will play discs in CD format but the discs will include motion video so special players are needed. A CD could store about 600 PAL 625 line colour TV frames. To play the data at TV frame-repetition rates, data delivery would need to be at a rate of at least 25 Mbytes per second and the disc would play for 24 seconds or less.

Since a CD-I actually delivers data at 170 Kbytes per second, special measures must be taken. A store in the player holds 1 frame of data which is scanned at TV rates for viewing, but new data is fed into it only when there is a change of information - quite unlike normal TV practice where the system always runs at the 25 Mbytes per second rate whether there is a change of information or not. A number of other coding and display techniques are used to overcome the data rate problem.

The launch of CD-I is expected in the US at the end of 1991 with 100 disc titles, and players with interactive control software will cost about $1000 each. One expected title is "a guide to photography" where a user adjusts his camera settings to photograph a subject, takes the shot, and then looks at a "print" to check the results. Another title displays "pages from a colouring book" and a child can fill in the colours.

DV-I (Digital Video Interactive)

DV-I is not in the "CD hierarchy" - it is currently an Intel product. However it builds on CD disc technology - a DV-I disc is basically a high capacity CD-ROM disc running on a CD drive. Until recently, motion video had to be recorded on a DV-I disc via a mainframe computer to compress it to 5 Kybtes per frame. The disc will then play 72 minutes of full-screen colour motion digital video (VCR quality 256 x 240 pixels).

Alternatively it will store and play 40,000 medium resolution or 10,000 high resolution (512 x 580 pixels, 750 Kbytes uncompressed per frame) still pictures, 40 hours of audio, 650,000 pages of text, or some pro rata combination.

Decompression is carried out by a 12 MIPS VLSI (Very Large Scale Integration) chip and a second chip handles the display.

However, astonishing advances in compression technique enabled Intel to announce in November 1990 the availability of plug-in boards for microcomputers with 80386 processors, containing chips with on-chip proprietary microcode capable of "mainframe" online compression rates. The microcode can be replaced so that DV-I compression/decompression algorithms can be made to comply with expected standards in due course. A DV-I player with a 30386 PC, keyboard, joystick, audio amplifier and loudspeaker sells for about £5000.

One consequence of this development is that with an Intel TV-rate frame-grabber board installed in the micro, motion video from a camera or a broadcast TV signal can be compressed and captured on removable hard disc in real time, the disc removed, and the recorded programme played back on someone else's micro. Current floppies have insufficient capacity so the most convenience removable "disc" could be the removable cartridge on a Bernouilli drive external to the PC.

REFERENCES

Anon.
  Addison-Wesley, Reading, Mass, 1988.
    Apple Hypercard script languages: the Hypertalk language.
Anon.
  Advanced Information Report 11, 13-14, August 1989.
    PC multimedia to be a $17 billion market in 1994.
Baird, Patricia.
  The Electronic Library 6(5), 344-353, 1988.
    Hypercard opens an electronic window on Glascow.
Begoray, John A.
  Int. J. Man-Machine Studies 33, 121-147, 1990.
    An introduction to hypermedia issues, systems, and application areas.
Bolt, Richard A.
  "Spatial Data Management" interim report. Architecture Machine
  Group MIT November 1977. DARPA contract MDA903-77-C-0037.
Bordogna, P., Carrara P., et al
  Journal of Information Science 16(3). 165-174, 1990.
    Pictorial indexing for an integrated pictorial and textual IR
    environment.
Brondmo, Hans Peter, Davenport G.
  Paper presented at the hypertext II Conference, University of
  York, June 1989.
    Creating and viewing the elastic Charles - a hypermedia journal.

Bulick, Stephen.
   The Electronic Library 8(2), 88-99, April 1990.
      Future prospects for network-based multimedia information retrieval.
Bush, Vannevar.
   The Atlantic Monthly, 101-108, July 1945.
      As we may think.
Bush, Vannevar.
   In Science is not enough. Apollo Editions, New York, 1969.
      Memex re-visited.
      Note. Both Bush's articles are re-printed in a more readily
      available publication - Cawkell, A.E., (Ed.). Evolution of
      an Information Society. Aslib, London. 1987.
Carey, James W.
   Journal of Communication 31(3), 162-178, 1981.
      McLuhan and Mumford; the roots of modern media analysis.
Cawkell, A.E.
   Critique 2(9), 1-12, July/August 1990. Aslib, London.
      Compression systems.
Clarke, Arthur C.
   In The View from Serendip. Random House, New York, 215-236, 1977.
      The second century of the telephone.
Coghlan, Andy.
   New Scientist, Page 31, 23rd February 1991.
      Magazine on screen.
Conklin, Jeff.
   IEEE Computer 20(9), 17-41, 1987.
      Hypertext: an introduction and survey.
Cook, Rick.
   Byte 15(2), 229-234, February 1990.
      Desktop video studio.
Cookson, Clive.
   Financial Times, October 11th 1990.
      First auditions for the multimedia show.
Dahmke, Mark.
   Byte, 9(7), 166-167, July 1984.
      An ideal video peripheral.
Doland, Virginia M.
   Hypermedia 1(1), 6-19, 1989.
      Hypermedia as an interpretive act.
Foss, Carolyn L.
   Information Processing & Management 25(4), 407-418, 1989.
      Tools for reading and browsing hypertext.
Fox, Jeffrey A., Smith, S.L.
   Dynamic rules for user interface design. Publication M89-22,
   May 1989. The Mitre Corporation, Bedford, Mass.
Frisse, Mark.
   Byte, 13(10), 247-253, October 1988.
      From text to hypertext.
Gale, John.
   In Proceedings of the 14th International Online Information Meeting.
   London. December 1990. Learned Information, Oxford & New Jersey.
      Multimedia - how we get from here to there.
Goddard, John, Armstrong, Peter.
   Trans. Inst. Brit. Geographers 11(3), 290-295, 1986.
      The 1986 Domesday project.

Guillaume, Jeanne.
  Can J. Information Science 5, 21-29, 1980.
    Computer conferencing and the development of an electronic journal.
Hardman, Lynda.
  Hypermedia 1(1), 34-63, 1989.
    Evaluating the usability of Glascow online Hypertext.
Landow, George P.
  Computers & the Humanities 23, 175-198, 1989.
    Hypertext in literary education, criticism, and scholarship.
Maekawa, Mamoru, Sakamura, Ken, et al.
  In Mason R.E.A. (Ed). Proc. IFIP 9th World Computer Conf.
  ("Information Processing 83"). Paris, September 1983, North
  Holland, Amsterdam, 1983.
    Multimedia machine.
Marchioni, Gary and Schneiderman, Ben.
  Computer, 70-79, January 1988.
    Finding facts vs. browsing knowledge in hypertext systems.
McKnight, Cliff, Richardson, A.D.
  The Electronic Library 6(5), 338-342, 1988.
    The construction of hypertex documents and databases.
McLuhan, Marshall.
  University of Toronto Press. Toronto. 1962.
    The Gutenberg Galaxy: the making of typographical man.
Meadows, Jack.
  New Scientist, page 69, September 3rd 1987.
    Whatever happened to the electronic journal?
Mumford, Lewis.
  Harcourt, Brace & World. New York. 1963.
    Technics and civilization
Nelson, Theodor H.
  Published by Nelson at P.O.Box 128, Swarthmore, Pa 19091.
    First Edition 1981.
      Literary machines.
      Note. Preceded by Nelson's first privately published book:
      Computer Lib/Dream Machines. 1974. Re-published by Microsoft
      Press, New York, 1987.
Nelson, Theodor H.
  Datamation, 83-86, December 15th 1986.
    The tyranny of the file.
Nielsen, Jakob.
  Hypermedia 1(1), 74-91, 1987.
    Hypertext bibliography.
Pournelle, Jerry.
  Byte, 15(12), 73-88, November 1990.
    Multimedia video.
Rada, Roy, Barlow, Judith.
  The Knowledge Engineering Review 3(4), 285-301, 1988.
    Expert systems and hypertext.
Rowe, Tony, and Rhodes, Cheryl.
  Que Corporation, Carmel, Indiana. 1990.
    Que's Macintosh multimedia handbook.
Schneiderman, B., Morariu, J.
  Report, Dept. of Computer Science, U. Maryland, June 1986.
    The Interactive Encyclopaedia System (TIES).

CHAPTER 29. THE INFORMATION SOCIETY
Concepts: Telecommunication Politics: Telecommuting:
Sociology: Health: Employment

What is it?

It is as hard to circumscribe the Information Society field as it is to circumscribe the Information Technology field; both have very fuzzy edges. Consequently the selection of topics to discuss and opinions about the topics vary. Although it's not easy to avoid political controversy when trying to expound Information Technology, it is impossible to avoid it when discussing the Information Society.

A sample of the various flavours to be encountered is provided here in the brief review which follows covering three recent books on the subject.

Lyon (1988) says that "to foresee the emergence of a new kind of society is to exaggerate the novelty of IT's social consequences and to neglect familiar factors and processes - such as the built in inequalities of the market system - which continue to be highly significant. At the same time, I do wish to stress that many of the social changes related to IT are truly far-reaching and do raise basic questions for social theory".

"...It is assumed that the new "kind of society" bought about by IT is generally desirable. This sort of optimism (not unknown in the history of technology!) is not warranted, or so I shall argue. Let me also say quickly that the alternative to such optimism is not scepticism or pessimism, still less despair. Such optimism about the socially beneficial effects of new technology is an abstraction".

Martin (1988) says:- "In publicising their case the optimists appear to have been the more effective with writers such as Bell, Naisbett, Toffler, and Matsuda attaining best-seller status. In Matsuda's view, society will undergo dramatic changes typified not by struggles, wars and revolutions but by systematic, orderly, transformation.

The pessimists tend to come from the Left of the political spectrum... IT should be seen as... a further stage in the subordination of social needs and values to technological rationalisation and the needs of the market. Garnham contrasted two forms of society: one based on social reciprocity and what he called the public essence of humanity: the other on the private world of commodity-based exchange and capitalist domination."

Cawkell (1987) does not need to get much involved in "is it good or is it bad?" arguments, except by failure of inclusion or exclusion, since the book is an attempt to offer a selection of articles about the subject. The included articles are about social and political change and about developments in IT systems. He includes both optimistic and pessimistic political articles, erring on the side of the former, but also comments upon and includes a range of technical articles, considering that outstanding technical achievements deserve equal recognition.

For example in the Preface, Cawkell asks of Shannon's "A mathematical theory of communication":- "why has this article about a seemingly mundane topic, had an impact which arguably exceeds any other in this book?", and responds to that question.

Origins of the concept

Most people agree that Fritz Machlup (1962), an American economist, started it all, although he called it "The Knowledge Industry" in his book **The production and distribution of knowledge in the United States.** Machlup made the rather sensational assertions that "Knowledge Production" amounting to 29% of the US GNP, was growing more than twice as fast as the average of other GNP components, and would soon reach 50%.

A number of articles and books followed but the next major boost came in 1973 with Daniel Bell's **The coming of the post-industrial society** (Bell 1973) which discussed the drop in agriculture and manufacturing industries and the rise in services with information as the main component.

However it was Professor Parker of Stanford University and his associate Marc Porat who, in 1975, appeared to confirm that the Information Society really was approaching (Parker 1975). Porat analysed the several hundred categories of occupational statistics about the US labour force provided by the Bureau of Labour and concluded that by 1975 half the US labour force would be engaged in "information processing" occupations.

Consideration of this work - the work which launched the Information Society concept in earnest - reveals that of the 29.5 million people said to be engaged in information processing activities, well over 17 million are office workers, managers, and teachers. Nothing different is likely to happen because these people have been re-labelled "information workers".

Somewhere within Porat's corpus exist the people who are recognisably information workers. Debons (1981) suggested that there were about 1.6 million "information professionals" in the US, and Cawkell (1985) suggested that there may well be up to about 300,000 of them in the UK. While there continue to be substantial increases in the number of people fully entitled to be called information workers, the numbers involved are only a fraction of those nominated by Porat, and it was his 50% claim which really hyped-up the Information Society concept.

In the UK there are about 30,000 librarians and other information professionals, most of whom classify, keep, search, or analyse information on behalf of others. But as pointed out by Gleave (1985), the major growth is provided by different people.

It includes those engaged in scientific publishing; authors and editors; planners, implementors, and managers of information systems and networks; most researchers; statisticians;, computer programmers and so on. As many of them are generating new information, they qualify to be labelled information workers at least as much as the Librarians and Information Scientists who are mostly providing access to existing information.

Notwithstanding this shaky start, hundreds of articles and books about the topic have appeared. A rather small number look forward to halcyon days, a larger number are full of gloom and foreboding, and a huge number set out the pros and cons and come to no conclusion but advocate the need for someone, presumably governments, to intervene so that we get it right.

For example Virgo (1983) considers that unemployment in the UK is a temporary phenomenon. He provides a table of well over 3.5 million potential new jobs in what he defines as the "information industries", well exceeding the then current unemployment total.

In contrast, Schiller (1984) has visions similar to those of E.M.Forster in his story "The Machine Stops", written at the beginning of this century. Forster describes an individual sitting in an armchair as "a swaddled lump of flesh - a woman about five foot high with a face as white as a fungus. There were buttons and switches everywhere....to call for food, for music, for a hot bath". Schiller's book "Information and the crisis economy" is a condemnation of the misuse of information - an indictment of Big Business, Privatisation, and Materialism in general and of the United States in particular.

The standard middle of the road argument is put rather well by Belkin and others (1983). Listing the benefits such as computers and networks to provide information for everyone, they also discuss loss of privacy, job elimination, social isolation etc., and advocate the need for a strategy - for instance the need to take account of public fears, the requirement of continuous monitoring of the informatization of society, etc.

Progress in a sub-divided society

We need to qualify that very broad word "Society". The financial and money movement sector could be re-named the Financial Information Society right now. Their tools are keyboards, telephones, display screens and telecommunication networks. The behaviour of the staff is totally different from what it used to be. This small society has been propelled into electronic offices because of its special occupational needs. It would be absurd to label Society at large an Information Society because of the unrepresentative activities of this group, or for that matter of any other small group.

Another sector deserving special mention is the Office Sector. Unlike many other sectors, productivity has increased very slowly. This factor, together with its sheer size, have been the reasons for its selection for special attention by the equipment suppliers.

In practice the suppliers have been the victims of their own over-ebullience. One disgruntled customer said way back in 1980:- "Watch out - vendors are there for one reason and one reason only. They are there to sell. They will sell as much as the floor will bear without collapsing". Exaggerated claims have made potential customers cynical. Here is one from that same year:- "Software architectures that integrate many new jobs are making computer systems at home with top management and clerical workers alike".

The real situation in today is rather different. Word-processors are in widespread use. Many so-called professionals, particularly in large companies, use stand-alone or mainframe-connected microcomputers, but the planning, implementation, measurement of results, and social consequences of changing from a conventional to an electronic office on any scale has proved to be loaded with formidable problems. A huge number of publications offering advice have appeared, presumably to satisfy the demands of an all too receptive market.

Determining its arrival

When the phrase "The Information Society", is used, presumably this means society as a whole. Is it possible to differentiate between entertainment and information and what events can be said to really signal the arrival of The Information Society?

The TV set incorporates a tube which may display signals which are broadcast, beamed by satellite, or received via a telephone line, cable system, or fibreoptic network. It may embody special circuitry or add-on units such as videotape machines, remote control units, hi-fi reproduction units or game-playing home computers. But it will probably still be used primarily to watch entertainment programmes, and only secondarily for information such as news, weather forecasts etc.

However a teletext, or viewdata TV set which includes a keypad, decoding, page storage, and other circuits, enables its owner to use services such as tele-shopping, and provides access to some additional information. A substantial number of people have either TV sets of this type, or are using microcomputers, so it might be said that the era of the Information Society is approaching.

At some point people who use their home equipment mainly for entertainment may decide to buy add-on units, such as modems so that they can connect to external services, magnetic disc storage, optical discs, printers, speech recognisers and synthesisers and other control devices. He or she will then be able to participate in on-line educational, medical and other information services, electronic mail, home security and energy control. The power of this system will enable activities otherwise done at the work-place to be done at home. If a substantial mumber of people reach this stage it would be hard to deny that the Information Society has truly arrived.

Constraints

Established-technology constraints limit the alternatives open to users and policy makers. This factor is called "The Technocultural Paradigm" by Moschowitz (1985). The most dominant and pervasive paradigm is the pursuit of technology to increase productivity. Some would argue that this policy will create as many social and economic problems as it will solve because of the "jobless growth" phenomenon.

There are many other less all-embracing examples. The computer industry pressed the well-tried but basically unsuitable Von Neuman program-sequential number-crunching computer design into use for data processing. Consequently software design and application performance were, and still are, constrained. Parallel processing computers are a quite recent development.

Cawkell discussed technical and other facets of the supposed socio-technological revolution in 1978. The only technical point I will make here is that physical limitations are unlikely to constrain the extraordinary rate of increase in chip speeds during the next decade. Spacing limits of about 0.1 microns (one tenth of a millionth of a metre) will have been reached implying clocking intervals of less than 1 nanosecond and more than one thousand million instructions per second. Beyond that quantum effect and optical techniques will arrive. In theory this should increase speeds by a further five powers of ten - that is up to 10^{-14} seconds or 10 femtosecond switching intervals.

Choosing the right moment is one of the problems facing the organisations which implement standards. In a rapidly changing field, an improved standard may take years to implement in the face of the vested interests which are still trying to recoup their investments based on last year's standard. On the other hand a standard which is prematurely introduced may fall into disrepute because it is quickly overtaken by technical progress. It may be ignored by manufacturers who want to compete with the latest, not the obsolete, technology.

Intensive standardisation programmes are in hand, but even if vested private and public interests were in total accord, the problem is daunting. Today one of the oldest and simplest data communication standards - V24/RS232 for data-terminal/modem inter-working - is still beset by variations and mis-interpretations.

Needs and markets

In 1987 about 75% of UK students left school with less than three "O" levels and 75% of about 28 million UK taxpayers earned less than £6000 a year after tax. Most members of one of these groups are probably also members of the other. Many of them may first notice changes at work, but the Information Society will not truly have arrived until their private lives and the lives of their counterparts in other countries, who we might call "ordinary people", have become part of it.

Ordinary people's need for information is primarily about living. In my nearest town the largest volume of enquiries at the information centres and the library are about housing, welfare and health, and consumer and legal matters. This information is free. At home, television is used primarily for entertainment purposes, although a good deal of information is also viewed.

Purchased sources are likely to be confined to a newspaper plus perhaps one or two magazines. Information ranks low as a good upon which disposable incomes are spent. Perhaps the acquisition of information beyond the needs of daily living has something to do with education with which also comes increasing curiousity.

Providers have not identified the information needs of ordinary people presumably believing that they do not constitute a market. There aren't any generally available easily accessible public information services about doctors, solicitors, accountants, or about drugs, child-care, do-it-yourself materials, garden centres, supplementary benefit entitlements, or garages.

Providers may also be discouraged by certain properties uniquely associated with information which make marketing difficult. The incentive to sell is coupled with the need to retain exclusivity until payment is received. Information is intrinsically difficult in this respect. Considerable expenditure on software patenting, copyright in databases and downloading, photocopying etc., testifies to the current interest although enforcement and the degree of protection provided by the law is still a grey area.

Home computers are quite widely used but the major US studies described by Dickerson (1983) indicate that adoption of them is likely to be limited to home owners with above average education and income. The installed base, said to be over 12 million in 1983, was used for games and to a lesser extent for education, all other uses totalling only 20% according to Baer (1985). However in the UK, according to the 1984 microcomputer census (BIS-Pedder 1984) 90% of the 2.5 million UK home computers are used solely for games and "it is hard to think of a single domestic application which can be cost justified". Evidently ordinary people, even if they have a home computer, are unlikely to use it for information retrieval.

Information services geared to domestic use are obtainable, provided suitable equipment is available, via services like Compuserve and more general information can be obtained via the over one million Teletext TV sets and the 30,000 Prestel sets in UK homes. The ordinary man's terminal is most nearly approached by the French Minitel which is in much wider use.

But regardless of income or education, many people are overwhelmed by an information overload of political claims, legislation, news, crises, drummed-up scares and general aggravation. When the next politician preludes his remarks with "the facts are....etc"., the long-suffering listener/viewer knows that nobody is going to check the fiddled statistics he has used to support his argument. They are forgotten in the next wave of extraneous information.

The difficulties we have are well put by Michael (1984). We live in a world where "everything is connected with everything else. Neat divisions of black and whites, either/ors, cause/effect, winners/losers disappear and with them the comfortable certainty of knowing what's going on and what to do about it. Pogo's discovery that "we have met the enemy and they is us" is hardly ever comforting". Not only are we overloaded with information, we are overloaded with the task of choosing the information to take our chances with".

Social effects

Social forecasts cover a huge range. On the one hand we have Kranzberg (1985) saying "The advances of the Information Age, if they follow previous patterns, could provide us with more goods and services, increased material well-being, and help do away with poverty and misery throughout the globe. By giving us greater knowledge of the human, social, and environmental consequences of our technical options it might help us avoid catastrophic assaults upon nature and upon our fellow human beings".

On the other hand Schiller (1984), with special reference to public information, considers that while library information access has greatly improved "this benefit is accompanied by the abandonment of the libraries' free access policy. The composition and character of its holdings change as the clientele shifts from the general public to the ability-to-pay users.

What hypothetically could become an information rich society is on the way to becoming a community divided into information haves and have-nots. The commercialisation of information knows no bounds. There is the spectacle of information deprivation in the midst of information abundance."

General unease about unauthorised access to networked files, telephone tapping, and other aspects of the invasion of privacy does not seem to be very great. For the information-haves there is certainly some unease about computer fraud, industrial and international espionage, and the acquisition of technical information by stealth rather than by Research & Development.

Futures

One of George Eliot's characters says In the **Mill on the Floss** "It is always chilling to say that you have no opinion to give. If you have to deliver an opinion at all it is mere stupidity not to do so with an air of conviction and well-founded knowledge. You make it your own in uttering it and naturally get fond of it". I cannot say that I am fond of any the forecasts which follow because they will probably be wrong.

Much has been said about The Information Society with an air of conviction, yet for most facets of this topic, supportive evidence is notable for its absence. The impact of a new kind of social structure - and it seems likely that eventually there may be one - has yet to be felt. Today, talking about the Information Society is still an exercise in forecasting.

We do have a track record for forecasting the underlying information technology. If these forecasts had been reasonably accurate we would feel more confident about making predictions about the very difficult area of societal changes. Unfortunately they have been hopelessly wide of the mark.

A 1970 article in **Computer Decisions** said "Small businesses are not going to have small computers: it's not a practical way to go". In 1979 a forecast was made for just one year into the future:- "There will be 100,000 Prestel sets in the UK in 1980 equally split between domestic and business".

Weitz (1990) supplies some interesting information about forecasting information trends. He suggests methods of assessment in the case of the future effects of Expert Systems, hoping to do better than a forecast made in a 1958 article in the Harvard Business Review that computer technology would "move into the managerial scene rapidly with a definite and far-reaching impact".

Growth markets were forecast for "Tooth decay vaccine (in 1968) - 10 years", "Rotary automobile engines (1971) - 4 years, and "Ultrasonic dishwashers" - 5 years. The primary reason for failure is an overvaluation of the technology, infatuation with technology for technology's sake, failure to assess benefit at a reasonable cost, and an inability to predict social or demographic changes.

Correct forecasts were made about "The Elderly market", "The Baby Boom market", "Personal computers", "Microwave ovens", and "Home pregnancy tests". "Correct forecasts tended to be demographic in nature, and those where fundamental market research was undertaken and where real benefit was offered for the price", says Weitz.

But even if Kalman Toth (1990) read Weitz's article he probably remains unabashed. Toth is founder and chief scientist of the Silico-Magnetic Intelligence Corporation. His forecast is that human intelligence will be surpassed by machine intelligence before the year 2000.

"Silico-Magnetic Intelligence" (SMI) will have some quite nasty/pleasant effects according to your viewpoint.

Toth obviously thinks that if you are going in for forecasting you might as well go the whole hog:- "The SMI revolution will differ drastically from the Industrial Revolution because it will eliminate all jobs including those of the industrial elite".

In passing I should mention that it usually takes at least ten years from first announcement of a new development to medium scale use. Packet switched networks took 15 years, optical fibres 14, satellites 30. The electronic journal was conceived in 1976 and no viable product is yet available. Continuous speech recognition may not be here for another 20 years.

There has been steady progress over the years in processes amenable to data processing such as accounting, inventory, and payroll. The idea of the Electronic Office involving the rest of the executive, professional, and secretarial staff has been heavily promoted, carried along on the success of word processing, but very little has really happened.

Promotional photographs of models smiling at their WP machines scattered among the potted plants, captioned "The Office of the Future" do not signify that office behaviour or the way work gets done have changed much. It is one thing to provide a tool to improve typing processes, and document production and quality, but quite another to make an impact upon the working day of administrators and managers. But the potential cost savings achievable by time-saving and decision-making aids for these people is large so there will be no let up in the effort.

During the next five years large organisations will continue to experiment, slowed down by telecommunication and incompatible machine problems, the absence of critical masses of people using the same services, and a lack of understanding in matching office behaviour to machine functions. It seems unlikely that the executive's working methods will have changed very much. However the productivity of certain professionals will have increased, following improvements in multi-purpose software packages, manipulative aids, graphics and displays.

Data communication facilities should improve greatly with the arrival of the Integrated Services Digital Network (ISDN). In 1986 is was stated that it would be in place nationally in the UK by 1990. It isn't. Similar developments are in progress in other countries. This means a gradual change from a network designed for telephone conversations into one which appears to be designed for high speed data transmission as well.

Expert systems and speech recognition will make good progress in the 1990s, and even better progress when the needed higher processing speeds come with electronic and optical parallel processing. However the bottleneck will be programming. Progress may well be dictated by the development rate of automatic programming. It will be a hard task to transform today's human-intensive unrecorded processes into items such as automatic compilers.

Many more small businesses are using multi-purpose micromputers but people will still believe persuasive salesmen and expect to buy it today and use it tomorrow. In the near future the long frustrating period of finding

out how it works and merging paper-based and machine readable data will ease
only slightly.

In retailing, Electronic Funds Point of Sale (EFTPOS), the use of
Smart Cards, and other systems for performing cash transactions electrically
will grow, also slowed down by incompatibility, but especially by
difficulties in deciding who benefits and who pays for costly installations.
Although there will be some social resistance, at least an understanding of
what needs to be done is less dependent on the need first to understand
human behaviour.

In articles about the Information Society it is often implied that
each member of it will have to pay for equipment, communications, and often
the information itself. But if "Information Society" is meant to apply to
Society in general, it involves the 5% of rich or relatively well off
people, the 20% with some disposable income, and the 75% which form the mass
of ordinary people with little disposable income.

The top 25% will be able to afford to add to their equipment and
telecom facilities for a bigger choice of entertainment and information. It
is from this group that the so-called telecommuters will emerge if they are
prepared to accept the social re-adjustments demanded by this working
method.

At present it is not at all clear at what rate service availability
will increase and charges will drop, or when a critical mass situation will
be reached. The top 5% of people by income in medium and large size
countries represent a large market.

The strongest controlling forces will be social. For instance
shopping can be a boring routine need or a pleasurable social activity.
People at the social-loner technology-minded end of the spectrum will be
happy to fiddle around and acquire expertise at their terminals. Those at
the gregarious non-technical end of the spectrum will not. Among the top
5%, their attitudes rather than their income, will determine how they prefer
to live, even if a wide range of electronic services are on offer.

The rate at which ordinary people become part of the Information
Society is likely to depend on state social priorities as well as upon
attitudes. So far, governmental subsidies have been mainly confined to
scientific services. In the US, Sputnik One provided the incentive. The
present trend seems to be to move towards a situation where information is a
good among many others to be purchased according to perceived values. State
money is not then wasted in propping up unwanted services.

Ordinary people's information consumption may increase when it is
associated with the consumption of other goods. Those temperamentally
inclined will go teleshopping if service costs are borne by the suppliers
and the necessary home electronics are incorporated in a slightly more
expensive TV set.

There is no reason to believe that ordinary people will re-evaluate
their priorities and up-rate information just because they hear that
electronic offices are all the rage. They will probably continue to rely on
what they get free or by a modest expenditure.

It seems likely that information and the associated facilities will steadily increase where there is an occupational need, the knowledge to use the facilities, and the money to pay for it. Current human-machine interface problems will gradually improve with the development of natural language expert systems. The majority of the population will not be included in this scenario so the gap between the information haves and have-nots will widen.

Will this information differential have undesirable consequences? There is a case for state intervention in some areas. For example what is the point in deciding that people need state assistance of whatever kind if obscure complex information denies them access to it? In the UK many people are denied help for this reason.

More important still is the availability of the background information which makes for the "well informed person". Inevitably the information-haves, having acquired a taste for the facilities and benefits of improved occupational information, and usually being within the top 20% by income, will extend these experiences into their home activities. On the other hand if the trend of charging ordinary people for information that is now free continues, then it will be harder for them to become well informed. An increase in this kind of unbalance is unwelcome, but quite likely to happen.

A very important aspect stems from that hackneyed but true phrase "Information is power". Un-noticed insidious changes can result in undesirable concentrations of power, but most people don't concern themselves with this intangible idea.

The information haves will accumulate more power, a trend which is unlikely to be arrested, least of all by governments of whatever complexion. Witness the promises made about reforming the Official Secrets Act before every election in the UK since the first world war, but never fulfilled by any incoming government - a classic example both of "information is power" and public unconcern.

TELECOMMUNICATIONS POLICY

> In the U.S. a woman takes to the telephone as a woman in more decadent lands takes to morphia. You can see her at morn at her bedroom window, pouring   confidences   into her   telephone, thus   combining   the joy of her innocent vice with the healthy freshness of breeze and sunshine.
> The Spectator, April 7th, 1906.

Telecommunications and information services infrastructures

A requirement for an "advanced" Information Society is a telecommunication-based information service infrastructure. It will consist of the same basic arrangement as now exists - information providers connected to user's machines via a telecoms network.

But the machines and software needed for the presentation of text, graphics, and illustrations in a variety of formats will conform to agreed standards. Information providers of information in any standard format will then be assured that any user's machine will reproduce their data exactly as intended. A user's machine must be very easy to operate.

User's will themselves be able to select any desired service, and their machine will then be automatically configured to the appropriate standardised data format needed for that particular service.

The inter-connecting network will not be a pressed-into-service telephone network designed for speech, but an end-to-end international network which will accommodate the information provider's data signals, whether representing text, illustrations, or motion video, assuring error-free transmission of the data at a specified speed.

Provider's will not need to incur large costs associated with their particular kind of data, nor need they be concerned with the means by which customers receive the service. Customers will not have to incur additional expenditure on their installation to receive it.

Such a system, representing as it does an enormous telecoms investment, the development of software of great complexity, and volume manufacture of machines to bring prices down, will take decades to develop. For such a system to be viable it will have to accommodate all data - that is both "entertainment" and "information" data.

The 50 year investment in a monopolistic global telephone network, its adaptation for the transmission of even simple data for which it is ill-suited, and the provision of alternative networks, limit the rate of progress. Cut-throat competition within private industry has produced a wide range of non-standard incompatible equipment to hook on to the telephone system, or on to the fragmented specialised networks.

The old technology is well entrenched. It has been developed by trial and error since 1455 - when Gutenberg demonstrated the feasibility of moveable type. A set of compromises in compilation, distribution, storage, display, aesthetics, convenience, accessibility and cost has emerged which serves us after a fashion.

The new technology has been developed during the last 50 years, but 90% of it during the last 15. In that time radio, television, automation and computers have been followed in quick succession by pocket calculators, home computers, online systems, word processing machines, video and optical disks, desktop publishing and multimedia, backed by a semiconductor technology proceeding at an unprecedented speed.

The general momentum of all this encourages the belief that almost anything is possible by the introduction of more technology. There is no shortage of people with vested interests in fostering that belief. However application takes time, as has been discussed already. Ordinary people get in the way. They have contra-beliefs generated both by innate conservatism and often by well-founded scepticism.

This scepticism is in part a reaction to sales razz-mataz, to the observed general mismatch between men and machines, and to the fact that for every prediction which turned out to be an under-estimate, there are several which turn out to be unduly optimistic or completely wrong.

Political reality means both concentration on the art of the possible with operations managed to take advantage of PTT or government policy instead of clashing with it. Current attitudes and actions in communications deregulation, particularly in the US and UK, obviously need close attention. What should governments do and what will they actually do? You may take the view that the less a government does, the better, you may think it should have a limited role, or you may think it should intervene at all levels.

I see little evidence that any government has had much success in intervening at the market level. It may result in a disaster - witness the rise and fall of Nexos in the UK some years ago. The financing and political pressures, followed by the sale of Inmos were not much better. In this area of rapid changes and emerging markets, bureaucratic involvement seems unhelpful.

All governments are more or less involved in several areas - particularly employment in the industry, control of telecommunications, and with privacy and security. Involvement in communications - because of the importance of what is communicated, particularly news - spills over into topics like data protection, the flow of information across borders, and the concern of undeveloped countries about this topic.

The government has a role in co-ordinating national and international standards. Perhaps it can best continue to do that by supporting organisations like NPL, British Standards and ISO in the UK, National Bureau of Standards and ISO in the US, and similar activities in other countries.

In the US the IEEE has succeeded in establishing standards which have become international such as the RS232 communications interface. Some manufacturers have established de facto standards such as IBM's SNA communication protocol. Europe often follows the US in this field although attempts by IBM to formally establish SNA in the UK by an alliance with British Telecom was frustrated by one of the first major acts of the then newly established UK regulatory body, OFTEL. In Europe, German DIN standards have been adopted in some fields (not in information technology).

The economics and politics of telecommunications

Governments are of course concerned about roads, medical services, police, railways, telecommunications etc., and the question of state control has always been controversial in democratic countries. In the US, telecommunications has been in the public eye for many years. In the UK, interest is more recent. Governmental interest in information technology has grown because it is seen as a way of generating new industries and services, increasing exports, and providing new jobs to replace those lost in decaying industries. UK governmental interest in cable systems is a particular example.

The present UK government takes more of an arm's length view than has formerly been the case - in other words it is attempting to set a climate which it thinks will encourage development, rather than becoming directly involved in it - hence its action in first liberalising and then privatising British Telecom, in granting licenses for cable franchises, and so on. In the US the trend is similar with the deregulation of AT&T. There are some signs of a move in this direction in continental Europe.

Inevitably governments have been and will continue to be involved in the provision of telecommunications through the PTT's (a European acronym which is used here to describe all telecom authorities). The creation of a suitable PTT network depends upon the actions of PTTs/governments.

The great advantage of the international PTT telephone network is that it exists. It is far from ideal for data transmission but can be pressed into service for that purpose. Most PTTs have also created, or are in the process of creating, purpose designed national data networks. They also collaborated in Europe under EEC auspices in setting up Euronet, a network consisting of interconnected host computers in different countries running databases for information storage and retrieval (mainly scientific information) for terminal-connected users.

The conversion of telephone networks into Integrated Service Digital Networks (ISDN) - a long term objective of many PTTs - will remove the distinction between the analogue telephone network and digital systems using an out-dated telephone network - the system will become all-digital.

Private Networks are composed of lines leased from the PTTs for inter-connecting the different sites of an organisation within a country, or may be to provide intra-organisation services for large companies, airlines etc.

Commercial Networks are mainly Value Added Networks (VANs) developed by private telecommunication companies in consequence of de-regulation in the United States, providing special services over lines leased from AT&T, or using satellite or terrestrial microwave communications. Some commercial network companies have been accorded the status of "common carriers", meaning that they are permitted to carry traffic for others without having to qualify as VANs. Large commercial networks have "nodes" - that is connection points - in Europe and elsewhere for local connection.

If these three kinds of network were interconnected so that any service available on any of them was available to any customer in such a way that there appeared to be a single network, then a big step towards universal communications would have been made. The critical mass of customers needed to encourage more services would appear, the system would grow, costs would fall and home services would become viable.

There are difficult technical and political problems to overcome but the main obstacles to this kind of common sense have been political. Most PTTs have rigidly applied their carrier monopoly. No organisation has been permitted to provide its own communication links between itself and customers without the partial or total involvement of PTTs. This may be a desirable objective for a universal telephone system, but the requirements for a universal network for information transmission are quite different.

A range of opinions, mainly by economists, about telecommunications politics are provided in a book edited by Snow (1986). You may agree with Edmund Burke's comment:- "The age of chivalry is gone; that of sophisters, economists, and calculators has succeeded", but there are some interesting articles in it.

Eli Noam considers that the European PTT's are shocked at the US "voluntary dismemberment" of the US monopoly. Their "perception has resulted in strong defensive actions, including an interpretation of American developments as rooted in political-ideological values rather than in engineering and technology, and thus as outside scientific rationality".

Jean-Paul Voge takes precisely this viewpoint. Having discussed late 19th century "unbridled competition" in the US and measures taken to curtail it such as the Sherman Antitrust Act, he continues "It is therefore rather astonishing to see these antitrust measures now weakened in the name of a deregulatory policy that pretends to be an attack on monopolies but that in practice eliminates the obstacles to dividing up the world market between cartels or the constitution of international trading companies of the Japanese variety".

Voge uncompromisingly concludes "In view of the preceding, French Telecom has little doubt of its ability in the coming years to continue reconciling the concept of a public service with economic dynamism and progress, without the need to modify the laws governing telecommunications in France" - a statement which seems to have been overtaken by events.

But another Frenchman - Gorges Anderla, one-time Director of the CEC department dealing with scientific and technical information - is scathing about current French telecoms policy. Writing not in the Snow book, but in the January 1987 issue of "Information World Review" he criticises Jacques Stern of Bull who states that competition in telecoms "would be a catastrophe for everyone".

Anderla suggests that comments made about Transpac - "infinitely superior, and by far, to its American competitors" should be taken with a grain of salt "...when remembering that a recent study (by EUSIDIC) showed that 49 out of 100 data calls did not arrive at their destination". Transpac is the French packet switched network.

He is also scathing about French company policy. He suggests that remarks about Bull's "spectacular turnaround" are premature. " Having accumulated losses of 3 billion francs it received a capital grant of 4.7 billion and a research grant of 1.5 billion. In addition, the government reserved major orders for Bull.. .without exception its mainframes are either Honeywell or NEC and two thirds of its other models are either imported or made under licence... in all of that where is France's real interest?" What goes on in France sounds remarkably like what goes on in the UK.

Returning to Snow's book, Charles Jonscher is one of the few people who has no unkind words for the old British Post Office. When they ran telecoms in the UK I always found the PO people to be very helpful, but the equipment they demanded from UK manufacturers was over-engineered and antiquated (hence the decay of the UK telecoms export business), and the curious legal framework under which the Post Office laboured was stultifying.

According to a well known authority, Ithiel de Sola Pool, government policy for the Post Office at that time "protects inefficiency, removes incentives for self-improvement, penalises consumers, and lowers the gross national product".

In regard to co-operation between PTTs and their national telecom industries Noam says:- "A variety of barriers are set to protect this cooperation; these include an unwillingness to procure foreign equipment, coordinated development of new technology, and PTT-organised setting of equipment standards. One consequence of this protective system is that European prices are said to be 60% to 100% higher for switching equipment and 40% higher for transmission equipment than prices in North America".

"The labor unions are in a similar position because PTTs are among the largest national employers, and because employees benefit from salary levels and job security that may not be sustainable under a competitive regime. Furthermore for unions as well as for the political left, the existing PTT system merits support not only for material but also for ideological reasons as a nationalised key industry".

"The frequently more pronounced political and class divisions in Europe lead to a strong feeling that a critical part of their superstructure, particularly one with such future importance in the information society, cannot be entrusted to private interests dedicated to the profit motive".

"Other members of the post-industrial coalition are the poor, the elderly, the farmers, and the small towns, all of whom support the PTT system because they fear that a liberalised regime would threaten the supply of their service".

Can the existing networks be coalesced, however administered, to provide the needs of the Information Society and how long is it likely to take? The "critical mass" problem mentioned previously could of course be resolved by further separation rather than coalescence. New separate networks can appear for inter-connecting a specific information source and its customers (subject to regulatory conditions) because the value of the specific information is believed to justify the specific service - the services available to stockbrokers in the City of London are an example.

A possible compromise would be multiple interconnected networks, each free to innovate (a huge unified network would tend to adopt communications new technology rather slowly), but with common interconnection standards and a payments clearing-house mechanism.

Private industry is unlikely to introduce networks or services unless it considers that the market will return an adequate short or medium term profit. For PTT monopolies this aspect is less important, consequently marketing skills are also of less importance to them.

The potential advantage of the activities of government agencies such as PTTs in establishing a network is that the system is imposed on the population by dictat which means that it ought to be possible to install it quickly. Whether it is done quickly is another matter - Euronet progressed very slowly. However the launching of Viewdata/Teletext in the UK and the associated standards was done relatively quickly. There was no public consultation.

The disadvantage is that in the absence of control by the market the taxpayer's money can be "invested" more or less continuously. Shut-down may become politically unacceptable and good money follows bad money.

It may be necessary to start up in this manner, but without commercial criteria, success yardsticks are absent. The Prestel (originally Viewdata) service would have been long since shut down had it been a commercial system since it turned out to be based on wrong expectations.

In the United States it is almost impossible to do things by dictat. Prolonged public discussion, lobbying, etc., is necessary before anything can be done. Considerable reliance is placed on market forces. That country also possesses a strong electronics industry, has a propensity to innovate, and contains a large number of people with disposable income. Together these factors may enable service infrastructures to get off the ground.

In 1980 information services to home computer owners were being operated by two companies, The Source and Compuserve. Compuserve's Micronet was interconnected with Tymnet. Charges were $5 per hour plus $2 for Tymnet. The Source and Compuserve then had about 8000 subscribers, mainly with TRS80's or Apple 2's. Compuserve offered micronet terminal programs for both machines and a videotex program for TRS80s.

The Source and Compuserve are also Information Providers. Compuserve provided a range of services included with its $5/hour fee - for instance an electronic mail service for all listed uses - but charged extra for special services like access to 32,000 continuously updated stocks in its Microquote service. Detailed information about a stock cost 5c. Compuserve had also signed up other information providers, including 13 daily newspapers, to provide current editorial information. A special service from AP was included.

Perceiving that it might have a customer base, a bank in Knoxville concluded an agreement with Compuserve and Radio Shack who supplied TRS80 microcomputers, and offered banking services for viewing statements, paying bills etc., by the page at $5 per hour.

The service included the provision of a special modem for use with a TRS80 into which a magnetic card carrying an encryption key had to be inserted. This provided a secure channel between the user and the bank. For those who did not already possess a TRS80, a service Company associated with the bank (UASC) would rent a TRS80 with the special modem at $25/month. At that time about 300 people used this service.

It was not clear whether prices for domestic users had dropped to a level which made continuing success probable. The fact is that a structure has been gradually assembled in which operational costs were shared by many. Consequently an information provider or customer could join at a low incremental cost. There was no public financial burden. The foundation of the undertaking was the existence of a corps of people with a common self-interest - they were computer buffs. However there is no reason why business and professional users could not use the common resource and some did.

This kind of approach prospered. By 1983 The Source, then owned by Reader's Digest had expanded greatly and Compuserve, a subsidiary of H&R Block, had over 20,000 subscribers. Each runs a "Chat" service with a directory of subscribers, for the exchange of typed messages with any other subscriber, also classified situations vacant and news services.

Compuserve offers an online encyclopaedia, and both have shop at home services listing 30,000 items in an online catalogue. The all-in price is about $21 per hour dropping to $6 per hour at off peak periods. Software on floppy disk for different microcomputers is available for auto-dialling, communications, moving data in or out, and printer control. Since then Compuserve has become an international provider offering hundreds of different services.

The United States; regulation in the 1930s

We may note, in passing, one unique aspect of the US telecoms scene; what the government or its agencies can or cannot do is set out in the Constitution, aspects of which set the whole scene. Sometimes the Constitution is directly invoked in telecoms regulation. For example freedom of speech and of the press referred to in the first amendment extends to electrically transmitted information (**Winters v. New York** 1948). This ruling was made during a hearing about cable systems. The court held that one person's entertainment may be another's doctrine.

In the communications area, regulatory issues set out in the 1934 Communications Act were, as one report put it, "adjudicated, investigated, prosecuted, negotiated, settled, or informally acted upon" by the Federal Communications Commission (FCC), and are reviewable by the court of appeals and ultimately by the Supreme Court.

The FCC was set up by Congress in 1934 to regulate communications, an action which must have been influenced by the earlier important **Smith v. Illinois decision** (1930). This made it mandatory for carriers to recover some of the cost of local calls by charging higher prices for long distance calls. The FCC now handles broadcasting, cable, common carrier, and safety and service matters in the United States. With the increasing complication of communication issues the regulatory procedures are laborious, costly, and time consuming.

Winds of change

In the 1960's the US telephone network started to be pressed into service for data transmission since it was the only ubiquitous network available. New requirements prompted the following questions. First, would consumer's needs be best fulfilled by entrusting all services to the traditional carriers, and second, was it rational to extend the monopolistic structure to the closely associated information processing technologies covering devices and services like modems, terminals, private line and microwave facilities, special data services, communication satellites etc?

The FCC held its first and second computer enquiries in 1971 and 1976. These enquiries had a great effect on the formulation of policy.

It became evident that the convergence of communication and computer technologies required that the business of a "common carrier", and the regulation applied to it under the 1934 Communications Act, needed re-assessment. Not only had it become extremely difficult to determine where communications ended and processing began, but carriers and processing companies are different animals.

The carriers adopt long periods over which to depreciate their equipment (the British Post Office depreciated plant and equipment over 25 years). The organisation's finances and price structures are arranged accordingly. Obsolescence in the computer/data processing industry, on the other hand, operates on a five year or less cycle, not because equipment has by then come to the end of its useful life, but because it needs to be replaced by something better and cheaper.

Steady as you go and reliable service are the watchwords of the carriers. The computer industry's are pace, rate of change, and attention to marketing.

The de-regulatory wind of change which first blew in the United States was not generated so much because the regulated monopoly principle for a telephone network was found wanting, although it had its critics, but because of converging technology. The answer to the question "Where have all the boundaries gone?" was "Stolen by engineers - every one!"

The telephone system, once a definable entity, was becoming an information system. The interwoven issues are complex and the outcomes are of the greatest importance, but, it was said, "commercial considerations indicate that the role of government lies in formulating generous and international telecommunication policies".

Action

A huge opinionated literature exists about ways to provide satisfactory communication services for all. One opinion, unsurprisingly from IBM (Branscomb 1979), is that "any entrepreneur should be permitted to purchase these facilities (electronic highways), utilize them to support any end application he has in mind, and offer the entire application to the public without any form of regulatory impediment".

The outstanding problem in the US has been in differentiating between data transport and data processing in order to formulate a regulatory policy appropriate to different kinds of organisation. Common carrier monopolies have a capital to annual turnover ratio of about 3:1 (Hartley's first law). The ratio for most industrial and commercial organisations is about 1:3. US tax laws relating to amortisation in the two cases is quite different.

Two paths to a solution have been sought. First, the monopoly of the carriers was allowed to be eroded. In 1968 the FCC allowed competitive devices to be connected to the existing telephone network (The **"Carterphone"** decision) and events were set in motion to allow Microwave Communication Inc. (MCI) to offer long distance links with distribution through local telephone lines. Liberalisation with cream skimming safeguards to ensure that the carriers offered a universal telephone service was starting to creep in.

Second, several attempts were made to re-write the 1934 Communications Act, but only relatively minor amendments were enacted until the passage of the Telecommunication Competition and Deregulation Act through the Senate in October 1981.

The relatively minor changes made during the period preceding the major changes introduced by this Act were highly controversial. For example AT&T's chairman of the board John de Butts (1977) said "By fragmenting responsibility for service, those (FCC) decisions jeopardise its quality. By encouraging wasteful duplication of facilities they add unnecessary costs to the nation's telephone bill. A continuation of these policies....will produce significantly higher charges - primarily for 68 million telephone users".

Raymond Kraus (1975), an ex-Bell employee turned consultant, waxes almost lyrical:- "The Bell Laboratories is the most unique, prestigious, and efficient communications organisation of its kind by several orders of magnitude. It has produced more Nobel and other award winners, more scientific discoveries and breakthroughs, more new apparatus developments, and more new systems and subsystems than all the other telephone laboratories in the world put together".

On the other hand ex-FCC bureau chief Walter Hinchman (1979) thinks that "The Bell system companies - under AT&T management - collectively enjoy control over every aspect of U.S. telecommunications service, equipment manufacturing and supply, local exchange service, and long-distance service. This bottleneck control is a major and growing threat to the increasingly vital information handling component of the American social, economic, and political system".

And with respect to allegedly selfish system development, Carlson Agnew remarked "AT&T favoured a low orbit (satellite) system...the equipment used in such a system would have been part of the company's base rate, thereby enabling it to earn a larger return than on a geostationary system... AT&T and Bell Labs had a substantial financial and even personal commitment to the low orbit technology (some would see this as evidence of the not-invented-here syndrome)...much of this behaviour is consistent with more general predictions as to the behaviour of regulated firms".

In August 1982 a Justice Department/AT&T anti-trust suit was settled by a decree issued after lengthy hearings under Judge Harold Green. It provided for the divestment by AT&T of its 22 operating companies. AT&T was allowed to provide equipment and services for the computer and data processing business, although it was not allowed to provide electronic publishing services, such as videotex, for 7 years.

A number of other conditions were included, but the general effect was to allow others to compete in areas where AT&T had a monopoly, while allowing AT&T to compete in fields which it was not allowed to enter previously.

This disentangling operation is the largest since the dismantling of the Rockefeller Standard Oil Empire decades ago. AT&T's revenues were nearly $65 billion in 1982, with assets at around $150 billion. The privatisation of AT&T's local operating companies placed $120 billion in the hands of shareholders during 1984.

One effect was expected to be an increase in the charges of local calls since the latter would no longer be automatically subsidised. Some repercussions soon emerged. A gentleman's agreement between AT&T and ITT was established many years ago whereby AT&T would not compete in ITT's overseas markets. In the new situation each turned its attention to what had been the other's preserve.

AT&T's chosen method of doing this relatively quickly was to join forces with Philips with the objective of joint production of a digital telephone exchange.

As Mayer (1980) says "This is an industry in a state of change with
many attendant uncertainties best resolved by proceeding with the market
tests that have been started during the last decade. So far the industry
has not crumbled because of these experiments....many ways can be
identified, moreover, to remedy any adverse developments if, by chance, they
do occur....there is considerable reason to believe that the market test
will end up where free markets usually do, with the most efficient
producers, and therefore consumers as well, all benefitting".

This last phrase suggests that Mayer's political pursuasions, are,
shall we say, to the right of centre - a thought confirmed by the complete
absence of any mention of the future for AT&T's employees. Perhaps Mayer
may consider that this is so assured that it needs no mention.

According to Judge Greene, who conducted the anti-trust trial:-

"With respect to all the important indicia - price, innovation,
quality, and broadening of the industry's base - divestiture is fulfilling
its promise... cost of both local and long distance service is down ...
hundreds of new businesses have sprung up ... MCI, US Sprint, and others,
have not gone under... (Greene 1989).

But Greene is also quoted as saying (Bell 1988) that the Baby Bell's
behaviour "does not inspire confidence that, should they be permitted to
enter other lines of business, they would treat competitors in an
even-handed manner". The Consumer Federation of America translates Greene's
remarks into "a complete slam-dunk of the regional holding companies which
have done everything errant monopolies would do". Five years after
divestiture Bell asks "have the goals been attained? On balance the answer
seems to be "yes" notwithstanding a few twists and turns on the way".

However workers in the industry take a poor view of the situation.
They "argue that the policy has led to increases in rates for individual
consumers and small businesses... and a poorer quality of service". When
asked who benefitted first from the change in a random sampling of 1062
people from the Canadian telephone industry workforce:- "1% said
themselves, 82% the company, 14% business customers, and 4% individual
customers" (Mosco and Zureik, 1988).

US Telecommunications after 1982

In 1982 the FCC proposed a "network access charge", tied to real
costs, to be levied on all new entrants. The cost of access would be
related to the value of the in-place equipment required to make a telephone
call, not the traffic-sensitive cost incurred by using the network, which is
small in comparison. The cost of using the network would be the same for
the incumbents and the new competitive services.

The FCC's first proposals were rejected by Congress on the grounds
that they would fall too heavily on residential and small business customers
who were already feeling the impact of higher prices in consequence of
deregulation. Larger businesses - bigger users of long distance calls -
were getting reductions. The access charge was limited to $2 per month.

Another reason for not setting the network access charge too high is
that it would encourage more competitors to provide direct-connections for
long distance service in order to bypass the local network; instead of

maximising the use of an existing resource, this arrangement simply duplicates it. The "duplication" may take the form of a microwave (radio) link from a customer to the nearest access point on the long distance network.

By-passing politics is a complicated bizarre on-going issue in the US. Briefly, AT&T's response to the FCC's freeing of microwave frequencies for private use in 1959 had been the introduction of the low-priced Wide Area Telephone Services (WATS) and Telpak private leased line services. This move successfully discouraged any competition from OCCs (Other Communication Companies) until 1975. In that year, MCI, approved with others as a carrier by the FCC in 1971, offered a competitive long-distance service.

AT&T countered by allowing OCC access to its switched network but increased its line charges; local access had, of course, to be via a Bell Operating Company (BOC), and this required a string of additional digits to be dialled by OCC users to make the necessary interconnections.

Both AT&T Communications and the OCCs pay an access charge to the BOCs, but the FCC have decreed that OCCs should receive a compensatory 55% discount - that is they are charged 55% less than AT&T. This discount is apparently a major factor enabling them to remain competitive. These extraordinary operations result in what economists would call a "welfare loss" since artificial pricing is distorting the market resulting in the under-use of existing resources.

If a way can be found of removing the extra digits so will the discount be removed - spelling disaster for some OCCs. Perhaps they have already seen the writing on the wall since some are reacting by diversifying. So far they have done quite well - MCI's 1986 revenues were 40% up on the previous year and US Sprint reported similar increases. AT&T and the BOCs may be subject to more direct competition and they may diversify further.

As will be noted later, most have already done just that - into such activities as "Yellow Pages" publications and mobile telecoms. They are flush with cash - the results of increases in local telephone tariffs. In 1988 the BOC's were allowed to carry, but not originate, information services.

In 1986 the FCC produced its **Computer III Report and Order** which seemed to change earlier policies of limited deregulation towards more complete deregulation, and included a further attempt to provide equal access. AT&T and the BOC's were no longer required to provide "enhanced" (i.e. "non-telephone") services through arms-length subsidiaries; they would be able to integrate enhanced services and POTS (Plain Old Telephone Service). In order that this should not provide unfair advantage against the competition they were also required to provide open access to the underlying transmission facilities and protocols.

The so-called "Dole Bill", introduced in June 1986, also seemed to encourage increases in the rate of de-regulation. It would transfer the responsibility for administering the provisions of the 1982 "modified final judgement" from the court of Judge Greene to the FCC. The FCC could then apply the "public interest" criterion when considering new competition.

Effects of de-regulation in the US

It is difficult to say what the outcomes of deregulation upon the main US players will be in the long term. Deregulation has produced three long-distance carriers - AT&T, MCI, and US Sprint - seven regional carriers, and hundreds of resellers of telecommunications capacity. Regulatory intervention including pricing which is not cost based, rate averaging, organisation separation requirements etc., still distort the market, and it is unclear what changes are likely.

For example a contributory factor to the success of the BOC's is that they receive 63% of AT&T's communication's revenue. This is a formalisation of the long-distance network internal subsidy for the local network when AT&T ran the whole network.

AT&T and the BOCs have been able to depreciate their equipment over many years and so enjoy low capital costs. Telecoms service is capital intensive so they have a considerable advantage over any new competitors. For this reason continuation of price regulation has been necessary simply to enable new entries to survive.

In September 1989 AT&T acquired the UK Company Istel spun off from British Leyland/Rover in 1987 where it had been the in-house communications and computer services provider. This may be a move to enable AT&T to expand into the European VANs market.

In August 1989 restrictions which stopped AT&T from using its own networks for special services expired. In January 1990 it filed plans with the FCC notifying its intention of using its network to allow large subscribers to access telephone number databases direct without having to go through operators.

Deregulation in the United States continues to evolve and Judge Greene continues to interpret the 1982 decree. His major task is to ensure that the regional carriers do not enter three forbidden areas - long-distance telecoms, equipment manufacture, and information services. However early in 1990 an appeals court ruled that Greene set up a screening process for the acquisition of other companies by Belcos in 1986 without conducting proper hearings. This will make it easier for the Belcos to acquire conditional interests - they will no longer have to first seek approval from the Department of Justice.

In February 1990 the terms of a draft Bill were announced proposing that the Belcos be allowed to offer certain information services through subsidiary companies outside their territories, and could offer various kinds of value added services on within-territory networks.

In January 1990 AT&T started to draft new rules for submission to the FCC, to remove restrictions imposed by that body in 1978 controlling tariffs. Those regulations do not apply to its competitors. However FCC is about to begin yet another enquiry about AT&T's still dominating influence in long distance telecoms, although its proportion of the market has dropped another 14% since 1984, to about 65%.

UK Telecoms after 1984: 1. British Telecom

The procedure in the UK for de-regulating telecommunications has been by statute and the issue of operating licences, not by judicial procedure. This method consumes far less time, There is little visible lobbying activity and very little public discussion. Discussion takes place in governmental committees and debates which are cut short if they do not fit the time-table.

The Office of Telecommunication, OFTEL, answerable only to the government, has wide powers to be exercised as it thinks fit. One of its actions was to direct BT to allow interconnections with Mercury at any point on favourable terms. Another early action was to rule that the price of BT's inland services could be increased only up to a level 3% below the Retail Price Index.

When privatisation was pending BT attempted to transform its image completely; until then it had spent little or nothing on marketing. It started taking full page advertisements in the national press and sent out a continuous stream of press releases announcing everything that moved from the appointment of Bloggs to be regional manager of Puddleby-on-the-Marsh to large-scale takeovers. Its 1983/84 results showed assets of £8500M, income at £6870M, and a profit of £990M. In the public share issue the price turned out to be too low; £3900M was raised without difficulty.

By the end of 1989 BT was able to report its continuing growth, having increased its business lines by 10.5%, its residential lines by 3.3%, and its inland calls to 11%, in that year, its total number of lines having increased to 24 million. Its profits increased from the £990M of 1984 to over £2000M and its assets from £8500M to over £13,000M.

In recent surveys it has been hard to find many with the exception of business customers who would say that the quality of service has improved since privatisation. The main complaints have been time taken to clear faults, the bad state of public telephone boxes, and slow service from telephone exchange operators.

However the speed with which directory enquiries are answered, including foreign enquiries, has improved by at least ten times since a computer storage and retrieval system was introduced. For the few hundred big business customers responsible for over one third of BT's profits, there have been new services and fast response to complaints.

As part of its image-building efforts, BT published a "quality of service report" for 1989 showing several percentage points improvement in network reliability, a small decrease in faults per line, and an increase in the rate of completion of orders. However customers have become more demanding and complaints about BT passed to OFTEL considerably increased in 1989. In response BT says it has now installed a £500M computer system integrating all information about each customer in one place which should enable it to provide a better service.

The UK and London in particular have become important telecommunications centres, partly because of the City's financial markets. BT's policy in driving down long-distance tariffs, and in getting competitive tenders for equipment supply have helped. Telephone charges to the US are 15% cheaper than the next cheapest European country (Sweden), and much cheaper than other major countries.

These factors, among others, have encouraged US Companies to site their European headquarters in the UK. Consequently UK is responsible for over one third of the European market for electronic information services. Germany has one fifth and France slightly less than one fifth. Of the 100 major European service companies, 25 are centred in London followed by Paris with 14. Associated with this growth is the growth of VANs. By 1987 over 800 licences had been granted - again the largest market in Europe.

In 1990 OECD produced a report about public telecommunications in its 25 member countries, and included some comparisons with countries outside the OECD. According to this report the UK's leased line charges are about one third of the OECD average, and substantially lower than in France and Germany. However for international business telephone charges although the UK is below the adjusted OECD average of $100, at about $90, charges in France are slightly less, and charges in the US are about 8% lower than in the UK.

British Telecom is steadily losing its share in the UK equipment market. Its share in PBXs, and also for the telephones purchased to go with them, fell to 45% and 66% respectively in 1986/87, and is likely to fall to 41% and 44% respectively. This is in spite of the fact that BT shops can now be found in the High Streets of many towns. The UK market for telephones grew to over 1.5 million in 1985/86, and is forecast to increase to over 3 million this year (1990), worth nearly £100M.

The UK press excels at bad news stories. Tired of reading a series of such stories about itself, BT has come back strongly, stating that its performance stems mainly from a legacy of under investment in the public sector, that it had been obliged by successive governments to buy from domestic suppliers who believed it had a bottomless purse, and that it was faced with unions with an industrial muscle which they believed was unchallengable. The fact that it had not so far succeeded in full was a measure of the size and nature of the task. There was no universal panacea to make everything come right at once.

In January 1990 a BT spokesman said that it had no qualms about further competition - an extension of the duopoly to three or four carriers was due to be announced in 1991 - provided "there is a level playing field". In March, BT's chairman, Ian Vallance, said that the government should sell its 49% holding in BT, currently worth about £8 billion, before the next election; the company wanted to expand overseas but foreign governments believed that BT was a quasi-governmental organisation. In 1991 the government announced its intention of doing just that.

So far as technical progress is concerned, BT took an early decision to go ahead rapidly with fibreoptic cabling, correctly foreseeing (unlike the Japanese) that "monomode" not "multimode" was the way to go. This jargon refers to the way light is propagated along the cable. For multi-line installations, apart from their much higher efficiency, once-expensive fibres are now competing favourably with copper.

In spite of its legacy and slow start BT has caught up with and is going ahead of others with digitising its exchanges and long distance traffic.

In 1986, anticipating the need for new business for its TAT-8 optical fibre transatlantic cable which was coming into service during 1988, BT announced new rentals for digital private circuits to the US. Customers outside London can connect to the UK end of the cable by Kilostream or Megastream links. The available speeds range from 56 Kbps to 2.048 Mbps. Assuming that data is being transmitted continuously, the rental charged is equivalent to 2p per Mbit of data at 64 Kbps, decreasing to 0.07p per Mbit at 2 Mbps.

UK Telecoms after 1984: 2. Cable & Wireless and Mercury

The Turnover of Cable & Wireless - the UK based international carrier - increased from £359M to £907M between 1982 and 1986 with profits before tax increasing from £89M to £295M in the same period. By March 1989 it had become the 11th largest British Company (by capitalisation) having increased its turnover to £1534M and its profits to £420M. The company now employs nearly 30,000 people.

C&W owns 26 satellite earth stations and provides external telecoms for 36 countries and internal for 19. It plans to offer round the world digital services via London, New York, Tokyo, and Hong Kong; this includes the existing transatlantic and the proposed transpacific fibreoptic cables. The PTAT transatlantic cable was laid by C&W and is owned by C&W and Nynex Inc. Licensed by the FCC it consists of two cables each with a capacity of 1260 Mbps. Cable & Wireless is the sole owner of Mercury, BT's telephone competitor.

Mercury now offers quite a wide range of services and the task of competing against BT is not all up-hill. One benefit of starting from scratch is that you can plan to attack your market and lay your network accordingly using the most suitable current technology free of the incumbrance of mixed ancient and modern fixed assets. Mercury did a deal with British Rail to lay its fibreoptic cables alongside BR tracks.

It also discovered other convenient "wayleaves" for its cables. Beneath the City of London lie the disused ducts of the London Hydraulic Power Company - once used for operating such systems as Tower Bridge, the curtain at the London Palladium and the lifts in Harrods, by water-conveyed hydraulic power. Optical and Microwave links also play a part in Mercury's "last mile" interconnections. Mercury started with a few large customers for long-distance telecoms.

In mid-1986 Mercury was able to offer local calls in the London area where 80% of its customers reside - undercutting BT for most of the day. Mercury's network now covers the country with a much larger network than its original "figure eight" system to large cities. A major company said recently that it expected to place £250,000 of long-distance telecoms with Mercury, reducing BT business to £25,000. One effect of Mercury's operations has been to force competitive bids from BT for special long-distance services, and so force down costs.

The service of greatest interest to small business and residential users is the 2300 service. All telephone calls except local telephone calls can be made with this service which uses the Mercury network where possible but relies on BT for the local connection at either end, and for other routes not covered. One subscriber - admittedly with an above average number of long distance calls - found that his telephone bills were cut by about 50%.

To use Mercury 2300, a subscriber needs to buy a special telephone costing £52 for joint Mercury/BT use and pay about £9 a year for an authorisation ID. To use Mercury you press the "M" button and dial. This takes longer because an access code and your ID must be dialled before the number. Mercury operates a range of other services including direct connection and Centrex for large customers, packet switched data services, telex, and electronic mail. Mercury supply a "Smart Box" for larger customers which analyses a normally dialled number and connects to Mercury or BT automatically.

In April 1988 Mercury said that it was unable to implement the 2300 service nationally, because BT would not provide the necessary links on the grounds that "the quality of calls would not then be up to international standards". It would appear that the person to make that judgement should be the customer, not BT; if the customer does not like the quality he can return to BT who provided the links responsible for the poor quality. The incumbent is indeed in an enviable position!

By 1989 Mercury had completed a large section of its fibreoptic network connecting London, Bristol, Brighton and Southampton, connected into Europe by an undersea cable to the Netherlands. Its connection to Bristol also enabled it to connect to the new private transatlantic PTAT cable which lands near Bristol.

Figures announced in February 1990 show that some PTAT circuits under-cut TAT-8 cable and Intelsat transatlantic half-circuit charges by up to 7%. Plans have also been announced by Mercury for further connections to Scotland, Southern England, and to Kent - the UK end of the channel tunnel.

UK viewpoints

Melody (1989) is rather disillusioned about the whole business. "The traditional model of public service monopoly has never worked very well in any country... on the other hand the competition that has been permitted in the United States to date is extremely limited and far from sufficient to seriously entertain the possibility of justifying deregulation in reality. The era of so-called competitive "de-regulation" in the United States has involved more detailed regulation than ever was applied in the period of regulated monopoly".

British Telecom was first liberalised and then privatised because, like AT&T, it was over-cumbersome, because it ran the telephone system for its own rather than for its customer's benefit, and because privatisation was the political philosophy of the Conservative administration. For some information about this fascinating, highly complex, controversial topic see Littlechild (1979), Meyer (1980), and Snow (1986).

Tsoi and Philip (1988) consider that:- "on the whole, privatization has benefitted only a small group of users. It has had little effect on a market with a vast potential; whatever impact that has come about is at the equipment end ... OFTEL (the UK regulating agency) is ineffective.

But Gillick (1989) attributes the effectiveness of competition "in benefitting users, the telecommunications industry, and the economy as a whole" to OFTEL, providing as examples "The range and variety of equipment available, wide selection of competitive VANs and data services, growing competition from Mercury and cable, greater benefits from telecom services".

The effect of deregulation on the average consumer is hard to assess, partly because whingeing at public services is a national pastime. Opinions of BT reached at all time low in 1987, since when there has been a steady improvement. BT retains at least 95% of the telecoms market. See Dyson (1986) for a comprehensive review of the politics of telecommunications.

Duopoly policy in the UK

The Telecommunications Bill, privatising British Telecom, became law in 1984. Kenneth Baker, Minister for Industry and Information Technology, addressing the committee considering the Bill in November 1983 said:- "we do not intend to license operators other than BT and Mercury Communications to provide the basic communications service over fixed links ... during the seven years following this statement".

This arrangement continued for the prescribed seven years so there has been plenty of time to consider its effectiveness. Telephone users must connect to BT's or Mercury's public networks and larger subscribers must use lines leased from them for site inter-connection.

Various deficiencies in the arrangements have prompted numerous suggestions for changes. Some of the arguments have been set out by Beesley and Laidlaw (1989).

They conclude that large users will not be allowed by the government to set up their own networks - for instance using microwave communications. Having excluded that possibility they summarise their recommendations for changes, the most important aspects being as follows:-

* License the resale of excess leased line capacity.

* Remove restrictions on provision of voice telephone by cable networks and allow their interconnection with other networks.

* License additional public networks.

* Permit resale of international private circuits.

Beesley and Laidlaw have come to the same conclusion for the UK as has Melody for the US - competition may be a good idea but we won't know until we have got it. What we have now is not real competition at all.

Later, Beesley and Laidlaw received a sharp rap over the knuckles from Pye (1990). "Beesley and Laidlaw attempted to start very early. As a result they suffered the embarrassment of dismissing as infeasible things that government has since implemented without waiting for the review... Resale was permitted by OFTEL at the end of last year... the UK government licensed three UK personal communication network operators ... the role of the expert should be to format and inform the debate, not to prejudge it. The government in the UK has abandoned all attempts to pick winners. So too should academics and consultants".

Local & global charges - an example of an intractable regulatory problem

The simmering question of competition and the charging for

international calls - a good example of the problems associated with
telecoms competition - came to the boil in April 1990.

According to the Financial Times of April 3rd, 1990:- "Telephone
users around the world are being overcharged by more than $10 Billion a year
for making international phone calls as a result of cartel-like arrangements
between the world's phone companies which keep prices at an artificially
high level".

Iain Vallance, Chairman of British Telecom (Vallance 1990)
explains:- "Historically the relatively high profitability of call charges -
particularly international calls, has been used by national monopolies
(normally state-owned) to subsidise local network costs, thus keeping down
exchange line rental charges ... This imbalance distorts the effect of
competition across the board because national operators have to subsidise
local networks by overcharging for calls".

And subsequently (Vallance 1990) "In the UK these decisions
(subsidising local networks) have been taken by the government and the
regulator. They are not in British Telecom's interest and we expect them to
be properly addressed in the forthcoming policy review".

BT inherited the "connected remote village" social syndrome - that
is that affordable telephones should be available for all. Desirable as
this may be, not many businesses are saddled with such concepts. However a
government decree removing the concept by allowing local call charges or
line rentals to be increased so that international (mainly business) call
charges may be reduced is unlikely to be a vote-catcher.

In July 1990, BT increased the cost of renting a line by 12%, but
according to Michael Bett, BT's Managing Director, line rentals would have
to be doubled for their costs to be fully recovered. More drastic increases
were rejected by OFTEL on the grounds that "this was not part of the deal
that OFTEL made with BT on prices two years ago. However a thorough
examination of the issues is needed as part of the November review" (Dixon,
1990).

In October 1990, Sir Bryan Carlsberg (Carlsberg 1990), OFTEL's
director, discussed a number of the issues and concluded with the following
remarks:- "... how should relative prices be determined? One relevant
consideration is the effect of different pricing structures on the use of
the telecoms network in relation to the incremental cost of changes in use.
Lower call prices may encourage the use of the network in a desirable way,
but higher exchange line rentals for everyone may discourage some people
from having a telephone to the disadvantage of other users of the network as
well as themselves".

"The pricing structure of other countries are also relevant. Some
businesses use telecoms intensively today and if UK businesses are in
competition with other countries internationally, they should have telecom
costs that enable them to compete effectively".

Key events in the run-up to the 1990 UK review

In 1988 the UK's Cabinet Advisory Council on Science and Technology (ACOST) proposed that a very large investment should be made in a National Wideband Fibreoptic network. Next, the White Paper "Broadcasting in the 90s: competition, choice and quality", appeared (November 1988) after two years of deliberation.

It proposed abolishing the Cable Authority which promoted placing Cable under a new Independent Television Commission (ITC), and encouraging TV microwave distribution for television, thus providing a cheaper solution than cable for the "last mile". This type of one-way microwave distribution cannot be used for interactive information services.

In December 1988 the "McDonald Report" about the regulatory future was provided by the Department of Trade and Industry. The DTI was influenced by a report which it had commissioned from PA consulting and Telecommunications. McDonald rejected the National Fibreoptic Network, estimated to cost £20 billion, for various reasons, but in particular that:- "technology continues to advance very rapidly. The UK might end up locking itself into a sub-optimal technical infrastructure.

Agreeing with the White Paper which encouraged competitive technologies including microwave delivery, McDonald hoped that cable franchise holders would subsequently compete with BT in providing two way services, and believed that BT would install fibre in the local loop anyway whether it was permitted to deliver entertainment TV or not.

Finally in 1988 a report from a House of Commons committee headed by Kenneth Warren which received unanimous support from its members, heavily criticised McDonald. Warren said that the government's refusal to support the fibreoptic network was a golden opportunity missed - a conclusion which appeared to be at odds with its other non-interventionist noises.

The 1990 Green Paper and the 1991 White Paper

The review - a Green Paper (for discussion) - was published in November 1990 (Anon C. 1990). Proposals for parliamentary consideration were due to be published in January 1991 but actually appeared on March 6th. Points for discussion included applications for fixed-link licences without BT or Mercury participation to be considered including cable company applicants, "equal access", price-capping on BT's international prices, and BT ultimately to be permitted to offer entertainment programmes.

In the event, the White Paper - for setting before parliament -(Anon 1991) confirmed most of these points. According to the Financial Times (Leadbeater 1991) it is "the product of a five-month power struggle. The main contestants were Mr. Peter Lilley, Trade & Industry secretary, Professor Sir Brian Carlsberg, director-general of OFTEL, the industry regulator, and Mr. Iain Vallance, British Telecom chairman".

The major points are :-

* Applications for new licences for fixed links (the "local loop" or the "last mile" at present totally dominated by BT) to customer's premises, to be considered.

* Cable franchisees permitted to provide fixed links not necessarily
  in conjunction with BT or Mercury, and adjacent franchisees
  allowed to interconnect.

* Mobile operators to be allowed to offer fixed links.

* Self-provision of private networks with connection to the PSTN, but
  resale of spare capacity not permitted.

* Customers to be allowed equal access to alternative trunk (long
  distance) telephone services.

* Licences to be made available for two way satellite services,
  but terminals must not be connected to the PSTN.

* BT prices to be reduced to Retail Price Index (RPI) -6.25%
  (existing is RPI -4.5%). Rebalancing between line-rental and
  connection charges permitted. BT's international charges to be cut
  by 10% from June 1991.

* BT and other public service providers to be allowed to provide
  entertainment in 10 years time, but reviewable in 7 years time.

Mr Iain Valence said, in a BT press release:- "We believe that,
taken as a whole, it is good for the customer and for the industry". The
proposals, particularly on pricing, presented a tough challenge to BT, but
one the company could accept.

Expectations and outcomes

From the run-up events, and from the White Paper, it is expected
that the UK will develop an improved telephone system by competitive trial
and error. How soon will we arrive at a "Universal Wideband
Data/Information Highway" by these processes? This was the thinking behind
the government's big push for cable in 1982 when it was asserted that
wideband information services would ride on a network responding to a demand
for entertainment.

The White paper embodies current UK governmental non-interventionist
policy and advance by competition. This policy also enables politicians to
avoid imaginative long range planning. It costs money, they might get it
wrong, there are no votes in it, and if they get it right but are thrown
out, some other political party will get the credit. So we have overloaded
roads and disused railway lines. Current business philosophy is to go for
relatively short-term profitability and the lower the risk the better.

On the other hand when the UK (and most other) governments become
more venturesome - as they would need to be to support a National
Fibreoptics Network - they often back losers. If the network turned out to
be a failure it would add to a list of financial or technical disasters such
as the ground nuts scheme, the abandonment of Blue Streak, the TSR2,
Concorde etc.

Even so I can't help thinking that provided the resources were made
available so that the job could be done quickly, and (with more difficulty)
if an engineer/organiser like Brunel or Hinton could be found to be put in
charge, a National Fibreoptic Network could become a successful fait

accompli years before anything else.

The arrival(?) of the Universal Wideband Information Highway

The White paper takes a line which confirms unfolding events. A network capable of transporting voice, text, graphics, halftone and colour pictures etc., is laboriously evolving, with the accent on voice communication. The industry obviously believes that voice has plenty of mileage to come - Mobile Cellular Radio has been a huge success.

Cellular Radio is an example of a winner in the network business. It managed to overcome the severe "critical mass" problem which inhibits the widespread adoption of any new network. A new network somehow has to get itself into a "take-off" situation which has long since been surpassed by the existing telephone system where potential subscribers know that they will be able to talk to most of the people with whom they wish to communicate.

The complexity of political, financial, and technical interaction between Cable, Direct Broadcast Satellite, Terrestrial Television, Fibreoptic Networks, Mobile Cellular, Telepoint, Personal Communication Networks, the ISDN and probably others which I haven't thought of, is such that it is bound to take years for winners to emerge. So far as voice is concerned, and in spite of the enthusiasm of the industry, it is not at all clear whether new forays into voice will be as successful as Mobile Cellular.

Alternative services and equal access

The objectives of the White Paper are to open up competition and limit the power of BT to throttle fragile newcomers. Paradoxically additional regulation will be needed to achieve what is hoped will become genuine competition.

The two major changes are in line with Beasley and Laidlaw's recommendations - more alternative telephone services with equal access, and construction of own networks. One recommendation which has not been adopted is the resale of spare capacity in private systems.

What happens when it becomes possible to present a telephone subscriber with alternative services for his or her choice? For most people reliability and cost are the prime requirements. The range of gimmicks offered when the local exchange is digitized are a minor consideration. But for business and high volume users a careful assessment of the offerings could be well worth while.

The angle chosen by Bradshaw (1990) in a piece about equal access in the U.S. is to highlight an activity called "Slamming" where subscribers are switched to a particular service without their consent. In that country subscribers can tell the local telephone company which long distance telephone company they want to use. There is supposed to be no local loop choice since that is provided by the local phone company monopoly. However "Bypassing" - for instance by microwave links - seems to be a national activity.

Bradshaw says nothing about the benefits of long distance choice to the subscriber. In a recent note (Anon D. 1990), attempts are made to counteract the UK "little old lady in the Shetlands losing her telephone argument" with "reassurances by recounting the american experience".

The note continues:- "since the breakup of the huge AT&T network into Baby Bells, many consumers have enthusiastically embraced the freedom to shop around for a carrier". I would be interested to find some evidence for that claim, but have not so far been able to unearth any. However prices for long distance - a market led by AT&T (65%), MCI (16%), and Sprint (10%) - have fallen.

In the UK if connection choices to and from your actual telephone are to become available, not just long distance choices via whatever local loop exists (which normally means BT), it seems most unlikely that they will be provided by digging up the road n times so you can have n different lines entering your premises.

More likely alternatives are Cable, if it passes your door, or microwave link to the nearest point of distribution owned by a competing telephone company. Such a link involves a very small dish on your premises with a line-of-sight path to the distribution point. Such a link could carry a number of channels.

There is one place in the UK where subscribers have a choice of long distance calls, but not for local service (which is probably not necessary because reports suggest that the local service would be hard to better), and that is in Hull. Hull is unique in somehow escaping the clutches of the Post Office earlier in this century. A subscriber who starts by dialling a 12 for out-of-Hull calls connects via BT, a 13 via Mercury. They get one bill from Hull.

However the idea of multiple choices both for local connection and long distance - a possible outcome if the Green Paper review is adopted - could introduce some severe practical problems. Among them are people's inertia if it is difficult to make a change, billing, and telephone numbers. For example what happens to your telephone number, your directory entry, and the ease with which others can be informed of your number should you change to a different local network?

"Equal access" depends on whether facilities are available at the local telephone exchange (in many exchanges they are not) so that a customer may be switched to his or her preferred service. Equal access has been in place in the U.S. since 1986. Some information is available about its effects from Cude (1989).

Cude says that :- "While consumers may benefit from a greater number of choices, many people are confused about the impact of deregulation". A survey was taken by selecting 1000 households at random in an area where equal access was available. 348 useable responses were received. Only 15 consumers had changed to a different carrier.

Cude's article turns on an analysis of the information obtained and considered to be necessary for a decision to change to be made. "Educators can help consumers to make the transition from viewing telephone service as an arena in which they are only passive participants to one in which they are knowledgeable, active, and effective decision makers".

But the survey took place only 8 months after equal access became available which seems far too short a time for the word to spread, "educators" or not. The idea that the average consumer might become a "knowledgeable decision maker" about changing to another telephone carrier sounds like a pious hope unless there is a substantial cost advantage. It seems reasonable to expect the average UK consumer to be just as lethargic as his US counterpart. It is businesses which at most likely to react and it's unfortunate that Cude did not include them in her survey.

Several contenders have emerged who would be well placed to provide alternative services. National utilities such as the Post Office, British Rail, and British Gas possess their own comprehensive telecom networks, or national strips-of-land networks, or both. Mercury already uses British Rail land for carrying a large portion of its fibreoptic network. British Rail formed a new company in September 1990 called British Rail Telecommunications and is said to be seeking partners and considering an investment of up to £400M.

The Cable companies find themselves in an eminently exploitable position. Although the number of cable subscribers has increased slowly, over 70% of the population of the UK is sufficiently closely passed by a cable belonging to one of the franchise holders to be able to be connected. Since entry to the market was eased in the early eighties, only about 100,000 subscribers have been acquired so a huge investment will be required for the large number of connections required to make Cable a viable telephone alternative.

Alternatively, Cable companies wishing to offer telephone services to non-Cable customers must connect via BT or Mercury. Presumably they will be able in future to use their networks, interconnected with the networks of other franchise holders, and complete the "last mile" with a microwave link instead of laying local cable.

The resale of excess network capacity, banned by the White Paper, and the purchase of it by an entrepreneurial company to form its own network to provide its subscribers with an "automatic best choice" is another idea which has been mooted. Sooner of later it will probably be permitted. Connections would be made via an automatically selected lowest price route and the company would provide a single bill. Problems of calculating the break-even point and the time to achieve it in order to justify the initial investment suggest that such a venture should not be undertaken by the faint-hearted.

In one respect BT's life may be eased - other telecom companies may be required to shoulder a part of its social burden. If the profits of BT's business services are appreciably reduced by the requirement that it must provide rural services at a loss, then competitors should be required to take on part of that burden or BT should be compensated in some other way. BT will not be allowed to put up local prices in order to reduce its tariffs for long distance.

In regard to competition from Cable, in which foreign companies now can invest and have invested strongly, BT says (Anon 1991):- "It is disappointing that the government plans to allow free entry to the UK market to foreign monopolies (meaning the Baby Bells, for instance) and has no apparent intention of using access to the UK markets as a lever to secure equivalent access to overseas markets for UK companies".

BT has a point - once the ban on foreign investment was lifted, foreign companies saw the possibilities of entry into the UK telephone market via the cable networks and invested heavily. They now own 90% of the franchises.

Continuing "If BT is prevented from setting retail prices which reflect efficient use of economies of scale, customers will pay inflated prices for the alleged benefit of market entry by overpriced competitors... in spite of the government's endorsement of genuine, effective, competition, it is in fact contemplating further and more extensive so-called "managed" competition which is another way of saying that it intends to continue the existing, and introduce new restrictions and handicaps on BT". With regard to these last remarks BT does not have a point. It should expect some restraints in view of its enormous head-start.

Mercury has had a hard time versus BT, and it appears as if the path of new entrants may be easier. It has been suggested that a new entrant is most likely to attack the same market - in other words attempt to cream off the most lucrative business telecoms.

Conclusions

Business users will benefit gradually but substantially when the White Paper is put into effect. The most likely consequences for the domestic subscriber are somewhat better service at prices gradually increasing at a rate mainly depending on OFTEL decisions.

It seems possible to peer at the longer-term future and make a general, if vague, forecast with some confidence. A whole range of services are now, and will increasingly, become available for medium and large organisations, but this does not solve the "Universal Network" problem.

The ISDN presents the best prospect for the creation of a critical mass of data and information service users. It is proceeding extremely slowly. Competitive possibilities such as cable or satellites are at a very early stage of development. I see no reason to alter my earlier forecast (Cawkell 1990) - "ISDN in the late 90s, Broadband early in the two thousands, SONET by 2020".

Deregulation efforts by the Commission of the European Community

The CEC hopes to implement its Green Paper setting out its reforming telecom measures (Anon 1987) in order to liberalise European telecoms.

The CEC uses diplomatic language to describe what it is trying to do - to put it bluntly they want to break the restrictive practices stranglehold of the PTTs. The Green Paper progress and objectives are re-stated in Anon. B (1989). Its interest is understandable since it estimates that about half the present global value of the "Information business" - about £500 Billion - is in telecoms (Anon. A 1989).

The CEC's major timed targets were an open market for all services, particularly VANs, except voice, telex, and datacoms by end of 1989, and free competition for terminals by end of 1990. Untimed proposals included tariffs to follow costs trends; separation of regulatory and operational activities; definition of "Open provisions" for leased lines, data networks, and ISDN; establishment of a Standards Institute (ETSI); guidelines for competition and a fair market; open PTT procurement.

The CEC is having a hard time. It cannot get agreement on VANs liberalisation; overdue by three years, it hopes to get a compromise agreement by the end of 1992. "Open provisions" have been put off. PTTs can get an extension of their leased line monopoly to 1996 if they can show that their packet-switched network is inadequate.

Exasperated by slow action in freeing terminals, the CEC invoked Article 90 of the Treaty of Rome to force compliance. An advocate to the European Court of Justice advised that the use of Article 90 should not be allowed. It had more success following the threat of legal action against a proposal by the CEPT (a PTT club), considered to be anti-competitive, to provide a managed data network. This was abandoned. The CEPT was also forced to abandon a cartel-like plan for fixing leased line tariffs.

Uniquely in Europe, the UK has usually been ahead of the CEC in its deregulatory ideas so the effects of CEC activities on UK telecoms are small.

The CEC's most recent endeavours are aimed at Satellite Communications.

The Green Paper on satellite communications (Anon 1990) aims at deregulation mainly in order to increase demand so that European suppliers can achieve the necessary economies of scale to compete. It points out that such economies can reduce satellite manufacturing costs by up to 40%. "The US manufacturer Hughes has sold more than 30 standardised satellites, charging up to 33% less than its competitors".

TELECOMMUTING

Working at home using a computer terminal connected to a central computer via a telecommunication link was discussed in the late sixties. In 1971 the US Academy of National Engineering decided to work on a special project to be called "The New Rural Society" to examine "....the application of telecommunications toward upgrading life in rural communities to encourage a voluntary decentralisation of people, business and government".

The idea was taken up by an engineer, Peter Goldmark, a Hungarian who was in charge of television at Pye, Cambridge, in the thirties, emigrated to the US, and subsequently invented a method of colour TV transmission and long playing records while at CBS in Stamford. Goldmark later formed his own company, Goldmark Communications, and became involved with "Audio Teleconferencing" and in a kind of "remote education" cable TV system (Goldmark 1976).

The words "Telecommuting" and "Teleworking" seem to have been used first in the early eighties, but the amusing thing is that today's announcements still not only inform us that the idea - 15 years after its introduction in the seventies - is "new", but that in the UK, the same two organisations - Xerox and F International (re-named the FI Group) - are now, as then, "typical examples". Could this be because people who write about the topic cannot find any others?

Telecommuting or Teleworking is used to describe employees or free-lancers who would otherwise be working in some central office, but who do work of a kind which enables them to do virtually the same work for their employer just as well at a remote point. In other words they simply employ a longer telecommunication link between their terminal and a computer. A case in point is a person working on computer programming.

The advantages for the employer are space saving and overhead reduction, but it is unclear whether the the absence of "face to face" management is a disadvantage or not. Perhaps the work done is of the kind which suffers least from the effects of "remote" management. Although there is the general advantage to employees of not wasting time and money on commuting, possibly very tiring commuting, other advantages would appear to accrue mainly to certain kinds of employees - for example to people with family commitments, those who would otherwise be made redundant, or those who will accept part-time telecommuting as a form of gradual graceful retirement.

The idea that telecommuting is the big growth area won't lie down. In a 1988 survey (Morant 1988) an article with the sub-title "Telecommuting from an office at home", gives us two paragraphs about the FI Group, and comments in the same sentence about a recent teleworking conference and a forecast from the Henley Centre that "4 million people will be working from home by 1995"; the rest of the article is about office equipment. There appears to be some confusion; 4 million people may be working at home, but how many of them will be telecommuters?

According to a 1984 report (Anon 1984) most of the homeworkers in a survey were computer professionals and most enjoyed the work. However pay levels were lower than average and there were few benefits or promotion prospects. The outstanding problem was social isolation.

British Telecom carried out a study on 250 sample households in 1983 and concluded that by 1995 about 14% of households would have people working from home of which about 20% would be using "electronic transactional services" (Wray 1983). In a report prepared for the National Economic Development Office (Bessant 1986) a response to this question was provided from a questionnaire circulated to "more than one hundred UK policymakers and informed sources". The mean result for a 1995 forecast was that 10-15% of the workforce would be engaged in "distance working", increasing to 15-20% by 2010.

In 1989 a new breed was reported (Bryant 1989) - the "Electronic Crofter" apparently reinforcing BT's forecast. The prototype Scottish crofter is a Dr. Krabshuis who lives in "a ramshackle overgrown cottage; a fire burns in the grate, cats curl up on overstuffed chairs, and history hangs low on cobwebbed beams". The give-away is a PC and "a huge black and yellow Excerpta Medica golf umbrella in the corner". Evidently Krabshuis does his online searching perched on the top of Ben Nevis. The word "telecommuter" does not appear once. For once telecommuting and home-working have not been treated as synonyms.

Undoubtedly much larger numbers of people are now working at home, but few of them are telecommuting - that is using a terminal in order to work for their employers over a telecommunications link instead of physically commuting. They are mostly self-employed.

Since telecommuters and home-workers usually seem now to be the same thing perhaps complaining about the need to separate them is merely being pedantic. However there is a difference. By definition, a telecommuter uses a telecoms link to his employer. That is why telecommuters are often mentioned in the "future telecommunications scenario" context.

In an exchange between Forester (1988) and Miles (1988), Forester makes a number of comments about the problems of self-management and family relationships. For the homeworker there may be a general problem of dividing "work" from "home" life. Telecommuting experiments have "usually been on a small scale and have often been abandoned. Time and again the same few examples crop up in the literature".

But most of Forester's article and all of Miles's are not about telecommuting at all but about IT in the home - the "Electronic Cottage". On this topic Forester ends with "It must be concluded that the electronic cottage is largely a myth". Miles goes along with much of Forester's coldwater, but considers that "he fails to give due weight to the role of new consumer technologies....where major challenges may be felt by collective services such as education and health".

In the absence of a cheap universal reliable telecommunication system, and because most humans are gregarious - a trait which will endure while technologies come and go - we may conclude that telecommuting is not a growth industry. There is as yet no evidence to suggest that the growth rate will speed up enough between now and 1995 for the figures in the above forecasts to be realised.

If there are by now millions of telecommuters anywhere it must have come to the notice of the telecoms authority. Each would probably need an extra telephone line. They would be prime targets for the integrated Services Digital Network (ISDN). It seems odd that I can't find anyone in the telecoms business who is the least bit interested in these millions.

NFAIS, Philadelphia offered a workshop on "telecommuting (work-at-home)" - a title confirming that these two activities are considered by some to be the same thing - for £285. But perhaps it is no longer a myth and something really is happening at last. Gil Gordon, who will preside at the NFAIS workshop, also publishes "Telecommuting Review", and claims that "we're seeing the same kind of growth curve with telecommuting as we did for personal computers".

Three out of the four articles under the heading "Telecommuting" - it's Home to Work We Stay" in a recent "Current Contents Press Digest" (ISI, Philadelphia) feature are about people working at home. One author claims that "55 to 60 percent of people he counselled who were losing their corporate jobs said that they wanted to work for themselves at home". We don't know whether they actually did. Another author firmly states that "over 26 million men and women, nearly one quarter of the labor force, have shifted part or all of their jobs from the office to the home". We don't know how many of them are telecommuters.

The "Current Contents" piece does not include what might be called the definitive article about the topic (Kraut 1989) - Kraut is manager of the Interpersonal Communications Research Group at Bellcore, Morristown, New Jersey.

To use the vernacular, Kraut takes the lid off telecommuting. The last of his 61 references is well known and remarkably appropriate. It is to "Zipf G., Human behaviour and the principle of least effort, Cambridge Mass. Addison-Wesley 1949". This reference comes in the section headed "Why - despite the popular image of telecommuting and the "electronic cottage" - have we seen so little employer-initiated workplace substitution"?

The telecommuting-hyper-uppers presumably don't believe it but Kraut succinctly expresses the obvious,:- "The defining component of the conventional office is the co-presence of other workers for a substantial part of the work day... physical proximity is the technology that organisations use to support the informal communication that underline much group work and the social relationships attendant upon this communication... it is frequently the basis of supervision, socialization, social support, on-the-job training, and the spread of corporate know-how and culture. Moreover the informal communication among co-workers helps provide the major satisfaction denied to home workers - socialising and friendly social interaction".

SOCIAL ASPECTS

Jeong (1990) considers that it is time to "derive a new classification model of a nation's economy... using an information level instead of an industrialization level. All nations in the world may be re-classified as "high information society", "middle information society, and "low information society", depending on the proportion of the information sector in each nation".

The social impact of the information Society has many facets including:-

* The man-machine mismatch
* Human factors
* The effect of machines on health
* The effects on life at work and at home
* Privacy, secrecy, security, and freedom
* Work, leisure, and unemployment
* The differential distribution of information - the
  "information rich" and the "information poor"

Machines, humans, and codes

A Frenchman observed "Je deteste ce qu'on pourrait appeler le "Macluhanisme", c'est a dire l'utilisation que l'on a faite des idees de MacLuhan pour justifier des choses injustifiables".

How many people find microform viewers or CRT screens acceptable substitutes for print on paper? So far as reading from a CRT screen is concerned he lapses into English - something a Frenchman does only when strongly provoked. He refers to Miller's "chunks of sense" and continues:- "Le processus de lecture ne progresse pas regulierement ligne apres ligne, page apres page. Cela n'est pas possible avec l'ecran".

In regard to mutual understanding, if a speaker or writer makes a syntactic slip or spelling error his listener or reader does not normally fail to understand but instead makes the obvious correction. The inability of current interactive systems to make such corrections is very frustrating for their human users.

An American complains that "Computer systems, and the abstract codes, detailed forms, unreadable reports and documents which they produce too often, are clearly a form of environmental pollution". Many computer people are insensitive to the fact that the tools that they design have to be used by non-computer people.

Forester et al (1990) draw attention to the increasing vulnerability of society as it becomes more dependent on computers, quoting several examples. A fire in Tokyo destroyed 3000 data communication and 89,000 telephone circuits resulting in business losses calculated at 13 billion Yen. A disgruntled employee at the Encyclopaedia Britannica tapped in to the database and made a few alterations - for example changing references about Jesus Christ to Allah, and so on.

On software engineering, Forester et al conclude that "the construction of software is a complex and difficult process... not as yet of assured quality and reliability... computer unreliability will remain a major source of social unreliability for some time to come.

Forester et al cite the case of 22 deaths in Blackhawk helicopter crashes because radio interference from external sources affected the on-board computer system. In 1986 Ray Cox and a month later Vernon Kidd received fatal radiation overdoses because of a malfunction in the computer controlling the linear accelerator being used for cancer treatment. "Accordingly we recommend that computers should not be entrusted with life-critical applications now, and should be only if reliability improves dramatically in the future".

Such arguments require to be made more plausible by comparing error and accident results in specific non-computerised and computerised activities before and after computerisation. Is there any evidence to suggest that computerisation made things worse?

Codes do not seem to receive the "humanisation" that they deserve. As an example consider the preferences of Bell personnel when rating coding schemes, scored 1 to 10. It was hardly surprising that the Bell people's preference rating for "732681 8518" as the code for "Canton, Ohio" was 2, but for "MK PHILA PA" (Market St, Philadelphia, Pennsylvania) it was 9. The BBC radio/TV licence number of about 38 digits is another example of the ridiculous lengths technologists will go to (and defend it with a letter to the Times).

It is hard to understand why the old UK telephone numbering system for London exchanges - for instance ABB 1234 (ABBEY 1234) - was replaced "for technical reasons" by all figure numbers. For UK postal codes such a changeover was not made (for "non-technical reasons"?). When more symbols were required, "WC1" (West Central 1), for instance, was extended to "WC1 2AA". A just sufficient number of symbols was added to existing meaningful information to provide the extra information needed.

If the UK owner of a terminal wants to obtain information from one of the many databases running in Europe or the United States, he can connect to it via the Public Switched Telephone Network (PSTN), British Telecom's International Packet Switched Service (IPSS) and a US network.

The string of alphanumeric symbols required to be typed absolutely correctly for online logging-on in the UK allows about 9.5×10^{32} host computers/databases to be addressed. Numbers like this may be of interest to astronomers but in this context they somewhat exceed requirements. (The world's population is about 4×10^9). The string of numbers is for engineering convenience. Evidently the idea of a small software package to reduce the number to say 6 digits has not been considered.

"Humanisation"

More (1990) illustrates the thrust of her article with some quotations:- "The message is clear. Previous attempts to apply and implement IT... have been doomed from the beginning because, typically, one crucial component has been mismanaged - people.

"No matter how obvious the importance of the social domain, it is largely ignored... although lip-service is paid to the "behavioural dimension" (e.g. user-friendly interfaces, user involvement and the like) little serious intention is given to the social domain... putting the matter very simply, there is little point in having hardware systems that can deliver megabytes of information that nobody can understand or make use of".

The need to humanise IT is discussed under a number of headings - management of organisational culture, politics and power rituals in the organisation, human communication, information richness of a media and problems of technological change.

According to an article by Iqbaria et al (1990) the need for "humanisation" also seems to be necessary to allay an emotion not discussed by More - anxiety. "The concept of computer anxiety which refers to the tendency of an individual to be uneasy, apprehensive , and phobic towards current or future use of computers, has been discussed in the popular press... The common theme has been that in spite of the potential of microcomputer-based management tools for productivity improvement, many people have resisted their adoption and acceptance, and actually avoid computer use".

The author's findings, following a survey, "emphasize the responsibility of those providing services for creating a supportive environment that is responsive to user concerns and needs".

In fact quite a lot of work has been going on in recent years on a closely related topic "Human Factors". Yates (1989) describing various aspects of the subject, says "Industrial relations, management/union consultations, bargaining for rewards etc., are all areas very close to the expanding boundaries of human factors. For the human factor worker, considerable satisfaction derives from the assurance that human factors knowledge is biased neither to managers or the managed, but is rather a total statement of all the factors existing in a workplace, and that the mutual consideration of these factors will lead to maximum benefit for all".

Another activity which, probably accidentally, assists the cause of humanisation is the Filofax. McMurdo (1989) says:- "Before filofaxes became culturally equated with yuppies, the main users of pocket personal organisers were rural clergymen and military officers, both displaying a need for a working information tool".

"As a personal, portable, retrieval sytem it may represent one milestone of an information society in which information work is a general, rather than a specialized activity... it introduces users to methods, dilemmas, and nuances of alphabetisation and amending, deleting, and inserting in indexed files - previously the province of professional filers... a key characteristic of the filofax is that it is configurable to personal requirements... despite English-only inserts, the Japanese, who account for 20% of Filofax plc sales, also have a textbook with sales of 30,000 copies".

Engineers are likely to be interested in a different aspect. Kobayashi (1990) says:- "The added value that semiconductor application products bring to society relates to the electronic functions of information handling... It is expected that the information industry will continue to produce Computers and Communications oriented products toward the 21st century as one of the necessary conditions for realizing true globalization of both industry and society".

Attitudes of IT professionals towards social issues are described rather well by Clarke (1988). He identifies the "adversarial approach" (computers are dangerous), and the "independent roles approach" (undertaking activities on unrelated social implications as well own main discipline). This second approach is "akin to the international arms dealer who commits some of his spare time to the local Boy Scouts troop".

Clarke is derisive about the "dual-specialist approach". "...As long as you maintain respectability in the mainstream, your proclivities for soft, socially responsible interests will not do you too much harm, and you can speak with authority in both of them". Few people have suffficient standing in IT and Sociology to adopt the "authoritative renegade approach" which "loses the individual some of his research grants, but protects personal integrity and public credibility".

Clarke's main conclusion is that "the moral responsibility of any professional must at least extend to an honest attempt to ensure that public debate is informed. Further, since the subject-matter is often obscure, the professional's role extends to ensuring that the debate takes place".

Haves and have-nots

Arguments about the merits of subsidised and for-profit information services seem to have died down. The trend on both sides of the Atlantic is towards treating information as a good to be purchased according to need - why subsidise unwanted services? But should some people be denied essential information because they cannot afford to pay for it? If access to essential information should be a right, then the supply of it, like the medical services in many countries, should be government funded.

These remarks cover different kinds of information. The first kind is usually occupationally related - for instance financial, scientific, or medical. The second kind, "essential information" for ordinary people, is usually about living - like consumer rights, housing availability, social benefits, or effective medical treatment.

"Essential information" is hard to define but sometimes it is self-evident. The information which a government must provide if it is going to get any applications for its social benefits is essential. This kind of information has to be, and is, free, so why is it that in the UK, and probably in other countries, a wide range of entitled persons don't receive their benefits? The answer is that the potential recipients are either unaware of their entitlement or are misled by the complexity of the information about it.

The barrack-room lawyers who understand the system get the benefits. The needy or inarticulate may not. Benefits may be funded but without clear supporting information they will not reach all those entitled to them.

Most people would probably agree that it is undesirable that there should be two kinds of people in any society - the well informed and the badly informed - although most governments believe that their responsibility ends with the provision of free education. But the process of becoming and remaining an "informed person" is an on-going process made possible only by continuous access to understandable affordable information.

The wealth-generating segment of the population - the "information haves" - provide the funding for all government aid. This essential segment is increasingly assisted by libraries. Noting their requirements and ability to pay, stocks and charging policies are adjusted accordingly. Libraries and government paymasters should see to it that the "have-nots" are also able to have access to information. The long tradition for the provision of free library services must be continued for their benefit.

HEALTH

Concern about the effects of Visual Display Units on health seems to have been expressed from about 1980 onwards, although interest in the effects of another kind of visual display - the microform reader - goes back at least to 1947 (Carmichael, 1947).

It's becoming quite hard to avoid articles about the subject which is discussed in an impressively scientific manner in medical and other learned journals, in an appropriately technical manner in the computer magazines, and in a suitably sensational manner in the newspapers. The approximately equal volume of literature reporting no connection whatsoever between VDUs and ill health receives very little mention.

Many writers need a "story" - and in this field (and in a good many others) it's the bad news stories which predominate. Who has ever heard of a balanced-view bad news story? That amounts to a contradiction in terms.

You could be easily convinced that you should go nowhere near your VDU, like not eating infected eggs, not drinking water which might be polluted, not eating meat because of the risk of mad cow disease, and not going out of doors in case you might get clobbered.

Five aspects of alleged "VDU effects" have received particular attention - radiation or emission effects, visual effects, postural effects produced by staring at the thing for long periods in a fixed sedentary position, effects on the arms and fingers, and the latest (first mention December 1990) - ultrasonic noise from scanning components.

An explanatory article about radiation/emission (the words are used as synonyms) from VDUs appeared recently in <u>Byte</u> (McGinnis, 1990). "You've probably heard about the controversy surrounding extremely low frequency (ELF) and very low frequency (VLF) electromagnetic emission from video monitors" says the author. "Whether the health hazards being blamed on such emissions are real or not, many manufacturers, especially those outside the US, have begun producing so-called low radiation monitors".

The "radiation" referred to is non-ionising radiated electric or electrostatic field radiation, or non-ionising radiated electromagnetic field radiation, not to be confused with ionising radiation such as that produced by radioactive materials. We can almost forget about the electric and electrostatic radiation since this is easily reduced by a thin conductive shield. Thus a plastic cabinet sprayed with a conductive material, and a CRT screen fronted by a thin-film conductive deposit - inexpensive remedies which are normally used - will virtually get rid of it.

It is more expensive to get rid of the electromagnetic radiation. VLF magnetic radiation is produced by the CRT's horizontal deflection scanning coils in the frequency range, according to McGinnis, "15,000 to 32,000 Hz". This is not quite correct since the range may extend up to 90,000 Hz, as in the Mitsubishi HL6605, HC3905, and other monitors.

Electromagnetic radiation is also produced in the form of ELF fields in the range 50 to 90 Hz from the vertical deflection coils and mains power supply components.

Both VLF and ELF magnetic radiation can be reduced by placing a screen of ferrous material between the source and the viewer. McGinnis provides an example of "a 0.254 mm thick iron sheet 10 cm from a 20,000 Hz emission source... attenuating magnetic emission by about 1000... but at 60 Hz (ELF) the attenuation for the above material is less than 3.

A more effective but more expensive remedy is to put the radiating component into an enclosure made of a high permeability material such as mumetal, forming a magnetic circuit in which the magnetic flux circulates instead of being radiated.

The second health aspect - visual effects - has also received considerable attention. In early studies, the observation of adverse visual effects seem to have come up as a by-product of subjective studies on such factors as symbol legibility, character design, viewing angle, and so forth.

The third aspect - bodily problems brought on by an incorrect posture in sedentary work - was studied in the nineteenth century. For example, Staffel (1884) noted the forward inclined benches favoured by coachmen and organists.

In recent years considerable work has been done - a representative selection from Leuder (1983), Life (1984), Bendix (1984), Corlett (1984) Grandjean (1984) and Yates (1988) is given in the references.

In his review citing 68 earlier articles Lueder (1983), mentions two techniques used for studying posture as an analytical tool for design:- "Habitual restlesness... associated with attempts to compensate for uncomfortable conditions" and "Evaluation of those postures assumed most frequently with different furniture".

Lueder (1983) concludes:- "The elusive relationship between performance and comfort is partially due to complexities inherent in the measurement of office performance. Office workers are information handlers who create symbolic end products. The further up the organisational hierarchy one ascends, the more abstract this end product becomes. Professionals and managers incur the greatest cost investment in the office, but the performance of these individuals is the most difficult to measure... little insight is available into the meaning of comfort".

Grandjean et al (1984), having observed the behaviour of 68 different operators in four different companies who were free to make their own adjustments, came to quite firm conclusions:- "A proper VDT workstation should be adjustable in the following ranges:-

Adjustment	Range (cms)	=	Approx Feet/inches
Keyboard height, middle row to floor	70 - 85		2/3.5 - 2/9.5
Screen centre above floor	90 - 115		2/11.5 - 3/9.25
Keyboard, middle row to table edge	10 - 26		0/3.75 - 0/10.25
Screen distance to table edge	50 - 75		1/7.75 - 2/5.5
Screen inclination to horizontal plane		88 - 105°	

"A VDT workstation without an adjustable keyboard height and without an adjustable height and distance of screen is, for a continuous job at a VDT, not suitable", say Grandjean et al..

According to Williams (1985):- "The rapid and widespread introduction of visual display technology in Australia has been accompanied by a large increase in disablement among operators of visual display units". Evidently people in the UK felt the same way. A note in the New Scientist (Anon, 1985) said that :- "A campaign for legislation to make safe the design of visual display units was launched this week in the House of Commons". Those in favour included the VDU Workers Rights Campaign, the Greater London Council, and six Labour MPs.

Furthermore, headaches and sore eyes are reported from Apex the UK white-collar union (Goodhart, 1985) and in a survey published by the Japanese General Council of Trade Unions it was reported that:- "Over one third of pregnant women working at VDUs have problems during pregnancy or at delivery" (Anon, 1985). Eyestrain or sometimes a painful or stiff neck or shoulders, muscular pain and backache are discussed by Bunker (1985).

Cooper et al (1985) found that the most significant stress factor for word processing operators was "lack of role clarity".

Doyle (1988) said that VDU workers "talk about their eyes swelling or being out on stalks, seeing pink spots, or their actual eyesight changing". The VDU Worker's Rights Campaign accused the UK Health and Safety Executive of "extreme complacency" in the matter.

In 1988 a World Health Organisation report said that "the visual discomfort experienced by many VDU users must be recognised as a health problem" (Hill, 1988). Patricia Little (1988) claimed that:- "researchers at the Kaiser Permanente Medical Care Programme (Oaklands, Ca.) noted that pregnant women working with VDUs for more than 20 hours a week suffered twice as many miscarriages as women doing other office work".

Morris and Barnacle (1989) provide 41 references and discuss aches and pains, eye discomfort, visual fatigue, stress, radiation, adverse pregnancy outcomes, static electricity, photosensitive epilepsy, migraine and skin rashes but without making any strong comments.

The FT reported in 1989 that "several UK trade unions are pursuing a number of claims for Repetitive Strain Injury (RSI) on behalf of their members and "operators of keyboards face high risk of limb disorders" - a finding of the Institute of Occupational Medicine in Edinburgh.

In 1989 a bill was proposed in California, which among other things, would set up a committee to establish guidelines for pregnant computer operators. But operators need more protection than this according to the UK Inland Revenue Staff Federation who find VDUs very taxing (Haughton 1990). After surveying 3,500 women members they found that "VDU workers were more likely to experience stress related menstrual problems, to drink and smoke heavily and to be dissatisfied with their working lives".

But help is on the way. An ergonomics standard is being prepared by the BSI and ISO which will have EC backing. It will specify measures to reduce the "countless complaints from computer users of illness or injury brought on by long periods in front of VDUs. In addition to repetitive strain injury - which can cause severe pain to arms and shoulders as well as wrists - migraines, blurred eyesight, eye strain and backache are among the ailments reported (Jones, 1989).

The fifth problem is "whisper-quiet sources of a tone which appear to cause stress among women" (Reed 1990). The "tone" is "the near ultrasonic noise produced by some computer monitors".

Alernative views are provided by Land (1985) "we can see no medical reason for recommending that pregnant women be exempted from working with visual display units". V. H. Reading et al (1986) found that:- "there was no significant difference in respect of eye strain or pain between full-time typists and VDU users", and Clark (1986) who "gave VDUs a clean bill of health" (Clark, 1986). concluded that "The possible health risks of VDU work have been much debated, haggled over, and exploited, but experts agree that any potential hazards can easily be avoided".

W. G. Nabor (1986) said "I have yet to measure any ionizing radiation from any CRT, old, new, colour, or monochrome... claims to the contrary are misleading to the point of fraud".

In a review of the subject, N. MacMorrow (1987) rebutts claims "that VDU's are connected with adverse pregnancy outcomes... none of the reliable studies shows any link, nor do "VDUs cause epilepsy... attention to the ergonomics of the workplace should avoid the development of such complaints as Kangaroo paw, tenosynovitis, writer's cramp, and carpal tunnel syndrome".

A spokesman for the Commputer and Central Telecommunications Agency (CCTA) is reported as saying in 1988:- "After hula hoops and skateboards, VDU health reports are the latest growth industry in the UK".

In late 1989 a New York City bill was vetoed by the departing Mayor Koch, and the Supreme Court struck down a law introduced in Suffolk County, NY. This law included mandatory 15 minute work-breaks every 3 hours, and company payments of 80% of the costs of annual eye checks. But the National Institute of Occupational Safety and Health is reported to have pointed out that "although more than 25 million VDUs are now in use in the United States, we are not aware of symptoms in large numbers of people". Campbell, 1989).

My personal experience, for what it is worth, leads me to the profound conclusion that certain measures and procedures need to be taken by anybody who does a sedentary job requiring concentration and continuous reading or inspection of detailed material - like sewing, soldering computer boards, reading small print, or using a VDU. Equally profoundly I conclude that these measures and procedures will be different from those adopted by people who do physically active work like athletes, travelling salesmen, and farmers.

Long concentration in a fixed sedentary position of visual detail of any kind without breaks is likely to be the cause of eyestrain and fatigue. It would seem reasonable that breaks in the job should be more frequent than breaks in mobile work requiring less concentration.

Nigel Heaton, University of Loughborough (1988), who studies these matters, says:- "If an employee's work is well designed, the job description is well defined, and you've still got problems, then, and only then, would you have to conclude that VDUs affect the user's health".

EMPLOYMENT AND LEISURE

Employment - facts and trends

General employment trends in industrialised countries can be deduced from official records. They have been well summarised by Rothwell (1981). The replacement of men by machines started to accelerate from around the middle of the eighteenth century - Arkwright invented his water-powered weaving machine in 1769.

Although there were periods of unemployment from then onwards, the demands of a growing population and the creation of new industries and services generated new jobs about as fast as men were replaced by machines until the first world war. Much later, scares about automation seemed to be unfounded.

Estimates are usually based on the analysis of post second world war trends. These trends are very obvious. In the period 1955 to 1975 agricultural employment continued to diminish ending at an average of about 8% of total employment in Japan, France, Germany, Sweden, Canada, US and UK. Industrial employment declined slowly to about 40% with the exception of Japan, but Service employment increased steeply from around 40% to 55%.

Productivity in the period also changed. In all EEC countries 1950-1965 was characterised by a 7% annual average increase in industrial output and 1% annual average job creation, but in 1973-1978 there was an average 1% increase in industrial output but a 1.8% decrease in employment annually.

Employment - theories.

Keynes proposed methods for stimulating demand to create employment **(The Aggregate Demand Theory)** but it appears from the above data that increased industrial output would not be accompanied by more jobs. Growth is now Jobless Growth. In the **Structural Change Theory** it is suggested that jobs are lost partly because industry in the home country cannot compete against imports, particularly technically advanced imports, and partly because the home industry responds by increased mechanisation of production.

In a more speculative idea called The **Kondratiev Wave Theory** (Kondratiev 1935) it was suggested that the formation of capital, investment in major technologies, growth, peak, obsolescence and depression, runs in 60 year cycles. There is some evidence to suggest that peaks occurred around 1813, 1872, 1918, and 1976. Schumpeter (1934) identified cyclic clusters of activity such as steam power, railways, and cars and electric power.

However Kuznets (1940) and de Solla Price (1963) consider that twentieth century science/technology-based expansion is best explained in terms of a symmetrical sigmoid (S shaped) curve. Growth starts from a floor, passes through a phase of exponential increase, and then inevitably hits a ceiling. Kuznets is interested in production, and Price in Science, Technology, R&D and scientists.

Kelly (1978) constructs a series of sigmoid curves to demonstrate the progress of several technologies e.g railways, cars, energy, armaments, etc. He concludes we are reaching a unique situation in which a number of dominant technologies are simultaneously losing momentum. A long period of R&D growth is also approaching a ceiling, as predicted by Price; the youngest technology - Information - uniquely offers the best potential, reaching maximum growth rate around the early eighties. Overall the position is bad because the outlook for successor technologies is gloomy, Information Technology excepted.

However the "common sense theory" demolishes these erudite explanations. Unemployment supposedly resulting from automation pre-supposes that there is only so much work available. But say prices come down - as with the pocket calculator. Large numbers of people can now afford to buy one without any increase in their wages. If a whole range of items fall in price because of cheaper mechanised production processes, purchasing power is increased, more goods are bought, so more have to be produced with more people employed to make them. In other words production technology creates demand.

Although many may be out of work because of general economic conditions, it is strongly suspected that a proportion of the 12 million jobless (1985) in EEC countries were jobless because of displacement by automation, so why doesn't the theory work? It is probably because the requirements for re-training re-employment and re-housing in a different location slow up the re-adjustment process so that people are removed from the pool of jobless at a slower rate than the people being added to it.

It may also be because £1 Billion of "automated" goods, say, bought because of the released purchasing power, require 50,000 people to make them, whereas 100,000 have been rendered jobless by the decay of old, non-automated, industries. Perhaps the "common sense theory" has some flaws, and things won't come right eventually without some kind of government intervention.

Another area which has received attention is the possibility of earlier retirement and a shorter working week. In fact a steady reduction in working hours has been going on since the 19th century - a fall of about 40% in life-time hours spent at work has occurred; since 1930 there has been a drop of over 20%. Suggestions of sharing a job to spread the work over more people is of limited value because it involves wage sharing as well.

"The evidence to support either "the nonsense of the threat to jobs" or "the collapse of work" - titles of articles about the topic - is nebulous. The availability of work will be determined, amongst other factors, by general economic conditions, replacement of men by machines, and efficiency and productivity of goods and services for internal use and export. History cannot tell us much because current economic conditions have no parallel in the past and the rate of change today is without precedent" (Cawkell 1981).

The rate of growth and competitiveness of an individual country and the state of its competitors will probably be a major factor determining the availability of work. The total number of available jobs will be higher in a "successful" country than in a "stagnating" one.

Even in the successful country, older people and those unable to contribute the new skills demanded in the new technology jobs becoming available may not find work when they are displaced by machines unless they are mobile and adaptable. In the stagnating country only the highly skilled are likely to find new jobs when displaced.

This generalisation is as about as far as you can go. I cannot see how anyone can separate out the effect of job losses or gains solely due to new technology. Nor can I see how anyone can put numbers to net job losses or gains from this cause since this will be the overall result of a wide range of winners and losers in many industries and services.

Henize (1981) comments on the arbitrary analytic methods which have been used as the basis for formulating policy. He rightly states that to determine the employment impact resulting from technological change, two basic problems have to be solved. The first is to determine the effect of change within individual industries. The second is to determine the end effect of all the separate influences.

The macro effects which result from the complicated interplay of all the various individual microlevel developments interacting together in various complimentary, conflicting, and continually changing ways are generally not well understood at all.

Another uncertainty is the amount of wealth to be created by new industries and services based on new technology and the distribution of it.

Nobody, so far as I know, has attempted to quantify this wealth which will probably be accompanied by jobless growth, nor has anyone suggested how it might be distributed without unpalatable side effects.

Employment, change, and chips - opinions

In the late seventies there was an extraordinary explosion of articles and books about the devastation likely to be caused in consequence of the arrival of "the chip".

Hines' "The chips are own" (Hines 1978) received wide attention in the media. Hines claimed in it that within the next few years vast sections of the industrial and service sectors would be automated and millions would lose their jobs.

In the following year a book was published (Barron 1979) which also commanded wide attention. It summarised a study carried out at the University of Sussex in which the possible effect of the widespread introduction of microelectronics was investigated in depth. It was concluded that in a society experiencing low growth and balance of payments problems we may be contemplating levels of unemployment around 10-15% of the labour force. Note the qualification about economic background conditions.

However there were still people who continued to be optimistic. Lepkowski (1980) considers that almost every major force in any human society is conservative. It seeks to preserve the status quo. You can look at law, politics, religion, tradition - they are all attempts to keep things the way they were.

New technology by its nature is anti-conservative. It's dynamic; it changes things. Every new idea upsets the status quo to some extent. In the long run, automation can be an enormous force for human freedom and for liberating the spirit. Without the invention of steam machinery we would still have slavery. Without the invention of the internal combustion engine we would still be on the farm working from dawn to dusk.

The Economist, addressing Englishmen in 1982 said "Go West young men", not to California, but to the heady atmosphere along the M4 motorway connecting London with Wales and the west country. The chips are up - high-technology companies in the area buck the trend by showing an average growth of 30% per annum and a similar growth in the work force in the three years ending 1981".

The Economist characteristically concludes that this has been happening quietly with more hindrance than help from governments. The marketplace has driven it along. "Moral: if planners seek to limit the natural growth of successful technological areas, their prosperity can quickly wither. Coventry was prevented from diversifying. It is now stuck in a ditch with the motor industry. Regional planners mark, learn, digest, and desist".

The interest in chips and unemployment waned when although unemployment went up and down, little evidence was advanced to show that microelectronics was playing a major part in it.

According to a report (Anon 1990) summarised in the Financial Times, fears of de-skilling and job losses have "proved unfounded". This is in spite of the fact that use of microelectronic technology in factories has grown from 7% in 1978 to about 70% today. Job losses from this cause were "dwarfed by job losses from other causes" and losses, primarily unskilled jobs, were three times higher in factories not using microelectronics than in those that were.

Many respondents, says the report, said that "new technology allowed major productivity gains without calling for either job losses or job gains".

Perhaps job losses in Information Technology will occur due to changes in Information distribution and not directly because of changes in Technology. It will be managers not factory workers who will go. Peter Drucker, when working for Arthur D. Little consultancy, is reported as saying (Mitchell 1990) that "a large multi-national manufacturer could cut out seven of its 12 levels of management". Companies will be information based so employees will do what needs to be done because "information will be available at all levels".

But Hepworth (1989) thinks that the ordinary worker will still get the thin end, and it's nothing to do with technology - it's the politics of regional information distribution in the UK - more like a Thatcherite plot:- "The ascendancy of the information worker.. and the disappearance of the old factory worker... go hand-in-hand with the rest of the labour market propped up by an abundance of "flexible job" opportunities, a dismal array of lower order service occupations, and in the UK at least, by the Thatcher governments numerous training schemes".

I don't recall this kind of political comment about aspects of the Information Society before, although Herbert Simon expressed some alternative views many years ago (Simon 1979):-

"Automation and computerization... eliminate mostly jobs that were already relatively routine... whilst service workers, sales personnel, and technical and professional workers increase, there will be a net increase in reported job satisfaction. Empirically we find no signs of a downward trend in work satisfaction, and when we look at the actual impact of automation at the workplace and the work force, we find no reason why such a trend should be expected. On the contrary, the newer technologies may even have a modest humanizing effect on the nature of work".

Another question "does it matter if there is a shift from manufacturing into services?" has been much discussed. It certainly does says Cohen (1988):- "There is absolutely no way that any advanced economy can lose control and mastery of manufacturing and expect to hold on to the high-wage service jobs that we are constantly told will replace manufacturing".

Cohen discusses the US Agricultural Industry by way of example:- "There was no shift out of agricultural production... we automated agriculture... As a result we developed massive quantities of high-value-added high-paid jobs in related industries and services such as agricultural machinery and chemicals. These industries and services owe their development, scale, and survival to a broad and strong agricultural sector".

"The process of creating wealth is not clear. There is not yet, nor is their likely to be a post-industrial economy. The division of labor has become infinitely more elaborate and the production process far less direct - involving ever more specialized services as well as goods and materials located far from the traditional scene of production".

Miles is more positive and has a more or less directly opposite opinion (Miles 1987):- The employment prospects of an information society appear to be extremely dependent upon the future of the services sector... If a major hope for employment creation is the establishment of new services, and the contribution of services in general to social and industrial innovation, this suggests that innovation policies should be directed at service firms - most are restricted to manufacturing or high-tech industries"

Women at work

The number of women employed in industrialised countries has grown steadily. The total number of women employed in the USA increased by 60% to 35.1 million between 1960 and 1976. Of the total male and female "White Collar" work-force of 43.7 million in 1976, about 23 million or two thirds were women. In Britain about 40% (about 10.5 million) of the employed total in 1980 were women. Of those about 3.5 million worked in offices. In 1971 only 17% of them were managers and the increase since then has probably been slow.

Over half the female paid workforce were (1977) concentrated in five occupations - clerical workers, sales assistants, stenographers and typists, housekeepers cooks and maids, and teachers. Over 50% of the female workforce were employed in "employment at risk" occupations, compared with 25.2% of the male. It is not claimed that anything will happen quickly, but when it does it will be bad for women.

Smith (1980) urges a policy of a wider range of non-traditional female subjects to be taught at school and that a wider range of employment opportunities might also be created for women by the provision of schemes for retraining on re-entry to the workforce.

The home

Much has been said about the use of microcomputers in the home but little about their use for importing information. Technical control functions in home entertainment and in the home environment seem to have had more discussion.

One problem in homes is the routing of information from a central computer or control device to the individual machines to be controlled. This can be done without the need for additional wiring or radio control by using the A.C. mains. Modulated signals are circulated between neutral and earth using the mains as a data bus.

Most reports come from the States and it is hard to judge whether anything actually happens, or whether the reports simply reflect the ebullience of that remarkable country. For example "A new concept in central heating and air conditioning control comes from Sensors & Systems Ltd. Programming is performed on a calculator type keyboard... all programs can be suspended for 99 days for holidays... but the Micro 8 still works to provide frost protection if the temperature falls below 5degrees ...the unit provides for two different hot water programs each of which can be programmed for any day of the week" - and that was back in 1980.

Philips (Veenis 1988) employ a group called the "Home Interactive Systems" (HIS) group. "The HIS products aim at making home and professional life more comfortable and satisfying ranging from entertainment and small business applications to home comfort and security. The market shows a rich potential. British market researcher MacIntosh estimates the world market in this area worth $18 billion by 1990".

REFERENCES

Amber, G.S.; Amber P.
  Prentice Hall. 1962.
    Anatomy of automation.
Anon.
  Society of British Telecom Executives, 102-104 Sheen Rd., Richmond,
  Surrey TW9 1US, England. July 1983.
    Liberalisation, privatisation & regulation. What future for British
    Telecom?
Anon.
  Report no. 1187. 1984. BIS-Pedder, York House, 199 Westminster Bridge Rd,
  London SE1.
    Microcomputer systems.
Anon.
  Report from the Low Pay Unit, 9 Poland St., London. 1984
    The new homeworkers.
Anon A.
  New Scientist, 106(1457), page 7, May 23rd 1985.
    Japanese miscarriages blamed on computer terminals.
Anon B.
  New Scientist, 108(1480), page 15, October 31st 1985.
    MPs back call for safer VDUs.
Anon
  COM(87) 290, Brussels June 30th, 1987.
    Towards a dynamic European economy - Green Paper on the
    development of the common market for services and equipment.
Anon. A.
  Report, contract number 17004.01 for DGXIIIF, CEC Brussels November 1989.
    Perspectives for advanced communications in Europe.
Anon. B.
  CEC Luxembourg, Publication no. CD-NA-12337-EN-C. 1989.
  Directorate General Telecoms, Information Industries and
  Innovation.
    Green Paper: report on the state of the implementation.
Anon.
  Policy Studies Institute, Park Village East, London. 1990.
    The employment effects of new technology in manufacturing.
Anon. C.
  HMSO London, November 1990.
    Competition and choice: telecommunications policy for the 1990s.
    Green Paper: report on the state of the implementation.
Anon. D.
  Datacom, page 10, November 1990.
    Two carriers bad.

Anon.
  Information Note P(90)85. CEC Brussels, November 14th 1990.
    Towards a free sky for a border-free Europe. Green Paper on
      Satellite Communications.
Anon.
 Zodiac, Number 38, 1990. (Cable & Wireless, London).
   A star is born.
Anon.
  British Telecom News Release NR10, January 17th 1991.
  Give customers a real choice says British Telecom.
Aylor, J.H.; Johnson B.W., et al.
  Computer, 35-40, January 1981.
  The impact of microcomputers on devices to aid the handicapped.
Baer, Walter S..
  In Guile, Bruce R. (Ed.). National Academy Press, Washington D.C., 1985.
  pps 123-153.
    Information technologies and social transformation.
Baker, T.W.
  Electronics & Power, 447-450, June 1982.
  The evolution of private communication.
Barron, Iann; Curnow, Ray.
  Francis Pinter, London, 1979.
  The future with microelectronics.
Beesley, Michael E., and Laidlaw, 1989.
  Institute of Economic Affairs, London 1989.
  The future of telecommunications.
Belkin et al.
  In Mason, R.E.A. (Ed.). Information Processing 1983. North Holland 1983.
  Pps 583-587.
    Mass informatics and their implication for everyday life.
Bell, Daniel.
  Basic Books, New York, 1973.
  The coming of the post industrial society.
Bell, Daniel.
  In Forester, Tom (Ed). The microelectronics revolution. Basil Blackwell,
  Oxford. 1980, pps 500-549.
    The social framework of the information society.
Bell, Trudy E.
  IEEE Spectrum 25(13), 26-31, December 1988.
    Bell breakup plus five: mixed reviews.
Bendix, Tom.
  Human Factors, 26(6), 695-703, 1984.
    Seated trunk posture at various seat inclinations, seat heights,
    and table heights.
Bessant, John et al.
  Report of the Long-term Perspectives Group of the IT Committee
  for NEDO, London, 1986.
    IT futures surveyed.
Bird, Emma, et al.
  Report, 1980, by Communication Studies and Planning Ltd for, and
  published by The Equal Opportunities Commission, Overseas House,
  Quay St., Manchester M3 3HN, England.
    Information technology in the office: the impact on women's jobs.
Boddy, David; Buchanan, David A.
  Omega 12(3), 233-240, 1984.
    Information technology and productivity: myths and realities.

Bradshaw, Della.
  The Financial Times, November 23rd 1990.
    Spoilt for choice by equal access.
Branscomb, Lewis M.
  Science 203(4376), Jan 12th, 1979, 143-147.
    Information: the ultimate frontier.
Branscomb, Lewis M.
  IBM Syst. J. 18(2), 189-201,1979.
    Computing and communications - a perspective of the evolving
    environment.
Bryant, Gayle.
  Information World Review, page 13, July 1989.
    The electronic crofter.
Bunker, Nick.
  Financial Times, 4th November 1985.
    Most VDU operators suffer eyestrain.
Campbell, Duncan.
  Personal Computer World, 144-149, December 1989.
    Vodes up, Doc?
Carlsberg, Bryan,
  Oftel News, 16, page 2, October 1990.
    From the director general of telecommunications.
Carmichael, L., and Dearborn, W.F.
  Houghton Miflin. Boston. 1947.
    Reading and visual fatigue.
Castell, Stephen.
  Telecommunications 63-67 July 1990.
    Data broadcasting and beyond.
Cater, Douglas.
  J.Communication 31(1), 190-194, 1981.
    The survival of human values.
Cawkell, A.E.
  Wireless World 84 (1511/1512), 38-42 69-74, July/August 1978. Reprinted
  in Forester, Tom (Ed), The microelectronics revolution. Basil Blackwell
  1980, and (in Russian) in Communication with databases. Znaniye public-
  ation No.12, Moscow 1979.
    The paperless revolution. Forces controlling the introduction of
    electronic information systems.
Cawkell, A.E.
  In Proc Aslib IIS LA Joint Conference, Sheffield, September, 1980; pps
  98-104. Pub. by The Library Association, 7 Ridgmount St.,London WC1E 7AE,
  England.
    The mismatch between converging information technologies and people.
Cawkell, A.E.
  Computer Weekly, July 1981.
    Micros will change our lives rather than destroy our jobs.
Cawkell, A.E.
  J.Info.Sci 8(1), 42-44, 1984.
    Economics of the information society.
Cawkell, A.E.
  Aslib Proc. 37(6/7), 287-288, June/July 1985.
    Inter-group connections in a structurally changing information society.
Cawkell, A.E.
  Aslib Proc. 37(8), 339-340, August 1985.
    Inter-group connections: the debate continues.

Cawkell, A.E. (Ed.)
  Aslib. London. 1987.
    Evolution of an Information Society.
Cawkell, A.E.
  Critique 1(3), 1-12, November 1988.
    Cheap, simple, universal communications - tomorrow.
Clarke, Sally.
  Computer Weekly, page 36, September 12th 1985.
    A deadly display?
Clarke, Sally.
  Computer Weekly, June 2nd 1986.
    Guide gives the VDU clean bill.
Clarke, Roger.
  MIS Quarterly 517-519, December 1988.
    Economic, legal, and social implications of information technology.
Clude, Brenda J.
  J. Consumer Affairs 23(2), 285-300, Winter 1989.
    Consumer response to telecommunications deregulation: the equal access
    decision.
Cohen, Stephan S. and Zysman, John.
  Siemens Review 2, 4-9, 1988.
    The myth of the post-industrial economy.
Cooper, Cary, L. and Cox, Anna.
  Stress Medicine, 1, 87-92, 1985.
    Occupational stress among word process operators.
Corlett, E.N. and Eklund, J.A.E.
  Applied Ergonomics 15(2), 111-114, 1984.
    How does a backrest work?
Daniel, W.W.; Stilgoe, Elizabeth.
  Broadsheet 572, October 1977. PEP Press, London.
    Where are they now? A follow-up study of the unemployed.
Debons, Anthony.
  Marcel Dekker,1981.
    The information professional: survey of an emerging field.
de Butts, John D.
  Telecommunications Policy 1(2), 112-118, March 1977.
    The US communications consumer and FCC policies.
de Sola Pool, Ithiel.
  In Proc. OECD Conf., Paris, February 1975. Published by OECD, 2 Rue Andre
  Pascal, Paris Cedex 15, France. Pps 281-308.
    Social implications of computer and telecommunications systems:
    background report.
de Solla Price, Derek
  Columbia University Press, New York, 1963.
    Little science big science.
Dickerson, Mary D., and Gentry, James W.
  J. Consumer Res. 10(2), 225-235, 1983.
    Characteristics of adopters and non-adopters of home computers.
Dixon, Hugo.
  Financial Times, July 19th, 1990.
    Hint of gloom in BT's price rise.
Doyle, Christine.
  The Daily Telegraph, page 11, July 26th 1988.
    Stress that stares us in the face.

Driscoll, James.
   In Landau, Robert et al.(Eds). Emerging Office Systems. 1982. Ablex
   Publishing Corp., Norwood. NJ C7648, USA. Chapter 16.
   Office automation: the dynamics of a technological boondoggle.
Drucker, Peter.
   Harper & Row, New York, 1968.
   The age of discontinuity.
Dyson, Kenneth and Humphreys, P (Eds).
   Frank Cass, London 1986.
   The politics of the communications revolution in Western Europe.
Eckart, Dennis R.
   Int. J. Women's Stud. 5(1), 47-57, 1982.
   Microprocessors, women, and future employment opportunities.
Engberg,Ole.
   Impact of Science on Society, 28(3), 283-296, 1978.
   Who will lead the way to the information society?
Forester, Tom.
   Futures 20(3), 227-240, June 1988.
   The myth of the Electronic Cottage.
Forester, Tom, and Morrison, Perry.
   Futures, 462-474, June 1990.
   Computer unreliability and social vulnerability.
Freeman, Christopher; Clark, John; Soete, Luc.
   Francis Pinter (London). 1982.
   Unemployment and technical innovation.
Godet, Michel.
   Futures, 120-123, April 1984.
   The technological miracle.
Gillick, David.
   Telecommunications Policy 13(3), 186-193, September 1989.
   The evolution of the policy and regulatory framework in the UK.
Gershuny, J.I.
   Futures 9(2), 103-114, April 1977.
   Post-industrial society: the myth of the service economy.
Gleave, D; Angell C; Woolley K.
   Aslib Proc. 37(2), 99-133, February 1985.
   Structural change within the information profession: a scenario for
   the 1990s.
Goldmark, Peter C., and B. Kraig.
   Report, Goldmark Communications, Stamford. November 19th 1976.
   Communications for Survival.
Goodhart, David.
   Financial Times, March 11th 1985.
    VDU health problems shown by surveys.
Grandjean, E., Hunting, W., and Nishiyama, K.
   Applied Ergonomics 15(2), 99-104, JUne 1984.
   Preferred VDT workstation settings, body posture, and physical
   impairments.
Greene, Harold H.
   Communications Week International, page 12, January 9th, 1989.
   An anniversary analysis.
Hecht, Jeff.
   New Scientist, "Inside Science" insert, October 13th 1990.
   Fibre Optics.
Henize, John.
   Technol. Forecast.& Social Change 20, 41-61, 1981.
   Evaluating the employment impact of information technology.

Hepworth, Mark.
  Belhaven Press. London. 1989.
    Geography of the information economy.
Hill, Simon.
  Computer Weekly, page 7, August 18th 1988.
    WHO backs up VDU user fears.
Hines, Colin.
  Pub. by Earth Resources Ltd, London, April 1978.
    The chips are down.
Hinchman, W.
  IEEE Spectrum 16(12), 42-48, December 1979.
    On Bell 1. Time for a change.
Horton, Emma.
  Computer Weekly, May 17th 1990.
    Tax women suffer VDU stress.
Huber, George P.
  Management Sci. 30(8), 928-951, August 1984.
    The nature and design of post-industrial organizations.
Igbaria, Magid and Chakrabarti, A.
  Behaviour & Information Technology 9(3), 229-241, 1990
    Computer anxiety and attitudes towards microcomputer use.
Jenkins, Clive; Sherman, Barrie.
  Eyre Methuen, London, 1979.
    The collapse of work.
Johnson, Deborah G.
  J. Social Issues 40(3), 63-76, 1984.
    Mapping ordinary morals on to the computer society: a philosophical
    perspective.
Jones, Keith.
  Computer Weekly, Page 32, October 12th 1989.
    Can your office measure up?
Kelly, Francis H.M.
  Report, Blyth Eastman Dillon Inc., 1221 Ave. of the Americas, New York, NY
  10020. June 1978.
    The Faustian delusion.
Kobayashi, Koji.
  NEC Research & Development 96, 1-9, March 1990.
    Information society and information technology.
Kochen, Manfred.
  In El-Hadidy, B., & Horne, E.E.(Eds). The Infrastructure of an
  information society. Elsevier 1984. PPs 26-40.
    A new concept of information society.
Kondratiev, Nicolai.
  Rev. Economics and Statistics, Nov 1935.
    The long waves in economic life. (Translation).
    For an interpretation see Freeman, C. In Proc. OECD Conf. Structural
    determinants of employment and unemployment. OECD Paris, November
    1977. Pub by OECD Paris. The Kondratiev long waves , technical change
    and unemployment.
Krantzberg. Melvin.
  In Guile, Bruce R. (Ed). Information technologies and social
  transformation. National Academy Press, Washington D.C., 1985. Pps 35-54.
    The information age. Evolution or revolution?
Kraus, Raymond.
  IEEE Communications, September 1975.
    Kraus responds to "another view of the AT&T anti-trust suit".

Kraut, Robert E.
  The Journal of Communication" 39(3), 19-47, Summer 1989.
    Telecommuting - the trade-offs of home work.
Kuznets, S.
  American Economic Review, 30, June 1940.
    Review of Business Cycles.
Land, Thomas.
  Financial Times, 13th May 1985.
    VDU screens cleared of threat to health.
Leadbeater, Charles.
  Financial Times, March 6th 1991.
    Lilley calls for more competition for BT.
Lepkowski, Wil; Bova, Ben, et al.
  Computers & People, 17-21, November/December 1980.
    The impact of automation upon people - Part 1.
Life, M.A. and Pheasant, S.T.
  Applied Ergonomics 15(2), 83-90, 1984.
    An integrated approach to the study of posture in keyboard
    operation.
Little, Patricia.
  The Sunday Times, August 7th 1988.
    VDU fears re-surface.
Littlechild, S.C.
  Peter Peregrinus (for the IEE, London). 1979.
    Elements of telecommunications economics.
Lueder, Rani K.
  Human Factors 25(6), 701-711, December 1983.
    Seat comfort: a review of the construct in the office environment.
Lyon, David.
  Polity Press, Cambridge. 1988.
    The Information Society.
Machlup, Fritz.
  Princeton University Press, 1962.
    Knowledge: its creation, distribution, and economic significance.
MacMorrow, Noreen.
  Aslib Proceedings, 39(3), 65-74, March 1987.
    Do VDU's make you sick.
Martin, William J.
  Aslib. London. 1988.
    The Information Society.
Maslow, Abraham H.
  Harper & Row 1954.
    Motivation and Personality.
Maynard, Geoffrey.
  Financial Times, January 29th 1986, Page 19.
    The UK's manufacturing deficit doesn't matter.
McGinnis, Bill.
  Byte, 15(10),445-452, September 1990.
    Of monitors and emissions.
McLuhan, Marshall; Fiore Quentin.
  The medium is the message: an inventory of effects.
    Bantam Books, New York, 1967.
McMurdo, George.
  J. Information Science 15, 361-364, 1989.
    Filofax, personal organizers, and information society.

Meade, James.
 J.Social Policy 13(2), 129-146, 1984.
  Full employment, new technologies and the distribution of income.
Melody, William H.
 J. Economic Issues 23(3), 657-688, September 1989.
  Efficiency and social policy in telecommunication: lessons from the
  US experience.
Meyer, John R., Wilson, Robert W., Baughcum, Alan., Burton, Ellen.,
 Caouette, Louis.
 Oelgeschlager, Gunn & Hain, Cambridge, Mass. USA. 1980.
  The economics of competition in the telecommunications industry.
Michael, Donald R.
 Technology Forecasting & Social Change 25, 347-354, 1984.
  Too much of a good thing? Dilemmas of an information society.
Miles, Ian.
 Oxford Surveys in Information Technology 4, 25-55, 1987.
  Information technology and the services economy.
Miles, Ian.
 Futures 20(4), 355-366, August 1988.
  The myth of the Electronic Cottage: myth or near-myth?
Mitchell, Amanda.
 Computer Weekly, April 12th 1990.
  Changes that spell death for the middle manager.
Moore, Nick; Kempson, Elaine.
 J.Librarianship 17(1), 1-16, January 1985.
  The size and structure of the library and information workforce in the
  United kingdom.
Morant, Adrian.
 Financial Times Survey of Office Equipment, Page VIII, Oct 19th, 1988
  A new way of working.
More, Elizabeth.
 J. Information Science 16, 311-320, 1990.
  Information systems: people issues.
Morris, Anne, and Barnacle, Stephen.
 The Electronic Library, 7(2), 84-92, April 1989.
  A human side of library automation.
Moschowitz, Abbe.
 Human Systems Management 5, 99-110, 1985.
  On the social relations of computers.
Mosco, Vincent and Zureik, E.
 Telecommunications Policy 12(3), 279-287, September 1988.
  Deregulating telecommunications: the worker's view.
Mourant, Ronald R., Lakshmanan, Raman, et al.
 Human Factors 23(5), 520-540, 1981.
  Visual fatigue and cathode ray tube display terminals.
Mumford, Enid.
 In Moneta, Josef (Ed). Proc 3rd Jerusalem Conf. on Information
 Technology, August 1978. Pub. by North Holland, Amsterdam. Pps 239-244.
  Human values and the introduction of technical change.
Nabor, William G.
 The Lancet, page 24, May 1986.
   CRT's are safe.
Northcott, Jim; Rogers, Petra.
 Available from Policy Studies Institute, 1-2 Castle Lane,
 London SW1E 6DR.
  Microelectronics in industry: What's happening in Britain. (1982).

768

Nussbaum E.
  Telecommunications Journal 57(4), 233-238, 1990.
    Public broadband networks in an information society.
Parker, Edwin B., Porat, Marc.
  In OECD Informatics Studies. Proc. OECD Conf. 1975 on computer and
  telecommunications policy. OECD Paris 1975. Chapter 2.
    Background report.
Philip, George, and Tsoi, S.H.
  Journal of Information Science 14, 257-264, 1988.
    Regulation and deregulation of telecommunications: the economic
    and political realities. Part 1. The United States.
Porat, M.U. (with M.R. Rubin for some volumes).
  Government Printing Office, Washington D.C., USA. 1977.
    The information economy (7 volumes).
Pye, Roger.
  Telecommunications Policy, 14(2), 99-104, April 1990.
    The UK duopoly review: status and issues.
Rajan, Armin.
  Institute of Manpower Studies Report. Gower, 1984.
    New technology & employment in insurance banking and building
    societies
Reading, V.M., and Weale, R.A.
  The Lancet, 905-906, April 19th 1986.
    Eyestrain and visual display units.
Reed, David.
  Byte 15(13), page 19, December 1990.
    Monitor noise causes stress, researchers say.
Robinson, Arthur L.
  Science 195(4283), 1179-1184, 1977.
    Impact of electronics on employment: productivity and
    displacement effects.
Rothwell, Roy.
  Int. J. Management 9(3), 229-245, 1981.
    Technology, structural change, and manufacturing employment.
Rothwell, Roy; Zegveld, Walter.
  Francis Pinter (London) 1982.
    Innovation and the small and medium sized firm.
Rumberger, Russell W.
  Technology in Society 6, 263-284, 1984.
    High technology and job loss.
Schement, Jorge R; Lievrouw, Leah.
  Telecommunications Policy, 321-334, December 1984.
    A behavioral measure of information work.
Schiller, Herbert I.
  Ablex Publishing, Norwood NJ, 1984.
    Information and the crisis economy.
Schumpeter, Joseph.
  Harvard University Press, Cambridge Mass., 1934.
    Theories of economic development: an enquiry into profits, capital,
    interest, and the business cycle.
Simon, Herbert A.
  Science 195(4283), 1186-1191, 1977.
    What computers mean for man and society.

Smith, Andreas W. et al.
  Daily Telegraph 10-11, Jan 29th 1985 and 7, Jan 30th 1985.
    Unemployment crisis 25 years in the making: eight proposals for
    reversing the trend.
Smith, Joy.
  The Australian Quarterly, 52(4), 415-431, Summer 1980.
    Developments in microelectronic technology and the impact on women
    in paid employment.
Snow, Marcellus (ed).
  Elsevier Science Publishers. 1986.
    Telecommunication regulation and deregulation in industrialised
    democracies.
Staffel, F.
  Zentr Allgem Gesundheitspflege 3, 403-421, 1884.
    Zur hygieine des sitzens.
Stone, Philip J.
  Scientia 115(1-4), 125-146, 1980.
    Social evolution and a computer science challenge.
Toth, Kalman A.
  The Futurist, 33-37, May-June, 1990.
    The workless society.
Tsoi, Hing Shao, and Philip, G.
  Journal of Information Science 14, 266-273, 1988.
    Regulation and deregulation of telecommunications: the economic
    and political realities. Part II. The United Kingdom
    and other West European countries.
Vallance, Iain.
  The Financial Times, April 5th 1998.
    Telephone rates and the UK review (Letter).
Vallance, Iain. (B)
  The Financial Times, April 18th 1990.
    Telecoms: the way to fair competition.
Veenis, Simon.
  Optical Information Systems, 127-131, May-June 1988.
    Home interactive systems: new media for an information society and its
    technological innovations.
Virgo, Philip.
  Information Age 5(4), 199-204, October 1983.
    Political aspects of information technology.
Weitz, Rob R.
  AI Magazine, 50-60, Summer 1990.
    Technology, work, and the organization: the impact of expert systems.
Williams, T.A.
  Human Relations, 38(11), 1065-1084, 1985.
    Visual display technology, worker disablement, and work organisation.
Wray, Donald.
  Aslib Proceedings 35(10), 379-388,October 1983.
    An exploration of the social and economic effects of information
    technology.
Yates, R.F.
  British Telecom Technology Journal, 6(4), October 1988.
    Human factors - an overview.
Yeong, D.Y.
  Special Libraries, 230-235, Summer 1990.
    The nature of the information sector in the information society: an
    economic and societal perspective.

CHAPTER 30. PRIVACY, FREEDOM, AND DATA PROTECTION

PRIVACY AND FREEDOM

What is Privacy ?

Huff (198) illustrates the character and importance of privacy with the story in Genesis of Noah's reaction in cursing his son, Canaan, upon finding out that Canaan had observed him in a drunken sleep, naked in his tent, and had told his brothers about it.

Privacy is to do with our ability to develop social relationships and intimacies enabling us to control what is known about us. This enables us to decide when evaluation of us is appropriate, expected, or invited. Thus Canaan's intrusion and disclosure had violated Noah's code of privacy.

Privacy invasions of this kind are at the heart of the uncomfortable feeling we have when we are treated as an object of gratuitous evaluation by others. Orwell describes The shape of Winston's living room in Victory Mansions. It provided a degree of privacy and enabled him to open his diary out of sight of the telescreen.

Most people's feelings in regard to the government's interest in us were pronounced at the time of the French Revolution (Simitis 1987):- "Chacun a droit au respect de sa vie privee". Saint-Just's famous statement "La liberte du peuple est dans sa vie privee; ne la troublez point. Que le gouvernement.. ne soie une force que pour proteger sa etat de simplicite contre la force meme" * - not only rejects an autocratic political order but also expresses the conviction that a society that considers the freedom of individuals to act as its paramount regulatory principle must distinguish clearly between private and public life and preserve the intimacy of the former".

* "The liberty of the people lies in their private lives: do not disturb it. Let the government... be a force only to protect the state of simplicity against force itself".

Similar sentiments are to be found in Judge Brandeis' remarks, made during the **Olmstead v United States** case, about the intent of the makers of the Constitution. "They conferred, as against the government, the right to be let alone - the most comprehensive of rights and the right most valued by civilised man".

The same rights are declared in article 8 of the European Convention on Human Rights "Everyone has the right of respect for his private and family life, his home and his correspondence".

But Simitis (1987) writes:- "Privacy is an old and venerable subject. Generations of lawyers and legal scholars have explored its different aspects. Yet "privacy research" was recently described as being in "hopeless disarray" and the whole debate characterized as "ultimately, futile". Indeed the more the need for a convincing definition of privacy based on criteria free of inconsistencies has been stressed, the more abstract has the language become".

An attempt was made in 1989 to introduce a privacy bill in the UK parliament. It was prompted by widespread indignation about press intrusion and the inadequacy of the Press Council in dealing with it. It failed to become law because the UK parliament, once again, showed its lack of interest. The vote was 98-1 in favour, but a private member's bill requires 100 votes in favour to make further progress, so it failed.

A great deal of information about freedom and censorship for many countries in the world is contained in D'Souza (1991) produced by an organisation called "Article 19" (After Article 19 of the Universal Declaration of Human Rights).

Information technology and privacy

Information technology has added the dimensions of computer-based information storage and retrieval of information about people, and access to it via communication networks. As the complexity of modern society has steadily increased so has the interest of the government in us, for better or for worse.
Can we still say in the UK that "An Englishman's home is his castle", or is the drawbridge gradually coming down? Where lies the balance between the interests of the individual and the legitimate interest of organisations and society? People are uneasy about the amount and correctness of information held about themselves in computer storage, and about the number of people who can get at it via proliferating networks.

The ubiquity of computer facilities introduces a tendency to obtain information by consulting records instead of asking. The Privacy Protection Commission (USA, 1977) observed:- "most record-keeping organisations consult the records of other organizations to verify information they obtain from an individual and thus pay as much or more attention to what other organizations report about him than they pay to what he reports about himself".

A different aspect of privacy, reviewed by Salton (1980), summarises the **Menard v. Saxbe, Anderson v. Sills** and other similar cases in the US. Menard took nine years and spent a great deal of money to get his record and finger-prints removed from the FBI file following his arrest and release without charges being brought. In these cases the opinions and dissentions of judges show that existing US legislation is not clear.

In one case a court ruled that the prospect of injury caused by the existence of a personal databank must be a real and immediate threat before a suit is brought; the chilling effect of such a file upon individuals is insufficient to warrant its destruction.

Surveillance and telephone tapping

The "Big Brother Syndrome" - the idea that the world might follow Orwell's predictions - still features in people's fears about surveillance. 1984 came and went; by and large the feared excesses were not justified.

But Gandy (1989) thinks that "... new technologies make the pursuit of information through surveillance more extensive, more efficient, and less obtrusive than former methods, because advanced electronics allows innovations not originally designed for surveillance to be integrated into the pool of surveillance resources".

"The U.S. government is both the largest user and the greatest supporter of the development of computer and telecommunications system's surveillance capabilities... it operated an estimated 27,000 large mainframe computers in 1985 serving some 173,000 terminals (Congress estimate). A survey of 12 cabinet-level departments and 13 independent agencies by the U.S. Office of Technology Assessment found 539 records systems with 3.5 billion records subject to the guidelines of the Federal Privacy Act, 1974".

"Bureaucratic practice and the incentives of managers to extend the reach and influence of their agencies have led to the eventual normalization of "exceptions" which soon became the bureaucratic paths around the legislative barriers. When a data protection or privacy commission is established, complacent citizens and politicians presume that the problem has gone away".

Improved technology provides the potential for automating telephone tapping - a once labour intensive activity. Speech can be automatically logged using a voice actuated recorder and many lines can be monitored by scanning (similar to "polling" where one line is used for transmitting data from many intermittently generating sources connected in turn to the line). The recording can be networked from a central interception point to "subscribing" agencies.

In the UK, assurances are given from time to time at Westminster that the restrictions and safeguards controlling government telephone tapping are the same today as they were in 1957 - the year of the Birkett Committee's re-assuring enquiry. There were then 159 taps in the entire year.

The value of these assurances can be assessed against the findings in a piece of 1980 investigative journalism by Campbell (1980). British Telecom operates the "Tinkerbell" telephone tapping service in a building in Ebury Bridge Rd., London, manned 24 hours a day for several customers including MI5 and the Special Branch, alleged Campbell. It probably has the capacity to monitor 1000 lines simultaneously and employs 125 executive engineers. The home and office numbers of union leaders are regularly tapped and during the Grunwick strike the organiser's office was tapped at the local telephone exchange.

When the Home Office was asked to comment on these allegations, the Director of Information replied that it was not in the public interest to supply details and that the Burkitt recommendations were carried out to the letter. Early in 1985 a former MI5 officer claimed (of course violating the Official Secrets Act) that Arthur Scargill, leader of the striking coal miners, members of CND etc., had their telephones regularly tapped.

But in 1985 the influence of the European Convention may have had some effect. In that year the Interception of Communications Act was introduced including further safeguards for phone tapping.

The United States

No government can be unaware of invasion of privacy dangers - for instance those associated with access to networked files containing personal information - but actions taken to deal with such dangers depend on style and political climate. Attitudes towards secrecy, or more particularly towards freedom, spread from the top downwards.

In the United States freedom of speech and of the press are referred to in the first amendment to the constitution, proposed by James Madison during the first Congress in 1789. It says :-

"Congress shall make no law... abridging the freedom of speech, or of the press; or the right of the people peaceably to assemble, and to petition the government for redress of grievance".

These rights have been argued and extended into other media - for example in **NBC v United States (1943)** ensuring the expression of diverse views and in **Winters v New York (1948)** dealing with entertainment and doctrine.

The climate in the US is further exemplified by the Privacy, Freedom of Information, and other Acts. Problems associated with the FOI Act include the many cases in which one or more of the nine exemption clauses have been invoked, according to Madans (1980). Administrative problems resulting from the 1974 amendments have been discussed by Peterson (1980). The two major "Sunshine" Acts illustrate some of the conflicting requirements in privacy legislation.

The FOI Act provides for an individual or "legal person" (e.g. a corporation) to request and be supplied with any non-exempt government record but not "private" records in certain defined categories. The Privacy Act permits an individual to inspect government records about him or herself, but about another only with another's written authorisation. Neither Act provides for information disclosure by private organisations. Inspection of credit ratings,etc., held in private files, is covered by other Acts.

According to Wise (1989):- ""President Johnson signed the FOI Act into law over the objection of just about every agency in government. The bureaucracy hated the idea of having to share information with the public".

The message from Congress to the agencies, implied from a number of amendments in 1974 to the FOI Act, was that:- "The Congress would not tolerate the executive branch's wholesale rejection of the policy initiative reflected in the FOI Act". The amendments provided for a judicial review. People then started to make a large number of requests for information.

The upholding of the Freedom of the Press, a related issue of great importance, also has its problems - for instance the delicate matter of "leaks" and the naming of sources as in the famous case of **The New York Times v US** (1971) (The "Pentagon Papers").

In short, the will exists in the United States to confront information and secrecy problems although more than the Acts mentioned above are needed to clarify rights of access and personal privacy. There has been much criticism about the absence of a national information policy.

The UK: a potted history of inertia

In some countries in Europe, and particularly in Britain, secrecy is pervasive. The UK climate is set by the Official Secrets Act, passed hastily in 1911 during a spy scare, and virtually unchanged since.

Conveniently for the government of the day the Press was fully occupied at the time with the Kaiser and the Agadir crisis. Governments take refuge behind this blanket measure, although before every election pledges are given to reform the Act.

Recommendations for the reform of the catch-all section 2 (forbidding government officials to divulge confidential information) appeared in a 1978 White Paper. The Labour government did nothing and was heavily criticised by the opposition. That opposition, now the governing Conservative party, found reform to be equally unattractive until very recently.

In February 1985 events connected with the sinking of the Argentinian warship the Admiral Belgrano demonstrated, once again, the need for reform. The restrictive nature of the Act prompted leaks which, among other issues, highlighted the question of the relationships between the government and the civil service. The parliamentary debate reflected no credit on anybody. It so happened that a Labour opposition berated a Conservative government about reforming the Act, but both displayed the same hypocrisy.

While the makers of the US Constitution tried to ensure that their countrymen would not be subjected to the tyranny of the Old Country, the rulers of Britain have never felt that much is amiss. The feelings of our mentors about secrecy in government are enshrined in the Official Secrets Act. Those feelings have been obvious over the years in lip service for more open government prior to elections, and no action when in power.

The Act has become a symbol of government inertia - extreme reluctance in getting to grips with data protection is one of many examples. The Act has been used by successive governments for their greater general convenience. To acknowledge a public "right to know" as opposed to a governmental "right to secrecy" requires a complete change of attitude.

Three bills introduced to the UK parliament in the late 60s to do with personal information and privacy failed to get a second reading. The 1972 Younger report concluded that there was no need legally to establish privacy rights. The 1970 Conservative manifesto contained a pledge to "review the operation of the Official Secrets Act so that government is more open and more accountable to the public". When elected, the Conservatives appointed the Franks committee to review the topic. It argued against a freedom of information law in its report, but suggested some reforms. Nothing was done.

The 1974 Labour manifesto contained almost the same words as the Conservative's. In 1978 Mr Mervyn Rees produced a White Paper with proposals to reform the Act but members of his own party thought it was "completely inadequate". Labour MP Mr Christopher Price said "the secrecy we have in Britain is a cancer which acts against everything which this Labour movement wants to carry out". His government obviously did not agree since again nothing happened.

Having quoted from remarks in the White Paper to the effect that a Freedom of Information Act would completely change the nature of the government's obligations, an article in the Financial Times, dated July 21st 1978 remarked "Of course it would - that is why it was in the Labour manifesto". The article continued "It is claimed that legislation along

Swedish or American lines would be inappropriate in the British context, where the policies and decisions of the executive are under constant and vigilant security by parliament. There could be few clearer examples of British hypocrisy than that statement".

The 1978 Lindop report to which the government again paid lip service, recommended legislation, including the establishment of a Data Protection Authority which would bring Britain into line with other countries. It had one encouraging provision although not completely explicit. The Data Protection Authority might employ a security-cleared inspector able to check that the government was not evading its responsibilities merely by shifting files into a "security" classification.

In 1980 a parliamentary statement prompted the headline "Go-ahead for privacy law". In March 1981 a Conservative Home Secretary, Mr. Whitelaw, announced that "legislation will be introduced when an opportunity offers". Perhaps he had Orwell's 1984 in mind as an ironically appropriate year.

The Offical Secret Act became discredited following several failures of application. In 1990 a new Act became law replacing part 2. Previously a private members bill attempting to allow unauthorised information disclosure in the public interest - that is where a crime or abuse of authority had occurred - had been defeated.

The new Act is a slight improvement in that it replaces generalised catch-all powers by specifically defined areas of protected information - defence, security and intelligence services, international relations, and confidential information entrusted to other states or international organisations. Servants of the Crown have to preserve confidential information for life.

There seems to be little public concern. The Crichel Down scandal (in which "vigilant scrutiny" was notably absent when civil servants deceived the public in the course of disposing of Crown held farmland) has long since been forgotten. Had the 1990 private members bill become law a civil servant releasing information about it would not have been prosecuted.

In the words of an American and an Englishman, quoted in a perceptive discussion of the issues by Michael (1973):- "The liberties of the people never were, nor ever will be, secure, when the transactions of their rulers may be concealed from them" (Patrick Henry, American revolutionary). "Persons who carry high responsibility in Britain tend to assume that they cannot be expected to explain their actions fully to ordinary people, who would be unable to understand even if they wished to. This is the residue of old-fashioned aristocratic principle which remains firmly embedded in British democracy." (Andrew Schonfield, English economist).

Archaic English laws

The absurdity of much of English law in this area has been well reviewed by Stevens & Yardley (1982). They point out that while the restraints which exist in the law resemble those in the European Convention (and doubtless the First Amendment too) the absence of a written constitution in the UK in which freedom of expression is afforded a degree of constitutional protection is very clear. The basic assumption is that

Parliament may make any laws it chooses - very different from the wording of the First Amendment - and that the courts are obliged to give effect to these laws.

The absence of a yardstick, such as that provided by the First Amendment, has meant that our judges have little to go on and instead have adopted the relatively easy course of simply following, literally wherever possible, the words of parliament, seldom enquiring into their spirit. Stevens & Yardley give two major examples of the way the law does less than credit to the English legal system. They cite first the extraordinary case in which Mrs. Whitehouse tried to prosecute for obscenity those responsible for producing the play "The Romans in Britain".

Because the Attorney General refused to bring proceedings, Mrs. Whitehouse brought a private prosecution against a Director of the National Theatre, where the play was shown, under the Sexual Offences Act 1967. This Act provides for imprisonment of up to 2 years for homosexual acts in public. When the case came to Court the judge felt that an act of gross indecency within the meaning of the Act had been shown in the play, but that having been established, Mrs. Whitehouse declined to bring any further evidence - consequently proceedings were abandoned.

Mrs. Whitehouse's action demonstrated that Parliament's intention was thwarted since the intention was that the Attorney General should have sole discretion about prosecutions in respect of theatrical performances.

Absurdities of the law had been demonstrated earlier during the "Ladies Directory" case of 1962 concerning a booklet of services with prices. The extraordinary conclusion of the House of Lords was that a person could be guilty of corrupting public morals whether or not he was guilty of an obscene publication, and whether or not his purpose was itself criminal - whether or not there was such an offence as "corrupting public morals"!

Earlier still, questions about the obscenity of Lawrence's "Lady Chatterley's Lover" were the subject of a notorious case in which bishops, critics, and experts were required to testify as to the merits of the book. "It is this sort of subjective judgement which gives rise not only to confusion of the law but a tendency for an articulate and aggressive minority to dictate the case of the majority" conclude Stevens & Yardley.

A Bill of Rights for the UK?

Without a written constitution or a Bill of Rights in the U.K., it is necessary for people to "take the long road to Strasbourg as a court of first instance". Article 26 of the European Convention says that all domestic remedies must be exhausted before the Commission can entertain an individual's petition. Remedies seldom exist in the UK. To change the situation a Bill of Rights was introduced by Lord Wade in September 1976. It was reintroduced in February 1981, but not enacted.

Article 10 of the European Convention on Human Rights protects freedom of expression and information but it has not been incorporated into UK law.

The British public do not seem to be concerned about the new-technology Big Brother Syndrome. In a 1982 Mori poll, two thirds of those asked disagreed with the statement:- "I'm suspicious about the possible effects of new technology", and only 4% disagreed with the statement:- "On balance new technology is a good thing". So far as I am aware privacy questions, with the exception of reform in the Official Secrets Act, have never been an issue at election time, so there is no political mileage in the subject.

The public have no right to know what is stored in the police computers in England. A policeman took the number of a car parked near John Peel's grave in the English countryside at the time of its desecration. Car numbers and other personal details of various groups are held in the central police computer. The policeman checked with the computer, found that the car owner was a member of the Anti Blood Sport League, and arrests followed. Nobody knows how many groups are listed in the machine.

A similar situation obtains in Germany with computers run by the German Verfassungsschutz (VFS - Office for the Protection of the Constitution). The VFS can interrogate various computers in addition to their own. In 1978 it was claimed that they could assess people's politics or tastes by checking the computerised lending files in public libraries.

Attempts to find out more about the use of the 20 gigabytes of MI5 computer storage by parliamentary questions have been abortive. In a 1975 White Paper it was said that there were exceptions to the general rule of not inter-linking government computers - doubtless MI5 would be among them.

DATA PROTECTION LAWS

Access to recorded data

The potential for errors and illegal access exists, so we should ask further questions about the content of computer files (and for that matter manually kept files), the use of those files, the possibility of obtaining unauthorised access to them, and the right of people to check that records about themselves are correct.

It may be more difficult to deal with print-on-paper files because of the scale and cost, policing problems, access rights etc. Many European countries lump computer and paper files together, so although the difficulties of dealing with data protection for such files may be considerable, and although they may think that computer-based files present greater dangers, they do not differentiate.

It is hard to disagree with the premises firstly, that the government and certain other bodies such as the police need information about people stored on computers (although some people may still advocate armies of clerks and acres of filing cabinets) and secondly that the public should be kept informed about what is going on.

Freedom gets eroded in imperceptibly small steps until there is a sudden concentration of power. The first act of a dictator is to take over communications and the dissemination of information. These days such a takeover would be much easier and far more effective.

The European experience of data protection

Belated action in the UK is based much more upon European than US experience. Data protection in Europe was set in motion following the 1970 census in Sweden and the use of computers to process the data. It was felt that the ease of manipulating quantities of information encouraged the collection of data about individuals, leading to the possibility of errors and misuse.

The Swedish 1974 Data Act required that permission be obtained from a Data Inspection Board before computer files containing personal information could be established, and that the Board should be able to supervise the files to ensure compliance with the provisions of the Act. Information should be used only for the specified purpose, and individuals would have certain rights of access at no charge and the right to have errors corrected not only on the file being checked but also on the files of any other party to whom the data had been communicated. Manual files are not covered by the Act.

Note that the abbreviation DP, used in this chapter, means "Data Protection" not "Data Processing". DP laws in Sweden seem to have brought about a change in climate, at least in credit enquiries. Credit bureaux record only debts proved in court, not those which have just been reported. Activities are more open; a copy of the reply sent in response to a credit enquiry from a trader is automatically sent to the subject of the enquiry.

The Council of Europe drew up a resolution in 1974 embodying principles similar to those adopted in Sweden. Protection laws were subsequently enacted in West Germany, France, Norway, Denmark, Austria and Luxembourg and later in Belgium, Finland, Iceland, and The Netherlands and Switzerland. In a number of countries, including Denmark, Finland, France, Germany, Iceland, and Norway, data protection covers manually kept records as well as records in computer systems.

All European countries operating Data Protection laws have established a DP authority. Originally most countries operated schemes where application had to be made by owners of computer files containing personal information, followed by registration. Now that experience has been gained and DP administration costs have been reviewed, there is a trend towards systems in which the file owner simply declares their existence to the authority and runs the files unless the authority intervenes.

Access and correction rights vary from country to country, but the expected workload in dealing with right of access requests has not materialised. The most controversial area is exclusion of public access to governmental files designated as "classified".

Transborder data flow, discussed later in this chapter, is permissible if (ideally) equivalent DP laws operate in the recipient country, but in practice it is allowed if a reasonable degree of protection operates there. There do not seem to be any instances where information transfer has been forbidden, but there have been cases where the DP authority has asked companies to reconsider their practices.

Legislation in Europe has created awareness and debate, evolved principles, and shown the need for adaptation of the laws.

The US experience

The main concern in the US has been with the record-keeping activities of the government about private individuals. There is no legislation in the US of the kind favoured in Europe. The 1966 Freedom of Information Act - about the right of public access to government information - was reinforced by the Privacy Act of 1974 which included measures for easing procedural barriers in public access.

The 1974 Act is the only comprehensive piece of privacy protection legislation, although there are several other Acts and a number of state laws, and there have been US government initiatives in this area.

Major US corporations were asked in 1981 and again in 1982 to endorse guidelines about the privacy of records covering customers, shareholders, and employees. 157 large corporations and trade associations did so. Senator Edward Kennedy (1981), active in this field, warned against attempts to change the Acts in order to limit freedom of access to government information on the grounds that criminal investigations were impeded.

He cites the information uncovered about the My Lai massacre, and about misuse of powers used to investigate political dissidents, tax evasion by Spiro Agnew, and million dollar expense payments in connection with contract lobbying as evidence of the value of the Acts as they stand.

Proposals covering the use of information in databanks and other matters were made by the Carter administration in 1979 but the outcome seems to be to have more of the same kind of legislation - for example the 1980 Privacy Protection Act which limits government search and seizure of documents from individuals.

Data protection in the UK

Data protection legislation is not universally approved. Some people think that it will be impossible to enforce. It can be argued that the necessary expensive procedures will be adopted by honest people, but the person who wishes to conceal could arrange for selected print commands to be excluded from a program. The complexity of, say, relational databases, is such that the most thorough inspector could not be sure that there had been no concealment.

A speaker at a UK parliamentary computer forum said "I use a computer network with nodes in 27 countries including a public call box in Peru. How can any data protection authority hope to find out what I am doing with my data?"

The UK Data Protection Act

The new version of the Data Protection Bill was published in November 1983. It had already been of immense benefit - to the lawyers who prepared it. It was littered with sub-clauses and sub-sections, encouraging sentences like "(3) where any such notice as is mentioned in paragraph (b) in subsection (1) above contains a statement by the Registrar in accordance with section 10(6), 11(5), or 12(7) above then....etc. Legalese is worse than Computerese.

The purpose of the bill was to implement the 1982 White Paper on Data Protection (Cmnd 8538) and to enable the UK to ratify the European Convention. Some would say it was grudgingly introduced for that purpose and for no other. It was enacted in July 1984.

It established eight data protection principles - fair and lawful processing; specific purposes; confidentiality; sufficient but not excessive data; accuracy and timeliness; keep no longer than is necessary; individual right of access and correction if necessary; proper security.

The Act set up a Registrar of data users and bureaux who hold or provide services involving personal data. Provision is made for enforcement and appeal and a tribunal was set up.

Several changes were made to the Bill during its passage through parliament. Data user's accounts and payroll were made exempt. Immigration information is no longer exempt from the provisions for subject access.

There is no provision for a security-cleared inspector to check whether the files specified as "classified" are legitimately so specified, or have merely been shifted into that category to avoid rights of access.

The exclusion of manual files from the Act presents the opportunity for the data user to shift files to paper should he wish to deny right of access. Other European countries (except Denmark) and the US, do not specify the media for files, and the rather small number of enquiries received have applied to printed files. In other words attention is focused on the data, not the method of recording it.

A governmental code of practice aimed at civil servants formalising the arrangements for confidentiality was published in June 1984. It emphasised this requirement during the widespread practice of data collection for statistical purposes only. It is hoped that this will allay public distrust.

The Act makes no mention of the need for data users to record transfers of information to other files. An error, found by a person requesting access, may therefore still be present on the transferred information. Problems have already arisen by the adoption in the Act of a definition of data as "information recorded in a form in which it can be processed by equipment operating automatically in response to instructions given for that purpose".

The above curious definition apparently applies to WP equipment, any type of computer and punched card equipment, and microform equipment if it embodies computer-controlled retrieval, but not if it doesn't.

In 1988 it was reported that (Kavanagh 1988) "nearly 100,000 people invoked their right to see information held on them in computer systems in the four months after this right became law".

The EC proposes a number of measures to harmonise data protection laws - control on providing data to third parties, rules for telecom companies, ban on sensitive data without consent of subject, appoint an EC DP commissioner, and include both computer and manual files.

Nicolle (1990) reports that Eric Howe, UK registrar, supports these

measures. Howe recently forced the Advertising Association to amend their
direct mail code of practice about right of access and passing personal
information to others.

Of 2500 UK complaints received by the registrar, 45% are about
direct mail marketing, 17% consumer credit, and 8% about refusal to grant
access. In the year ending May 1990 there were nine enforcement notices and
14 registraton application refusals. The registrar took legal action
against 30 users winning all those cases heard so far. A major case is
pending - it concerns certain information stored by the Halifax Building
Society during 1987.

DATA PROTECTION BY ENCRYPTION

The principle weapon against the interception of data in electrical
transit is encryption. Diffie (1979) has provided a comprehensive treatment
of the subject; the cloak-and-dagger politics and possibilities of
code-breaking have been discussed by Sugarman (1979).

Gebhardt (1990) reviews the precautions taken in public telecom
networks for several countries, drawing attention in particular to ISDN
networks where security at a number of points are needed. The ISDN contains
subscribers terminals and installations, subscriber lines, ISDN exchanges,
gateways to foreign countries, stored program processing computers,
electronic mail, videotex, voice mail etc,. processing computers, operation
and maintenance computer centres, and so on.

A code is simply the substitution of codewords for plain language,
while the two major types of cypher - transposition and substitution - are
operations on individual characters. Cyphers and cryptography (from the
Greek kryptos, hidden, and graphein, to write) are used to prepare secret
messages.

The two major encryption methods in use today are the DES or Data
Encryption Standard and the PKA or Public Key Algorithm. They provide
protection against the theft of tapes or disks, or against the interception
of data in the course of transmission.

The DES specifies an enciphering algorithm for the high speed
processing of data by computer hardware. A 56 bit key is used for multiple
permutations of blocks of plain text composed of 64 bits inclusive of 8
error-detection bits. To decipher, it is only necessary to apply the same
algorithm to an enciphered block using the same key. Everyone knows the
algorithm but only the sender and receiver know the selected key.

There are 72 quadrillion possible keys and there has been some
controversy about the effort and cost needed to produce a computer capable
of breaking the algorithm, with charges of collusion between the US National
Security Agency and IBM who developed it - real space age cloak and dagger
stuff.

The PKA, however, embodies an additional factor to nullify the
possible effect of the security risk inherent in the DES; with DES,
information about keys could be intercepted en route to perhaps many
correspondents. PKA uses two separate keys - a public enciphering key and a
different secret deciphering key. The inverse of the enciphering functions

cannot be derived even if the enciphering functions are known.

The distribution of information about keys to the message recipient is not necessary because of the "trap-door" method of using one way enciphering and inverse functions. The PKA also embodies a signature to authenticate the sender as actually being the person he is purporting to be.

In September 1990 IBM announced several new security measures including fast encryption for data transmission using an "Integrated Cryptographic Feature" (ICRF). It supports cryptographic standards for PIN numbers, the DES, and the Data Encryption Algorithm (DEA).

Cane & Keyhoe (1990) point out that various restrictions on the export of encryption technology are enforced - the "cloak and dagger" aspects, mentioned above, endure. Indeed that very phrase is used as the title for Grehan's (1988) explanatory article about codes and ciphers. Interest is centred on the chip which embodies the encryption processes. The use of IBM's new encryption options are only available to specified classes of user. The UK government does not want DES to become widely used.

Other computer manufacturers and European governments see too close an association between encryption methods and the US military. France, Holland, West Germany, and the UK are putting forward proposals called Information Technology Security Evaluation Criteria (ITSEC).

A computerised encryption scheme somewhat resembling a one-time pad, widely used during the last war, seems to be emerging as a new contender.

The key in the "one-time pad", invented by G.Vernam in 1917, is a sequence of randomly generated bits, held by both message sender and recipient. The message to be sent, coded into bits, is "XORed" with the key. The recipient XORs his received message with the same key to decypher the message.

An Xor (Exclusive or) logic device has two input terminals, X and Y, and one output terminal. Its operation can be expressed as "X or Y but not both"- i.e. identical inputs produce a 0 output, non-identical a 1.

Thus:- 0,0,= 1 0,1,= 0, 1,0,= 0, 1,1,=1.

As used in the 39-45 war, the one-time pad "key" was contained in a pad of numbered pages containing lines of columnised randomly generated decimal numbers held by message sender and recipient. The letters of a message to be sent were first encoded into numbers using a simple substitution code. The sender subtracted each number, without borrowing, from a one time pad number, starting at a particular column and line on a particular page, and the result was transmitted. The message contained a group at the beginning telling the addressee where to start on his pad.

The recipient, starting at the place indicated by the sender on his copy of the same one-time pad, subtracted each received number from his one-time pad number, without borrowing, thereby de-cyphering the message, and then changed the numbers back to the original letters using the same substitution code as used by the sender. Provided each new message was encyphered using a part of the pad never used previously, the method was perfectly secure.

The new version is more like Vernam's, and was invented recently by Robert Mathews, also the science correspondent of the Daily Telegraph. It overcomes the inconvenience of distributing keys to intended message recipients in advance. It includes a device which always generates the same set of random numbers when triggered by the same triggering number. Each new message contains a new triggering number which generates a new set of random numbers.

Actually the system as just described could not work because a truly random number list cannot be repeated. The numbers are "pseudo-random", generated by electronic circuits capable of generating the same set of pseudo-random numbers when triggered by the same triggering number, but sufficiently different from any other set of pseudo-random numbers generated by different triggering numbers to make cypher-breaking almost impossible.

The design background to such systems are discussed by Zeng et al (1991). The only way to determine the randomness, and hence the undecypherability of a message using a particular system design, is to subject messages to "Merciless attacks" using the armoury of known cypher-breaking techniques to see if the system can resist them.

A different solution, as described by Walker (1980), is needed for the case when a large computer, connected to a communications network, contains files of different security classifications, and it is desired to make the installation available to a number of people who themselves are within different security categories.

Machines can embody a security "kernel" or interface between the operating system - that is specialised software controlling computer functions - and the hardware. The function of the kernel is to check the access rights of each user to any information-containing system element. It may, of course, be necessary to encrypt data flowing through the network as well.

HACKERS

Hackers have been viewed as "folk-heroes" - for example the teenager in the film "War Games" - but "When someone tampers with someone else's data or programs, however clever the method, we all need to recognize that such an act is, at best, irresponsible and very likely criminal" (Parrish 1989).

In the UK, one reaction to hackers was a private members's anti-hacking Computer Misuse Bill which started on its passage through the House of Commons in 1989. It became law in September 1990. The Act makes it an offence to attempt to gain unauthorised access to a computer, punishable by six months imprisonment, or a maximum fine of £12,000. Damaging a computer's memory is punishable by up to five years in prison.

Curious forms of "co-operation" between hackers and hacked, with the hacker sometimes acting semi-benignly, have hitherto deterred the labelling of hackers as criminals. When Schifreen and Gold broke in to British Telecom's system, Schifreen reported this failure in security to British Telecom. BT's response was to prosecute, but both were acquitted on a point of law.

Three West German Hackers were arrested for espionage and given suspended sentences for hacking into military networks. One of the "Chaos Computer Club", as they were called, was trapped by bait set by Clifford Stoll of Berkeley Labs who had noted that someone was using a computer, but had no address to which bills should be sent. He allowed the hacker, Markus Hess, to roam networks and find a package containing fictitious data about Star Wars. Hess was so interested that he stayed on the line long enough for his terminal location to be backward-tracked through the networks.

According to Schwartz (1990), hackers are typically "young somewhat immature individuals who are looking for adulation. To carry out their intrusions silently and without record... is much like asking a good fisherman not to tell you about the really big one he just caught"

COMPUTER VIRUSES AND WORMS

A Virus is a stored program, a copy of which is transferred from one computer to another via a floppy disc or telecoms network, designed to create confusion or destruction in each new host. A Trojan horse is a variation fed into a program to do damage to that particular program. A Worm is rather different; it usually re-writes itself in memory and gets transferred to different parts of the system as a kind of challenge, generating a message on a screen.

One of the first viruses to receive publicity spread through the ARPA network in the United States on October 27th 1980, and brought it to a halt. It took three days to get rid of it. It worked by saturating network nodes on the network. Worms also appeared around 1980. The Cookie Monster Worm spread through a system at MIT and displayed messages such as "I'm a worm, kill me if you can".

A major invasion of viruses started in 1987. The (C) Brain virus was extraordinary. It changed the volume label of a disc and when a machine was first switched on displayed the message "Welcome to the dungeon. Beware of this virus. Contact us for vaccination" followed by an address and telephone number in Lahore, Pakistan. The virus alters command files. According to the New York Times when the number was called, a person expressed surprise that the virus had travelled so far. This virus has no known cure.

Dozens of other viruses and trojan horses appeared such as the Bell Labs virus, the Israeli virus, the Lehigh virus, the MacIn virus, the Scores virus, the Xmas Card Trojan, etc.

One of the most elaborate was The Scores virus which appeared in April 1988 and penetrated Mac machines belonging to Apple sales offices, computer magazines, and a US Senator, among others. It lies dormant and becomes active at intervals of several days watching for a particular application to be run, then causing disc writing to fail. It recognizes attempts at deletion and modifies its memory location and re-names itself.

In 1989 thousands of users in several countries received a floppy disc purporting to contain a computer-based assessment of the recipients risk of AIDS infection. When loaded into a microcomputer it commenced destroying programs and data (Cane 1989). The virus originator, Dr. Joseph Popp, was arrested by an FBI agent (Fawcett 1990). Fawcett contains accounts of a number of different viruses.

Friday the 13th virus starts up on that day, creating damage. The

Datacrime virus come in two parts; anyone using a package designed to find Datacrime 1 won't find Datacrime 2 which contains a code difference. In February 1990 British Rail's machines were infected with the 1813 virus.

McGourtey (1991) reports that at the beginning of the year a destructive virus appeared in the House of Commons library computer system. It upsets the file allocation table. The virus affects only part of the network, but the extent of the damage is not known.

This virus is believed to be the work of the "Dark Avenger", a member of the Bulgarian virus factory which has produced 120 different viruses. It is similar to Evil, Phoenix, and V800, also written by the Dark Avenger.

For a review of viruses, Trojan horses, and Worms, see Hawkins (1989).

Madsen (1990) provides a hypothetical example of "a malicious attack upon the world's networked infrastructure... by entering a worm into the Dutch Datanet 1 public network from a terminal somewhere in Holland... Within ten minutes hundreds of computers in the Netherlands crash. The worm is transmitted to other public data networks round the world via international gateways and bridges, spreading through Tymnet, Telenet, Infonet, and the Compuserve networks. As the business day begins in the US it hits the New York teleport and brings about a crash of the Clearing House for Interbank Payments... invades the Euronet packet-switched network... the Japanese teleport... etc.

More limited interruptions have already occurred. A virus injected at Darmstadt in 1987 moved via Bitnet into IBM's worldwide network, gridlocked it, and "infected hundreds of IBM mainframe computers round the world".

A number of anti-viral software packages are available in the UK - for example Virex for Macs at £69, Virus-Pro for PCs at £49, and Disk Defender for PCs at $250. Most are designed to detect the presence of a virus so the user can erase an infected file, replace it, or attempt to repair it using the detection software.

Sophos offer a package called Vaccine (£99.50) which will detect the presence of a virus by looking for changes in file contents and attributes, for new files or file disappearance, and changes in certain other items. Sophos's Sweep package contains code enabling it to detect any of 350 different viruses, and delete infected files. It is up-dated monthly (Price £295 per annum).

Work is in progress to defeat or limit the effect of viruses by introducing file access rights at several levels (McLean 1990).

Precautions to take against infection include buying software only from reputable sources, being suspicious of public domain and shareware packages, testing new software before use, and being meticulous about back-up to ensure that copies of all files are available.

TRANSBORDER DATA FLOW

The ease of access to a computer in another country via international communications and the country to country beaming of information via satellites bring with them many complex new issues.

Consider two simple but dramatic actions which, in a crude way, highlight new-technology political implications.

At a 1978 colloquium a Hughes engineer admitted that the Indonesian Palapa satellite, Hughes designed and NASA launched, could be turned off by Hughes or by the US department of defence. The title of an article by Jacobson (1979) about this topic - "Satellite business systems and the concept of the dispersed enterprise; an end to national sovereignty" - spells out the implications.

In 1979 the British Post Office was successfully demonstrating Prestel at an international exhibition in Paris, but the competing French Didon videotex system was not working. Shortly after a tour by the French telecommunications minister both of the Prestel connections to London were cut off. The exhibition organisers improvised another line but that too was cut off. The exhibition was held at the French PTT headquarters, but a French service engineer was unavailable. No other exhibitors had telephone line problems.

The most important issue seem to stem from the realisation that we are heading for the Information Society (having left the Industrial and Post-Industrial Society behind us), that the United States dominates the technology of information distribution, and that he who dominates the technology can control content and even modify local culture.

"It is ironic that Reuters, the European news agency, once glorified English and French progress, but told the world about lynchings, crime, and the risk of attack from Indians while travelling in the United States, but that now the "free flow of information" is seen as a license to swamp the universe with made-in-America cultural/media artefacts" says Dizard (1980).

It has been suggested that Western agencies (Reuters, AFP, AP, UPI) and the Russian Tass agency generate news about but not for the third world; the distribution technology is also under their control. For example an Indian may well note that his country receives good coverage for its natural disasters and social problems at the expense of news about its doubling of food production and elevation to the eighth largest industrial country.

There are a number of related issues centred round a "Third World Information and Communication Order", and the UNESCO McBride report - an attempt to rectify the West's news domination. Recommendations made in it were considered to be a threat to press freedom by Western journalists.

Fears expressed before the 1979 World Administrative Radio Conference about a reversal of the "first come first served" satellite slot "policy" (in other words appropriation by the US or the USSR) at that conference also bear on the same issue. The fears were that scarce communication satellite slots might be shared out but not taken up because of technological inability or lack of need. Decisions on this issue were postponed. Recommendations about satellite broadcasting have also been made by Unesco but the US foreign service fears international censorship.

Transborder flow restrictions are also seen as a way of curtailing the transfer of lucrative data processing business out of the home country. According to Dunn (1979), European attempts to implement all-embracing privacy laws could be an indirect but perhaps obvious way of curtailing US dominance - "...a tourniquet applied by foreign governments to the data flow essential to modern business".

The point here is that privacy laws could be used not to keep out cultural influences but to keep in revenue ".....it's most often discussed in pious terms of concern for individual privacy...but the real issues involve such materialistic matters as balance of payments and the opportunity to tax data transmission".

In a 1987 review (Mendelsohn), the author says:- "It is significant to note that most of the arguments against the use of privacy legislation as a trade barrier have been made by the Americans, in that the United States is the most developed nation in the area of information processing and has a vested interest in maintaining this position".

"Thus while the purpose of domestic privacy legislation and documents encouraging such legislation (such as the OECD guidelines and the CoE Convention) is outwardly to protect personal privacy and facilitate international information flow, the effect has been the opposite. The question arises as to whether this inhibitory effect is deliberate or accidental, and if deliberate, what its purpose is". On the other hand the lack of privacy legislation, as in Britain until recently, could lead to the loss of business because foreign companies will not use data processing facilities in a country which does not provide adequate protection for their data.

The export-import of data brings me back full circle to the man using his terminal from Peru and the datastream complexity problem - that is that it will be impossible to police dataflow. Instead, remedies should be sought through enforceable regulations aimed at systematic patterns of illegal behaviour where many kinds of evidence may be available, thinks de Sola Pool (1979). He also argues (with reference to "Swedish bogeymen") that there is no evidence yet that there is any need for a bureaucracy to control transborder flow, nor is there yet a single indication that anyone has been hurt by it.

Transborder flow takes many forms. Television distribution by satellite in Europe is controversial. West German newspaper companies wanted to transmit to Germany via a Luxembourg transmitter outside the control of the German government. It was thought that this might enable publishers to gain excessive control over the media at the expense of the German public corporation monopoly, upsetting a carefully preserved media balance.

The United States has been particularly active sometimes successfully, sometimes not, in reducing foreign confidentiality regulations (Madsen 1989). It negotiated treaties giving it right of access to bank and business data held in the Bahamas and the Cayman Islands which over-ride the confidentially regulations of those countries.

Other countries, including the UK, South Africa, and Australia, reacted sharply against attempts by the US Department of Justice to obtain access to confidential data. The UK passed the Protection of Trading Interest Act enabling the prohibition of the supply of certain data to foreign countries. Switzerland "was successfully leant on" (Madsen) to reveal bank records if specially requested, while Liechenstein refused such access.

FURTHER READING

Campbell, Duncan.
  New Statesman, Feb 1, 1980
    Big Buzby is watching you.
Cane, Alan.
  The Financial Times, December 29th, 1989.
    Avoidable fate of AIDS disk victims.
Cane, Alan, and Keyhoe Louise.
  The Financial Times, September 13th 1990.
    Data encryption - a new munition.
Charles, Dan.
  New Scientist, 24-25, January 26th 1991.
    Can we stop the databank robbers?
de Sola Pool, Ithiel; Solomon, Richard J.
  Telecommunications Policy, 3(3), 176-191, September 1979.
    The regulation of transborder data flows.
D'Souza, Frances (Ed.)
  Library Association Publishing Ltd. London. 1991.
    Information, Freedom, and Censorship.
Diffie, Whitfield; Hellman, Martin E.
  Proc IEEE 67(3), 397-427, March 1979.
    Privacy and authentication: an introduction to cryptography.
Dizard, Wilson P.
  Journal of Communication, 30(2), 157-168, Spring 1980.
    The U.S. position - DBS and free flow.
Fawcett, Neill.
  Computer Weekly, 28-29, July 12th 1990
    There's a nasty bug going around.
Gandy, Oscar H.
  J. Communication 39(3), 61-76, Summer 1989.
    The surveillance society: information technology and bureaucratic
    social control.
Gebhardt, H.P.
  Telecommunication Journal 57(1), 37-44, 1990.
    The legal basis of data protection, and protection in telecommunic-
    ation in seven countries: Switzerland, France, the Federal Republic of
    Germany, the United Kingdom, Sweden, the United States and Japan.
Grehan, Rick.
  Byte, 15(6), 311-324, June 1990.
    Cloak and Dagger.
Hawkins, Corinne C.
  Telecommunications, 42-44, July 1989.
    What users should know about computer viruses.
Huff, Thomas.
  Washington Law Review, 55, 777-794, 1980.
    Thinking clearly about privacy.
Jacobson, Robert E.
  Media Culture & Society 1, 235-253, 1979.
    Satellite business system and the concept of the dispersed enterprise
    - an end to national sovereignty.

Kennedy, Edward M.
   Harvard Civil Rights - Civil Liberties Law Rev.16(2), 311-317, Fall 1981.
      Foreword: is the pendulum swinging away from freedom of information?
Madans, Alan S.
   Duke Law Journal 1980, 139-169, 1980.
      Developments under the freedom of information act 1979.
Madsen, Wayne.
   Information Age 11(3), 131-137, 1989.
      Effect of transborder data flow upon information security and integrity.
McGourty
   The Daily Telegraph, January 28th, 1991.
      Computer bug hits the House.
McLean, John.
   Computer 23(1), 9-16, January 1990.
      The specification and modelling of computer security.
Mendelsohn, L.D.
   Information Services & Use 7, 43-49, 1987.
      Legislation for personal privacy: its impact on transborder flow.
Michael, James.
   Social Audit, 1, 53-64, 1973.
      The politics of secrecy, the secrecy of politics.
Nicolle, Lindsay.
   Computer Weekly, July 26th 1990.
      EC calls for data law harmony.
Parrish, Edward A.
   Computer 22(1), page 98, January 1989.
      Breaking into computers is a crime, pure and simple.
Peterson, Trudy H.
   The American Archivist 43(2), 161-168, Spring 1980.
      After five years: an assessment of the amended US freedom of
      information Act.
Salton, Gerard.
   Journal of the American Society for Information Science, 31(2), 75-83,
   1980.
      A progress report on information privacy and data security.
Schwartz, Melvin.
   Communication & Computer Product & Software News 1,8, March/April 1990.
      The bottom of the iceburg.
Simitis, Spiros.
   University of Pennsylvania Law Review 135, 707-746, 1987.
      Reviewing privacy in an information society.
Stevens, I.N; Yardley, D.C.M
   Basil Blackwell Oxford. 1982.
      The protection of liberty.
Sugarman, Robert et al.
   IEEE Spectrum 16(7), 31-41, July 1979.
      On foiling computer crime.
Wise, Bob.
   Government Publications Review 16, 425-428, 1989.
      Electronic information and freedom of information - moving towards
      policy.
Zeng, Kencheng, Yang, C-H, et al.
   Computer 24(2), 8-17, 1991.
      Pseudorandom bit generators in stream-cipher cryptography.

CHAPTER 31. THE VALUE OF INFORMATION

> The top entrusts the lower circles with an in-
> sight into details, while the lower circles
> entrusts the top with an insight into what is
> universal: thus they mutually deceive each other
> ....a hierarchy of bureaucratic information.
>
> Karl Marx

> Why is it, if information is power, all those
> people such as librarians, who have it, are
> powerless and all the people who have power
> really don't have it by reason of the infor-
> mation that they acquire?
>
> Trevor Howard, University of Birmingham

The economics of information

Some years ago, prompted by the comment that "**Current Contents** is rather expensive (Fletcher 1976), I wrote: "We information protagonists are faced with the problem of arguing the benefits of an intangible resource in difficult times when funds are more likely to be allocated to activities with tangible and easily measured outcomes" (Cawkell 1977). On an earlier occasion, following a trial after which 92% of **Current Contents** users decided to continue with it, a medical librarian concluded that: "relative economy is the primary advantage of this type of current awareness" (Matheson 1971).

One year earlier E.B.Parker had said under the heading "Information is Power":- "eventually theorists may be able to devise an economic theory appropriate in the information age" (Parker 1976).

One of the earliest articles which broached the subject came from Robert von Hayek (1945). Highly theoretical, it dealt with uncertainty caused by imperfect information in a system comprising markets, prices and money. Wider interest in the Economics of Information was aroused by three Americans who published seminal articles, with some differences of emphasis, within two years of each other in the early sixties.

Kenneth Arrow (1962) was concerned with problems associated with inventions as property - "no amount of legal protection can make a thoroughly appropriable commodity of something as intangible as information", Arrow wrote. "There is a fundamental paradox in the determination of demand - it's value to the purchaser is not known until he has it ".

George Stigler (1961) investigated how market prices are established. He discussed the consequences of imperfect information about goods in the market and the consequential benefits to price-conscious buyers prepared to conduct searches. It was Stigler who said later, with reference to the attention devoted to information economics by academics, that "information is a valuable resource: knowledge is power. And yet it occupies a slum dwelling in the town of economics".

Both Arrow and Stigler received the Nobel Prize for their work on

Economic theory.

For some years it has been believed that economic theory should be taken much more seriously by information scientists. Following a discussion about the economics of information organized by the American Society for Information Science, Kochen (1972) launched an appeal for articles for the ASIS journal and suggested that a prize should be offered for the best paper on the topic. He considered that "economics....is a discipline which has a great deal to contribute to the information sciences".

Others felt the same. King (1981) quotes a comment made by Vladimir Slamecka - a very well-known specialist in the information field - "the development of a pragmatic measure of information utility (value) must rank as the most important task of information science research in the next decade".

Information theory

The cost of the electrical transportation of "information", discussed in a seminal article by Claude Shannon (1948), should be mentioned in this chapter, although it is discussed in more detail elsewhere in this book.

Shannon's work enabled Channel Capacity - that is the maximum data transmission rate with some arbitrary number of errors - to be theoretically calculated. This work, together with certain coding and statistical considerations incorporating the notion of "amounts of information in bits", at least as important as the explanation itself, gave rise to "Information Theory".

After the receipt of an almost correct message containing a set of purposefully selected symbols, "information" has been communicated - each time a symbol is correctly identified out of a repertoire of possible symbols, uncertainty is diminished. "Communication theory" would have been a better title - a correctly received set of symbols need have no meaning, and meaning is usually considered to be an essential ingredient of "information". "Information" in the Shannon sense differs from its everyday meaning.

Shannon's work was soon wrongly applied to "meaningful information" - an application easily debunked by Howard (1966):-

> "The early developers stressed that the information measure was dependent only on the probabilistic structure of the communication process. For example, if losing all your assets in the stock market and having a whale steak for dinner have the same probability, then the information associated with the occurrence of either event is the same. No theory that involves the probability of outcomes without considering their consequences could possibly be adequate in describing the importance of uncertainty to the decision maker".

However Shannon's article stimulated statistical work, word frequency studies (as for example in natural language and so in indexing codes (Garfield 1961) and in symbol manipulation in systems - as pointed out in great detail by Jacob Marschak (1971).

But "an economic theory appropriate to the information age" has not appeared. Nor has any assistance yet been provided to respond to questions such as "what percentage of my time/budget should be spent on the acquisition of occupational information?" or "how can I assess whether information service x is likely to represent better value for money than service y?" Very little help has come from the economists.

The value of information 1. Cost Effectiveness and Cost/Benefit

In the late sixties it looked as if some answers might be forthcoming because the "computer-based information service" euphoria started to run out. It was time for the Sputnik-engendered rate of expenditure to be examined and attention shifted towards value for money, particularly in regard to government subsidised services.

Hyslop (1968), referring to the 1967 ASIS meeting, said that "speakers were asked again and again about costs and almost invariably the question was politely sidestepped". Two phrases now started to appear – "Cost Effectiveness", meaning the cost incurred to meet the specified goal of an information service, and "Cost/Benefit", meaning the value in monetary terms, of the benefit of the information supplied.

Some years earlier, following a survey among scientists in the UK, Martyn (1964) estimated that avoidable duplication of research might be costing at least £6M annually, but this "negative value of the inadequate dissemination of information" line of approach was not immediately pursued.

Martyn's note was one of only three references provided in a 1969 report (Anon 1969) to the American Chemical Society Corporation associates about cost-effectiveness – one of the earliest to appear. The report suggested that an information system might "save time... improve access to the literature... make available a given body of literature in a given time... stimulate a new idea... help prevent duplication of research... provide specific information for a new project".

Time saving and improved literature coverage might be measurable although "not the worth of a brilliant idea that results from improved access to the literature". Nearly 1400 responses were received to a questionnaire sent to research and non-research industrial chemists in an attempt to find out more. The average time spent in literature retrospective searching and current awareness was found to be 11.8 hours per week. Specifically in response to questions about computerized services (440 responses), the estimate of time saved per week averaged 2.3 hours. The "lower-bound value" of time saved for 100 chemists, based on salary and overheads of $20 per hour, would then work out at $250,000 per annum, or $2500 per chemist.

Numerous articles appeared in the early seventies along the same lines, often by librarians wishing to justify their existence – as spelled out in the title of one of them (Kramer 1971). In this case it was stated that an average of nearly 9 hours of an engineer's time at a Boeing library was saved per hour spent by library staff in fulfilling literature search requests.

In 1974 the Office of Scientific and Technical Information (OSTI), later to become the British Library's research division, commissioned Professor Flowerdew and Dr. Whitehead of the London School of Economics to "critically survey previous research on cost-effectiveness and cost-benefit measures of scientific and technical information....to identify promising areas for future research".

Earlier work was comprehensively reviewed, the problems were clearly stated and defined and a primer on costs as viewed by economists and accountants was included. The earlier work was, by and large, considered to be unsatisfactory, collected data was inadequate, and recommendations were made for more studies (Flowerdew 1974).

It may be noted, in passing, that economists attach much more importance to marginal costs (in this case for information services) - that is the incremental cost of servicing one extra user - than to sunk costs such as the cost of Research & Development needed to devise the service.

R&D costs are also nearly always ignored in articles by information service designers enthusing about the cost effectiveness of their services. This works out conveniently for everyone because had the final R&D costs (which notoriously over-run) for information services been known at the outset, the service probably would have been still-born.

Martyn (1981) reported in a review that the response to the British Library's request for proposals following Flowerdew & Whitehead, was disappointing. Two were funded. One was unsatisfactory, and the other was not a cost/benefit study. Martyn recommended further studies, concluding with the comment "on the question of the value of information, unfortunately at this point only a case-history approach seems likely to produce any useable results".

Urquart (1976) formerly director general of the British Library's lending operations ("BLLD"), a rather efficient economically viable unit, bluntly told us what he thought about further work in this area:-

"The truth is that scientific activity can be likened to that of a gaggle of geese, some of which sometimes lay golden eggs. It is impossible to say which goose will lay a golden egg or when...if you have a number of geese of the right kind, and if you give them adequate accommodation and food and a plentiful supply of information, some will lay golden eggs....Perhaps it is time for the British Library to support some research on the economics of economic research in the information transfer field".

King (1981) reports on data collected from Department of Energy and other users of the Energy Database. The overall costs to the DOE, including users time in reading 6.6 million technical reports and 7.1 million journal articles in 1981, was estimated to be $500M, representing what the users would have paid on the basis of a break-even service. Although much of this material yielded no savings, the part that did was estimated to have yielded $590 per article and $1280 per report savings on average. The total value of the savings to DOE in 1981 was estimated at $13 billion.

Lamberton (1984), in a review with well over 100 references, quotes only one example of work relevant to the topic of interest here. Dunn et al (1982) suggest that user cost is the determinant of a single user's use of information services and is given by "the sum of the service's market price and its unit monetary time cost to the user - the latter being the product of the user's value of time and   the time taken to use one unit of the service. Lamberton considers this to be "a major improvement". Unfortunately it relates only to costs not to cost/benefits.

I came across quantifiable "time-saving" cases in discussions following seminars organised during the seventies. In one instance a research biochemist at the Clinical Research Centre, Harrow, England, told me how he avoided time-wasting ATP enzyme assays by consulting an early edition of the **Science Citation Index.** He decided to check application validity and looked up "Cori's assay" paper (O.Cori et al., Biochem.J. 70, 633, 1958), describing a frequently used method. He found that in 1961 it was cited by J.Morrison (Biochem J. 79, 433, 1961) in a paper stating that the method was too insensitive for the frequent assays he required.

Another example is shown in Figure 31.1. Part of an article by Egozcue is shown at the top. He says that Prieto and himself had anticipated

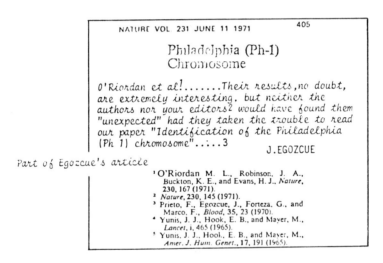

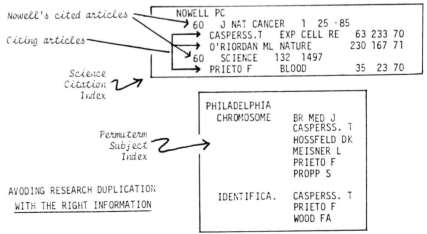

FIGURE 31.1. RESEARCH DUPLICATION

the research recently claimed to be novel by O'Riordan. We may surmise that this caused O'Riordan some embarrassment.. It may also mean that several weeks of O'Riordan's time was spent on an unnecessary project. The question is how could O'Riordan have found out Prieto et al's work and so have received the quantifiable benefit of not incurring weeks of wasted time?

The excerpt from the **Science Citation Index** (SCI) in the Figure shows that Nowell was cited by O'Riordan in his **Nature** article. If O'Riordan had used this index and it had occurred to him that others like himself who cited Nowell could well be engaged on similar work, he would have found Prieto's article in **Blood**.

A search in the **Permuterm Subject Index** section of the SCI (bottom of Figure) - an index to words in titles of articles in the **Source Index** section (middle of Figure) - under "Philadelphia" - would also have shown that Prieto's article, and another by Caspersson were worth investigation.

The Value of Information 2. Demand and Price

Flowerdew et al's report cited earlier was followed by another report by the same authors (unpublished 1976), financed by the Commission of the European Communities, in which the demand/price relationship for online information services - in other words the "elasticity of demand" - was investigated. "Elastic demand" means that a relatively small price change brings about a relatively large change in demand.

This report was associated with the implementation of Euronet - a CEC/PTT (a PTT being a national telecoms authority) sponsored trans-European network inter-linking host computer databases and user's terminals. Presumably the uncertainties for Euronet growth projections, as discussed in the report, made publication politically imprudent.

Flowerdew and Whitehead showed in an appendix that they need not have been quite so uncertain about the elasticity of demand for scientific information in the main text. They mention that the introduction of charges in 1970 for medical information searches using MEDLARS caused a fall from about 60 searches a week to about 17. 80% of the users were educational, and for them a small cost of £6 per search was enough to cause a substantial drop in demand for this hitherto free service. Commercial users were charged £10.

Huston (1979) reports a drop in demand from 645 to 147 search requests per year from physicians using a Pennsylvania information centre when a fee of $5 per search was introduced. "This reduction is particularly significant since physicians obviously possess the ability to pay this modest fee and, one would assume, would be professionally motivated to be fully informed", comments Huston.

She also reports on the Lockheed DIALIB study in which searches dropped from 2000 to 750 when patrons of the public libraries in California had to pay a small charge. More than half had to pay $10 or less (Huston's article appeared after the Flowerdew report).

Hyslop's paper (1968) was something of a watershed. The pioneering American Society of Metals information service, originally known as the Western Reserve University system, and then as Metals Abstracts, foreclosed when support from the National Science Foundation ended.

According to Arrow/Stigler economics, information's intangibility and the absence of "commodity-like" properties makes valuation, and therefore price-setting difficult. Although the establishment considered it to be a "good thing" worthy of support with public money, the ASM service could not survive the price/demand test in the market place.

From this and the other examples of demand it seems that in Science the cost of supplying information as identified, selected, retrieved, and delivered by systems designed for the purpose, often exceeds the price which must be charged for the service to be successful in the open market.

These cases tell us something about the elasticity of demand for **particular information services** used by **particular** communities. They do not tell us much about the **intrinsic value** of **Information** to a user. It might be that the information was not very timely, not easily extracted from the literature, not necessarily relevant when found, supplied but not used when it was free, or inadequate for a host of other reasons.

The Value of Information 3. How can an information user assess it?

Presumably the economists did not have simple factual information in mind when they grappled with intangibility. Curiously enough we may be unable to assess the value of facts **qua** facts - that is when they are correct - but we may be able to value a fact if it is wrong.

How can we assess the value of the factual information "the 9.0 bus from Victoria to Gatwick connects with the 10.30 flight to Rome?" But if the leaving time is really 8.30, and we miss the bus and have to take a cab, our loss is £25 - the difference between the bus and cab fares. We certainly would not have paid £25 for the correct information in the first place, but it could be worth £25 to the bus company if (taking an extremely naive view of legal processes) we sued them and were awarded £25 damages because they had incorrectly printed the time-table.

The growth, price, effectiveness etc., of online information services are usually linked together for comment and marketing purposes in the literature and at exhibitions. The differences in the kind of information supplied are as large as the difference between bus time tables, and scientific information. Moreover we can roughly rank-order the occupational need of their users. It is likely to be related to the degree of tangibility of the information.

It would not be difficult for a dealer on the money market to work out the diminished value of an online display of current exchange rates if the screen was up-dated every 30 minutes instead of every 30 seconds. Nor would he find it difficult to estimate the total value of the service since it fulfills his occupational needs. Such an information-user would come near the top of our need list.

Engineers are said to be less information conscious than scientists, but that is too sweeping a generalisation. The need for up-to-date information when designing, say, a steel deck for a suspension bridge, would be of paramount importance. The latest advances in bridge design, which draws heavily on aeronautics, need to be known, but much data on the properties of steel would also be needed. A knowledge of current work in surface physics when assessing the effectiveness of protective finishes, would not come amiss either.

Returning to scientific information, how can a user evaluate his information needs and sources and adjust his expenditure accordingly? Does the conceptual, as opposed to the factual, nature of much of the information make this difficult? How important is timeliness and comprehensivity? To avoid an overload, can a cut-off point be set for the receipt of information below some arbitrary level of importance?

How much time should be allocated for **regularly** reading the stuff? Unless this latter point is properly managed, the task simply becomes a pile-of-paper reduction chore instead of an enjoyable session of knowledge acquisition. Once browsed or read, how much effort should be devoted to filing the material for easy later access?

It seems that there are two main processes here differing both in nature and in considerations of cost. First, there is the requirement of identifying the information sources covering the field of interest - an exercise mainly in cost effectiveness. Having chosen the sources some direct out-of-pocket expenditure will probably be required to use them. Then there is the question of "utilisation functions", mainly associated with transforming the information into new knowledge - probably a more expensive operation because of user's time consumption - but also in the form of overhead costs which can be more easily swept under the mat.

But what advice has been given in this chapter to help a user to actually allocate a plausible monetary value to these processes so that they may take their proper place in budgets?

We may conclude that although no "theory appropriate to the information age" has emerged, there are several points of some interest. For scientists, the value as judged by the price they are prepared to pay for a source supposed to cater for their needs, seems inordinately low. The case of the drop in demand to less than one quarter when physicians were required to pay $5 per search is absurd.

The most likely explanation seems to be that the nature of the information or the manner of its delivery fulfilled almost no needs. Surely, for example, an up-dating service devoted to the introduction, effectiveness, and side-effects of, say, new drugs would have been valued more highly? (Perhaps the drug manufacturers have pre-empted a competitive service).

Alternatively, are traditional information sources such as journal-browsing, invisible colleges, reprint exchanges, conference attendance etc., considered to be good enough to make yet another source superfluous? Services based on a large database with a well designed search system for needle-in-haystack-finding should compare favourably with some of these more time-consuming methods.

Most information providers will make arrangements for free test services for a period. For a "product" like information, first-hand comparison testing like this is much better than reliance on "Which" type reports by others on tests carried with the help of "typical" users.

The most compelling, if not completely satisfactory, idea seems to be the "Insurance Analogy" approach. There is sufficient evidence to show that an information service which matches a user's needs will produce a dollar cost in time-saved which is greater, sometimes much greater, than the dollar cost of the service.

There is also an insurance analogy in the processing of "paper-based information found and filed for a possible future need" - that is in maintaining an effective personal information system rather than storing papers in folders in a filing cabinet; most of them will exist as potential but not realisable information. This, of course, is in addition to "information of great immediate interest when first found, then filed for future reference". Such a personal system fufills the dual functions of information discovery and information recovery.

The insurance notion has been frequently mentioned. For instance Garfield (1968) suggested that ISI's **ASCA** service should be so regarded. McMullen (1973) briefly reviewed the situation during the "Cost Effectiveness" phase mentioned earlier, concluding that "information is not free, you cannot spin gold from straw... Information is like insurance".

"Information is valueless except when you need it, when it become priceless. In this respect it is like insurance, 99% of the time one does not need insurance but for the other 1% the need is critical". For insurance "we recognize the value of paying a relatively small sum now so that we have access to a relatively large sum in the future if we need it. Surely this is precisely what we do in building up a library of information resource".

The size of the premium is a matter for personal judgement. In my experience an information premium is very like an insurance premium - unless careful regular attention is given to it, you will probably be under-insured and the policy will not be sufficiently comprehensive.

Recent work

Interest in the value of information in the context of this book has lapsed during recent years, although work continues in the "market" field.

For example "Consumer researchers have studied patterns of information people acquire and use in making purchase decisions. This treats information in the broadest information-theory sense as uncertainty reduction... the absolute amount of information search appears rather low, even for costly product searches. For example, only about half of consumers visit more than one outlet, or consider more than one brand for expensive products such a automobiles and appliances (Ward 1987)".

Repo covers similar ground to that covered in this chapter in a recent review (Repo 1989) but cites little recent work. He also discusses one or two approaches which have not been discussed here. Of the "Decision Theory Approach" he says:- "Fascinating ideas are almost useless in practice... the approach does not have any possibilities of offering a general framework for assigning value to information". And of the "Cognitive Approach":- "... does not allow of a full assessment of the value of information. It does not comprehend the values of information products in the market".

Continuing "There is even less to say about the other approaches... it seems that the case-study approach is the only means available for studying the value of information deeply enough... It is not possible to develop a general model for studying the value of information".

Bawden (1990) says "We have seen how difficult is is to quantify effectiveness, let alone benefits, except in the simplest comparison of systems... or by finding surrogates for cost, such as time saved. Though far from satisfactory, this is about the best that can be managed at present. The basic problem, after all, is that no one has any realistic way of quantifying the value of information".

But wistful hopes are still expressed, in this case by a librarian who should have studied the literature:- "Both education and industry could benefit from the rise of a specialization in the economics of information similar to that in the economics of medicine which appeared in the 1950s or thereabouts... certainly valuable work awaits qualified scholars' attention in this area(Govan 1991)". Would that it did!

REFERENCES

Anon.
  Unpublished Report to American Chemical Society Corporation
  Associates, May 20th, 1969.
    Cost-effectiveness of information systems.
Arrow, K.J.
  In "The rate and direction of inventive activity: economic
  and social factors" National Bureau of Economic Research,
  Princeton University Press, 1962, 609-626.
    Economic welfare and the allocation of resources
    for invention.
Bawden, David.
  Gower Publishing Company. Aldershot. 1990.
    User-oriented evaluation of information systems and services.
Cawkell, A.E.
  Int. Social Science J., 29(3), 533-538, 1977.
    The value of citation indexes - a comment.
Dunn, D.A., and Fronistas, A.C.
  In Goldberg, R. (Ed). The economics of information proces-
  sing. Volume 1. Wiley Interscience, New York, 1982.
    Economic models of information services.
Fletcher, J.
  Int. Social Science J., 28(3), 563-571, 1976.
    Secondary information services in economics.
Flowerdew, A.D.J., and Whitehead C.M.E.
  Report to OSTI (London) on project S1/97/03. London School
  of Economics and Political Science, October 1974.
    Cost-effectiveness and cost/benefit analysis in
    information science.
Flowerdew, A.D.J., Thomas, J.J., Whitehead, C.M.E.
  Unpublished Report, July 1976.
    Demand for online information services as a function
    of the charges.
Garfield, E.
  J. Chem. Doc., 1, 70-75, 1961.
    Information theory and other quantitative factors
    in code design for document card systems.

Garfield, E.
  "The Information Scientist" in Current Contents December
  24th 1968.
    ASCA...insurance for readers.
Govan, James F.
  In Trani, Eugene P. (Ed.). Proc. Conf. University of Wisconsin, September
  1989. Occasional papers University of Illinois Library School, Nos. 188/
  189; the Future of the Academic Library. 1991.
    Ascent of decline? Some thoughts on the future of academic libraries.
Howard, R.A.
  IEEE Trans. Systems Science & Cybernetics SS2(1),
  22-34, 1966.
    Information value theory.
Huston, M.
  Library J., 15, 1811-1814, September 1979.
    Fee or Free: the effect of charging on information
    demand.
Hyslop, M.R.
  Proc. 31st Meeting ASIS, 5, 301-3C, 1968.
    The economics of information systems - observations
    on development costs and the state of the market.
King Research Inc.
  Technical Report DOE/TIC-4608, June 1981.
    US Department of Energy Technical Information Center;
    Energy database: subject coverage, literature
    coverage, data elements, and indexing practices.
Kochen, M.
  Journal of the Amer. Soc. for Information Science, 281-283,
  July-August 1972.
    On the economics of information.
Kramer, J.
  Special Libraries 62, 487-489, November 1971.
    How to survive in industry: cost justifying library
    services.
Lamberton, D.M.
  In Williams, M.E. (Ed)., Annual Review of Information Science
  and Technology. Volume 19. Knowledge Industry Publications
  White Plains, New York, 3-30, 1984.
    The economics of information and organisation.
Marschak, J.
  J. Amer. Statistical Assoc. 66(333), 192-219, March 1971.
    Economics of information systems.
Martyn, John.
  New Scientist 21 , 338, February 1964.
    Unintentional duplication of research.
Martyn, John.
  Report, Aslib research & consultancy, Aslib, London, October 1981.
    Studies of the economics of information:
    a commentary.
Matheson, N.W.
  Bull. Med. Library. Assoc., 59(2) 304-321, 1971.
    User reaction to Current Contents Behavioral,
    Social, and Management Sciences.

Mc Mullen. R.M.
  Journal of the Amer. Soc. for Information Science 24(5),
  404, 1973.
    Information - value and cost.
Parker, E.B.
  In "OECD Informatics Studies II." OECD, Paris, 1976,
  pps 87-117.
    Background report for social implications of
    computers and telecommunications.
Repo, Aatto J.
  Journal of the American Society for Information Science 40(2), 68-85,
  1989.
    Value of information: approaches in economics, accounting, and
    management science.
Shannon, C.E.
  Bell System Technical J. 27(3), 379-423 (July), and
  27(4), 623-656 (August), 1948.
    A mathematical theory of communication.
Stigler, G.
  J. Political Economy 69(3), 213-225, 1961.
    The economics of information.
Urquart, D.J.
  J. Documentation 32(2), 123-125, June 1976.
    Economic analysis of information services.
von Hayek, F.A.
  American Econ. Rev., 35, 519-530, 1945.
    The use of knowledge in society.
Ward, Scott.
  In Berger, Charles R., and Chaffee, Steven H. (Eds.). Handbook of
  Communication Science. Sage Publications, Newbury Park, 1987. Chapter 21.
    Consumer behaviour.

CHAPTER 32. COPYRIGHT AND PATENTS

"The Founding Fathers of the US were at their deliberations
in 1788 nine years before J.M. Jacquard would unveil the
world's first programmable machine. Article 1, section 8,
clause 8 of the Constitution had no programs in mind when
giving the Congress power to "promote the progress of
science and the useful arts, by securing for limited time
to authors and inventors the exclusive right to their respective writing and discoveries".
                    Hugh Kenner (Kenner 1990) quoting Anthony Clapes

COPYRIGHT

Interest in copyright from the information technology viewpoint
centred, until recently, on the rights of authors and publishers because the
invention of the Xerox machine (and upon the expiry of the Xerox patents,
many other similar machines) had enabled photocopying to be carried out on a
large scale. There is now also considerable interest in the application of
copyright law to the protection of less tangible information resident in a
computer as author's text or software, and to the protection afforded to
database producers.

Copyright protection goes back to Queen Anne's Statute to protect
the rights of book authors in England, introduced following pressure from
the Stationer's Company in 1710. Similar laws were enacted in many
countries according to the local background - whether based on Roman or
Anglo-Saxon tradition. International agreement came with the Berne
Convention of 1886.

Since then there have been many changes, notably at the Universal
Copyright Convention, Geneva, 1952, and the Paris 1971 revisions taking
special account of the needs of developing countries.

A copyright subsists in an "original work of authorship fixed in any
tangible medium of expression" (US Copyright Act 1976), extending for the
life of the author, usually plus 50 years, the same term as in the UK.

International copyright

(Anon. 1990) provides a chart for 64 countries showing whether
subject matter copyright protection is available under the national law of
each country, and also each country's membership of the Berne, Universal
Copyright, and Paris conventions. If national law protection is available
in any pair of countries and they have a mutual Convention membership, then
there is mutual protection.

For example Canada, France, West Germany, Hong Kong, Japan, Spain,
United Kingdom, and the United States operate protection under their
national laws, and all these countries are members of all three conventions.
China, for example does not operate national copyright law and is a member
only of the Paris convention, however it does intend to pass a software
copyright protection law. For a review of international copyright law see
Cornish (1989).

Copyrightable items

Fletcher (1991) provides a general summary of items subject to copyright:-

Text   Exclusive rights.
Graphics   Copyright when fixed in a medium.
Software   Source and object code usually covered by program's
                copyright.
Music   Composer, publisher, recording Company, and musician
                have rights over a recorded program.
Film.   Every frame copyright.

Abuse of copyright

Pagell (1990) provides a list of what he considers to be areas of abuse for a number of products:-

Books.   Photocopying, translating, reprinting.
Journals   Photocopying.
Computer programs   Copying, cloning, translating.
Machine readable data   Copying of Citation records, abstracts, full
                          text articles, CD-ROM data & software
                          copying.
Cassettes   Duplication for sale.
Trademarks/patents   Counterfeiting, cloning.

He also lists "country issues". Western copyright laws may not make sense when the following factors for a country are taken into account:-

Income of population.
Cost of materials relative to income.
Time taken to obtain a copy.
Market size (people who could actually use the information).
Language. Need for translations.
Information infrastructure.
Culture.

Pagell suggests that attempts could be made to alter the situation in such countries with International Conventions and Treaties; trade sanctions: contractual agreements; better education; patience and understanding.

Copyright reform 1. The United States

Referring to the quotation at the beginning of this chapter, "do not hasten to acclaim our Congress-critters" says Kenner (1990) "for by 1980 they had enacted a most equivocal law which:-

1. Defined a "computer program".
2. Said that if you owned a copyrighted program you were not
   infringing if you used it in a computer or made an archival
   copy.
3. Deleted the "prior law" clause of 1976 which was meaningless
   anyhow.

... and that's where things stand today"

However in 1983 the Court of Appeals held that Object Code embedded in a ROM is subject to copyright protection, and in 1984 the Semiconductor Chip Protection Act was introduced creating a new intellectual property law protecting chip masks from being copied.

Copyright protection in the US extends to collective works - that is where a number of independent works are assembled into a collective whole. This is thought to cover full text databases such as Lexis even though this database is a compilation of public domain material. If this kind of information is, in fact, protected, databases containing the full text of articles not in the public domain contributed by separate authors, would also seem likely to be covered.

Copyright reform 2. The UK.

Two documents proposing reforms were published in the UK - the Whitford Report (Anon. 1977) and the 1981 "Green Paper" (Anon. 1981). Whitford was in favour of blanket licensing for photocopying whereby an organisation like the US Copyright Clearance Centre (CCC) would collect royalties and distribute the proceeds to publishers with no exceptions as are now provided for research purposes. But the Green Paper proposed that the exceptions should be retained "with some tightening to control abuse". Neither the British Library nor the Publishers were happy with the Green Paper, the publishers considering that the approach to photocopying was inconclusive.

However the UK Copyright, Designs, and Patent Act 1968, became law on August 1st and 1989, replacing the out-dated 1956 Act.

The main changes, with some comments about some earlier items still retained, are listed below.

* All the following are subject to copyright:-

   Original literary, dramatic, musical, or artistic works
      (copyright still lasts for 50 years beyond author's death).
   Sound recordings, films, broadcasts, or cable programmes (50
      years from first release or relay).
   Typographical arrangements of published editions (still 25
      years).
   Microforms.

   NOTE. "Films" include video recordings. "Literary Works" include computer programs. "Literary Works" or "Cable Programs"
   or both may define databases.

* Copying restriction includes electronic storage in any medium.

* A "Rental Service", such as a company which produces sound
   recordings, films, and computer programs in electronic form etc.,
   must obtain a "Rental Right" by seeking a licence and making
   royalty payments during the 50 year copyright period.

* Copyright for the work of a programmer or his employer, as a
   "Literary Work" author, lasts for life plus fifty years. If the
   creator is the producer he or she automatically gets Rental Right.

* There are certain changes in multiple copying for educational
  purposes, and in other matters, confirming that an educational
  establishment is not a public audience.

* Certain limitations on "prescribed library" copying for research
  or private study ("fair use") are introduced.

Warner (1990) points out that:- "The collocation made in the 1988
Act by subsuming documents in ordinary written language and computer
programs within the single category of literary work can be read to imply,
but does not state, that they are mutually connected by the presence of
writing, and as the product of intellectual labour. Such a connection seems
to be simultaneously implicitly denied by the retention of a concept of a
document as a deposit substantially unaltered since 1842".

Photocopying

The 1972 Williams & Wilkins v. United States case is a landmark in
this area. The US Court of Claims commissioner recommended that a
publisher, Williams & Wilkins, was entitled to compensation for the
photocopying of its journal articles by the National Library of Medicine
(NLM). In 1970, NLM handled 120,000 photocopying requests. 18 months
later, in a 4 to 3 decision, the Court rejected the commissioner's
recommendation, finding no evidence of economic harm to Williams & Wilkins.
This decision was upheld by an equally divided Supreme Court in 1975.

One consequence of this decision was a re-defining and formalising
of the manner and extent of photocopying in libraries in the US 1976
Copyright Act. In 1978 the Copyright Clearance Centre (CCC) was set up to
handle royalties accruing from library photocopying in excess of the
permitted quantity. Journals print the royalty due on the title page of
each article. The CCC soon ran into difficulties because the royalties
collected did not cover the processing costs. However things improved in
1980 when royalty collection increased to $300,000, compared with $57,000 in
1978.

The same issue - that is the conflict of interest between libraries
and publishers - is exemplified in an exchange of articles in the UK in
1976. In the piece by Line (1975) from the British Library Lending Division
(BLLD which photocopied nearly one million articles in 1974) containing many
facts and figures, it was concluded that "in the absence of any evidence to
the contrary the economic difficulties experienced by journal publishers and
the increased demand on the BLDD are unrelated".

This was followed by an exchange of letters between the publishers
association and BLDD (Line 1976). The publishers claimed that the BLDD
article was an attempt to whitewash large scale free use of articles. This
was firmly rebutted by BLLD.

Fair Use

In many countries provision is made for taking a copy of a journal
article for "research or private study" which is considered to be "fair
use". Section 7 of the UK 1956 Copyright Act, for example, says this may be
done provided that the person taking the copy signs a declaration that the
copy is for this purpose only.

The UK Society of Authors and Publishers suggest that re-publishing of an extract, or multiple extracts of a work not exceeding 10% of the length of the work, might not infringe copyright. If this be so then the re-publishing of short abstracts or bibliographic references certainly would not infringe.

Fair use is to continue under the 1988 Act with a tightening up of certain aspects of photocopying in libraries such as "one copy of the same article per person" and "allowing photocopying of no more than a reasonable portion of a book". In view of the difficulty of policing self-service photocopying machines to be found in all libraries these points seem unrealistic.

Fair use of copyright material is similar in several countries. It usually covers the limited use of the material for comment, criticism or review, teaching and research. Warwick (1984) defines the four tests for fair use in the US and considers them as applied to "downloaded" material – that is data transferred from a database, following a search, to a user's usually local computer via a telephone line.

The tests are: purpose and character of use, nature of the copyrighted work, amount and substance of the portion used, and the effect on the market for the copyrighted work or the value of the work.

Databases and downloading

For downloading, Warwick (1984) suggests that after the fair use of the work, the copy of it stored in memory should be erased. With respect to the nature of the work of the provider, he points out that the effort required to load data into a database having limited specialised use may be just as great as loading it into a heavily used database.

Warwick considers that there is no limit to the number of records which may be downloaded but the number of copies which may be made of the records without copyright infringement is not clear. It will be difficult for the downloader to satisfy the supplier that he is not having an effect on the market. For example the user could repeatedly search the downloaded material instead of repeatedly paying the supplier for online searching.

In addition to the rights of authors of material stored in databases, there are the rights of producers who have expended time and money in compiling them. Such producers, when drawing up agreements with users, spell out conditions of use in an attempt to make the users believe that they may be sued if they transgress certain conditions. In particular they warn against the sale of any part of a database in any form to a third party.

In 1989/1990 a controversy developed about ambiguity in the UK 1988 Act for databases and downloading (Oppenheim 1989, 1990, 1991, Wall 1989, 1990). Is a database download a "cable program service", with no allowance for fair use, or is it a "literary work" allowing for fair use, or could it be both?

Downloading from a CD-ROM does not normally involve telecoms of any kind so presumably cannot be a "cable program service". Downloading from a remote database via a telecoms connection might be covered by "cable programs containing literary works". Once downloaded, the data might be the owner of the copyright in that material. If he or she then asks for a repeat download or offline prints he is acting as the copyright owner.

Computer software

It is still not entirely clear whether computer software is best protected by a patent, assuming the application can be worded in such a way that it is accepted by a patent examiner, or by copyright.

"In many countries the trend is for software to be covered by the subject matter protection provided by existing copyright law. Generally copyright laws provide protection for the expression of an idea but not for the idea itself. For software this typically means that the computer program in both human readable and machine executable form and the related manuals are eligible for copyright protection, but the methods and algorithms within a program are not protected expression" (Anon 1990).

According to Anon (1990) "the trend around the world appears to be against patent protection for object code or source code per se, but in most jurisdictions the opportunity does exist for protecting software as part of an apparatus invention or in the form of a process invention, where the invention claimed is neither a mathematical algorithm nor a mere mental step".

Whether or not software may be patentable (see under "patents" below), it is copyrightable - like poems, books, or sheet music. The controversial aspect is whether just the software code should be protected, or whether "effects" i.e. patterns of words and images on the screen can and should also be protected.

One way of finding out how software works is by "reverse engineering". A program can be "de-compiled" from machine code to object/source code. Some think that this is theft. Starting with source code to extract as much information as possible is not. An EC working party is currently considering this practice (Gannon 1990).

A series of events known as "look and feel" appear to have been set in motion by a patent ruling.

"In 1981 the Supreme Court ruled in the Diamond vs Diehr case that a computer-controlled rubber moulding process, including the software, was patentable. The ruling established a precedent on which hundreds of software patents have been applied for... there are a seemingly endless number of possible software patents based on previous examples... with the potential for further limiting the techniques and tools of the programmers trade. (Levitt 1990).

As a consequence of the granting of software patents, Levitt continues, "Apple has been sued by Quickview Systems for using its patented arrangement of scrollable objects "easily programmed using any modern windowing system.... it may soon become nearly impossible to write a non-trivial programme without using some patented techniques".

One of the first copyright cases was Apple vs Franklin (1982) in the US, where Apple's case was upheld on appeal. The judge asked "Could Franklin have simulated the Apple operating system without copying it line by line?" If idea and expression merge, Apple has no valid copyright because that amounts to copyrighting an idea, and that can't be done. The line between the two, said the judge, must be pragmatic. She was not presented with a case for "not copying except where necessary" but with a case of "line-by-line" copying". Instead of reaching a decision she hinted that Apple and Franklin should settle out of court. (Kenner 1990).

More recently, Lotus Development won a case against Paperback Software in a US District Court. It was ruled that Lotus 1-2-3 command structure is copyrightable (source and object code were not involved) - "Copyright protection should be extended, clearly and unequivocally, to those nonliteral elements of computer programs that embody original expression".

This seemed to open opportunities for suing for "look and feel" copying. Look and feel refers to the screen presentation where human and machine interact - the "human-machine interface". After winning against Paperback, Lotus sued Borland and Santa Cruz. Apple sued Microsoft and Hewlett Packard for windows imitation. Ashton Tate is suing two other companies for dBase imitation.

"I haven't met a single programmer who thinks that Apple had any right to sue Microsoft after they essentially borrowed the technology lock stock and barrel from Xerox", said a computer scientist. Xerox obviously agree with these comments. In January 1990 they sued Apple for $150M.

An organisation called SAGE has been formed to represent US major software groups backed by the US government in Brussels to lobby for protecting the human-machine interface.   Opponents say this would make it harder for European companies to compete. The ECIS European group support source and object code copyright but not interfaces. (Charles 1990).

Marketplace aspects

An EC memorandum, issued in December 1990, says that Authors, performers, and producers should be entitled to authorize or prohibit rental and lending of copyright works - mainly with reference to CD and cassette copying.

Elias (1989) addresses a number of practical issues in regard to databases:- "It is important to notice that at a number of points in the evolution of copyright, protection was awarded not only to the created work, but also to its performance and display. When one examines the process as a schematic the statutory protection on which we base our business is derived from an original creative act. This property base is then subjected to a variety of processes which may themselves be creative.

The subsequent act and its effect on the original property is the cause of our concern in database licensing since these acts are limited only by ingenuity. For our purpose they can be grouped as media, distribution, and software technologies.

Database licensing thus involves the adaptation of copyright/ownership concepts to the processes and uses to which the database must be subjected. In addition the licence must provide for the normal business understandings that are involved in any contract".

Oppenheim (in AIR 1991) points out that the Provider of a database, or any other information product, may be liable for the accuracy of the information provided. Dun & Bradstreet were successfully sued by Greenmoss Builders because D&B held inaccurate information about Greenmoss.

PATENTS

A patent or "letters patent" grants a monopoly in an invention for a limited period. The procedures vary in different countries although there was unification in Europe, to which Britain contributed, with the 1977 Patent Act. A major change was the requirement that a patent should exhibit "absolute novelty" involving the furtherance of knowledge by an "inventive step". There is a delay between the filing of a patent and its publication - usually about 18 months in the UK, and a further delay until the actual granting of the patent. A diagram from a famous patent is shown in Figure 32.1

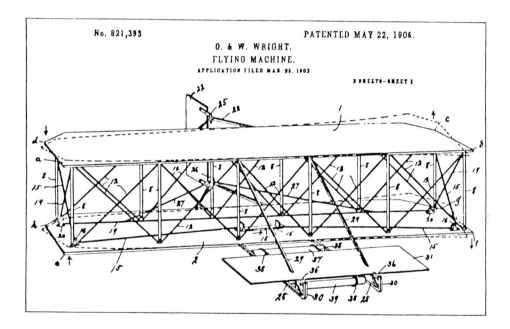

FIGURE 32.1.   DIAGRAM FROM A FAMOUS PATENT

In the USA a patent covers an invention or process for 17 years during which the patentee has a monopoly, and in the UK the maximum period is twenty years.

There is no such thing as "world patents pending" - a phrase often applied to new products. The European Patent Convention, established in 1978, grants a patent covering 14 countries if the application is successful, from the European Patent Office (EPO) in Munich. The more states included, the higher the cost. Under the proposed 1993 Community Patent Treaty a single application will cover all EC states automatically.

Anon (1990) points out that in the US the "first to invent" establishes invention priority, and an application may be filed up to one year after commercialisation, remaining secret while pending.

In nearly all other countries priority is established by "first to file". There is a "period of grace" between filing date and commercialisation, with a routine delay between filing and publication.

If a competitor uses the invention between publication and granting, the owner of the patent cannot do anything until the patent is granted. He can then sue the infringer with regard to the infringer's activities back-dated to the publication date.

It is sometimes considered that the uncertainties, costs, and delays associated with patents make it better, at least for smaller fast-moving organisations, to keep their inventions secret and get into production quickly, preferably with the "Mark 2" version up their sleeves. In other words make hay while the sun shines.

Liebesny (1973) points out that patents are useful sources of information per se. Their main purpose is of course to protect inventors who traditionally have a hard time. One irate inventor took out a patent for packaging the British patent office and blasting it into space with a rocket.

It is the companies to whom employees or other persons assign their patent rights which mainly benefit, after applying their production and marketing experience to exploit a patent. During the last war the EMI Company took out a number of patents on circuit inventions by Alan Blumlein. Blumlein was killed while flight-testing one of his inventions. The patents were so drafted that it was almost impossible to construct any piece of digital electronic equipment without infringing a Blumlein patent. At one time EMI employed a large staff, whose main activity was negotiating royalties for the use of Blumlein patents.

But it seems unlikely that a certain patent taken out in the US in 1895 proved to be remunerative. It described a method for avoiding head-on railroad collisions. All trains had lines running along the top of the carriages sloping down to rail-level at the back and front. The sloping part at the front for trains running in one direction was adjusted to be at a slightly different height above the track from trains running in the other. Two trains could not, of course, collide because one would simply run up and over, and down the other side in perfect safety. No information is available about the testing of this device.

Current interest in IT patents seems to be mainly centred on attempts to get computer software defined in such a way that existing definitions about what is patentable may also apply to it.

In the UK, software patentability seems unlikely in view of the dismissal, on appeal, of Merrill Lynch's 1989 application to patent a novel computer-based shares trading system. The judge ruled that the system was "a way of doing business". In 1991, Norman Gale applied for a patent for software in a ROM chip which was initially accepted, but then rejected by the Patents Office Court. Gale wanted to appeal to the House of Lords but decided he could not afford to.

There is considerable interest in the USA concerning Intel's refusal to licence AMD to produce a clone of its successful 386 processor. AMD ignored the refusal and produced the AMD386 just the same. A Federal judge denied Intel's request for an injunction. Intel is still challenging AMD's use of its microcode.

IBM's patent portfolio gives the company freedom do use other's inventions by cross-licensing. "Only companies having access to patented technologies will be able to compete in later 90s" said an IBM spokesman. IBM made over 100 patent applications in 1989.

REFERENCES

Anon.
  Cmnd 6732, HMSO London 1977.
    Report of the committee to consider the law of copyright and designs.
    (Chairman The Hon. Mr.Justice Whitford).
Anon.
  Cmnd 8302, HMSO London, 1981.
    Reform of the law relating to copyright, designs, and performer's
    protection ("Green Paper").
Anon.
  Report. Fenwick, Davis & West, Washington DC. January 1990.
    International legal protection for software.
Charles, Dan
  New Scientist 44-48, September 29th 1990.
    Rights and wrongs of software.
Cornish, Graham P.
  Interlending & Document Supply 17(4), 117-123, 1989.
    Copyright law and document supply: a worldwide review of developments
    1986-1989.
Elias, A.W.
  Information Services & Use 9, 347-361, 1990.
    Copyright, licencing agreements, and gateways.
Fletcher, Paul.
  Personal Computer World, 216-220, April 1991.
    Copy protection.
Gannon, Paul.
  Computer Weekly, July 19th 1990.
    Piracy battles stir.
Kenner, Hugh.
  Byte 15(4), 352-354, April 1990.
    Advise and compute.
Kutten, L.J.
  Mini-micro Systems, 249-253, September 1984.
    Can copyrights protect all forms of software?
Levitt, Jason.
  Unix Today, 50-51, September 17th, 1990.
    Programming freedom at risk.
Liebesny, F; Hewitt, J.W; Hunter, P.S. et al.
  Report. School of Lib., Polytechnic of N.London, Holloway Rd.,
  London N.7. July 1973.
    The scientific and technical information contained in patent

specifications.

Line. Maurice B., Wood, D.N.
  J.Doc 31(4), 234-245, Dec.1975
    The effect of a large scale photocopying service on journal sales.

Line,M.B., Wood, D.N.
  J.Doc.32(3), 204-206, Sep.1976
    Photocopying and journal sales.

Oppenheim, Charles.
  Journal of Information Science 15, 377, 1989.
    Letter; Databases and copyright.

Oppenheim, Charles.
  Aslib Information 18(1), 22, 1990.
    Letter (Copyright and online).

Oppenheim, Charles.
  Journal of Information Science 16, 401-402, 1990.
    Letter; Copyright and Downloading.

Oppenheim, Charles.
  Advanced Information Report (Elsevier, Oxford), 1-4, January 1991.
    Should information providers be liable for the information they
    provide?

Pagell, Ruth A.
  Database, 5-9, June 1990.
    International copyright issues: a personal view.

Van Tongeren, E.
  J.Doc.32(3),198-204, Sep.1976.
    The effect of a large scale photocopying service on journal sales.

Wall, Raymond A.
  Aslib Information 17(11/12), 264-267, November/December 1989.
    Copyright and online.

Wall, Raymond A.
  Journal of Information Science 16, 139-140, 1990.
    Copyright and downloading.

Wall, Raymond A.
  Journal of Information Science 16, 401, 402-403, 1990.
    Letters: Copyright and downloading.

Warner, Julian.
  Journal of Information Science 16(5), 279-289, 1990.
    Writing, literary work, and document in United Kingdom copyright.

Warwick, Thomas S.
  Online 8(4), 58-70, July 1984.
    Large databases , small computers, and fast modems: an attorney looks
    at the legal ramifications of downloading.

CHAPTER 33. BROADBAND ISDN

David G. FISHER
Fort Communications Technology Ltd.
Harpenden, U.K.

This chapter explains the Integrated Services Digital Network (ISDN) concept and outlines its evolution to provide Broadband capabilities. Network architecture, services and implementation technologies are discussed. Related standards are indicated and comments made on their status.

Network management plays an increasingly important role and is the basis for the future "Intelligent Network". Evolution planning is considered particularly in the European context in which there are a number of important initiatives including the "RACE" programme.

The ISDN Concept

Public telecommunications services are provided today by a combination of a General Switched Telephone Network and a number of Dedicated Networks for particular services such as telex, packet switched data, circuit switched data, mobile telephony etc. The result is that users face bewildering choices between alternative means and network operators have to implement complex interworking mechanisms.

The solution to these problems is seen as a universally accessible digital network capable of providing a very wide range of telecommunications services using a limited number of powerful network capabilities. This is the ISDN concept.

It is being standardised by the International Telecommunications Union through its CCITT Study Groups. This work is published in the 1988 Blue Books in which the I series of Recommendations relate to ISDN. The main focus of standardisation has been services (I.200 series), User-Network Interfaces (I.400 series) and Network Capabilities for Interworking (I.300 and I.500 series). In addition the I.100 series gives a general introduction and the I.600 series discusses maintenance principles.

ISDN implementation is expected to follow the sequence:

a)   -   conversion of the General Switched Telephone Network to digital switching and inter-exchange transmission (Integrated Digital Network);

b)   -   provision of digital transmission over existing copper pairs for the customer's connection to the network (Integrated Digital Access);

c)   -   end-to-end digital connections at 64 kbit/s (64 kbit/s ISDN);

d) - upgrading of user access to broadband capability using optical fibres (Broadband Access);

e) - end-to-end broadband switched services (Broadband ISDN).

Network Architecture

Architectural models of networks provide a framework for the definition of their component parts, the interfaces between them and interfaces for user access. These interfaces are specified using layered protocols following the Open Systems Interconnection (OSI) 7 layer model as described in the X.200 series Recommendations. The architectural model for ISDN is shown in Fig. 1.

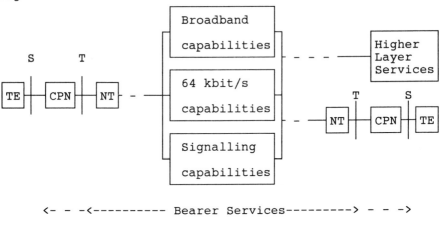

TE = Terminal Equipment
CPN = Customer Premises Network
NT = Network Termination

S and T are
Reference Points

Fig 1 ISDN Network Architecture

The diagram shows the partition of the network into its major blocks and the location of key Reference Points (S and T). These Reference Points are the locations of user - network interfaces. The S interface is for terminal connection and the T interface for connection of Customer Premises Networks such as Private Automatic Branch Exchanges (PABX) or Local Area Networks (LAN).

The public network comprises network terminations (NT) on customers premises together with the transport and signalling capabilities provided within the network. Transport capabilities are sub-divided into 64 kbit/s and broadband as the latter is seen as an overlay network. The signalling network serves both types of transport network and also provides user-to-user signalling as a special service.

Telecommunications "Bearer Services" are provided between user-network interfaces at S / T Reference Points. They are limited to the lower three layers of the OSI model. The lower three layers contain physical transmission, data link and network protocols.

Teleservices include the higher layer capabilities of layers four to seven (transport, session, presentation and application). These functions are located either in terminals or special service facilities located at the edge of the network. This functional separation is consistent with the achievement of a high degree of transparency in the network leading to the flexibility needed to accommodate a wide range of services.

User Services

The CCITT I.200 series Recommendations covers ISDN service definitions. In the Blue Book versions several Teleservices, bearer services and supplementary services have been defined in detail.

Teleservices and bearer services are defined by means of their attributes as follows:

Transfer mode	eg. circuit, packet
Transfer rate	eg. 64 kbit/s
Transfer capability	eg. speech, data, video
Structure	eg. 8 kHz integrity
Establishment of communication	eg. switched, permanent
Communication configuration	eg. point-to-point, point-to-multipoint
Symmetry	eg. unidirectional, bidirectional
Access channel and rate *	eg. B channel 64 kbit/s
Signalling access protocol	eg. Recommendation I.420
Information access protocol	eg. Recommendation X.25
Connection control protocol	eg. Recommendation Q.931
Supplementary services	eg. I.250 series
Quality of service	eg. Level of speech distortion
Network performance	eg. Bit error rate
Interworking possibilities	eg. With telex networks
Operational and commercial	(not yet defined)
Type of user	eg. speech, sound, video
Higher layer protocol	eg. Teletex

* (see section on user-network interfaces)

Bearer services are grouped according to transfer mode. In the Blue Book, 8 circuit mode and 3 packet mode bearer services have been defined as follows:

Circuit mode
- 64 kbit/s unrestricted
- 64 kbit/s speech
- 64 kbit/s 3.1 kHz
- 64 kbit/s alternate speech / unrestricted
- 2 x 64 kbit/s unrestricted
- 384 kbit/s unrestricted
- 1536 kbit/s unrestricted
- 1920 kbit/s unrestricted

The variety of 64 kbit/s bearer services is required because of the need for special interworking treatment of speech or data carried on 3.1 kHz telephone type circuits using modems.

Packet mode
- Virtual call with permanent virtual circuit
- Connectionless
- User signalling.

These bearer services support a range of Teleservices any of which are at the user's discretion according to the terminal facilities that he chooses to equip. Several, however, are standardised for public interoperability. Those included in the Blue Book are:

- Telephony
- Teletex
- Telefax 4 (group 4 fax)
- Mixed mode
- Videotex
- Telex.

All bearer service and teleservice specifications are limited to essential features but can be complemented by a series of supplementary services. Definitions have been produced for the following:

Number identification services
- Direct In-dialling
- Multiple subscriber numbers
- Calling line identification presentation
- Calling line identification restriction
- Connected line identification presentation
- Connected line identification restriction
- Malicious call identification
- Sub-addressing

Call offering services
- Call transfer
- Call forwarding on busy
- Call forwarding on no-reply
- Call forwarding unconditionally
- Call deflection
- Line hunting

Call completion services
- Call waiting
- Call hold
- Call completion to busy

Multiparty services
- Conference call
- 3 party call

Community of interest services
- Closed user groups
- Private numbering plan

Charging services
- Credit card
- Advice of charge
- Reversed charges

Added information services
- User-to-user signalling.

The two major new aspects in the broadband era are the inclusion of distribution services (eg for cable TV) and the possibility of interactive video-communications (eg video-conferencing). Services are classified in the following way:

Interactive services

Conversational services
Messaging services
Retrieval services

Distribution services

Broadcast services
Distribution services with user individual presentation control

Some examples of new broadband services are :

- High quality broadband video telephony
- High quality broadband video conference
- Existing quality and high definition TV distribution
- Broadband videotex

Many existing services will also benefit in quality and economically from broadband network capability. Fig. 2 shows the bandwidth requirement for a number of service types.

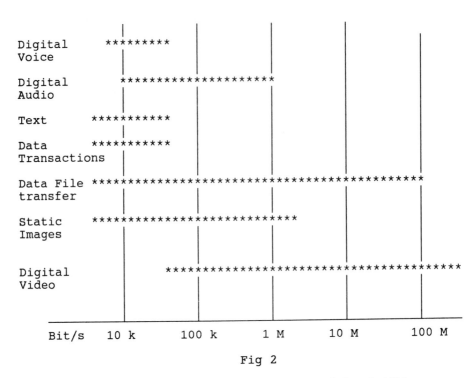

Fig 2

Relationship between services and bandwidth

The important point to note is the large range of bandwidths that could be used for each type of service. The selection of a point within the range is a trade-off between quality and cost. The economics will involve decisions on the appropriate level of bandwidth compression through the use of signal processing techniques. Clearly different applications will lead to different choices and the optimum for each will move with time.

Digital voice is mainly carried at 64 kbit/s but improved coding techniques such as ADPCM allow comparable quality to be obtained at 32 kbit/s. Where bandwidth is limited, for example when using the radio spectrum, acceptable quality can be obtained at 16 kbit/s. This rate will be used in the Pan-European digital cellular mobile telephone network due to start operation in 1991. Higher quality may be made available at 64 kbit/s and above. For Hi-fi stereo music rates of about 1 Mbit/s are required.

For the various kinds of data communications services the information transfer rate depends on data volume and required response times. In many cases these parameters can be adjusted by the application software to achieve the best balance between transmission cost and overall system performance. Level of database distribution and local or remote searching are examples of these options.

Static images have similar traffic characteristics to other forms
of data transmission but involve larger blocks of information.
Video (moving pictures) however imposes stringent real time
constraints particularly when used in an interactive mode
(videophone). The scope for data compression by sophisticated
coding techniques depends on the level of spatial and temporal
redundancy. Head and shoulders pictures with static backgrounds
on a small size screen can be compressed to 64 kbit/s. At the
other end of the range High Definition entertainment TV on large
screens requires in excess of 100 Mbit/s.

This emphasises the importance of bandwidth transparency which is
the main advantage of the ATM technique.

Asynchronous Transfer Mode (ATM)

ATM involves the partition of user information into fixed length
blocks for transfer across the network. Each block is identified
by means of a label contained within an associated header. An ATM
"cell" thus comprises a header and an information field.
Multiplexing ATM cells is a form of time division multiplexing
which can be distinguished from the conventional Synchronous
Transfer Mode (STM) in that channel separation is not dependent on
a reference to a clock. The difference is illustrated in Figures
3 and 4.

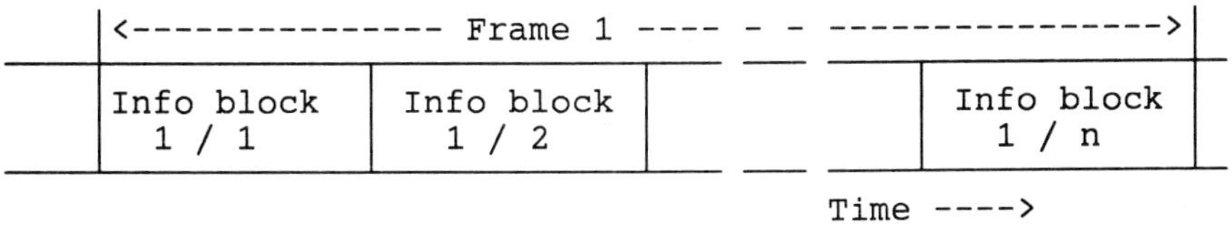

```
 |<--------------- Frame 1 ---- - - ---------------->|
_____
| Info block  | Info block  |        |  | Info block  |
|    1 / 1    |    1 / 2    |        |  |    1 / n    |
_____
                                    Time ---->
```

Fig 3 Time Division Multiplexing using
      Synchronous Transfer Mode

```
 _____
 || Info block | Info block ||     |  || Info block  |
 ||    1 / 1   |    1 / 2   ||     |  ||    2 / 2    |
 _____
                                    Time ----->
```

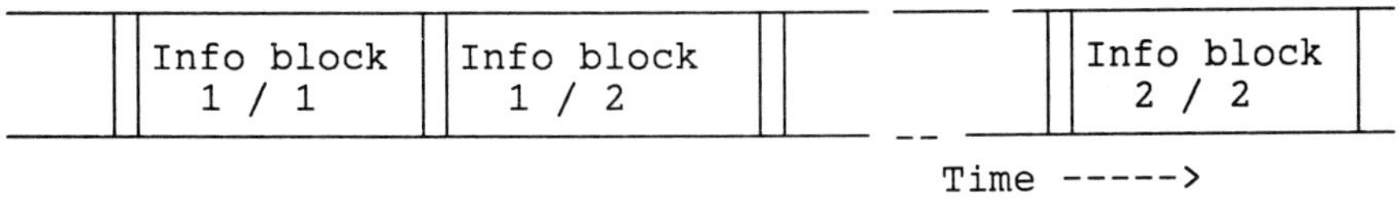

Fig 4 Time Division multiplexing using
      Asynchronous Transfer Mode

The above diagrams indicate that STM uses frames defined by clocks
to indicate the allocation of information blocks to channels
(1 / 2 denotes block 1 of channel 2). Thus the number of channels
per frame is fixed as is the block repetition frequency (ie
channel bandwidth).

With ATM the channel association is by means of the label (denoted
by the double line at the beginning of each block). A sequence of
ATM cells with the same label value constitutes a "virtual
channel". The transfer mode is asynchronous in the sense that the
rate of transmission of cells within a particular virtual channel
can be variable and depends on the source rather than any clock
reference within the network. Consequently, an ATM-based network
is bandwidth transparent. The benefits of this characteristic can
be summarised as :

- the ability to handle dynamically variable mixtures of
  services at different bandwidths;

- the ability to introduce new services in a gradual manner;

- insensitivity to inaccuracies in predictions of the mix in
  service demand;

- the ability to handle variable bit rate traffic; and

- inherent statistical multiplexing.

ATM is intended to accommodate the complete range of
telecommunications services. Consequently, it is supported by
very simple, highly efficient mechanisms. The transport
capability of a broadband ISDN based on ATM can be represented by
the layered model shown in Fig. 5.

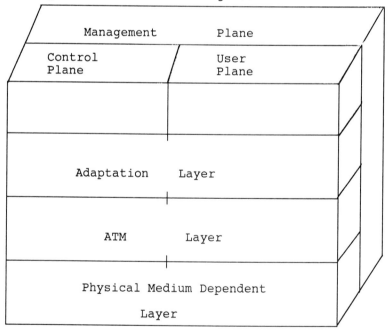

Fig 5 Layered model for ATM

This model demonstrates that ATM may be supported by any digital transmission system (Physical Medium Dependent Layer). Such systems could be synchronous, plesiochronous or fully asynchronous. The ATM layer provides a unique means of supporting the whole range of telecommunications services. Its characteristics will be matched to the requirements of particular services by means of functions in the Adaptation Layer. For example Adaptation Layer functions will segment and reconstitute (packetise / depacketise) information streams for continuous bit-stream oriented services. Alternative protocols at the adaptation layer permit the network to handle the circuit or packet mode bearer services, outlined earlier, as well as offering new capabilities.

Control and management information transfer use the same transfer mechanisms and network resources as the transport of user information. This improves overall network efficiency and avoids the cost of dedicated, specially designed equipment.

ATM is sometimes described as "fast packet switching". There is a similarity between the techniques in that both have the important characteristic of bandwidth transparency. However, there are a number of significant differences associated with the need for ATM to support services requiring time transparency (short and stable delays in transmission). The key aspects are minimal header functionality and short cell length.

The ATM cell structure was agreed by CCITT Study Group XVIII as a potential world-wide standard in June 1989. This structure is shown in Fig. 6.

The ATM cell comprises a 5 octet header and a 48 octet information field. The principal header function is the identification of the communications channel to which the information field belongs. This identification is subdivided into a virtual path and a virtual channel within that virtual path. The virtual path represents a semi-permanent route between channel switching nodes and can be established by means of ATM cross connection devices or ATM multiplexers. The virtual channel is established in response to user service requests by a separate signalling process. This indicates that ATM is essentially a connection oriented technique. It can however be used to support connectionless services.

Subsidiary header functions include generic flow control which is used to support multiple user access, payload type indication which discriminates between user and network overhead information in the information field and header error control which performs a cyclic redundancy check on the header field.

822

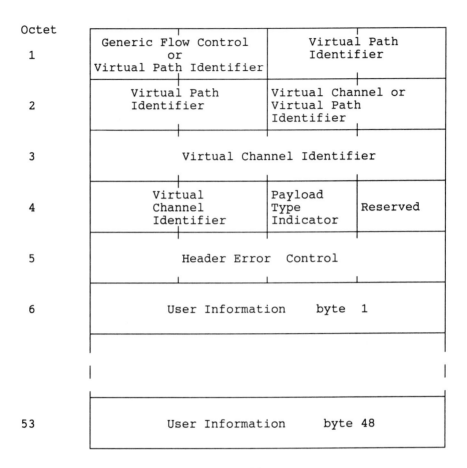

Octet

Generic Flow Control or Virtual Path Identifier	Virtual Path Identifier	

1

| Virtual Path Identifier | Virtual Channel or Virtual Path Identifier | |

2

| Virtual Channel Identifier | | |

3

| Virtual Channel Identifier | Payload Type Indicator | Reserved |

4

| Header Error Control | | |

5

| User Information   byte 1 | | |

6

| User Information   byte 48 | | |

53

Fig 6   ATM Cell Structure

Stages of Evolution

It is generally accepted that ISDN will evolve gradually to
incorporate broadband capabilities. This means that the new
technologies discussed above must coexist economically with
today's technologies and those that will be introduced prior to
the establishment of the IBCN. It is expected that many PTOs will
invest heavily in transmission facilities based on the new
Synchronous Digital Hierarchy (SDH). This technology provides for
high bit-rate channels to be transmitted on optical bearers.
Flexible multiplexers allow for variable combinations of channel
rates together with drop/insert and channel rearrangement
(grooming) capabilities. SDH based Digital Cross Connect devices
can switch partitions of the transmission payload between ports.
These new capabilities can be used together with network
management to provide a high capacity and flexible transmission
network capable of supporting broadband services. Such networks

will be used in the early stages of evolution to provide leased
broadband circuits and flexible access to broadband switches on an
overlay basis.

An example of this type of managed transmission network is British
Telecom's City Fibre Network in London.   In its initial
implementation conventional plesiochronous transmission systems
are use together with a Digital Cross Connect based on an ISDN /
Digital Telephone exchange (System X).   This scheme is being
further developed into a more general Flexible Access System which
provides business users with a variable mixture of switched
network access and leased line services.   The system is
illustrated on Fig. 7.

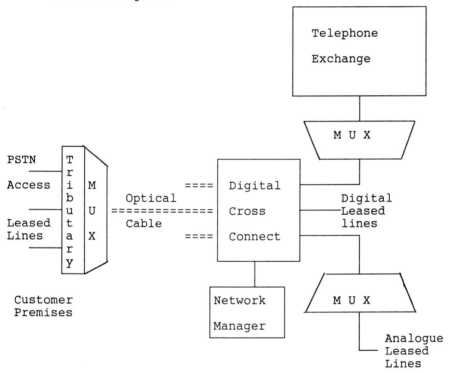

Fig 7   City Fibre Network

This example shows one particular strategy for the start of
introduction of broadband capability into the network.   In this
case it is strongly oriented towards the needs of the business
customer.   Other strategies will undoubtedly be appropriate in
different areas according to market and political forces.

Synchronous Digital Hierarchy

Schemes of the type described above are effective in providing
broadband transmission capabilities to businesses and other large

communications users. With conventional digital transmission equipment individual services are effectively limited to bandwidths upto the ISDN Primary Rate (2 Mbit/s in Europe or 1.5 Mbit/s in the USA). Extension to higher rates on a leased line basis can be achieved through the use of synchronous multiplexing and digital cross connection techniques.

The first initiatives in this area were taken in the USA under the title of Synchronous Optical Network (SONET). The CCITT standard version of this system accommodates both digital hierarchies and is called the Synchronous Digital Hierarchy (SDH). It is defined in Blue Book recommendations G.707, G.708 and G.709.

SDH is intended to take advantage of the bandwidth available on optical fibres and envisages transmission rates of:

- 155.52 Mbit/s   (Synchronous Transport Module 1)

- 622.08 Mbit/s   (Synchronous Transport Module 4)

- 2488.32 Mbit/s (Synchronous Transport Module 16)

The inputs to an SDH transmission network are "containers" which comprise combinations of user channels and their associated end-to-end overheads. The following containers are accommodated:

C 11   1544 kbit/s

C 12   2048 kbit/s

C 21   6312 kbit/s

C 22   8448 kbit/s

C 31   34368 kbit/s

C 32   44736 kbit/s

C 4   139264 kbit/s

SDH equipment allows combinations of these containers to be formed. Such combinations are called "virtual containers". The assembly process allows containers to be dropped or inserted. This gives flexibility to allow one optical fibre to be used to serve a number of physically separate locations. A related function is that of "grooming" containers into "administrative units" which can be manipulated as single entities by SDH digital cross connection equipment. The use of these capabilities is illustrated in Fig. 8 which shows an example SDH transmission network.

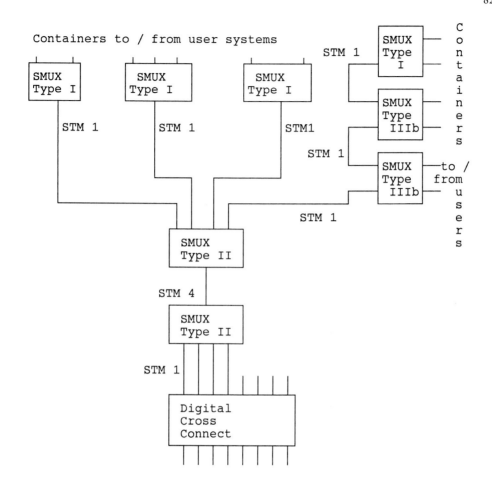

Fig 8 Example Synchronous Digital Hierarchy Network

In the example network we see some of the ways in which
containers, at any of the bandwidths listed above, can be combined
into Synchronous Transport Modules (STM) for onward transmission.
Synchronous multiplexers (SMUX) are being classified in a series
of Recommendations due for approval by CCITT in summer 1990. The
classes and their capabilities are as follows:

SMUX Type I   Multiplexes containers into an STM

SMUX Type Ia   As type I but with flexible container assignment

SMUX Type II   Multiplexes STM n to a higher level STM m

SMUX Type IIa   As type II but with flexible allocation of VC-3/4
                 virtual containers

SMUX Type IIIa Multiplexer with STM n input and output and the
ability to add or drop one or more containers

SMUX Type IIIb As type IIIa but adding or dropping an STM n

Type IIIa multiplexers on the right hand side of the diagram
illustrates the use of drop / insert capabilities to distribute
the capacity of a single 155 Mbit/s STM 1 over several sites. The
combination of 4 STM 1 systems onto one STM 4 system at 622 Mbit/s
shows the application of type II multiplexers. Interconnection of
groups of containers is effected through the digital cross
connect. In the diagram it is assumed that all digital cross
connect inputs are at the 155 Mbit/s STM 1 level but cross
connection can be made of lower level groups of containers.

Clearly this arrangement offers new flexibility in network design
as well as the capability to support broadband services on a
leased line basis. The SDH standards include powerful means for
network maintenance and management.

Optical Technologies

The use of optical fibre in the local network leads to an
examination of alternative network structures and topologies. Of
particular interest is the use of optical couplers to construct
Passive Optical Networks. This allows construction of tree and
branch type topologies similar to those used in coaxial cabled
CATV networks. Fig. 9 illustrates such a network showing how
several customers share sections of the fibre distribution cable
and the opto-electronics at the exchange end.

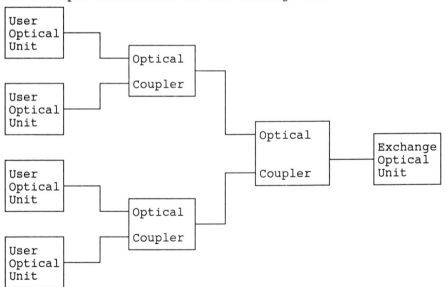

Fig 9 Passive Optical Network

In the passive optical network shown in Fig. 9 the optical units at user and exchange ends contain optical transceivers. The optical couplers are very simple passive devices. Time division multiplexing is used to separate the individual user channels. Downstream channels are transmitted to all customers sharing the same fibre each one picking off its preassigned time slots. Time Division Multiple Access techniques, similar to those used in radio and satellite communications, are used in the upstream direction. The bandwidth of each user channel is limited by the multiplexing technique and the number of users sharing the system. For broadcast applications optical multiplexing can be used to provide broadband capability.

Wavelength division multiplexing in the optical regime is likely to find more general application particularly in the local access part of broadband networks. A number of different possibilities exist ranging from the use of separate optical windows for the two directions of transmission on a single fibre, through more extensive multiplexing using direct detection to very high density multiplexing using coherent detection.

Optical switching is also a possibility but unlikely to be sufficiently mature to be used as a general solution within the foreseeable future. It is however likely to find specific application in such areas as protection switching.

Broadband ISDN

We have seen how telecommunications network development is taking advantage of digital electronic and optical technology to improve its service capability and overall efficiency. The elements required to provide full Broadband ISDN capabilities are:

    i   high capacity access transmission based on optical
          fibres

    ii   broadband switching based on ATM

    iii   standardised user-network interfaces

    iv   control and management with associated signalling.

Optical technology is available and already being deployed where economically justified. In the first instance this is likely to be for business communications for large scale users. In a number of cases optical fibres are being used for distribution of entertainment in CATV networks. Broadband ISDN provides the means of integrating interactive and distributive services and hence consolidate these demands.

The principles of ATM have been outlined earlier in the chapter. The use of these principles to realise switching equipment involves routing of cells from switch inputs to outputs based on the header content and translation of the header to a new value on the output port. A number of experimental ATM switches have been

demonstrated in the laboratory and in field trials. Examples are
Prelude (France Telecom), the Orwell Ring (British Telecom) and
Berkom field trial in Berlin (Siemens). All three have broadband
capability.

The final two elements are questions of standardisation rather
than technology. An outline recommendation on B-ISDN (I.121) is
included in the 1988 Blue Book. Its main provisions are:

-      support of services over a wide range of bit-rates up to about
       140 Mbit/s;

-      provision for distributive services (eg. cable TV) as well as
       communicative services;

-      adoption of ATM as the transfer mode in the target network;

-      specification of a number of values or narrow ranges for
       broadband user channel rates (H channels);

-      outline structures for user/network interfaces at about
       150 Mbit/s and 600 Mbit/s.

Since that time further work has been done to elaborate the
standards and reduce the variations permitted in I.121.

User - Network Interfaces

One of the main areas in which standardisation work has progressed
is the structure of the user-network interface where five
varieties in I.121 have been reduced to the two shown in Figures
10 and 11.

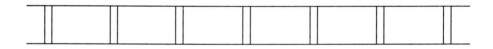

Fig 10 User-Network Interface based on Pure ATM

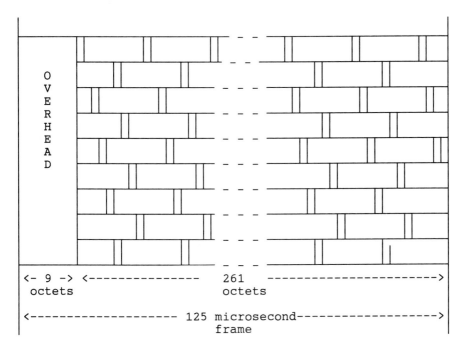

Fig 11 User-Network Interface based on ATM in an SDH Frame

The two forms of interface structure shown are both provided at
155 Mbit/s. Higher levels using similar structures are envisaged
in due course. In the pure ATM case, the structure consists of an
uninterrupted stream of ATM cells as shown in Fig 10. In this
case all overhead functions for maintenance, synchronisation etc.
must be handled by the ATM cells. In the alternative case, shown
on Fig. 11, these overheads are accommodated by a dedicated
portion of the SDH STM 1 frame. This frame arrangement and the
implementation of overhead functions is fully compatible with the
SDH synchronous multiplexer and digital cross connect network
outlined earlier. This is an obvious convenience from the
viewpoint of network evolution. It will therefore be implemented
at an early stage in several networks. In the longer term
migration to the pure ATM format is envisaged.

Since, in both cases, the interface definition is based on ATM for
all user information there is full flexibility for any combination
of bandwidths of user virtual channels subject only to the total
capacity of the interface. In due course specially constructed
terminals will be able to take advantage of this flexibility
directly. In the early stages of Broadband ISDN implementation it
is likely that the main usage will be by conventional fixed
bandwidth terminals. Most particularly combinations of the
circuit switched ISDN channel rates will be found frequently.

These are

```
B channel      -      64 kbit/s
H 12 channel   -    1536 kbit/s
H 21 channel   -    1920 kbit/s
```

In addition the 64 kbit/s ISDN provides a packet organised D
channel at either 16 kbit/s or 64 kbit/s. This is used primarily
for signalling but can also carry user packet switched data.

Signalling

ISDN uses common channel signalling for connection control and for
the transport of management information. Between exchanges CCITT
No. 7 signalling is used as defined in the Q.700 series
Recommendations. The signalling is carried in a 64 kbit/s channel
which may be routed over a different path from the call that it
controls. This is known as the quasi-associated mode. HDLC
protocol is used at layer 2 of the OSI model. The CCITT
specification separates layers 1, 2 and part of layer 3 into a
"Message Transfer Part". The upper portion of layer 3 comprises
the "User Part" of which there are a number of varieties. There
is a specific Integrated Services User Part for the control of
ISDN connections.

For ISDN user access signalling a new digital subscriber
signalling system (DSS 1) has been designed and is described in
CCITT Recommendation Q.931. It is a common channel signalling
system with many characteristics similar to those of CCITT No 7.
The main differences are simplifications in error control
mechanisms and message routing features since it is designed to
operate on single point-to-point links. The message repertoire is
tailored to ISDN user access functions.

In the UK the British Telecom pilot ISDN service uses and early
intercept version of digital access signalling called DASS 2.
While it is only a temporary solution for ISDN access signalling,
it is of continuing interest in its private network form Digital
Private Network Signalling System (DPNSS).

Private ISDNs

Digital PABXs with ISDN facilities can be interconnected to form
private ISDNs. This interconnection can be performed most easily
by leased 2 Mbit/s digital lines. If the PABXs are from the same
vendor then proprietary signalling schemes can be used for
interworking. An open scheme requires the definition of a private
digital network signalling system. DPNSS fills this purpose at
present in the UK but is still only an informal standard agreed
between a group of PABX manufacturers and British Telecom.

If the interconnection of PABXs is performed by the public
switched ISDN then a Virtual Private Network is realised. The
name indicates that the interconnecting links are established as
required rather than being permanent. This gives more economic

operation and flexibility to change the size and location of inter-PABX links. The public ISDN, however, has to know and interpret the private network numbering plan.

Intelligent Networks

The operation of virtual private networks and the implementation of the supplementary services outlined earlier in the chapter place significantly increased demands on information processing and storage capabilities in the network. Early ISDN implementations are providing these capabilities through the stored program control facilities in the digital switching systems employed. In this situation the implementation is vendor specific leading to bottle-necks due to the limitations in their software engineering resources. Also the processing and storage capabilities of the switching system control complexes become strained as the number and complexity of service offerings increases. Thus distributed processing and database solutions are being considered.

The realisation of Intelligent Networks is the subject of standardisation activity to ensure open architectures allowing multi-vendor participation and inter-operability between end user systems. Network Databases with associated processing facilities are separated from digital switches by standardised interfaces using CCITT No 7 signalling. In the longer term it is envisaged that users may have direct access to the facilities enabling them to design their own service packages.

Network Management

As the service and traffic handling capacity of the switching and transmission components of a network increase it becomes more important to manage their use effectively. This involves monitoring their status and usage in order to control their most effective disposition to optimise service performance under the particular conditions of service demand and any equipment irregularities.

Management includes operational, maintenance and administration aspects of the network. Requirements in these areas are often very dependent on the organisation, policies and practices of the network operators. Consequently the level of standardisation is low. The increasing complexity is however creating more interest in the area. A new concept for a Telecommunications Management Network (TMN) is contained in Blue Book Recommendation M.30. This gives a reference configuration separating operations systems from the network elements that they monitor and control. Mediation devices may be included to provide a standardised (Q3) interface to the operations system. Rapid progress is now being made on the standardisation of interfaces and protocols for the operations system (Q3) and the network elements (Q1 and Q2).

In addition ISDN maintenance principles have been established in Rec. M.30 and for maintenance of subscriber installations and access in the I.600 series.

Implementation Plans

ISDN implementation is harmonised technically by the standardisation work of CCITT. This is necessary but not sufficient to ensure that consistent development of service offerings to end users. The standards offer so many options for network features and do not deal comprehensively with terminals which are increasingly seen as open to innovation by their suppliers. The need for coordination is clear. In Europe the Commission has launched a number of initiatives to harmonise telecommunications service and network evolution. For Broadband ISDN the most important initiative is the RACE programme.

RACE stands for R & D in Advanced Communications technologies in Europe. Its objective is to contribute to the introduction of Integrated Broadband Communications (IBC) progressing to community-wide service by 1995. It started in 1986 with a one year definition phase. A number of competitive contracts were let for initial studies leading to the construction of a work plan for the main 5-year programme which started at the beginning of 1988. Two calls for proposals have led to the award of about 100 R & D contracts. Each project involves a consortium of companies representing at least two different European countries. Virtually all European PTOs, the larger equipment manufacturers and several representative potential users are participating.

The RACE programme covers three general areas:

-      service and network development strategies,

-      technology

and -   verification of the above including pilot user applications.

Conclusions

In this chapter we have briefly reviewed Broadband ISDN concepts, service capabilities and implementation technologies. The opportunities are many but their exploitation requires greater cooperation between network operators, equipment suppliers and users.

CHAPTER 34. ELECTRONIC DISPLAYS

K.G. FREEMAN
Philips Research Laboratories
Redhill, U.K.

Introduction

Although man, like many creatures in the natural world, makes considerable use of sound to communicate information it can be argued that like them he makes even greater use of visual perception. It is therefore hardly surprising that visual displays are so important for human communication. Just as the development of printing made possible the dissemination of the written word on a scale impossible with laboriously handwritten manuscripts so, within a few decades, has the advent of a variety of electronic displays enabled man to create and distribute images of text and pictures virtually instantaneously.

With a single refreshable display device and some form of high-speed communication channel he now has instant access to almost unlimited information from anywhere in the world and, using space probes, from even far beyond. On the television receiver in his home he can observe events as they happen and with the now widely-used teletext facility he can obtain up-to-the minute information on such vital matters as the weather forecast, sports results and the state of his stock-market investments. Bank terminals accessible almost round the clock enable him to carry out financial transactions even on his way to work, and if he commutes by rail large, refreshable displays at mainline stations will tell him when and where to catch his train home. At work he will probably use a computer terminal to rapidly peruse and process vast amounts of data or to send and receive messages. The list of possibilities is virtually endless. Electronic displays are now a vital component of almost every information system and an integral part of our daily lives.

These displays all have one thing in common. By some means or other they produce an artifical image which differs in a number of ways from the images of the natural world to which the human visual perception mechanism has adapted over hundreds of thousands of years. The nature and quality of the image we perceive when looking at an electronic display is thus a complex function of the intrinsic properties of the display itself, of the spatial and temporal parameters involved in the generation of the image (including in many cases the characteristics of the communication channel used to deliver the information) and of their interaction with the characteristics of the human visual process in the eye-brain system. If all the components in this chain are not properly matched the end result may be at best unsatisfactory and at worst disastrous, even for those of us who have what may be termed 'normal' vision.

The purpose of this contribution to the Handbook of Information Technology is therefore two-fold. First, it will review those features of electronic displays and the associated characteristics of the visual perception process which determine the final appearance of the displayed image and hence its acceptability or legiblity. Second, it will summarise the current state of the art in electronic display technology (particularly as it meets, or fails to meet, the required objectives) and attempt to indicate likely developments in the near future.

Visual Characteristics of Electronic Displays

This Section examines those features of an electronic display which determine the quality of the displayed image. As we shall see, some of these features are inter-related, but as far as possible they will be treated separately. Ideally, the performance of a display should be so good in all respects that the perceived image quality is determined solely by the limiting characteristics of the human visual perception mechanism. In practice, of course, cost and available technology will result in inevitable compromises. The task of the display designer is therefore to arrive at a solution which is an optimum for the chosen application. To achieve this calls for an understanding of the many factors which are involved.

Brightness

This display characteristic is closely linked with contrast (see below). Strictly speaking, the term brightness refers to the subjective appearance of a self-luminous object, which is very much a function of our state of visual adaptation. Thus stars invisible in normal daylight appear very bright when we are adapted to the dark night sky. For reflective displays we should really use the term lightness to describe their appearance, though this has a rather more specific significance. Neither of these parameters provides an objective measure of the light produced by a display. At the same time physical measurement of the light power reaching the eye does not take account of the fact that it is not equally sensitive to all visible wavelengths, but has a maximum at wavelengths in the region of green.

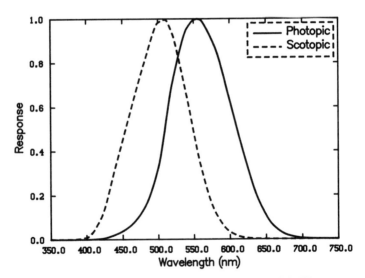

CIE STANDARD LUMINOSITY CURVES
FIGURE 1

Based on the behaviour of an average normal observer, the CIE (Committee Internationale de l'Eclairage) therefore defined standard luminosity curves to describe the response of the eye at high (photopic) and low (scotopic) light levels. These are shown in Fig.1 and provide the basis for objective measurements of display performance. The psycho-physical parameter which results is known as luminance and is usually measured in candelas/m^2 (cd/m^2). Not surprisingly, the terms brightness and luminance are often loosely inter-changed!

Clearly the image of any useful display must be bright enough for its information content to be satisfactorily seen in relation to the surrounding illumination, especially if the image contains intermediate 'grey' levels. Early monochrome CRT displays used for home television had low luminance - little more than the few cd/m^2 of a typical cinema screen - and could only be viewed in subdued levels of ambient illumination if they were not to appear dim and of low contrast. Nowadays, even colour CRTs readily achieve a highlight luminance of several hundred cd/m^2, which is acceptable under normal domestic viewing conditions. Indeed, the luminance may be so high as to cause flicker (q.v.) or to give unacceptable glare if the ambient is low. Displays based on other technologies may not achieve such a high luminance, particularly if a large screen image is being generated, e.g. for tactical command purposes or for the entertainment of large audiences.

The increasing use of displays in outdoor situations where the eyes may be obliged to adapt to high ambient light levels can place severe demands on their light output, and pose severe problems, even for those with substantially normal vision. Since in the last resort brightness is a subjective parameter it will depend not only on the display luminance, but also on the state of adaptation of the eye and its intrinsic sensitivity, both absolutely and as a function of wavelength. Even small departures from the response of the hypothetical 'normal' observer can cause problems, as witness the difficulty many people encountered with the red LED displays used in early pocket calculators. Since some 8% of all males have defective colour vision, with around 4% effectively having only dichromatic (two-colour) vision this is not a trivial problem!

Contrast

The visibility and quality of display images is also highly dependent on contrast. This can be defined in a number of ways, but following normal TV practice it will be defined as the simple ratio of the maximum and minimum luminances produced by the display. Here we should distinguish between large and small area contrast, and between the intrinsic contrast of the display itself (some displays such as liquid crystals may be rather poor in this respect) and the degradation of contrast by the reflection of ambient illumination.

Small and large area contrast are very much a function of the display technology. For example in a CRT small area contrast can be degraded by the scattering of electrons or light itself within the phosphor layer, whilst larger area effects may be caused by the scattering of electrons from high-brightness areas of the image. On the other hand in a liquid crystal display, which makes use of light modulation by photographically-defined cells, the small area contrast may be good, but because it is not practicable to reduce the transmission to zero on blacks the large area contrast may be poor and very dependent on viewing angle.

The effect of ambient illumination can be reduced by careful siting of the display, by the use of a shading hood and/or anti-reflection coatings and by using neutral density filters, which are either added to or are an integral part of the display. Many CRTs, for example, have a darkened faceplate glass with a transmission as low as 50%. This reduces the reflected ambient light by a factor of four times whilst the peak display brightness is only halved - thus improving the contrast. However, since the image brightness is reduced relative to the surround to which the eye is at least partially adapted, this technique cannot be taken too far or the image will appear unacceptably dim. Note that the contrast may also be a function of the flatness and reflectivity of the screen and any faceplate and will be degraded by the accumulation of dust and fingerprints, particularly for off-axis viewing. Finally, we must not forget that the perceived contrast can be affected by scattering and diffraction effects in the eye itself.

For single colour displays which only provide easily perceived information such as alpha-numeric characters a low contrast ratio may be acceptable - perhaps 10:1 or less. However, for colour displays, especially those involving half-tone information, much higher values are necessary. This is because unwanted light, however produced, has the effect of reducing the intensity of saturated colours and hence the ability of the eye to distinguish differences. For high-quality reproduction of television images it is generally accepted that the large area contrast-ratio should be at least 50:1!

Gamma

For most displays the light output is not a linear function of the drive voltage. For many, such as the CRT, it can be approximated by a power-law having an exponent between 2 and 3. By analogy with photography, this is generally known as the 'gamma'. For colour television this parameter has such an important bearing on the reproduction of half-tone material and hence on the final appearance of the picture that it is well-established practice to provide pre-correction of the source signals so that the overall 'gamma' from the original scene to the displayed image is approximately unity (Fig.2). Considerable attention must also be paid to accurate matching of the transfer characteristics of the individual red, green and blue channels, typically within a few percent, if mid-grey tones are not to be noticeably coloured and flesh tones obviously wrong.

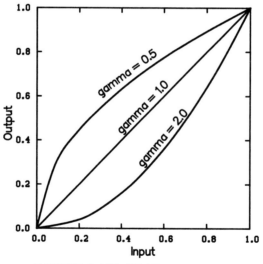

POWER-LAW CHARACTERISTICS
FIGURE 2

For many information displays, even those using colour, operation is often only of the ON-OFF kind, to produce alpha-numerics or simple diagrams. In this case, of course, 'gamma' correction and matching may not be necessary.

Sharpness

By this term is meant the amount of image detail apparent to the viewer. This will be a function of the intrinsic resolution of the display, e.g. the picture-element (pixel) or spot-size depending on the type of display, and of the detail in the incoming information - which will in turn depend on the number of raster lines and the signal bandwidth used to convey that information. The perceived sharpness will, of course, also depend on the image size and viewing distance and the limiting acuity of the eye.

According to the well-known Rayleigh-Helmholtz criterion the eye can distinguish two point sources of light, such as stars, if they are separated by an angular distance of about 1 minute of arc. This is therefore usually taken as the resolution design target for high-resolution displays, but, of course, for many applications much lower resolution may be sufficient, However, it should be remembered that for text etc. the number of pixels used to create the characters and the choice of character fount may have an important effect on the legibility.

Colour

Since whole books have been written on the complex subject of colour perception and the use of colour in displays there is not space here to do more than summarise the most important points.

To begin with it must be emphasised that colour perception is a very subjective phenomenon. Attention has already been drawn to the fact that a significant proportion of males have defective colour vision, which can have serious implications for the use of colour displays in information systems. Less well-known is the fact that even for those with normal vision the perception of the colour of an object is affected by a large number of factors including the nature of the colours in the rest of the image, the colour and brightness of the surround illumination etc. It is therefore not possible to quantify colour in an absolute way.

If for the moment we consider a broadcast colour television system, we could, of course, describe the colour of each pixel in the image by measuring its energy distribution throughout the visible spectrum and re-creating this with the display. This would be a formidable undertaking. Fortunately, it turns out to be unnecessary.

Maxwell discovered by experiment more than a century ago that it was possible to match most colours by mixing the light from three primary colour sources, viz. red, green and blue. Subsequently, using three spectral primaries, matching experiments with a number of observers enabled the colour of any object or light source to be described in terms of these standard 'trichromatic' primaries. Because of some strange anomalies in our colour perception this was soon replaced by a representation in terms of imaginary 'supersaturated' primaries X, Y and Z. From this, in 1931 resulted the CIE diagram shown in Fig.3 which describes the 'chromaticity' of an object in 'psycho-physical' colour space in terms of two normalised co-ordinates x and y. The luminance, or brightness, being the third dimension, has its axis perpendicular to the page.

The horse-shoe shaped boundary represents the locus of pure spectral colours and the lower straight line the purples, which exist only as a subjective sensation produced by a mixture of red and blue. Between them these boundaries enclose all possible chromaticities. However, it should be remembered that colour is a

838

three-dimensional phenomenon. For example a chromaticity which appears orange when it has a high luminance relative to its surround will appear brown when its relative luminance is low!

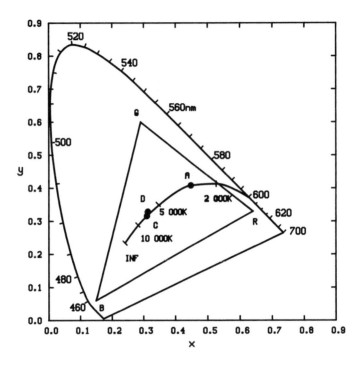

1931 CIE xy CHROMATICITY DIAGRAM
FIGURE 3

Also shown on the diagram is the locus of colour of a black body as its temperature is increased, together with the points of a number of standard 'white' illuminants. Illuminants A and C are respectively typical of tungsten lamps and northern daylight, whilst D is that chosen by agreement as the reference white to which colour television systems and displays are balanced in Europe.

This method of representation of colour enables us to specify it and to measure it with instruments. We can plot on our diagram the red, green and blue primaries of our display (R, G and B), which may be produced by emissive light sources such as the electron-excited phosphors in a CRT or by back-lights and transmissive colour filters as in a liquid crystal display. The triangle joining them indicates the gamut of colours which they can reproduce. We can also determine the result of mixing them in terms of the x and y chromaticity co-ordinates and the luminance (L). It is a useful feature of this diagram that for additive mixtures of two colours (not to be confused with the subtractive mixing process which occurs with paints) the resultant lies on the straight line joining the x,y co-ordinates of the components. Less useful is that equally perceptible colour differences are not represented by the same distance in different parts of the diagram. Various transformations, such as the 1960 u,v diagram, have therefore been devised in an attempted to deal with this and other limitations. Further details can be found in the Bibliography at the end of this chapter.

However, although this subjectively-based method of quantifying colour is extremely useful and allows us to specify colours and measure them with suitable instruments, it does not precisely describe what we actually *see* in subjective terms, since as indicated above, this depends in the last resort on many aspects of the viewing conditions. Nor, incidentally, does it tell us how we differentiate between colours. This is not the place to discuss this fascinating subject in great detail, but we need to appreciate some important facts which are extremely relevant to displays. First, although our colour perception almost certainly involves red, green and blue sensitive elements in the eye (the cones) the subsequent processing of the information means that when we look at objects we assess their colours not in terms of the amounts of red, green and blue light present but in terms of their brightness and chromaticity, which in turn are differentiated into hue, or dominant wavelength, and saturation, or purity. It has long been known that the eye cannot resolve fine detail in highly-coloured areas unless it also contains high-frequency luminance information: less well-known is the fact that both our visual acuity and colour discrimination are functions of chromaticity. In just the same way as some artists (e.g. Raoul Dufy) have used this fact to good effect by adding a coarse overlay of colour to a fine pen-and-ink drawing, so it has made possible an acceptable bandwidth-saving colour television systems, by transmitting high-resolution luminance information and two low-resolution colour-difference signals.

Now since the colours we perceive are defined and measured, albeit rather approximately, by the co-ordinates on the CIE colour diagram of Fig.3, it should be apparent that two colours, whether primaries or mixtures, can appear the same even though their spectral energy distributions are quite different. This phenomenon, which is known as metamerism, is really what makes colour television possible, since it is then only necessary for the system analysis and display primaries to have the same appearance.

For most information display systems the high-quality colour reproduction of a television picture is not required. However, this does not mean we need not pay careful attention to the use of colour - there are still many pitfalls for the unwary. Colour in printed material is usually on a white background, whereas electronic displays for various reasons, often employ black or coloured backgrounds. This may significantly affect legibility. The choice of colours for text characters can also be crucial. Since the response of the eye falls off at long and short wavelengths the use of red and blue primary colours for these, whilst desirable for good picture colour gamut, can result in poor character visiblity and sharpness. The choice of red characters on a blue background or vice versa is a particularly bad one since it is also affected by dispersion (variation of refractive index with wavelength) in the eye itself. This can even make the text and its background appear to be in different image planes!

Artefacts

In a sense any perceived feature of the image which makes it appear different from what was intended may be called an artefact, but the term will be used here to describe those defects or effects which arise because of the intrinsic structure of the display or of the way in which the information is processed or transmitted. Obviously, the way in which the display is made will have an important bearing on the appearance of the image. This is best illustrated by considering the shadowmask colour CRT (see below). Since this comprises 3 separate electron beams which are used to excite a mosaic of red, green and blue light-emitting phosphor dots, the quality of the image will clearly depend *inter alia* on the size of the phosphor dots, which should be small enough to be imperceptible at normal viewing distance, and on the accuracy with which the 3 electron beams are made to land at the same point on the screen.

Probably the most familiar artefact in image displays is large area flicker. This perceptual response of the visual system to an intermittent light source is a function of the image-brightness, the repetition rate and the display persistence. For broadcast television the field-scan repetition rate is chosen to be close to the frequency of the supply mains (50Hz in Europe and 60Hz in North America) to avoid stroboscopic effects due to studio lighting or power supply ripple. The critical brightness is a logarithmic function of frequency, so that for present day CRTs this is a much more serious problem in Europe. Larger displays are also worse than small ones because of the greater sensitivity for peripheral vision. Another problem with broadcast television is that in order to conserve bandwidth all existing systems use interlaced scan in which alternate image lines are transmitted on alternate fields, so that each picture element is only refreshed at 25Hz. This gives rise to a noticeable interline 'twitter', especially on horizontal edges. For data displays, where signal bandwidth is less of a constraint these problems can be overcome by use of a higher field rate (e.g. 70Hz), sequential (i.e. non-interlaced) scan and the use of longer persistence display mechanisms.

A familiar example of a signal processing artefact is the cross-colour effect in colour TV receivers. This results from the frequency-multiplexing of the luminance and chrominance signal by the colour-transmission system and gives rise to coarse colour patterning on fine luminance detail. The effect therefore also occurs with home-computers designed to give an output suitable for feeding directly into the aerial socket of a conventional colour receiver. For information display systems the system can and should be designed to avoid such artefacts.

Information Display Devices

Cathode Ray Tubes (CRTs)

The cathode ray tube is the most well-known and to date most widely used display available. It comes in a wide range of sizes, in both monochrome (viz. white, green or amber) and full colour. Developed to a high-degree of refinement for entertainment in the home it is a key element of the information technology scene. Until the recent advent of low-power lap-top portable computers with non-CRT displays it has been a vital component of almost every computer system, either to display information about programmes, data or text being processed by a local or remote operator or to monitor the progress of the computer itself, particularly in a time-shared main-frame system.

Its bulk apart, the CRT is an almost ideal display. Using one or more electromagnetically-deflected electron beams, to excite high-efficiency light-emitting phosphors at very high writing speeds, the single envelope, direct-view display is capable of high-brightness (up to 500 cd/m^2 or more), excellent intrinsic contrast of around 100:1 and very high resolution. For large-screen applications, e.g. for command and control systems, it can be used as the building brick for projection displays. For direct-view applications with a screen diagonal of up to about 0.75m, colour versions based on the shadowmask principle and operating at a final screen voltage of 25kV or more now yield images with excellent colour quality and high-resolution data/graphics tubes intended for computer-aided design of integrated circuits etc. are now capable of displaying in excess of a million pixels.

Recent years have seen progressive improvements in the conventional CRT, such as shallower envelopes, flatter screens, more precise and stable registration of the primary colour images, etc., but for both domestic TV reception and for many information systems applications its bulk, weight and power consumption have remained disadvantages. A number of manufacturers including RCA, Philips and Matsushita have therefore pursued research on CRTs based on some from of flat, thin technology. However, although some experimental displays have been demonstrated, their commercial realisation is still very uncertain.

Although their use is as yet much more limited, the use of 3 separate red, green and blue CRTs and projection optics to produce a large screen image deserves mention. Since they offer a means of providing wide-screen high-definition entertainment television, there is now considerable development activity on them and the problems of poor resolution and brightness are steadily being overcome. We can therefore expect them to be more widely used for large screen information systems in the future.

In connection with CRT displays, although not in principle confined only to these we may note the availability of touch screens as one way of providing very 'user-friendly' data access systems. When combined with a system of menu-based operation they can offer a facility which requires very little skill on the part of the user, who may be a member of the general public. For the not-insignificant fraction of the population who suffer from some form of manual or visual handicap this may be an extremely valuable feature.

Vacuum Fluorescent Displays

These are similar to CRTs in that they use electrons to excite phosphor screens. However, addressing is not by means of electron-beam deflection but by means of spatially extended electron sources such as hot wire filaments, with a matrix of control electrodes. These may be located between the electron source and the screen, which is generally viewed from the incident electron side. The image structure thus consists of an array of small areas of light, which can be used to form alpha-numeric characters. For simple displays, where segmented characters are sufficient, the control can be effected by switching the voltage applied to areas of the phosphor screen itself.

Versions are now available in sizes up to about 0.25m diagonal and with 640x400 pixels or more. With a screen potential of no more than 100V or so they are often surprisingly bright, but are generally only available in a single colour, namely blue-green, although low-brightness full colour displays have been demonstrated. So far their use has been largely limited to the display of a few lines of text and simple graphics, for which other display technologies, particularly liquid crystals can now be used. Only a few manufacturers are active and the prospect of large, high-brightness, high-resolution full-colour half-tone displays seems rather unlikely.

Plasma Displays

The production of light by means of an electrical discharge in neon has been known for a long time and the ability to modulate its intensity was exploited by Baird in the early days of his attempts to produce television pictures using the Nipkow disc scanning system. In the last 25 years considerable effort and ingenuity has gone into developing very thin matrix displays based on this principle, which requires drive voltages in excess of 100V to strike and maintain the discharge. As with any matrix display, addressing is by means of an array of horizontal and vertical conductors. For this device these are arranged to be on opposite sides of an array of cells containing neon, which may be combined with a small quantity of argon or xenon. By successively addressing rows and columns each with half the voltage necessary to create a discharge it is possible to activate (or not to activate) the cell at each crosspoint in turn without lighting up cells elsewhere on the rows and columns being addressed. By sequentially 'scanning' the rows and columns it is thus possible to access each display point in turn. Various ingenious techniques have been used to ensure that the discharge occurs immediately the pixel is addressed.

For simple displays the discharge is maintained only while the relevant pixel row and column lines are actually being driven. Consequently, the duty cycle is inversely proportional to the total number of pixels in the display. With continous cycling of the drive sequence the brightness thus also decreases with the total number of cells. For small alpha-numeric displays, such as those which are now quite common for supermarket check-outs etc., this may not be too serious, but it severely limits the brightness of displays with a large number of pixels. Fortunately, considerable advantage may be be gained by making use of the unusual voltage-current characteristics of the discharge, which can be maintained by a lower cell voltage than that which is required to actually start the discharge. This characteristic can also be exploited by driving the cells with an a.c. voltage instead of a d.c. one. The cells can then be driven via coupling insulators and having a lower capacitance can be maintained in an excited state so that when addressed a smaller voltage is required to make them produce light. Another technique which can be used instead of, or as well as, this is to drive the columns via a shift register so that all the cells of a single row can each be driven with the relevant information for the whole of the time that the row line is being addressed. This 'line-dumping' process can also have advantages for the drive circuits.

Using techniques such as the above, larger displays have been developed for computer terminals and very large ones (more than $1m^2$) for military applications. However, for many applications the plasma panel has serious disadvantages. The principal ones are colour gamut and efficiency. The intrinsic neon discharge produces light only in the red-orange part of the spectrum. Attempts to produce other colours by adding other materials to produce other colours, or to produce ultra-violet light which can be used to excite different colour phosphors, have met with limited success. For the neon discharge the light-generating efficiency is typically no more than 1 lumen/watt. Very large bright panels therefore dissipate considerable power in the form of heat and are thus capable of doubling as wall-heaters!

Electroluminescence

Electroluminescent displays have a number of similarities with plasma displays. They produce light as the result of an intense electric field and use a matrix addressing system. However, instead of a plasma these displays use a layer of powder material, generally zinc-sulphide doped with manganese. The exact mechanism, though long known, is not fully understood.

Although low-voltage versions driven with d.c. have been developed for some applications, the need to avoid polarisation effects and the fact that more light is obtained by exciting the material with a high-frequency alternating voltage of the order of 100V has tended to favour a.c. driven displays. At present only a limited choice of colours is available having reasonable efficiency and even these are much less efficient than CRT phosphors. There is also a question mark about life. Their main application is therefore for small annunciator panels or for displays where their thinness and lightness are prime considerations. Work is in progress aimed at producing full-colour displays, but seems likely to decline in view of the success of liquid crystal displays

Light-Emitting Diodes (LEDs)

Light-emitting diodes produce their light by an energy transition at a low-voltage semi-conductor junction, which gives rise to essentially monochromatic light. Single diodes were first introduced as tiny indicator lamps and as single-character dot matrix or segmented alpha-numeric displays for the first pocket calculators. These were based on gallium arsenide phosphide and produced red light with an energy peak at a wavelength of about 660nm, i.e. near the edge of the visible band. Consequently some people with apparently normal vision had difficulty seeing and reading them due to their poor sensitivity at that wavelength.

Subsequent development of hybrid materials has yielded more acceptable reds and some other colours such as green are now possible, but their lumen efficiency is well below that of the red devices, which are not much better than plasma displays in this respect. Since the junction operates at only about 2V, the low lumen efficiency, which is partly the result of poor coupling of the light generated at the junction to the outside world, each element requires quite a large operating current. These devices are therefore not very well suited for large matrix-driven displays where the power used to drive the elements must be supplied via the addressing lines. They therefore tend to be used as single character dot-matrix building bricks for anything from small multi-character displays up to very large bulletin boards, where their high-brightness capability can be utilised without the dissipation of excessive power. However, the pursuit of mdium sized monolithic character displays still continues.

Liquid Crystal Displays

Liquid crystals are a class of materials which, within a limited, but sometimes quite wide, temperature range, exhibit a behaviour having characteristics between those of true isotropic liquids and those of a solid with a regular crystalline structure. They are optically active and under the action of an electric field can modify the nature of the light passing through them. Three basic types of material can be identified viz. smectic (Gr. soaplike) in which the molecules are arranged in layers, with their long axes perpendicular to the layers, nematic (Gr. thread-like), in which the molecules are arranged with their long axes parallel as for smectic, but not separated into layers and cholesteric (from their similarity to cholesterol) which also have a layered structure but with the long axes of the molecules lying in the plane of the layer.

Many variants of these basic types have been discovered but the one which has received most attention in recent years is the so-called 'twisted nematic' effect. In displays based on this effect a thin layer of liquid crystal (typically a fraction of a mm) is sandwiched between two flat glass plates coated with thin films of a transparent conducting material such as indium tin oxide (ITO). Application of a low-voltage (typically as low as 3 or 4V) between these closely spaced electrodes then produces an intensive electric field in the liquid crystal material. By suitably treating the inside surface of the plates with directional layers the molecules near to the glass surface can be made to take up a particular orientation. If these are chosen to be different then in the absence of an applied field the liquid crystal will have a twisted structure. This is optically active and can therefore be made to rotate the plane of polarisation of any transmitted light. When the electric field is applied then, because the liquid crystal material is dielectrically anisotropic, the molecules will align themselves parallel to the field and the twisted structure and hence the optical rotation will be lost. Hence by adding polarised optical filters to each side of the cell we can modulate its light transmission by means of the applied voltage.

For simple black and white or single colour displays we can shape and segment the ITO layer so that we can generate characters or parts of characters by suitable application of voltages. If there is sufficient ambient illumination the display can be used with a reflective surface behind the cell so that the light passes twice through the cell and no backlight is required. This arrangement is commonly used in digital watches and pocket calculators, since the power needed to actually switch the cells is very small and good battery life is possible. It is therefore also an attractive solution for multi-row displays for use with portable lap-top computers.

The main problem with these displays is their rather poor contrast especially under relatively high levels of ambient light. Their transmission in the 'ON' state is not high and in the 'OFF' state, which usually corresponds to a black character being 'ON', it is not zero. Viewing in low illumination will obviously also present problems. For many applications a back-light is therefore added.

For large dot-matrix displays there are further difficulties. The power required to generate the light for a bright, back-lit display becomes significant. The maximum light required for each pixel must be provided whether or not the pixel is intended to be illuminated and a high-duty cycle for the 'ON' transmission state is increasingly important. Computer alpha-numeric displays therefore usually have bright characters on a nominally-black background. For direct-view full-colour displays for data terminals, particularly those with graphics capability, as for colour television display the requirements are particularly exacting. Such displays must have an active-matrix operation. e.g. by associating some form of storage with each pixel so that its state is maintained between successive addressing. Moreover, for a multiplexed array of cells of different colours, the individual colour filter elements must be chosen in conjunction with a suitable broadband backlight so as to yield satisfactory primary colour points. When we also take into account the not-less-than 50% loss of light due to the the polarisers it turns out that even a small display requires a back-light power of many tens of watts.

Although picture quality is not yet as good as that for a CRT in respect of resolution, brightness, contrast, colour saturation, speed of response and useful viewing angle, the attraction of thin flat light-weight displays has led to tremendous investment in research and development, particularly in Japan. Direct-view colour and monochrome displays with a diagonal of up to 14″ already exist. For larger displays, projection using one or more small (2-3″ diagonal) arrays is an attractive solution since it offers high brightness without loss of resolution. We can therefore expect liquid crystal displays to play an increasing role in information technology in the future.

Other Technologies

It is not possible in the space available to review all the possible techniques which exist or which have been proposed for displaying data or televison images. Attention has therefore been concentrated on those which have or may be expected to have the greatest impact on the information technology scene. For specialist applications other displays may have a place. These may range from simple flip-element displays, such as may be used for railway terminal announcement boards to highly-sophisticated laser projection flight-simulator displays which have been developed for training fighter pilots in aerial combat. Whatever the application, in the last resort all information displays have to interface with the visual system of the human observer. It is therefore hoped that this review will have given insight, not only into some of the more important displays currently available or likely to be so in the near future, but also into the major characteristics of the human peception mechanism on which their successful use ultimately depends.

Bibliography

The Measurement of Appearance - R S Hunter & R W Harold - Wiley 1988

Measuring Colour - R W G Hunt - Wiley 1987

Television Engineering Handbook - Blair Benson (ed.) - McGraw-Hill 1985

Light & Colour Principles - IBA Technical Review No.22 - Nov 1984

Colour Science in Television & Display Systems - W N Sproson - Hilger 1983

CHAPTER 35. THE TRANSFORMATION OF COLOUR PRINTING

Andrew TRIBUTE
Attributes Consultancy Ltd.
Godalming, U.K.

Developments in the use of systems of colour origination in printing

During the mid to late 1980s the printing industry has seen significant changes in terms of computerising the processes of page creation. What we have seen in this time is a move by the various principal system vendors to use off the shelf computer hardware and software, instead of creating their own hardware and developing their own specific operating systems and application software.

This move has not stopped companies developing specialised application software. What it has done is to make use of much of the excellent off the shelf software that has been available in the mainstream personal and mini computer markets, linked into specialised applications software. This is seen particularly in the area of newspapers where, in the early and mid 1980s, most of the systems that were available were highly proprietary, and made use of specialised operating procedures. They made little use of anything available in the mainstream computer market.

The change now is that the majority of newspaper and magazine systems are becoming available built around absolutely standard off the shelf personal computer systems or Unix workstations, and make use of standard operating systems and very often much off the shelf computer software.

The Impact of DTP

The best example of this is the growth of desktop publishing. This phenomenon started in the mid 1980s, when we saw a growth of the use of the Apple Macintosh for handling the layout of relatively complex pages. The development of desktop publishing has been one of the most interesting phenomena of the personal computer market in recent years. What we have seen is the use of such software changing the whole face of publishing.

At the time of the introduction of desktop publishing most of the principle vendors of publishing systems regarded it as a low quality irrelevant development. One or two however were more farsighted, and saw this as a real change in the way that people would use systems. Desktop publishing, they saw, was going to enable users to take the responsibility for the creation of pages, and be responsible for their own deadlines and costs, rather than being totally reliant upon professional printing organisations. As the 1980's went on this evolving structure became more and more apparent. Now in the early 1990's we see desktop publishing as being the most significant large scale publishing medium available. It is being used by a very large number of professional publishing organisations who previously would have bought expensive proprietary solutions or used outside services. We are also seeing it being used as a feeder system into some of the most expensive complex colour systems. Desktop publishing in this case becomes the design element of such systems, and more and more people are using it to handle the creation of the layouts, the origination of the text, and the positioning of elements prior to passing them into the still complex area of colour.

This brings us to the real phenomena that we are going to see in the 1990's. The changes that we saw in desktop publishing in the late 1980's applied predominantly to the monochrome text and graphics area. The production of colour was always a much more complex task than monochrome, and one that has not yet been adequately cracked by these lower cost systems. We will find many of these low cost desktop publishing systems particularly Quark Express, Letraset's Design Studio or the market leader Aldus Pagemaker, being able to handle colour for such elements as type and background tints, as yet not being seen as appropriate for handling the complex, large scale colour images that are an element of quality colour production.

At the present time if we want to handle such items we really need to use an expensive high end colour system. These colour systems are still largely built around proprietary hardware and software, and come mainly from three or four large scale suppliers selling at a high cost. We would expect to find a full scale colour system used for producing high quality reproduction work aimed at the magazine and advertising markets, selling for £1 million and above. We have yet to see the low cost or medium cost colour systems break into this high quality area.

The Influence of the DRUPA Exhibition

Within the printing and publishing industry, developments go in phases, and these phases tend to be built around specific industrial exhibitions. The predominant one happens every four years in Germany and is called DRUPA. This is thought to be one of the world's largest industrial shows. It goes on for a period of two weeks, and has in excess of half a million visitors from around the world who come to see the state of art and developments on the printing and publishing market. At DRUPA in Germany in May 1990, we saw the start of a really significant change for colour and graphics handling in the printing and publishing world. For many years the major high-end colour suppliers have dominated the colour market. DRUPA 1990 saw a real challenge coming to them from more than one area.

The first of these areas is the mainstream text systems suppliers who are being gradually pushed out of the conventional text area by the rise in desktop publishing. These suppliers are now moving into the colour area with relatively impressive high functionality systems. These colour systems tend to cost approximately one third to one half of the equivalent high-end colour systems.

At the same time we see a rise in desktop publishing adding more and more colour functionality. We see new programs arriving on the scene specifically for the handling of large scale colour images. The functionality of these programs appears to be comparable to those systems costing many hundreds of thousands of pounds or more from the traditional high end suppliers. The main difference is not in their ability for handling complex colour manipulations, but more in the ability of desktop computers to handle the very large size files that these images require. It is not uncommon in the high quality colour market to find images requiring in excess of 30 Megabytes. To expect to manipulate this image in reasonable speed on screen is somewhat beyond the power of desktop systems at the moment.

So what did we really see at DRUPA and what was the impact of it? The first thing was that from the traditional high end vendors we saw an emphasis on increasing productivity and a move down market by some of them to counter the threat from the new vendors in this area. However these systems really showed little change in their functionality. What we saw was a change in the functionality of colour systems coming from the typesetter vendors and from the desktop publishing vendors, and a reduction in other functions and price.

We could say that we are now starting to see the same level of change within the colour market that we saw within the monochrome market in the mid 1980's. At that time we saw a move from the use of proprietary systems to standard platform systems.

Up to now we have seen little of this impact in the high end of the quality colour market, and most companies that operate in this area use proprietary systems that have been specifically built for this task. For example we find very specialised computer processors for moving large graphical files from disc into memory at very high speeds, and for panning and zooming these images around the screen. These systems often use powerful array processors to manipulate large graphical files to handle the various transformations that are required on the data that they hold.

Standard Hardware and Software Solutions for Colour

With the new systems we saw for the first time at DRUPA the use of standard computer hardware and software for handling large colour images. One difference is the lowering cost of mass memory. It is not uncommon now to find a standard system, predominantly a Unix workstation such as a Sun Sparcstation system, with 64 Megabytes of memory as standard. Even Macintoshes, with modifications to the operating system, can address this amount of memory.

In order to facilitate faster processing of images, graphics processors are being added, often using RISC technology, sometimes operating in a parallel mode. We are also seeing in this evolving colour area, software for very sophisticated levels of publishing functionality. Some new programs like Adobe's Photoshop or Letraset's ColorStudio give very impressive colour editing of graphics files, with a comparable level of functions to systems that in the past would have been cost at least £200,000.

Today these new systems allow companies using them to compete in many areas with those who have been using very expensive high functionality reproduction systems from the traditional suppliers. The new systems built around off the shelf computer hardware and software have a similar level of functionality in many areas to the older more expensive systems. Where they perhaps have limitations is in areas of performance, and possibly in areas of quality.

One fundamental difference between the way the new systems work and the older systems, is that many of them are built around the use of PostScript[1] as their graphics language. PostScript is a way of defining any kind of element that can form a page, whether it be monochrome or colour. PostScript has always had the functionality of being able to output colour, but up till now there have been major limitations in some aspects of its performance and imaging quality, particularly in colour.

What we are seeing now is that many of the new vendors have found ways to improve the quality of the output of PostScript and also its speed of operation. Performance has certainly been rather slow, particularly when large images are being handled, and one often hears of output times for A4 pages taking many hours. While high speed PostScript is not yet completely here, we are now seeing some very much faster applications of the PostScript language from both the initial developer, Adobe Systems, and from many of the alternative, or so called clone developers.

At DRUPA we saw some advances by Adobe with their new range of Raster Image Processors (RIPs), that are being offered by many of the Adobe licencees. Adobe do not manufacture RIPs themselves, but licence their technology for incorporation into systems manufactured by third parties. These were showing impressive levels of performance that can be anything up to five times faster than we have seen before.

1. Postscript is a registered trade mark of Adobe Systems Inc.

There are other vendors of PostScript – the cloners – who are also showing impressive levels of speed. The U.K. company, Hyphen, predominates. Hyphen have always been seen as the speed kings in the PostScript area, and have had great success in the past year as the only act in town offering really impressive speeds of PostScript output. This has been particularly demanded by newspapers. What we also are now seeing are improvements in the PostScript language for handling better quality screening with data compression of large colour images. Such developments of PostScript ensure that it is becoming more and more viable as the only means of output for colour in the long term future.

The Growth in the Colour Market

The change in structure of colour systems is most appropriate to accompany the growth of the colour market. We are going to see an increase in the level of colour being used in all forms of publication. We can see this in the near future in newspapers, where there has been a massive increase in purchases in recent years of colour presses. In order to feed these colour presses, fundamentally improved and fast colour systems that are easy to use and are lower in cost, are needed. The new generation of colour systems seen at DRUPA look as though they are appropriate for this growth in the colour market.

One of the reasons for this is that users of colour systems will also be the colour originators – the publishers – rather than companies who simply process the work for others, as in the current structure of the colour reproduction industry. What we are likely to see in the future, is a wide range of off the shelf software packages for handling complex quality colour, in the same way that a very wide range of software is currently applicable at low cost for handling monochrome and text. Amongst these new offerings are the impressive illustration packages such as Adobe Illustrator, Aldus Freehand and Corel Draw – perhaps the best product available on the IBM PC/PS. The others are mainly Macintosh packages. This software, linked in with the packages for handling scanned images, makes personal computers a real challenger for the evolving colour markets.

Does this therefore mean that colour is going to be just one of those other applications that anyone can do on a personal computer? This is unlikely, since we are talking about work that requires significant volumes of memory and computer power, plus high resolution colour monitors, together with a high level of skill to get the real quality that is necessary in publishing. There is a limited market for the so called "good enough colour". We are going to see an increase in functions bought about by artificial intelligence that will permit many of the skilled tasks that are required today, to be handled more as automated tasks in the future. As we progress into the mid 1990's artificial intelligence functions are likely to take over many of the skilled tasks that are an element of publishing at present. We will still need artistic creativity. Much of the work that can be automated is built into people's experience and we can expect to see some of it incorporated into an artificial intelligence structure in the future.

It is likely that the 1990s will see a growth in the use of colour in many different areas. The first of these is through the use of more colour presses, and a greater demand for colour in almost every type of publication. That will put an increasing pressure on the skilled colour staff who are currently in control of the generation of colour. The skilled staff's understanding of colour and the recognition of colour and its make up, has developed through experience in working with specific colour systems. Such people can look at any colour, and instantly indicate the required make-up of that colour on the printing press, as the percentage of each of the four constituent yellow, magenta, cyan and black printing inks that are used.

There are, however, not enough such people around, so there is a need for a replacement of staff by systems that can eliminate much of this skilled approach to the work. Many of these skills, particularly in assembling the page element together, are readily incorporated into computer based systems and these systems can be used by a different type of staff. Other skills, such as colour assessment, are less easy to assimilate. In these areas we are looking to a contribution from artificial intelligence.

Artificial Intelligence (AI) in Colour Systems

At DRUPA one of the interesting developments was an increase in the use of AI structures in the systems coming from the traditional high end colour suppliers. The use of AI is specifically designed to simplify the operation of complex colour scanners, devices that historically have required high levels of understanding of colour and its make up. If the skill of the staff can be ported into AI structures, one of the major barriers to colour for the masses will have been eroded. In the meantime the traditional suppliers are doing what they can to maintain their position as the custodians of quality in colour, and the more they can bring staff into working in this area the longer they think they will be in control.

What we are expecting to see in the 1990's is a change in the users of colour that will be similar to the changes in monochrome in the late 1980s. At present colour origination for printing is handled only by dedicated specialised skilled staff. The customers for these companies are the designers and writers of the copy that is to be converted into colour. We can expect the handling of colour in the 1990s to move from the specialist to the user. This means that a magazine designer will in future use a terminal to design the publication and process the colour images. These images will either come from existing camera systems, but are more likely to come from video based systems – either as still video, or as images from High Definition Television (HDTV).

We can expect that publishing on paper and in electronic form, such as television, will come closer together, and the data formats will be somewhat similar. The use of the same data for advertising on television and on paper is very likely, and the systems are likely to be operated by the design community rather than the specialist. In this we will see almost every designer, editor, and journalist working with electronic means of publishing. They will handle the complete make up of pages in colour with a system that will convert a scanned image or an image grabbed from video format into the required format for quality printing. It will be the specialised program using AI techniques that will enable this to happen, rather than a change of the skills of the user.

The structure of colour graphics for printing will allow people to work in the same style that they do at present, without having to learn new skills – assuming that they already work with a computer, rather than directly with paper. This requires more than just a learning of new skills, but also an acceptance of the idea that the computer can be used as a creative tool.

Universal Colour Space Management

To allow this to happen we will need new standards for defining the manner in which a computer sees and understands colour. We will need a universally accepted colour space management and control structure that is independent of any specific system. This will mean that colour shown on one system will be the same when used on a totally different system without the user having to understand anything about the complications of the colour management system. It will mean that the internal colour space will be calibrated against a range of peripheral devices, so the effect of seeing the colour on any specific colour monitor or proof printer should be the same. It means that a system used by the designer of an advertisement will allow the designer to see the same result as the designer of the magazine making up the page containing the advertisement which will have been electronically transmitted to him. The same effect should also be seen on the printed page of the magazine after the image has been converted to a printable form.

Independent colour space management is something that is being worked upon by a large number of organisations at present, and many of these are developing to the standard controlled via the CIE (Commission Internationale de l'Eclairage). This was evolved in 1931 by an international committee working on illumination, and consists of a set of equations that convert the spectral data into measurements of visual colour based on the perception of an average person.

There have been various developments to make this scheme more suitable for handling printed colour, but as yet there is no internationally agreed standard. The established colour systems suppliers base their colour management around the four process printing colours of yellow, magenta, cyan and black (YMCK), whereas suppliers of video based system use a red green blue (RGB) colour model. The reason for this is that although one cannot construct as wide a range of colour from the four process printing inks as from an RGB model, only colours that can be created from a YMCK structure should be allowed.

Most of the new entrants to the colour printing area are building their systems around an RGB model, with restrictions on the generation of colour to identify colours that cannot be printed from YMCK. As yet there is little agreement in coming to a universal colour space management system, so we will have to wait some further time for this to happen, if it every does. It is interesting that this was one of the major areas of discussion at the two major printing and publishing technology conferences being held in the USA in September and October 1990. Universal colour space is being pushed far more by the new entrants to the colour market, as well as companies whose background is in consumables, like Kodak and Agfa, rather than by the established colour vendors.

Other Standards for Colour

The colour standard discussed above is just one of the standards that are becoming more and more important in colour. There are now agreed standards for holding image data for transfer between systems. These standards do not have an independent definition of colour but relate more to the basic data structures. The most popular at present are the TIFF (Tagged Image File Format), of which there are a number of variations, and EPSF (Encapsulated PostScript) which is a PostScript file which can be placed within another PostScript page without being modified. Both of these formats have come from the desktop publishing area, and are now fully accepted in the high-end of the colour and monochrome publishing markets. The standards from the high-end of the market, particularly the DDES data transfer format, are not being used in the desktop markets, nor are the formats by which the high-end systems allow other systems to input data and layouts into them.

The most popular of these is the Scitex Handshake format which allows a number of systems to pass data into, and take data from a Scitex system. Hell and Crosfield, two of the other three high-end colour suppliers, have their equivalent, but with different structures. One of the trends for the future for desktop level systems is to transfer data into high-end systems for swapping low resolution for high resolution images, but maintaining the text and layout structures. This can be done via a structure called OPI (Open Pre-press Interface) - an extension of the PostScript commands. Again OPI has come from the desktop area and is being adopted by the high end of the market as their means to live with the growth in the desktop area.

Data Compression

We see further standards evolving for the storage and compression of colour images, which are generally very large. Here there is substantial joint work between the video and professional colour publishing industries in developing a compression standard. The one being now discussed is the JPEG (Joint Photographic Experts Group) standard. Having evolved and been proven in software it is now being committed to silicon chip level for very high performance. With the silicon implementation we can expect to see decompression of low resolution images in the 1/30th second refresh time of a video screen, and of high resolution images in a manner of seconds. The benefits are in data storage, speed of transmission of images around networks, and in wide band communications. We can expect the JPEG chips when widely available, to be included in a range of controllers including those for disc drives, networks, printers, video screens etc., as well as in all forms of video device including still and moving video cameras and recorders. There are still some doubts about the JPEG standard as a means of handling quality images. The technology used does sometimes show major image aberrations if too much compression is applied. The cell-like structure applied by the compression algorithm becomes visible.

Changes in the Use of Colour

The trends we can see coming about in the 1990's are a move of colour to the user from the specialist, and a far greater acceptance of the use of colour in all forms of publication and information distribution. Users will want to have control of colour production to give themselves the immediacy of having editable colour data that can be used in a multimedia structure. It will no longer be appropriate to look at data being used for only one type of work.

Colour data in future will become a universal product that is applicable over a wide range of uses. When this happens we can logically talk about the arrival of multimedia, and the digital world. In the colour printing market we are now making the first steps in this direction. There will have to be many changes before it really arrives, but at least we have made a start to move colour back to the originator. As we move forward into the 1990s we will find that system improvements enabling us to use colour data will give us a better form of publishing, with more originality and flexibility and a new generation of creative users who will have a major impact in changing the style of publishing.

CHAPTER 36. DESIGNING HYPERTEXT SYSTEMS

Cliff McKNIGHT, Andrew DILLON and John RICHARDSON
HUSAT Centre
Loughborough University, U.K.

What is hypertext?

The ideas underlying hypertext are extremely simple — 'non-linear' text in which *nodes* of information are connected by *links*. This view is typically contrasted with the allegedly 'linear' structure of printed texts, a conception of text which is currently all pervasive (see, for example, Duncan, 1989; Cooke and Williams, 1989; Trigg and Irish, 1987; Beeman *et al.*, 1987) and seems to rest on the surface characteristics: words are arranged in a specific order to yield sentences, sentences similarly ordered to produce paragraphs and paragraphs sequenced, in turn, to make successive chapters, and so forth. This gross simplification of the structure of text takes no account of the lengthy evolution of text formats and reading skills which allow us to transcend the apparent limitations of the medium. Text designers (authors and publishers) can make use of a host of devices to provide non-linear access to text (see Jonassen, 1982, 1985). Similarly, readers' skills have become increasingly sophisticated and this allows them to use suitably constructed text in ways that are anything but linear.

At the semantic level expository text is rarely linear. As Collier (1987) indicates, the logical relationships between themes and the rhetorical relationships involved in their treatment make text inherently inter-connected. In this sense, hypertext has been around for hundreds of years and the humble footnote provides a good example. The body of text on a page can be considered as a node of information, the footnote is another related node, and the footnote marker in the text provides the link or pointer between the two nodes. Other kinds of links are scattered throughout written text: 'as mentioned earlier'; 'as we will discuss later'; 'see also page 27' are all typical phrases used to suggest connectivity between the ideas expressed in the text. Thus very few written texts contain the pure linear structure which the previously mentioned authors suggest is 'imposed' on text by the linear nature of the printed medium. So, if many traditional texts are non-linear, how is hypertext different?

Probably the most important difference is that in hypertext systems the links are 'active' in the sense that selecting them (usually by a pointing device such as a mouse) causes the linked node to be presented. For example, Figure 1 shows a screen of a hypertext on wine in which the node on display discusses the idea of 'sweetness'. The fact that the word 'fermentation' is printed in bold text indicates that it is a link to a node of information about this subject, and clicking the mouse on this word causes the fermentation node to be displayed. There are no strict rules about how a link should operate. Hence, in some systems selecting a link causes the related node to replace the present node, as in the wine example which was produced in Apple's HyperCard. In other systems (like Xerox NoteCards), another window may open containing the linked text, allowing the reader to see more than a single node at a time. In yet other systems (e.g., the Guide system), the related text 'unfolds' from 'behind' the hot-spot or 'button'. However, all share the

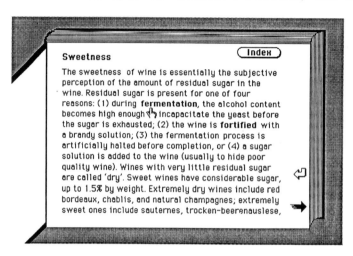

Figure 1: The bold words indicate links to other nodes.

feature that the link is active and it is this feature which makes hypertext so attractive for a number of reasons.

Links are arbitrary in that there are no fixed rules to govern what gets linked to what. Such decisions are part of the author's responsibility, as they always have been, although as we have suggested elsewhere (McKnight *et al.*, 1989) hypertext highlights the importance of such decisions. The implied and explicit links in a printed text are supported by the reassuring context of the physical presence of the book and some fairly well established conventions concerning book formats — e.g., there is frequently an index and it is likely to be at the back of the book. There are few conventions concerning the format of hypertexts and the creator consequently has a greater responsibility for providing 'support' for the reader.

It is the active nature of links which can be seen to have slowed the development of hypertext. For example, Bush (1945) — often considered to be the modern founding father of hypertext — describes a 'memex' system which contains all the essential elements of hypertext but which was conceived in terms of microfilm technology. While that technology might well have been able to support the storage of the information, the retrieval of it via the links was not feasible.

Thus, while even the earliest texts might have contained the basic ideas behind hypertext, its full implementation has had to wait for an affording technology. The recent growth, and hence interest, in hypertext systems is a direct result of the popularisation of computing. It is only now that microcomputers with sufficient power (speed, memory and processing capability) and ease of use (sophisticated graphical interfaces) to support hypertext applications are becoming affordable. Computer-based implementations of hypertext have existed since the 1960s, but these were mounted on large mainframe computers which in turn tended to be restricted to use by computer specialists. The rise in availability of the microprocessor has led to the development of desktop computers which have brought computer power out of the data processing departments. It is the ability of such machines to support the linking in hypertext which has led to its popularity.

A hypertext node is also arbitrary in the sense that there are no rules governing its size or content. Certain systems — particularly the card or frame based systems such as Hypercard, KMS and NoteCards — tend to contain nodes which are less than a given window size or screenful, but this is a design choice and is in no way inherent in the concept of hypertext. A node can vary from a paragraph to an article, or indeed from a line diagram to a photograph or even speech, music or moving images. The fact that the information can be held on different media and that such systems usually integrate the use of such media gives rise to the term 'hypermedia'. However, for present purposes we will continue to use the term hypertext since the principles involved are the same.

The fact that links are supported electronically is insufficient to define a system as hypertext. For example, modern database systems can have links of various kinds, notably relational and object-oriented links. It might be possible to build a free-form relational database resembling a hypertext database, but such systems usually emphasise 'selection against criteria' and 'reporting' rather than reading and browsing.

Similarly, the inverted file common in information management systems could be seen as a set of links allowing any word to be accessed. However, in such systems a word is simply an alphanumeric string, the basis for a search operation rather than a unit of meaning. A sophisticated system will allow the user (or, more typically, the 'database administrator') to define synonyms in terms of links between equivalent terms in the inverted file, and a thesaurus of words and phrases arranged according to their meaning could be constructed with the inverted file terms as the base level. However, the operation is still essentially one of searching rather than linking on the basis of meaning.

If it is possible to build a database which ostensibly resembles hypertext, why are such constructions not *really* hypertext? What differs is the underlying purpose for which such systems were designed, and consequently the effort involved in producing such a database and supporting changes to it. The situation is analogous to a graphics package with a text facility; such a package could be used to produce a paper document indistinguishable from the output of a word processing package, but the effort required is related to the purpose for which the package was designed. You *could* write letters with a drawing package, but you *wouldn't*.

Thus the second defining characteristic of hypertexts is that they should support browsing with as much ease as is possible. It is generally held that this consideration should maximise the utility of the tool for a variety of reasons. Browsing — as opposed to formal querying — allows a greater range of people to search the knowledge base. Relatively naïve users can access the information without the need for intermediaries or formal training in Boolean searching. Browsing facilities also broaden the range of tasks for which hypertexts can used.

Having said this, there is an emerging typology for hypertext based on different applications. Hypertext systems designed for organizing information (perhaps prior to traditional publishing) such as NoteCards, are strong on facilities which allow multiple views and easy rearrangement of the hypertext network. This is usually achieved by way of a 'graphical browser' — a representation of a portion of the hypertext with selectable nodes and their relationships displayed graphically. Hypertexts designed for the presentation of technical documentation, such as KMS for example, may contain no graphical browser at all, the design philosophy being that the consistent hierarchical structure and rapid system response time obviate the need for one. A third major area of hypertext applications resides in the teaching domain (with Brown University's Intermedia being the most well-known system in this area) and such systems emphasise the rôle of reader as author — adding/deleting links and creating new sections of the hypertext.

This diversity in hypertext conception and application has a direct correspondence to our experience of printed books. An encyclopedia, dictionary, philosophical treatise, undergraduate course text or even a detective novel are very different in structure and usage but we have no particular difficulty in describing them all as books.

General system design considerations

The literature on system design is replete with guidelines which give general advice to the would-be designer (see for example Smith and Mosier, 1986). However, in the present chapter we will not follow the trend for a variety of reasons. These reasons centre on what we consider to be fundamental problems with any set of design guidelines and we discuss them below.

What's wrong with guidelines?
Guidelines are inherently general and as such require interpretation in any specific application. This is not strictly a problem with guidelines but with the conditions under which they tend to be used. That is, a skilled human factors (HF) expert can make the necessary situational interpretation, but guidelines tend to be used by designers with little or no human factors training. The fact that they are frequently written in

general terms gives the mistaken impression that they are easy to understand.

Guidelines tend to be treated as the sum of all human factors knowledge by computer scientists. They therefore trivialise HF and lead designers to think that they can grasp HF by reading a set of guidelines in much the same way as they can grasp an argument or algorithm or structured program.

Guidelines, like any generalisations, often contradict each other and are therefore potentially misleading. We are not alone in this view of guidelines. Hammond *et al.* (1987) cite Barnard's (1983) paper as containing examples where guidelines can be misleading. They go on to say:

> "Since guidelines are simple statements about user behaviour, they … cannot fully describe the interaction between system and user. If behaviour results from an interplay of factors, so will the ease of use of an interface. These interdependencies are hard, or even impossible, to capture in simple statements. A guideline which is true in one context may well be misleading in another. While for many purposes it would seem that guidelines do provide a useful simplification, the more complex the interface, the less plausible it is that guidelines will help." (p. 41)

Guidelines misrepresent HF's strengths which are evaluative rather then prescriptive. In other words, good design is an iterative process. The development of prescriptive models of user behaviour and system usability is a major research effort in itself which will not be discussed here. Interested readers wishing to read the alternative viewpoint are referred to Polson (1987).

Designers don't use guidelines (Hannigan and Herring, 1987). The caveat might be that, as noted above, they don't use them properly as they lack the skills and experience required to interpret them correctly.

There is no reason to assume that designers of hypertext systems will be any more effective with guidelines than designers of word processors, spreadsheets or other databases. However there are some differences that might prove relevant. In particular, where users are likely to be modifying the document to suit themselves the distinctions between designer/user and author/reader blur. In this context some "designers" might be end-users who know very well how to design for their own needs. Such users might well make good use of guidelines. What we are saying here though is that the traditional designer, i.e., the one who builds the application in the first instance for other end-users, is not likely to be significantly different in this respect from those who design more traditional application software.

Constructing the hypertext

There are two main routes in constructing a hypertext document or database: moving an existing paper document to hypertext, and originating a document in hypertext. In fact an intermediate route might be to take a collection of 'related' pieces of existing information and bring them together in a hypertext document. This was done recently with the Glasgow Online hypertext (Baird and Percival, 1989) in which a large amount of information concerning the city of Glasgow was structured using HyperCard in order to produce an information resource for visitors to the city. However, the principles involved in producing such a document are the same as those we will discuss in relation to the two 'pure' routes. In the case of moving an existing document to hypertext there are sources of information available to the designer wanting to know about how he should proceed. In the case of originating a document in hypertext such sources are less accessible. In the following section we consider how knowledge of people's uses of paper based information can be a source of practical guidance for design.

Understanding the usage of paper-based information
Psychologists have long recognised the complex nature and range of skills involved in text usage (see for example Huey, 1908). On the physical side, the apparently simple operation of lifting up a text provides the reader with information on size, age, and assuming an informative cover, the likely quality of the contents. Manipulatory skills, acquired by readers early in life, support jumping back and forth to various parts of the text. Furthermore, these physical skills are transferable across most reading situations.

Cognitively, with little obvious effort, the reader is capable of scanning the text rapidly to decide upon relevance to current needs, range of issues covered, depth of coverage and level of detail. Evidence suggests that the reader builds a mental model of both the author's message and the organisation of the text itself (Johnson-Laird, 1983; Rothkopf, 1971) In the former case it is a matter of comprehension, in the latter, it is a case of appreciating the way this message is organised through the presentation medium. Both provide useful information for navigational and manipulatory purposes.

The physical and cognitive aspects of reading are inter-related. Without the ability to manipulate texts physically, many of the reader's cognitive demands would be unfulfilled. This may seem a trivial point but in the design of hypertext systems to facilitate reading it is important to identify and support both kinds of needs. Presenting black text on a white background on a high resolution screen may satisfy some human factors needs (Gould *et al.*, 1987) but will lead to user rejection if suitable manipulatory facilities are not available, or only partial use if optimal text structures are not considered.

In an attempt to analyse people's views of texts in a way that would lead to informed design decisions being made with respect to hypertext developments, Dillon and McKnight (1989) used the repertory grid technique (Kelly, 1955) to categorise texts. The results indicated that readers distinguish between texts in terms of three meaningful attributes:

- **How** they are read: e.g., serially, selectively, rapidly, etc.
- **Why** they are read: e.g., for work, leisure, specific information, etc.
- **What** type of information they contain: e.g., grahics, text, technical, etc.

For example a novel may be classified on these dimensions as being read serially, in depth, usually for leisure, and containing fictional text-based material. This distinguishes it from, say, a magazine which would probably be classified as read non-serially, for leisure interest and containing non-technical, general interest material of both a textual and graphical nature.

Such an approach can also distinguish between superficially similar texts. For example, two magazines may be read very differently according to the reader's motivations and the type of information they contain. In this way *The Observer Colour Supplement*, for example, is not the same as *PC User*. Though both may be called "magazines" and contain similar amounts of text and graphics, they are likely to be read for different reasons and in different situations.

This analysis provides a simple representation of the factors influencing readers' perceptions of texts. Characterising text according to How, Why and What variables offers a useful means of understanding the manner in which a given readership is likely to respond to a text and thus quickly facilitates sensible decisions about how they should be presented. Ultimately, these aspects indicate what readers see as important in their use of text and therefore, what should be considered by developers of hypertext systems. This point will be developed further in the case study.

Creating new document types in hypertext
When we speak of originating a document in hypertext we do not just mean using a hypertext package to author the document but rather the creation of a document type that has no equivalent paper form. In this instance we cannot necessarily gain direct information on likely usage by observation and task analysis of users with the paper version as described above.

However, this need not be an insurmountable obstacle. A general understanding of humans interacting with computers combined with an awareness of the important issues in information usage can be fruitfully applied to the design of new hypertexts. What will users want to get from their interaction: specific information about a problem or general advice that needs studying and interpretation? Will they be experienced or naïve computer users? Will they want to add information or links to the document or out to other documents? Even approximate answers to these questions can constrain the design space sufficiently to rule out certain options. For example, if the target users are naïve the designer cannot assume that basic knowledge of interactive principles are understood and users will need explicit instructions from the outset. If experienced, an assumption that users will undertand the concepts of linked nodes and non-serial structures may be justified and the designer can concentrate more on optimising manipulation and navigation facilities. If the document needs to be 'locked' or 'read-only' in order to maintain its integrity (as in the case of a public access resource like Glasgow Online), questions of user-added links can be ignored.

Likely problems in this instance are failing to structure the information in a suitable manner, providing access mechanisms that support certain tasks but are unsuitable for others, and not providing usable navigation facilities, to name but a few. However, the risks of designing such errors into the system can be minimised by adopting an iterative design process.

Design iteration
The importance of involving target users in the design process through consultation, and the use of simulations and prototypes to evaluate potential designs, cannot be over-emphasised. No application should ever be designed in ignorance of the target users. To do so will lead to certain failure. There are a number of techniques and methodologies for system design that offer prescriptions for inputting human factors into the design process. We will not detail these here because all too frequently they assume the existence of an idealised design process consisting of discrete stages from specification to evaluation that supports structured inputs. Our experience suggests that in the real world it is rarely so straightforward.

However, human factors can have an impact on product development no matter how a design proceeds. Ideally user issues should be considered early and frequently. This means identifying the potential users and their goals in using such a system, testing designs on such users with prototypes and simulations. No amount of "expert" opinion (usually the developer's own biased intuitions!) can substitute for feedback from real users. The moral might be: "If you think you know what your users want, then design the exact opposite — you probably stand a better chance of being right!". Those who carry out evaluations regularly will confirm the inevitable surprises that result from watching users interact with new software. If there are bugs, users will find them. If you think it natural for users to behave one way, half of them will behave another way. If you think you've considered all possible interactions, prepare to be shown some more.

These are not staggering design principles but they are effective. We have yet to see a user model or design tool that can offer better guidance than feedback from users. The drawback to this approach is time and effort. Any simulation must be realistic enough to afford users the opportunity to offer sensible feedback[1]. It assumes a willingness on the part of designers to alter a design on the basis of feedback. If developers cannot admit they are wrong they will never get it right. This design philosophy is embodied in the case study described below.

The Hypertext Database: a case study

Many small-scale demonstration hypertexts have been produced, and these have generally been held to support hypertext implementation. However, in many cases the efficacy of hypertext in the 'real world' has yet to be determined. The decision to build a hypertext database was taken with the specific aim of investigating real world issues — would a hypertext database be of significant use to the people who would normally use the paper-based version of the information? In the environment in which researchers work, the various professional journals form the largest single paper-based resource and so this was selected as a realistic target.

In order to evaluate the possibilities of a journal in hypertext format it was decided to create an electronic version of the journal Behaviour and Information Technology (BIT). This journal publishes papers concerning the human factors issues associated with the introduction of information technology and its readership is typically composed of psychologists, ergonomists and computer scientists. The academic sub-discipline of human-computer factors is relatively recent and the majority of relevant papers are published in only a handful of journals. Thus by creating an electronic version of just one of the journals an appreciable proportion of the literature could be made available for experimental investigation using actual readers and realistic tasks.

Following the granting of limited copyright permission from the publishers, all the back issues of BIT were scanned and the resulting computer files subjected to optical character recognition (OCR) processing. Thus the full text and graphics for all the articles were made available for presentation as a hypertext database.

The first step in developing such a system was to identify the characterstic manner in which this material was used by the target recipients of the database: researchers. The issues considered, analytic techniques employed and implications drawn for the development of the system are outlined below.

How Are Journals Used?
In the first instance a study of journal usage by the present authors looked at a sample of regular journal readers interacting with a variety of articles (full details are published in Dillon et al., 1989). The results indicated that

---

[1] This does not mean that it must be sophisticated or fully functional but rather it must be obvious to the subjects/users that it represents a system they might work with. Thus, it might be a paper based simulation rather than a computerised model. The metric is the extent to which the users appreciate the representation.

readers develop strategies for scanning an issue of a journal in order to look for salient articles, e.g., searching the list of authors for familiar names or lists of titles for relevant topics. Furthermore, the journal articles themselves are subjected to relatively consistent forms of use by readers. When an article of interest is identified, then the reader opens the journal at the start of the relevant paper and adopts one of three reading strategies.

In the first case the abstract is usually attended to and a decision made about the suitability of the article for the reader's purposes. At this point most readers reported also browsing the start of the introduction before flicking through the article to get a better impression of the contents. Readers reported attending to the section headings, the diagrams and tables, noting both the level of mathematical content and the length of the article. Browsing the conclusions also seems to be a common method of extracting central ideas from the article and deciding on its worth.

The second strategy involves reading the article in a non-serial fashion to rapidly extract relevant information. This will involve reading some sections fully and only skimming or even skipping others. Typically the method and results sections of experimental papers are skim read while the introduction or introductory sections and the discussion/conclusions are read fully.

The final strategy is a serial, detailed read from start to finish. This was seen as "studying" the article's contents and though not carried out for each article that is selected, most subjects reported that they usually read selected articles at this level of detail eventually.

While individual preferences for a strategy were reported, most readers seem to use both the second and third strategies depending on the task or purpose for reading the article, time available and the content of the article. Original and interesting work is more likely to be read fully than dull or routine papers. Reading to keep up with the literature requires less "studying" of articles than that required in attempting to understand a new area. However, even when reading at the third level some subjects still reported skimming particular sections that were not intrinsically relevant to their particular needs at that time.

Thus, readers perform a variety of tasks with journal articles, from scanning for specific information to studying the contents in depth, and these tasks require interactions with the text lasting a few seconds to an hour or more. Manipulations of the paper may be simple (e.g., turning a page) or complex (jumping to a particular section while keeping a marker in another). Electronic documents are likely to offer some improvements for particular task scenarios but none in others. For example, electronic storage and retrieval should make access to material easier and faster, thus offering a distinct advantage over paper. However, at the article level, merely reproducing the linear format of the text on screen is unlikely to encourage use and paper will certainly be preferred. Structuring the presentation on screen in ways not available on paper may be the answer, which brings us to the consideration of readers' models.

Readers' models of text structure

It was clear from comments made by subjects in the previous study that as readers, they are very aware of how an article is typically structured, how the argument is built up and where they are likely to find certain types of information. This concurs with work on memory for, and comprehension of, text (van Dijk, 1980; Johnson-Laird, 1983) which suggests that readers develop a model of text organisation or structure that facilitates manipulation and comprehension of the contents. Presumably this model develops with experience of certain text types and is more sophisticated for people who read a lot than those who do not. The extent to which this concept is important in the domain of hypertext is difficult to assess, but if one accepts that lessons learned from other areas of human-computer interaction such as user navigation of databases and menu hierarchies are relevant (i.e., users get lost in a maze of electronic information very easily), then it is likely that such models have a very real application.

Two studies by one of the present authors (Dillon, 1989) investigated this concept. In the first of these, subjects were presented with cut-up paper versions of two journal articles and their task was to assemble each article into a cohesive whole. To avoid referential continuity cues every second paragraph was removed and in one condition only the basic level headings were provided (Introduction, Method, Results and Discussion). Subjects found little difficulty in piecing the articles together in a general sense, i.e., mean accuracy rates were higher than 80% for correct placement of a paragraph in a major section. The main difficulty involved deciding where to place the secondary headings and the specific ordering of paragraphs within a section. This suggests that experienced journal readers are capable of distinguishing isolated paragraphs of text according to their likely location within a complete article. Interestingly this could be done without resorting to reading every word or attempting to understand the subject matter of the paper.

In the second study, subjects read a selection of paragraphs from two articles on both paper and screen and had to place each one in the general section to which they thought it belonged (Introduction, Method, Results or Discussion). Again subjects showed a high degree of accuracy (over 80%) with the only advantage to paper being speed (subjects were significantly faster at the 5 per cent level in the paper condition) which is probably explicable in terms of image quality. Taken together, these results suggest that readers do have a model of the typical journal article that allows them to gauge accurately where certain information is located. This model holds for information presented on paper and on screen.

These findings have direct relevance to the development of hypertext articles in that they suggest that drastically

altering the structure of the text would not aid the reader.
Rather the reader's model should be supported by the hypertext
version as a way of aiding navigation and manipulation of the
text. In conjunction with the findings from the earlier studies
on how articles are used, these results suggest that hypertext
articles may support several of the tasks readers perform and
greatly enhance the rate of access to stored material.

The structure of the database
     The database is composed of two distinct hypertext modules:
a 'front-end' structured in HyperCard and the body of journal
articles which are formatted as individual Guide documents. The
database architecture reflects the two distinct components of
reading identified in the journal usage study: an initial period
of searching or browsing at the title and author level which
typically results in a decision to read a piece of text (perhaps
only briefly). The text is then sampled repeatedly until a
higher order decision can be made with a degree of confidence
concerning its suitability for a particular information
requirement ("this text does/does not contain the information
that I want"). At this stage a more continuous style of reading
is likely to be adopted for particular sections of the text, or
the article will be abandoned and the reader will return to the
top level, possibly to repeat the process.

The database front-end
     The initial view of the database consists of a graphical
representation of a library shelf with the spines of various
selectable volumes visible (see Figure 2). Such a representation
has the advantage that it draws on a wealth of experience which
users already have — everyone understands a library shelf at a
local level. However, the categorisation of books often seems
arbitrary to non-librarians and can result in semantically
related books being distributed across widely separated shelves.
Thus, this simple visual metaphor is not necessarily the optimum
form of representation and would not be appropriate for a much
larger database. For this reason, alternatives such as concept
maps or semantic nets should be experimentally evaluated. Access
to a search option is offered at the top level, which allows a
string search of the author and title fields and the full text
of the journal articles (see Figure 3).

     Selecting a volume from the shelf leads to the display of a
schematic browser for the complete contents of the journal in
terms of the various volumes and parts (see Figure 4). Two means
of accessing the individual articles are offered at this stage:
a series of volume indices which alphabetically list the authors
and titles; or issue/part contents lists which present the
author and title details in the same order as the paper
original. Selecting an article from either display results in
the 'launch' of the Guide software and the presentation of the
top level of the chosen article.

The structure of the articles
     The individual articles are organized hierarchically and
the top level consists of the title page details plus the major

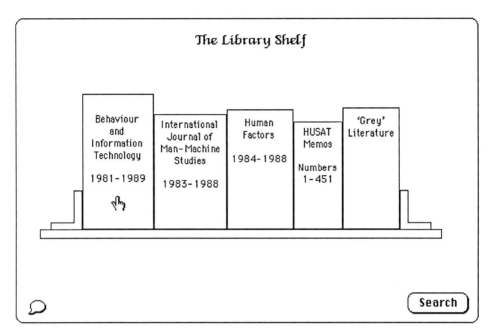

Figure 2: The library shelf from which journals can be selected.

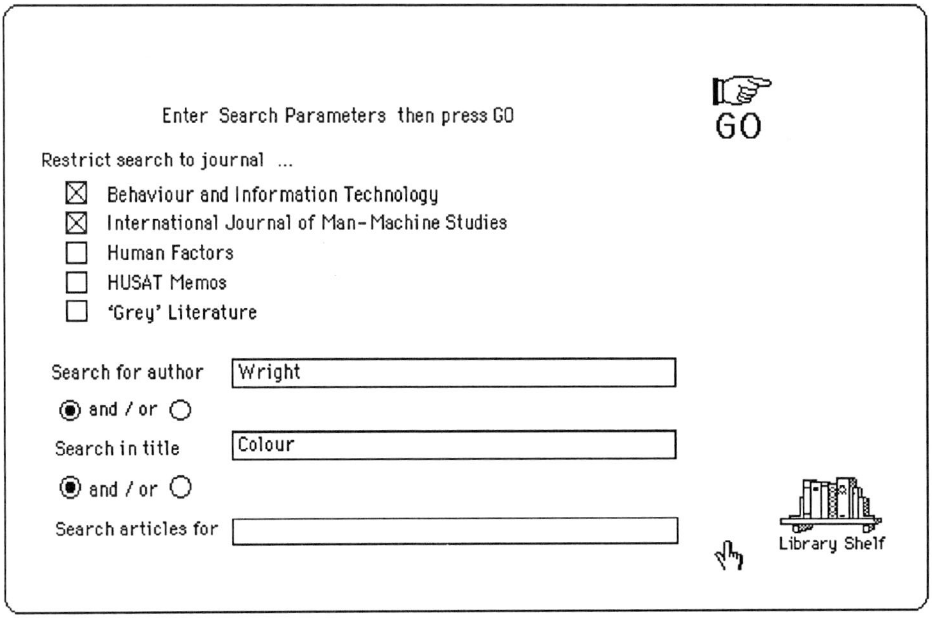

Enter Search Parameters then press GO

☞
GO

Restrict search to journal ...

☒ Behaviour and Information Technology
☒ International Journal of Man-Machine Studies
☐ Human Factors
☐ HUSAT Memos
☐ 'Grey' Literature

Search for author   Wright

◉ and / or ○

Search in title   Colour

◉ and / or ○

Search articles for

Library Shelf

Figure 3: The search facilities operate across the entire database.

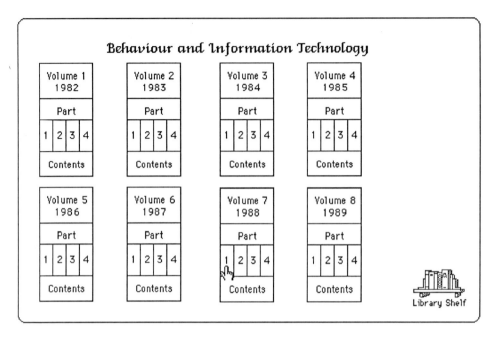

Figure 4: The available volumes of the selected journal.

headings of the article (see Figure 5). With the exception of
the title all these items are selectable. Choosing an item with
the mouse causes the text 'folded' underneath to be displayed at
that point and the length of the document increases
proportionally. The text that is unfolded may itself contain
further 'buttons' (subheadings, figures and tables) and this
process can therefore be repeated until the full text of the
article has been unfolded and is displayed on screen as a
linear, scrollable document. A second type of embedding is used
to display the equivalent of electronic footnotes. Selecting any
of the references in the text causes a window to temporarily
appear on the screen with the full bibliographic details of the
reference displayed (see Figure 6). If a reference is made to
another article in the database then selecting it results in a
separate window being opened and the display of the article as a
new Guide document. If the reader quits from Guide then all the
documents are closed and the reader is returned to the top level
HyperCard browser.

The interface for accessing the documents and the structure
of the individual articles are designed to support and enhance
the reading strategies identified in the paper journal usage
study. Readers can rapidly scan the contents lists in the same
way as they do with paper journals but they also have the
ability to search the complete set of authors and titles to
find, for example, a specific article when only a few details of
the title or authors are known; all the papers by a given author
or all the papers with a specific keyword in the title and,

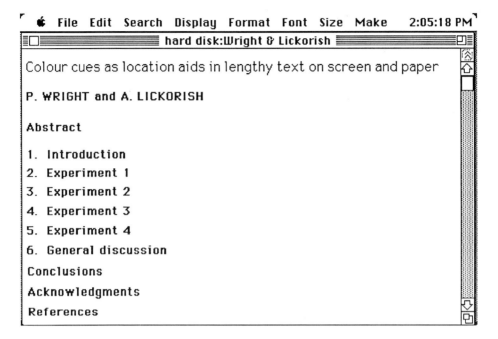

Figure 5: The top level of the selected article. Each heading is a 'button'.

finally, any article which includes a given term in its text. The first strategy is simple but laborious using the paper version but the last strategy is totally impractical without an electronic version.

Similarly, the hierarchical structure of the journal articles is designed to support the reader while 'manipulating' the document. It is not true that "readers access most text in serial order" (Jonassen, 1986) except at the obvious sentence level. The journal usage study indicated that readers very rarely read articles serially, preferring to 'jump about' from section to section, typically from the Introduction to the References or Discussion.

The Guide format allows readers to access directly the sections of the document that are of particular interest without the possible distraction of having to search through the entire text. Thus a reader can select and the skim-read the abstract, conclusion or even only the references. If more detailed reading is warranted then not only is the full text available but it is also possible to follow up references to other papers immediately to check on the author's interpretation of the results or even the experimental details themselves.

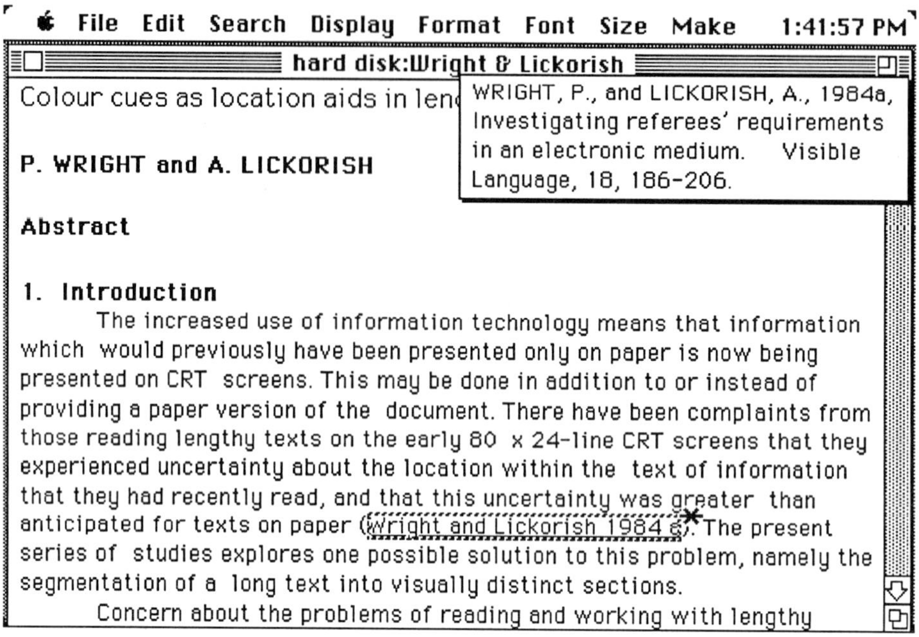

```
  ⌐  🍎  File   Edit   Search   Display   Format   Font   Size   Make      1:41:57 PM ⌐
 ┌────────────────────── hard disk:Wright & Lickorish ──────────────────────┐
 │ Colour cues as location aids in len│ WRIGHT, P., and LICKORISH, A., 1984a,│
 │                                     │ Investigating referees' requirements │
 │                                     │ in an electronic medium.     Visible  │
 │ P. WRIGHT and A. LICKORISH          │ Language, 18, 186-206.                │
 │                                     └───────────────────────────────────────┤
 │ Abstract                                                                     │
 │                                                                              │
 │ 1.  Introduction                                                             │
 │         The increased use of information technology means that information   │
 │ which  would previously have been presented only on paper is now being       │
 │ presented on CRT  screens. This may be done in addition to or instead of     │
 │ providing a paper version of the  document. There have been complaints from  │
 │ those reading lengthy texts on the early 80  x 24-line CRT screens that they  │
 │ experienced uncertainty about the location within the  text of information    │
 │ that they had recently read, and that this uncertainty was greater  than      │
 │ anticipated for texts on paper (Wright and Lickorish 1984 a). The present     │
 │ series of  studies explores one possible solution to this problem, namely the│
 │ segmentation of a  long text into visually distinct sections.                 │
 │         Concern about the problems of reading and working with lengthy        │
 └──────────────────────────────────────────────────────────────────────────────┘
```

Figure 6: Bibliographic details appear in a pop-up window (top
          right).

Testing the design

   The design of the database has been the subject of some
pilot evaluations on samples of the target users. Typically
these have involved a small sample of the target user population
familiarising themselves with the database and/or performing
small tasks. Such trials were deemed more relevant than more
formal experimental trials at this stage of the design process.
In the first instance the evaluations have been primarily
concerned with whether or not people can use it sensibly (i.e.,
can they use it for a task they wish to perform). These have
indicated that the design is easy to learn and to use for
individuals with some experience of Macintosh-style WIMP
interfaces. This initial success is attributable to the manner
in which the system embodies the user's natural style of
interaction with this type of text as detailed in the task
analysis.

   The ability to access instantly the total contents of a
journal from one's desk is seen as a major advantage. However,
as we have noted elsewhere (Richardson *et al.*, 1988),
individuals have difficulties with search facilities and this
limits their use of such a system. Jumping to other articles is
an issue that requires investigation because it is not always
the case that readers want the full contents of another article;
an abstract or relevant section of the selected text may be
sufficient. Also, the current implementation of the database is
weak in terms of the navigation information required to support
jumping between articles. This is the first area for re-design.

At this stage we know that we are on the right lines. Minor modifications and evaluations of the search facilities would be a logical next step. Obviously further evaluations must be carried out before we can be confident that this system is viable. The next major test is to offer the database as a resource in the HUSAT library for use by human factors researchers to see how it is used in real task situations. Ultimately we envisage readers accessing it on their desktop via the computer network but only after we have demonstrated its usability and utility to intended users. The design process enters another iteration!

Conclusions

Hypertext systems offer great potential as information storage and retrieval mechanisms. Using hypertext structuring techniques allows a range of user tasks to be supported, including some tasks which would not be feasible using only the paper medium. However, in designing hypertexts it is important to consider not only specific task requirements but also the appropriate human factors principles. Furthermore, it is important to test the design on potential users and to modify the design in the light of user feedback. Design is a process, and the design of a complex hypertext structure holds many pitfalls. For hypertext to achieve its potential, good design is essential.

Acknowledgements

This work was funded by the British Library Research and Development Department and carried out as part of Project Quartet. We are also grateful to Taylor & Francis for permission to use the journal Behaviour and Information Technology for research purposes.

References

Baird, P. and Percival, M. (1989) Glasgow On-Line: database development using Apple's HyperCard. In R. McAleese (ed.) *Hypertext: Theory into Practice*. Oxford: Intellect.

Barnard, P.J. (1983) Applying the products of research on interactive dialogues. In M.J. Elphick (ed.) *Man-Machine Interaction*: Proceedings of the Joint IBM/University of Newcastle Seminar.

Beeman, W.O., Anderson, K.O., Bader, G., Larkin, J., McClard, A.P, McQuillan, P. and Shields, M. (1987) Hypertext and pluralsism: From lineal to non-lineal thinking. In Proceedings of Hypertext '87 Workshop, Chapel Hill, NC.

Bush, V. (1945) As we may think. *Atlantic Monthly*, July, 101-108.

Collier, G.H. (1987) Thoth-II: Hypertext with explicit semantics. In Proceedings of Hypertext '87 Workshop, Chapel Hill, NC.

870

Cooke, P. and Williams, I. (1989) Design issues in large hypertext systems for technical documentation. In R. McAleese (ed.) *Hypertext: Theory into Practice*. Oxford: Intellect.

van Dijk, T.A. (1980) *Macrostructures*. Hillsdale, NJ: Lawrence Erlbaum Associates.

Dillon, A. (1989) Readers' models of text structures: some experimental findings. HUSAT Report, HUSAT Research Centre, Loughborough University.

Dillon and McKnight (1989) Towards the classification of text types: a repertory grid approach. *International Journal of Man-Machine Studies,* (in press).

Dillon, A., Richardson, J. and McKnight, C. (1989) The human factors of journal usage and the design of electronic text. *Interacting with Computers*, 1(2), 183-189.

Duncan, E.B. (1989) A faceted approach to hypertext. In R. McAleese (ed.) *Hypertext: Theory into Practice*. Oxford: Intellect.

Gould, J.D., Alfaro, L., Finn, R., Haupt, B. and Minuto, A. (1987) Reading from CRT displays can be as fast as reading from paper. *Human Factors*, 26(5), 497-517.

Hammond, N., Gardiner, M.M., Christie, B. and Marshall, C. (1987) The role of cognitive psychology in user-interface design. In M.M. Gardiner and B. Christie (eds.) *Applying Cognitive Psychology to User-Interface Design*. Chichester: John Wiley.

Hannigan, S. and Herring, V. (1987) Human factors in office product design: European practice. In G. Salvendy (ed.) *Cognitive Engineering in the Design of Human-Computer Interaction and Expert Systems*. Amsterdam: Elsevier.

Huey, E.B. (1908) *The Psychology and Pedagogy of Reading*. New York: Macmillan. Reprinted in 1968 by MIT Press, Cambridge MA.

Johnson-Laird, P.N. (1983) *Mental Models*. Cambridge: Cambridge University Press.

Jonassen, D.H. (1982) *The Technology of Text. Vol I. Principles for Structuring, Designing, and Displaying Text*. Englewood Cliffs, NJ: Educational Technology Publications.

Jonassen, D.H. (1985) *The Technology of Text. Vol II. Principles for Structuring, Designing, and Displaying Text*. Englewood Cliffs, NJ: Educational Technology Publications.

Jonassen, D.H. (1986) Hypertext principles for text and courseware design. *Educational Psychologist*, 21(4), 269-292.

Kelly, G.A. (1955) *Personal Construct Theory*. New York: Norton.

McKnight, C., Richardson, J. and Dillon, A. (1989) The Authoring of Hypertext Documents. In R. McAleese (ed.) *Hypertext: Theory into Practice*. Oxford: Intellect.

Polson, P.G. (1987) A quantitative theory of human-computer interaction. In J.M. Carroll (ed.) *Interfacing Thought: Cognitive Aspects of Human-Computer Interaction*. Cambridge MA: MIT Press.

Richardson, J., Dillon, A., McKnight, C. and Saadat-Samardi, M. (1988) The manipulation of screen presented text: experimental investigation of an interface incorporating a movement grammar. HUSAT Memo Nº 431, HUSAT Research Centre, Loughborough University.

Rothkopf, E. Z. (1971) Incidental memory for location of information in text. *Journal of Verbal Learning and Verbal Behaviour*, 10, 608-613.

Smith, S., and Mosier,J. (1986) Guidelines for Designing User-Interface Software. Report 7 MTR-10090, Esd-Tr-86-278, Mitre Corp. Bedford MA.

Trigg, R. H. and Irish, P. M. (1987) Hypertext habitats: experiences of writers in NoteCards. In Proceedings of Hypertext '87 Workshop, Chapel Hill, NC.

CHAPTER 37. NETWORK & PC DEVELOPMENT: THE SECURITY PROBLEMS – AND A FEW ANSWERS

Ken SLATER
Touche Ross, Management Consultants
London, U.K.

The Technology

During the 1980's two major developments in computing have increased the expectations - and in some cases - the satisfaction of the users of IT services. Both of these:

-       the use of increasingly complex networks

        and

-       new developments in microcomputing

carry the promise of more effective business use of IT facilities. However, a number of new or increased security implications lurk among the inevitable problems caused by any new development, and the potential risks must be understood in order to instal the necessary countermeasures.

IT networks have increased dramatically in size and complexity, and many varied services are available. One communications system can carry applications data, Funds Transfer messages, electronic mail, Telex and Fax data, while access to a complex variety of information data bases and Value Added Data Services (VADS) is available to businesses and individuals. User workstations may be connected using a Local Area Network (LAN), which may in turn be linked to large corporate facilities on a national or international basis.

A variety of users now have access to information over public communications networks. National and international databases provide fast access to text services, financial data and quickly-changing information such as Stock Market prices. Individuals and the business community can transfer money and financial messages using such systems as SWIFT, CHAPS, CHIPS, Link or Matrix. The use of ATM's or EFTPOS facilities is increasing, and the ordering of goods or services via Prestel and Minitel terminals is expected to develop rapidly.

The data being transmitted via communications networks may be extremely sensitive or confidential; a substantial loss of income - or, equally important - business credibility - could be incurred if it were disclosed, lost, amended or delayed. In order to provide the appropriate level of assurance that the service will retain the necessary degree of confidentiality, integrity and availability, security measures are required - but these must be seen to be practical and helpful, rather than bureaucratic and negative.

The development of solid state microcircuitry and the
miniaturisation of storage media led in the 1980's to the
increased use of cheap, compact computers which can operate in
individual user departments. As the decade has progressed
they have become increasingly powerful and flexible, and their
use and application has increased dramatically. Originally
intended as standalone machines performing simple tasks in a
user environment, personal computers (PCs) are now
increasingly being linked to each other and to mainframes,
performing complex business activities and downloading and
manipulating sensitive corporate information.

The cheapness of standalone microcomputers often led to their
being purchased without the control and monitoring procedures
established in most organisations for capital spending
projects. Indeed, many powerful PC's were purchased using the
office petty cash, which required a comparatively low level of
authorisation. However many of these machines are capable of
full scale processing and can operate with real time systems
and databases. They have the potential to cause as many
problems as mainframes while, in many cases, being operated by
personnel who have little knowledge of the controls and
disciplines required in a large IT department.

As standalone PC usage has increased other needs have been
identified. These include:

-       a requirement for many users to access the same data or
        use the same peripherals;

-       the need to download data from a mainframe to PC's for
        further local processing, possibly followed by the
        return of the results to the mainframe.

Parallel developments in network processing have created the
technology to satisfy these requirements.

A Local Area Network allows facilities such as processing,
storage, printing, information retrieval and electronic mail
to be shared by multiple PC's in a comparatively small
geographic area. The network can, in turn, be linked using
'bridges' to create a Wide Area Network (WAN) in which a user
can access data on any of the component LAN's.

The improved cost-effectiveness of using a microcomputer to
perform some processing while allowing quick access to vast
quantities of information on the host mainframe has been
demonstrated in many organisations, and can be seen as an
attractive business option. Many PC software packages can
directly access data and facilities running on the mainframe.
A database 'front-end' can be held on a PC, linked to a more
comprehensive 'back-end' on the mainframe, allowing selection
and manipulation of central data via the users machine.

Further developments are taking place. Optical disks can now provide storage in gigabytes, providing massive databases which can be shared using networks. Fax gateways allow users to fax files to individuals or all members of a specific group.

The development of microtechnology has created a wide variety of tangible benefits. Business users are finding that flexible, cost effective computing is available, and in many cases control of processing has reverted to the user after many years of remote, apparently bureaucratic and sometimes arbitrary decision making by a central Data Processing Department.

However, the benefits of micros - from standalone PCs to complex networked environments - are accompanied by a wide range of security problems. Increased risk and vulnerability is inherent in:

-       the technology;

-       the methods used to develop the techniques and applications;

-       the way in which the systems are operated.

In many cases one person - particularly in a standalone environment - will have responsibility for operating the machine, retaining the files and distributing the output. The same person was probably responsible for choosing the machine and its software, and writes any necessary programs on an ad hoc basis. The segregation of duties expected in a mainframe installation will probably not exist and there may be no control section or media library.

If the security objectives cannot be met by segregation the major control over the computing functions will be provided by supervision. Even though the 'supervisor' may not be a specialist he will be the recipient of control reports which must be produced by all systems. The reports will cover such areas as:

-       exception conditions identified by the system;

-       machine usage statistics;

-       reconciliation reports.

The dangers of the 'one man band' should be identified and guarded against:

-       back up staff should be trained and regularly tested in practice;

-       all systems and operating procedures should be documented and copies held at a remote site;

-       fall back systems (manual if necessary) should be
        available;

-       fall back equipment should be purchased.

Despite the low cost of these machines it is essential that
the organisation should have a co-ordinated policy for their
purchase and use, and that this should be adhered to.

It must be stressed that the necessary level of security
depends on what the computer is expected to do, not how much
it costs or who is running it. From a practical point of view
effective control need not be costly when set against the cost
of recovery from a disaster (or even from a mere problem!).

What is Security?

A widely-accepted definition of security in any IT environment
specifies an organisation's need for assurance that:

-       computer facilities are available at all required times;

-       data retains its integrity during processing and while
        in storage;

-       access to data is restricted to those with the
        necessary authority.

If this definition is accepted, security can be seen to be
concerned with the following issues:

-       continuation of processing in the event of hardware or
        software breakdown;

-       protection of stored data and software from corruption,
        loss or deliberate amendment;

-       assurance that authorised work is correctly processed;

-       privacy of confidential data and software;

-       protection against unauthorised use of computer systems
        and equipment.

These concerns apply to the PC environment to the same extent
as to larger machines and networks. The adoption of adequate
security measures must be preceded by an assessment of the
risk involved, since only when this is complete can a
realistic understanding of the security requirements be
achieved. Requirements will vary from system to system,
depending on such aspects as:

-       the sensitivity of the data being processed, stored and
        transferred;

-       the technical complexity of the system;

-       the vulnerability of the system components.

A true understanding of the vulnerability of the business to security failures will be reached in terms of, for instance:

- financial loss;

- loss of business;

- loss of public confidence or goodwill;

- legal liability;

It will then be necessary to assess the effectiveness of existing security measures, and identify the need for additions or enhancements. The security measures could be provided by:

- physical devices;

- procedures;

- software packages;

- application or system software coding;

- the organisation of the business.

The security requirements of most organisations will require a combination of measures from each of the above categories. The ideal approach to security is one in which the failure of one aspect does not leave data or systems completely unprotected - another security measure will take the strain.

Even in the most technical environment, security measures are not only technical - they will typically be found in such areas as:

- departmental and business organisation;

- personnel recruitment, training and control procedures;

- physical security over access to premises, and measures which inhibit theft and destruction of equipment;

- data security;

- software development and maintenance procedures;

- purchase, use and maintenance of equipment or packaged software;

- operations and network control;

- authorisation, encryption and key management;

- password control;

- job control and scheduling.

Network Security

The security requirements of a network will be determined by a number of factors, including:

- the type of data transmitted;

- the services available to, and used by, the network;

- the complexity of the network;

- national and international standards;

- the volume of network traffic.

The level of security achieved will similarly depend on a variety of factors including:

- the type of cable used;

- the physical security of terminals, nodes, cable and cabinets;

- access control software;

- password procedures;

- encryption and authentication techniques;

  and - of course

- the honesty and ability of employees.

Planning for network security should, if possible, take place at the same time as that for network development or enhancement. Not only will costly mistakes be avoided but cost savings may occur as security is integrated into network components from the outset. Fire and water protection for all cables is vitally important and must be planned from the outset. The protection and location of the main telecommunications interconnection cabinets is vital, since they guard the communications lifeline of the organisation to the outside world.

The Threats

Systems, networks and data can be threatened by a number of different activities, which can be deliberate or accidental. These activities can, in various different ways, provide the following headaches:

- loss of confidentiality of messages;

- loss of accuracy of message contents;

- incorrect message destinations;

- loss of availability of service.

Every network has the potential for direct or indirect action which will produce:

-       loss of service;

-       incorrect transmission of messages;

-       corruption or loss of data;

-       unauthorised disclosure of messages;

-       interference with message text.

One aggravating factor may very well be a lack of resilience or contingency planning which could turn a small problem into a major tragedy.

The Methods

Most of the methods can be categorised under the following headings:

Accidents

This group includes natural hazards - ranging from fire and flood to plagues of locusts - but also includes failures of equipment and software. The effects are similar - disruption and unavailability to a greater or lesser extent. They share this effect with some deliberate attacks, such as sabotage or industrial action.

Physical Attack

This group covers theft or damage to equipment, and can be caused by:

-       unauthorised people gaining illegal entry;

-       or staff who are authorised to be there doing unauthorised things.

Electronic Attack

The system can be attacked electronically or logically in the same ways:

-       by an unauthorised hacker gaining entry to the system illegally;

-       or professional staff using their official access to express a grudge, or make a profit.

Examples of hacking, unauthorised interception and modification of messages, introduction of bogus messages, viruses and illicit program changes are included in this group.

Interceptors could record message traffic on the network, together with details of associated parameters, such as dates and times of transmission and the location of each circuit. This line-tapping may be followed by the introduction of spurious messages to be delivered to users or host computers. The spurious message may be invented by the attacker or it may be a retransmission of a previous valid message.

Disruption of service can be disastrous to organisations which depend upon the timely communication of data. The disruption may take the form of a selective loss or delay of legitimate messages, or a complete breakdown of communications. The attack may be achieved simply by occupying a communications line at the expense of a legitimate user, even though the attacker may be incapable of creating legitimate transactions. Another form of disruption is the deliberate modification of legitimate messages, either for the benefit of the attacker, or for purely malicious purposes.

A spoofing attack is performed by connecting an illicit terminal to the network and masquerading as a legitimate terminal to the host system, or as the host system to other users.

The most obvious effect of any of these is financial. There are many other consequences, many of which have indirect financial implications, but where other considerations must also be taken into account.

Some examples are:

-       loss of business;

-       loss of reputation or public confidence;

-       contravention of laws or other regulations such as:

        .   the Financial Services, Banking or Building
                Societies Acts;

        .   the Data Protection Act;

        .   even the Health and Safety Act;

-       even-in extreme circumstances - injury or loss of life.

880

LAN Security

Risks to a LAN are similar to those for the wider data
communications networks, although the level of technology
required by an attacker for full penetration of a LAN may be
considerably higher. A LAN normally operates at 10 million
bits per second, compared with 64,000 bits per second for a
wide area data communications network. The security of
terminals and workstations are, however, the same for both
types of network. The threats associated with LANs are
similar to those of other networks:

-       introduction of false messages into the LAN;

-       eavesdropping;

-       disruption of service;

-       attaching an illicit terminal or node to the LAN;

-       re-routing of messages to fraudulent terminals or nodes;

-       illegal access via gateways.

Information related to cabling, including details of physical
access, is not normally available in the case of
telecommunications services supplied by the national carrier.
However, with LANs the introduction of false messages,
eavesdropping and disruption of service is simpler because
internal staff have ready access to the cabling itself and to
details such as type and location.

LAN's can be tapped on the cable directly or by accessing the
termination or connection points, so the cable should be
physically protected but capable of being regularly
inspected. The use of fibre optic cable will reduce the
vulnerability, although the increased cost must also be
considered.

One of the major advantages of most LAN's is that extra work
stations can be easily connected. Unfortunately this means
that unauthorised terminals can also be connected, allowing
viruses, Trojan Horses and other illicit instructions into the
LAN and, if the necessary connection exists, into WAN and
mainframe facilities.

Security Techniques

The major technical security measures used in any network are
those which have been used throughout the 80's, although their
application and methods of use have developed. Since there is
obviously a cost involved, each will only be used if its
necessity is dictated by the risk. They include:

-   Dial back systems: these allow the system to restrict
    dial in facilities only to those users and locations
    with the necessary permission;

-   Encryption Techniques: These take different forms, and
    allow data to be transferred without endangering its
    confidentiality. There are three methods;

    .   link-by-link encryption;

    .   node-by-node encryption;

    .   end-to-end encryption.

    The three modes have their individual advantages and
    disadvantages. In some cases a combination may be used;

-   Digital Signatures: can be used to verify the identity
    of the sender and/or the receiver of the data;

-   Authentication: used to confirm the accuracy of message
    contents;

-   Identification: many different techniques can be used
    to verify the identity of a remote user;

-   Resilience: duplication of network features to ensure
    uninterrupted network service;

-   Closed User Groups: will restrict access to authorised
    users on a packet switched network.

These are some of the technical security measures. Some
controls are not technical at all. In a network environment
every computer security manager must be able to inspect and
obtain full information on the following:

-   location of all internal data and telecommunications
    cabling;

-   location and accessibility of the main
    telecommunications interconnection box, which has
    usually been installed by an outside organisation
    (probably the PTT);

-   the type and nature of all connections to the network
    cabling.

This requirement should include details of the cable connecting the network to a mainframe's front-end data communications computer system.

Micro-Mainframe Links

As mentioned earlier, the downloading of mainframe data can be a cost-effective business option. However, transferring sensitive data from a secure mainframe database to a less secure micro environment is a major risk, and great emphasis should be placed on security. In addition to mainframe and network security measures there should be:

- an adequate level of physical access control;

- an effective level of management and supervision;

- monitoring of all processing and associated clerical procedures;

- sufficient trained staff to ensure that 'one man bands' do not develop in the area served by the microcomputer;

- standard procedures for the purchase and use of micros and packaged software.

Since processing may take place on two or three systems the overall application will not be visible to the host mainframe, which is therefore incapable of logging all of its activities. The mainframe can log its own activities, but the microcomputer may not generate a similar log. Even if it does produce a log, the act of combining and analysing the information from all sources will be extremely complicated. Compiling a comprehensive report of system activities as an audit trail or security tool can therefore prove extremely difficult.

Data transferred to a microcomputer is valid only at that point in time. Any update taking place after the transfer will not be notified to the micro user, who must take this into account when using the information received. If this is not allowed for, far-reaching business decisions may be made on the basis of currently invalid, inconsistent data.

VAD's and VAN's

Value Added Network Services (VANS) and their successors Value Added Data Services (VADS) are prime targets for a variety of attacks ranging from large scale fraud to simple mischief. The user-friendliness demanded by legitimate users provides a major benefit to the attacker. Since attacks on dial-up communications networks can be launched from remote locations physically distant from the premises of the service providers, the perpetrators can be very difficult to track down. Even leased line VANs usually offer dial up back-up.

The major security risks derive from the fact that users belong to a different organisation to the service provider. Aspects of this problem include the following:

- the service provider has little control over the correct operation of user procedures;

- terminals may be located in insecure premises such as shops, or even the users' homes;

- it can be difficult to determine responsibility when something goes wrong.

The potential damage falls into three categories:

- loss of service revenue;

- claims from users or even third parties;

- loss of public confidence, leading to loss of business as the service loses credibility.

Security aspects of a VAD system will include:

- the control of passwords and access privileges in the service providers' DP Operations and Systems Development organisations;

- physical access to premises housing parts of the system where sensitive data is held in clear, or which may be a target for malicious damage;

- control of service operations and maintenance;

- the use of remote diagnostics;

- backup and resilience;

- disaster recovery plans;

- clarity and comprehensiveness of the contract between the user and the service provider;

- encryption and key management where appropriate.

Conclusions

In this article I have briefly described the ways in which a small number of IT developments have expanded the quantity and quality of services available to users. The benefits are many and varied, and can be used to great advantage by large and small businesses as well as, in many cases, by individuals. However, an extension of the 'caveat emptor' warning must apply. If effective assurance of an acceptable level of security is to be achieved the buyer, the user and the supplier must beware! All parties to an IT service must understand the threats to the system and their own vulnerability to those threats. Understanding by itself is not, of course, enough. The security measures necessary to counteract these threats must be installed. However, these measures are not all of an expensive or technical nature, and many simply rely on performance of the organisational and procedural controls which a well-run business always needs.

CHAPTER 38. LANGUAGE TRANSLATION BY COMPUTER

Geoffrey KINGSCOTT
Praetorious
Nottingham, U.K.

Experiments in using computers to translate natural language have been going on since the late 1940s but, although there are now a number of commercial systems available, nearly all of the translation in the world is still being done by human translators. This, however, is likely to change in the course of the 1990s.

Although the terms are frequently used loosely, in a general sense, computer translation (CT), also called machine translation (MT), is strictly speaking reserved for the automatic translation by computer of a whole document, normally carried out in batch mode. Computer-aided translation (CAT), also called machine-aided translation (MAT), is strictly speaking applied only to those systems where the computer produces the translation in short sections, usually a sentence at a time, for the translator or post-editor to work on in interactive mode.

Computer translation and computer-aided translation should not be confused with what are called machine aids to translation, for use where the translation itself is produced and input directly by human translators; such aids include word processing programs specially aimed at translators, the ability to use foreign language character sets, access to remote terminology data bases by modem, machine-readable glossaries and dictionaries which can be brought up on screen during the translation process, and spelling, style and grammar checkers. Such machine aids are outside the province of this article.

It must be emphasised that at the present state of the art it is not often possible to use translations automatically generated by computer, where natural language is used for the source text, without subsequent human editing (post-editing), except for very rough information scanning. However, experiments have shown that much better computer translations can be obtained by re-writing the source text (pre-editing).

The electronic digital computer, it will be recalled, had its first major applications during the Second World War, for mathematic calculations and code breaking. Immediately after the war further applications were sought. W. John Hutchins, of the University of Essex, the world's leading authority on the history of computer translation, has traced the first serious suggestion that computers be used for the translation of natural language to a conversation which took place in New York on June 20, 1946, between UK computer pioneer Andrew D. Booth and US scientist Warren Weaver.

In the early years there was a widespread notion that translation was essentially a matter of word substitution using a bilingual dictionary, which is how the layman thinks of translation, even human translation, to this day.

In fact natural language is of almost infinite complexity, and often the actual textual information, the words on a page, gives only a partial clue to meaning; the human translator usually has no difficulty in deducing the meaning, using his non-textual knowledge. Take the phrase (one of the first signs the visitor sees on arriving at Heathrow): "No electric passenger carrying vehicles allowed past this point". The human mind visualises the correct meaning almost instantly, because of inferences made from external knowledge; otherwise the message that would be conveyed would be that electric passengers were prohibited from carrying vehicles past the point in question.

Of course, it could be argued that if the sentence were given a verb, as it ought to be in continuous text, and if a hyphen were inserted between passenger and carrying, so that the sentence would read: "No electric passenger-carrying vehicle is allowed past this point", all ambiguity disappears. Which is why the pre-editing of text for translation results in an enhanced computer translation quality.

In the history of computer translation, the early word for word substitution quickly gave way to the writing of paradigms to allow parsing and semantic analysis to take place, and the first operational systems began to emerge.

Although individuals and institutions in various countries had been involved in early machine translation projects, by the end of the 1950s and early 1960s most of the development was concentrated in the United States, largely because of the availability there of ample funding. The launch of the first Soviet Sputnik on October 4, 1957, had made an enormous psychological impact on American thinking: it was a revelation that Soviet technology was so far advanced that it had been the Soviet Union, and not the United States as everyone expected, which had succeeded in launching the first spacecraft.

Suddenly there was a realisation that it was important to peruse Soviet scientific literature, and funds were made available for translation systems that could assist in this. The impact of the Sputnik is clearly reflected in the concentration, in the 1950s and 1960s, on systems to translate from Russian to English.

There was a wave of enthusiasm, which waned as experiments showed that the problems of processing natural language were more intractable than had been supposed. By the mid-1960s there was a widespread feeling that machine translation was not getting anywhere, and this mood was reflected in the ALPAC report of 1966.

ALPAC is an acronym for Automatic Language Processing Advisory Committee of the United States Academy of Sciences, and the committee had been established in April 1964 to study the existing demand, supply and costs of translations. It concluded that the supply of human translators exceeded the demand, and that machine translation had progressed from the "deceptively encouraging" early results to "uniformly discouraging" results by the time of the report.

The effect of the report on the availability of funding for, and major industrial interest in, machine translation, was devastating. Many projects were suspended or abandoned, and by late 1975 machine translation research in United States had reached its lowest level since 1950.

One result of this was that advances in machine translation after 1966 came from maverick individuals and organisations, who chose to be uninfluenced by the report, or from outside the United States. As the history of machine translation development after ALPAC was to a large measure the history of individual initiatives, until the emergence of the Eurotra project in Europe and various collaborative measures in Japan, in the late 1980s, we shall now proceed to examine individually those initiatives which led to working systems or promising developments.

Research in Canada was to some extent uninfluenced by the ALPAC report, since developments in Canadian society had revealed a huge requirement for translation which it was felt might be beyond the scope of human translators. The language consciousness of the French-speaking part of Canada had been growing for years, and if the country were to be held together official bilingualism seemed to be called for. The first Official languages Act was passed in 1969, and brought home to many Canadians the huge volume of latent translation.

The Canadian government had supported from first the Montreal University TAUM (Traduction Automatique de l'Université de Montréal) project, one of the results of which was TAUM-METEO, one of the first machine translation systems to work cost-effectively.

TAUM-METEO was commissioned in 1975, the prototype demonstrated in 1976, and the production model put into operation in June 1977. Improvements led to a new version, METEO2, in 1983.

With a relatively small dictionary of some 2,000 words and expressions, the system translates, from English into French, hourly weather forecasts for Environment Canada's meteorological stations in Vancouver, Edmonton, Calgary, Regina, Toronto and Halifax. The system handles an average of 30,000 words a day, or 8.5 million words a year.

In 1988 METEO translated 49,694 weather forecasts, totalling 10,508,893 words. The editing rate was calculated at 3.74%, and the average turn-round for a text, not including communications, was 27 minutes.

In 1989 a new French to English system, translating forecasts from the meteorological station in French-speaking Montreal, was introduced.

According to consultant John Chandioux (October 1989) the METEO system is now estimated to do the work of ten full-time translators, and has already processed one hundred million words.

In the United States, one of those who disagreed with the conclusions of the ALPAC report was Dr Peter Toma, who had worked on some of the earlier experimental systems. He persevered with machine translation development, and created systems called Autotran and Technotran, which were forerunners of a more sophisticated system called Systran, which he was able to produce in an operational form by 1970. He delivered his first system that year to the United States Air Force Foreign Technology division at Wright Patterson Air Base, where Systran is still being used today - 20 years later - for translation of scientific and military information from Russian to English. The current throughput is some 100,000 pages a year.

The use made of Systran at the Wright Patterson Air Base is for information scanning, that is to obtain a rough or raw translation of the original material, so that the scientists can get a general idea of Soviet activity in their particular domains.

The next major advance for Systran came in 1976, when a contract was signed with the Commission of the European Communities for its use and development. This acquisition required a change in application, since the Commission were interested in the translation of texts for distribution and possible publication, and that meant that texts had to be produced, either by the system alone or with the help of post-editing, to a higher standard than that required for information scanning.

Currently (end of 1989) a team of 35 people, either employed by the Commission or contracted to it, are working on the development of Systran in 12 language pairs, English into French, Italian, German, Dutch, Spanish and Portuguese; French into English, German, Dutch and Italian; and German into English and French. German is notoriously a difficult language for machine translation (many nouns and verbs have a wide spectrum of meaning), and it was not until 1987 that development work really got under way on German as a source language.

The Commission has greatly contributed to the development of Systran, and its versions have become steadily more modular over the years, with source language analysis now completely independent of target language generation, even in respect of the basic dictionary. Dictionaries have been enlarged, in some cases considerably so, and this, combined with the greater modularity, has made the system more directly useful.

Translations are generated at a rate of about 500,000 words an hour, and the number of work stations in the Commission which can access Systran is growing steadily. It is estimated that some five million words a year are translated through Systran at the Commission.

Other users of Systran in the public sector include the Nuclear Research Centre at Karlsruhe in Germany, NATO headquarters at Brussels, the German national railways (Bundesbahn), the International Atomic Energy Authority at Vienna,

Since 1979 Systran has also been sold to a number of major industrial companies in the private sector, such as the Xerox Corporation, General Motors, Aerospatiale, Dornier GmbH and Festo KG. The approach used by Xerox is to use the system to translate the same text out of English into several target languages; for this purpose the writing of the source text is strictly controlled, using what is called Controlled English.

World rights in the private sector are now owned by a French industrial company, Gachot SA, which works closely with the Commission on the development of the system. Gachot, which has bought out Dr Toma's interests, in addition to offering Systran installations, also offers raw Systran output on line through the telephone network, by modem, or even through the French Minitel system, which has three million installations, most of them in private homes.

Gachot is currently offering from its centres at Soisy sous Montmorency, near Paris, and its subsidiary in La Jolla, California, 12 language pairs: English to Arabic, French, German, Italian, Spanish and Dutch; French to English, Dutch and German; German to English and French; and Russian to English.

The long history of Systran has equipped it with a large program base – it has been calculated that it now consists of several hundred thousand lines of programming, and dictionaries which can contain up to 140,000 terms per language pair. In the 1970s and for much of the 1980s dictionaries were often developed by users, while various Systran companies in different countries worked on the software modules. As Systran is essentially a lexicon-driven system, there were divergences, but since the world conference of Systran users, held in Luxembourg in 1986, and more particularly since the various former scattered Systran companies came under the centralised control of the Gachot organisation, divergence is giving way again to convergence.

Another long-running practical application of machine translation is the SPANAM and ENGSPAN systems used by the Pan-American Health Organisation (PAHO) in Washington DC for translation between English and Spanish. It is now the principal mode of translation between those two languages, which account for much of the organisation's work; that is to say more translation work is processed by machine translation than by human translators. In the person of its director, Dr Muriel Vasconcellos, and in the early development of SPANAM, the systems have an ancestry going back into the early days of machine translation research at Georgetown University, Washington. Work on SPANAM was begun in 1976 and the system was ready for implementation in late 1979; an updated version came into use in November 1988. The English to Spanish system, ENGSPAN, constructed on somewhat different principles, came into use in 1984.

The SPANAM system was produced by outside consultants, but in 1980 the source codes were handed over to PAHO, and since then responsibility for the continued development and operation of the system has lain directly with the PAHO translation staff, which is still an unusual arrangement in the machine translation world, where developers and users normally keep to their distinct roles.

Another application which has been in use since the 1970s is TITUS, a text-specific system (i.e., like METEO, described above, it deals only with restricted subject matter). TITUS is used by the Institut du Textile de France for translation between French, English, German and Spanish of abstracts of articles on various aspects of textiles. TITUS requires rigorous pre-editing of the source text, with considerable simplification of sentence structure, although with the introduction of TITUS4 in 1980 the range of structures which the system will accept has been extended.

When work on most machine translation development ceased in the United States as a result of the impact of the ALPAC report, one of the organisations which ignored the report's findings was the Mormon Church, which was interested in financing machine translation with a view to using it to translate Mormon religious literature. Eventually, however, the research work, at Brigham Young University in Utah, was wound down, but two commercial companies emerged and hired many of the programmers who had worked on the development. These two companies were Weidner and ALPS (Automated Language Processing Systems).

Weidner was established in 1977, and by 1980 an English to French system was being marketed. The first systems (MacroCAT) were on mini-computers, but quite soon a version (MicroCAT) on personal computers was made available. Language pairs available include English to French, Spanish, German, Portuguese and Italian; French to English and Spanish to English plus, on MacroCAT only, English to Arabic and German to English.

The Weidner system was purchased by a number of industrial companies including, in the UK, Massey Fergusson of Kenilworth, and Perkins Engines of Peterborough. Perkins Engines have developed a way of writing the source text in English, using a set of parameters they call PACE (Perkins Approved Clear English), which allows for easier translation (in a similar way to how Xerox use Systran).

In the mid-1980s the Weidner company, which had changed its name to World Communications Corporation (WCC), was acquired by the Japanese company Bravice International Inc. In 1986 Bravice closed down the WCC offices in the United States and Europe, and the future of the system is, at the time of writing, subject to uncertainty.

The ALPS system is unusual, in that it can function on three different levels, the higher levels encompassing all the features of the lower. Automatic translation as such is only performed at the highest level (the other two levels provide sophisticated translation aids), and this translation is interactive, that is to say the computer offers a proposed translation to the translator sentence by sentence, with questions displayed on screen asking the user to elucidate ambiguities.

In 1988 the ALPS company, in a change of marketing strategy, switched their priority from selling software systems to operating a translation bureau service, and they took over the three largest translation bureau companies in Canada, the United Kingdom and the Federal Republic of Germany.

Logos is another American machine translation company, and the actual system development began in the 1960s. A version for translation from English to Vietnamese was introduced in 1971 for the translation of military equipment maintenance manuals, the United States being then heavily involved in the Vietnam war. At the end of the war the company turned its attention to producing a German to English system, running on Wang computers, and this was sold to a number of users in Europe, particularly in the Federal Republic of Germany.

Language pairs currently offered are German to English and French, and English to French, German and Spanish. It is claimed that the system will translate, in batch mode, up to 100 pages an hour.

In addition to its offices in the United States and Germany, Logos is now also based in Canada, and experiments are being carried out using Logos by the office of the Canadian Secretary of State, one of the largest governmental users of translation services in the world.

Another system used in Canada is the Smart system, marketed by Smart Communications Inc., of New York. This company, which also has a system for writing manuals in clear English (Smart Editor), markets Smart Translator. This, it is claimed, can produce raw translations at a speed of 200,000 words an hour when running on mainframes. Smart's largest customer is the Canadian Ministry of Employment and Immigration, which uses the system to translate job descriptions from English to French, which can be displayed within minutes of being generated (with rapid post-editing) at the Ministry offices in Ottawa to any of the 3,500 terminals installed in employment exchanges throughout Canada.

The University of Saarbrücken in Germany has long been involved in machine translation, and though its main system, SUSY (Saarbrücker Übersetzungssystem) has not yet had any major application, its influence has been felt, in particular in the German work on the Eurotra project (see below).

The present ongoing SUSY project dates back to 1972, and was at first concerned with translation from German into Russian. During the following years components for the language pairs French into German and English into German were added. Some research work has also been done on Esperanto into German, Danish into German, Dutch into German, German into English and German into French.

Although work is continuing with a view to using offshoots of SUSY, such as SATAN (Saarbrücker Automatische Text-Analyse) for automatic indexing, SUSY-BSA (restricted test applications at the Bundesprachenamt), SUSANNAH (incorporation of outside terminology information) and MARIS (Multilinguale Aspekte von Referenz-Informations-Systeme), SUSY is still generally thought of as an experimental system.

There is a small independent Canadian company marketing a system called SOCATRA (Société Canadienne de Traduction Assistée) for the language pair English to French, but the company places its marketing emphasis on using the system itself and selling raw machine translation or post-edited output.

METAL (Mechanical Translation and Analysis of Languages) derives from a project first established at the Linguistics Research Centre of the University of Texas, with United States government funding, in 1961 for the translation of German into English. The project dwindled with the reduction of Government funding after the ALPAC report, but was revived, and received a considerable boost when the West German company Siemens began to support it. Since 1980 Siemens has been the sole sponsor, and developments in the system have been tested at Siemens main offices in Munich.

METAL is now commercially marketing the language pair German to English; there are said to be 12 installations already using it. Work is also going on in French to Dutch at the University of Leuven in Belgium, German to Spanish at a site in Barcelona, and German to Danish at a site in Kolding, Denmark.

A number of new systems have come on to the market in recent years, including the only system developed in Israel, Tovna, which was unveiled at the London Translating and the Computer conference in November 1987. Its creator was a software expert, Dr Daniel Cohen, and the first pilot operational system, for translation from English into French, has been installed at the World Bank in Washington DC, United States. An English to Russian pair is being developed, as is a French to English pair.

One of the surprise entries to the machine translation market in recent years was that of Linguistic Products, an American firm with a European sales base in Nice, France. The surprise was that they were offering a machine translation system, PC-Translator, at $985 for the first language pair, a fraction of the cost of other systems on the market. They have sold a number of their products for the language pairs English to French and English to Spanish, and are developing a number of other combinations. The system is linguistically unsophisticated, but it is easy to enter new terms and even whole phrases; some observers consider it more a powerful phrase dictionary than a machine translation system as such.

Another recent low-price entry into the market, at around $2,000 for a language pair, comes from another American company, Globalink. A few systems are said to have been sold in the United States, and at the end of 1989 they were actively looking for a European distributor.

One system that has not been a success is Gigatext, in Regina, Canada. The company was set up in response to a huge demand, as a result of a court decision, for translation from English into French of 100 years of provincial legislation in the Canadian province of Saskatchewan. The Saskatchewan provincial government put some money into the company ($4 million according to some reports), but became concerned when no translations appeared, long after the initial deadlines had been passed. In November 1989 it was announced that the company was to be closed down.

Latest news on commercially operational systems in the West at the time of writing was that Winger 92, an English to Danish translation system was due to be launched by another new company in the machine translation field, Winger Holdings A/S, of Virum, Denmark.

Japan came comparatively late to the machine translation field, after three decades when most of the advances had been in the United States, but is rapidly making up for lost time. As might be expected, systems in Japan are overwhelmingly for the translation of English into Japanese and Japanese into English, but there is a widening of the horizons taking place, with interest in translating between Japanese and the other major languages of South-east Asia, such as Chinese, Korean and Thai.

A breakthrough occurred when Bravice introduced its Mini-Pack Japanese to English system in 1984, to run under Unix on a DEC microcomputer, followed a few months later with a microcomputer version, the Micro-Pack.

Meanwhile work was already well advanced on the research project supported by the Japanese government, the Mu project, with which Professor Makoto Nagao, today recognised as one of the world's leading authorities on machine translation, was closely involved. This was a four year project, 1982-1986, and has been succeeded by the Japan Information Centre for Science and Technology (JICST) project. Test operation of this system is scheduled to start within the next few months, and it may be possible to start practical operation in the early future.

Many of the big names in the Japanese electronics industry are marketing, producing or developing machine translation systems, among them Oki Electric (PENSEE), Canon, Sanyo Electric (SWP-7800), CSK, Sharp (DUET), Toshiba (AS TRANSAC), NEC (PIVOT), Hitachi (HICATS), Fujitsu (ATLAS II), Mitsubishi Electric (MELTRAN) and Ricoh (RMT). In addition to its English to Japanese (ATLAS I) and Japanese to English (ATLAS II), Fujitsu is also working on a Japanese to German system.

There is also an ambitious project to create a machine translation system for Asian languages. This is being developed by the Centre for International Cooperation for Computerisation (CICC), which uses an interlingual approach, i.e. each language is translated into an artificial language, the "interlingua", and then the target language is generated from the representation as it is found in the interlingua. The languages involved are Japanese, Chinese, Malay and Thai.

Another collaborative project is the creation of a Japanese electronic dictionary for English and Japanese, where many of the companies developing machine translation, named above, are collaborating, in order to save themselves individual dictionary-building effort. The project is strongly backed by the Japanese government.

Another project which has won heavy Japanese government backing is the long-term development of a system for the automatic interpreting of telephone calls between English and Japanese, using speech recognition and speech synthesis. The system, started in 1984 and scheduled to take 15 years, will represent one of the most extraordinary machine translation developments of all if it can be brought to successful fruition, but little information has been made available on progress so far.

There is little doubt that the Japanese investment at both government and company levels is quite large. Because of the relative inaccessibility to foreigners of the Japanese language (in contrast to the position of English in the world), and because of their need to export worldwide, the Japanese are convinced that a key to future success in all domains lies in machine translation. One estimate is that currently some 800 or 900 people are currently engaged in research and development of machine translation systems in Japan, of which some 60% are working in commercial companies.

Meanwhile in Europe the biggest research effort is the Eurotra project of the Commission of the European Communities. The aim is to lay the foundations for the development of a system for multilingual high-quality translation between all the nine official languages of the Community, namely Danish, Dutch, English, French, German, Greek, Italian, Portuguese and Spanish.

For political reasons research has been decentralised to units in all the countries of the Community, with only a comparatively small central unit at Luxembourg, and this decentralisation has made administrative coordination difficult. The project has not been without its critics, since there has been little movement towards producing an operational system, but against this can be set the fact that the stimulus to research has been considerable.

While most operational systems in the world today are either American or Japanese, some other countries, such as France (with its GETA project at the University of Grenoble) and the Soviet Union, maintain research projects. There are also two interesting private research projects proceeding in the Netherlands, DLT and Rosetta.

The DLT (Distributed Language Translation) is an interactive multilingual system using an intermediary language or "interlingua", based on the 100-year old international artificial language Esperanto. It is intended for use by monolingual speakers, using networked terminals, and is therefore more for multilingual communication than for machine translation as such, although the system uses machine translation technology. The developers, BSO, of Utrecht, demonstrated a prototype model in December 1987. In an interesting new development they are now said to be introducing into the system a Bilingual Knowledge Base (BKB), which uses discourse analysis and statistical probability to assess target language meanings.

Rosetta is an experimental project being carried out by the major Netherlands electronics firm Philips, of Eindhoven. From its inception in 1980, until 1985, it was conducted on modest lines, but in 1985 the project was expanded and experimental translation work was carried out between Dutch and English, and English and Spanish. This phase, known as Rosetta3, is now drawing to a close and researchers are expected to begin work on Rosetta4, a phase which is designed to lead to an operational system.

The long-term aim of the French GETA project is a multilingual system, and its current version is known as Ariane. It has been tested on a wide range of languages, such as Malay and Thai, though often only in small-scale experiments. GETA is also involved in the French national project, financed partly from public funds, and involving companies in the aerospace and data processing fields, to create systems known as Calliope-Aero and Calliope-Infor respectively, the first for the language pair French to English and the latter for English to French.

In the Soviet Union systems, such as ANRAP for translation into Russian from English and German, at the Soviet Centre for Translation in Moscow, and SILOD, for translation into Russian from English, French and Spanish, and vice versa, at the Leningrad State Pedagogical Institute, still appear to be at an experimental stage. An English to Russian system, called ETAP-2, limited to electrical engineering texts, has now reached the stage of experimental testing.

Little work has been done on using machine translation for languages which are not major commercial languages, but mention should be made of the CADA (Computer Assisted Dialect Adaptation) approach which has been under development since 1979 by David Weber of the Summer Institute of Linguistics of the United States (heavily involved in translation of the Bible into tribal languages), and colleagues in South America. The method homes in on the differences between languages, and is for use only between closely-related languages. It has been mainly used for the translation of texts into South Amerindian languages, such as Quechua.

One of the universities most closely involved in machine translation research in the United States is the Carnegie-Mellon University, which has a Center for Machine Translation, where work is going ahead on a knowledge-based system (i.e. one that incorporates Artificial Intelligence techniques).

In the United Kingdom, which played such a major role in machine translation in the initial years, there is no major developer or project, but the University of Essex and the University of Manchester Institute of Science and Technology (UMIST) are both involved in the Eurotra project (see above). UMIST is also working in collaboration with the University of Sheffield, which has a strong Japanese teaching department, on research into an English to Japanese automatic translation system (NTRAN), and Japanese to English (AIDTRANS).

The much-publicised British Telecom speech translation system for business telephone messages, on which work began in 1984 and which was announced in August 1987, is of limited application, since it cannot handle natural language (i.e. continuous speech). The system is designed to recognise up to 400 common business phrases involving some 1,000 words in total, with each phrase taken in isolation, and generate the foreign language equivalent.

The University of Lund, in Sweden, is working on an experimental Swedish/English system, SWETRA. At the same University successful experiments in the use of machine translation to translate information in Japanese data bases into English have been carried out. The development of an English to Norwegian system (ENTRA) at the University of Bergen in Norway, in collaboration with the World Communications Corporation and using the Weidner system, appears to be suspended for the present.

The richest source of information about new developments in machine translation is obtained at conferences on the subject, some of which publish their proceedings.

The conference series which has recently emerged as the major forum on the subject, in particular for the exchange of information between Japanese and Western developers, is called the Machine Translation Summit. MT Summit I was held in Tokyo in 1987, and MT Summit II in Munich in August 1989. MT Summit III will be held in North America in 1991, and will almost certainly see the creation of an International Association for Machine Translation, a project now being actively discussed.

The theoretical side of machine translation is discussed at the COLING (International conference on computational linguistics) conferences, held since 1976 every two years. The last was held in Budapest in 1988, and the next is due to be held in Helsinki in 1990.

In the UK the information science organisation Aslib, in conjunction, first with the Translators' Guild, and later with the Guild's successor organisation, the Institute of Translating and Interpreting, organises an annual conference on "Translating and the Computer" in London. The series started in 1977.

What is almost certainly the largest archive in the world concerned solely with machine translation is held in the UK, having been personally created and built up as a personal venture by W. John Hutchins, assistant librarian at the University of East Anglia, Norwich. Mr Hutchins' book "Machine Translation, Past, Present, Future", is generally recognised as the definitive history of the subject up to 1986.

News of current developments in machine translation are to be found in the language news journal, "Language International" and in the computer applications journal "LT/Electric Word" (formerly "Language Technology"), while theoretical articles on machine translation can be found in the journals "Computers and Translation" and "Computational Linguistics".

FURTHER READING

W.J. Hutchins: "Machine translation: past, present, future", published by Ellis Horwood, Chichester, 1986.

J. Lehrberger and L. Bourbeau: "Machine translation: linguistic characteristics of MT systems and general methodology of evaluation", published by John Benjamins BV, Amsterdam, 1988.

J. Slocum: "Machine translation systems", published by the Cambridge University Press, 1988.

Dan Maxwell, Klaus Schubert and Toon Witkam: "New Directions in Machine Translation", published by Foris Publications, Dordrecht, Netherlands, 1988 (contains an article by W.J. Hutchins bringing his 1986 history up to date).

Proceedings of the Translating and the Computer conferences, 1984, 1985, 1986, 1987, 1988, published by Aslib, London.

Proceedings of the COLING conferences, 1984 (published by Stanford University) and 1986 (Bonn University).

Andrew BRAID
The British Library
Boston Spa, U.K.

0. Synopsis

This chapter deals with the changes that may occur in the process of document supply in the next 10 years or so. The changes will be driven by advances in technology but it will be market forces which will control the pace. The elements of document requesting, storage and delivery are examined; the barriers which may prevent or delay progress are discussed. Certain key events are required to happen before real progress can be made.

1. Introduction

This chapter is concerned with the process of document supply. As a result of technological advances in other library processes, there may be further changes which in turn affect document supply; conservation is one which comes to mind. These are not covered in this chapter. Please note two caveats. First, I would not claim to be a "guru" in forecasting technology. However, I would not be the first person to get things badly wrong[1]. Second, the views presented here are personal ones and should not be taken to be those of the British Library.

The term "document supply" is relatively new to library vocabulary[2]. It is generally taken to mean the supply of a surrogate of an original article, report, paper etc. which is required at a remote location. Today the majority of these surrogates are produced by making a photocopy of the original item and despatching it to the requester by conventional methods. The widescale introduction of photocopy machines in the 1960s was the main cause for the rapid growth in the supply of surrogates. Before then copying of material was a time consuming, sometimes even messy, operation. But there is much more to document supply than the photocopying of an item and mailing it. Much of the process is inseparable from a much older library practice, that of inter-library loan (ILL)[*]. For this reason the terms are sometimes used interchangeably.

Libraries have always relied upon each other to fulfil requests in areas where they were not self-sufficient. But within the last 20 or 30 years libraries have become far more dependent upon

---

[*]ILL was probably first practised between monasteries in the 12th century or even earlier. It was used for borrowing manuscripts in order to copy them.

ILL. The reason for this is not difficult to understand.
Libraries are facing ever increasing financial problems.
Acquisition spending is the largest non-staff element of library
budgets. Also, acquisition costs are rising at a rate higher than
general inflation. Thus, acquisitions have to take the lion's
share of any cut in expenditure. If libraries wish to maintain
the same level of service to their clients, they have no recourse
except to place greater reliance upon ILL. Some libraries have
tried to solve this problem in other ways. There are schemes for
cooperative acquisition or resource sharing, these are often
limited in some way and rarely offer the comprehensiveness of
ILL.

It is, therefore, somewhat ironic that the process of ILL in
many libraries is something of a "Cinderella" service. Libraries
have invested over the past few years in a variety of automated
systems for many basic library processes, acquisition,
cataloguing, circulation control, etc. Until very recently little
investment has been made in the automation of ILL and document
supply procedures. Recent advances in technology should allow the
document supply process to catch up with, and possibly overtake,
other library processes. Imagine the scene in a research
laboratory in a few years time.

> A researcher requires some information on a particular
> subject. He (or she) enters a brief description in
> free text into a workstation. Within a few seconds a
> facsimile image of an article appears on the high
> resolution screen of the workstation. The article does
> not seem to be exactly on the subject but one of the
> references seems to contain the required information.
> The workstation's mouse highlights the reference and
> within a few seconds the new article appears on the
> screen. This article is relevant, the printer produces
> a copy of high quality. The article may also be of
> interest to other workers in the research group and so
> it is transmitted over the internal network to other
> workstations.

Technically, most of that described above can be done today.
This chapter describes the current state of developments and
examines the barriers to achieving the above scenario.
Librarians should take comfort from the fact that it is unlikely
to happen within the next 15 years. When it does, they may be
all out of a job!

2. The Current State of Document Supply

There are four stages in the document supply process
1. selecting the required document
2. requesting the document
3. storing documents
4. delivering the document.

Information on books, articles, conference proceedings, etc. has been available in electronic form for some time. Over 25 years ago the National Library of Medicine's MEDLARS database was the first non-military use of a computer based information retrieval system. Today information is available on-line on every known topic; there are literally hundreds of databases mounted on hosts throughout the world[3]. The majority of this information is in the form of extracts or abstracts. The original full text version is available in an on-line version in only a few cases. The majority of these full text systems are in areas where the information changes rapidly, eg financial databases, and where the user can afford to pay for the higher cost of this type of database.

As far as automation is concerned, the remaining elements have received little attention until very recently. Developments in telecommunications have led to the ability to request documents very quickly, but it is by no means a universal method of requesting. The method of processing requests within supply centres is, with one or two notable exceptions, a manual process. The delivery of documents relies on the postal service in the vast majority of cases. It is only recently that facsimile transmission has started to be used.

2.1 Selection of Documents

Surveys have shown that surprisingly little use is made of databases to search for documents[4]. References from other articles and personal recommendations are far more common ways of gaining information. This makes the application of technology to the first part of the supply chain more difficult. Even for those items which are selected by means of a database search there are problems. Is the journal held in the local library? If a search has been made on more than one database, are there duplicate entries? Technology can now provide answers for this type of problem. Matching algorithms can be used to detect duplicates and also to match references against lists of holdings. But if the reference has come from a more traditional source it is necessary to use either manual methods or else to convert the request into machine readable format.

2.2 Ordering of Documents

Once it has been established that a reference is unique and that the article is not held locally, it is necessary to locate a source from which the required item may be ordered. Machine readable catalogues of holdings now exist in various forms as well as union lists. The largest example of a union list is the OCLC database of over 20 million items[5], although ILL is not its prime purpose. One of the newer forms of technology, CD-ROM, is also finding a niche in this area. CD-ROM is an ideal medium for catalogues of this type which do not need frequent updating. With some supply centres it is not necessary to carry out this step. They work on the principle of holding, or having access to, any item that is likely to be requested. As systems become more mechanized this method of working will become more difficult. Automated systems are not able to cope with speculative locations for items as easily as with known locations.

When a possible source for an item has been established, an order has to be placed with the supply centre. The most efficient way of doing this today is to transmit requests electronically. Most supply centres can accept requests in electronic format. Reply messages, for items which are not immediately available, can also be transmitted back to the requester in the same manner. In this way a process which using mail may take several days or even weeks, can be reduced to a few hours or less. Systems which can manage requests as well as transmit them are now available[6]. Many of these employ standard database management packages and run on microcomputers. To standardize the ordering of documents there is now a draft proposal for an International Standard for ILL requesting, ISO DP 10160 and 10161.

It is also possible to combine the searching and ordering of documents into a single operation. Many of the on-line database hosts offer the facility to transmit down-loaded citations to supply centres. This has great benefit in terms of convenience, but could lead to the ordering of items held locally unless checks are made. Some database providers have introduced systems to supply the documents held on their database[7].

2.3 Storage of Documents

This is the area that has received least attention to date. The electronic processing of the full text of books and journals is much less advanced than the methods for either requesting documents or delivering them. This is due to the nature of the material itself. The majority of requests are for articles from learned journals. The requesters of these articles want to see either the original article or a true facsimile copy. The loan of the original item or a photocopy of it are, at the present time, the only acceptable methods of providing this facility. In order to store and transmit such true copies electronically, it is necessary to use the technique of facsimile encoding.

2.3.1 Facsimile Encoding

This is the only feasible method of electronically reproducing all the text, diagrams, illustrations, graphs, etc. which an article may contain. A drawback of this technique is the very high volume of data that is generated. With conventional character encoding, such as ASCII, a typical page from a scientific journal may contain up to 10,000 bytes. Note, however, that it is impossible for character encoding techniques to cope with anything but the simplest of non-textual material. The quality of an image in facsimile encoding is directly proportional to the number of bits that are used to specify that image. The resolution of an image on a standard CCITT group III facsimile machine, at normal resolution, is approximately 200 lines per inch in the horizontal plane by 100 lines per inch in the vertical plane. (The eye is less sensitive in the vertical plane and does not notice the loss of quality as much as in the horizontal plane.) For a DIN A4 sized page this resolution results in a total of approximately 1.75 million bits. Whilst the normal resolution of CCITT group III facsimile machines is adequate for office applications, it is not for scientific material. Most scientific and technical literature contains small text in footnotes etc., and small point sizes in sub- and super-scripts. These often form an essential part of an article. A resolution of 400 lines per inch gives an acceptable result for scientific articles. This allows as low as 4 point text to be resolved. Also the human eye cannot resolve much more than the equivalent of about 400 lines per inch. However, the volume of data for facsimile encoding increases to about 16 million bits for a DIN A4 page.

The result of the encoding process is a bit stream, often called a bit-map; this can be manipulated using data processing techniques. Data compression is one technique that can be used. Data compression algorithms can reduce the volume of data by as much as 100 times. The methods used in commercial facsimile machines are not so efficient and they only achieve between 5 and 20 times compression. Thus, to store or transmit a page in compressed format at 400 lines per inch can require anything up to 1 million bits (125 kilobytes). At normal CCITT group III resolution this reduces to the order of 175 kilobits (22 kilobytes). The majority of scanning and compression techniques which are used have been developed for textual material. When half toned images are scanned the volume of data can increase considerably. Some compression algorithms can even increase, rather than reduce, the volume of data when photographs are scanned and the data compressed.

An article in a scientific journal can be quite lengthy, up to 10 pages is quite typical. Thus, for an average article even at low resolution over 200 kilobytes are required. At a resolution of 400 lines per inch up to 1 Megabyte of data is generated. It is only relatively recently that storage and transmission technology has been able to cope with such large volumes of data.

2.3.2 Optical Storage

Optical storage is one of the most cost efficient methods of storing large amounts of data. There are a variety of optical storage systems now available using both analogue and digital encoding techniques[8]. There are also two classes: those which can have data read from them and written directly to them and those which are of the read-only (ROM) type. In many cases the former are not erasable, but can be written to once only - the WORM (Write Once Read Many) disk. The two types of storage that are used predominantly in document delivery applications are WORM disks and CD-ROMs. WORM disks are usually used in applications where the supply centre has decided to scan and store material for internal use (See section 2.3.5). CD-ROM is used in publishing applications when several copies are required.

2.3.2.1 ADONIS

One of the most successful trials to date for the storage of documents in electronic format is the ADONIS project[9]. This involved the scanning in facsimile encoded format of some 200 biomedical journals and storing them on CD-ROMs. Articles are retrieved from the CD-ROM using a relatively simple workstation. This decompresses the image and either displays it on a high resolution screen or else prints it on a laser printer. The trial covered journals published in 1987 and 1988 and the system was tested, in 12 centres throughout the world, during 1988 and 1989. In 1989 the ADONIS Consortium of publishers decided to launch the ADONIS system as a commercial service. This is not planned to start until 1991 and details of the service are not available at the time of writing. Meanwhile, a technically similar service has been launched by University Microfilms International (UMI). They have used the same technique of scanning journal pages in facsimile mode and storing the pages on CD-ROM. A slight difference is that in the UMI version the index of the articles is stored on a separate CD-ROM instead of on the magnetic hard disk of the microcomputer as with ADONIS.

2.3.3 Disadvantages of Facsimile Encoding

One of the disadvantages of facsimile encoding is that the information is not directly searchable. To retrieve information it is necessary to produce an index of the images. For journal articles there is no universally accepted method to describe an article, in the same way that a International Standard Book Number (ISBN) can describe a book. (The serial equivalent, the International Standard Serial Number [ISSN] only describes to the serial title level.) There are two standards to describe articles, the Serial and Article Identifier (SAID), draft NISO standard Z39.56-198X, and the Bibliographic Identifier (BIBLID), ISO 9115. Neither of these standards has been used in practice and the recent DOCMATCH report has shown that they may not be unique identifiers[10]. ADONIS developed its own identifier but this was assigned at the time of indexing and thus was not known in advance. It is planned to make this identifier more widely available in future. At present, articles have to be described by conventional means, serial title, year, volume number, page number, article title and authors. This makes searching a fairly laborious process.

The creation of the index for this method of searching is a very staff intensive process and can be more expensive than the cost of scanning. In some cases it is possible to use indexes that have been created for other purposes. An example of this was the use of the PASCAL database with the TRANSDOC trial at the Centre National de Recherche Scientifique (CNRS) in France[11] and the use of an internal database in the large Optical Disk Program at the Library of Congress[12]. Often when the database is created for other purposes as well, there can be a delay before it becomes available. ADONIS tried to overcome this problem by creating the index at the time of scanning. Even so there were delays of up to 3 weeks from the reception of the journals to the production of the discs. This is not acceptable for journals in areas of science, technology and medicine where currency is very important.

A further disadvantage of facsimile encoding is the large volume of data that is created. The capacity of a CD-ROM is over 500 megabytes; but with the resolution used in these applications, normally 300 lines per inch, it means that between 6,000 and 7,000 pages only can be stored per disc, (compared with as many as 250,000 character encoded pages.) The number of pages is reduced considerably if there are many half tone pictures contained within the documents. This was the case with ADONIS and during the two year period of scanning 84 CD-ROMs were produced. This number is difficult to handle manually; some form of assistance is required. For ADONIS this led to the development of a CD-ROM jukebox[13]. This was specified by the British Library Document Supply Centre (BLDSC), as was the ADONIS workstation, with the help of a partial grant from the European Commission. The capacity of the jukebox is 240 CD-ROMs, any one of which can be accessed in less than 10 seconds. After building a carousel type of jukebox, the developers, Next Technology of Cambridge, UK, developed a stacking version. The advantage of this version is that it allows more than one CD-ROM drive to be used and this, in turn, can allow multiple user access to the CD-ROMs in the jukebox. This version of the jukebox, named Voyager, is now available commercially.

2.3.4 Alternatives to Facsimile Encoding

From the above it is obvious that neither facsimile encoding nor CD-ROM are entirely suitable for the storage of the full text of documents. Yet there are several systems now available using both these technologies. Facsimile encoding is used because it is currently the most effective way of capturing all the text and non-text material on a page. It is also the only method that is capable of recreating a true facsimile image of a page. This is likely to remain the case until there is agreed standardisation and common implementation of page mark-up systems. Even then the incorporation of half tone pictures will be a problem. The importance of half tone pictures in journals, particularly medical material, should not be overlooked. It is

likely that methods to overcome the drawbacks of facsimile
encoding will be sought before looking for alternatives. For the
commercial service, ADONIS is proposing to have a higher
compression ratio and store about 15,000 pages per CD-ROM. The
use of jukeboxes which allow access for multiple users to a
single database may also be attractive.

It is probable that both facsimile encoding and the use of CD-
ROM are transient technologies for full text applications.
Speculation about their successors is rife. Market forces will
determine which of the many technologies which could possibly
replace them will prevail. Market forces will also determine the
timing of such changes. At the present time, as improvements are
continually being made to the current technology, they may well
have at least another 10 years of life; perhaps even longer for
facsimile encoding. The reason for this is the widespread use
for document transmission. One of the more attractive
alternatives is the storage of the computer type setting tapes
which are used to create the journals. This option was rejected
by ADONIS as these tapes are not standardised and often do not
contain the entire contents of an article. A research project in
the UK, Knowledge Warehouse, has examined the problem in more
detail but has not yet reached the trial implementation stage[14].

2.3.5 Alternatives to CD-ROM

CD-ROM was originally chosen for two reasons. First, the
equipment to retrieve data is relatively cheap. CD-ROM
technology is based on audio CD technology. This has the benefit
of a mass market and players are inexpensive. CD-ROM drives are
much cheaper than any other form of optical disk drive. The
price differential is now reducing but when ADONIS took the
decision to use CD-ROM the difference was almost a factor of 10
greater for WORM drives. The second advantage of CD-ROM is that
it is a cheap and simple process to make multiple copies. This
is of great benefit for publishing applications. The
disadvantage is that initial production costs for CD-ROM are
relatively high.The data has to be stored on an intermediary
medium and then process it before disc manufacture and
duplication. However, duplicating WORM disks can be a lengthy
and expensive process. A balance needs to be struck, therefore,
if multiple copies are required. In 1986 ADONIS decided that,
with less than 20 copies required, CD-ROM was the answer.

In cases where multiple copies are not required, WORM disks are
financially more attractive. There have been several
experimental projects involving the use of WORM disks for
document supply applications. In particular at the Library of
Congress in the USA and at CNRS in Paris. The latter went as far
as to experiment with the direct transmission to remote
facsimile machines. At the Library of Congress use was limited
to workstations for readers. The future of the Library of
Congress project is unclear and may concentrate on conservation

rather than document delivery aspects. CNRS, in their new home
at Nancy in eastern France, have recently announced plans for
the large scale use of electronic storage using facsimile
encoding and WORM disk storage.

2.4 Electronic Document Delivery

Facsimile transmission is one of the oldest examples of
electronic communication technologies in every day use. It was
developed, in the early 1840s, as a spin-off from trying to
solve another problem. (At that time the problem was
communication between railway signal-boxes.) In its earliest
form facsimile transmission had to rely on the telegraph
network. The development of the telephone and the telephone
network was still some time away. Consequently, early use of
facsimile transmission was limited. It was used over the
developing radio network in the early 1900s but its use over the
telephone network was very limited until the 1920s. Then, it was
limited to specialised applications, mainly for the transmission
of newspaper pictures and weather maps. It was not until the
1960s that any real progress was made. This was mainly due to
the Japanese. As well as expertise in office equipment, the
Japanese realized the benefits of facsimile for electronic
transmission of the Kanji alphabet. This is extremely difficult
to convert into character encoding. Developments in facsimile
transmission then took place at a tremendous rate. After over a
century of virtual inactivity in just 12 years (1968 to 1980)
there were no fewer than three international standards developed
and implemented. A fourth recommendation followed 4 years later
(see section 2.4.2). Today there are so many facsimile machines
in the world that nobody counts them any more - probably
approaching 10 million in total. All of them are manufactured in
the Far East, mainly in Japan and almost half of them are also
used there. The simultaneous development of the public switched
telephone network (PSTN) on a world wide scale, with automatic
switching, means that it is now possible to transmit documents
to any one of the millions of facsimile machines now in
existence. An exception is those machines connected to private
circuits.

2.4.1 The CCITT Group III Facsimile Standard

It was inevitable that facsimile transmission should be used for
document delivery. The first use is not recorded but it was
probably not until the late 1960s[15]. Even then it was little
used. It was slow and expensive in transmission as well as
equipment costs. The introduction of the CCITT Group III
standard in 1980 was the first universal standard. Machine
prices began to fall and transmission times improved. There is
a lot of confusion about transmission times. Most manufacturers
base it on a "standard" page. The pages of learned journals have
far more data per page which increases the transmission time.
Many experiments with the use of group III machines took place

in the early 1980s. A typical experiment was that between the BLDSC and the Chalmers University of Technology in Gothenburg, Sweden. In the first quarter of 1982 over 1,000 pages were transmitted. Transmission time averaged 2 minutes per page and about 25% of pages had to be retransmitted because of quality problems. The machines used were expensive, over £5,000 each.

Today the use of group III transmission has increased. For example, BLDSC is transmitting over 1,000 pages per week to customers all over the world. But there are inherent disadvantages in the use of group III facsimile machines for document delivery purposes. These include:

1. Transmission times still in excess of one minute per page and transmission is, therefore, expensive for multi-page articles.
2. Most machines work on the hopper feed principle and it is necessary to make a photocopy of articles in bound books. This is time consuming, adds additional expense and leads to loss of quality.
3. The majority of machines use thermal paper in the printer. The archival qualities of this paper are very limited.
4. The normal resolution is 200 lines per inch by 100 lines per inch (although 200 by 200 lines per inch, fine resolution, can be supported). Even the fine resolution is not adequate for some of the small text, particularly sub- and super-scripts in formulae.
5. Until recently there was no error correction; even now it is limited.

Machines are now available which will overcome some of these problems, eg. machines with laser, as opposed to thermal, printers and machines with flat-bed platens. The problems of speed and resolution have not yet been overcome except in a proprietary way. Error correction and detection have now been added to the group III standard although not all machines are able to support these improvements.

2.4.2 The CCITT Group IV Facsimile Standard

The group IV facsimile standard was ratified by the CCITT in 1984. It has several advantages as far as document delivery is concerned. A page is transmitted in about 10 seconds. The machines use laser printers as standard. 200 by 200 lines per inch is the minimum resolution which is supported and resolution can be up to 400 by 400 lines per inch. Full error correction is incorporated in the protocol. In combination the result of these improvements means that the quality of a transmitted page is indistinguishable from a photocopy.

A major disadvantage of the group IV standard is that it requires a digital rather than analogue transmission medium. This is available on a private point-to-point basis or on the infant Integrated Services Digital Network (ISDN). It will be

some years before ISDN becomes widely available, but prototype
networks have been available in limited areas for some time. In
the UK a pilot network, IDA, became available in 1985. The BLDSC
decided to experiment with group IV machines using the IDA
network. The first page was transmitted from BLDSC at Boston Spa
in Yorkshire to University College, London in September 1986.
This was probably the first commercial use of group IV facsimile
transmission over a public switched network anywhere in the
world. Network problems limited the value of the trial but
results were encouraging when the system was operational. The
introduction of ISDN has not occurred as quickly as originally
expected. Trials have been very limited. The problem of a flat-
bed platen has only recently been resolved with the introduction
of a Fujitsu machine in place of the NEC machines used
originally in the trials at BLDSC.

Apart from its high quality, a further attraction of group IV
is its low transmission cost. In the UK at present, ISDN has the
same tariff as PSTN, although connection charges are higher for
ISDN. The effect of this is that an average 10 page article can
be transmitted over ISDN for the same cost as a single page
using group III transmission. Depending on circumstances this
means that an article can be transmitted more cheaply than using
conventional methods. In the UK the group IV transmission cost
of a 10 page article in the local call area at off-peak rates is
£0.05. At peak rate and long distance, the cost rises to about
£0.50. For comparison, the cost of postage and packing of a
photocopy at BLDSC is about £0.75. Thus, the high cost of group
IV machines (currently at least double the price of group III
machines with comparable features) and the high cost of
connection and line rental of ISDN still make it financially
attractive compared to group III transmission, and even the use
of postal services, provided the volumes are high.

The ability to scan and transmit high volumes must be resolved
before group IV transmission can be used extensively for
document supply applications. The production versions of group
IV machines currently on the market are simply duplicates of
group III machines from an operating point of view. The
potential of group IV allows far more than just scanning a
document, transmitting it and printing it at the receiving end.
Group IV machines work on the store and forward principle. All
the pages of a document are scanned into the memory of the
machine before transmission begins. Thus, transmission is not
dependent upon the time taken to scan a page. Similarly, at the
receiving end, the printing takes place after the whole document
has been received. This mode of operation allows for scanning,
transmission and printing to be separated to a much greater
degree than is possible with the method of operation of most
group III machines.

If it is assumed that scanning and compression takes twice as
long as transmission then the transmission line is idle for 50%

of the time. Thus, a single line could support two scanners. This is not possible with the current design of machine and would require a much larger buffer store than those used at present. If the transmission line were to be used for 24 hours per day, then in a single 8 hour shift it would be possible to employ up to 6 scanners. This is technically feasible as the store and forward method allows for delayed transmission. There would be a great increase in line productivity. Also at the receiving end it is not necessary to print documents immediately on reception. With a suitably enlarged buffer store it should be possible to store documents electronically on reception and print them on demand. It should also be possible to call them up over a local area network for viewing on a screen at the end-user's workplace.

2.4.3 Solutions to the Problem

The decoupling of the processes of scanning, transmission and printing for facsimile transmission could be achieved with group III, as well as group IV, machines. Group III machines now exist which work using the store and forward method. In addition, fax cards are available for use with microcomputers. These allow documents created on a microcomputer to be transmitted directly to a facsimile machine. Some cards also allow for a document scanner to be connected and images to be transmitted. Most of these cards are rather slow and the quality of the image is not very good. Proposals have been made to increase the transmission speed of group III. Some group III machines also allow higher resolution, up to 400 lines per inch, on a proprietary basis. Thus, in future, it may be possible to achieve the quality of group IV transmission with group III machines. In order to achieve this it will be necessary for machines for both transmission and reception to be similarly upgraded. This may prove to be as expensive as using group IV equipment.

Group IV is, in some aspects, over specified. It has full error correction which is used on a transmission medium, ISDN, which itself is virtually error free. The quality and transmission speed of group IV are adequate but the machines are expensive and currently do not meet the needs for document delivery applications. Theoretically, it should be possible to use a scanner connected via a micro-computer to ISDN and thence to a laser printer via a second micro-computer. This would enable the quality and speed of transmission of group IV to be achieved but at lower cost. Whilst it is possible to do this using group III fax cards at present; these are not yet available for group IV.

2.4.4 Direct delivery from full text databases

It is theoretically possible to transmit images from a facsimile encoded, full text database to a remote facsimile machine. In practice, this proves to be rather difficult. To date, most full text databases have used the resolution of 300 lines per inch.

This has been chosen as a compromise between the large amount of data generated at the preferred resolution of 400 lines per inch and the inadequate resolution of 200 lines per inch. Although 300 lines per inch is quoted in the CCITT group IV standard as one of the optional resolutions which can be supported, there are currently no machines which do support it. Thus, in order to transmit from a full text database it is necessary to convert the resolution to one which is supported. Techniques for doing this conversion do exist but at present they tend to be slow and often lead to a loss of image quality. This should improve in the not too distant future with the advent of more powerful processing power.

3. Necessary Developments

In the above description of the current status of document delivery there are several key steps which must take place before real progress can be made.

3.1 Selection of Documents

A better method of selecting documents will be necessary if automation is to be employed. Asking for a green book published last year on a certain topic may succeed (just) in a local library today. It is unlikely to do so for much longer. Searching on-line databases is a fairly expensive operation. For this reason it tends to be done by information specialists rather than end-users. There are signs that the advent of databases on CD-ROM, with no associated transmission or on-line use costs, may change this. At present most CD-ROM databases employ the fairly complex searching methods that were designed for rapid retrieval from on-line databases. This should change in time to a system of using free text searches which can be more easily understood by end-users. The direct methods for ordering from on-line databases which exist today will be extended to allow direct ordering from CD-ROM databases. Technology will provide more time saving methods. For example, the system outlined in section 1 above is based on the ability to scan citations using optical character recognition (OCR) techniques. The resulting data can be analyzed, formatted into fields and a request made to a supply centre.

3.2 Ordering of Documents

It will be possible to use the automatic matching and sorting techniques within supply centres only for those requests which are in machine readable format. It is possible that conventional, postal requests could be converted by supply centres into machine readable format using OCR techniques. Such techniques can now cope with handwritten as well as well as printed text. Problems may arise with the automatic formatting of text converted by OCR. This problem should be resolved in the not too distant future.

3.3 Processing of Requests

In order to provide faster turnaround times, documents will have
to be stored in electronic format. With the current methods of
storing documents in facsimile encoded format, large data stores
will be required. As discussed above there may be developments
in this area, but there will always be a need for some form of
mass storage. Note that it is not essential to provide immediate
access. Surveys of readers needs have shown that this is not
essential[16]. In many cases overnight delivery is quite adequate.
For this reason some form of sequential storage could be used.
An example of this is the recently announced digital paper tape.
Requests could be automatically sorted into order and processed
within a matter of minutes of receipt. On demand scanning of
material not held in electronic format will be available but may
mean further delay whilst documents are retrieved and prepared
for scanning.

3.4 Delivery of documents

The essential item is the development of ISDN. There will almost
certainly be improvements in communication using PSTN but these
will not give all the advantages that ISDN will provide. These
include a public, switchable, digital network which provides a
transmission rate of 64 kbits/second and which is widely
available. This will revolutionize document delivery. If ISDN is
further delayed in its implementation other methods of achieving
broadband transmission are possible. It is quite feasible to
provide such circuits using satellite transmission. Indeed, an
attempt has already taken place to achieve this[17]. This attempt
failed for financial, rather than technical, reasons. The
development of direct broadcast satellite (DBS) transmission may
a more viable alternative. DBS can transmit data as well as
television signals. The receivers required for DBS television
are relatively cheap because of the mass market they enjoy. The
receivers for data are exactly the same as for television
signals, the only difference is that an extra decoder is
required. Although not ideal for point-to-point transmission,
signalling systems can be developed so that documents are only
received at a single station. This is effectively the same as a
circuit switched channel.

4. Barriers which may delay or prevent progress

Many of the activities outlined above exist today, but few of
them are in common use. The principal reason for this is that,
as stated above, library budgets are coming under increasing
pressure. Although libraries may wish to invest in automation,
it is becoming increasingly difficult for them to find
sufficient money to do so. There are exceptions and progress has
been made by some institutions. But, even when money is
available for libraries to make investments, other problems
arise.

As far as document delivery is concerned, copyright is probably the most contentious issue at present. For many years publishers have been concerned about the systematic photocopying of journals. ADONIS is an attempt to counter that threat. The widespread use of electronic storage and transmission presents an even bigger threat than photocopying. But technology also provides a means of control. ADONIS was developed with such a thought in mind. In the ADONIS system, as articles are requested their use is recorded automatically. This is a simple matter to organize and control in a workstation. But the supply of single copies of articles is not financially attractive for publishers. In the proposed commercial phase of ADONIS, it is planned that the use fee for making copies from the electronic version will be related to whether or not the user also subscribes to the hard copy version. A lower fee will be charged for journals which are also held in printed format. In this way publishers hope to preserve their income. Whether such a system will be attractive to users remains to be seen. Casual use will presumably be left to be satisfied by supply centres. They too will be required to pay a use fee. A further premise of ADONIS was that an automated system would be cheaper to operate than a manual system for supply centres. The saving would be shared between the publisher, as a use fee, and the supply centre. Use of the trial ADONIS system has shown that in order to realise these savings it is necessary to automate the entire process of supply, not just the retrieval from the shelf and photocopying operations.

Electronic storage is relatively easy to control. If pages are scanned on demand and then transmitted to remote locations, it is more difficult to exercise control. It will soon be possible for supply centres to transmit articles using either group III or IV facsimile machines to a recipient who does not immediately print out the article, but stores it in electronic format. It could be stored for reasons of expediency, but it could be stored for archival purposes. This could entail use by several users and the possibility of multiple copies being made. This is clearly in contravention of the fair use for purposes of research or private study as permitted by UK and other copyright legislation. A close degree of cooperation is required between publisher, libraries and user. Publishers will not give their rights away, nor should they be expected so to do. Agreement will be required for such use. It is not at all clear who should be responsible for such agreements.

Solutions to this and other problems concerning copyright will be needed before major advances can be made. Problems of a technical nature will not be a barrier to progress. Indeed, technology must assist rather than hinder progress. If one technical solution does not work, then another one will quickly be found. Those which offer a cheap solution, *vide* CD-ROM and facsimile machines, will continue to occupy a substantial market share. This may prove difficult to shift in time.

5. Conclusion

Through the advent of various forms of technology, many of which are available today, document supply looks set for major changes in the course of the 1990s. The pace of these changes is very difficult to predict. There seem to be two changes, those of high speed electronic document delivery and optical storage, which will have most impact. The first will be delayed until ISDN is widely available. It is not clear, in spite of the effort being put into it, when this will happen. The timing of the second is less easy to predict, market forces will be the determining factor.

It is also difficult to predict which of the two technologies will predominate. In one sense, the two are complementary. That is, documents which are stored in electronic format can be easily transmitted. In another sense, the two are in competition. It is not necessary to transmit documents which are held locally in electronic format. The proposed ADONIS service provides a good example of the quandary. The service is to be aimed at high volume users of those journals which are held on the system. Depending on the price charged for use of the ADONIS system, the potential customers may find it economically more attractive to cancel their subscriptions and obtain the documents electronically, and virtually instantaneously, from a supply centre. If this did happen, publishers would need to rethink their strategy. An easy option would be for publishers not to make the material available in electronic format. The technology is fast approaching the point where, if the publishers did not publish the material in electronic format, somebody else would. At least if the publishers are responsible for the electronic format they have some form of control over it. If a third party scans and stores journals, the publishers may lose all control. This could lead to the demise of the publishing of learned journals in conventional, or any other, format.

It is not in anybody's interest that this should happen. But very soon high use material will be available in electronic format. The source of the material could either be in-house from cheap mass storage or else from a remote source on demand via facsimile delivery. The real question is whether it will be cheaper to store documents electronically in-house or will it be cheaper to request them on demand and have high quality copies delivered in a matter of hours? The signs at present are that the user interface for this type of technology will be the same. A user workstation, based on a desk top microcomputer, will be capable of performing both tasks. It will not matter whether a document is held locally or remotely. The same workstation will be capable of either displaying documents on a high resolution screen or printing them on a high quality printer. Such a workstation may be able to decide automatically where a particular document is held. This could be linked with a pricing algorithm. Documents would always be obtained from the cheapest source; or it could be an algorithm based on speed of supply, documents would be obtained from the fastest source of supply.

There is also the possibility that changes in other library functions may lead to changes in the process of document supply. For conservation purposes facsimile scanning may prove to be the most cost effective course of action. (For archival purposes the storage media used is not of great importance. Once the material is captured electronically, it is fairly easy to convert from one medium to another.) Articles would then be available in electronic format for document supply purposes.

There may be a change in the method of publishing. There seems to be little possibility of this happening within the next 10 years, unless publishers find a way of protecting their revenue. Indeed, over 10 years ago predictions were made concerning the use of electronic publishing in the early or mid 1980s.[18] These have proved to be wrong, there seems little reason to think that they will come true in the next 10 years.

Of course, there may be some technological breakthrough that occurs before this book is published which renders every thing above obsolete overnight. I shall not speculate what that breakthrough might be. If I could prophesy what it may be, I would not be writing this chapter! Even if such a dramatic change does occur there seems little likelihood that paper will be eliminated. The paperless office is still a distant dream. The photocopy machine began a trend of duplicating paper, the facsimile machine not only duplicates at the touch of a button but also spreads copies all around the world. Electronic storage will facilitate obtaining paper copies rather than reducing the volume of paper. Further advances in technology will make these processes even easier in future.

References

1. CAWKELL, A. E. Progress in Electronic Publishing Related Technologies and Some Prophecies. In: Mastroddi, F. ed. *Electronic Publishing: the New Way to Communicate* London CEC/Kogan Page 1987 Publication No EUR 10978 EN ISBN 1-85091-263-7 pp. 253-264

2. The first recorded use of the term appears to be: LINE, M. B., Document supply: an essential support to science and technology. *Journal of Scientific and Industrial Research (India)*, **38**(2) 1979: pp. 53-57

3. *Directory of Online Databases*, quarterly, Cuadra/Elsevier

4. GOOD, B. and BARDEN, P., *Information Flows into Industrial Research*. Centre for the Exploitation of Science and

914

Technology and the British Library Document Supply Centre, UK, 1989. ISBN 0-712-32065-2

5. BOUCHER, Virginia, The impact of OCLC on interlibrary loan in the United States. *Interlending and Document Supply,* **15**(3) 1987: pp. 74-79

6. ADAMS, R., Development of the automation of interlending by microcomputer (AIM) system at Leicester Polytechnic. *Program,* **19**(1) 1985: pp. 48-58

7. BERGER, Mary C. Document delivery by database producers - closing the loop. *Information Services & Use,* **8** 1988: pp. 195-200

8. HENDLEY, A. *Videodiscs, Compact Discs and Digital Optical Disks.* Hatfield, Cimtech, The Hatfield Polytechnic, 1985, 208p. (Cimtech publication 23)

9. CAMPBELL, R. and STERN, B. T., ADONIS- the story so far. In: Oppenheim, C. ed. *CD-ROM Fundamentals to applications.* London, Butterworths, 1988 ISBN 0-408-00746-X pp. 181-219

10. YANNAKOUDIS, E.J., and RIDLEY, M.J., The DOCMATCH Project: automating document delivery by linking references to full text databases. *Outlook on Research Libraries,* 11 (9) 1989: pp. 3-7

11. SOULE, J., TRANSDOC, European programme for electronic storage and document delivery. In: Ahmed, H. and Joachim, W. eds. *International Library Cooperation. Proceedings of the 10th Essen Symposium, Oct. 19-22 1987.(Publications of Essen University Library Vol. 10)* ISBN 3-922602-11-8 pp. 264-279

12. PRICE, J., The optical disk pilot program at the Library of Congress. *Videodisc and Optical Disk,* Nov-Dec 1984: pp. 424-432

13. BARDEN, P., Developments in a CD-ROM jukebox for the ADONIS system. *Program,* **23**(4) 1989: pp. 437-441

14. BUCKINGHAM, M., The Knowledge Warehouse: technical issues. *The Electronic Library,* **6**(1) 1988: pp. 6-9

15. ANAND, Havelin. Interlibrary loan and document delivery using telefacsimile transmission. Part 1 Preliminary study. *The Electronic Library,* **5**(1) 1987: pp. 28-33. Part 2 Telefacsimile projects. *op. cit.* **5**(2) 1987: pp. 100-107

16. FJALLBRANT, N. What the user wants in a document delivery service. In: *Proceedings 8th International Online Information Meeting,* 1984, London pp. 533-539.

17. RAITT, D. I. and CASAS, J. M. The applications and implications for APOLLO for satellite document delivery. *Space Communication and Broadcasting,* **4**(5) 1986: pp. 375-383

18. LANCASTER, F. Wilfred. *Towards paperless information systems.* New York and London, Academic Press, 1978.

CHAPTER 40. LIBRARY SYSTEMS

Lucy TEDD
Consultant
Aberystwyth, U.K.

Introduction

Computer systems are now comparatively commonplace in many libraries
all over the world. They are used to assist in the management of the
"housekeeping" functions of libraries, such as keeping track of who has what
book out (circulation control), maintaining and providing access to the items
in the collection (cataloguing), obtaining new items for the collection
(acquisitions) and looking after periodicals (serials control). The
importance of, and therefore problems related to, these functions vary in
different types of library. For instance in a special library much of the
key information will be found in serial publications and so much of the
library's budget will be involved in acquiring, housing, circulating serials;
this contrasts with a public library which may be involved mainly in lending
stock and keeping details of these loans. Computers are also used in all
types of library for "information retrieval" generally and for assisting with
general administrative tasks. This Chapter, however, will concentrate on the
housekeeping or library management aspects.

Generally speaking computer-based systems are introduced to libraries
in order to provide a better service at a lesser (or not greater) cost or to
provide added benefits; in essence to help provide a more effective and
efficient service. However this will not happen automatically and, as with
any information technology that is introduced to the workplace, staff need to
be adequately educated and trained in its use for the new service to be
successful. Dyer and Morris[1] have produced a guide looking at the reasons
why library automation may be inefficient and suggesting some solutions
relating to the human aspects of library automation.

Brief historical aspects

In the mid-1960s the Library of Congress (LC) in the U.S. started to
experiment with the production of MARC (machine-readable catalogue) records.
In Britain the then British National Bibliography (BNB) co-operated in the
development of the MARC record structure, the aim of which was to enable
bibliographic descriptions to be communicated in a machine-readable form
which could then be reformatted as necessary for any particular application.
Between 1968 and 1974 the use of MARC at LC and the BNB was experimental and
several libraries received copies of MARC records on magnetic tape for use in
the production of local catalogues. Since the mid-1970s the MARC record
structure has been used in many countries for the production of national
bibliographies. A universal MARC format, known as UNIMARC, was produced by a
working group containing representatives from Australia, Austria, Belgium,

During the early 1960s several libraries in North America and Britain
began to experiment with using computers. In the U.S. much of this work was
carried out in special libraries and university libraries; for instance the
Douglas Aircraft Corporation started to produce catalogue cards by computer.
In Britain public libraries have always been as involved as academic and
special libraries in developing computer-based systems. In 1965, the
metropolitan boroughs of London were reorganised and several (e.g. Barnet,
Camden, Greenwich and Southwark) decided to use computers to assist in the
problems of producing unified catalogues. Eighty-column punched cards were
used with the resulting catalogue being printed on line printer paper.

Canada, Denmark, Finland, France, German Democratic Republic, Federal
Republic of Germany, Great Britain, Hungary, Ireland, Netherlands, U.S.S.R.,
U.S.A. and Yugoslavia; this was designed to facilitate the international
exchange of bibliographic data between national agencies.

During the early 1970s libraries began to use their parent body's
computer system and 'local' systems were designed, programmed and implemented
by staff at the organisation's computer centre. In those days computers were
large, general purpose, expensive machines requiring a large staff of
programmers, systems analysts and operators. Most of the library systems
developed during this phase were designed to deal with a single application.

The 1970s saw a growth in co-operative services and resource sharing
amongst libraries. In the U.K. the two major co-operative systems which
emerged, after initial government funding, were BLCMP (Library Services) Ltd.
(formerly the Birmingham Libraries Co-operative Mechanization Project) and
SLS Ltd. (formerly SWALCAP (South-Western Academic Libraries Co-operative
Automation Project) Library Services). BLCMP developed a co-operative
cataloguing service based on a database of U.K. and LC MARC records as well
as MARC records compiled by members of the co-operative for materials not
already in the database. SLS initially developed a circulation system for
its member libraries. Both BLCMP and SLS have continued developing their
systems and services and their current inhouse stand-alone systems will be
described later. There are also many examples of co-operative systems in
North America. The largest of these is OCLC, originally the Ohio College
Library Center and now known as the Online Computer Library Center. OCLC was
set up in 1967 with the two main objectives of sharing resources and reducing
the rate of rise of library costs in 50 academic libraries in the state of
Ohio. By the late 1980s there were several thousand libraries covering North
America, Europe and Australia gaining access to OCLC's large database of MARC
records. UTLAS, the University of Toronto Library Automation System, is a
Canadian-based co-operative. It developed from an online catalogue support
service using MARC records at the University of Toronto. Apart from U.K. and
LC MARC records the database contains Canadian MARC records, Fichier MARC
Québecois (the database of the Bibliothèque Nationale du Québec) and
Japan/MARC records from the National Diet Library in Japan. Recently[2]
UTLAS has been involved in the processing of Chinese characters as many
libraries in Asia as well as in Canada and the U.S. make use of its services.
Other North American co-operatives that started to be developed in the 1970s
were the Washington Library Network (WLN) and the Research Libraries
Information Network (RLIN). WLN offers shared cataloguing, authority
control, ordering, fund accounting and interlibrary holdings records to its
member libraries, most of which are located in the Pacific North-West of the
U.S.. The software developed by WLN for its services has proved to be very
portable and has been used in various academic libraries as well as the
national libraries of Australia, New Zealand, and Singapore. RLIN was set up
to offer the four main research libraries in the U.S. (Columbia University
Library, Harvard University Library, New York Public Library and Yale
University Library) shared access to their databases of bibliographic records
and which offer various cataloguing support services and related products.
Saffady[3] surveys the services offered by six bibliographic utilities
(including OCLC, UTLAS, RLIN and WLN) in North America.

In the late 1970s several libraries started to supplement the
computing facilities available from their parent authority by having a
minicomputer installed in the library. The trend for libraries to be in
charge of their own computing facilities accelerated in the 1980s with the
availability of microcomputer systems and with the development of packaged

918

hardware and software (or turnkey) systems for library housekeeping purposes. Such systems will be described. A review of computer-based library systems since the 1960s is provided by Tedd[4].

Library housekeeping systems

Over the years the use of computers to assist with the management of a single housekeeping function has developed into a variety of large, multi-functional, integrated systems being produced specifically for libraries. Manson[5] defines the basic requirements for a system to be integrated as:

- there should be consistency and integrity of data across all applications. Where data are copied, say from the cataloguing file to a circulation file, this is carried out by the system which will maintain the links between the two files. Typically, the librarian would only be permitted to add or to update records via the cataloguing module and the system will see that these changes are reflected in the acquisitions and circulation databases.

- transactions, such as placing an order or recording a loan, should update the status of an item and this change in status should be immediately viewable in the catalogue module or in the database enquiry module.

- there should be easy movement between the functions, especially between say enquiry and reservation in a circulation module.

Leeves[6] provides a guide to the various organisations providing hardware and software products for library management purposes.

Cataloguing

A basic function of any library is to keep records of items in the collection. Many of the current computer-based systems used incorporate the following features:

- allow online access to a database of potentially needed bibliographic records. With many national agencies using the MARC format to produce national bibliographies the 'intellectual' task of cataloguing need not be replicated in all libraries. Thus many libraries acquire their records in machine-readable form from national agencies, bibliographic utilities or other similar organisations.

- allow for records to be input online, perhaps using formatted screens for items that are not available elsewhere.

- provide online authority control to ensure consistency of search terms or phrases. A linked function is the ability to maintain the authority file by creating and amending headings and associated references.

Most of the packages are flexible and allow the librarian many options in the setting up of the catalogue database. It is important that any librarian takes into account the needs of the users of the catalogue in deciding which data elements or fields be included in the bibliographic record. The MARC format is a very full format, as might be required by a national bibliographic agency, but it would probably not be needed in its entirety by any particular library. A number of systems include the use of

MARC, perhaps for the input of records from an external source; sometimes these records are converted to an internal record structure for processing. Record suppliers sometimes provide an interface for MARC records to be downloaded into a local system. For instance, the British Library Automated Information Service (BLAISE) which supports an online search service giving access to U.K. and LC MARC records (and a variety of other bibliographic data) has developed BLAISE RECORDER, a software package to run on an IBM PC microcomputer for the downloading of records.

Interest in authority control has increased dramatically during the 1980s and many of the integrated systems provide facilities for this as detailed by Johnston[7]. Authority control is usually provided by having a separate authority file which controls headings added to the main bibliographic file. Some systems provide a thesaurus function which incorporates broader terms, narrower terms, related terms and so on.

Access to the catalogue

Most of the early computer-based catalogue systems relied on the actual catalogue being prepared on to some physical medium such as catalogue cards, line-printer paper, typeset into a book or on Computer Output Microfiche (COM). The use of catalogue cards as a form of output was much more used in North America than in Britain where COM fiche tended to be the most used form. When a catalogue is to be made available in some physical form the rules by which the records are to be filed (letter by letter or word by word etc.) need to be decided as well as the access points to the record (author, classification number etc.)

During the 1980s online public access catalogues (OPACs) began to appear. The developments in computer technology enabled many of the library systems to support access by several workstations so that the catalogue database could be searched directly. Many of these OPACs provide facilities, similar to those available from the online search services, such as Dialog, for searching by keywords or phrases from various fields of the cataloguing record and to link the search terms using the boolean operators of AND, OR and NOT. Some OPACs are menu-driven whilst some use a mixture of menus, commands (or function keys) and prompts. The British Library Research and Development Department (BLR&DD) has funded a number of projects related to OPACs; one of these OKAPI[8] at the Polytechnic of Central London aimed to provide extreme ease of use with effective searching. The Centre for Bibliographic Management (formerly the Centre for Catalogue Research) at Bath University organised several conferences on OPACs during the 1980s but in 1989 the focus changed slightly so that OPACs were viewed in the context of international bibliographic access; the proceedings[9] provide details of current developments in OPACs as also does Hildreth[10].

In Britain, by 1989, some 42 OPACs at university and polytechnic libraries were available to the higher academic community via JANET - the Joint Academic Network[11]. These OPACs are individually available, via local area networks at their institutions and also, through JANET which is aimed at linking the computing facilities generally in British academia. It is now possible for a searcher in one academic library to carry out an online search of the catalogue of a remote library.

A further development in OPACs has been influenced by the developments in CD-ROM technology. In the 1980s the compact disc-read only memory (CD-ROM) evolved from the developments in optical discs so that by the end of the decade there were many CD-ROM products of relevance to libraries.

Desmarais[12] provides a general overview of this area. One particular
development links OPACs and CD-ROM as some suppliers now offer libraries the
possibility to produce a 'local' CD-ROM of their catalogue, sometimes
referred to as a CD-ROMcat. Such a catalogue would be searched using a CD-
ROM player attached to a microcomputer-based workstation rather than using
the main computer system (although it may be dedicated to library work) that
is controlling all the housekeeping systems. The Library Corporation's
Bibliofile, is one example of this type of product. Bibliofile was launched
in North America in 1985 and, since librarians have enthusiastically accepted
CD-ROM as a viable storage and delivery medium, by 1989 there had been over
1000 sales. Beiser and Nelson[13] provide a detailed comparison of seven CD-
ROMcat systems available in 1989; these include Bibliofile, the General
Research Corporation's Laser Guide, Brodart Automation's Le Pac and UTLAS'
CD-PAC. CD-ROMs are of particular use in developing countries since there is
no reliance on telecommunications to access remote databases. Wright[14]
describes, amongst other CD-ROM applications, the use of Le Pac for producing
a catalogue at the University of Technology in Papua New Guinea. CD-ROMs can
also be used in the production of shared bibliographic databases; Parkes and
Wade[15] report on the first CD-ROM catalogue product in Australia, a shared
database of 670,000 bibliographic records.

Acquisitions

When computer-based acquisitions systems were first developed in the
1960s there were few options available to the designers of these systems;
most developed programs inhouse which were run in batch mode on the computer
of the library's parent organisation. Now there are a variety of
organisations such as booksellers, bibliographic utilities, national
libraries, turnkey producers whose services may be used in the design of an
acquisitions system.

The basic functions of an acquisitions system include receiving
recommendations of items to be purchased and establishing that the item is
not already on order, preparing order notes to be sent to booksellers,
maintaining details of items on order or in process, generating claims to be
sent to the bookseller for items not received, maintaining the accounts,
accessioning the items on arrival in the library and keeping statistics. An
extensive checklist of the functional capabilities of acquisition systems
available in the mid-1980s can be found in Boss et al[16]. In an integrated
system the librarian would be able to retrieve existing catalogue data to
create order records for similar or updated items and details of the progress
of an order might form the basis of the initial record in the catalogue
database.

There are often links between a given library and an outside agency,
such as a bibliographic utility or co-operative, the national library or
booksellers for the input of the basic bibliographic record related to a
particular item. In the case of the utilities a search using the ISBN
(International Standard Book Number), a unique identification number for a
given book title, will retrieve (hopefully) a record which can then be
downloaded to the local system. Such a search would usually be undertaken
using telecommunication links between the given library and the remote
utility. National libraries, have for many years enabled MARC records from
their databases to be identified, edited and then downloaded for local use.
A current development is for the national bibliographies to be produced on
CD-ROM so that they can then be searched locally. Smith and McSean[17]
describe the stages involved in planning and producing the British National

Bibliography on CD-ROM which was undertaken as a joint project with Bibliothèque Nationale in France. Following on this work a consortium also involving the national libraries in the Federal Republic of Germany, the Netherlands, Denmark and Portugal has been set up to further the compatibility and exchange of bibliographic records via CD-ROM for the benefit of libraries in the European Economic Community.

Various commercial organisations are also now using CD-ROM technology to assist in their services to libraries. Whitaker's, a British firm, launched its Bookbank CD-ROM service in 1988. This provides details of nearly 500,000 titles of books published in Britain using information collated from 13,000 publishers and has proved to be very successful in British libraries. Bowker's Books in Print CD-ROM is a similar product covering American publishing output. A standard, known as TRADACOMS, is being developed for electronic data interchange in the book world. The standard would take into account commercial messages (e.g. orders), details of publishers bibliographic databases, sales data statistics, short title records and standard address numbers[18].

Circulation systems

One of the basic features of a computer-based circulation system is the recording of details about the item on loan and to whom it is loaned. In the early systems of the 1960s this was often achieved by having the book details recorded on an 80-column punched card and borrower details on a special badge, similar to a credit card. In the 1970s many libraries, especially in the UK, began to use more sophisticated equipment for identifying books and borrowers such as bar-coded labels and light pens. Initially the manufacturers of these data collection devices solely provided the equipment and libraries had to be responsible for developing their own software. The resulting batch processed systems which were prevalent in the early-mid 1970s provided fast and reliable collection of data, eliminated the need for filing and automatically printed overdue notices but they did not provide immediate access to the files and had to rely on print-outs. By the late 1970s and early 1980s several organisations, including some which had produced data collection devices, started to market turnkey circulation systems and these in turn have developed into fully integrated systems.

The general features of a circulation system involve being able to issue and discharge items quickly and accurately, determine and locate particular titles, prepare overdue and recall notices, enable items to be reserved, indicate over-borrowing, deal with fines and produce the necessary statistics. Integrated systems enable links between the circulation system and the catalogue so that, for example, a search of an OPAC for a particular item can follow on with a statement of the availability of that item.

Serials

The basic requirements of a serials system are similar to, but more complex than, those for controlling a collection of monographs; these include selecting and ordering titles, receiving issues and claiming for issues not received (check-in), keeping current and accurate details of holdings (cataloguing), providing access to the catalogue of serials, allowing individual issues to be circulated, organising for the binding of completed volumes and assisting in the control of the financial aspects. In special libraries spending on serials accounts for much more than spending on books and so the serials control module is often the dominant one in an integrated system aimed at special libraries.

Several suppliers of serials have set up their own computer-based systems and some are now marketing systems to libraries. Blackwell's, for instance, a large British serials subscription agency with many overseas customers has developed ISIS, the Integrated Serials Information System. ISIS is a software package that can be run on a local IBM PC microcomputer and then be linked in to Blackwell's computer system in Oxford for orders, claims or cancellations. Faxon, an American subscription agency has developed a stand-alone system, Microlinx for serials control in individual libraries. Hunt and Dyer[19] compare Microlinx with the serials control module of an integrated system, Bookshelf. A general overview of serials automation is provided by Heitshu[20].

Computer systems for large-ish libraries

The following two sections cover the use of computer systems in large-ish and small-ish libraries respectively. It is difficult to draw the line accurately between the two. The first section deals with computer systems that may be used in university, polytechnic or public libraries whereas the second section deals more with microcomputer-based systems that may be used in special or college libraries.

Blunden-Ellis[21] provides an analysis of the market for large library automation systems in Britain; it is based on a similar analysis of the American market[22]. The first stand-alone, turnkey integrated system was installed in the U.K. in the late 1970s. In the following years many libraries have installed such systems and some are now in the process of upgrading their original system or replacing it with a newer system. Batt[23] reports on the use made of information technology generally by the 167 public library authorities in Britain; for instance 113, by 1989, reported that they used computers to manage circulation in at least some of their libraries. Most of these systems, 80, were stand-alone systems.

McQueen and Boss[24] report that by 1988 some 1250 commercial, integrated library systems had been installed in American libraries with perhaps 20% supporting multiple libraries. These systems were supplied by at least 39 vendors ranging from small specialist companies to large general purpose companies.

The computer systems which are now briefly described allow libraries to define their own parameters for variables such as loan periods for different categories of borrowers, fields in the bibliographic record, indexing options menus (and sometimes the language of the dialogue), printed output formats and so on. The costs in these descriptions are taken from Leeves[6] and may be used as a rough guide.

ALS ALS is a system manufacturer that has been involved with library automation since the late 1960s. As the technology has developed the company has developed suitable products for the library market. Its System V integrated stand-alone system was developed in the late 1970s. ALS has also developed a special label reader for its circulation system; this device enables books to be slid over the reader without having to be opened. ALS' current product, System 88, uses Intel 80286 processors with parallel processing to access the 320 Mbyte hard discs; Hertfordshire County libraries has installed this system. ALS has some customers in Europe.

Hardware from £40,000
Software £7,000 – £9,000 per module.

BLCMP BLCMP currently supplies automated systems to over 50 public, academic and special libraries in Britain and Ireland. The stand-alone system BLS now covers a variety of functions (the initial stand-alone system, CIRCO, of the early 1980s just covered circulation control). Users of BLS can access BLCMP's centralised database of 7.5 million MARC records[25]. BLS runs on the Data General range of 32-bit mini and microcomputers.

Hardware from £20,000 (not including terminals, light pens, telecommunications)
Software license fee £7,500

CLSI Computer Library Services International (CLSI) has been involved with library automation in America since 1971. During the 1980s CLSI started to market its products in other parts of the world and there are now about 1,500 libraries using CLSI in seven countries; examples include the National Library of China, Le Reseau des Bibliothèques de la Ville de Paris, the Helsinki Metropolitan Library network as well as several university and public libraries in Britain. In late 1988 CLSI adopted UNIX as its operating system and much of the software has been rewritten in the C programming language. CLSI was one of the first suppliers of integrated systems to provide a CD-ROMcat option – CD-CAT[26]. The CD-CAT system was written for CLSI by Online Computer Systems of Maryland, U.S.A.; this firm's software is also used for Bowker's Books in Print CD-ROM and by many of the national libraries' CD-ROMs.

For very large library systems parallel processing using Sequent Computers is used whereas in smaller libraries the Altos Series 2000 computers are used.

Hardware: £30,000 to over £1m.
Software: £25,000 to over £150,000

DS DS is a British firm which was set up, mainly by ex-Plessey personnel, when Plessey withdrew from the library market in 1983. DS' Galaxy system has proved particularly popular in British public libraries, many of which have up-graded from one system to another following on from Plessey's original data capture system, using bar-coded labels, of the early 1970s. The central computer is based on the Concurrent Computer Corporation (formerly Perkin-Elmer) 3200 series.

Hardware: central £60,000 – £350,000
          branch £3,000 – £25,000 per branch
Software: £15,000 -£80,000

Dynix The Dynix system was originally developed in the U.S. in 1983 and has been marketed in Europe since the late 1980s. Dynix uses the PICK operating system and so runs on a range of hardware including the Ultimate, Prime and Hewlett Packard. Dynix was designed as a fully integrated system accessing a common bibliographic file. Anley and Muller[27] describe the selection of of Dynix (which was chosen to replace a Plessey off-line circulation system) and its implementation using Honeywell Bull hardware at the Royal Borough of Kensington and Chelsea libraries in London. There are over 200 users of Dynix worldwide.

Hardware: £35,000 upwards

Software: £12,000 (cataloguing and circulation) –
£50,000 (all modules)

Geac Geac is a Canadian firm which developed a turnkey circulation
system that was first used in the university libraries of Guelph and Waterloo
in Canada in 1977. Each module within Geac operates using its own database
with the transfer of records between modules being transparent to the
user[28]. The original system uses Geac's own 8000 and 9000 series computers
and proprietary software. In 1988 Geac acquired an American company,
Advanced Libraries and Information Inc., which had developed a PICK-based
system for the University of Hawaii. Geac is now marketing this system,
known as ADVANCE[29], which runs on a range of machines from PCs upwards,
alongside its Geac Library Information System. Users of ADVANCE include
Boise State University, Idaho, San Francisco State University and the
Polytechnic of the South Bank in London as well as several sites in France.
There are many universities (e.g. Aston, Bangor, Dundee, Durham, Edinburgh
and Sussex) using the main Geac system.

System   ADVANCE from £50,000
(hardware and   Geac   from £200,000
software)

IBM IBM's integrated system DOBIS/LIBIS was developed by IBM in
conjunction with Dortmund University (Federal Republic of Germany) and Leuven
University (Belgium), and was first available in 1978. It runs on IBM
mainframe computers under various operating systems, such as IBM DOS/VSE or
(MVS), most of the applications are written in PL/1. DOBIS/LIBIS is now used
at about 130 libraries world-wide. Chaudhry and Ashoor of the King Fahd
University of Petroleum and Minerals Library (the IBM support centre for
DOBIS/LIBIS in Saudi Arabia) compare DOBIS/LIBIS with MINISIS[30].

Hardware: from about £110,000 for up to 300,000 records
from about £230,000 for up to 750,000 records
Software: about £60,000
or   £1,243 per month

McDonnell Douglas McDonnell Douglas' URICA system originated as a
system using a relational database structure for catalogue and enquiry
functions. In 1981 Amalgamated Wireless Australasia developed modules for
circulation, acquisitions, serials and an OPAC. The system was then taken
over by Microdata, a firm which was duly acquired by McDonnell Douglas.
URICA uses the REALITY operating system (the original PICK operating system)
and was designed as a fully integrated system[31]. There are nearly 100
users world-wide of URICA in countries such as America, Australia, New
Zealand, Singapore, Switzerland as well as almost 20 users in Britain.

Hardware: £25,000 -£600,000
Software: £15,000 – £65,000

NOTIS NOTIS the Northwestern Online Total Integrated System is an
example of an integrated system that has been around for many years having
been first developed at Northwestern University in the U.S. in 1967. All the
modules of NOTIS have evolved steadily as new hardware has become available
and as new needs were identified. For instance, a general online public
access module LUIS (Library User Information Service) was added in the 1980s
as described by Veneziano[32].

OCLC   During the 1980s OCLC developed a system for local processing known as LS/2000. LS/2000 is used by many libraries world-wide. However, in the late 1980s, OCLC Europe (OCLC's marketing organisation in Europe) decided not to market LS/2000 actively. Many libraries make use of OCLC's vast database of 20 million records both for current cataloguing and for retrospective conversion. OCLC offers various services for this:

RETROCON - a customised total conversion service carried out by OCLC staff.

MICROCON - using special workstations to create search keys and add local holdings details offline. Requests are batched, sent to OCLC and the resulting records are supplied on tape.

TAPECON - using an existing machine-readable file on tape to be matched against the OCLC database with resulting "hits" being output on to tape.

Crawford et al[33] describe their experiences in using RETROCON; it cost just over £74,000 to convert 81,590 records to machine-readable form.

SLS   SLS Information Services Ltd. developed from its co-operative services a stand-alone integrated library management system, LIBERTAS, in 1986. The system has a particularly sophisticated OPAC module being based on some of the research work carried out by Mitev et al[8]. LIBERTAS runs on the Digital Equipment Corporation's VAX series, from a Micro VAX 2000 to a VAX 6340. LIBERTAS was designed as a fully integrated system accessing a common bibliographic file. Most of the sales to date have been to British academic libraries (e.g. University of Bristol, Open University, Leeds Polytechnic, University College of Wales, Aberystwyth and several colleges within the University of London); some of these libraries were previous users of SWALCAP's services.   The Swedish Business School Library in Stockholm has also recently acquired LIBERTAS.

Hardware: £50,000 - £500,000
Software: £50,000 - £80,000

VTLS   The Virginia Tech Library System (VTLS) was developed at the Virginia Polytechnic Institute and State University in the U.S. as an integrated system incorporating all the usual modules. It runs on Hewlett Packard 3000 series computers[34]. There are over 100 users of VTLS world-wide; examples include the University of the West Indies at St. Augustine, Lund University, Sweden and the National Library of Scotland, which is one of the largest VTLS sites.

Computer systems for small-ish libraries

As could be deduced from the previous section the integrated turnkey systems for the large-ish libraries often cost hundreds of thousands of pounds taking into account all the workstations, networking software as well as the central library computer system and the library management software. Housekeeping systems for small-ish libraries cost a lot less.

By the late 1970s several libraries started to supplement the computing facilities available from their parent authority by having a minicomputer installed in the library. The minicomputer was used for a variety of functions with a popular one being the provision of online access to some of the files in a computer-based circulation system. The trend for libraries to acquire their own computing facilities accelerated greatly in

the 1980s with the appearance of microcomputer systems. The initial systems
of the early 1980s (Commodore PET, TRS 80, Apple) with perhaps 32K or 64K of
main store and perhaps 0.5 Mbyte of floppy disc storage ran under the CP/M
operating system. These microcomputers were used initially to provide
"intelligent" terminal access to remote online search services (e.g. Dialog)
or to other computers within the organisation. General database management
systems (e.g. dBase family) were used for some library housekeeping
functions, then single function systems for single users appeared and by the
late 1980s integrated systems providing modules for the major housekeeping
functions and including networking software for multi-user configurations
were developed. Many of the latter are designed to run on the IBM PC or PS/2
series of microcomputers (or compatibles). A general overview of the
software available is provided by Manson[5]; Leggate and Dyer's paper[35] was
the first (in a series of six) which formed an introduction to microcomputers
with particular reference to their use in smaller libraries.

The comparative low cost of microcomputer systems has meant that many
smaller libraries, as well as many libraries in developing countries, have
acquired systems which make use of various PC techniques such as windowing,
colour and graphics.

The following descriptions give a "flavour" of some of the packages
available for small-ish libraries; this time they are ordered by name of
package (sometimes the suppliers change). Again prices, where available,
have been taken from Leeves[6].

ADLIB/ADLIB 2. The original ADLIB package was developed in the mid-
1970s as a database management tool for individual libraries to build their
own library management system. ADLIB runs on a full range of Prime computers
and much re-writing of the original software took place during 1989. ADLIB
is now supplied by Databasix. Databasix has also produced ADLIB-OPAC which
offers input, storage and retrieval of text and pictures online using an IBM-
PC or compatible. In 1988 the UK rights to develop an ADLIB-based system to
run under UNIX was given to Digital Design and has resulted in ADLIB 2.
Examples of British users of ADLIB include Celltech, Royal Naval College,
Greenwich and BioCommerce Data Ltd; there are also users in Europe and
Australia.

```
Hardware:  ADLIB   £ 25,000 upwards
           ADLIB-2 £6,000 - £400,000
Software:  ADLIB   £12,000 upwards
           ADLIB-2 from £16,500 for all modules on a PC-based
           system
```

BOOKSHELF/BOOKSHELF PC. Bookshelf was originally designed by Logical
Choice (Computer Services) Ltd., in conjunction with the Cairns library at
the John Radcliffe Hospital in Oxford, and was installed at the Cairns
library in 1984. In 1985 the marketing of the multi-user package was taken
over by Specialist Computer Systems and Services whilst Logical Choice
continued to market a single user version known as Bookshelf-PC. Bookshelf
is now being developed by SCSS independently of Logical Choice. Bookshelf
runs on any computer supporting PICK. Most Bookshelf users are in medical,
government or special libraries in Britain (e.g. Barnado's, City of London
School for Girls, Royal College of Nursing, and Leeds General Infirmary).

CAIRS-LMS. CAIRS (Computer Assisted Information Retrieval System)
was developed by the Leatherhead Food Research Association in Britain in the
mid-1970s. A microcomputer version micro-CAIRS became available in the 1980s

and both proved to be popular systems in special libraries. In 1987 a library management systems, CAIRS-LMS, was developed to complement the information retrieval system[36]. CAIRS-LMS runs on a variety of mainframe, mini and microcomputers including IBM-PCs and compatibles for which a networked multi-user version is available for about £3,600. CAIRS-LMS is sold in Australia and New Zealand as well as in Europe.

CALM. CALM (Computer Aided Library Management) was initially developed in Israel in 1982 and by the late 1980s was being used in about 120 libraries world-wide, including 60 U.K. libraries. Out of Britain it is sometimes called LMS - Library Management System. In 1984 CALM started to be distributed in Britain by Pyramid Computers Ltd. and in 1988 DS Ltd. (producers of Galaxy) acquired a majority shareholding in Pyramid. CALM runs under MS-DOS on IBM PCs and compatibles.

Software (all modules) £5,600
Serials stand-alone   £1,750

LIBRARIAN. LIBRARIAN was developed in 1982 by a British firm, Eurotec Consultants. There are three modules available: cataloguing and enquiry, circulation and acquisitions with serials control being planned[37]. The system has been developed using a proprietary database management system which is then tailored to each customer's requirements. LIBRARIAN runs under a variety of operating systems on a range of hardware from a single-user PC to large multi-user systems; it is used mainly in British special and small academic libraries.

Software: £500 - £10,000

MANDARIN. MANDARIN is a library management package developed in Canada with modules for cataloguing, enquiry and circulation; an acquisitions module is planned[38]. MANDARIN is used by over 300 libraries, most of which are either school or college libraries in North America. In Britain the firm 20-20 Electronics is an agent for MANDARIN. MANDARIN runs on IBM-PCs, or compatibles, under MS-DOS; it can be networked.

MINISIS and CDS/ISIS. MINISIS was developed by the International Development Research Centre (IDRC) of Canada and is a minicomputer version of ISIS (Integrated Set of Information Systems) which was developed at the International Labor Office in Geneva. MINISIS is designed for use on the Hewlett Packard 3000 series of minicomputers and is used by about 140 libraries throughout the world. Chaudhry and Ashoor[30] describe its use for library housekeeping functions and compare it to DOBIS/LIBIS. Unesco has developed a microcomputer version of MINISIS which is known as CDS/ISIS. This is a general 'information retrieval' type program (i.e. users can define record structures, enter and edit records, generate indexes, search, sort, display and print records). CDS/ISIS is available with the menu dialogue in English, French, Italian and Spanish. CDS/ISIS is used extensively in developing countries as Unesco makes it available free of charge in these countries.[39]

PC/PALS. PC/PALS is a microcomputer version of the mainframe package PALS developed by Sperry in conjunction with Markato State University in the U.S.A.. In 1987 Sperry and Burroughs merged to form Unisys which markets PC/PALS. The PC version was written in conjunction with the British firm Information Management and Engineering (IME), developers of TINlib. PC/PALS runs on Unisys personal computer workstations. A UNIX version U/PALS is also being developed. PC/PALS is used mainly in Europe and North America.

Hardware: from £2,000 for a PC workstation
Software: from £5,000 for the integrated system

Sydney Library System. Sydney Library System has developed from
MicroLibrary, a microcomputer version of an integrated system (Easy Data
Integrated Library System) designed to meet the specific needs of the Exxon
libraries. Sydney has been modified over the years to meet the needs of
college and academic libraries as well as special libraries. The marketing,
support and development of this package in Europe is carried out by Soutron
Ltd. The Sydney system runs on IBM PCs or compatibles as well as the DEC
VAX range of computers. There are about 450 users of this system world-wide
with about 80 in Britain. Soutron also markets Standard, a product aimed at
smaller libraries, with limited budgets and a straightforward set of
requirements. Standard provides for an integrated catalogue with thesaurus,
OPAC, acquisitions and circulation control.

TINlib. TINlib comprises a range of modules for library housekeeping
purposes which are based on the TINman database management system developed
by Information Management and Engineering in 1983. TINman incorporates
relational database techniques and TINlib is an integrated system with
bibliographic data elements distributed round the database and shared by all
modules. There are other products such as TINlend (interlending) and TINterm
(thesaurus management) which can be used by themselves or be interfaced to
TINlib. TINlib runs on IBM PC's or compatibles; it was originally developed
to run under MS/DOS but a UNIX version is now also available.

Software: Total for single-user DOS £6,450
UNIX from £16,750

Conclusions

As can be deduced from the foregoing there have been many
developments in computer-based housekeeping systems over the past thirty
years. However all that has been described relates to the hardware and
software and not to the other aspects related to setting up a computer-based
library system. Data creation and maintenance is a major aspect and steps
have to be taken to ensure appropriate backing up policies. As with any
computer system the human element is a very important factor and staff must
be adequately trained, educated and informed as appropriate. A number of
papers on management techniques in library automation are included in
Kirkland[40]. Evaluating systems once they have been implemented and running
for a while is of course good practice with any system and Caswell[41]
describes some measures for this.

In the early days of library automation plans, hopes and desires were
written up in the library literature; then came descriptions of successfully
implemented systems and now we are beginning to see some truthful accounts
e.g. "we didn't foresee the need for a database analyst", "we were amazed at
the unexpected and wide-ranging skills required for a system
administrator"[42].

References

1. H. Dyer with A. Morris, Human aspects of library automation. Aldershot: Gower, 1989.

2. J. Cain, The development of Chinese ideographic processing for a shared cataloguing system. Program vol.24, no.2, April 1990.

3. W. Saffady, Six bibliographic utilities: a survey of cataloguing support and other services. Library Technology Reports vol.24, no.6, Nov.-Dec. 1988, pp.723-839.

4. L.A. Tedd. Computer-based library systems: a review of the last twenty-one years. Journal of Documentation vol.43, no.2, June 1987, pp.145-165.

5. P. Manson, Integrated automated systems for cataloguing, circulation and acquisitions on microcomputers: an overview of functions and products on the U.K. market. Program vol.23, no.1, January 1989, pp.1-12.

6. J. Leeves, Library systems: a buyer's guide. 2nd ed. Aldershot: Gower, 1989.

7. S.H. Johnston, Current offerings in automated authority control: a survey of vendors. Information Technology and Libraries, vol.8, no.3, September 1989, pp.236-264.

8. N. Mitev, G. Venner and S. Walker, Designing an online public access catalogue: OKAPI, a catalogue on a local area network. Library and Information Research Report 39. London: British Library, 1985.

9. International conference on bibliographic access in Europe. London: Taylor Graham, 1989.

10. C. Hildreth (ed.) The online catalogue: developments and directions. London: Library Association, 1989.

11. J.A. MacColl, JANET: a free source of online information for the academic library community in Online Information 89: Proceedings of the 13th International Online Information Meeting. pp.537-565. Oxford: Learned Information, 1989.

12. N. Desmarais, The librarian's CD-ROM handbook. London: Meckler, 1989.

13. K. Beiser and N.M. Nelson, CD-ROM public access catalogs: an assessment. Library Technology Reports vol.25, no.3, May-June 1989, pp.281-452.

14. S. Wright, Application of CD-ROM technology to libraries in developing countries. Program vol.24, no.2, April 1990.

15. J. Parkes and R. Wade, CLANN CD-CAT: the CLANN database on CD-ROM. Lasie vol.19, no.6, May-June 1989, pp.120-131.

16. R.W. Boss, S. Harrison and T. Espo, Automated acquisitions. Library Technology Reports vol.22, no.5, September/October 1986, pp.481-634.

17. R. Smith and T. McSean, Planning and producing the British National Bibliography on CD-ROM. Program vol.23, no.4, October 1989, pp.395-413.

930

18. Babel II: an account of the second conference on data standards for electronic data interchange in the book world. Vine no.75, October 1989, pp.10-12.

19. C. Hunt and H. Dyer, Automated serials control: a view of Microlinx and Bookshelf Computers in Libraries vol.9, no.5, May 1989, pp.18-21.

20. S. Heitshu, Serials automation: past, present and future in M. Tuttle and J.G. Cooke (eds.) Advances in serials management vol.2, pp.95-115. Greenwich, Connecticut, JAI Press, 1988.

21. J. Blunden-Ellis, A U.K. market study of large library automation system vendors (to January 1989). Program vol.24, no.1, January 1990, pp.59-71.

22. R.A. Walton and F.R. Bridge, Automated system marketplace 1987: maturity and competition. Library Journal vol.113, no.6, May 1988. pp.33-44.

23. C. Batt, Information technology in public libraries, 1989 Winchester: Public Libraries Research Group, 1990.

24. J. McQueen and R. Boss, Interfacing products for libraries. Library Technology Reports vol.24, no.4, July-August 1988, pp.511-603.

25. P. Stubley, BLCMP: a guide for librarians and system managers. Aldershot: Gower, 1988.

26. CD-CAT: Catalogue output on CD-ROM. Vine no.72, November 1988, pp.3-8.

27. C. Anley and K. Mullner, Dynix at Kensington and Chlesea libraries. Program vol.23, no.3, July 1989, pp.231-246.

28. D.R. Westlake, Geac: a guide for librarians and system managers. Aldershot: Gower, 1987.

29. ADVANCE: Geac's new PICK-based system. Vine no.75, October 1989, pp.13-19.

30. A.S. Chaudhry and M.S. Ashoor, Potential of DOBIS/LIBIS and MINISIS for automating library functions: a comparative study. Program vol.24, no.2, April 1990.

31. K.A. Jones and G.A. Rea, URICA: a guide for librarians and system managers. Aldershot: Gower, 1989.

32, V. Veneziano, The "new" NOTIS/LUIS indexes. Information Technology and libraries vol.8, no.1, March 1989, pp.5-19.

33. J.C. Crawford, J.A. Powles and J. Gilmartin, Database creation and management at at Glasgow College. Program vol.24, no.1, January 1990, pp.33-48.

34. D. McGrath and C. Lee, The Virginia Tech Library System (VTLS). Library Hi Tech vol.7, no.1, 1989, pp.11-28.

35. P. Leggate and H. Dyer, The microcomputer in the library: 1 Introduction. Electronic Library vol.3, no.3, 1985, pp.200-209.

36. CAIRS-LMS: a library housekeeping system based on CAIRS. *Vine* no.74, August 1989, pp.11-18.

37. LIBRARIAN: an overview. *Vine* no.72, November 1988, pp.21-25.

38. MANDARIN: a PC-based system from Canada. *Vine* no.75, October 1989, pp.25-27.

39. P. Jacso, A. Szucs, and S. Varga, Micro-CDS/ISIS: a bibliographic information management software from UNESCO. *Microcomputers for Information Management* vol.3, no.3, 1986, pp.173-198.

40. J. Kirkland (ed.) The human response to library automation. *Library Trends* vol.37, no.4, Spring 1989, pp.385-542.

41. J.V. Caswell, Performance evaluation of computerised library systems in J.A. Hewitt (ed.) *Advances in library automation and networking* vol.2, pp.95-118. Greenwich, Connecticut: JAI Press, 1988.

42. J. Drabenstott (ed.) Truth in automating: case studies in library automation. *Library Hi Tech* vol.7, no.1, pp.95-111, 1989.

Robin MANSELL
Science Policy Research Unit, Sussex University
Brighton, U.K.

INTRODUCTION

International and supra-regional organisations have an increasingly important role to play in the global restructuring of telecommunication markets. Telecommunications is no longer a domestic affair where national policy can be developed in isolation from the policies of other countries. If telecommunications is to be an effective tool of corporate strategy and if it is to link social, economic and political communities across national boundaries, policies must be developed in concert. A growing emphasis on transnational communication in the European Community (EC) requires that existing organisational relationships be modified. Changes must keep pace with developments external to the EC and they must promote the economic, social and political goals for the development of the EC marketplace.

The Commission of the European Communities (CEC) believes that:

"..information, exchange of knowledge, and communications are of vital importance in economic activity and in the balance of power in the world today. Telecommunication is the most critical area for influencing the 'nervous system' of modern society. To flourish, it has to have the optimum environmental conditions...Telecommunications must now be seen as the major component of a conglomerate global sector comprising the management and transportation of information." (1)

The Commission is moving to restructure the telecommunication market and to create a new institutional environment. Its actions need to be considered in the larger framework of international negotiations on the terms and conditions of market development. The International Telecommunication Union (ITU) and the GATT Uruguay Round of Trade Negotiations on Services provide two of the major fora for these negotiations. Both are influential in creating external constraints to the Commission's ability to introduce changes in telecommunications that contribute to its economic and social goals.

Together with the CEC, these international organisations are creating new 'rules of the game' for telecommunications. Steps are being taken in the policy, trade and standards fields which aim to create a more open, competitive marketplace for global equipment, network and service supply. Inevitably there are conflicts among those supporting the 'old' monopolistic order and those favouring a new, more competitive regime.

Technical innovations in telecommunications and computing are pushing forward the frontiers of service applications. New ways of reducing barriers of space and time in the conduct of business are being devised with the more widespread use of advanced business services, e.g. electronic data interchange, electronic mail, video and computer conferencing, etc. The need to provide these services across international boundaries has created a parallel need for institutional adjustment. These adjustments carry opportunities and threats for the EC marketplace.

A CONVERGENT POLICY ENVIRONMENT?

The telecommunications markets of the 1990s will continue to be characterised by tensions between technical opportunity and political and economic objectives. These tensions are influencing the direction of technical development, inter and intrafirm strategies, regulatory patterns and trade policy. In each of these areas there is a tension between the appropriation of telecommunications as a strategic competitive tool by large corporate users and as a tool for implementing widely accessible public services.

In the **technical** area, several major waves of innovation have radically affected the use of telecommunications. Electromechanical devices created possibilities for a transition from step-by-step and crossbar switching to automatic switching. Use of the radio frequency spectrum for microwave transmission, together with multiplexing techniques, led to improved transmission. Advances in microelectronics ultimately will lead to the complete digitalisation of telecommunication switching and transmission. Continuous innovation in software design supports an ever-growing array of service applications. Innovations in optoelectronic technologies have stimulated the use of optical fibre cables for transmission and, in the future, will make optical switching commercially viable. In computing, the cost of processing power that drives many telecommunication applications is declining at exponential rates.(2)

In the face of these developments, policy-makers are searching for ways of creating an institutional environment that encourages the incorporation of new technologies into networks and services. Their objective is to stimulate the supply of more efficient, diverse and lower cost services. But they encounter many options, each with different implications for the future costs of network and service supply and the types of advanced service applications that are likely to be provided. These options range from the expansion and upgrading of standardised public networks to the proliferation of private proprietary networks and services. Different alternatives imply varying degrees of competition in the supply of terminal and network equipment, in services and in the ways in which public telecommunication operators (PTOs) comply with their responsibilities to provide public or universal services.

Inter and intrafirm strategies with respect to the supply and use of telecommunications are increasingly important ingredients that must be reflected in telecommunications policies. Suppliers and users have varied competencies and incentives to apply new telecommunication services. These variations affect their competitiveness in domestic, regional and global markets. Policy-makers need to consider whether public intervention in the equipment or services market will support or hinder firms' attempts to maximise the potential of telecommunications and to benefit from productivity gains.

These considerations have led the EC into a continuous process of developing methods of 'regulating' the telecommunications marketplace.(3) These methods are directed to achieving a compromise among the disparate economic and political actors. Telecommunications historically has been supplied in a monopoly environment. Today there are pressures, internal as well as external to telecommunications, to introduce competition. How this should be done and what methods should be used to achieve a workable form of competition is an issue on the agenda of the CEC, the ITU and the GATT Uruguay Round of Trade in Services Negotiations. Which organisations should be responsible for determining policy, for implementing and enforcing it? How should national, regional and international organisations relate to each other? What are the enforcement mechanisms for policies once they have been established?

Trade policy is fundamental to the future prospects of the EC telecommunications market. Policy decisions here will affect whether firms can benefit from economies of scale and scope in the production of equipment and services. A key theme in the CEC's efforts to complete the internal European Market in 1992 is to enable European-based firms to take advantage of a wider market and thereby establish a more competitive position against global players from Japan and the United States.

Multilateral negotiations which aim to restructure the telecommunications environment are carried out in a wider context that is characterised by two main factors. First, national, regional and international government and industrial actors are not always fully informed of each other's concerns. They have varying levels of expertise and different priorities in the telecommunications field. For some, trade liberalisation is a high priority. For others, a gradual transition to a market structure that supports the competitiveness of the major players is more important. For still others, social policies and public service mandates take precedence. This unevenness has created considerable flux and turbulence in negotiations among suppliers, users, and governmental representatives.

Second, organisations that have coped adequately with technical change in telecommunications in the past are frequently not well-positioned to resolve policy issues and conflicts in the face of increasingly rapid technical change. There is a continuing 'mismatch' between technical potential and organisational competence. As Freeman has noted, in a period of rapid technical change:

> "..the established social and institutional framework no longer corresponds to the potential of a new techno-economic paradigm. Structural crises of adjustment are thus periods of experiment and search and of political debate and conflict leading ultimately to a new mode of regulation for the system."(4)

A **mismatch** between technology and organisational competence is a permanent fixture of any economy. Structural change and the emergence of new organisational forms are inevitable. Policy-makers must assess how existing and new organisations are shaping market outcomes at any particular point in time. In telecommunications, a major question is when and how to intervene in a market which is characterised by elements of monopoly and competition. Decisions to require technical standardisation and rules concerning the structure of markets and the behaviour of suppliers and users may be **irreversible**. They may limit future possibilities for implementing policies. Nevertheless, policies must often be negotiated in the face of uncertainty with regard to technological trends and the economic viability of service applications.

There is a tension that pervades virtually all negotiations on telecommunications in international fora. On the one hand, equipment, networks and services are components of the infrastructure which provides valuable public services. Certain services (e.g. voice telephony, telex) need to be provided economically and on a widespread or universal basis. Policies need to ensure that residential and small and medium-sized firms benefit from the introduction of advanced services. They must also ensure that traditional voice telephony services reach a reasonably high level of penetration. On the other hand, efficiency in the use of telecommunications by the business community is needed to improve the competitiveness of industry. Used as a 'strategic weapon', telecommunications can offer a vital competitive edge to firms seeking to expand their markets. Thus, the pattern of telecommunications development is vitally important to industrial as well as social policy.

NEW RULES FOR TELECOMMUNICATIONS MARKETS

The global restructuring of telecommunications will work to the advantage of European suppliers and users only if workable competition results. New entrants and existing suppliers need assurances of relative stability in the rules affecting the marketplace if they are to undertake substantial new investment. The Telecommunication Network-based Service market extends to include traditional and advanced services. It is defined as:

936

"All services that combine information production, manipulation, storage and/or distribution, with the use of telecommunication facilities and software functions".(5)

Chart 1 shows that the suppliers in this market can come from multiple industry segments. These suppliers need assurances if they are to exploit the full potential of telecommunications markets. Potential entrants need to be assured that they will not be unfairly disadvantaged by incumbent firms (i.e. PTOs) who retain substantial market power and a monopoly in segments of the service market. New "rules of the game" are emerging from multilateral negotiations in regulatory and trade policy arena.

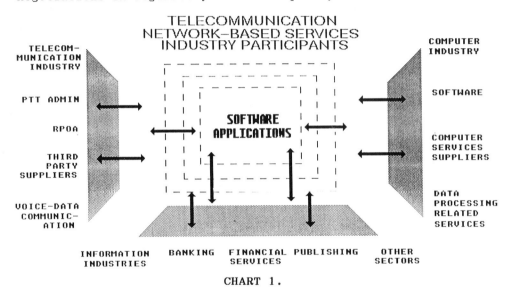

CHART 1.

The International Telecommunication Union

The ITU represents 166 countries and its regulations carry the status of international treaty law. Members of the ITU are government officials, representatives of PTOs (Administrations) or Recognised Private Operating Agencies.(6) Each of the member states of EC is individually represented in the activities of the ITU.

The ITU aims to "maintain and extend international cooperation between all members of the Union for the improvement and rational use of telecommunication of all kinds...and the development of technical facilities and their most efficient operation, with a view to improving the efficiency of telecommunication services, increasing their usefulness and making them, so far as possible, generally available to the public."(7)

The regulations for telecommunications, in effect since 1972, were superseded in July 1990 by a new set of 'International Telecommunication Regulations'. The text was finalised at an ITU Conference in Melbourne, Australia in December 1988.(8) The regulations provide a general framework of principles for the structure and organisation of global telecommunication markets. They carry implications for the restructuring of the EC market because they can be interpreted as encouraging bilateral agreements to establish telecommunication services.

With technical change and greater competition in international telecommunications, the ITU regulations have become increasingly controversial. The growing number of suppliers of international services had forced the ITU to reexamine the question as to who and what should be regulated. For example, should competitive non-PTO suppliers of international networks and services be subject to international regulation? Should these suppliers be obligated to implement the ITU's recommendations on standards and tariff principles or should they be free to develop proprietary networks and services? What are the implications of different regulations for suppliers and users within regions such as the EC?

The 1990 regulations secured a compromise among the divergent views of the role that the international regulatory apparatus should play. Some felt that the new regulations should provide an administratively centralised, detailed, and economically restrictive regime which would maximise the PTO's responsibilities and provide strong support for public service objectives. Others felt that an administratively decentralised, general and economically permissive regime would maximise opportunities for private network and service suppliers to compete in all segments of the telecommunication market.(9)

The new regulations embody a compromise which protects the rights of national governments to approve the operation of competing suppliers. However a compromise was reached that permits special arrangements between suppliers and users to meet specialised (corporate) international telecommunication needs.(10) This was aimed at encouraging telecommunication suppliers to become more responsive to business demand.

The 'Melbourne package', as the various clauses of the regulations came to be called, has been seen as a victory for operators and users of private networks since they can now negotiate 'special arrangements'. But others see the new regulations as a major defeat. They believe the door has been opened to widespread international competition which could jeopardise the ability of PTOs to meet their public service obligations.

These regulations attempt to recognise the need to balance public service and industrial policy objectives. But the ITU leaves to its members the responsibility for implementation. It has no powers of direct enforcement and there is no 'regulatory agency' to ensure that a common interpretation of the regulations is achieved. Members of ITU are free to negotiate bilateral agreements with suppliers and users wishing to enter their domestic markets. Given the multiplicity of EC telecommunication markets, the ITU regulations could provide a stimulus to divergent market development as each member state initiates separate agreements for service supply with external actors.

GATT – Uruguay Round of Negotiations on Services

Whereas the ITU regulations provide little incentive for convergent market development, the GATT Uruguay Round of trade negotiations on services provides a counteracting set of incentives. The CEC is empowered to act on behalf of the member states in matters of commercial policy and the GATT rules establish the rights of producers in almost 100 countries to sell their products in other member countries.

The United States has led pressures to include services in the current round of negotiations which is scheduled to be completed at the end of 1990. The Uruguay Round of negotiations was initiated in 1986. A two track negotiating process on goods and services was established and the Group of Negotiation on Services (GNS) agreed in December 1988 to consider services (e.g. financial, telecommunication, consultancy, tourism, etc) in their discussions.

The negotiation of an agreement on services has required detailed examination of the applicability of goods-related trade concepts to telecommunications services. Concepts including national treatment, right of establishment, non-discrimination, and transparency as well as goals such as market access have been considered.(11)

International trade in information, computer and telecommunication services requires that competing suppliers be able to access and use national telecommunication networks on an equitable basis. But the dividing line between 'competitive' services and 'monopoly' services differs among the member states of the EC. The problem for trade negotiators is to decide whether these differences amount to 'unfair' restraints to trade in which case they should be changed, or whether they do not constitute barriers to trade and should simply be made more transparent to enable suppliers to trade fairly.

In May 1989, the GATT secretariat produced a background paper which implied that all telecommunication services would be considered in the context of trade liberalisation. The paper suggested that Telecommunication Network-based Services (TNS), defined as above, could be placed on the bargaining table for trade negotiations. The GATT secretariat noted that:

"The concept includes all services which are being modified by continuous technical change. The TNS concept is flexible and dynamic. It reflects technological change and the shifting boundaries of traditional industries involved in the supply of TNS. It includes existing, and admits future, services and it ignores boundaries implied by 'value-added' service definitions."(12)

Thus the starting point for negotiation in the current round of trade negotiations is to include services such as voice telephony as well as advanced business applications in the deliberations. This does not mean that the draft of a General Agreement on Trade in Services (Gats) which is produced in July 1990 will include references to all these services, or even to telecommunications. Nevertheless, an eventual agreement on services liberalisation could include services such as voice telephony which the EC countries wish to provide under monopoly conditions.

Although the CEC negotiates on behalf of its members and can put forward a coherent view in its objectives for services liberalisation, the member states themselves remain divided over the scope of competition in the European Community market. In trade negotiations, debate has focused on the forms in which trade in telecommunication services should occur, the alternative modes of service delivery between countries, the structure of markets, and domestic and international treatment of network access and tariff practices.

Since the current round of trade negotiations is unlikely to produce a clear definition of which services should be subject to liberalisation, this could strengthen the hand of large telecommunication users and competing suppliers who wish to establish flexible, specialised services and the global opening of markets may create problems for the implementation of the CEC's plans for the Internal Community Market. These plans aim to achieve public service objectives as well as greater efficiencies in the supply and use of business telecommunication equipment and services.

Thus, the development of a viable EC telecommunications market and an appropriate regulatory framework is urgently needed. This is as much the result of internal factors relating to the creation of a Single European Market by 1992, as it is the result of the need to ensure that global processes of restructuring in telecommunications do not threaten European actors. Threats could arise from the entry of foreign competitors in the individual member states as a result of bilateral agreements that go substantially beyond the Commission's framework for liberalisation.

RESTRUCTURING THE EUROPEAN COMMUNITY MARKET

Greater competition in equipment procurement, network and service provision is envisaged as a result of the CEC's actions with respect to telecommunications. The degree of competition varies substantially from the United Kingdom where the duopoly in network provision is being reconsidered, to countries such as Greece, France, Belgium and Italy where there is continuing reluctance to liberalise the provision of some advanced services.

The Commission's 1987 'Green Paper on Telecommunications' is being implemented with the aim of creating a more open internal European market from 1992. The "overriding aim is to develop the conditions for the market to provide European users with a greater variety of telecommunications services of better quality and at lower cost, affording Europe the full internal and external benefits of a strong telecommunications sector".(13) Forecasts suggest that telecommunications could account for some 7% of the Community's gross domestic product by the year 2000. Regardless of the accuracy of such forecasts, there is virtually no argument as to the widespread impact of innovations in telecommunications.

A variety of mechanisms are being used to move toward the introduction of competition. These include directives under Article 90(3) of the Treaty of Rome, Council resolutions and recommendations and the encouragement of Memoranda of Understanding among PTOs on matters such as the implementation of Integrated Services Digital Networks (ISDN). Table 1 shows the mechanisms that have been used to urge or require the member states to move down the road toward market liberalisation.

The Commission's actions on telecommunications are directed to three main concerns - concerns which are also at the core of debates in the ITU and GATT negotiations. First, there is the problem of liberalising the use of networks. This has led to directives designed to introduce competition in terminal equipment and service markets, excluding the basic or 'reserved' markets for voice telephony and telex services. These markets currently generate approximately 90% of the PTO's revenues, but it is the data, image and text markets that are expected to grow. The PTOs and competing service providers are eager to capture these markets.

TABLE 1

EUROPEAN COMMUNITY RECOMMENDATIONS AND DIRECTIVES: TELECOMMUNICATIONS

-- Implementation of Harmonization in the Field of Telecommunications: Council Rec. 84/549/EEC.

-- First Phase of Opening up of Access to Public Telecommunications Contracts: Council Rec. 84/550/EEC.

-- Definition Phase for a Community Action in the Field of Telecommunications Technologies - R&D Programme in Advanced Communication Technologies for Europe (RACE): Council Decision 85/372/EEC

-- Use of Videoconference and Videophone Techniques for Intergovernmental Applications: Council Resolution: 86/C160/EEC.

-- Initial Stage of the Mutual Recognition of Type Approval for Telecommunications Terminal Equipment: Council Directive 86/361/EEC.

-- Community Programme for the Development of Certain Less Favoured Regions of the Community by Improving Access to Advanced Telecommunication Services (STAR): Council Regulation 86/3300/EEC.

-- Adoption of Common Technical Specifications of MAC/Packet Family of Standards for Direct Satellite Television Broadcasting: Council Directive 86/529/EEC.

-- Standardisation in the Field of Information Technology and Telecommunications: Council Decision 87/95/EEC.

-- Coordinated Introduction of the Integrated Services Digital Network (ISDN) in the European Community: Council Recommendation 86/659/EEC.

-- Coordinated Introduction of Public Pan-European Digital Mobile Communications in the European Community: Council Recommendation 87/371/EEC; Availability of Frequency Bands to be Reserved for the Coordinated Introduction of Public Pan-European Digital Land-Based Mobile Communications in the European Community: Council Directive 87/372/EEC.

-- Introduction of a Communications Network Community Programme on Trade Electronic Data Interchange Systems (TEDIS): Council Decision 87/499/EEC.

-- Community Programme in the Field of Telecommunications Technologies - R&D in Advanced Communications Technologies in Europe (RACE): Council Decision 88/28/EEC.

-- Competition in the Markets for Telecommunications Terminal Equipment: Commission Directive 88/301/EEC.

-- Development of the Common Market for Telecommunications Services and Equipment up to 1992: Council Resolution 88/C257/01.

-- Procurement Procedures of Entities Operating in the Telecommunications Sector: Proposal for a Directive COM(88)378.

-- Establishment of the Internal Market for Telecommunications Services through the Implementation of Open Network Provision: Proposal for Council Directive COM(88)825.

-- Strengthening of the Further Coordination of the Introduction of the Integrated Services Digital Network (ISDN) in the Community up to 1992: Council Resolution, 27 April 1989.

-- Standardization in the Fields of Information Technology and Telecommunications: Council Resolution, 27 April 1989.

-- Coordinated Introduction of Pan-European Land-Based Public radio Paging in the Community: Proposal for Council Recommendation COM(89)166; Frequency Bands to be Reserved for the Coordinated Introduction of Pan-European Land-Based Public Radio Paging in the Community: Proposal for a Council Directive COM(89)166.

-- Approximation on the Laws of the Member States concerning Telecommunications Terminal Equipment, including the Mutual Recognition of their Conformity: Proposal for a Council Directive COM (289)

Second, the Commission has sought to establish a consensus on who should be able to participate in these expanding markets. A consensus has been reached that will enable the PTOs to enter any market where they believe that they have the expertise. The PTOs will compete with third party service suppliers, e.g Istel UK; PTOs from other countries who expand into international service markets, e.g. British Telecom; as well as a host of other service suppliers, e.g. IBM, GEIS Co., EDS, etc.

Third, the full participation of the PTOs will require a clear separation between regulatory and operational functions. This will be necessary to ensure that PTOs are unable to exploit their dominant market position to create barriers to entry by manipulating tariff structures or failing to establish effective network access for competitive suppliers.

These steps have been taken in the name of innovation, efficiency and competitiveness. Telecommunications traditionally involved the production of a relatively homogeneous product, e.g., voice, telex, and data transmission. The PTOs offered an end-to-end service which involved little customer choice as to equipment or service applications. Technical change in telecommunications and computing has called forth increasing heterogeneity in the services demanded especially by the largest customers.

THE NEW TELECOMMUNICATIONS CUSTOMER

The 1990s will see the further development of three parallel trends in the evolution of the telecommunication infrastructure. The **first** is the upgrading of public networks to support ISDN and 'intelligent' business service applications. The **second** is the growth of in-house corporate networks and third party services. The **third** is the hybrid network which includes public and private services in a complex interconnected web of standardised and proprietary applications for business customers.

Public switched networks are being upgraded to introduce services for both the corporate and the residential community. Nevertheless, a major incentive for investment in public networks stems from the PTOs' attempt to persuade the larger corporate users to mount their service applications on public switched networks. This strategy is also reflected in the development of 'intelligent network' services that aim to simplify network management and operation by combining digital signalling with computerised databases. In the longer-term, new services will be introduced through enhancements to databases, rather than through costly reconfiguration of switching facilities. The PTO's plans for the introduction of intelligent networks aim to offer services that large corporate users require without the disadvantage of having to maintain or operate private corporate networks.

The development of public networks needs to be considered in the light of the parallel development of private corporate networks and services provided by third party suppliers. Since the 1970s, this second trend has seen the larger corporate users leasing capacity from PTOs and configuring their own applications. The growth of these networks in Europe has been slowed by disparate national regulations which affect private and public network use. In most countries private network operators have been required to limit their services to 'closed user groups', e.g. banking, automobile, etc.

Since the early 1980s, the UK has retained its status as the most liberalised market for private networking within the EC. Liberalisation, privatisation and the removal of restrictions on the use of networks have accelerated the growth of private networks. In 1987 there were approximately 11,060 private data networks in Western Europe with the UK market representing some 28% of all data networks and 45% of installed equipment.(14)

Larger corporate users also turn to third party suppliers such as Istel, GEIS Co., and IBM for services that are far more advanced than those available directly from PTOs. Third party suppliers can reduce problems associated with complex software, network management, skills shortages and the hidden costs of running a private corporate network.

The third main trend in telecommunication infrastructure is

the 'hybrid' or mixed solution. Larger users opt for a combination of public and private networks to meet their needs. As regulatory restrictions on network use in the EC are relaxed, this alternative is likely to become the predominant pattern. The hybrid alternative has implications for PTO investment strategies. In their efforts to capture the most advanced customers, PTOs have moved to develop costly business applications, sometimes at the expense of allocating resources to service development for consumers and smaller businesses who represent a more risky market.

The patterns of infrastructure development that emerge over the next decade, together with the new ways of organising and regulating telecommunication markets, will have a major impact on the efficiency of telecommunication supply and use by the corporate user. The direct costs of private corporate networks arise from the development and implementation of 'intelligent' software applications and from the costs of the underlying transmission facilities. The corporate user's evaluation of efficiencies associated with public or private networks has to be considered alongside dynamic improvements in public networks, changes in the firm's pattern of internal and external communication needs and its competitive strategies.

Even where control and management problems can be met by the public network, the firm must consider the responsiveness of the PTO (and its suppliers) to its particular telecommunication needs. For firms using networks to develop new forms of quasi-integration (i.e. long-term contractual agreements between formally independent firms), proprietary private networks are an important element in their success. For other companies, public networks that can deliver access to widely dispersed suppliers and customers may offer a better solution.

Case studies of advanced applications in the airlines, automobile and financial services industries suggest that new services are not substantially altering pre-existing economic relations.(15) Many applications simply speed up information flows at various stages of the production and marketing chain. Typically, where smaller firms have been dependent on orders from major firms, they remain so. In fact, they can experience increased costs due to the need to respond more rapidly to requests for changes in design, batch size, etc.

While the larger users can often choose between public and private networks, the range of choice for smaller firms and consumers is far more restricted. Even in the UK where competition in the provision of local exchange services is being actively encouraged, few subscribers perceive that they have alternatives. Mercury, British Telecom's major competitor, has yet to effectively target the smaller business market. Cellular radio services are far from becoming price competitive and the newly announced Personal Communication Networks in the UK are expected to levy charges for usage in excess of 20% higher than a normal voice telephone call. For the vast majority of telephone subscribers in the EC, there is unlikely to be realistic competition for traditional voice services for some time even with widespread market liberalisation and competition.

CONCLUSION

The ITU is an international organisation with a mandate to give consideration to public service and efficiency objectives, but its regulatory powers are delegated to its individual members. Within the GATT framework, the emphasis is on the steps which can be taken to reduce or eliminate barriers to trade in telecommunication services and on creating incentives for greater efficiency, innovation and competition in international services. The CEC is concerned with social, industrial and competition policy dimensions.

Telecommunication markets are being shaped by multilateral negotiations and there are complex problems as the transformation of telecommunication markets becomes increasingly widespread. If the CEC wishes to present a common face to external actors it will need to develop its own internal institutions. The social and economic role of telecommunications is important to the EC's wider industrial and social agenda. The evolution of the technical system cannot be left to market solutions or to the incentives that arise from multilateral negotiations within the ITU or GATT.

One analyst of the 'networking economy' in the United States has forecast that:

"The future network is one of great institutional, technical and legal complexity. It will be an untidy patchwork of dozens or even hundreds of players, serving different geographical regions, customer classes, software levels, and service types, with no neat classification or compartmentalisation possible. To the tidy mind of the traditionalists this will be heresy. Carriers will be engaged in multiple functions, although there will be no shortage of official attempts to establish order by segmentation.."(16)

The major issue for EC policy is whether it has the political and economic powers to encourage the development of a marketplace that works to the advantage of European-based suppliers and the widest spectrum of telecommunication users. A representative of British Telecom has forecast that by the end of the 1990s there will be four or five telecommunication operators who dominate in the global provision of services.(17) Unless European PTOs compete successfully in the international market and increase their responsiveness to their customers, the future will be dominated by AT&T, KDD and other non-European competitors.

For the telecommunications suppliers and users, the key question is "who will be in the business?". For EC policy-makers the question is how to remedy an inadequate institutional framework which copes uneasily, if at all, with the globalisation of information networks.

REFERENCES

1.   CEC (1988) "Implementing the Green Paper on the Development of the Market for Telecommunication Services and Equipment." COM(88)48 final, February.

2.   See R. Mansell (1990) "Rethinking the Telecommunications Infrastructure: The New 'Black Box'", Research Policy, forthcoming Summer 1990.

3.   See H. Ungerer and N. Costello (1988) Telecommunications in Europe, The European Perspectives Series, Brussels.

4.   C. Freeman (1988) "Preface" in G. Dosi et al. (eds.) Technical Change and Economic Theory, London, Pinter Publishers, p. 11.

5.   OECD (1989) Telecommunication Network-based Services: Policy Implications, ICCP Report No. 18, Paris; and R. Mansell (1988) "Telecommunication Network-based Services: Regulation and Market Structure in Transition," Telecommunications Policy, September, p. 246.

6.   RPOA are private network and service providers so designated by their governments. RPOA status enables participation within national delegations to ITU meetings.

7.   ITU (1989) Convention, Nice.

8.   See, ITU (1988) "International Telecommunication Regulations, Final Acts", Melbourne, December.

9.   See W. J. Drake (1989) "The CCITT: Time for Reform?" in Reforming the Global Network, International Institute of Communications, London.

10. For greater detail see, R. Mansell et al. (1990) "European Integration and Telecommunications: Restructuring Markets and Institutions", Prometheus, forthcoming Summer.

11. See OECD (1990) Trade in Information, Computer and Communications Services, ICCP Report No. 21, Paris.

12. GATT Secretariat (1989) "Multilateral Trade Negotiations, The Uruguay Round", MTN.GNS/W/52, 19 May 1989, UR-89-0062.

13. CEC (1987) "Green Paper on the Development of the Common Market for Telecommunication Services and Equipment", COM(87) 290 final.

14. Logica UK Ltd. (1987) "The Wide Area Network Market", Telematica.

15. See K. Morgan and A. Davies (1989) "Seeking Advantage from Telecommunications: Regulatory Innovation and Corporate Information Networks in the UK," Final Report, OECD/BRIE Large Telecommunication User Group Project, Brighton, September 1989.

16. E. Noam (1988) "The Public Telecommunications Network: A Concept in Transition," <u>Journal of Communications</u>, Winter.

17. D. Dey, (1990) Remarks to Plenary Session of the 8th International Telecommunications Society Conference, Venice, Managing Director, British Telecom.

Hitoshi WATANABE
NEC Corporation
Tokyo, Japan

Introduction

No one can predict what office systems will be like a decade from now. If one were pressed to make a guess, however, the answer should be based on two questions: in what directions are the desires of users heading, and in what directions is the technology developing? The answers to these questions are important because the course of future development will be determined by the extent to which technological progress will be able to fulfill the desires of users.

As Dr. Koji Kobayashi, the Chairman emeritus of NEC Corporation, has previously stated in his book (1), the future information society will see the support of human creative and intellectual activities through the fusion of Computers and Communications (C&C). He refers to this as "modern communications," and calls the resulting society supported by modern communications "Man and C&C." The most desirable office systems of the future will be achieved primarily by the implementation of modern communications, a C&C system unifying computers and communications, in the office.

Essential Requirements for Future Office Systems

What might an information worker in a modern office regard· as the most important factors involved in performing his duties creatively and smoothly? Of the many contributing factors, the following three might be the most vital:

- Multimedia Human Interface;
- Networking among Human-Beings; and,
- Response Time in Networking Environment.

These are described in detail below.

Multimedia Human Interface

Why is multimedia information important for information workers? First of all, humans perceive information about the outside world and attempt to communicate thoughts with others by utilizing the five senses. In fact, it is difficult to fully express human thoughts and ideas through information that can be conveyed only by a single medium. Using a combination of all media perceivable by humans to understand the thoughts and ideas of others is not only completely natural, it fits the very essence of human nature. If one carries this premise to the extreme, one could not refute the statement that telephones are only for blind people and that Video Display Terminals (VDTs) are only for the hearing-impaired.

How, then, are human thoughts and ideas communicated to other people through multimedia? To answer this question, let's propose a new concept of "Information Spectrum", which means the total range of accumulated information.

There are two important types of "Information Spectrum" defined below.

1) *Idea Expression Spectrum*: The amount and range of information needed to express a thought or idea is called the *Idea Expression Spectrum*. This contains the spectrum of characteristics that express each idea.

2) *Medium Spectrum*: There is a certain limit to the ability of a particular medium to convey information. This characteristic maximum information expression spectrum of each medium is called the *Medium Spectrum*.

In general, it is not easy to handle human ideas with information systems, but by introducing new concepts it is possible to make the characteristic expression spectrum of an idea the object of manipulation.

The Idea Expression Spectrum of an idea is difficult to decompose into a set of small pieces of information having different attributed values, and to observe directly from the outside. However, there are several ways of expressing a part of the Idea Expression Spectrum, in what we call multimedia, such as data, text, voice, graphic, image, gesture, etc.

This situation is analogous to the color of an object, where reflecting light from the object is composed of certain spectrum of light-wave-lengths. One can recognize this object through such light-spectrum. However, it is not necessary to recognize the object using the full range of light-spectrum. Instead the object can be recognized almost exactly through three principal colors (light-spectra), that is, red, green and blue.

Unlike light-spectra, there are no principal colors (light-spectra), representing the original Idea Expression Spectrum, through one can define a part of the Idea Expression Spectrum expressed by a medium as a Medium Spectrum. It is clear that every medium has its own native limitation of expression capability and that no single medium can express all kinds of information. So in many cases the original Idea Expression Spectrum can be represented approximately by the proper combination of several media spectra. Therefore, it is quite natural to use multimedia when one wants to communicate his idea more exactly.

Each medium spectrum is transferred, processed and manipulated through the C&C system, then those media spectra are recombined into an expression spectrum, which approximates the original Idea Expression Spectrum.

In the recombination phase, coherence of those media spectra is very important. If those are out of phase, the entire figure obtained from them becomes hard to grasp.

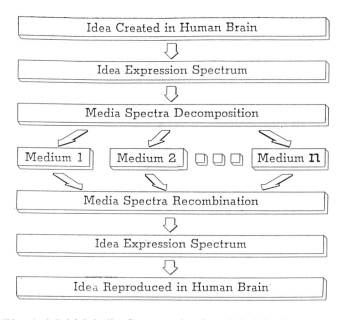

Fig. 1 Multi-Media Communications Model, through which
a Created Idea is Transferred

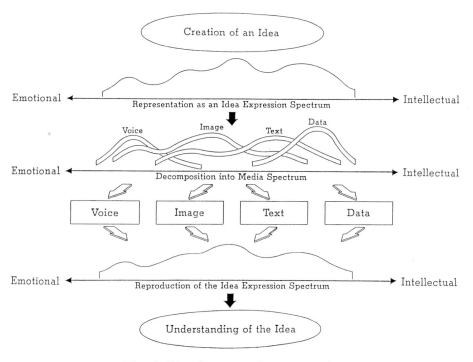

Fig. 2 Idea Spectrum Representation

They should be integrated so that the original idea is clearly presented. Thus the decomposition and the integration technology of multimedia spectra with coherence is the key to good use of multimedia.

In *Figs 1 and 2*, an idea is expressed as a spectrum, which is decomposed into several media spectra, and transmitted to the destination. Received media spectra are combined and they reproduce a spectrum, which approximates the original idea.

Networking among Human-Beings

In this paper, "Networking" is used with the following meaning:

> The establishment of a reciprocal relationship among a group of people with a common interest or task that makes the smooth distribution of necessary information and thus the sharing of information (knowledge, wisdom, ideas) possible.

This concept of networking is becoming increasingly more important as the basic concept of the future information society. Networking is especially playing a vital role in the performance of general work in integrated offices, which are actually early prototypes of the information society.

The most important and basic work that is common to any division in an office, such as accounting, R&D, engineering design or production control, is pursuing of problems, their formulation and the direction of efforts to solve them. This work can be called intellectual and creative activities. These types of activities normally entail the following steps: collection of information related to the problem, analyzing the information, performing several insightful investigations, evaluating the results and preparing a proposal for the solution that is regarded as optimal. These sorts of activities may be performed through reasoning by a single person communicating with others through a workstation, or by several people working together, exchanging opinions and investigating problem areas. The process of circulating a design proposal or plan among the concerned parties for their opinions and approval is one form of this type of activity.

If this activity is performed by gathering in a single room, it could be called a normal conference. If networking, however, allows people to work as needed without having to gather at certain times in certain places, its effect on the importance of working at an office and the improvement of results is incalculable. Therefore, by expanding the concept of the normal conference, one could propose a new concept, "The Intelligent Distributed Conference (IDC)," as a new general format for performing office work.

> IDC is the realization of an environment for problem solving by sharing necessary information (knowledge, wisdom, ideas) among the participants of a conference through a network.

This is a general concept that encompasses all office work and is a realized form of networking.

The IDC can be classified according to the number and location of people taking part. These classifications are as follows:

1-Conference: These classifications are one person resolving problems by exchanging information individually through his workstation.

2-Conference: Two people at two different locations take part in problem-solving by exchanging and sharing information through their workstations.

n-Conference: "n" people at "n" different locations take part in problem-solving by exchanging and sharing information through their workstations.

1G-Conference: One group at a single location resolve a given problem by exchanging and sharing information through a group workstation (if necessary).

2G-Conference: Two groups at two different locations take part in problem-solving by exchanging and sharing information through the group workstations located at each site.

mG-Conference: "m" groups at "m" locations take part in problem-solving by exchanging and sharing information through the group workstations located at each site.

Table 1 The Intelligent Distributed Conference (IDC)

Conference Type Classification		Examples	
		Real Time	Non Real Time
DESK-TOP 1-Conference	One Person using a WS	Interactive Processing	Information Retrieval, Database Service
2-Conference	Two Persons thru WS's	Telephone Conversation Remote Co-working	Electronic Messaging
n-Conference	n Persons thru WS's	Desk Top Conference	Document Circulation BBS(Bulletin Board Service)
CONFERENCE ROOM 1G-Conference	One Group of Participants	Decision Room	DSS (Decision Support System)
2G-Conference	Two Groups	Teleconference	Nationwide Information Dissemination
mG-Conference	m Groups	Multi-site Teleconference	Worldwide Information Dissemination
MIXED (n, mG)-Conference		Distributed Panel Discussion Remote Lecture	Remote Research Lab.

With regard to time, this expanded concept of the conference can be separated into two categories: communications between two or more parties that take place in real time (all parties are at their workstations at the same time), and non-real time communications (some parties are at their workstations at different times). The former is close to an expanded concept of traditional communications while the latter includes the form of general business. However, IDC, the embodiment of the concept of networking, should be used without distinguishing between "real time" and "non-real time." These different groupings are shown in Table 1.

Response Time in Networking Environment

In order to produce the best results for the mental and creative activities involved in office work, an integrated office system, designed to assist in human intellectual activities, should be used to create an environment that provides the necessary information and services when requested at all times. At the same time it is vital to avoid hindering other tasks while concentrating on solutions to the problems that people face. If a response from the system comes slower than the user expected, no matter how small the difference, the concentration of the user, and thus his creative and intellectual abilities, is hindered to some extent. With this in mind, the response time of integrated office systems must obey the following principle:

> The response time of an integrated office system (Tc) must be less than the response time of the human user (Th)
>
> $$Tc < Th$$

Although the human beings response time Th will be changed on past experiences, abilities or adaptiveness of individual users, it is classified into three categories.

Class A: User can predict the result completely and proceed to the next step without confirming the result.

Class B: User can predict the greatest part of the result, but not completely, and has to spare time to confirm details.

Class C: User cannot predict the main part of the result, and has to spend time to understand the result.

Class A is the so-called "rapid reaction task." People always prefer a rapid interaction, if the task is simple and easy. The response time of "0.2 seconds" is set, since the blinking of eyes takes this time.

Class B is the so-called "smooth reaction task." Many tasks belong to this class. The response time of "2 seconds" is set, since the human brain's short memory can temporarily hold chunks of information for 2 seconds. In many experiments a "2 second response time" is shown to be an acceptable time for people to wait on the display terminal.

Class C is the so-called "slow reaction task." Lengthy response times are generally detrimental to productivity, increasing error rates and decreasing satisfaction. The response time of "20 seconds" is set, since the error rates increase rapidly above a 20 seconds response time in experiments.

Table 2 shows the description of each task class and corresponding response time guideline.

Table 2 The Response Time Guideline

Class	Response Time (sec.)	User Expectation	Data Handling Complexity	Examples
A	<0.2	Easy to predict	Less(1)	Text Editing
B	<2.0	Hard to predict	Little(10)	Information Retrieval
C	<20	Not predictable	Large(100)	Numerical Computation

Progress of Technologies Creating the Future Office System

The path along which information communication technologies will develop over the next ten years is agreed upon in detail among specialists. More specifically, the field of electronic devices, the very basis for future development, will enter the age of ULSI (Ultra-Large Scale Integration), when chips will contain tens of millions of gates on a single chip, and also become correspondingly faster. Because of that, telecommunications will enter the age of Broadband ISDN.

Computers will also become increasingly more compact and have more powerful functions due to the introduction of logical elements with millions of logic gates per chip, 64M byte DRAM chips and others. Therefore, we can safely say that the integrated office system will have the potential capability to completely fulfill the desires of their users.

The Integrated Office System of the Future

The Target and The Fundamental Structure of
The Integrated Office System

The office is first and foremost a place for each information worker to independently perform mental and creative activities. But that is not all, for it is an organizational enterprise. A business organization is a hierarchy made of different levels of authority and responsibility, which, at the same time, has a network structure regarding information. From the viewpoint of the former structure, the hierarchy, the work of individuals is unified into an accomplishment of the work group. Then, those work groups are regarded as elements of the next higher level of work group (department, corporation) in the hierarchy as shown in Fig. 3.

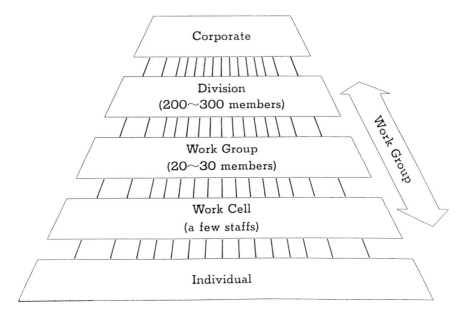

Fig. 3 Hierarchical Representation of a Business Organization

In this structure, authority and responsibility are designated, orders are made and obeyed, and briefings are conducted. In this way, information flows through the hierarchy, and is changed qualitatively. From the viewpoint of the latter structure, the network, the work groups on each level work together to mutually advance their work. In this structure information is disseminated by persuasion and understanding, and its value increases through creativities. Both of these structures can be regarded as overlapping.

In such an office situation as this, a facility is needed for assisting intellectual and creative activities as well as a facility to support the collection of the products of each work group as well as support cooperative efforts by different work groups. An information worker involved in information handling as mentioned in the section on essential requirements for future office systems, would request the following three points:

1. Integrated handling of multimedia information
2. Implementation of networking (IDC)
3. Observance of response time guidelines.

From this point on, the requirements of the office of the future will be for a combination of the hierarchical and network structures, with an eye to the three points listed above. In short, the target will be the integrated office system of the future, aiming at the "realization of IDCs that can handle multi-media information in an integrated fashion and observes the response-time guideline."

In reference (2), the author, et al., have already presented a unified philosophy of such an integrated office system as the "C&C Office System." As described in the reference, the basic structural elements, Fig. 4 of which such an integrated office system should be composed, are the following:

- A desktop multimedia workstation to support the intellectual and creative activities of individuals;

- Integrated information equipment or C&C Boxes for integrating the results of individual activities in work groups; and

- Intra premises wiring scheme linking each desktop workstation with the work group's C&C Box.

The C&C Box mentioned above is a sophisticatedfunction box which includes the functions of both work group computers and PBXs and integrates these information processing and networking functions.

958

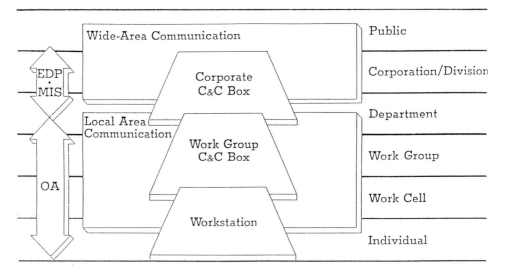

Fig. 4 Roles of Major Components of the Integrated Office
with Respect to Corporate Organization

The Basic Guiding Principle for The Integrated Office System

How should information be handled in an office system composed of desktop workstations and C&C Boxes? To develop an answer, the author would like to advance, as a basic guiding principle that comes from the universal nature of human society, the following;

"The Principle of Here, There, and Over There"

This refers to the idea that humans are physically and emotionally interested primarily in their immediate surroundings, that is, the area within arms' reach. After that, they may be concerned with the area within a very short walking distance, and finally places that are comparatively far. This is a principle which can be applied to human relationships, organizational relationships and societal relationships. If one considers this principle in terms of *space*, it can be seen to be a fundamental principle of the IDC described previously, whereas, from the standpoint of time, this principle provides a foundation for the response time guideline. If this principle is applied to informational relationships in human activities and applied to an integrated office system, the result seems quite natural:

> The appropriate arrangement of information support functions *here* (immediate surroundings), *there* (nearby), and *over there* (distant locations) in order to meet the requirements for system response time.

From this we can conclude that the integrated office system should have a *distributed system architecture*.

In other words, with a distributed architecture, desktop workstations would be installed for each information worker, and information of immediate concern for each individual ("here") would be quickly stored/supported in accordance with the response time guideline (within 0.2 seconds). A C&C Box would be installed for each work group, linked with workstations within the work group, and would be used to store/support information relating to that work group ("there") with only a minimal delay (less than 2 seconds). Information related to the corporation as a whole ("over there") would be stored/supported on the corporate C&C Box, and perform its services for each desktop workstation via the C&C Boxes on each level of the hierarchical structure, within a reasonable response time. This state of affairs is depicted in Figs. 5 and 6.

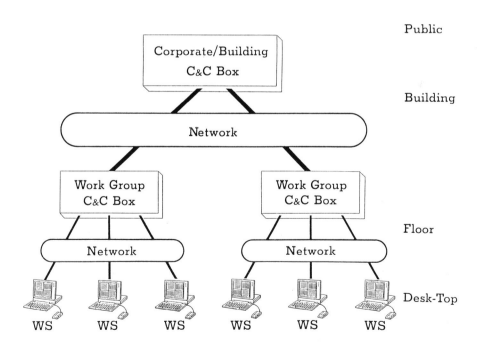

Fig. 5 Distributed System Architecture

960

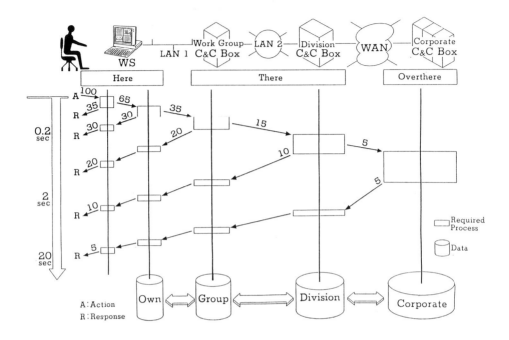

Fig. 6 Illustration of the Principle of Here, There and Over There

The Integrated Office System at the Individual,
Work Group, and Corporate Level

The Integrated Office at the individual level is realized through the installation of an appropriate integrated multimedia workstation at each individual's desk in accordance with his position, duties, and type of work. These workstations, as described earlier, are meant to provide an excellent human interface in order to convey human ideas through multimedia communications. The core of the realization of this interface is the multimedia processing functions supported by Artificial Intelligence (AI) technology. Some current examples of such multimedia processing are data/text processing, data base retrieval, CAD and CAI, but with advances in AI technology, such new services as translation, text/voice conversion, browsing and decision support systems can be expected. Future workstations including such core functions must also provide a user-friendly advanced human interface and multimedia communication interface as described in Fig. 7.

At the level of the work groups, composed of individuals bearing the same level of work responsibilities, the workstations of all the members of a work group are

Future Workstations
—Multi-Media and Artificial Intelligence—

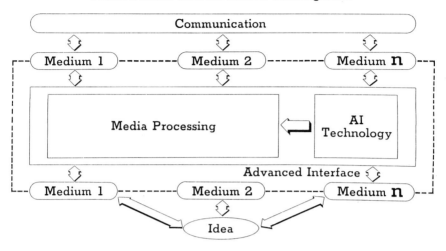

•Conventional Media Processing: Data/Text Processing, Data Base, CAD, CAI
•Intelligent Media Processing: Translation, Dictation, Browsing, Consultation, Decision Support
•Multi-Media Communication: Narrow/Broad Band ISDN

Fig. 7 Future Workstations

linked together, and in cooperation with those, a C&C Box is installed to handle information in an integrated fashion. This C&C Box is an information processing equipment designed to:

- Gather/Distribute;
- Process/Support; and,
- Store/Retrieve

multimedia information necessary for the whole work group. The gathering and distribution functions are expansions of functions that have been handled by conventional PBXs and LANs. The processing and support functions and the storage and retrieval functions are expansions of functions that have been handled by ordinary computers until now. The C&C Box must perform three major functions;

- Gathering/Distributing multimedia integrated information from/to each member's desktop workstation belonging to a work group.

- Processing/Handling necessary information for the problems under consideration in a work group.

962

• Storing/Retrieving appropriate information upon demands.

Based upon these major functions, the C&C Box will be able to carry out various advanced office activity supports such as; multimedia intelligent distributed conference (IDC), hyper-media management, business utility support or knowledge base management. The mutual relations on three major functions and four important applications of the C&C Box is illustrated in Fig. 8.

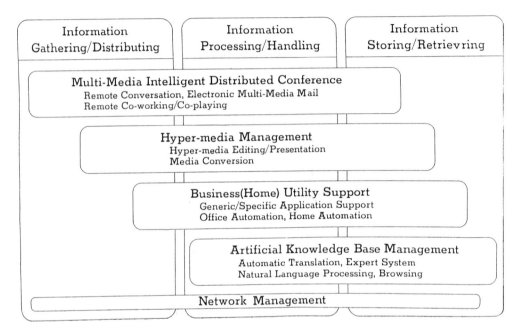

Fig. 8 Major Functions and Important Applications of C&C Box

It is hard to implement these functions and applications with a simple computer and a communication equipment. Rather, new functions brought about by a fusion of the capabilities of a computer and a communication are required. A conceptual configuration scheme of such computer and communication function box, C&C Box, can be expressed as indicated in Fig. 9.

With such a C&C Box at each level of an organization, they can be linked together by private information communication networks to form a building-wide integrated office system. Going one step further, by linking integrated office systems in different locations through a wide area network, a global integrated system can be developed.

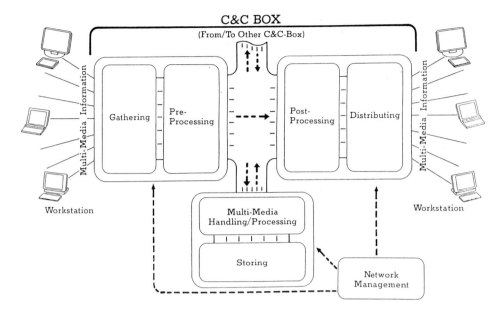

Fig. 9 A Conceptual Configuration of C&C Box

Conclusion

In the integrated office of the future, each information-worker will have at least one desktop workstation to handle multimedia information. Each work group will be furnished with at least one C&C Box, which will be connected with its subordinate workstations. By linking the C&C Boxes hierarchically through communication network, a corporate, and ultimately, a global information network can be constructed. In a future office in this sort of environment, every information worker: will freely share and exchange information through IDCs while performing creative intellectual activities. People will definitely be able to enjoy humanity and full office life.

In order to realize this office of the future, many technological problems, such as the development of advanced network technology (standardization, distributed resource management, network operation management, network-OS etc.), multimedia processing technology and, most importantly, human interface technology, must be overcome. With the tremendous potential capabilities of technological development, there is no doubt about progress in ULSI and the possibilities of miniaturization and increases in the speed and capacity of many devices. Although there are many difficulties in the research and development of system technologies, application techniques and management techniques, under the guidance of strong desires for the integrated office system of the future, it is expected that steady progress will be made through constant trial and error, bringing about the eventual realization of the integrated office system described in this paper.

References

[1] Koji Kobayashi, *Computers and Communications-A Vision of C&C*, The MIT Press, 1986
[2] Hitoshi Watanabe and Nobuhiko Shimasaki, *"Overviews of the C&C Office System — Structure of Office System,"* NEC Research & Development, Special Issue on C&C Office System, pp, 3-15, May 1985.
[3] Special Issue on ISDN, *NEC Research & Development*, February 1987.
[4] Hitoshi Watanabe, *"Integrated Office Systems: 1995 and beyond.* December 1987 — Vol. 25, No.12 IEEE Communications Magazine

CHAPTER 43. THE ARTIFICIAL INTELLIGENCE SOCIETY

C.J. HINDE and J. EDWARDS
Department of Computer Studies
Loughborough University, U.K.

Abstract

We introduce the concept of Artificial Intelligence and discuss its interpretation and possible limitations. We draw the distinction between Artificial Human Intelligence and the concept of Artificial Non-Human Intelligence. A potentially Artificially Intelligent system must obtain information and knowledge about the world it occupies and we see that it must be fully integrated into the various aspects of its life. In our example of a manufacturing facility the information is produced as a result of the systems earlier life and experiences. We conclude that the knowledge embodied in the system is obtained not as an afterthought which would require extensive knowledge engineering but as part of a society within which the system would be integrated. For an Artificially Human-Intelligent system to exist it must similarly have the environment, experiences and integration into society that a real human enjoys; hence we use the title Artificial Intelligence Society.

Outline of Artificial Intelligence

First of all, let us start with an ad-hoc definition of Artificial Intelligence, what it is and what is its history. We may break it down by analysing the two words separately. Artificial is really quite easy and we may define it as human-made or constructed by Artificial means. Intelligence is more difficult to define and there is no adequate definition of what we mean by it. Barr and Feigenbaum [1] define Artificial Intelligence as "the part of computer science concerned with designing intelligent computer systems, that is, systems that exhibit the characteristics we associate with intelligence in human behaviour". We thus start with a concept allied to Artificial Human Intelligence. This is superficially reasonable as the only example of intelligence we are all prepared to agree upon is that based on Human Intelligence, it is perfectly adequate for an informal discussion but falls down in several important respects if taken too seriously.

Research in Artificial Intelligence or pursuit of an Artificial Intelligence has shown that many of the skills we associate with a high degree of intelligence are easier to reproduce by artificial means than those which we associate with everyday activity. It would seem that the more elementary or basic the skill the harder it is to reproduce artificially. An early attempt at connected speech recognition [13] taken together with an earlier system concerned with quite sophisticated chemistry [11,14] underlines this point.

Intelligence tests have been used for a long time to test the intelligence of human beings but tended to rely on knowledge associated with a particular culture or language. For example a set of symbols may be presented and the examinee asked to provide the symbols which follow. If these are numbers then a formula of a particular type may be fitted to the numbers provided and then used to derive the next number.

Example
1,2,3,5,?

Fitting a polynomial to this gives the following:

$$\frac{n^2}{6} - n + \frac{17n}{6} - 1$$

substituting n=5 to get the next term gives us 9.

This is also a fibonacci sequence formed by adding the previous two terms together, the next number in the fibonacci sequence is 8. The term after is 16 for the polynomial but 13 for the fibonacci sequence.

We may fit other models to symbols and use the model to predict the next symbol such as

S,S,M,T,W,?
can be interpreted as
Sydney's Sorting Method Transformed William's Data.
giving D as the next symbol whereas
Sat, Sun, Mon, Tues, Wed, Thurs.
gives T and has a more universal acceptance.

A similar set of symbols such as

    S,D,L,M,M,?

can be interpreted as the initials of the days of the week in French and so gives

Samedi,Dimanche,Lundi,Mardi,Mercredi,Jeudi.

giving J as the next symbol.

In the preceding examples we see that the same set of symbols may be interpreted in two different ways, one way resulting in the following symbol being D is intuitively unsatisfactory but is none the less a 'valid' interpretation of the symbols. On the other hand we have an entirely different set of symbols eliciting the same model, days of the week, but in another language. The 'most reasonable' interpretation within a particular context of a set of ambiguous symbols is clearly what is required. This requires an understanding on the part of the machine of the context within which it must operate and also of the expectations of the questioner or user.

The ability to interpret a set of symbols in a particular way comes up in several areas of Artificial Intelligence especially speech [13] and pattern recognition [57]. We may hear only part of a sentence and yet be able to deduce the remainder from other clues such as context, similarly with vision. Most computer programs leave the machine in no doubt about what is required and as such appear to be almost unbelievably pedantic in their requirements, we accept such behaviour from machines but would be unwilling to tolerate it from other humans.

Robotics

For the purposes of this paper we will define robotics as the study of how to make robots or manipulators do whatever we want them to do. Typically this is done by using a 'teach' box to take the robot through the required task, this sequence is then stored until required and then replayed. This usually removes the robot from productive work which is sometimes very expensive, and can also create a bottleneck in production lines.

One solution is to program the robot 'off-line' and so keep the device in productive use while new programs are developed. This is an attractive solution and would be relatively easy to implement if all 'identical' robots were in fact identical; in practise each device has slightly different geometry and will also not necessarily be mounted in the same position. In order to make better use of 'off-line' programming, robots must be calibrated so that these differences in geometry can be eliminated, this in turn can involve some quite complicated mathematics.

Having designed an apparently suitable program for a robotic device or manipulator, this program will require testing and validation. This will typically take the robot out of productive use but for less time than if the robot was used 'on-line' for development and testing of the program.

Simulation

There would generally be several phases involved in debugging a robot program, the first few being involved with getting the basic ideas correct without worrying to much about the detailed movements. There are several systems or packages [51,52] which allow the user to simulate a robot program and to check visually whether the program does as it should. These vary in sophistication from those that take a wire frame model of the robot through the program so gross errors may be determined, to solid 3D modellers such as NONAME [55] developed at Leeds University which gives a realistic view of the assembly robot, and can offer facilities such as automatic clash detection etc. None of these packages can completely debug a robot program as the geometry of the actual robot will differ slightly from the model and unforeseen failure modes will need to be tested on the actual robot. No readily available robot programming system as yet understands that slippery objects require different handling to non-slippery objects and other objects may not be as accurately dimensioned as first thought. The task of loading a rough casting into a machining centre clearly involves manipulation of objects with imprecise dimensions.

Feedback and Sensors

In more sophisticated systems there are sensors attached to the robot which allows the device to determine its own relative position and also those of the objects to be manipulated thus partially eliminating some of the calibration required. The robot is therefore able to gather information about its current context in a predefined manner. Given such a system then the programmer can be freed from some of the tedium of manual calibration. Similar procedures exist in machining systems with calibration and inspection machines to measure the tools which are then used to derive a precise machining sequence from a parametrised sequence. In machining the 'tool' offsets are entered as parameters to the part program, special devices to measure accurately the appropriate tool dimensions are available and can be linked into the overall machining process. In this example we see that the robot is able to determine some of the information required to program itself from interacting with the environment and only the 'basic' program needs to be input from the user. We could not call such a system intelligent, but it knows more about its environment than a robot which requires manual calibration.

In other tasks the sensors are used as part of the task itself, and so the taught task needs to incorporate the actions required under the various conditions that the robot might encounter. This requires the teacher to anticipate all the conditions that might arise during the performance of the task. The teacher will inevitably only incorporate those conditions that he can foresee. It would be much easier if the robot could take 'reasonable' corrective action without being told. This would involve storing the relevant 'failure' modes with appropriate actions as a backup library. This 'knowledge' of what to do in relatively unforeseen circumstances is the beginnings of the incorporation of Artificial Intelligence at the robot task level.

Object Level Programming

In the previous sections we have explored the idea of programming a robot 'off-line' and so keeping the robot in productive use for much longer periods. In such systems we still need to know quite a lot about the robot that is to perform the task such as the manufacturer and model number at least. We could certainly not normally substitute a 5 axis machine for a 6 axis or a conventional robot for a Selective Compliance Assembly Robot Arm (SCARA) if we had relied on the compliance properties of the latter. What we have done is told the robot which motors to run, when and for how long, not what it is to do. Object level programming with systems such as RAPT [49,50], short for Robot APT allows us to specify the task without reference to a particular robot arm and without normally worrying about fixing the base component.

RAPT uses the relations between the objects to reason about the actions required to complete the assembly. For example; suppose an assembly consists of the three parts illustrated in figure 1. which need to be

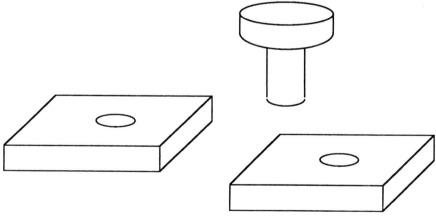

Figure 1. Three components of an assembly.

970

assembled to produce the component shown in figure 2.

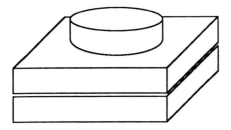

Figure 2. Showing the complete assembly.

The RAPT programmer can concentrate on the order of assembly without worrying about which robot to employ for the actual task. In our example the robot programmer has become an assembly designer and can deliberate whether to place the two plates one above the other before inserting the pin or to insert the pin in the top plate before placing the sub-assembly onto the lower plate. Only when the order of assembly has been decided and the ramifications explored, need a robot be actually selected; this can be in the light of much fuller information than might be the case if the robot is selected before the task has been designed. In the case of a complex assembly this would be a significant advantage. RAPT itself is not an example of Artificial Intelligence but to make good use of Artificial Intelligence the system needs to be able to reason about objects, as RAPT does.

Expert Systems

The study and development of Intelligent Knowledge Based Systems (IKBS) and Expert Systems is a branch of Artificial Intelligence. However, it is one area that has shown practical benefit in many areas. The two terms are often used synonymously; very few if any Expert Systems are not Knowledge Based but very many IKBS are not Expert Systems. The difference is not in the systems themselves but how they are formed. An Expert System is a deliberate model of an acknowledged expert or the coding of a body of expert knowledge and as such is a Knowledge Based System. A Knowledge Based System is just that and may not be a deliberate attempt to mimic an expert. The prefix of Intelligent adds little extra meaning to KBS but does emphasise the original goals of Knowledge Based Systems.

The first IKBS to obtain widespread publicity was the Heuristic Dendral program by Feigenbaum, Buchanan et. al. [11,14,15]. The word heuristic had been around in Artificial Intelligence circles for some time before Heuristic Dendral came into being. Heuristic has the same root as 'Eureka' meaning 'I have found it' and means roughly 'serving or helping to find'. Dendral originates from Greek again and means tree so Heuristic Dendral is essentially a 'helping tree'.

Expert Systems are typically rule based and the programs are coded as a set of "condition - action" pairs or a variation of this.

    i.e.

    IF Condition

    THEN perform Action.

The rule which has its condition true will be executed and this cycle can be repeated, potentially forever. Examples of expert systems include medical diagnosis [12,58] language and speech analysis [13]. The relative success of these systems indicates the perversity of AI problems, tasks capable of being accomplished easily by most 3 year old children such as connected speech understanding are harder to implement successfully than skilled tasks such as medical diagnosis and chemical analysis.

The Heuristic Dendral was also designed as a vehicle for experiments in scientific theory formation and as such had an accompanying program called 'Meta-Dendral' [11,14] which was capable of solving problems about (meta) the Heuristic Dendral.

Expert Systems not only attempt to give the same answer as an expert in their chosen domain but also attempt to reason in the same way giving an explanation for any conclusion reached. Whereas conventional programs will tend to take each instruction in some predetermined sequence, an expert system will apply rules where appropriate so the sequence of rule invocations and application is largely determined by the problem under consideration.

The rules may be added to without interfering with those already present, however this must be done fairly carefully and any additions must be consistent with the old rules. An outstanding problem in IKBS work is the problem of maintaining consistency in the Knowledge Base given that there may be several hundred rules, or even more, and possibly many experts contributing to that Knowledge Base. An early example of a system for maintaining consistency in the knowledge base was Teiresias [16] which helped the expert to enter consistent rules into a medical knowledge base associated with the Mycin system but unlike Meta-Dendral did not induce rules from examples [36,37,38,39].

A typical rule for mass spectrometry as used in the Heuristic Dendral [14] is given below:

IF	the spectrum for the molecule has two peaks at masses X1 and X2 such that:
	a. $X1 + X2 = M + 28$
AND	b. X1 - 28 is a high peak
AND	c. X2 - 28 is a high peak
AND	d. at least one of X1 or X2 is high
THEN	
	the molecule contains a ketone group.

This is in contrast to a representation of the same fact in a conventional programming language which would tend to be imperative rather than declarative. The above declares a piece of knowledge about Mass Spectrometry but not what to do with it, this is the job of the organisational part of the expert system. Many tasks have been coded as IKBS including medical systems, the most successful being those with a fairly well established body of knowledge. The rule shown above for Mass Spectrometry is exact and if the conditions specified are matched then the conclusion is clearly true, there is no doubt about it. Other systems are less exact and the conclusions reached embody some aspect of uncertainty. There are several types of uncertainty, the best known being probability; even within probability there are two types of probability: epistemic and aleatory [23]. Aleatory probability is the one most commonly analysed by mathematicians and is the one concerned with the frequencies of events given some experimental evidence. Epistemic probability is the one concerned with belief and does not necessarily require any evidence; as such it is not a chance function but a statement of belief in a particular outcome. Another type of uncertainty is based on fuzzy logic [64,66,67] where we are able to make statements such as "Don Bradman is a good batsman" and also make some deductions under such uncertainty. We are also able to make statements about the probability of a fuzzy event [65] by asking questions such as " What is the probability of the next person coming into the room being tall?". This question has components of a chance function in the request for probability and the uncertainty engendered by the adjective tall. We are not able to classify people into two crisp sets 'TALL' and 'NOT TALL' without destroying the essential concept of tallness.

PROLOG [17,18,19,20] is a language often cited as an IKBS design language and although it has considerable representational power it has no explicit mechanism for handling uncertainty such as probability. Hinde [65] reports a development of Fuzzy Prolog which deals with symbolic uncertainty in a Prolog environment. It is therefore possible to build Expert Systems in PROLOG and also to incorporate some uncertainty. The dialogue with APES (A Prolog Expert System) [18] can be quite readable and given a little practice the rules can be easily understood.

Bratko [19] describes the PROLOG code for a very simple expert system to determine properties of a set of animals. An example rule is as follows:

IF   Animal isa animal
AND   Animal gives milk
OR   Animal has hair
AND   Animal has warm_blood
THEN
            Animal isa mammal.

Two features typically found in Expert Systems are an Explain facility and a Why facility. The Explain facility will explain why a certain conclusion has been reached, the Why will state why a particular question has been asked and so is supplying context to the question. An example may be, we have diagnosed that there is a sticky float chamber needle in the carburettor because 'Explain' the engine is flooding with fuel. Associated with the diagnosis might be a remedy for the fault so this would tell us to remove the carburettor and replace the float chamber needle. The terminology can vary somewhat so it is worth while checking the meaning of a particular term when assessing any particular system. Many workers in the field insist that the Explain facility is necessary for a program or collection of programs to be an Expert System although it would not be so for it to be an IKBS; to be an IKBS it must be knowledge based and for the knowledge to be separated from the procedures that use it. PROLOG is more than a tool for building Expert Systems, it is also a general purpose programming language so Expert Systems built using PROLOG as a base can offer powerful facilities. This does not mean that a 'layperson' could come along and use PROLOG to build an Expert System any more than they could write a CAD package in FORTRAN. This is changing as more 'user friendly' tools are developed [53]. Clearly there is room for an Expert System builder endowed with some level of Artificial Intelligence, Meta-Dendral is one such system in a limited domain.

974

Medical systems are less precise and tend to have a more uncertain body of knowledge. For example, a runny nose and slight fever usually indicate a cold, however, it may also indicate the early stages of measles. MYCIN [12,21] was the first published medical expert system and was concerned with bacterial blood infections. It was pre-dated by Heuristic Dendral, which was one of the first IKBS, but was the first Expert System as an expert's knowledge was deliberately coded.

More recently the type of knowledge used in systems such as Mycin has been supplanted by more explicit knowledge about disease models. The idea of models or frames was introduced by Minsky [44] as a representational mechanism for sets of statements or properties which were grouped together naturally; such a set would be all the properties of a motor car but would also include methods for calculating dependant items such as the total weight of the car from its components. In practise a disease model based diagnosis system [58] would have slots containing attributes of the disease as well as rules for exploring and manipulating the models of the disease and so deducing the results from more fundamental evidence. In order to update a procedural system to include a new disease we might have to undergo extensive rewriting, a system like Mycin would need the rules checked for interactions and so would still require considerable checking. Teiresias [16] helps the user to enter consistent rules to the Mycin system. The model based approach has rules which cater for the interactions between models and so the introduction of a new disease model is relatively straightforward. A more recent example of the use of the model based approach used in training needs analysis is given in Shepherd and Hinde [59]. A general theory relating to the manipulation of models is given in Sowa [46] under the title of conceptual graph processing.

Expert System Shells
Shells are commonly used to develop prototypes of Expert Systems quickly, they are thus non specialised and tend to have inadequate user interfaces.
They are typically developed from a particular application which is then generalised to form a basis for other applications; as a result they tend to perform well on applications that are similar to the original one. The tendency now is towards more sophisticated toolkits such as ART [61] which are more like programmimg languages or systems and therfore tend to require some expertise to use. This is not to denigrate the, sometimes relatively cheap, general purpose commercial shell for small applications but the uninitiated should beware of expecting something magic; if it takes some time to train a human to do the expert's job it will not necessarily be easy to recode the expert's knowledge into the form required in the Expert System overnight. Final working or production systems are often coded specially for a job from the specification derived from the prototype shell. Such a system, developed initially using two different shells is described in [26], the translation system

described in [27] falls somewhere in between the two approaches.

Clark & McGabe [18] report the use of PROLOG as a language for building expert systems and as such we could take the view of PROLOG being an Expert System shell. Many of the points they make are concerned with the structure of Expert Systems and the representation of rules using classical logic. They also illustrate how uncertainty can be incorporated into the model using the standard constructs available in PROLOG.

Allwood, Stewart, Hinde and Negus [53] evaluate a selection of commercially available shells in the context of civil engineering. As the subject area of Expert Systems develops then so the number of products on the market increases giving interested parties a wider but more confusing choice.

Expert System shells are formulations of theories of knowledge and as such may be viewed as general problem solving systems. Many problem solving systems [62] are based on theorem provers so they will prove that it is possible to achieve a certain goal and as part of that proof will deliver a method of achieving the set of requirements or goals. The theorem provers are also generally built using rule based systems.

Languages for developing theorem provers and expressing the rules in a natural way include LISP [28], PLANNER [29], CONNIVER [30] and more commonly in the UK PROLOG [17,19]. An important point to be made regarding such systems is that the diagnoses or recommendations are the result of a proof procedure and as such is a verified or proven implementation of the goal statement or specification provided that the underlying knowledge is correct.

Types of knowledge
In this section we explore two types of knowledge 'shallow' and 'deep', both of which may be satisfactory in different situations. Shallow knowledge relates to mimicking the behaviour of an expert and is quite widespread in the production of Expert Systems; in many cases it is quite sufficient and is almost always easier to extract and will run quicker than a much deeper understanding. The other extreme, deep knowledge, is based on the internal models of the expert which are then used to drive the expert system. The shallow knowledge based systems may perform stunningly in a demonstration but fall down badly when presented with something novel which the expert can solve but has not 'cropped' up in the behavioural knowledge elicitation. We illustrate with an example taken from the pastime of crosswords.

Suppose we have a clue '3D picture of small house, firewood and butter' then there may be many explanations of this clue. Given that we have the following letters already available in the crossword from solving other clues: $H \_ L \_ \_ R \_ M$ then we may explain the answer (HOLOGRAM) in several ways.

Shallow
Only word in the Chambers dictionary that fits

Deeper
a.	3D picture	HOLOGRAM
b.	Small house	HO
c.	Firewood	LOG
d.	Butter	RAM

By deep knowledge we mean the knowledge embodies an understanding of the field which can refer to the tangible parts in the field. A shallow knowledge would still be able to solve a large number of problems in the field but only by being 'told' the answer. An example of shallow knowledge would be diagnosis by symptom fault pairs. This kind of diagnosis may be more sophisticated in that the symptoms and faults are linked by a complex network and may have text associated with the links but it would not understand the workings of the mechanism being diagnosed. A deeper understanding of diagnosis would be present if the two parts of knowledge were separated, i.e. knowledge of diagnosis and knowledge of the mechanism and its variations.

Another way of explaining this is to compare two ways of solving problems, firstly by rote. Some schoolchildren can do 'sums' quite well by just following the method that the teacher has shown them, others will understand more about numbers and will therefore understand what they are doing. In many cases their behaviour will be indistinguishable until their knowledge is to be extended. Those with only the behavioural knowledge will need to be taught almost the whole new process whereas those with a deeper understanding will be able to add the new knowledge to their existing knowledge in a more constructive fashion.

Process planning software systems [48] give examples of shallow and deep knowledge. Variant process planning exhibits shallow knowledge as it merely stores the previous parametrised plans and uses a, sometimes sophisticated, lookup system to retrieve them. Generative planning may exhibit deeper knowledge. The variant system is not trivial to implement and also requires considerable input of parametrised plans. Chang and Wysk [48] describe them as follows:

"A pure variant planning system is a pure retrieval system and is analogous to planning based on experience. In a variant planning system, standard plans are stored based on component shape. These plans are then retrieved based on the similarity of a coded part... A generative system, however, makes processing, tooling, and other decisions via software program logic".

There are very few process planning systems which come any where near a purely generative approach, however, a variant process planning system will capture much of the methodological or behavioural knowledge of a human process planner. It is clear though at this stage that the intuition of a good process planner is very difficult to capture, if not impossible.

An optimised system would be able to use both types of knowledge but a system with generative capability would only need to have the machines redefined if the factory were updated whereas a variant system may need to have a whole new set of plans and sub-plans defined if it is to make full use of the new machines. In this sense the generative system exhibits deeper knowledge than the variant system as it is easier to transfer the generative knowledge than the variant into new circumstances.

An example of a process planning system which has attempted to address some of the deeper issues in automated process plan generation is reported in Hinde et al. [56]. The knowledge extraction process in that system [63] was a longish apprenticeship to an expert process planner. Although they did not deliberately set out to extract knowledge following any particular methodology they found that comparing different process plans for the same component gave them insight into the goals of the process planner; this in turn enabled them to understand some of the behaviour observed. Typically the behaviour of an expert can sometimes appear inconsistent and the knowledge engineer has to make the best of this; they found that the observation of inconsistency can sometimes lead to greater insights providing some degree of empathy can be established with the expert.

In the context of systems already described the Heuristic Dendral program [11,14] uses a model of molecular cleavage and would be closer to a deep knowledge system than Mycin which has its knowledge of physiology implicit in the rules rather than explicitly stated. Again, the system may be able to behave in a manner which appears intelligent merely by copying the behaviour of its teacher but in order to become as knowledgeable as the teacher it needs to have the underlying models available.

Planning

One property of intelligent behaviour is to be aware of the consequences of any action or sequence of actions. Given a goal to achieve we may plan a sequence of actions which will accomplish that goal and then execute that sequence of actions. The goal may be described as a set of properties to be obtained after a sequence of actions which is to be determined. As goals may be broken down into subgoals we then link the properties required by one action to the results of a previous task. The previous task provides the necessary pre-conditions for the succeeding task.

The major difference between a proof procedure in a 'logic' system such as PROLOG and a planning procedure is the presence of significant interactions between the effects of the various operators. This is illustrated by the simple planning system outlined below.

The planning tasks may be performed by a problem solving system and the plan then executed by an executor.

Our paradigm is this:

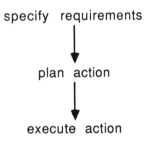

With feedback loops incorporated this may be repeated ad infinitum or until the final requirements are met. Problem solving systems are typically based on theorem provers so they will prove that it is possible to achieve a certain set of requirements or goals and as part of the proof will deliver a method of achieving that set of goals.

One formulation of the planning problem which is adequate in many respects, suffers from several major deficiencies but illustrates the process, is described by Nilsson in [31,32] and employs pre-conditions, operators and post-conditions. The operator is any system which can effect changes on the world and as such may be either human or machine. In this formulation some of the pre-conditions for the operations match some of the post-conditions, so some properties of the world are unchanged by application of the operator. Another way of describing the situation is by using additions and deletions, after an operator has been applied then the state is changed by adding some properties and deleting others. By examining the post-conditions and comparing them with the goal statement we may decide which, if any, operator to apply. The operator typically reduces the difference between two states and in many respects may be regarded as being driven or chosen by the differences. This may also be likened to the use of manufacturing form features in the process planning and machining world where the feature is the result of a machining operation. If more than one operator is applicable then several branches of the search tree are generated and explored in turn. Each problem on the search tree may be specified by a triple consisting of the initial conditions, the set of operators and the goal or desired conditions. It is worth while noting at this stage that the operator definitions are in the rule based form we outlined earlier.

The process employed in the theorem provers is similar to the syntax analysis phase of a compiler or translator used in computing and the answer extraction process is also similar. Each problem suggests a set of 'key' operators which will reduce the difference between the initial state and the goal state and will generate two subproblems associated with attaining the pre-conditions required to apply the operator and attaining the goal state from the post-conditions. The paths expand until the graph is solved and can result in various solutions. The answer extraction process delivers the plans accordingly.

The foregoing is a very simplified explanation of the way in which some planning systems work. There is considerable work going on in both academic establishments and industrially based concerns towards more sophisticated, robust and user-friendly planning systems [56].

Integrated Systems

We have outlined several areas where Artificial Intelligence might be applied to a Robot system, however, we have not yet addressed where the robot is to obtain its information. The information required to enable Artificial Intelligence techniques to play a part is itself a significant problem. In many cases the information exists in another part of the factory or has been produced as part of an earlier design process. This knowledge is generally lost giving rise to a 'sawtooth' form of information gain and loss [54] shown in figure 3. Typically this can occur as the evolving product is passed from the design office where functional attributes are considered to production engineering where machining and assembly procedures are determined.

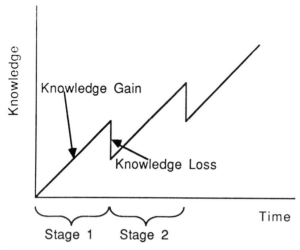

Figure 3. Showing knowledge loss between design stages.

If all the knowledge is kept from stage to stage the later stages will have the benefit of knowing why a particular decision was made and therefore how critical it is to the function of the product. A drawing may be produced and annotated so that any operation without a specified tolerance is to be machined or assembled to 'standard' tolerances. The designer may be signalling that 'standard' tolerances are sufficient or that much looser tolerances could be acceptable and still meet the functional and aesthetic considerations. Figure 4 illustrates the ideal of integration where all the information or knowledge arising from earlier decisions is kept and is made available to all stages of the product's pre-delivery life.

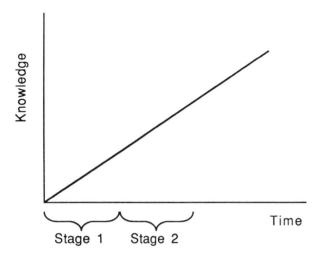

Figure 4. Showing smooth knowledge gain throughout the product cycle.

As Artificial Intelligence techniques may be applied with effect at any stage of the product life cycle then the maintenance of an uptodate information base to support all stages of design and manufacture becomes more cost effective. The integration of all the accumulated knowledge allows decisions made in the preliminary stages to be more accurately assessed in the later stages of development and also to have their intended effect.

Finally we come to true integration of design and manufacture. At the design stage the design engineers will consider possible manufacturing processes and will use their knowledge of manufacture to design a product that is not unduly difficult to manufacture. Given an Expert System to advise on the ease of manufacture or assembly of any particular product the designers can be more aware of the effects of their decisions on later stages. Similarly ease of maintenance and reliability of various components can be more easily incorporated early in the design process before the design is 'fixed'.

We now illustrate two simple paradigms for production, the first in figure 5 illustrates a sequential view of the product's life as it is designed.

982

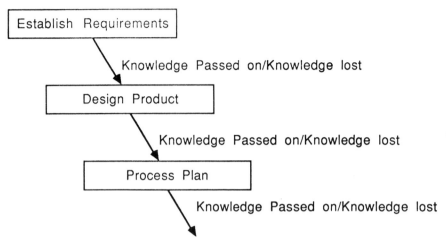

Figure 5. Illustrating a sequential view of the overall design process, incorporating knowledge loss at the various stages.

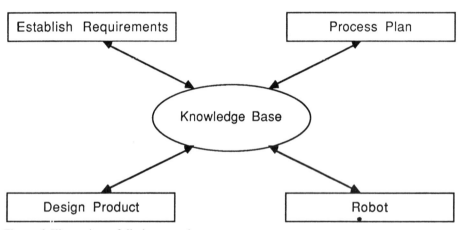

Figure 6. Illustrating a fully integrated system.

Figure 6 illustrates a fully integrated system but with only a few of the components shown where decisions on any aspect of the product may be made at any time. The robot is also included with a two way information or knowledge flow; to the robot is the robot's instructions or program and from the robot is feedback about the success or otherwise of the assembly plan. This feedback may be incorporated into any or all of the decision processes accordingly.

Given an integrated system as described above the robot or manipulator can be more aware of the intentions of the designer and can therefore interpret the 'ambiguous' and possibly very general instructions given by a supervisor; for example "assemble the motors before connecting the gearboxes" could be quite unambiguous instructions to a skilled person but a robot would not yet be expected to make any sense of this.

Conclusions

Having started with the human-robot interface we have placed many software systems between the person programming the robot or manipulator and the device itself. Each stage has taken the user further away from the actual details of the programming task and brought him closer to the real problem of manufacturing and assembling products. One possible result of high investment in automation would be a reluctance to change the shop floor layout or the machines and robots used, as the accompanying reprogramming would be expensive and extensive. Artificial Intelligence techniques can help to make the investment in knowledge rather than programs and as such deep knowledge would be applicable to new situations with a minimum of retraining or reprogramming. A first rate engineer will not require retraining in the basic skills on the introduction of new machinery but will be able to apply those skills to the new system with a minimum of unproductive time. We have proposed that the knowledge of the task the robot is to perform is available not as an afterthought which would require manual input after the product has been designed but as part of a factory wide integrated system concerned with the whole product life cycle.

For a computer to behave in a humanly intelligent manner it must be integrated into the society in which it is to 'live'. It must share the experiences of its colleagues and have some degree of empathy. It may be made to behave very similarly to a human but would lack the deeper knowledge which is the privilege and characteristic of humans [4,5].

984

Further reading, references and bibliography

[1]   Barr A.& Feigenbaum E.A.(1981) Handbook of Artificial Intelligence, Vol. 1. Pitman.

[2]   Barr A.& Feigenbaum E.A.(1982) Handbook of Artificial Intelligence, Vol. 2. Pitman.

[3]   Cohen P.R.& Feigenbaum E.A.(1982) Handbook of Artificial Intelligence, Vol. 3. Pitman.

[4]   McCorduck P.(1979) Machines Who Think,W.H. Freeman.

[5]   Weizenbaum J.(1976) Computer Power and Human Reason: From judgement to calculation,W.H. Freeman.

[6]   Bobrow D.(1968) Natural Language Inputs for Computer Problem Solving Systems. In Minsky M.Semantic Information Processing,M.I.T. Press.

[7]   Minsky M.(1968) Semantic Information Processing,M.I.T. Press.

[8]   Bundy A.(1983) The Computer Modelling of Mathematical Reasoning, Academic Press Inc. (London).

[9]   Bundy A., Byrd L., Luger G.,Mellish C., Milne R., and Palmer M.(1979) Mecho: A Program to Solve Mechanics Problems, Working paper 50.Dept of Artificial Intelligence, Edinburgh.

[10]   Winograd T.(1971) Computer Program for Understanding Natural Language., M.I.T. PhD. Thesis.

[11]   Buchanan B.G.,Feigenbaum E.A. & Lederberg J.(1971) A heuristic programming study of theory formation in science,IJCAI 2,40-50.

[12]   Shortliffe E.H.(1976) Computer-based Medical Consultations MYCIN, American Elsevier.

[13]   Reddy D,R., Erman L.D,, Fennell R.D., and Neely R.B.(1973) The Hearsay Speech Understanding System: An Example of the Recognition Process. In IJCAI 3 pp 185-193 (Stanford, CA).

[14]   Buchanan G., & Feigenbaum E.A.(1978) Dendral and Meta-Dendral: Their Applications Dimension, Journal of Artificial Intelligence 11,5-24.

[15]   Buchanan B.G.(1982) New Research in Expert Systems, Machine Intelligence 10, pp 269-300, eds. Hayes J.E., Michie D. and Pao Y-H.,Ellis Horwood, Chichester.

[16]   Davis R.(1977) Interactive transfer of expertise:Acquisition of new inference rules,IJCAI 5 pp 321-328 (Cam. Mass.).

[17]   Clocksin W.F. & Mellish C.S.(1981)Programming in PROLOG, Springer-Verlag.

[18]   Clark K.L. & McGabe F.G.(1982) PROLOG: a language for implementing expert systems,Machine Intelligence 10, pp 455-476 eds. Hayes J.E., Michie D. and Pao Y-H.,Ellis Horwood,Chichester.

[19]   Bratko I. (1986) Prolog Programming for Artificial Intelligence, Addison-Wesley.

[20] Sterling & Shapiro E.Y. (1986) The Art of Prolog, M.I.T.Press.

[21] Buchanan B.G. and Shortliffe E.H.(1984) The MYCIN experiments, Addison Wesley.

[22] Warren D.H.D.(1977) Implementing PROLOG - Compiling predicate logic programs, Dept Artificial Intelligence Edinburgh University Research Report Nos.39,40.

[23] Shafer G.(1976) A mathematical theory of evidence,Princeton NJ:Princeton University Press.

[24] Duda R.D.,Gashnig J.G. & Hart P.E.(1979) Model Design in the PROSPECTOR Consultant systems for mineral exploration, in Expert Systems in the Microelectronic age, ed. Michie D. Edinburgh University Press 153-168.

[25] Duda R.D., Hart P.E. & Nilson N.J.(1976) Subjective Bayesian Methods for Rule Based Inference Systems.In Proc. 1976 Nat. Computer Conf. (AFIPS Conf. Proc.) 45 1075 - 1082.

[26] Hinde C.J., Owen G. & Winch D.(1984) An Expert System to diagnose faults in a Communication Network., Unpublished M.Sc. projects.

[27] Hinde C.J. and Mawdesley A.(1984) An Interlingual English to French Machine Translation System.,Dept. Computer Studies Loughborough University Internal Report No. 218.

[28] Winston P.H. & Horn B.K.P.(1981) LISP,Addison-Wesley.

[29] Hewitt C.(1971) Procedural Embedding of Knowledge in Planner, in Proceedings 2nd IJCAI.

[30] Sussman G.J. & McDermott D.V.(1972) From PLANNER to CONNIVER - A genetic Approach. Fall Joint Computer Conference 1972.

[31] Nilsson N.(1980) Principles of Artificial Intelligence, Springer.

[32] Nilsson N.(1971) Problem Solving Methods in Artificial Intelligence, McGraw-Hill .IP30 Barstow R.A.(1979)Knowledge Based Program construction,North Holland.

[33] Samuel A.L.(1963) Some studies of machine learning using the game of checkers.In Feigenbaum E. & Feldman J.Computers and Thought, McGraw-Hill.

[34] Samuel A.L.(1967) Some studies of machine learning using the game of checkers 2,IBM Journal Res.Dev 11.

[35] Feigenbaum E. & Feldman J.(1963) Computers and Thought, McGraw-Hill

[36] Shapiro E.Y.(1982) Algorithmic Program Debugging,M.I.T. Press.

[37] Bundy A.,Silver B. & Plummer D.(1983) An Analytical comparison of some rule learning programs,Expert Systems 83.

[38] Quinlan J.R.(1981) Discovering rules by induction from large collections of examples.In Michie D.Expert Systems in the Microelectronic Age, Edinburgh University Press.

[39] Gaines B.R.(1976) Behaviour structure transformation,Journal of Man Machine Studies 8 337-365.

[40] Gloess P.Y.(1981) Artificial Intelligence,Alfred Handy Guide.

[41] Hofstadter D.(1979) Godel, Escher Bach An Eternal Golden Braid, Penguins Books.

[42] Michie D.(1981) Expert Systems in the Microelectronic Age, Edinburgh University Press.

[43] Boden M.A.(1977) Artificial Intelligence and Natural Man, Harvester Press.

[44] Minsky M.(1975) A Framework for Representing Knowledge.In Winston P.H.,The Psychology of Computer Vision,McGraw-Hill.

[45] Winston P.H.(1975) The Psychology of Computer Vision,McGraw-Hill.

[46] Sowa J.F.(1984) Conceptional Structures,Addison-Wesley.

[47] Winston P.H.(1977) Artificial Intelligence,Addison Wesley.

[48] Chang T-C. and Wysk R.A.(1985) An introduction to automated Process Planning,Prentice Hall.

[49] Popplestone R.J. (1978) RAPT- A Language for Describing Assemblies, The Industrial Robot 8 No. 3 131-138.

[50] Ambler A.P. (1982) RAPT: An Object Level Robot Programming Language, D.A.I. Research Paper No. 172, Department of Artificial Intelligence, University of Edinburgh.

[51] Bonney M.C., Edwards P.J., Gleave J.A., Green J.L., Marshall R.J. and Yong Y.F. (1984) The Simulation of Industrial Robot Systems, OMEGA Int. J. of Mgmt. Sci. 12 No. 3 pp 273-281, Pergamon.

[52] Edmonds E.A., Clarke A.A. (1987) Investigation into the Provision of Man-Machine Interfaces for a System to Program Robots Off-Line, Final Report SERC Grant GR/D 87505.

[53] Allwood R.J., Stewart D.J., Hinde C.J. and Negus B. (1985) Survey of Expert System Shells for Construction Industry Applications, Final Report SERC Grant GR/C 94865.

[54] Smithers T.M. (1985) The Alvey Large Scale Demonstrator Project "Design To Product", Proceedings of the Technology Assessment and Management Conference of the Gottlieb Duttweiler Institute Ruschlikon, Zurich, Switzerland.

[55] Staff of the Geometric Modelling Project, (1983) NONAME Documentation, Geometric Modelling Project University of Leeds.

[56] Hinde C.J., Bray A.D., Herbert P.M, Launders V.A. and Round D. (1989) A Truth Maintenance Approach to Process Planning, in ed Rzevski G. (1989) Artificial Intelligence in Manufacturing, Cambridge, England.

[57] Tou J.T. & Gonzalez R.C. (1974). Pattern Recognition Principles, Addison-Wesley: Massachusetts.

[58] Aikins J. (1983) Prototypical knowledge for expert systems, Artificial Intelligence Vol 20, pp. 163-210.

[59] Shepherd A. and Hinde C.J. (1989). Mimicking the training expert- a basis for automating training needs analysis. in Bainbridge L. & Quintanilla. (1989) Developing Skills with Information Technology, John Wiley:Chichester.

[60] Gabrielides G. (1988). A system that learns to recognise 3-D objects,Ph.D. Thesis: University of Technology Loughborough.

[61] Clayton B.D. (1985). ART programming Tutorials. Ferranti Computer Systems, Bracknell.

[62] Newell A., Shaw J.C., & Simon H.A. (1959) Report on a General Problem-solving Program. Proceedings of the International Conference on Information Processing, Paris, pp. 256-264.

[63] Hinde C.J. (1989) Loughborough University Manufacturing Planner: L.U.M.P., One day meeting of the British Computer Society's Specialist Group on Expert Systems: M.E.D.C. Paisley. Nov. 1989.

[64] Zadeh L.A. (1973). Outline of a new approach to the analysis of complex systems and decision processes. IEEE Transactions on Systems Man and Cybernetics 1 pp. 28-44

[65] Baldwin J.F. & Pilsworth B.W. (1979). A Theory of Fuzzy Probability. Proceedings of the 9th International Symposium on Multiple-Valued Logic. Bath England. IEEE Computer Society Publications Office.

[66] Zadeh L.A., Fu K.S., Tanaka K. & Shimura M. (1975) Fuzzy sets and their application to cognitive and decision processes. Academic Press. New York.

[67] Baldwin J.S. (1979). A new approach to approximate reasoning using fuzzy logic. Fuzzy sets and Systems 2 pp. 309-325.

ABREVIATIONS AND ACRONYMS

ADPCM Adaptive Differential Pulse Code Modulation
ADTV Advanced Definition Television
AFIPS American Federation of Information Processing Societies
AI Artificial Intelligence
ALU Arithmetic Logic Unit
AM Amplitude Modulation
ANSI American National Standards Institute
APOLLO Article Delivery Over Network System
ARPA Advance Research Projects Agency
ASCII American Standard Code for Information Interchange
ASIC Application Specific Integrated circuit
ASLIB Association of Special Libraries & Information Bureaux (new title is The Association for Information Management)
ASSAS-SIN A System for Storage and Subsequent Selection of Information
ATM Automatic Teller Machine
AT&T Automatic Telephone & Telegraph
Au Angstrom Unit = 10^{-10} metres
Baud Unit of signalling speed 1 Baud = 1 sig. element/sec.
BBC British Broadcasting Corporation
BCPL Basic Combined Programming Language
BDLC Burroughs Data Link Control
BDOS Basic Disc Operating System
BIOS Basic Input/Output System
Bit Binary Digits; unit of information content
B-ISDN Broadband Integrated Services Digital Network
BLLD British Library Lending Division
BMA British Medical Association
BNB British National Bibliography
BOC Bell Operating Company
Bpi Bits per inch
BPO British Post Office
Bps Bits per second
BS British Standard
BSC Binary Synchronous Communication

BSI British Standards Institute
BT British Telecom
Byte Usually 7 data bits + parity
CAD Computer Aided Design
CAFS Content Addressable File Store
CAV Constant Angular Velocity
CB Citizen's Band
CCD Charge Coupled Device
CCIR International Committee of Rediffusion
CCITT Comite Consultatif Internationale de Telegraphie et Telephone
CD Compact Disc
Cd Candela
CD-I Compact Disc Interactive
CD/MA Collision Detector/Multiple Access
CD-ROM Compact Disc Read Only Memory
CD-V Compact Disc Video
CEC Commission of the European Community
CEPT Conference Europeene des Administrations des Postes et des Telecommunications
CGM Computer Graphics Metafile
CGROM Character Generator Read Only Memory
CIM Computer Input Microfilm
CIO Chief Information Officer
CISC Complex Instruction Set Computer
CLV Constant Linear Velocity
C-MAC C(Sound)-Multiple Analogue Component
CMOS Complimentary Metal Oxide
CNRS Centre Nationale de la Recherche Scientifique
COAX Co-axial cable
COBOL Common Business Oriented Language
CODEC Coder-Decoder
COM Computer Output Microfilm
CP/M Control Programme for Microprocessors
CP/NET Control Programme for Networks
Cps Characters per second
CPU Central Processing Unit
CR Carriage Return
CRC Communication Research Centre
CRT Cathode Ray Tube

CS	Circuit Switched OR Chip Select
CSMA/ CD	Carrier Sense Multiple Access/Collision Detection
CUG	Closed User Group
C&W	Cable & Wireless
DAT	Digital Audio Tape
dB	Decibel
DBMS	Database Management System
DBS	Direct Broadcasting Satellite
DDC MP	Digital Data Communications Message Protocol
DEA	Data Encryption Algorithm
DEC	Digital Equipment Corp
DES	Data Encryption Standard
DIANE	Direct Information Access Network Europe
DIP	Dual in-line package
DMA	Direct Memory Access
DMS	Data Management System
DNA	Digital Network Architecture
DOI	Department of Industry
DP	Data Protection OR Data Processing
DRAW	Direct Read After Write
DRCS	Dynamically Redefinable Character Set
DSS	Decision Support System
DTL	Diode Transistor Logic
DV-I	Digital Video Interactive
EBCDIC	Extended Binary Coded Decimal Interchange Code
ECL	Emitter Coupled Logic
ECMA	European Computer Manufacturers Association
ECOM	Electronic Computer Originated Mail
ECS	European Communications Satellite
Ecu	European Currency Unit
EDI	Electronic Data Interchange
EDI-FACT	Electronic Data Interchange For Administration Commerce and Transport
EDTV	Extended Definition Television
EFT	Electronic Funds Transfer
EFTPOS	Electronic Funds Transfer from Point of Sale
EIA	Electronic Industry Association
EIES	Electronic Information Exchange System
EIRP	Equivalent Isotropically Radiated Power

EISA	Extended Industry Standard Architecture
EL	Electroluminescent
EM	Electronic Mail
EMS	Electronic Message/Mail System
EMS	Expanded Memory Specification
EPC	Editorial Processing Centre
EPLD	Electrically Programmed Logic Device
EPROM	Erasable Programmable Read Only Memory
EEPROM	Electrically Erasable Programmable Read Only Memory
EGA	Extended Graphics Adaptor
EIS	Executive Information System
ESA	European Space Agency
ETSI	European Telecommunications Standards Institute
FAX	Facsimile
FCC	Federal Communications Commission
FDDI	Fibreoptic Digital Data Interface
FDM	Frequency Division Multiplexing
FEP	Front End Processor
FET	Field Effect Transistor
FM	Frequency Modulation
FORT-RAN	FORmula TRANslator
FRG	Federal Republic of Germany
FSK	Frequency Shift Keying
FT	Financial Times
GAs	Gallium Arsenide
GCR	Graphics Code Recording
GHz	Gigahertz (thousand million Hz)
Giga-	Thousand million
GKS	Graphics Kernel System
GNP	Gross National Product
GSP	Graphics Signal Processing
GUI	Graphics User Interface
HDLC	High Level Data Link Control
HDTV	High Definition Television
HEMT	High Electron Mobility Transistor
HEX	Hexadecimal
HIT	Retrieved item which matches query
HMOS	High Speed Metal Oxide Semiconductor
HP	Hewlett Packard

Hz	Hertz ("cycle")	LCD	Liquid Crystal Display
IBA	Independent Broadcasting Authority	LC/H	Lines of code per hour
		LED	Light Emitting Diode
IBM	International Business Machines	LPC	Linear Predictive Coding
		Lpi	Lines per inch
IC	Integrated Circuit	LQ	Letter Quality
ICI	Imperial Chemical Industries	LSI	Large Scale Integration
ICL	International Computers Ltd	M	Million
IDA	Integrated Digital Access	MARC	MAchine Readable Catalogue
IEEE	Institute of Electrical & Electronics Engineers	Mbits	Million bits
		Mbps	Million bits per sec.
IFIP	International Federation for Information Processing	Mbytes	Million bytes
		MCA	Micro-Channel Architecture
IIS	Institute of Information Scientists	MCGA	Multi-Coloured Graphics Adaptor
INRIA	Institut National de Recherche en Informatique et Automatique	MED-LARS	MEDical Literature Analysis and Retrieval System
INTREX	Information TRansfer Experiment	MED-LINE	MEDLARS Online systems
I/O	Input/Output	Mega-	Million
IPS	Instructions Per Second	MESFET	MEtal Semiconductor Field Effect Transistor
IPSS	International Packet Switching System or Service	MFLOPS	Millions of Floating Point Operations Per Second
IR	Information Retrieval	MFM	Modified Frequency Modulation
ISBN	International Standard Book Number	MHz	Megahertz (million Hz)
		Micro	Millionth
ISDN	Integrated Services Digital Network	Mil	One thousandth of an inch
		Milli-	Thousandth
ISI	Institute for Scientific Information	MIPS	Million Instructions Per Second
		MIS	Management Information System
ISO	International Standards Organisation	MIT	Massachusetts Institute for Technology
ISPN	International Standard Program Number	mm	Millimetres
		Modem	Modulator/Demodulator
IT	Information Technology	MODFET	Modulation Doped Field Effect Transistor
ITA	Independent Television Authority		
		MOS	Metal Oxide Semiconductor
ITDM	Intelligent Time Division Multiplexing	MOSFET	Metal Oxide Semiconductor Field Effect Transistor
ITT	International Telephone and Telegraph Co	MPEG	Motion Picture Experts Group
		MP/M	Multiprogramming Control Program for Microprocessors
ITU	International Telecommunication Union		
		ms	Millisecond
ITV	Independent Television	MS DOS	Microsoft Disk Operating System
I^2L	Integrated Injection Logic		
JPEG	Joint Photographic Experts Group	MTA	Message Transport Agent
		MTBF	Mean Time Between Failures
K	Thousand		
Kbits	Thousand bits	mu	Microsecond
KBS	Knowledge Based System	MUSE	Multiple Sub-Nyquist Sampling Encoding
KWIC	Key Word in Context		
KWOC	Key Word Out of Context	Mux	Multiplexer
LAN	Local Area Network	Nano-	Thousand Millionth
LC	Library of Congress	NAPLPS	North American Presentation Local Protocol Syntax
Lc	Lower case		

NCC	National Computer Council	PTT	Post Telegraph & Telephone administration
NCR	National Cash Register		
NLM	National Library of Medicine	RAM	Random Access Memory
NLQ	Near Letter Quality	R&D	Research & Development
NMOS	n-type Metal Oxide Semiconductor	RISC	Reduced Instruction Set Computer
		RJE	Remote Job Entry
NRZ	Non-Return to Zero	RLIN	Research Libraries Information Network
Ns	Nanosecond		
NUI	Network User Identifier	ROM	Read Only Memory
OCC	Other Communications Company	R/W	Read/Write
OCLC	Ohio Computer Library Centre	SAA	Systems Applications Architecture
OCR	Optical Character Recognition		
ODA	Office Document Architecture	SBS	Satellite Business Systems
ODBS	Optical Disk Based System	SCI	Science Citation Index
OEM	Original Equipment Manufacturer	SCSI	Small Computer Systems Interface
		SCVF	Single Channel Voice Frequency
OFTEL	Office of Telecommunications	SDI	Selective Dissemination of Information
OPAC	Online Public Access Catalogue		
OROM	Optical Raad Only Memory	SDLC	Synchronous Data Link Control
OS	Operating System		
OSC	Operating System Command	SECAM	Sequential Couleur a Memoire
OSI	Open System Interconnections	SGML	Standard General Markup Language
OTS	Orbital Test Satellite	SLIC	Subscriber Line Interface Circuit
P	Pica (million Millionth)		
PABX	Private Automatic Branch Exchange	SNA	Systems Network Architecture
		SPL	Sound Pressure Level
PBX	Private Branch Exchange	SQL	Structured Query Language
PAD	Packet Assembler/Disassembler	SRAM	Static Random Access Memory
PAL	Phase Alternation Line	SSSO	Special Service Satellite Operator
PARC	Palo Alto Research Centre		
PC	Printed Circuit OR Personal Computer	STATDM	Statistical Time Division Multiplexing
		STD	Subscriber Trunk Dialling
PCM	Pulse Code Modulation	STDM	Synchronous Time Divison Multiplexing
PCNET	Personal Computer NETwork		
PDI	Picture Description Instructions	STI	Scientific & Technical Information
PDN	Public Data Network	T	Tera (million million)
Pel	Picture element	TDM	Time Division Multiplexing
Peta-	Thousand Million Million	Tera-	Million million
PIN	p-i-n photodiode	THz	Terahertz (million million Hz)
PIN	Personal Identification Number	TPA	Transient Program Area
PIRA	Printing & Packaging Research Association	TRE	Telecommunications Research Establishment
Pixel	Picture element	TTL	Transistor Transistor Logic
PKA	Public Key Algorithm	TTY	TeleTYpewriter
PLP	Presentation Level Protocol	TV	Television
PMOS	p-type Metal Oxide Semi-conductor	TVRO	TeleVision REceive Only
		TWT	Travelling Wave Tube
POTS	Plain Old Telephone System	u	(Greek) Micro (millionth)
PROM	Programmable Read Only Memory	UA	Uer Agent
		UART	Universal Asynchronous Receiver and Transmitter
PSI	Permuterm Subject Index		
PSS	Packet Switching System/Service	UNESCO	United Nations Educational Scientific and Cultural Organis.
PSTN	Public Switched Telephone Network		

UNISIST	United Nations International Scientific Information Systems	**VSAM**	Virtual Sequential Access Method
us	Microsecond	**VSAT**	Very Small Aperture Terminal
USART	Universal Synchronous/ Asynchronous Receiver and Transmitter	**VTAM**	Virtual Telecommunications Access Method
USPS	United States Postal Service	**WAN**	Wide Area Network
VADS	Value Added Data Services	**WARC**	World Administrative Radio Conference
VANS	Value Added Network Services	**WATS**	Wide Area Telephone Service
VAT	Value Added Tax	**WFP**	Wideband Flexibility Point
VCR	Video Casette Recorder	**WIMP**	Windows, Icons, Mouse, Pull-Down Menus
VDU	Visual Display Unit		
VGA	Video Graphics Adaptor	**WORM**	Write Once Read Many
VHD	Video High Density	**WP**	Word Processing
VHSIC	Very High Speed Integrated Circuit	**WYSI-WYG**	What You See Is What You Get
VLSI	Very Large Scale Integrated circuit	**WUI**	Western Union International
		X-OFF	Transmitter Off
VME	Virtual Machine Environment	**X-ON**	Transmitter On
VRAM	Video Random Access Memory	**XOR**	Exclusive Or

GLOSSARY

ACOUSTIC COUPLER
    A modem incorporating receptacles for the microphone and earphone in a telephone handset. When the handset is placed on the acoustic coupler, which is connected to a computer communications port, tones representing data may be sent and received. Since the telephone is connected to a telephone line, no other direct connection to the telephone network is needed.

ALGORITHM
    A set of step-by-step rules for solving a problem.

ALPHA-GEOMETRIC CODING
    A scheme for transmitting control codes and displaying videotex frames, providing for a wider range of colours, character sizes, and character sets than are provided in alpha-mosaic coding.

ALPHA-MOSAIC CODING
    A scheme for transmitting control codes and displaying videotex frames built up from a repertoire of symbols stored in the receiver. The selection and positioning of the symbols in small areas on the CRT screen are controlled by coded data. The repertoire consists either of characters, occupying the whole of the small area, or smaller elements occupying all or part of the area, which can be combined together. A combination of small elements is used to construct graphics having a rather coarse structure. This method of coding, with variations, is used in most videotex systems, Telidon being a notable exception.

ALPHA-PHOTOGRAPHIC CODING
    A scheme used for controlling individual picture elements with as much within-receiver storage as may be necessary to display high resolution pictures on all or part of the screen. See Picture Prestel.

AMPLITUDE MODULATION
    The variation of carrier signal strength (amplitude), as a function of a data signal.

ANALOGUE SIGNAL
    A voltage or current varying in proportion to a change in a physical quantity - as produced, for example, by a microphone.

ANALOGUE-TO-DIGITAL CONVERTER (ADC)
    A device for converting analogue data into digital form.

ANISOTROPIC
    See ISOTROPIC.

ANSWERBACK
    A reply message from a terminal to verify that the correct terminal has been reached and that it is operational.

ANTIOPE
    Generic name for French videotex systems e.g.Didon and Titan.

ARCHITECTURE
The design and philosophy of both the hardware and software of a computer system.

ARQ
Automatic Request for Repeat. A method of error correction in which each block of data - a block is some fixed number of data elements - is checked at the receiver and if an error is detected a request for a repeat is automatically sent to the transmitter.

ASCII
American Standard Code for Information Interchange - a code widely used for the transmission of text. It is a 7 bit (plus 1 parity bit) code providing for 128 alpha-numeric and other symbols.

ASSEMBLY LANGUAGE
A computer language using symbols, often mnemonics, which is translated by the assembler conversion program into machine code. It enables a programmer to work in a language more like English instead of having to work with the bit patterns of machine code. For example if the assembly symbol for register C is C and the symbol for the ASCII code for K is "K", then the assembly language statement MV C, K would mean "Move the ASCII code for K to register C". In microcomputers each proprietary CPU has its own assembly language according to the nature of its architecture.

Assembly language may appear to be "of higher level" than machine language and so qualify as a high level language, but it is not so regarded because it does not have all the features of higher languages; a single instruction in a high level language often translates into a series of sub-routine and/or machine code instructions.

A Cross-Assembler is a program which translates an assembly language program written for one type of microcomputer into a machine code for another computer.

ASYNCHRONOUS
A method of defining the start and end of a code group with a special code - the code group is not time-defined.

ASYNCHRONOUS DATA TRANSMISSION
Data transmission in which receiver and transmitter are not synchronised, each code group representing a character being defined by a special code preceding and terminating it.

ATM
Asynchronous Transfer Mode. A method to be used for transporting all data over the B-ISDN in the same format. This format bears some resemblance to the format used for packet switching.

ATTENUATION
The decrease in amplitude of a signal, usually measured in decibels.

AUTOMATIC FALLBACK
An automatic decrease in the speed of transmission of a facsimile signal if the transmission channel is unable to sustain the existing speed.

AUTODIALLER
A device for automatically dialling telephone numbers, for instance by pressing one key, which may be under software control. Often many different numbers may be typed in by the user for permanent storage to be recalled by the software for single key "dialling".

AUTOMATIC SHIFT-DOWN
See AUTOMATIC FALLBACK.

BACKUP
To make a copy of stored data in case the original data is lost because of a computer malfunction.

BANDWIDTH
The range of signalling frequencies which can be conveyed by a communications channel with some defined small amount of attenuation and distortion.

BASEBAND
The transmission of a digital signal without the use of a carrier, i.e. without modulation.

BASIC
Beginners All-purpose Symbolic Instruction Code. A high level language developed by Kemeny and Kurtz at Dartmouth College, USA in 1964. It was the first language to become very widely used in microcomputers and still is widely used.

BATCH MODE
Computer processing of data in one operation from start to finish.

BAUD
One signalling element per second.

BAUDOT
A 5-bit data-code commonly used for low speed transmission over telegraph and telex circuits. The International Telegraph Alphabet number two (ITA2).

BILDSCHIRMTEXT
A viewdata-type service in use in The Federal Republic of Germany.

BINARY DIGIT
In the binary notation either of the characters 0 or 1. "Bit" is the commonly used abbreviation for binary digit. The basic unit of data with which the computer works. The bit can take the form of a magnetised spot, an electronic impulse, a positively charged magnetic core, etc. A group of bits forming a code are used to represent a character in a computer. See also BYTE.

BISTABLE MULTIVIBRATOR
A multivibrator in which one transistor is on and the other off until the states are changed over by a triggering pulse.

BIT
Abbreviation for BINARY DIGIT (q.v.). In data transmission, if one signalling element contains one unit of data, one bit per second equals one baud. In multi-level signalling, more than one unit of data may be sent per baud. For example if 8 level signalling is used, 8 bits are sent per baud, and the signalling rate is $\log_2 8 = 3$ bits per second.

BIT MAP
A technique for providing a screen display in which every pixel on the screen corresponds to an addressable pixel in memory.

BLOCK
A contiguous sequence of BYTES (q.v.).

BRIDGE
See GATEWAY.

BROADBAND
Of wide bandwidth. Implying the ability to transport data at high speed.

BUFFER
A storage unit organised to act as a reservoir for data being moved between a source and a destination which operate at different data rates.

BUS
A set of electrically conducting lines between data sources and destinations.

BYTE
A group of 8 bits, which may include a parity bit, forming a code to represent data.

CABLE TELEVISION
A system that delivers TV by wire (cable) to a subscriber's TV receiver, often by a number of selectable channels. Many cable systems cable can carry other services such as data transmission and telephone services.

CACHE MEMORY
A relatively small fast storage buffer unit organised to handle data called from disk on a "probability of need" basis which can be transferred into main memory faster than from disk into main memory.

CAPTAINS
A videotex system developed by Nippon Telegraph & Telephone (NTT) in Japan capable of handling Kanji (Chinese) and Kana symbols which are reproduced by dot patterns in 8 x 12 blocks. Control signal and dot patterns are transmitted. In order to cope with the bandwidth/time problem a relatively high transmission rate is used with data reduction techniques.

CEEFAX
A teletext service offered by the British Broadcasting Corporation via its television channels. Data is broadcast during an interval within each frame unoccupied by "conventional" TV signal data.

CELLULAR RADIO
A mobile radio telephone system comprising a large number of short range base stations linked to the PSTN, controlling a small area. As a vehicle moves from one cell to the next it is transferred automatically to the new cell's base station.

CENTRAL PROCESSING UNIT (CPU).

A set of computer circuits, usually at least an Arithmetic and Logic Unit (ALU), and a Control Unit, which interpret and execute instructions.

CENTREX
Remote PABX facilities provided by a telecoms authority which appear to the subscriber as if there is a PABX exchange on his premises.

CHANNEL
The electrical link between data communicating devices. The near synonym "circuit" when used in this context is, perhaps, better reserved for individual data-communication paths within the channel. A channel may contain one or more circuits.

CHANNEL CAPACITY
The maximum rate of data transfer that is possible in a given channel.

CHARGED COUPLED DEVICE (CCD)
A semi-conductor element in which data is stored as an electrical charge which may be transferred to an adjacent element by a control pulse. In a CCD image sensor, a charge is generated when light is focused upon it. Sensors may be arranged in the form of a strip of CCD elements associated with an electronic transport system. After a given light exposure time, the charges are shifted by the transport system along to an output terminal where they represent a bit-by-bit serial representation of the light reflected from a strip of the image.

Such an Image Sensor is manufactured like other integrated circuits, the strip consisting, for instance, of 1728 elements spaced at 0.127 mm, with about 8 elements per mm or about 200 per inch. The output from such a strip represents a strip of the image 0.127 mm wide and about 21.9 cm long (0.005 x 8.6 inches).

CIRCUIT
1. A set of interconnected electronic components.
2. A connection between telecommunicating devices.

CIRCUIT SWITCHING
A technique of switching in a data network whereby a physical route or a fixed data path is dedicated to the two interconnected devices for the duration of the connection. Sometimes called line switching.

CLOCK

A master timing device to provide timing pulses for synchronising the operation of a system.

CLOSED USER GROUP

An arrangement giving designated users exclusive access to part of a system - for instance a videotex data base.

COAXIAL CABLE

A central core of signal wire, contained within an outer metallic tube but separated from it by a low loss insulating material. The form of construction provides a wideband telecommunications channel.

CODE

A system of symbols representing data. Thus a "7 bit binary code" could represent up to 128 data elements. Sometimes coded data may be recoded. For instance in facsimile systems, re-coding is used to transform data derived from scanning the image into a suitable form for transmission.

COMPATIBILITY

A word used to indicate that one device can exchange "information" with another.

COMPILER

A program which translates a program in a high level language into a low-level one (usually in machine language).

COMPRESSION

A method of reducing amounts of data.

CONCENTRATOR

Generic name for devices which organise the transport of data in two or more circuits within a single telecommunications channel without mutual interference.

CONFIGURATION

A particular grouping of hardware/software elements designed to meet a particular requirement.

CONTENTION

A condition on a communication channel or in a peripheral device when two or more stations try to transmit at the same time, or when access to a resource is simultaneously required by two or more users.

CSMA (CARRIER SENSE MULTIPLE ACCESS)

A data link control protocol for networks in which all stations can receive all messages. A station can detect the presence of a transmitted message by sensing the carrier of the transmission. When a station wishes to send a message it first waits until no other station is transmitting. When two or more stations try to send messages concurrently, collisions may occur since a station will not receive another station's signal until after it has begun transmitting. A collision detection (CD) mechanism detects the collision, causing the stations to terminate their current transmissions, and they try again later.

COUNTER
An electronic circuit which generates an output pulse after receiving a given number of input pulses.

CP/M
Control Program Monitor, the most widely used microcomputer early operating system. It was developed by Gary Kidall of Digital Research in 1975. A large number of versions of it have been written, CP/M 80 1.4 being well used for 8 bit microcomputers but then moving on to other versions including CP/M 86 for 16 bit machines (which was somewhat less successful), and a multi-user version called MP/M.

DAISY WHEEL
A type of impact printer printing-head comprising a rotating spoked wheel with an embossed character at the end of each spoke. When printing, the required spoke is positioned over the paper and pressed against it through an ink ribbon.

DATA
Plural of Datum.
1. Symbols assigned a meaning in order to convey "information".
2. Data, as in a message, as opposed to speech, images, text etc., although all of these are, in fact, also "data".

DATABASE
Files of data organised so that users can access a pool of information.

DATA CAPTURE
The collection of data, usually with a view to storage and "information" access.

DATA COMMUNICATION EQUIPMENT (DCE)
The data network side of a telecoms interface, usually a modem. See also DATA TERMINATING EQUIPMENT.

DATAGRAM
A self-contained package of data sent independently of other packages.

DATA REDUCTION
See COMPRESSION.

DATA TERMINAL EQUIPMENT (DTE)
The user's side of a data network interface such as a computer terminal, teleprinter, or office workstation. See also DATA COMMUNICATION EQUIPMENT.

DEBUG
To remove program errors.

DEBUGGING
The detection and correction of program faults.

DECIBEL (dB)
A measure of relative magnitude (as power, current, or voltage). The number of decibels equals 10 times the log (to the base 10) of the ratio of the measured power to the reference power level, or 20 times the log of the ratio of the voltage or current to the reference voltage or current level.

DEDICATED LINE
A line permanently assigned to specific data terminals and not part of a switched network. Also called a private line.

DES
Data Encryption Standard. Transformation adopted by the US Government for the protection of data.

DESCRIPTOR
Synonym for TERM

DIDON
French teletext system similar to British teletext but using a different code and character repertoire requiring a degree of extra complexity.

DIGITAL
Data represented as a series of coded pulses having only two possible states "on" or "off", "1" or "0", etc. Digital signals can be more easily stored, processed, regenerated, and transmitted than ANALOGUE data (q.v).

DIGITAL TRANSMISSION
A method of signalling by coded pulses. Its advantages are that impulses which become weak may be regenerated without adding noise (as is added in amplifiers for ANALOGUE (q.v) signals; signals may be stored, processed etc., by cheap mass produced semiconductor circuits; forms of coding, and error correction may be used effectively.

DIRECT BROADCASTING SATELLITE (DBS)
A geostationary satellite which picks up broadcast signals from an earth station and then retransmits them back to earth. The signal is powerful enough for it to be received direct (by the consumer) by means of a domestic dish aerial fixed to the roof (or in the garden) measuring as little as 90cm in diameter.

DISTRIBUTED SYSTEMS
A computer complex made up of separate networked co-operating computers at different locations as opposed to a centralised system.

DOWNLOADING
Moving data from a source to a destination computer, usually through a telecommunications link.

DPNSS
Digital Private Network Signalling System. A signalling system used between most PABXs made in the UK,for control purposes.

DRIVER
A small program of routines for port input/output control.

DUOBINARY SIGNALLING
A method of signalling in which two level impulses, 0, 1, are encoded into three levels 0, +1, and -1. The signalling element rate remains the same but more information is transmitted per element.

DUPLEX SIGNALLING

Data transmission in both directions at once. A receiver can interrupt a transmitter without waiting for the conclusion of transmission.

DYNAMICALLY REDEFINABLE CHARACTER SET (DRCS)

A scheme for transmitting control codes and displaying videotex frames built up from a range of patterns transmitted or stored at the receiver either to form characters, or to be combined to form graphics with good resolution. The graphics are formed from combinations of patterns such as Line, Arc, Polygon, etc., or by specifying a shape pixel by pixel.

ECCLES-JORDAN CIRCUIT

A bistable multivibrator.

EDI

Electronic Data Interchange - the exchange of invoices, orders and other transactional documentation transferred in a standardised manner between the computers of trading companies.

EDIFACT

EDI (q.v.) for Administration, Commerce and Transport. EDI standards developed within the UN/ECE WP4, and now an International Standard - ISO 9735. Intended to provide a generic national and international syntax and message set able to accommodate many current standards.

EGA

IBM's enhanced colour graphics "standard" (640 x 350 pixels, 16 colours). Widely supported by other manufacturers.

ELECTRO-ETCH RECORDING

A obsolete recording method in which the stylus at a receiver scans the surface of sensitive paper in synchronism with the transmitter's scanner. Contact is made when a "black" signal element is received, and a current passes across the contact point producing a mark on the paper.

ELECTRONIC FUNDS TRANSFER (EFT)

Transfer of funds by electronic means e.g. from a purchaser's to a vendor's bank account, or bulk fund transfers between banks.

ELECTRONIC FUNDS TRANSFER AT POINT OF SALE (EFTPOS)

Automatic transfer of funds from a purchaser's account to a retailer's in consequence of a message sent to the purchaser's bank from a point of sale terminal.

ELECTRONIC MAIL (E-MAIL)

A system for the delivery of messages from networked computer terminals to storage at addressee's terminals for retrieval on demand.

ELECTROSTATIC RECORDING

A recording method in which a "writing" element charges a point on the surface of non-conductive paper or intermediate drum, corresponding to a "black signal" element. A liquid or particle "toner" then adheres to charged points and is fixed permanently by heat.

EMULATION
The use of programming techniques and special machine features to permit a computing system to execute programs written for another system. A particular example is where a microcomputer with the addition of special hardware and/or software can be made to act as a terminal compatible with a mainframe computer.

EMULATOR
A program to make a computer run programs written for a different type of computer or (more widely) to make a computer behave as if it were another computer.

EQUALISING
A method of compensating for distortion introduced by a communications channel by adjusting circuit elements externally connected to it.

ERLANG
A unit used for defining the volume of telephone traffic, measured as the connection rate of calls multiplied by their mean holding time.

ETHERNET
A widely used Local Area Network conforming to the provisions of the Open Systems Interconnection (OSI q.v.) seven layer model.

EXPONENT
The power to which the number base is raised e.g in 10^3 and 2^8, 3 and 8 are the exponents.

FACSIMILE ("FAX")
A system for transmitting a copy of an image on a piece of paper from one fax machine to another via a communication channel, usually the PSTN.

FIBREOPTIC CABLE
A cable containing one or more strands of special glass capable of conveying light modulated by a data signal over long distances with only a small amount of attenuation. Semiconductor devices at either end convert electrical into light energy or vice versa. A major purpose of using light as a telecoms media is its inherent extremely wide bandwidth.

FIELD
A part of a record designated for a particular kind of data. For example each record in a car part file might contain a field for the name of the part, a field for the manufacturer's name, a field for the part number, etc.

FILE
A named collection of computer records, usually with common attributes - for example descriptions of car parts. The name enables the file to be stored and recalled as one unit.

FIRMWARE
A program which is permanently stored in a computer hardware device, often as a circuit which always performs the same functions when triggered.

FLATBED SCANNING
A scanning procedure in which an illuminated document is moved on rollers driven by a stepping motor past a photo-sensor strip so that it is flat when opposite the strip.

FLIP-FLOP
A bistable multivibrator.

FLOATING POINT NUMBER
The representation of a number by integer(s) multiplied by the radix raised to a power e.g. 105 becomes 1.05×10^2. This form or representation is more convenient for computer handling.

FOOTPRINT
Of a Direct Broadcasting Satellite. Geographical area over which a satellite signal can be received.

FORTRAN
FORmula TRANslation, a high-level computer programming language developed by IBM.

FREQUENCY DIVISION MULTIPLEXING (FDM)
A type of multiplexing where the band width of a transmission channel is divided into separate subchannels or circuits, separated by guard-bands.

FREQUENCY MODULATION
A method of varying the frequency of a carrier of fixed amplitude above and below the normal carrier frequency at a rate corresponding to changes in a modulating signal .

FULL DUPLEX
Transmission of data in both directions at the same time.

GATEWAY
1. A communications processor connected to at least two networks which enables messages to pass between networks and therefore between stations connected to different networks.
2. An interconnection between two or more host computers established so that an online user can easily access databases available at any host.

GEOSYNCHRONOUS ORBIT
A satellite orbits the earth at a fixed distance from it when its velocity, which tends to carry it away from the earth, is exactly balanced by gravitational pull. When positioned over the equator at a height of 35,860 Kms moving in the same direction as the earth, it completes one orbit in the same time as the earth takes to complete one rotation. It then appears to be stationary over a point on the earth's surface and is said to be in geosynchronous orbit.

GREYSCALE
The representation of a tonal scale from black to white. For a digital representation, each of 256 shades, for example, could be represented by an 8-bit number.

HALF DUPLEX TRANSMISSION
Transmission possible in both directions alternately but not simultaneously, compare full duplex (simultaneous 2-way) and simplex (one direction only)

HAMMING CODE
A code in which extra bits are automatically inserted into a code group by a transmitting device so that a receiving device capable of carrying out the necessary checking procedures can detect and correct single bit errors.

HANDSHAKE
An exchange of information between inter-communicating devices to establish compatible operating conditions and procedures.

HARD COPY
A "print-out" of data on paper. A printed copy of data (text, image, etc) output from a machine in human-readable form.

HARDWARE
A general term used to describe the electronic or mechanical components of a communications system: e.g. satellite, computer terminal, TV set. etc.

HDLC
High-level data link control. An international standard communications protocol developed by ISO in response to IBM's SDLC.

HERTZ (Hz)
The unit of frequency equal to one cycle per second. Cycles are now referred to as Hertz in honour of the experimenter Heinrich Hertz.

HIGH LEVEL LANGUAGE
A language enabling programs to be written relatively quickly in which each instruction embodies two or more instructions of a lower level language - e.g. assembly or machine language. A programmer writing source programmes will usually use a high level language, but parts, and occasionally all of a program will be written in assembly language for special purposes. Instructions in a higher level language take longer to execute than in assembly language.

HOST COMPUTER
A host computer in a network is a computer that provides services and facilities that may be used via other computers and/or terminals on the network.

HUFFMAN CODE
A form of run length one dimensional code. A modification of it is recommended by CCITT for data reduction in group 3 facsimile machines.

HOME BANKING/TELEBANKING
Term used to describe a service for calling up information about a bank account, transfer money from one account to another, pay bills, etc., from a home terminal by means of an interactive videotex or cable system.

HOME SHOPPING/TELESHOPPING
A service for viewing, ordering, and paying for goods from home using a microcomputer or terminal and an interactive videotex or cable system.

IMAGE SENSOR
See SENSOR

INFERENCE ENGINE
Expert system software embodying a set of rules for solving problems using data from a knowledge base.

INFORMATION
1. The reduction of uncertainty.
2. A collection of meaningful data usually assembled with the objective of increasing the knowledge of a human who assimilates it.

INFORMATION PROVIDER
An organisation that supplies the information stored on the computer of a public videotex or private "value-added" data service, e.g. banks, news agencies, mail order firms, travel agencies, and database hosts.

INKJET PRINTER
A printer in which a jet of ink is broken up into charged fine particles which are steered on to paper by an electrostatic field.

INPUT
The data to be input. The transfer of data from a peripheral device into a computer.

INPUT/OUTPUT
A general term for the peripheral equipment used to communicate with a computer, commonly called I/O. The data involved in such operations.

INTEGRATED CIRCUITS
Complete complex electronic circuits on small chips of semi-conductor material formerly made up of separate components occupying a very much larger volume.

INTEGRATED SERVICES DIGITAL NETWORK (ISDN)
A CCITT project for telecommunication networks employing digital transmission and able to handle digitized voice and data on an "end-to-end" (subscriber to subscriber) basis.

INTELLIGENT NETWORK
A term, coined by the Bell Organisation, indicating that a range of easily selectable services will be available over a network. It may include the provision of a Private Virtual Network, that is a switched network of the type normally only available in a private line system, but whose costs are closer to the costs of a public network. Such a network would include the facilities of an ISDN network, with enhancements.

INTERACTIVE MODE
Computer processing which proceeds in steps with human intervention to observe, modify, or input new data according to results or requirements.

INTERFACE
The boundary between computer or telecom hardware devices or functions. The word may be used to cover details from plug and socket pin connections to quite complex control software.

INTERPRETER
A program which fetches and executes an instruction in a high level language before proceeding to the next instruction.

INTERRUPT
A signal generated in a computer system to indicate a requirement to the CPU with some previously assigned priority rating. For example a signal may be received from a printer port to indicate that the printer is ready to receive data. The CPU may then interrupt the program currently running if the interrupt has a higher priority, supply the data, and then return to the program.

IPSS
International Packet Switched Services. A service offered by British Telecom for connecting data from the UK to the North American Telenet and Tymnet and other networks.

ISDN. See INTEGRATED SERVICES DIGITAL NETWORK.

ISO
International Standards Organisation. An organisation established to promote the development of standards for the international exchange of goods and services, also to develop mutual cooperation in areas of intellectual, scientific, technological and economic activity.

ISOTROPIC RADIATION
Radiation with equal intensity in all directions. A radio transmitting aerial (antenna) designed to provide a service to the area surrounding it would radiate isotropically. A satellite dish aerial beamed at some area of the earth is an example of anisotropic radiation.

KEYFAX
A teletext service introduced by Field Electronic Publishing, Chicago. It is transmitted via satellite to cable TV companies for distribution to their subscribers.

KEYPAD
A small device resembling a pocket calculator containing miniature keys. For example a keypad is used for controlling a television receiver. A videotex receiver keypad embodies keys numbered 0 to 9 and three or four control keys.

KNOWLEDGE BASE
The data base in an expert system, input by a human subject expert .

KU BAND
The microwave frequency band 12-18 GHz, used by both line-of-sight radio links and communication satellites.

LEASED LINE
A line reserved for the exclusive use of a leasing customer without the necessity for exchange switching.

LIGHT PEN
A miniature photo-electric device mounted in a pen holder, used to interact with a program by "writing" on a computer monitor screen; also used at point-of-sales terminals for "reading" bar codes.

LOCAL AREA NETWORK (LAN)
A data communications network used to interconnect data terminal equipment distributed over a limited area, typically up to 10 square kilometres.

LOCAL LOOP
A term (of American origin) used to describe the telephone lines between a subscriber and the telephone exchange.

MACHINE LANGUAGE
A set of binary-coded instructions for execution by a particular computer. Machine language instructions are directly executed by the computer so machine code may often be the object or target code which is produced by a higher level language (q.v.). These days it is unlikely that machine code will also be the source code - that is the code used by the programmer to write the program.

MACRO
A named series of source program lines which are inserted en bloc by an assembler program when named. A macro is a programmer's time-saving aid since a frequently used series of instructions can be added without the need to write out the full code.

MANAGED DATA NETWORK SERVICES (MDNS)
Network connections provided and managed by the supplier on behalf of their customers.

MANTISSA
The significant integers of a number raised to a power. Thus in the floating point number 6.8×10^3, the mantissa is 6.8.

MAP
Manufacturing Automation Protocol is a detailed paper specification of communications protocols, enabling integration of computerised machines.

MENU
A computer-displayed page offering a number of choices. Typically each choice is numbered and a particular choice is executed by depressing a numbered key.

MESSAGE
Symbols in a series of more or less unlimited length, which convey information. The symbols in a message may signify text, graphics, illustrations etc. "Message" as used in telecoms does not mean "a brief communication".

MESSAGE SWITCHING
A method for transmitting messages over a network, often implying a "store and forward" technique. For example a series of telex messages could be input to a message switching terminal which is already sending messages, to be stored and queued for transmission to addressees listed in headers.

MICROPROCESSOR
The integrated circuit elements on one or more chips which form the Central Processing Unit of a computer.

MICROWAVE
Very short wavelength radio waves which are used for high capacity terrestrial point-to-point and satellite links.

MODEM
(MOdulator/DEModulator). A device that converts computer signals to audio signals that can be sent over an analogue telephone line, and converts audio signals received over the telephone to digital signals suitable for computers. It follows that a compatible modem is required at each end of the telephone network to allow two computers to "talk" to each other.

MODULATION
A method of converting data from the form in which it is generated into a different form which enables it to be transmitted through a channel unable to convey the data in its original form. For example data pulses may be changed into audible tones which can be conveyed by the telephone network.

MONITOR
A visual display unit (VDU) on whose screen data is displayed; the display part of a computer or data terminal.

MP/M
A multi-user operating system for microcomputers, derived from CP/M.

MS/DOS
Microsoft Disc Operating System, a microcomputer operating system introduced by Microsoft in 1982. It incorporates some improvements compared with CP/M particularly in respect of transportability - that is the ease with which it can be used on different types of machine. MS/DOS is being widely used with programs using "windows". A version of it - PC/DOS - is used on today's most popular microcomputer - the IBM PC.

MULTI-ACCESS
The ability for several users to communicate with the computer at the same time, each working independently on their own job.

MULTI-DROP LINE
A communication system configuration using a single channel on-line to serve multiple terminals. Use of this type of line normally requires some kind of polling mechanism, addressing each terminal with a unique ID. Also called multipoint line.

MULTIPLEXER
1. A device which organises the data from two or more circuits to be transported in a single telecommunications channel.

2. An electronic switch used in computers successively to connect a number of sources or destinations to a single bus. The switch may be multi-pole - for example it may connect data from any of several 8-line sources to an 8-line bus.

MULTIVIBRATOR
An electronic circuit consisting basically of two transistors with the output of each coupled to the input of the other producing positive feedback. The on-off states of the two transistors depend on the coupling method.

NARROWCASTING
Term used to refer to the aiming of programmes at specialised interest groups. It involves a step beyond "broadcasting", where programmes have to contain a mass appeal, and is technically feasible in broadband cable systems.

NETWORK
1. Electrical. General term used to describe the interconnection of devices (telephones, data terminals, exchanges) by communications channels, e.g. public switched telephone network (PSTN), packet switched data network (PSDN), local area network (LAN), and wide area netework (WAN).
2. Library. Co-operative arrangements between libraries, for example for book loans.

NODE
A computer or switching device situated at the connection point of a communication network to monitor, switch, or attach communication channels.

NYQUIST RATE
Sampling at a rate equivalent to twice the bandwidth needed for a signal - a requirement for satisfactory analogue to digital conversion.

OBJECT CODE
The machine code used for running programs on a computer. Programs are not now written in the object code. They are automatically translated from a higher level language which is converted into the object code when a program is run. See also COMPILER.

ODA
Office Document Architecture standard, an ISO recommendation related to X4G0 and compatible with it. ODA caters for the efficiently coded representation of multimedia documents having pages which are a mixture of text, and raster or bit map images such as graphics or illustrations.

ODETTE
Organisation for Data Exchange through TeleTransmission in Europe which controls automotive industry EDI message standards and file transfer protocols. Now being adopted in allied industries.

ONLINE
Connected to a computer.

OPCODE
An instruction for an operation to be carried out in a computer program.

OPERAND
The quantity or function upon which an operation is performed in a computer program.

OPERATING SYSTEM
An operating system consists of a suite of utility programs which perform computer management functions and organise and allocate the resources of the machine to deal with Jobs. A job is simply a sequence of processes several of which may be in progress concurrently - for example an overlapping of computational and input/output processes. The operating system handles peripherals and interrupts and deals with errors. It controls the computer system, manages the memory, and provides for file operations and file maintenance. Other important functions include management functions in a microcomputer development system and in machines on which several programmers can work simultaneously ("multi-user" machines).

OPTICAL CHARACTER RECOGNITION (OCR)
A process where a device scans printed or typed characters and converts the optical images into machine readable data, usually ASCII code.

OPTICAL FIBRE CABLE
Optical fibre is the most expensive type of cabling. It has a very wide bandwidth enabling high transmission speeds. Fibre provides a high degree of security along with immunity from environmental factors such as an electrical noise. Users need equipment to convert electrical signals to light pulses and back again. See also COAXIAL CABLE and TWISTED PAIR.

ORACLE
A teletext system offered by Independent Television (ITV) companies in the UK via their television channels. Data is broadcast during an interval within each frame unoccupied by "conventional" TV signal data.

OSI
Open Systems Interconnection. A framework or model recommending standardised methods for interconnecting different systems. All computer systems conforming to the model would be able to communicate with each other regardless of the manufacturer, operating system, etc. The model consists of a hierarchy of "layers", each of which represents a set of functions.

PACKET
A group of bits including data control elements which is switched and transmitted as a unit. The data is arranged in a specified format.

PACKET SWITCHING
A method of transmitting data through a network via computer-controlled store and forward nodes to ensure efficient error-free transmission. Nodes are usually interconnected by at least two telecom channels. A message is split into a number of relatively short blocks of data each comprising header, data, and checking tail. It is stored and despatched through any network path that may become available. Upon arrival at the node to which the addressee is connected the headers and tails are removed and the separate parts are re-constituted into the original message.

PARALLEL PROCESSING
Concurrent execution of two or more programs in the same computer.

PARALLEL TRANSMISSION
The simultaneous transmission   of data along parallel conductors. It is faster but more expensive than serial transmission.

PARITY BIT CHECK
A form of error checking where a bit is added to a bit-group in order to make the bit total always an odd or always an even number (as agreed between sender and recipient). If such a total is not produced when the bits are added at the receiver, an error is present.

PARSER
Software used in natural language expert systems for breaking down a sentence into its component parts with reference to stored grammatical rules.

PASCAL
A high level language developed by Nicholas Wirth at the University of California (San Diego) in 1970. It became used after 1978 when compilers became available. It is gradually displacing Basic since it has a well defined standard and is designed specifically for programmers.

PEL
Picture element.

PHOTOELECTRIC SCANNING
The original form of image scanning in which light reflected from the image is picked up by a photoelectric cell.

PHOTODIODE
A type of photosensor used in image scanners in a similar manner to a CCD element. A photodiode is a semiconductor device in which the reverse current varies according to the incident light.

PHOTOSENSOR
A device which converts light energy into electrical energy.

PICTURE PRESTEL
A system developed by British Telecom for transmitting and receiving high resolution pictures. It exhibits various compromises in data transmission speeds, coding, receiver storage capacity, and percentage occupancy of the screen area by a high resolution picture.

PIPE-LINING
A method of speeding up the execution of a computer program by fetching and executing instructions in the same machine cycle.

PIXEL
Picture element, the smallest discrete element making up a visual display image.

POINT TO POINT
A limited network configuration with communication between two terminals points only, as opposed to multi-point and multi-drop.

POLLING
A method of interrogating a number of transmitting devices with the intention of triggering data transmission if they have data to send. In facsimile, polling means one facsimile machine calling another and receiving a facsimile transmission from it having initiated the transmission with a password.

PORT
The place provided on a computer for the connection of some peripheral device such as a printer, modem, etc.

PRAGMATICS
The study of the useage of a language.

PRESTEL
The viewdata service provided nationally in the UK by British Telecom. A network of interconnected geographically distributed computers are used so that local telephone call connection can be made by users. Page by page information is supplied by a number of information providers.

PREXTEND.
A system developed by British Telecomm to demonstrate the feasibility of using more complex coding compatible with Prestel software.

PRIVATE AUTOMATIC BRANCH EXCHANGE (PABX)
An automatic private exchange with a number of exchange lines and a large number of subscriber lines providing for the transmission of calls to and from the public telephone network, often with each subscriber having his own diallable telephone number.

PRIVATE BRANCH EXCHANGE (PBX)
A manually operated private exchange with a number of exchange lines and a large number of subscriber lines providing for the transmission of calls to and from the public telephone network.

PROGRAM
A sequence of instructions to perform a computational process.

PROOF
Primary Rate ISDN OSI Office Facilities. An Esprit project, due to be completed in 1992, for investigating ISDN-linked LANs.

PROSODIC
Patterns of stress and intonation in a language.

PROTOCOL
A set of rules to control data handling in a communications system.

PSS (PACKET SWITCH STREAM)
The public packet network of the UK's PTT, British Telecom; it offers a national packet switched data service and has been available since 1981. It uses the X.25 interface protocol, providing full duplex working at a range of speeds up to and including 48,000 bps. It can also provide inter-communication between data terminal equipment operating at different speeds. Connections to other public packet networks can be made.

PULSE CODE MODULATION
    A method of coding an analogue signal into digital form.

PVN
    Private Virtual Network. A private switched network similar in effect to a public switched network, but provided by a telecoms authority at a price much lower than a network using leased lines.

QUANTISATION
    Process in which the amplitude range of a signal is divided into a finite number of smaller subranges, usually in digitizable steps.

QUEUED PACKET SYNCHRONOUS EXCHANGE (QPSX)
    A packet switching system devised by the University of Western Australia, likely to be adopted in SONET.

RANDOM ACCESS MEMORY (RAM)
    A form of electronic memory that allows data to be both written to or read from any location independently of others.

RASTER
    The pattern of scanning lines on a CRT screen produced by a spot which traces out a line and then rapidly flies back to trace another adjacent line until the whole screen is traced.

READ CODE
    Relative.Element Address Designate code - a two dimensional code of Japanese origin used in some facsimile machines.

RECORD
    A collection of items containing data with common attributes - for example descriptions of car components - together forming a file.

REDUNDANCY
    Information in a stream of meaningful data which may be excluded without affecting the meaning. Redundant information may be added to a message to make reception more certain. Data may be removed, possibly with some sacrifice in certainty, in order to permit greater efficiency during storage or transmission. For example much redundant information is present in human languages; if all the vowels are removed from a message in English, the meaning of the message may still be understood. Another example is the addition of codes to each code group before transmission to enable devices at a receiver to perform checking, and in some cases automatically to correct an erroneous code group. An increase in the probability of correctness has been achieved at the expense of an increase in redundancy.

REGISTER
    A computer storage circuit usually to store the bits in one word.

REMOTE JOB ENTRY (RJE)
    A system by which work/data is input via a communications link.

REPEATER
    A device used to regenerate (increase and restore) signals in a communications link.

RESOLUTION, IMAGE

The maximum number of discernible elements. Vertical resolution is usually specified in lines per inch or lines per millimetre, horizontal in pixels or lines per inch or millimetre. In facsimile systems when manufacturers specify resolution details, they may also specify the time taken to transmit average density text on A4 paper. More details are shown in the table.

Mode	Transmission Time	Vertical Resolution	Horizontal Resolution
High speed	15 secs	57 lpi(2.66 lines/mm)	200 lpi (7.94 lines/mm)
Standard	22 secs	100 lpi(3.97 lines/mm)	200 lpi
Fine detail	36 secs	200 lpi(7.94 lines/mm	200 lpi

Note the trade-offs between resolution and transmission speed.

RESPONSE TIME

The time a system takes to react to an input.

RS232

EIA standard for terminal-modem serial data transmission interface, equivalent to CCITT V24. Current revision is RS232C.

RUN LENGTH CODING

A code in which a sequence of identical data elements, each of which would normally be individually coded, are collectively coded. The net effect is a considerable reduction in the number of codes required.

SCANNING, IMAGE

The operation of examining the reflected light from an image, usually on paper, point by point and line by line in an ordered sequence. This enables the image to be represented by a stream of data emanating from a photosensor which may be electrically communicated to a remote machine where the image may be reconstructed on paper by a synchronous scanning/printing process. See also CCD.

SCRATCHPAD

A type of memory that usually has small capacity but very fast access.

SDLC

Synchronous Data Link Control. A data link control protocol developed by IBM, superseding BSC.

SEMANTICS

The principles which govern meaning in a language.

SEMICONDUCTOR

A material, such as silicon or germanium, whose conductivity increases with temperature, and may be made to be more conductive permanently by the introduction of other chemicals.

SENSOR, IMAGE
A device for detecting a change in light intensity and converting it into an electrical signal.

SERIAL TRANSMISSION
The transmission of data, one bit at a time, down a single communications wire. See also PARALLEL TRANSMISSION.

SHELL
1. Inference engine software in an expert system which is domain independent. A general purpose set of rules which should be able to solve problems and derive conclusions from different kinds of knowledge data.
2. A structured way of containing data.

SHIFT DOWN
See AUTOMATIC FALLBACK

SIDEBAND
A band of frequencies resulting from a modulation process and displaced from the carrier frequency.

SILICON CHIP
A wafer-fragment of pure silicon, only a few millimetres square, upon which an integrated circuit is printed.

SIMPLEX
Transmission in one direction only.

SINK
Synonym for Destination.

SNA
IBM's standard for information processing networks. It defines the logical structure along with the formats, protocols and operational sequences used for transmitting data through a network. It consists of a set of products which conform to the structure and implement the rules.

SOFTWARE
The collection of programs used on a computer including accompanying paperwork such as instruction manuals and documentation for recording design, coding etc.

SONET
Synchronous Optical Network. A SONET standard has been agreed internationally for the transport of data in optical form. Sonet takes account of the fact that optical communication channels will need special interfaces for the inter-conversion of electrical data at very high rates and that special synchronising and multiplexing arrangements will be needed. Signalling rates are expected to be from about 5C Mbps upwards, using a packet-switched system called QPSX.

SOURCE CODE
The code of the high level language in which a program is written. It is translated by a compiler program into the object code - the machine code in which the program is actually run.

SPOOLING
Queueing. A Spooler is a scheduling program for resources such as disc or printer, whereby processes are queued and take their turn.

STAR NETWORK
A network in which each terminal and computer is linked to a central computer. Because of this structure, all communication between various computers and terminals takes place through the central computer.

STATISTICAL MULTIPLEXER
A statistical multiplexer divides a data channel into a number of independent circuits in such a way that the total capacity of the circuits is greater than the total capacity of the undivided channel. The data is distributed so that all circuits always work at near-maximum capacity.

STORE AND FORWARD
Any electronic device for storing data and transmitting it later. A facility available on some facsimile machines for transmitting one or more documents to one or more addresses automatically at a pre-chosen time. The transmitting and receiving machines need not be attended during transmission and reception.

SWITCHED NETWORK
A network which is shared among many users any one of whom can potentially establish communications when required.

SYNCHRONISATION
The action of maintaining the correct timing sequences for the operation of a system.

SYNCHRONOUS
Occurring at the same instant.

SYNCHRONOUS TRANSMISSION
A communications method that eliminates the need for start and stop bits to define each character. A clock runs continuously at the receiver at a rate close to a clock at the transmitter and is pulled into synchronism by clock-controlled transmitted signal transitions. Since each character is of fixed duration the receiver is able to separate characters by timing circuits.

SYNTAX
The rules governing the grammar of a language.

SYSTEM X
A family of digital telephone exchanges controlled by computer software manufactured by GEC/Plessey.

TCP/IP
Transmission Control Protocol/Internet Protocol. A US industry standard for communication between different types of computer.

TELESOFTWARE
A system for storing programs on pages in a teletext database so they can be captured by any user with the right equipment and fed into (downloaded) microcomputer storage via a communications channel for execution.

TELECONFERENCING/VIDEOCONFERENCING
A conference between people at either end of a telecommunication link using television equipment to simulate a face-to-face meeting.

TELEMATICS
An extension of services beyond voice, to data and video communications. It signifies the totality of techniques involving the marriage of telecommunications and computing.

TELETEL
The national videotex service in France.

TELETEX
An ill-chosen name used for a text transmission system which has nothing to do with teletext. The system, comprising machines and protocols, is being supported by PTTs to provide a faster and generally improved form of Telex. It seems unlikely that it will survive.

TELETEXT
A class of videotex system in which a sequence of numbered information pages ("Magazine") is broadcast cyclically usually over a shared television channel. User interaction is limited to "frame grabbing" - the required page number is set on a dial and the page is captured the next time it is transmitted, typically 12 to 20 seconds later on average, and "frozen" for viewing.

TELEX
The public switched telegraph data network.

TELIDON
A viewdata-type system developed by the Department of Communications, Ottawa,Canada. It uses dynamically redefinable character sets (DRCS) which enables finely structured graphics to be constructed and displayed with some degree of extra cost and complication.

TELSET
A videotex service being tested in Finland using the viewdata system.

TERM
A descriptive name, expression, or word. In information systems the label accorded to items in a record so that the record may be retrieved by using that label.

TERMINAL
A term used to describe equipment that displays data, usually on a screen, and enables data to be input, usually by a keyboard. A data input and output device.

THERMAL PRINTER
A printer embodying a strip of transistor/resistor elements which are heated and make marks on heat sensitive paper. It provides better quality than electro-etch recording. Improvements made by replacing the elements with thin film print heads enable a page to be printed with a 200 elements/inch dot structure in 15 seconds. Thermal transfer printing was introduced later still using a ribbon between heads and paper so that plain paper could be used. The ink melts on to the paper, but the cost of the ribbon offsets the cost of the cheaper paper. Colour printing becomes possible by using ribbon with colour bands.

TIME DIVISION MULTIPLEXING (TDM)
A method of sharing a transmission channel among multiple sources by allocating specific time slots to each source. Both synchronous and asynchronous TDM is used. Synchronous TDM wastes time slots if a device has no data to send. More refined methods require devices to reserve their time slots ahead of time or allow devices to use time slots of other devices that were unused on the previous cycle.

TITAN
French videotex system similar to viewdata requiring a degree of extra complexity, but using a different code and character repertoire accommodating accented and other special characters.

TOKEN RING
A network architecture configured on the basis that each station (node) on the ring awaits arrival of a unique short sequence of bits (a token) from the adjacent upstream node, indicating that it is allowed to send information toward the downstream node. The network is configured in a manner that ensures that only a single token is present on the ring at one time.

TRANSCEIVER
A single device that is capable of both sending and receiving data.

TRANSDUCER
A device which accepts signals in one form and changes them into another - for example optical to electrical, electrical to acoustical etc.

TRANSPONDER
A receiver/transmitter on a satellite which receives signals from a ground station and re-transmits them to another ground station.

TRANSPUTER
A chip made by Inmos embodying communication links so that a number of inter-communicating transputers can provide parallel computing.

TREE STRUCTURED INDEX
An index designed to enable a user easily to locate particular information in a series of steps progressing from the general to the particular, usually by a succession of multiple choice "menus".

UHF
Ultra High Frequency. The range of frequencies extending from 300 to 3,000MHz.

UNIX
    An AT&T-designed computer operating system for telecommunications and multi-user environments.

VALUE-ADDED NETWORK SERVICES (VANS)
    A combination of communications and computers providing a wide variety of information and transaction services, e.g. electronic mail, videotex services, and reservation and billing services.

VGA
    IBM's graphics "standard". (Resolution of 640 x 480 pixels and 16 colours.

VERY HIGH FREQUENCY (VHF)
    The range of frequencies between 30 and 300MHz.

VIDEO-CASSETTE RECORDER
    A recorder which records and plays back video and audio signals.

VIDEOPHONE
    An "audiovisual" (sound plus sight) communication system where subscribers can see and talk to each other.

VIDEOTEX
    Generic name for information storage and transmission systems enabling pages of information to be displayed in response to simple commands. Videotex systems are usually simpler to use and less expensive than other kinds of computer based information systems. The two main types of videotex systems are teletext and viewdata.

VIDEOTEX STANDARDS
    The international videotex standards situation is complex. At present there seem to be two pseudo-standards. The first, CEPT, adopted by virtually all European PTTs under CCITT aegis, is a compromise solution to national differences in codes and character sets. It provides for a degree of standardisation leading to the possibility of mass producing receivers and terminals. The US situation seems to be in the hands of AT&T who have introduced a de facto standard, NAPLPS - an adaptation of Telidon.

VIEWDATA
    The name chosen by the British Post Office (now British Telecom) for a videotex system which it developed. The components of viewdata are a central computer containing pages with a tree structured index, the PSTN, and modified television receiver "terminals". The TV receiver modifications include the means of connecting the receiver to a computer via a dial telephone line and a keypad. A menu command display and the tree structure of the index enable any page to be quickly and easily retrieved.

    The viewdata service provided by the BPO was re-named Prestel, as "Viewdata" was found to be unregistrable. The word viewdata is still used as a generic word for describing systems of this type.

VIEWTEL
        A viewdata-type system developed and offered as a service by Online Computer Library Center, in Columbus, Ohio, USA. It started as a home library service and other services were added later. It is sometimes referred to as "Channel 2000" - the number of the channel to which a user's modified TV receiver is tuned.

VIEWTRON
        A viewdata-type system developed by AT&T and introduced by the Knight-Ridder publishing group for users in Coral Gables, Florida, USA.

VISTA
        An experimental viewdata-like system developed by Bell Northern, Canada.

VISUAL DISPLAY UNIT (VDU)
        A device for displaying textual or graphical information. When used with a keyboard, as is usually the case, "VDU" is virtually synonymous with "terminal".

VOICE-GRADE CHANNEL
        A telephone channel of sufficient bandwidth to permit the transmission of the human voice (typically 300Hz to 3400Hz).

VOICE MESSAGING SYSTEM
        A system for the capture, storage, and re-transmission of voice messages in digitized form. A means for recording telephone messages for later retrieval by the addressee.

V21
        The CCITT 300/300 bit/sec. full-duplex PSTN modem interface standard.

V22
        The CCITT 1200/1200 bit/sec. full-duplex PSTN modem interface standard.

V22bis
        The CCITT 2400/2400 bit/sec. full-duplex PSTN modem interface standard.

V23
        The CCITT 600 or 1200 bit/sec., 2-wire half-duplex, 4 wire full duplex standard

V24
        The CCITT recommendation for the terminal-modem interface for serial data transmission. The only universally accepted and implemented CCITT recommendation.

V35
        CCITT standard definitions for higher-bit rate DTE-DCE interface circuits

WHITE SPACE SKIP

A compression system fitted on many facsimile machines for substituting a short code for a succession of white elements as commonly encountered between lines of characters and elsewhere. The code signals to the receiving machine that it must re-insert a given number of white elements.

WIDE AREA NETWORK (WAN)

A communication network distinguished from a local area network (of which it may contain one or more) because of its longer-distance communications, which may or may not be provided by a common carrier or PTT The term is sometimes used as another name for the public packet network of a particular country or region.

WINDOW

A program controlled bounded space displayed on a CRT screen to contain information which may be manipulated independently or in association with information contained within other windows displayed at the same time. In order to provide sufficient flexibility, bit-mapping is usually used to construct windows within which text and graphics may be displayed.

WORD PROCESSOR

A computer, usually with a printer, on which software is run for office document processing and printing.

WORKSTATION

A computer equipped with comprehensive facilities for dealing with a specific complex task - for example Computer Aided Design. Because of the increasing facilities provided in microcomputers and a tendency in the industry to move terms originated for "high end" products downwards and apply them to "lower end" products for hyping-up purposes, there is a fuzzy boundary between micros and workstations.

X-SERIES

The CCITT standards for data transmission over digital data networks. See separate entries.

X25

A CCITT recommendation for the interface between data terminal equipment and circuit terminating equipment operating in packet switched networks.

X50

A CCITT recommendation for the format of streams of 64 Kbps subscriber data in a multiplexed interconnection between synchronous data networks.

X400

A series of CCITT recommendations for message handling protocols used when interconnecting computer-based message handling systems.

X500

A CCITT/ISO standard for an address specification and global directory. One of the major intentions of the standard is that it should be used in conjunction with X400.

Acronyms which have become names, e.g. "FORTRAN", are used as indexing terms. Others are usually spelled out, e.g. "Cathode Ray Tube" (CRT).

ABATON halftones   115
Accumulator
ACE
        Computer   30
        Language   112
Acoustic Coupler   135
ADOBE ILLUSTRATOR   110 603
Address Register   37
ADONIS   274
ALDEN   227
Algorithm   40
Aliasing   116
Allophone   301
All-in-one   386
American Standard Code for
        Information Exchange   8
AMIGA   693 701
AMSTRAD   449
AMPS   151
Analogue
        To digital convertor   43
        Transmission   125
Angstrom unit   7
ANSI X3.131 standard   56
Anti-Aliasing   116
APOLLO   210
APPLE
        Communications   501
        DTP   589
        History of-   446
        Lisa   95
        Operating system   483
        Macintosh   95 445
        Multimedia   692 701
        Printer   112
ARCNET   169
Arithmetic Logic Unit   37
ARPA network   290
Artificial Intelligence
        Chaining   308
        Domains   308
        Effects of   523
        Expert Systems
                Description   312
                Information Retrieval,
                        for-   317
                Online Systems, for-   426
                Products   313
        History   306

Inference   308
Knowledge Base   308
Lisp   310
Natural Language   307
Neural Computers   315
Prolog   310
Shells   308
Social Aspects of-   416
Vision System   311
ASSASSIN   385
ASTON Campus Network   171
ASTRA   213
Asynchronous Transmission   134
Automatic Indexing   355 358
AUTOMATIC TELEGRAPH &
        TELEPHONE CO   123
Avalanche Diode   201

BABBAGE, CHARLES   29
Backplane   456
Bandwidth   124 128 229
        Effects on TV   650
Bank -s -ing   565
        Futures   570
        Home   571
        Security   572
BANYAN   170
Barcodes   569
BARNSLEY, MICHAEL   80
Barrel Shifter   100
BASIC   39 484
Baud   126
BBC Datacast   223
BELL, ALEXANDER GRAHAM   122
BELL, DANIEL   710
BELL Laboratories   123
BELL TELEPHONE CO   123
Benchmarks   464 467
Bibliographic Coupling   357
Binary
        Arithmetic   35
        Coded Decimal   43
        Synchronous Communication   175
        System   4 42
Bipolar semiconductor   15
Bit
        Mapping   62
        Plane   94
BLUMLEIN, A.D.   30

12

Boolean Algebra   35
Break-in Box   136
Bridge   492
BRITISH AEROSPACE   221
BRITISH LIBRARY   269
BRITISH TELECOM
    Deregulation of-   730
    Gold   552
Broadband ISDN   159
BSB   213
Buffer   44 142
Building Societies   568
Bus   455

Cable
    Configuration   618
    DBS versus-   621
    Europe, in   626
    Information Services   620
    Interactive-   617
    Inter-city-   202
    Introduction   615
    Qube   617
    Satellite
      distribution, for-   619
    Technology of-   616
    Transatlantic-   202
    United States, in   622
      Deregulation   623
      Finance   624
      Growth   623 626
    United Kingdom, in
      Deregulation   631
      Futures   635
      Hunt Report   630
      Politics of-   629 740
      Services   218
Cable & Wireless   733
Cache memory   44
Cathode Ray Tube   91
    Resolution   64
    Screen   94
    Sizes   98
    Speed   94
        SEE ALSO:
            Displays
            Monitors
C-CUBE Compression   79
CD-ROM
    SEE Compact Disc
Charge Coupled Device   44 66
Character presentation   64
Cellular Radio   151
    CELLNET   152
    Subscribers in Europe   153

Central Processing Unit   35 453
Centrex   148
Channel Capacity   127
CHAPS   567
CHERRY
    Digitizer   61
    Voicescribe   302
Chip   13
    Politics   26
Circuit
    Assembly   11
    Performance   14
    Switching   14 168
Citation Index   354
CLARKE, A.C.   208
Classification   334 339
    Methods   339
C Language   484
CLEVERDON, CYRIL   332
Clock   34 45
CMOS Technology   16 20
Code -s -ing   129 746
    Trellis   139
COLOSSUS   30
Colour   593
    Display Standards   96
    Printing   66 71 111
    Reproduction   65
    Scanning   70
Combination Logic   33
COMITE CONSULTATIF INTERNAT-   156
    IONALE DE TELEGRAPHIE ET
    TELEPHONE
COMMISSION of the EEC
    Telecommunications Policy   742
COMMODORE   704
Communications
    SEE UNDER Telecommunications
Communication theory   5
    SEE UNDER Information Theory
Communication Science   409
Compact Disc
    Interactive (CD-I)   705
        Players   264
        Compression   264
    Read Only Memory (CD-ROM)
        Databases   263
        Drives   263
        On-line, versus-   263 429
        Players   262
        Review of-   260
        Standards   260
        XA   263 705
    Video   265
    SEE ALSO Digital Video
        Interactive (DV-I)

Compiler   39
Complimentary Metal Oxide
    Semiconductor   17 34
Compression   75-80 129 264 282
    BLTZ   129
COMPUSERVE   436 571 724
Computer -s
    Conferencing   559
    Digital   29
    Files
        SEE UNDER Files
    History of-   41
    Libraries in-   365
    Mainframe   41
    Neural-   315
    Output Microfilm   665
    Personal
        SEE UNDER Microcomputers
    Viruses   784
    Virus Protection   785
    Worms   784
COMSHARE   524
Concentrator   142
Contention Network   169
Contrast   91
Co-processor chip   21 457
Copyright
    Databases, for   806
    Downloading   806
    Fair Use   805
    International-   802
    Items & Abuse   803
    Photocopying   805
    Software   807
    UK, in   804
    US, in   803
Counter   45
Crossbar switch   146
CROSFIELD Scanners   70 117
CSMA/MD   492
CT2   154
Cyphers
    SEE UNDER
        Security
Data
    Network   167
    Protection Act   779
        Effects of-   781
        Europe, in-   778
        Laws   777
        US, in-   779
        UK, in-   779
    Under voice   150
Database -s   431
    Copyright   806

Full text   434
    Growth of-   432
    Hypertext-   680
    Management systems   388 558
    Relational-   558
    Users of-   433
Decision Support System   320
Default value   403
DENDRAL   306
De-regulation
    Telecommunications of
    SEE UNDER
        Telecommunications
            Policy
    UK Cable, of   634
    US Cable, of   623
Desktop Publishing
    ADOBE Illustrator   603
    Applications   605
    Colour in   593
    Equipment   594
    Examples   606
    Growth of-   590
    History   598
    Indexing with   610
    INTERLEAF   601
    Introduction to-   586
    OCR, in   83
    Page Formatting Software   108
    PAGEMAKER   601
    Page layout   596
    Printers for -   112
    QUARK EXPRESS   601
    Systems   603
    Typography   590
    VENTURA   601
    Zooming   600
DIALOG   144 424
Digital
    Audio Tape   57
    Exchanges   147
    Network Architecture   176
    Telephone Network   147
    Transmission   125
    Video Interative   80 265
Direct Broadcast Satellite   212 215
Disc
    Drives   54
    Emulator   57
    Formats   55
    Hard-   55
    History of-   50
    Sizes   53
Display   401
    Functions of-   457

HDTV-   655
    Microcomputers for-   444
    SEE ALSO
        Monitor
        VDU
Dither printing   68
Divider   36
DOCDEL   275
Document delivery system
    ADONIS   274
    DOCDEL   275
    Facsimile   227
    LIBRARY OF CONGRESS   275
    Methods   268
    NATIONAL LIBRARY OF
        MEDICINE   276
Document Image Processing
                    System
    Equipment   278
    Indexing   280
    Markets   284
    Page Handling   281
    Workflow   283
DOMESDSAY Project   257 688
Downloading   427 806
Downloading Trailblazer   139
DTI
    Office System Tests   508
Dual Inline Package   12
Duplex Transmission   134
DV-I   705
Dynamic Random Access Memory 20   26

Edge-notched card   346
Edge Detection   73
EDIFACT   555
Electrically Programmable
    Logic Device   23
Electroluminescent Display   102
Electronic Books   322 580
Electronic Data Interchange
    (EDI)   554
    EDIFACT   555
    Growth of-   555
    ODETTE   555
    TRADANET   555
Electronic Funds Transfer   567
Electronic Funds Transfer at
    Point of Sale   568
Electronic Journal   576-579
    Sociology of-   579 678
Electronic Mail   550
    BT GOLD   552
    History of-   551
    Useage of-   553

Electronic Publishing   573
    Authors, by   575
    Industry   575
    Media   574
    Print Production   574
    Print, versus-   581
    SEE ALSO
        Desktop Publishing
Emitter Coupled Logic   34
Employment
    Conditions, working   530
    Effects of-   757
    Facts & Trends   754
    Homework   759
    Theories   734
    Women's   759
Encryption
    SEE UNDER
        Security
Enhanced Small Device
    Interface   57
ENIAC   30
Erasable Programmable Read   20
    Only Memory
Ergonomics   240
Error correction   134 139
    Rate   128
Executive Information Systems
    SEE UNDER
        Management
Expert system
    SEE UNDER
        Artificial Intelligence
Exponent   32
Eyestrain   404

Facsimile
    British library   272
    Buying   238
    Coding   229
    Compression   72
    Ergonomics   240
    Futures   241
    Groups   232
    Group 4   240
    Halftones   245
    History of-   227
    Library system   270
    Machine facilities   244
    Machines, typical   239
    Mobile   245
    Noise in-   234
    PC fax   246
    PC fax cards   248
    Speed of-   233

Resolution 229
Standards 231
Storage 243
Test document 230
Transmission 228
FAIRTHORNE, ROBERT 326 331
FARALLON 698
Feature Analysis 85
FEDERAL COMMUNICATIONS
  COMMISSION 622 725
Fibre Distributed Data
  Interface (FDDI) Standard 180
Fibreoptic 168 195
  Cable 196
  Cost of- 198
  Inter-equipment links 205
Field 49
  Effect Transistor 15
File -s 49 349
  Inverted 350 418
  Management 558
  Searching- 351
  Sequential- 351
  Transfer 491-497
Flicker 91
Flip-flop 34 37 45
Floating point number 32
Floppy Disc 51
Flowchart 40
Fonts 546 592 598
Forecasting 715
FORTRAN 484
Fractals 80
Frame Grabber 72
France 163
Frequency
  Spectrum 124
Frequency Division
  Multiplexing 142
FUJITSU Reprographic Machine 113
Full Text Indexing 343
FULLWRITE 108

Gallium Arsenide
  Semiconductor 16
GARFIELD, E. 331
Gateway 427 493
Germany 163
Glyph 592
Graphics 402
  Kernel System 98
  Metafile 98
  Signal Processor 21 99
Greeking 597

Greyscale
  SEE UNDER
    Halftones
Group Coded Recording 55

Hackers 783
Half Duplex 134
Halftone 245
  Dithered 597
  Printing 113
  Reproduction 63 69
  Scanning 113
Hard Sector 52
HARPY 290
HDTV
  SEE UNDER:- Television
HEMPT Semiconductor 16
HENDRIX OCT 81
HEWLETT PACKARD 536
High Level Data Link Control
  (HDLC) 175
High level language 39
HOLLERITH, HERMAN 30
Home Banking 571
Home Computer 759
Home Control Systems 759
HUGHES GALAXY 219
Human Aspects
  SEE UNDER
    Man-Machine
    Information Society
Hypermedia
  SEE UNDER
    Multimedia
Hypertext
  Applications 675 684
  Browsing 682
  Compositions, for- 679
  Database 680
  Electronic journal 678
  HYPERCARD
    Arrangement 675
    Authoring 677
    Buttons 677
    Messages 677
  Indexing 682
  Introduction 674
  Multimedia, in 694
IBM
  PC 447-448
  PS/1 451
  PS/2 449-450 548
  TANGORA Speech Recog-
    nition 293

IEEE		180
Image		62
Compression	6	18
Processing		73
Setter		116
Studio	69	115
IMPERIAL CHEMICAL INDUSTRIES		536
Index -ing		337
Alphabetising		341
Associative		369
Automatic	355	357
Citation		354
Conceptual		337
Co-ordinate		344
Document Image Processing Systems, in-		280
Edge notched card		346
Exhaustivity		341
Factual		337
Full text	117	343
Hypercard		682
Meaning, and-		326
Offices, in	344	353
Online systems, for	342	417
Peek-a-boo card		345
Personal		338
Searches	348	351
Specificity		341
Thesauri		347
Vocabulary control		338
Information		
Classification	334	339
Management		511
Assets		563
Background of-	516-518	
Competitive advantage		515
Concepts	512-515	
Current issues		520
Politics of-		518
Successes		521
System trends		523
System reviews of-		524
Manager's understanding of		521
Recall & precision	335	337
Retrieval		334
Science		326
Society		
Arrival of		712
Constraints		712
Definition of-		709
Future of-		715
Haves-and-have-nots		749
Health		
SEE UNDER		
VDU		
Humanisation of-		746
Needs		713
Origins of-		710
Progress of-		711
Social effects of-	714	716
Theory	5 327	332 791
Value of-		
Cost benefit		792
Cost effectiveness		792
Demand & price		795
Economics		790
Recent work on-	796	799
Inkjet printer		110
INMOS		33
Input system		60
Instruction manuals		396
Instruction set		37
Integrated Circuit		12
Integrated Services		
Digital Network (ISDN)	155	658
Basic		158
B-ISDN		159
Broadband	159	184
Electronics		166
Europe, in-		163
Futures		182
Japan, in-		164
Primary		157
Standards		164
UK, in-		162
US, in-		160
INTELSAT	211	216
Interface, man-machine	392	407
INTERLEAF		601
INTERNATIONAL BUSINESS MACHINES		
INTERNATIONAL COMPUTERS LTD		
International Packet Switching System		
INTERNATIONAL STANDARDS ORGANISATION		
Interpreter		39
INTREX		
Inverted file		350
JESSI		27
JK Flip-Flop		46
Jobs		
SEE UNDER		
Employment		
KERMIT		493
Keyboard	60	459
Key system		149
KILDALL, GARRY		443

KODAK KIMS   278
KONDRATIEV Wave Theory   735

Language
    Computers, for
        SEE UNDER Name of
        Language
LAP-M Error Detection   139
Laser
    Error Detection   139
    Jet Printer   107
    Transmitter   199
LASERVISION
    SEE UNDER
        Videodisc
Latch   37
Latency   50
Librar -y -ies
    Acquisitions   361
    Catalogues   359
    Circulation   361
    Computers in-   359
    Facsimile in-   270
    Future of-   366
    Integrated systems   362
    LIBRARY OF CONGRESS   275
    Networks   363 406
    OPACs   360
    Science   327
·Light
    Pens   62
    Transmission   199 253
Light Emitting Diode
    Display   31 103
    Transmitter   199
Linear Predictive coder   302
LINUS Handwriting Pad   61
Liquid Crystal Display   102
    Supertwisted   103
Local Area Network   169
    Fiber   202 204
    File transfers in-   496
    Protocols   180
    Token ring   495
Local Loop   156
Logic   32
LOTUS   557
LOVELACE, LADY   29
LUHN, H.P.   355
Luminance   91

MACHLUP, FRITZ   710
MACINTOSH   213 445 700
MACROMIND DIRECTOR   698
Magnetic Storage   49

Management
    SEE UNDER:-
        Information
Man-machine interface   392
    Dialogue   410
    Human aspects   407
    Systems   407
MARC   359
MATHTYPE   611
MATS-E   151
Meaning   326
Measuring units   6
MEGADOC   279
MEMEX   90
Memory
    Chips   20
    DRAM   460
    Extended   461
    Management of-   461
    RAM   460
    Refreshing   460
Menu   393 398
MERCURY   733
MESFET Semiconductors   16
Metal Oxide Silicon   15
METAPRAXIS   524
Metropolitan Area Network   169
Microcomputer
    Benchmarks   464 467
    Choice of-   468
    History of-   440 443
    Information retrieval,
        with-   473
    Libraries, in   365
    Maintenance   469
    Purchasing   470
    Speed of-   444 464
    8080   442
    SEE ALSO:-
        Names of - & functions of-
Micro -film -form
    Advantages   670
    Applications   664
    CIM   607
    Costs of-   665
    Colour   666
    COM   606
    Current developments in-   672
    Disadvantages   671
    Fiche   666
    Film   666
    History   663
    IBM   699
    MNEMOS   667
MICROPAD   60

Microprocessor 17 46
MICROWRITER 60
Minicomputer 4
MINITEL 643
MIT 685
MNEMOS 668
MNP Error Detction 139
Mobile Telecoms 151 245
    SEE ALSO:-
      Cellular
Modem -s
    Choosing a- 139
    Problems 136
    Prices of- 138
    DOWTY Trailblazer 139
MODFETs Semiconductors 16
Modified Frequency
        Modulation 54
Modulation 130
    Transfer Function 93
Monitor -s 96 596
    Table of- 97
    Auto-tracking 698
MORSE, SAMUEL 122 138
Mouse 462
MP/M 479
MSDOS 471 480
MUIRHEAD 227
Multimedia
    AMIGA 700
    CD-I 705
    CD-ROM XA 705
    COMMODORE CDTB 704
    Definition of 674
    DOMESDAY Project 688
    DV-I 705
    Encyclopaedia 687
    FARALLON Sound 696
    Future of- 689
    Hardware 692
    History of- 684
    MACINTOSH 700
    MACROMIND DIRECTOR 698
    MEDIAMAKER 700
    MIT 685
    Motion Video 697
    Software 693
    Voice & music 694
Multiplexers 36 46 141
Multivibrator 47
MUSE 651
MYCIN 306

NATIONAL LIBRARY OF MEDICINE 276
NETBIOS 493

Network -s
    Neural 41 315
    Library 363 496
    Telecommunication
        Data 167
        Managed 169 172
        Managing 497
        Metropolitan Area 698
        Policy of- 721
        Private 171
        Universal- 173
        SEE ALSO:-
          Integrated Services
          Digital Network
          Local Area Network
Node
Noise
    Facsimile 234
    Telecommunications 126
Numbering systems 4
NYQUIST, H. 128

OBERON OCR 82
Object code 38
ODETTE 555
Office -s
    Document Architecture 536
    Documents 531
    Managers 511
    Productivity 531
    Records 353
    Systems
        Assessment of- 509
        DTI tests of- 508
        Effectiveness of- 560
        Expenditure on- 563
        History of- 507
        HP NEW WAVE 536
        ICI 535
        Modelling 532
Official Secrets Act 774
Operating systems 472
    Addressing 476
    APPLE 483
    Communication functions 500
                  of-
    CP/M 477
    DOS 4.0 548
    MP/M 479
    MSDOS 477 480
    OS/2 482
    UNIX 480
On line system
    Costs of- 420
    Example of- 424

Indexing in-
Expert-   426
Full text   343
Migration from print to-   430
Search example of-   424
Searching   348 365
Services   417 420
Session   423
Vendors & Producers   435
Versus CD-ROM   429
Opcode   37
Open System Interconnection   177
Operating system
Operational amplifier   47
Operand   38
Optical disc
Erasable   267
Recordings   253
SEE ALSO:-
Compact
Digital
Optical Read Only
Videodisc
Worm
Optical Character Recognition   81
Software   84
Functions   84
Tests on-   86
Optical Read Only Memory (OROM) 266
OPTIRAM   82
OPTRONICS Scanner   67
OS/2   482
Output technology   90

Packet switching   142 168
Tariffs   144
Page formating software   108
PAGEMAKER   601
PALENTIR   82
PANAMSAT   216
Paper sizes   8
Parallel processing   41
PARC   411
Parity   132
PARKER, EDWIN   710
Parsers   318
PASCAL, BLAISE   40
Pascal language   40 484
Patents   807 809
PATSEARCH   256
Pattern Recognition System   81
Peek-a-boo card   345
PERMUTERM SUBJECT INDEX   346
Personal Information System
Basics of-   375

Current developments   387
Document ordering for-   374
Examples of-   377
Indexing in-   373
PRIMATE   376 378
SCIMATE   379
Phoneme   301
PHONEPOINT   154
Photocopying   805
SEE ALSO UNDER:-
Copyright
PIN Diode   201
Pipelining   41 462
Plasma display   101
Plotter   104
Pointer   419
Point Sizes   8
PORAT, MARC   710
Port   36
Postscript   109
Clones   112
Post Office   123
Precision   335
PRESTEL   640
PRIMATE   578
Print -er -ing   66 104
Dithered   597
Dot matrix   546 596 598
Laser   546
Privacy
Bill of Rights   776
Discussion of -   770
IT, &-   771
Official Secrets Act   774
Surveillance   771
UK, in   773
US, in   772
Private Automatic Branch
Exchange   146 149
Program   454
Counter   37
Programmers Hierarchical
Graphics System (PHIGS)   98
PRODIGY   647
Protocol   173 180
Pulse Code Modulation   77 126
Pulse rise time   15

Quadrature modulation   139
Quantisation   77 126
Raster   91
QUARK EXPRESS   601
QUBE   617
Query by Example   394
Quickcapture Frame Grabber   73

RACAL REOS   278
Radiation, VDU   405 750
Radiopaging   153
RAMAC   50
Random access memory   2C
Raster   91
Reading from a CRT   100
Recall   335
Record   49
Reduced instruction
    Set Computer (RISC)   18 463
Redundancy reduction   77
Reed relay switch   147
Refreshing CRT   94
Register   36
Related records   358
RENDERMAN   99
Research duplication   794
Resolution   12 92
Response time   352 400
Rise time   15
Run length   130

SALTON, GERARD   355
Satellite
    Beam   211
    Business systems   214
    Deregulation   214
    Direct broadcast-   212 621
    Frequencies   210
    History of-   208
    Information delivery by-   218
    Japanese-   217
    List of-   209
    Power of-   211
    Transatlantic-   216
    TV distribution by-   619
    UK licences for-   217
Scan -ner -ning   278 595
    Colour   70
    Halftones   67
    Software   68 73
    Standards   74
SCIENCE CITATION INDEX   354 794
SCIMATE   379
Scrolling   402
SDI Services   421
Secrecy
Security
Seek time   50
Semiconductor   10
Sequential logic   34
Series-parallel convertor   46
Server   494
SGML   539

Shadowmask tube   93
SHANNON, CLAUDE   127 328 332 791
Shift register   47
Signalling System No. 7   165
Silicon wafer   14
SI system   6
Single instruction multiple
    datastream   41
SITA   555
Small Computer System
    Interface (SCSI)   56
Smart card   25 570
SMART system   318
Sociology of Science   579
Soft sector   52
Source code   38
SPARC chip   19
Spatial frequency   92
Speech
    Recogn -ising -ition
        Applications   295
        Assessment of-   289
        BELL TELEPHONE   292
        Current progress in-   297
        HARPY   290
        IBM TAGORA   293
        Machines/Cards/Boards   295
        Methods of-   291
        Typewriter   294
        VODIS   292
    Synthesis   315
        Methods   300
        Systems   302
        VOCODER   301
Spreadsheets   557
Standards
    CCITT   137
    Electronic Mail   552
    Fibre Digital Distributed
        Interface (FDDI)   180
    IEEE   180
    Integrated Services
        Digital Network   164 180
    High Definition TV   664
    Speech compression   77
    Modem   137
    Videotex   641
Statistical Time Division
    Multiplexing   142
STATUS IQ   355
Streaming Tape   58
STROWGER switch   146
Supercomputer   41
Surface mounting   12
SWIFT   555

Switch, electronic	13	Japanese	651
Synapse	42	MUSE	651
Synchronous		Standards	654
Data link control	176	US	653
Optical network	186	Standards on videodisc	255
Transmission	134 494	**Telex**	150 249
System Network Architecture	176	**Text**	
		Processing	
Tablet, handwriting	60	Reproduction of-	63
TCP/IP	176	SEE ALSO UNDER:- Word	
Telecommunications	146	Processing	
Bandwidth	124	**Thesauri**	347
Channel	124	**THORN-EMI**	524
Channel capacity	127	**Time Division Multiplexing**	142
Forecasts	187	**Timing circuits**	36
History	122	**Tiny Aperture Terminal (TAT)**	214
Noise	126	**Token Ring**	169
Policy		**TOME SEARCHER**	356
Equal access	739	**Touch sensitive screens**	61
European Commission	742	**TRADANET**	555
Infrastructure	718	**Transborder flow**	786
Monopolies	721	**TRANSDOC**	275
Network-	721	**Transform coding**	77 79
UK, in	730	**Transistor**	10
BT tariffs	736	Logic circuits	34
CABLE & WIRELESS	733	**Translation by machine**	316
Changes, 1990	736	**Transponder**	210
Duopoly	735	**Transputer**	23
MERCURY	733	**Trellis coding**	139
Outcomes, 1990	737	**TRUVEL scanner**	72
Viewpoints	734	**TURING, ALAN**	306
US, in	725	**Type face table**	7 8 592
AT&T	727	**Typography**	590
Effects of-	730		
Tariffs	140	**Unemployment**	
Telecommut -er -ing	743	SEE UNDER:- Employment	
Teleconferencing	559	**Units of measurement**	6
TELENET	687	**UNIX**	480
TELEPAD	60	**User's needs**	397 406
Telephone system	146		
Exchange	147	**Value Added Network**	172 188
Exchange switch	146	**Vector**	
Network	147	Display	92
Telepoint	154	Drawing	95
Teletex	151 250	Processing	41
Teletext	223 638	**VENTURA**	601
Television		**Very Large Scale Integration**	
Distribution methods	619	(VLSI)	13 17
Frame grabber	72	**Very Small Aperture Terminal**	
Frame line data	223	(VSAT)	213 219
High definition	648	**Videodisc**	254
Bandwidth	651	Applications	256
Displays	655	Standards	255
European	652	Training, for	248
Introduction	649	**Video random access memory**	21 100

Videotex	638
MINITEL	645
Politics of-	642
Private	646
PRODIGY	647
Successes	644
Teletex	638
PRESTEL	
Indexing for-	643
Standards	641
Viewdata	639
Visual display unit (VDU)	123
Health factors	403 750
Radiation from-	405 750
Vocabulary control	336
VOCODER	301
VODAFONE	151
VODIS	292
Voice	
Messaging	299 554
SEE UNDER:- Speech	
VON NEUMANN	30
V-series standards	137
Wavelength to Frequency table	7
Wait states	464
Wide area network	169
Winchester disc	50
Windows	485 490
Word lengths	455 476
Word processing	
Benefits	545

Graphics	548
History	541
Learning	549
Menus	403
Operations	542
Printers for-	546
Systems	543
WORD PERFECT	544 587 599
Work	
SEE UNDER:- Employment	
Workstation	132
Write Once Read Many (WORMS)	266 278
XENIX	481
XEROX STAR	545
XON-XOFF	495
X-series standards	179
X25	176
X400	552
X500	552
X Windows	491
ZIPF'S Law	331
Zooming	600
3290 display	102
3340 disc	51
3370 disc	51
34010 processor	22 99
68040 ..	18
80286 ..	17
80486 ..	25
80860 ..	19

L.-Brault   DATE DUE   BRAULT